GLOBAL SOCIOLOGY

2nd edition

Global Sociology

Second edition

Robin Cohen

and

Paul Kennedy

First edition 2000
Second edition 2007

Published by
PALGRAVE MACMILLAN
Houndmills, Basingstoke, Hampshire RG21 6XS and
175 Fifth Avenue, New York, N.Y. 10010
Companies and representatives throughout the world

PALGRAVE MACMILLAN is the global academic imprint of the Palgrave Macmillan division of St. Martin's Press, LLC and of Palgrave Macmillan Ltd. Macmillan® is a registered trademark in the United States, United Kingdom and other countries. Palgrave is a registered trademark in the European Union and other countries.

ISBN-13: 978–1–4039–4844–1 hardback
ISBN-10: 1–4039–4844–5 hardback
ISBN-13: 978–1–4039–4845–8 paperback
ISBN-10: 1–4039–4845–3 paperback

This book is printed on paper suitable for recycling and made from fully managed and sustained forest sources.

10 9 8 7 6 5 4 3 2 1
16 15 14 13 12 11 10 09 08 07

Printed in China

For Selina and Sue

Contents

CHAPTER 9

CHAPTER 10

CHAPTER 11

PART THREE EXPERIENCES

CHAPTER 12 TOURISM: SOCIAL AND CULTURAL EFFECTS

CHAPTER 13 CONSUMING CULTURE

CHAPTER 14

MEDIA AND THE INFORMATION AGE

CHAPTER 15

SPORT IN A GLOBAL AGE

CHAPTER 16

GLOBAL RELIGION

CHAPTER 22

CONTESTED FUTURES   527

List of Illustrations

MAPS

FIGURES

List of Tables and Boxes

Global Thinkers

Acknowledgements

We would like to take this opportunity to record the premature and sad death of Paul Kennedy's colleague in Manchester, Angela Hale. Both as a valued scholar and as a leading figure in the INGO, Women Working Worldwide, for many years, Angela's struggles to work for a fairer world have been an inspiration to us and many others. We also recall and value her help both on the first edition of this work and the present one.

Many people gave advice and support to the authors in the Herculean task of writing then rewriting this rather lengthy text. Robin Cohen would like particularly to thank Jim Beckford, David Chidester, Richard Higgott, Richard Lampard, Ali Rogers, Jan-Aart Scholte and Steve Vertovec. Paul Kennedy would like particularly to thank Colin Barker, Adam Brown, Tim Dant, Peter Forsland, Susie Jacobs, Geraldine Lievesley, Phil Mole, Gabe Mythen, Jonathan Purkis, Peta Turvey, Geoff Walsh and Derek Wynne.

Both of us are grateful to Selina Cohen for her editorial input and Jason Cohen for drawing the graphs. Andrew Parker supplied a helpful critique of our chapter on sport. Our previous editor at Macmillan, Catherine Gray, and her successor at Palgrave Macmillan, Emily Salz, have been helpful and supportive. Catherine provided a continuous stream of creative comments and searching queries and greatly improved the shape and structure of the book. Sheree Keep provided useful liaison while Sarah Lodge handled many queries with calm and assurance. Tulasi Srinivas provided a photo of her father and reminded us about his important concept of 'sanskritization'. Caroline Thomas was an effective photo editor. Adrian Arbib released a number of his invaluable photographs (see permissions below for a detailed list). The team at Aardvark Editorial undertook the meticulous editing and correction of the manuscript and developed the effective design of the book.

The feedback given by lecturers and other users of the first edition of this book was generally gratifying and also highly educative. We have responded positively to many of their suggestions and apologise that occasionally our response has been limited, especially where we were dealing with contradictory comments. The anonymous reviewers of the manuscript were meticulous and constructive in their evaluations and we extend our thanks to them too.

The authors and the publisher wish to thank the following for their help in obtaining images and their permission to use these:

Ari Sitas for Figure 1.1; Magdalena Gutierrez/Acervo Pr. FHC for Figure 1.2; Tulasi Srinivas Ph.D for Figure 1.3; Adrian Arbib for Figures 5.1, 8.1, 16.1, 17.2 and 19.1 (all © Adrian Arbib); akg-images for the picture of Max Weber (photo by akg-images); CORBIS for the pictures of Emile Durkheim (© Bettmann/ CORBIS) and Michel Foucault (© Bettmann/CORBIS); CORBIS for Figures 2.1 (© Kevin Schafer/CORBIS), 2.2 (© Louise Gubb/CORBIS SABA), 3.1 (© Bettmann/CORBIS), 3.2 (© Werner Forman/CORBIS), 4.1 (© Bettmann/ CORBIS), 4.2 (© Martin Rogers/CORBIS), 6.2 (© Bettmann/CORBIS), 7.2 (© Kapoor Baldev/Sygma/CORBIS), 9.3 (© Bettmann/CORBIS), 10.1 (© Bettmann/CORBIS), 10.2 (© Bettmann/ CORBIS), 12.2 (© Reuters/CORBIS), 12.3 (© Louie Psihoyos/ CORBIS), 13.1 (© Macduff Everton/CORBIS), 13.2 (© Robert Holmes/CORBIS), 14.2 (© Strauss/Curtis/CORBIS), 15.1 (© Hulton-Deutsch Collection/CORBIS), 15.2 (© Marc Serota/Reuters/CORBIS), 16.3 (© Warren Clarke/epa/CORBIS), 17.1 (© Peter Beck/CORBIS), 18.1 (© Charles Plateau/Reuters/CORBIS), 18.2 (© Peter Macdiarmid/Reuters/ CORBIS), 20.1 (© Robert Maass/CORBIS), 21.1 (© Lewis Alan/Sygma/ CORBIS), 21.2 (© Reuters/Str/CORBIS) and 22.1 (© Ted Spiegel/CORBIS); The Holberg Prize, University of Bergen/Florian Breief for the picture of Jürgen Habermas; iCube Solutions for Figure 11.1 (photo by iCube Solutions); Marxists Internet Archive (www.marxists.org) for the picture of Karl Marx; Mary Evans Picture Library for Figure 6.1; Panos Pictures for Figure 8.3 (© Fernando Moleres/Panos Pictures); Peter Seglow for the picture of Norbert Elias (© Peter Seglow); Still Pictures for Figure 7.1 (photo by J. Maier); Harvard News Office for Figure 8.2 (© Jon Chase), United Nations High Commission for Refugees for Figure 10.3 (photo by A. Hollman, © UNHCR) Caroline Thomas for Figure 11.2 (© C. Thomas); Jean Olivier Irisson for the picture of Pierre Bourdieu (http://jo.irisson.free.fr/ drawing.html); Maggie Smith for the picture of Manuel Castells.

The following authors kindly supplied their own photographs for the Global Thinkers boxes: Martin Albrow, Zygmunt Bauman, Howard Saul Becker, Walden Bello, Cynthia Enloe, Anthony Giddens, Ulf Hannerz, David Harvey, Roland Robertson, Sheila Rowbotham, John Urry and Immanuel Wallerstein.

Abbreviations and Acronyms

24/7	twenty-four hours seven days a week
9/11	11 September 2001 terrorist attack on twin towers in New York
ABC	American Broadcasting Corporation
ACS	automated clearance systems
AFL–CIO	American Federation of Labour and Congress of Industrial Organizations
AIDS	acquired immune deficiency syndrome
ANC	African National Congress
AOL	America Online
APWD	Asia-Pacific Forum on Women, Law and Development
ASA	American Sociological Association
BCCI	Bank of Credit and Commerce International
BIP	Border Industrialization Program (Mexico)
BJP	Bharatiya Janata Party
CBN	Central Bank of Nigeria
CBS	Columbia Broadcasting System
CCTV	closed-circuit television
CEDAW	Convention on the Elimination of All Forms of Discrimination against Women
CFC	chlorofluorocarbon
CLADEM	Latin American Committee for the Defence of Women's Rights
CND	Campaign for Nuclear Disarmament
CNN	Cable News Network
CO_2	carbon dioxide
CPC	Communist Party of China
CSGR	Centre for the Study of Globalisation and Regionalisation
CSR	corporate social responsibility
DAWN	Development Alternatives with Women for a New Era
DEVAW	Declaration on the Elimination of Violence Against Women
DIY	do-it-yourself
DNA	deoxyribonucleic acid
DVD	digital video disc
ECHR	European Court of Human Rights
EPZ	export-processing zone
EU	European Union
FAO	Food and Agricultural Organization
FDI	foreign direct investment
FM	frequency modulation
G7	group of seven (advanced industrial nations – now the G8)

GATT	General Agreement on Tariffs and Trade (now the WTO)
GCIM	Global Commission on International Migration
GDP	gross domestic product
GM	genetically modified
GNP	gross national product
GSM	global social movement
GUM	Gosudarstvenny Universalny Magazine (state department store, Russia)
HIPC	heavily indebted poor country
HIV	human immunodeficiency virus
IAAF	International Association of Athletics Federations
ICC	International Criminal Court
ICT	information and communication technology
IDP	internally displaced person
IGO	international governmental organization
ILO	International Labour Organization
IMF	International Monetary Fund
IMR	infant mortality rate
INGO	international non-governmental organization
IOC	International Olympic Committee
IOM	International Organization for Migration
IPCC	Intergovernmental Panel on Climate Change
IQ	intelligence quotient
ISDN	integrated services digital network
ISIS	International Women's Information and Communication Service
IT	information technology
IVF	in vitro fertilization
IWRAW	International Women's Rights Action Watch

IWTC	International Women's Tribune Centre
MAD	mutually assured destruction
MCA	Music Corporation of America
MCP	male chauvinist pig (slang)
MDB	multilateral development bank
MTN	Mobile Telephone Network (South Africa)
MTV	Music TeleVision
NAFTA	North American Free Trade Agreement
NATO	North Atlantic Treaty Organization
NBA	National Basketball Association
NBC	National Broadcasting Company
NFL	National Football League
NGO	non-governmental organization
NIC	newly industrializing country
NIDL	new international division of labour (theory of the)
OECD	Organization for Economic Cooperation and Development
OPEC	Organization of Petroleum-Exporting Countries
PEN	international writers' lobby
PIN	personal identification number
PRD	Pearl River Delta
R&D	research and development
RAN	Rainforest Action Network
RTL	Radio Television Luxemburg
SAP	structural adjustment programme
SARS	severe acute respiratory syndrome
SD	sustainable development
SEWA	Self-Employed Asian Women's Association
SSA	Sub-Saharan Africa
TB	tuberculosis
TNC	transnational corporation
TRIPS	Agreement on Trade-Related Aspects of Intellectual Property Rights

UN	United Nations		VCR	video cassette recorder
UNCED	United Nations Conference on Environment and Development		VHP	Vishna Hindu Parishad
UNCHR	United Nations Centre for Human Rights		VoIP	voice over internet protocol
UNEP	United Nations Environment Programme		WB	World Bank
UNESCO	United Nations Educational, Scientific and Cultural Organization		WCED	World Commission on Environment and Development
UNGA	United Nations General Assembly		WFS	Women's Feature Service
UNHCR	United Nations High Commissioner for Refugees		WHO	World Health Organization
UNICEF	United Nations International Children's Emergency Fund		WLUML	Women Living Under Muslim Laws
URL	universal resource locator		WSF	world social forum
USSR	Union of Soviet Socialist Republics		WTO	World Tourism Organization (in Chapter 12 'WTO' refers to this organization)
			WTO	World Trade Organization (elsewhere in the book 'WTO' refers to this organization)

Introduction

CONTENTS

1

Since the publication of the first edition of *Global Sociology*, we have witnessed a number of dramatic events of global significance. This should not obscure the underlying processes of global transformation we continue to document. These processes include the further shrinking of distance by better, faster and cheaper communications (what is called time–space compression), an increased pace of cultural, human, financial and trade flows and the enhanced interconnectedness of economic and social life.

These continuities were, however, punctuated by four events that were momentous in terms of their actual and likely future impact. In chronological terms they were:

1. The major protest mounted by the anti-globalization movement against the World Trade Organization (WTO) in Seattle in December 1999 and since followed by a blaze of similar protests in locations such as Prague, Barcelona and Genoa.
2. The merciless destruction of the World Trade Center in New York on 11 September 2001 unleashed by the Islamic al-Qaeda terrorist network followed by subsequent attacks on civilian targets in the West and elsewhere.
3. The collapse of the mighty Enron corporation, one of America's largest companies, also in 2001.
4. The commencement of a US-led war against Saddam Hussein's Iraq in 2003, followed by further military involvement by powerful Western forces in Afghanistan and the reigniting of old conflicts in the Middle East in 2006.

Although it is difficult to measure the ultimate impact of these events, in this edition we try to show in what ways they have challenged or confirmed our major arguments. An analysis of these events permeates the text, a quick summary of which is provided below.

THE ANTI-GLOBALIZATION MOVEMENT

We are not seers, yet we can claim to have anticipated the increasing salience of global social movements in the first edition of this book. The anti-globalization movement is, of course, itself a global social movement in that it organizes on a global scale for global concerns. 'Anti-globalization' should be understood as 'against corporate-led and US-dominated forms of globalization'. The anti-globalization movement is also highly diverse – being made up of a multitude of currents involving every kind of concern and interest – green, anarchist, socialist, feminist, trade unionist, religious, alternative development and human rights, to name but a few. Moreover, governments of some poor countries have often been sympathetic to these protests because many feel excluded from the mainstream of world decision-making and marginalized within the global economy.

Protests have been directed not only at the leading governments, the most powerful intergovernmental organizations (IGOs) such as the World Bank (WB), the International Monetary Fund (IMF) and the WTO, but also at the gigantic transnational corporations. The demonstrations have brought together collaborative protest streams from many countries and world regions, and have evidenced campaigning tactics that cut across diverse issues. While some groups have, on occasions, resorted to violent acts, the great majority of those participating have demonstrated peacefully and with a firm commitment to democracy and reform rather than to revolution. The protesters want to highlight issues concerned with the environment, human rights, poverty, world inequality, fair trade, indebtedness, peace, cultural autonomy and democracy.

THE AFTERMATH OF 11 SEPTEMBER 2001

What of the appalling destruction wrought in New York and the Pentagon on 11 September 2001? As Calhoun (2002: 87) has argued of the USA: 'One need be no friend to terrorism to be sorry that the dominant response to the terrorist attacks has been framed as a matter of war rather than crime, an attack on America rather than an attack on humanity.' The chance to press forward on a number of key global concerns was thereby lost. The establishment of an international criminal court looks further away than ever. The Bush government backed off pressuring Israel to bring peace to the Middle East and instead aligned itself totally to the counterterrorist activities of the Sharon and later the Olmert governments, a stance that was bound to escalate tension in the area.

Across the world there was sympathy for the victims of 9/11, but this sympathy was tinged with hopes that the government and the people of the USA would realize that other people had also experienced dreadful catastrophes and we are all now vulnerable to the dangers of a new kind of instant, portable, ever-present violence. In some places, Osama bin Laden was turned into a hero. In northern Nigeria, for example, Yusuf Sarki Mohammed (2002: 51) recorded that bin Laden's image was printed on posters and T-shirts to satisfy 'a seemingly insatiable demand'. However, Mohammed continued: 'People hoped the attacks would also burst the bubble of American self-importance and make it more reflective when dealing with the rest of the world.' In the midst of their grief and anger, it may be that it was too much to expect that the American people would ask, let alone answer, this question: Does the growing inequality both within and between the nations of the world, coupled with a one-sided exercise of power by a few actors go some way towards explaining why violent and abusive acts are perpetrated by criminal and terrorist gangs against innocent citizens?

THE CRITIQUE OF AN UNREGULATED MARKET

The third momentous event that needs discussion is the naked exposure of the frailty of speculative capitalism. While Japan and a number of other countries were mired in no-growth or low-growth economies, from which they have just emerged, the US stock market experienced a run of good fortune for nearly 15 years. Was this too good to be true? By the turn of the century, a number of commentators were worried that reckless speculation would lead to dramatic collapse and bankruptcies. So it proved. By early 2002, US$4 trillion had been lost in the value of US shares. The most dramatic example of failure was the case of the energy supplier Enron, one of the 50 biggest public companies in the USA, which recorded over US$100 billion in sales and US$1 billion in earnings in 2001. Within six months, the company was bankrupt, with a loss of US$90 billion in market value. What was shocking was not so much that this massive company had collapsed, but that its managers and auditors knew about the financial position of the company and sought to conceal it from investors and employees. Company executives and board members quietly unloaded shares, while Arthur Anderson, the previously respectable global accountancy firm, shredded evidence that demonstrated its awareness or complicity in these transactions. About 25,000 employees lost most of their savings.

If we were convinced Marxists, we might shrug our shoulders at such evidence of corporate malfeasance, saying that, 'it is only to be expected'. But powerful critiques of such conduct have been mounted by far more unlikely sources. Take, for example, the views of Felix Rohatyn, a former governor of the New York Stock Exchange, managing director of the financiers Lazard Frères and Co and the US ambassador to France from 1997 to 2000. For him, 'a large proportion of the stock market was becoming a branch of show business and it was driving the economy instead of the other way around' (Rohatyn 2002: 6). Similar arguments have been mounted by George Soros (2002) on a global scale. If left alone, as the neoliberals want, financial markets would go to extremes and would eventually break down, argued Soros. The IMF and other international agencies should be used, he argued, to regulate the global marketplace and promote the flows of capital to emerging markets. Again, the source of this critique is instructive. Soros, who now wishes to be a global thinker and intellectual, was, in an earlier incarnation, a financial speculator who made a great deal of money from the deregulation of the markets in the 1980s. In late 2002 he was on trial in France for insider trading. For many political commentators and intellectuals, the Enron collapse marked the moment when an unrestrained market ideology had exhausted its positive possibilities.

WAR WAR NOT JAW JAW

The Bush administration has ignored such introspective thoughts and instead has aggressively advanced militarist and unilateralist policies abroad, while restricting civil liberties at home (Harvey 2003). The sentiments of the White House are ameliorated by some in the administration itself and by a number of its longtime allies. Yet it is difficult to contain the 'arrogance of power'. US military expenditure is 40 per cent of the world's total, while its share of gross world product (though declining) remained at 30 per cent in mid-2002. The US, in short, is hegemonic in military and economic terms and has the capacity to win any 'hard war'. It won the first round of war against the Taliban in Afghanistan. In 2003, it annihilated Saddam Hussein's armed forces in a few weeks. Yet continuing conflict in Afghanistan and Iraq and the reigniting of war in the Middle East in 2006 has raised a large question mark around the wisdom of the current foreign policy of the USA and its allies. While being able to win any hard war, the Bush administration seems to have lost the 'soft war' – the war of ideas, credibility and sympathy. Perhaps they should have taken heed of a Gallop poll of 10,000 interviewees in Muslim countries in 2002. Surprisingly, most did not even believe that Muslims carried out the 9/11 bombings. Interviewees 'overwhelmingly' described the USA as 'ruthless, aggressive, conceited, arrogant, easily provoked and biased' (*Guardian Weekly,* 7–13 September 2002).

FUTURE IMPLICATIONS

A corporate, market-led – quintessentially American – way of life has now spread throughout the world, but this particular manifestation of globalization has generated strong opposition from those who oppose rampant individualism, the trivializing obsession with consumerism and the endless search for distracting entertainment. Such opposition comes from two principal sources:

■ From those who see corporate capitalism as creating or perpetuating economic and political inequalities, violence and conflict. Organized in progressive social movements in many societies, such 'discontents' do not wish to be told how to live their personal and everyday lives, while at a social level, they seek to protect the environment and foster peace, social cooperation, responsibility and equality (Neale 2002).
■ From family heads, religious and political leaders in many countries who fear a future dominated by the loss of cultural identity, social disintegration and an empty materialism where money has become the sole measure of all things and people. They and their followers wish to preserve family and community values along with respect for traditions, the elderly and, above all, for the realm of the sacred.

We should not exaggerate the potential power of global social movements. Few individuals living under today's global condition can escape being influenced by glimpses of the dazzlingly seductive lifestyles lived by the world's celebrity figures, or by the temptations of other people's cultural repertoires. This is because of our ceaseless exposure to the flows of ideas and information through the media, or because of migration and the stories and souvenirs brought by returning travellers. There are opportunities and excitements that come from exposure to global variety, creativity and openness. Again, we should not minimize the oppression that can be wrought by those slavishly following conservative ways of life. Old male patriarchs often perpetuate gender inequality and suppress personal freedoms.

But we also cannot ignore the signs that the forces unleashed by corporate-led globalization have brought fear, uncertainty and the threat of diminishing cultural integrity for many societies. The leaders of the advanced industrial countries neglect the soft war, the war for hearts and minds, at their peril. The current danger is that the aggressive posture of the Bush government will drown out the sensible voices that argue that corporations have to be made more socially responsible, markets have to be regulated and the link between crime, politics and big business broken. As important is a viable settlement of international flashpoints like the Middle East and addressing glaring global injustices. (Much of the world is poor; nearly 50 million are ravaged with HIV/AIDS.) As we argue elsewhere in this second edition of *Global Sociology*, for our own long-term survival and prosperity, those lucky enough to be living in the advanced industrial societies (and educated elites everywhere) need energetically to tackle the contradictions and inequalities that afflict our planet.

■·■·■·■·■·■·■·■ ORGANIZATION OF THIS BOOK

This book is divided into four parts, each of which has five or six chapters. The themes of the book include:

- the *interpretations* that have been used to explain our increasingly globalizing world
- the differential impact of global changes that have reinforced inequalities or generated new *divisions*
- the ways in which global changes have generated different *experiences*
- the *dynamics and challenges* generated by contemporary globalizing tendencies.

There are a number of ways of understanding changes at a global level. We often need to refurbish old and develop new concepts, theories and perspectives to advance our understanding. These are discussed in Interpretations (Part One of this book) and summarized below.

THE MAKING OF GLOBAL SOCIOLOGY

In Chapter 1, we discuss how sociology as a discipline evolved, what it explains and some of its limitations. We show that some of the building blocks of the discipline, like the notion of 'community', worked well at a local level; others, like 'society', were more or less synonymous with the nation-state. As social, cultural, economic and political changes began to assume a global character, late twentieth-century sociologists had to adapt some of their ideas and perspectives to a global scale. We find that some of the insights of the founders of the disciplines in fact operate on a much larger canvas than the local or national level and can be deployed in developing a global sociology. Of course we cannot merely evoke past achievements, so sociologists are also deeply engaged in generating fresh theories and gathering new information.

In Chapter 2, we draw you into our understanding of two key concepts, *global-ization* and *globality*, necessary direction finders for our long intellectual journey. The first concept has now spread into common usage and is often found in magazines and newspapers. It refers to the ways in which the world is being knitted together by the increased volume and speed of cross-border transactions. Many popular accounts focus on the transnational flows of goods and money, or *economic globalization*. But there are many other aspects of globalization. For example, various parts of the world are drawn together by the increased density and lower cost of travel and communications. Globalization is therefore also about social and cultural connectivity. Images, ideas, tourists, migrants, values, fashions and music increasingly flow along global pathways.

The globalization of such social and cultural activities leads to the elaboration of a second and less well-rehearsed concept, the idea of globality. Whereas glob-alization refers to the objective, external ties that bind us together, globality alludes to the subjective, personal awareness that many of us share, and are increasingly likely to share – a common fate. Of course a good number of people, normally but not only those in poor remote areas, continue to experience lives marked by an indifference to or a conscious detachment from the world around them. But such insensibility is increasingly difficult to maintain. Jet planes and helicopters fly overhead, travellers appear as if from nowhere, roads are cut into the interior, mobile phones ring, the world's music pulsates from cheap transistor radios, while friends, neighbours and families share what they have seen on the ubiquitous TV screens.

MODERNITY AND WORLD SOCIETY

A major theme of this book (and an abiding concern of sociology) is how social change arises and becomes diffused. Despite the ubiquity of contemporary means of transport, globalization and globality have not been dropped from the sky by passing aircraft. They are the outcomes of a long evolutionary process whereby small isolated societies and large civilizations came to relate to one another. In Chapter 3 we situate the moments when humankind became increas-ingly capable of understanding itself collectively. Contacts arose from long-distance trade, from the spread of world religions like Islam, Buddhism and Christianity and from the force of colonialism and imperialism. The idea of a universal humanity was developed particularly by European Enlightenment thinkers who, though they recognized that there were 'backward regions', thought all were capable of reaching the end state of *modernity*.

There was an undoubted arrogance in this view, which implied that what obtained in eighteenth-century France and Germany was the preferred destin-ation of all humanity. The power of ideas, the success of the European economies and finally the force of military imperialist expansion propelled many areas of the world into an uneasy association. This juxtaposition also involved the effects of *industrialization* and *capitalism*, both key historical processes discussed in this chapter.

THE CHANGING WORLD OF WORK

In Chapter 4, we depict substantive changes in the world of work. Rapid and unprecedented technological change and intensifying international competition have led to economic insecurity and the *internationalization* of work. The more vulnerable position of women has led to the *feminization* of work. The development of flexible labour markets has also led to the *casualization* of work. For the winners, particularly those with portable skills in growing sectors like the information-related industries, these changes herald 'new times' – offering opportunities for greater individual freedom and self-realization and a more democratic, decentralized, less hierarchical workplace and society. The losers see only 'hard times' – dominated by fragmenting businesses, labour redundancies and part-time and poorly paid jobs. The rise of subcontracting and home-working in this emerging economic order will also be discussed.

NATIONHOOD AND THE NATION-STATE

The *nation-state* is a relatively recent political organization, dating in its complete form from the French Revolution. Nation-states replaced multinational kingdoms, principalities, religious domains and empires. Nationalists wanted their group identities to be protected by exclusive access to a territory. The rulers of nation-states often dealt harshly with minorities, diasporas and indigenous peoples, pressing them to assimilate into the dominant group, or isolating and excluding them from the mainstream of social and political life.

It will not be long before there will be 200 'recognized' nation-states. (Not all states are recognized by the UN, in international law or by other nation-states.) Yet, the number of peoples demanding autonomy or statehood is perhaps twenty times as great. The growth of religious, ethnic or other subnational sentiments threatens the nation-state system from below. The increasing pace of globalization also threatens it from above. The changing role of the nation-state in coping with these local and global pressures is considered in Chapter 5, in which we also introduce debates on citizenship and political power.

Global changes are overlaid on prior inequalities between people and also serve to introduce new lines of dominance and subordination. These changes are discussed in Divisions (Part Two of this book) and summarized below.

SOCIAL INEQUALITIES

Sociologists have always given much thought to the problem of how to conceptualize and explain the forms of inequality found in all societies and the ways in which these vary both between societies and over time. The unequal distribution of power, wealth, income and social status between individuals and groups is not randomly distributed but is patterned or structured. Some groups are marginalized, others enter the charmed circle of privilege and security.

Although we should definitely not forget forms of social inequality based, for example, on age, civic status, religion, immobility and disability, in general we can say that structured exclusions operate along the three main axes of *gender*, *race/ethnicity* and *class*. Each of these generates its own structure of unequal practices, giving rise either to institutionalized sexism, racism or class divisions and conflict respectively. Gender, race and class also crosscut each other in various complex ways, sometimes reinforcing and at other times weakening the impact of existing inequalities. In Chapter 6 we explore the ways sociologists have grappled with various schemes to understand how these forms of inequality and disadvantage arise and are perpetuated, modified or enhanced by global change.

CORPORATE POWER

Transnational corporations (TNCs) are dominant players in global affairs. They profit from the increased level of economic globalization and indeed can be said partially to cause this outcome. Are these ubiquitous organizations the Trojan horses, or perhaps the battering rams, of international capital? Such is their power and influence that they are often accused of dictating to rich and powerful states, while completely overwhelming poor states. Is this kind of characterization merely evoking an imagined demon rather than constructing a real social science? What are the origins of these organizations? Have they, in fact, escaped their national origins? What is their economic role in integrating the global economy? What are the social consequences, positive and negative, of the TNCs' activities? Do they exercise power without responsibility? Is the new emphasis on *corporate social responsibility* a positive sign of the TNCs' commitment to think of people as well as profit, or a fig leaf designed more for public relations purposes? In Chapter 7 we consider these questions.

UNEVEN DEVELOPMENT: THE VICTIMS

How do we account for the extremes of poverty and wealth, power and powerlessness in today's world? According to some theorists, whose views are examined in Chapter 8, the system is rigged to protect the interests of the leading players. Can those who lose out ever alter their place in the feeding chain? Could it be to the ultimate benefit of the powerful that the poor achieve some upward *social mobility* and raise their standards of living? Can social uplift be induced from the top, for example through the actions of benign social democratic politicians? Alternatively, will the only redress come from oppositional social and political movements emanating from the grassroots level?

Those who die from famine or in civil wars or natural disasters are the ultimate global losers, but other groups are also highly vulnerable. As the race gets
faster, those at the back – groups like the unskilled, the unemployed, those who
experience discrimination and the urban poor – appear to be trailing even further
behind. In Chapter 8, we probe the condition and possible trajectories of some
of the victims of recent global changes.

CRIME, DRUGS AND TERRORISM

Just as globalization and the deregulation of many national economies have
allowed banks and TNCs to profit from more open borders, so too have the
opportunities for cross-border terrorism and crime blossomed. Cross-border
crime may involve white-collar computer fraud, tax evasion or the smuggling of
people and goods. However, the cutting edge of global crime is the illegal drugs
trade, worth an estimated US$500 billion a year. Those who principally profit
from the trade are the 'drug barons', the smugglers and the dealers. But it is difficult to eliminate the trade while it forms so vital a part of the cash income gained
by poor farmers in countries like Afghanistan, Nepal and Jamaica and while the
demand for recreational and addictive drugs in rich countries seems insatiable.

Who can forget the endless replaying of the television footage of hijacked
aircraft ploughing into the World Trade Center on 11 September 2001? For
many in the USA, who had not experienced large-scale terrorism before, this was
a deeply traumatic event, after which nothing would ever be the same. Certainly
'9/11' marked the moment from which US state power was mobilized to wage a
global 'war on terror'. In Chapter 9, we provide a wider context in which to
understand the origins and character of terror and terrorism.

POPULATION AND MIGRATION

To both popular opinion and concerned policy-makers, population growth is
one of the most critical problems facing the world. Under intense pressure,
politicians have sanctioned or encouraged extreme measures to control population. But, as we argue in Chapter 10, we need to distinguish evidence about
population growth from prediction, projection and prejudice and we need to
question whether measures to control migration and population growth are
appropriate and effective.

Only a small proportion of the world's population (about 3 per cent) consists
of international migrants, defined in terms of someone born in one country but
who has been resident for over a year in another. But numbers alone are not the
major driving force to control and restrict global migration. International
migrants can bring highly motivated labour, economic skills and cultural renewal
to many countries. They fill gaps in the labour market, particularly in affluent
Western countries where the population is ageing and fertility is low. Nonethe-

less, they have managed to inflame public sentiments in many countries and politicians have consequently sought to control and restrict their movement.

HEALTH, LIFESTYLE AND THE BODY

We only have to think about the spread of HIV/AIDS, SARS or avian flu to see that the increased connectivity produced by globalization can transform the incidence, patterns and reach of infectious diseases. In Chapter 11 we consider the changing epidemiology of diseases, the privatization of healthcare and the ways in which lifestyle choices have led to new forms of ill-health. The diseases of affluence – strokes, heart conditions and obesity – exist alongside the tantalizing prospect of attaining a body beautiful, one that is lean, sexually desirable, fit and enduring. The body itself has become a locus for regulation and improvement by priests, governments, health professionals, quacks and the health industry.

In the poor countries, the incidence of infectious and waterborne diseases, mainly associated with poverty and economic backwardness, fell until 1980. However, some positive health indices have gone into reverse in many countries, particularly among the least advantaged groups. At the same time the chronic Western diseases of affluence have become established, especially among those in the developing countries exposed to strong modernizing influences; for example, with increasing affluence, roughly two-thirds of men in China have taken up or continued smoking, probably the biggest single source of self-inflicted illness.

Certain social processes can no longer be understood by a state-centric approach. For example, the unsettling effects of the flows of tourists, international communications, the development of new forms of transnational urban, cultural and sporting life, and the more intense globalization of many religions on people in all nation-states and across national frontiers are analysed in Experiences (Part Three of this book) and summarized below.

TOURISM: SOCIAL AND CULTURAL EFFECTS

One of the ways in which the boundaries between nation-states are becoming blurred is through the travellers, tourists and leisure-seekers who wish to gaze at all societies and potentially assimilate all of us into a 'global playground'. As we show in Chapter 12, instead of missionaries, explorers and anthropologists, tourists are now cutting their way into the diminishing protected spaces of previously isolated societies. Does the differential impact of tourism have something to do with the character of the tourists themselves? Or is the distinction between *mass tourism* and *alternative tourism* too cut and dried? Many travellers act like cultural warriors for the rich, powerful states, others are like the pilgrims of old, seeking renewal and enlightenment. Yet others, like sex tourists, simply exploit weaker, poorer people. Tourism exposes nearly everyone to a multicultural world where the boundaries between societies and between insiders and outsiders blur. In particular, international tourism compels both hosts and guests to rethink their own identities.

CONSUMING CULTURE

Drink a cup of coffee or tea and you instantly connect to the global marketplace. The list of world goods that arrives in this way is formidable and grows all the time. World goods are products that in whole or part are grown, processed, packed, manufactured, recorded, filmed or staged in a multiplicity of locations often far from the place where we finally purchase and experience them. In Chapter 13 we look at the effect of multiple sourcing. In particular, we ask whether we have become easy targets fot those who wish to sell us consumer goods or whether consumers have been empowered by the choices available in the global marketplace. We are increasingly aware that our purchases and possessions also carry various meanings – from the discreet logos of an exclusive brand to the 'in your face' messages that many consumers emblazon on their T-shirts. These meanings are associated with the wider cultural beliefs, values and orientations that we share with others. Drawing on this pool of common meanings enables us to communicate with groups that share our ideas and values – so they become markers to set off one group against another. Producers respond to this tendency by scaling down (so-called 'niche marketing') and also try to keep their sales of volume goods high by scaling up – thus fostering a global culture of consumption, linked together by advertising, envy and emulation.

MEDIA AND THE INFORMATION AGE

Girding the globe are lines of communication that snake along the sea bed, stretch across the land and bounce from satellites to earth. As we look at the ubiquitous television screens, our sense of distance from other places and other societies suddenly shrinks into insignificance. We live, in a famous phrase, in a 'global village'. As is made clear in Chapter 14, who controls the media and channels of communications and for what purposes provide important sociological data. We also discuss the significance of the telephone, particularly the mobile telephone, as a mass consumer good, together with the arrival of linked computer networks. These have rocketed information – its processing, storage, creation and distribution – to a central place in the national and global economy.

The capacity to share information and generate interactive communication also has social and cultural effects. Many social groups are concerned that negative representations of their group will lead to discrimination, or even violence directed against them. Some of these concerns are misplaced because they assume that we rather naively accept the messages that have been 'injected' into us. In fact, the effects of the media are more complex and often involve a reflexive critique of the film, news story, feature or programme. At the same time it is an exaggeration to see media consumers as 'semiotic guerrillas', accepting, discarding or refracting the message as they choose. We assess the effects of the '24/7' media revolution and wonder whether its impact has been exaggerated despite the proliferation of publications, programmes and stations.

SPORT IN A GLOBAL AGE

Like music, dance and art, the enjoyment of and participation in sport is not limited by speaking or reading different languages. Skill, competition, training the body, fair play and the fun that can be derived from sport allow it to cross borders and nations easily. In Chapter 15 we look at how different sports have spread far beyond their originating contexts, but also how governments have adopted (or rejected) certain sports in order to assist in the process of nation-building. From the middle of the last century, sport has also been appropriated by the TNCs who use it, its equipment, staging and broadcasting as a core business. Think, for example, of News Corp or AOL Time Warner. Business sponsorships also associate successful sports personalities with their corporate brands to build a positive image of their activities.

These crucial transformations have altered the nature of sport experiences for participants and spectators. They also contribute significantly to globalization, taking sport far away from its origins in village contests. Some observers also point to powerful trends towards the possible homogenization of sporting practices and the declining ability of sponsored, commercialized sport to engage meaningfully with the everyday lives of ordinary people, particularly those who are less well off. However, we must also remember that the mass world audiences who participate in mega sporting events such as the Olympics can, if only momentarily, enjoy a unity of feeling that contributes towards globality – our consciousness of the world as a single shared place.

GLOBAL RELIGION

For sociologists, the key issue is not whether religion is 'true' or 'false', but why it manifests itself in all societies, what meanings are invested in religion and what social functions it provides. Other pertinent questions that may be asked by a sociologist include whether there is a long-term tendency towards secularization (the normal finding that is still accepted by many sociologists), or whether we are experiencing a significant and long-term revival of religious sentiments and organization. Are particular forms of conduct in the secular world (for example business acumen) linked, as Weber surmised, to a particular religious affiliation? We have all recently become acutely aware of the small number of Islamic *jihadists* who have turned to terrorism to express their fervent beliefs. But why have they done so, and is Islam in general a threat to 'Western civilization'? In Chapter 16 we review what sociologists have contributed to the study of religion, consider why religion has claimed so powerful a place in contemporary life, examine how the global claims of religion are advanced and ask whether the practice of religion provides a threat to social cohesion or one means of attaining that condition.

URBAN LIFE

For much of human history, life was rural. In the year 1800, 97 per cent of the world's population lived in rural areas. Wind the clock on 200 years and we find that 254 cities each contained over one million people. The forms of settlement and the ways people lived in cities became the sites of study by some of the world's most eminent sociologists. Durkheim described the transition from 'mechanical' to 'organic' forms of solidarity, Simmel saw large cities as inducing anonymity, loneliness and the sense of being a stranger, while Park and Burgess at the University of Chicago looked at the 'ecological patterning' and spatial distribution of urban groups.

As we explain in Chapter 17, in the current era certain cities, called *global cities*, are becoming more detached from their hinterlands and other national cities as they take on the functions of servicing the global economy. Global cities are not only important phenomena in their own right, they are important because of their relationship to each other. Increasingly, many wealthier people living and working in global cities, or travelling there, find that they share conditions of life, attitudes, behaviour patterns and tastes with equivalent residents of other global cities. They downgrade their national culture or downgrade it in favour of an international and cosmopolitan culture. As once the local yokel was to the town, so the inhabitants of provincial cities may be to those of the global city. However, not only the wealthy make up the population of the global cities. In this chapter we also look at urban processes of social exclusion and in particular at the sociological debate about whether there is a so-called 'underclass'.

All too often, the literature of globalization assumes that people are mere chaff in the wind, unable to influence the nature and direction of social change. In Part Four, titled Dynamics and Challenges, we question this assumption and show how global social movements have emerged or been re-energized. These movements connect struggles at different levels, attempt to reshape the emerging world order and seek to create democratic and participatory possibilities.

GLOBAL CIVIL SOCIETY

In Chapter 18 we show how the public sphere is gradually widening as an informed citizenry uses access to information and the growing possibility for mobilization to develop organizations that are both free from state interference and able to challenge its authority. Having such a *civil society* is properly regarded as a sign that people are, at least potentially, capable of taking on state power and globalization, both often depicted as inanimate forces playing out their logic without human intervention. When social organizations are involved in creating links and networks to advance their particular causes, they are called *social movements* and, when they operate transnationally, *global social movements*.

It has become cheaper and easier to engage in networking activities over large distances, so that the fragmentation and diversity of non-governmental organizations (NGOs), which had been their weakness, can be offset or even turned into a source of strength. Coalitions can bridge North–South divides and mobilize people for such causes as protecting the environment, advancing human rights or mobilizing for charitable causes like helping victims of hurricanes, earthquakes, famines or the Asian tsunami. Of course global social movements often act in concert with international organizations like the United Nations (UN) or with national governments, in which case they can be effective in lobbying for more committed engagement by official bodies in the particular cause they espouse.

CHALLENGING A GENDERED WORLD

One important way of constructing 'globalization from below' is found in the rise of various women's networks that have moved to a global scale of activity, a phenomenon described in Chapter 19. The women's movement has been particularly effective in shifting from small, participatory, consciousness-raising sessions to such events as the international women's conferences in Kenya in 1985 and in Beijing ten years later. There is hardly a country in the world where gender relations have not been profoundly altered. Moreover, the timescale for this transformation has been impressively short; most of the force of the movement having been evident only since the 1950s. In addition to its successful grassroots organization, it is probable that the reason why this movement spread so fast is that the speed and density of communications allowed the global transmission of images that changed the consciousness of both women and men. Seeing women in new roles as police officers, pilots, astronauts or doctors, or seeing women standing up to men in popular 'soaps', questioned conventional stereotypes and gendered divisions of labour.

TOWARDS A SUSTAINABLE FUTURE: THE GREEN MOVEMENT

One of the most influential and visible global social movements is the environmental or green movement, discussed in Chapter 20. The development of an environmental movement is a major reversal of the prevailing nineteenth-century idea of unquestioned progress and civilization, perhaps best symbolized by a white man hacking his way through the Amazonian jungle to bring commerce and Christianity to the benighted natives. Instead, the central idea of the 'greens' is that planet earth is a fragile ball floating in space. The movement seeks to bring home the extent of the damage inflicted on the planet by human beings, referring particularly to the value of biodiversity, the stabilization of population growth and the need to resist the commercialization of agriculture. The increased consciousness of the threat of global warming has finally mobilized the leaders of some powerful nation-states into effecting international agreements to control CO_2 emissions and making largely rhetorical commitments to protect the environment. However, the power of the energy lobby in the USA and the massive use of non-sustainable energy consumed by China in its breakneck thrust to industrialization are both important constraints in developing a viable, global environmental strategy to protect our vulnerable world.

IDENTITIES AND BELONGING

The creation of strong social bonds is one of the most powerful of human impulses and, as we have seen, an abiding concern for sociologists. Paradoxically, for some the threat of globalization often reinforces family, kinship and other local attachments, ethnic sentiments and religious beliefs. Many people seem to need to belong to close-knit groups that protect their sense of self and provide a feeling of well-being and security. This tendency is usefully understood as *identity formation*, a process that happens at a number of levels. Often identity formation can be benign, for example in looking after the welfare of one's family, including infants or vulnerable seniors. However, the subnational level, where ethnic groups (sharing a common descent, religion or language) are mobilized, often generates enormous tensions. This is particularly the case where claims for autonomy or separate statement create 'high intensity' conflicts, sometimes civil war. We need think only of Rwanda, Burundi, Sudan and Bosnia to recall distressing scenes of ethnic intolerance. In March 1999 the leaders of the North Atlantic Treaty Organization (NATO) ordered an intensive and controversial bombing campaign of Serbia in retaliation for Serbian military and police attacks on the civilian population in Kosovo. This raised the question of whether military intervention in defence of human rights is justifiable.

The global age has thus produced an unexpected and even perverse outcome. Despite, or perhaps because of, the pressures to come together, fierce struggles have ensued to keep people apart. Although we lay emphasis on 'localism' (to encompass movements based on religion, race, ethnicity and subnational sentiments), in Chapter 21 we also consider states, groups, organizations and individuals that recognize diversity and difference and seek to foster creative and positive bonds between peoples of different backgrounds. Some are creating ties between themselves that anticipate the development of a transnational and cosmopolitan consciousness.

CONTESTED FUTURES

In our concluding chapter we consider the continuing controversies and emerging debates in global sociology. Perhaps the most persistent debate revolves around the extent of globalization and the differing reactions to it. Some sceptics say it is all 'globalony' (an American slang word suggesting that those who talk about globalization are reciting, parrot-like, a fashionable slogan without much content), but we use some convincing empirical research to show that globalization is indeed a powerful and growing force in the contemporary world. There are those who support, decry or wish to reform aspects of globalization. Others remain as outsiders to many developments, whether by choice or global social exclusion.

While reviewing this debate, we also suggest that it can serve to obscure some of the key changes at a global level. For example, is the USA going to engage further with the world as it seeks to protect market share, retain access to diminishing oil supplies and wage a war against terror? Or is it going to retreat into a new isolationism as military interventions fail and it loses ground in the 'soft war' – the battle of ideas and the attempt to win 'hearts and minds'? Again, what will the increasing economic power of China and India signify in areas other than world trade? Which social groups will gain and which will lose as global changes become consolidated? How will cultural change arise and, in particular, will we see dominance by a small group of cultures or the *hybridization* and *creolization* of the world in the form of dynamic mixed cultures? What will happen to monochromatic societies, including those in the West, as they increasingly absorb a widening range of cultural experiences? How will our faiths, ideas and other forms of social behaviour evolve as transnational flows of information, images, people, sounds and styles proliferate? These and other questions will occupy global sociologists for many years to come.

Using this book

- At the end of the chapters, you will find some advice on further reading, some suggestions for class work, some questions to think about and some web links.

- Key concepts in sociology are displayed like this – THIRD WORLD – and are defined in boxes headed like this key concept .

- Key historical events, and difficult words and ideas, often from disciplines other than sociology, are displayed in the text like this – *French Revolution* – and defined in the margin.

- In case you don't remember where you have read a definition or explanation, turn to the index. The page numbers in **bold** will tell you where to find the main discussion again. The Glossary on the companion website supporting this book (www.palgrave.com/sociology/cohen/) will list all concepts and explanations alphabetically.

- A good student will read more than appears in a single sociology textbook, however bulky it is. Use the Further Reading at the end of each chapter as a guide to your reading – a full list of all the sources referred to in *Global Sociology* appears in the References at the end of the book.

- Many, though not all, universities and colleges will teach a course through the use of a weekly lecture together with supporting classes or seminars. For you and your instructors/tutors, we make Group Work suggestions for interesting ways in which to analyse and discuss the material.

- You may want to try your hand at answering some of the Questions to Think About. You can use these as a way of structuring your revision, as essay titles or as a way of preparing for your examinations.

- Finally, most of us are now used to using the web for culling additional material, often accessing it through Google or a similar search engine. The trouble is there is too much out there and much of it is junk. At the end of each chapter, we provide a small, selective list of sites, concentrating on those that are portals to other information, those that are filtered for quality by social scientists and those that have original information. Occasionally, we have thrown in a wackier one for your amusement. Remember, too, that you need to acknowledge your source and show quotation marks around material you have copied from the Web (just as you do for printed books and journals).

We trust you will enjoy the course!

PREPARATORY WORK

1. Prepare yourself for this course by:
   - thinking about whether you can afford another book as well as this one
   - examining your library's online catalogue to see what books they have, using the Further Reading at the end of each chapter in this book as your guide
   - surveying what other resources are available, for example foreign newspapers, good weeklies (like *The Economist*) or CD-ROMs.
2. Take a guided tour of your library.
3. Look round carefully at the first small group of students you meet taking this course. There will almost certainly be some from other regions, cities or countries. Try to get to know them. They will be an invaluable resource in your understanding of the different facets of global society and they may also turn out to be friends.
4. Read at least one chapter ahead of each week's scheduled lecture. Start with Chapters 1 and 2 now. Chapter 2 is a tough one. If you can crack it, you should not have too many subsequent difficulties.

PART ONE

Interpretations

CHAPTER 1

The Making of Global Sociology

CONTENTS

Sociology involves the systematic study of the character and patterns of human interaction. Human behaviour is often structured by historical events, beliefs and social influences acting on an individual, a family or a wider social group. The outcomes are experienced at a number of levels – local, national, regional and global. In trying to explore these processes and levels, sociologists sometimes are able to use insights from the other social science disciplines – notably economics, political science, anthropology and history. However, certain theories and methods are intrinsic to the discipline itself and have evolved for over 150 years. Many teachers in the discipline insist that students should gain a good grounding by understanding the evolution of the ideas of the pioneers of sociology. In your discussions at college and university you will hear a lot of favourable comments about the virtues of 'interdisciplinary' and 'multidisciplinary' perspectives. We also like this idea in principle, but think that you can do it much better if you can first command the fundamental theories, methods, findings and sensibilities of your chosen discipline.

In this chapter we will look at some of the key starting points for sociologists, some milestones in the development of sociology, the changing contexts of the discipline, the construction of national sociologies that inhibited transnational outlooks, and finally the origins of global sociology. It should be stressed that global sociology is still a fledgling enterprise and not all sociologists would agree that this should henceforth be the central preoccupation of our discipline. However, as you follow us through all 22 chapters of this book, we hope to convince you that further developing a global sociology is indeed a vital and necessary direction for the discipline.

KEY STARTING POINTS IN SOCIOLOGY

What is distinctive about sociological analysis? After all, there are many ways of assessing people's motives and observing how they behave. In just 28 lines of *As You Like It* (Act 2, Scene 7), Shakespeare takes us through 'the seven ages of man', changing from an infant, a schoolchild, a lover, a soldier ('Jealous in honour, sudden and quick in quarrel'), a judicious middle age, old age and back to tooth-less infancy. At each stage we play roles, as if, as he puts it:

> All the world's a stage,
> And all the men and women merely players;
> They have their exits and their entrances;
> And one man in his time plays many parts …

Brilliant creative writers can touch our hearts, dazzle us with their command over language and illuminate our understanding of human conduct. Likewise, philosophers may probe the meaning of life and assess whether it is virtuous by the standards set out by classical philosophical writing. Psychologists might investigate the unconscious or concealed reasons for our actions or seek to modify them if they are making us unhappy or causing harm to others. Any historians worth their salt will tell you 'we have been here before' and give you numerous exotic examples of supposedly similar phenomena, though how similar they are is always a moot point. Many economists will tell you that human conduct is motivated by rational choice and material self-interest, while the bulk of political scientists will tell you that if you understand power all else will follow. Sociologists cannot do everything, nor should they. However, they have carved out a valuable and distinctive place in describing and theorizing cultural and social worlds, in framing social policy (generally called 'public policy' in the USA) and in developing critiques of conventional wisdoms and social practices that stifle human potential.

SOCIOLOGY AS SCIENCE

Sociology evolved partly by positioning itself with some disciplines and against prior bodies of knowledge, like theology. With economics and politics, sociology became aligned to an emerging body of secular scientific thought known as the Enlightenment (see Chapter 3). Auguste Comte (1798–1857), the person who first coined the term 'sociology', argued that all branches of knowledge passed through three stages. In the first, the theological stage, supernatural beings were held responsible for all phenomena. In the second, the metaphysical, abstract thought was possible, but only in the third phase, the positive stage, would a higher order of scientific reasoning become possible. The gradual understanding of scientific laws applied to what Comte called the 'statics' and 'dynamics' of societies would make sociology the governing science that glued all the other forms of science together. For him, the 'abstract theoretical sciences' formed a hierarchy, the apex of which was sociology. He wanted to use observation, experiment, comparison and history to enhance the scientific claims of the discipline (Kreis 2000).

A strong cohort of sociologists, known after Comte as 'positivists', still follow his lead and seek to minimize normative (that is, value-laden) comments. They endeavour instead to discover, measure and analyse regularities and patterns in social behaviour from a neutral point of view. Those who want to press the scientific claims of the discipline acknowledge that they have one major difficulty compared with natural science – namely that it is ethically impossible to conduct controlled experiments on people in the same way that laboratory scientists can rely on the manipulation and destruction of objects, or on the dissection of living creatures held to be inferior to humanity. However, we should not exaggerate how free natural scientists are. Many people object to experiments on animals or living organisms – protests against the cloning of sheep and stem cell research are two cases in point. Moral objections also proliferate about the sort of pure research that can lead to destructive herbicides, pesticides, chemical warfare, global warming or nuclear fallout. By contrast, using very large data sets (for example from censuses and aggregate data on income and expenditure), through complicated statistical calculations (like multivariate analyses) and by systematic temporal and spatial comparisons, sociologists have been able to offset (though not completely obviate) some of their initial scientific disadvantages.

THE COMPARATIVE AND UNIVERSALIZING ASPECTS OF SOCIOLOGY

Nearly all humans live collectively in what is generally termed 'society'. Of course there were and are some examples of hermits. Peter France (1996: Chapter 1) has some wonderful stories about the Greek hermit philosopher Diogenes (412–322 BC), who had an unbeatable line in being difficult. When Alexander the Great visited and asked what he could do for an impoverished philosopher, Diogenes replied 'Get out of my sunlight.' When he was banished from his birthplace, Sinope, he responded by declaring 'The Sinopeans have condemned me to banishment; I condemn them to stay at home!' There are many other hermits discussed in France's account, but the general import of his examples is clear. It is rare for hermits to disappear on their own forever; they usually seek a period of spiritual renewal and purification, often by depriving themselves of food, sleep and human company, in order later to re-engage in spiritual and social life with their fellow human beings. Perhaps we should also make the obvious point that if we all dispersed to live by ourselves, humankind would disappear.

So we are *social* creatures, and because of this we share certain attributes and behave in certain common ways that do not rely on our individual beliefs, nationalities, age, gender, status or wealth, important as these and other factors are in describing how we differ. Elias (1978: 107) puts it this way: 'The central unalterable factor in all societies is human nature.' However, the fact that we are dealing with *human* nature, not nature in general, means that we cannot assume that our nature is immutable. Indeed, Elias continues: 'One unique aspect of humanity is that human beings are in certain ways changeable *by nature*.' This has profound implications. We do not have to experience biological change (understood in the Darwinian sense of evolution) to experience and adjust to large-scale changes, for example in the move from preindustrial to industrial society, or in the phenomenon that interests us, the move towards a more global society. We can record our actions, recall our history, reflect backwards and project forwards. We can stick to old ways or adopt new ways. This makes the tasks of sociologists more complicated and different from those of biologists, who can assume that animal behaviour is largely limited by inherited characteristics (Elias 1978: 108). To get at our more complex subject matter, we therefore have to look at how particular societies have evolved, compare them with others (of similar or dissimilar appearance) and consider which social changes and behavioural patterns seem to be universal or, by contrast, which seem to be particular to one society or a cluster of societies.

SOCIOLOGY AS IMAGINATIVE UNDERSTANDING

Even alluding to the human aspect of human nature and the variations in social conduct between societies raises questions of whether the scientific sociologists are going to be able to pick up all the fine grain of human behaviour and social interaction through formal methods and statistical techniques. That is, of course, not to diminish the real achievements of positivist sociologists in accumulating reliable information, developing testable concepts (called 'hypotheses'), refining research techniques to ensure greater reliability and producing a body of social policy that has helped those in government. Everything from the causes of crime, football hooliganism, birth rates, sexual conduct and misconduct, family patterns, social mobility (how people move up and down the class and occupational structure), the extent of religious adherence, to the value of educational attainment and many other sociological issues have been illuminated by rigorous sociological research in the positivist tradition.

Despite massive gains in our knowledge of the social world, many sociologists would argue that there is a missing dimension to such studies. Generally, this omission can be described as 'the self' or 'the subjective' in society, but we allude more particularly to the *meaning* of a particular act – the meaning, that is, to the social actor, to other social actors or to an outside observer, who may or may not be a sociologist. To address this issue, the great German sociologist Max Weber (in Coser and Rosenberg 1976: 213–14, 219) called for *Verstehen* – loosely translated as 'understanding', but in one sense better thought of as 'insight' or even 'empathy'. *Aktuelles Verstehen* is a form of superficial, immediate understanding, while *erklärendes Verstehen* probes motivations, intentions and context to give a deeper meaning or possible interpretation. Helpfully, Weber provides an example. We can observe that a man is firing a gun (what is actually happening), but is he doing so because he is a member of a firing squad (therefore acting under compulsion), is he fighting against an enemy, is he doing it for sport or is he engaged in an act of revenge? The last is perhaps the most interesting possibility as it suggests irrational conduct that may have been 'provoked by jealousy, injured pride or an insult', and these additional possibilities allow us to include in our interpretative sociology both rational *and* irrational acts. To understand the act of firing a gun (or a host of more complex social acts), we therefore need to understand the subjective meaning of an act and its context in order to develop a rounded sociological analysis.

Subjective or interpretative sociology gained its most powerful expression in what is known as 'symbolic interactionism', a label that was applied to a group of sociologists working in Chicago, who followed Weber's emphasis on *Verstehen*. As Rock (1996a: 859) explains, symbolic interactionists argue that knowledge is not a simple mirror of an object. Rather, 'people actively create, shape, and select their response to what is around them. Knowledge is then presented as an active process in which people, their understanding and [external] phenomena are bound together.' Sociologists working in this tradition seek to get inside people's skins, as it were, and see how situations are understood, symbolically and literally, by the social actors themselves (as well as the others around them). This is particularly important when the subjects are not respectable or conventional citizens and are the objects of all manner of prejudices and stereotypes. The social worlds of criminals, prostitutes, drug users, sexual deviants and gang members have been notably explored by sociologists working in this tradition.

SOCIOLOGY AND THE SEARCH FOR KNOWLEDGE

Honesty and integrity are at the heart of any genuine search for knowledge. This means that sociologists, like any other scientists (*scientia* is simply the Latin word for 'knowledge' so there is no reason to be diffident about using the expression), cannot start by assuming the answer. We have to let the facts speak for themselves, honestly report the answers given by our respondents, faithfully record our observations and not twist arguments to suit our private purposes and political positions. For positivist sociologists this is so self-evident it is barely worth mentioning. Those working on comparative and historical sociology and those in the interpretative tradition also seek to follow scientific procedures and methodologies. However, some sociologists have suggested that honesty and integrity in research do not necessarily imply value neutrality. Precisely because we are human and are engaged in research on the human condition, we may find ourselves 'taking sides' and declaring to the world (or whoever will listen to us) that this or that public policy is ineffective, destructive, producing unintended consequences or is ethically indefensible.

We are sure that you can immediately sense we are skating on thin ice here. Let us take some examples to make the argument clearer. Suppose you were 'Yasmin Khan', an environmental scientist. Your routine measurements of the size of the polar ice cap suggested that it was shrinking rapidly. Global warming was a likely consequence and this could result in freak weather, hurricane damage, flooding and massive destruction to human and animal habitats. Presumably, most people would agree that as a responsible citizen it would be critically important that our fictional environmental scientist should share her knowledge with colleagues (by publishing it in a journal that used established academics to scrutinize the argument and data before accepting it), try to find powerful policy-makers to take her findings seriously and (though not all scientists will wish to do this) bring her arguments to the attention of the wider public. Dr Khan may even march with a placard in a demonstration to protest against a particular government policy that would, in her informed judgement, make the situation even worse.

However, here is the crucial point. In the design, execution and publication of her research, our virtuous fellow scientist did not fake her results or distort the truth. Sociologists are required to have similar standards. Let us suppose you are a researcher with strong feminist views and most of the people you question say they love to look glamorous and depend greatly on the attentions of enraptured males to make them feel good about themselves. Suppose again you are a sociologist with Marxist views and your working-class respondents say that they have no interest in their fellow workers. In fact, many cannot wait to make enough money to send their children to posh schools so they can escape their class background. You may not like these answers, but you have to report them faithfully. Nor should you at any point prompt or suggest an answer. If you do, you may get the answer you want to hear (many people being friendly or perhaps just wanting to get rid of you), but you would thereby be engaged in an ideological, not a sociological, exercise. Because we are human and dealing with human behaviour (not something like CO_2 emissions, atomic matter or molecules), it is even more important that we do not cheat!

SOCIOLOGY AS CRITIQUE AND ITS PUBLIC RESPONSIBILITY

If sociologists have to be careful to ensure their evidence and research methods reach a standard that is above reproach, does that mean that they are prevented from commenting on the great moral issues of our time – issues like war, poverty or inequality? The answer is 'no' and to help us through this tangled argument, we will rely on the 2004 presidential address given by the president of the American Sociological Association (ASA) Michael Burawoy, which was regarded as so important that it was published twice – first in the *American Journal of Sociology*, then in the *British Journal of Sociology*. Burawoy (2005: 260) recognizes that many sociologists were drawn to the discipline because of their passion for social justice, political freedom and human rights – in short, for a better world than the one we see around us. The majority of sociologists thus often find they are engaged in a critique of the existing order as well as a description and analysis of it. This is not because we always look on the negative side of life, but because many of us wish to find those structures, practices and possibilities that can release human potential, not crush it.

This ethical dimension of many sociologists' lives has led to passionate debates at sociology conferences. How far can we express our ethical selves and do such stances contradict our professional standards? Burawoy (2005: 262) recalls two contradictory resolutions at the annual conferences of the ASA. In 1968, when asked to support a resolution decrying American involvement in the Vietnam War, two-thirds of the membership *opposed* the ASA, taking this position on the grounds that it was professionally inappropriate, even though a narrow majority (54 per cent) of the members were against the war when individually polled. This conformed to the proportion in the population who were against the war. In 2003, a similar resolution against the war in Iraq resulted in two-thirds of the members *favouring* the resolution, when at the time (May 2003), 75 per cent of the American population supported the Iraq War. (Two years later, public opinion moved much closer to that of the members of the ASA.) This account is illustrative and suggests that the ASA is currently more representative of the more radical drift of the 13,000 career sociologists in the USA, who include more women, ethnic minorities and, in its leadership, the generation radicalized by the 1960s.

Clearly, sociologists are somewhat divided. Some centre their work on professional recognition and do not venture far outside the academy, others work with policy-makers. Others again feel the need to engage with the public and maintain that engagement is a legitimate extension of their roles as sociologists. Burawoy avers that though there are some overlaps between these categories and some of us move between them, in effect, we now practise four kinds of sociology – professional, critical, policy and public (Table 1.1).

TABLE 1.1	**Burawoy's four types of sociology**

Type of sociology	Common cognitive practices	Target audience
Professional sociology	Advanced theoretical and empirical work, explicit scientific norms	Peers, those who read professional journals
Critical sociology	Foundational and normative, driven by moral vision	Critical intellectuals, those who engage in internal debates about sociology
Policy sociology	Empirical, concrete, applied and pragmatic	Policy-makers in government, business and the media
Public sociology	More accessible/relevant theoretical and empirical work, lectures and media appearances	Designated publics including students, the local community and religious groups

SOURCE: Adapted from Burawoy (2005)

As seen in Table 1.1, one of Burawoy's 'designated publics' is our students – you. He is one of the few prominent sociologists who have recognized that sociology students are now an important force to be considered in their own right. There are a lot more sociology students for a start – 23,000 graduate with sociology 'majors' in the USA each year, while in 2004 about 22,000 applied for sociology degrees in the UK. Even in a small country like Hungary, nearly 2,000 sociology students are enrolled. Moreover, we cannot continue to think of our students as if we were the masters/mistresses and they the passive apprentices – blank slates upon which we etch our mature reflections. Instead, Burawoy (2005: 266) asserts:

We must think of [our students] as carriers of a rich lived experience that we elaborate into a deeper self-understanding of the historical and social contexts that have made them who they are. With the aid of our grand traditions of sociology, we turn their private troubles into public issues. We do this by engaging their lives, not suspending them; starting from where they are, not from where we are. Education becomes a series of dialogues on the terrain of sociology that we foster – a dialogue between ourselves and students, between students and their own experiences, among students themselves, and finally a dialogue of students with publics beyond the university.

SOME MILESTONES IN THE HISTORY OF SOCIOLOGY

We have mentioned the 'grand traditions of sociology' and, indeed, the discipline of sociology is much older than many of its students believe. It has its roots in the period after the **French Revolution**, when political conflict, rapid urbanization and social turmoil convulsed European societies.

The **French Revolution** was a series of social upheavals that began in 1789 with peasant revolt, monarchical collapse and moderate middle-class leadership. From 1793 to 1795, the urban poor of Paris and other cities, led by radicals such as Robespierre, pushed the revolution in a more violent and nationalist direction. An increasing involvement in European wars also led to the successful mass mobilization of citizen armies and the centralization of power.

Intellectuals sought to explain both the bewildering chaos and the new possibilities around them. Karl Marx saw the French Revolution and the European revolutions of 1830 and 1848 as harbingers of a new revolutionary order that would be ushered in by a class-conscious and politically motivated working class (he called workers 'the proletariat' after the dispossessed class of ancient Rome). By contrast, Herbert Spencer, Marx's contemporary, was more interested in how a social order was re-created after dramatic events like the French Revolution and how long-term evolutionary change could be reaffirmed. This historical corrective reminds us that sociology has important conservative roots and was often used to find traditional solutions to what was seen as moral decay, social breakdown and the loss of respect for old ways and old customs.

Sociology students are often shocked to learn that sociology departments were, occasionally, used for explicitly repressive purposes. The most notorious case was the 'sociological department' founded by Henry Ford, the great car manufacturer, in his River Rouge plant in Michigan in 1913. The plant was innovative – indeed, it was described as an 'industrial cathedral' – and Ford paid good wages, US$5 a day, twice the minimum wage. But the wage was still insufficient to stabilize the very rapid labour turnover of the largely immigrant workforce. Ford decided that surveillance was necessary and the sociological department was instructed to monitor workers' conduct at home and at the factory. Those who joined the union, drank excessively, had health problems or gambled were fired. Workers were told how to manage their household finances and lead a life of disciplined sobriety. Even their sexual conduct was monitored by the 1,000 informers who reported to the department. Above all, they were taught to be 'Americans' – to drop or downgrade their prior ethnic affinities and accept the American way of life (Hooker 1997).

We mention Ford's department not because it is typical – it is hardly that – but because we need to alert you to the complexity and multiple roots of the discipline, its use and possible abuse. To get a sense of the evolution of the discipline since the middle of the nineteenth century, we provide a timeline (Box 1.1) of some salient events.

Box 1.1	Timeline in sociology

1842 The publication of *Positive Philosophy* by **Auguste Comte** (1798–1857) (see Comte 1853). He was the first to use the word 'sociology'. Comte wanted to find regularities, even laws, in social life that resembled Newtonian physics. He allied sociology to the scientific models of the Enlightenment. His ideas were linked to those of scholars in the other two major social sciences – economics and political science. They dismissed philosophy as too speculative, theology as the rationalization of superstition, and history as too subjective and superficial. These writers saw themselves as champions of a new way of understanding reality. They wanted to establish general laws of human behaviour, to formulate hypotheses that could be tested and to develop strict scientific methods (Wallerstein 1996: 31).

1848 The publication of *The Communist Manifesto*, by **Karl Marx** and **Friedrich Engels** (1967), who argued in this influential pamphlet that:

'The history of all hitherto existing society is the history of class struggles.' They saw an increasing impoverishment of the workers, whom, they thought, would become class conscious and throw off the yoke of capitalism. Karl Marx (1818–83), who worked in Germany, France and Britain, saw the waves of rebellion in 1830 and 1848 as ushering in a new era of social revolution. He was consequently interested in class conflict and the dynamics of large-scale social change. He sought to be international in his outlook. Marx wrote on India and the USA and, as his socialist ideas caught hold, he found himself in dialogue with revolutionaries from Russia to Cuba. His daughter, **Eleanor Marx**, became a pioneer feminist thinker and agitator.

1874   The publication of **Herbert Spencer's** (1820–1903) *Principles of Sociology* (see Spencer 1902). He proposed an organic theory of society (likening it to a living organism) and was preoccupied with slow, long-term evolutionary change. His work paralleled Charles Darwin's writings on the animal and plant worlds. (Incidentally, it was he, not Darwin, who coined the expression 'the survival of the fittest', a notion that resonated well with the unregulated capitalism of the period.)

1892   The foundation of the first department of sociology in the USA. Three years later, the *American Journal of Sociology*, still the leading journal in the field, was established. The discipline was often concerned with the adaptation of new immigrants to their new settings, with urban settlement patterns (the 'Chicago School' produced celebrated studies in this field), industrial relations and community studies.

1898   In France, the renowned French sociologist **Emile Durkheim** (1858–1917) founded the *Année Sociologique* in this year. It contained a mix of material on law, customs, religion and social statistics. Durkheim himself concentrated on the elements that bind societies together, an issue close to the heart of a society that had experienced the disintegrating effects of revolution and an invasion (in 1871) by Prussia. Durkheim understood that his discussion of how social order and consensus were to be reached necessarily involved comparison with other groups. He tried to understand the religious practices of the Australian Aborigines and systematically collected statistics from a number of European countries to undertake his famous study of suicide.

1891–1903 Over these years, **Charles Booth's** surveys *Life and Labour of the People of London* were published (Booth 1967). These surveys covered the 'unoccupied classes', inmates of prisons and workhouses and recipients of 'outdoor relief'. By interviewing several thousand people, rich and poor, Booth provided a convincing picture of life in Britain and the desperate plight of the poor. His surveys are often cited as classics of this type of sociological enquiry.

1907   **L. T. Hobhouse** was elected to the first chair in sociology in Britain, at the University of London. Hobhouse was an important inspiration behind the social reforms of the Asquith government and made fundamental contributions to the evolving theory and method of the discipline. His book *The Elements of Social Justice* (1922) is a useful statement of his guiding ideas.

1920–21 The publication in German of **Max Weber's** (1864–1920) best-known book *The Protestant Ethic and the Spirit of Capitalism* (1977). In addition to work on his native Germany, Weber wrote on Spain, Italy and ancient Rome and was fascinated by the different ways in which religious belief facilitated or inhibited the development of capitalism. He was the first sociologist of comparative religion, having examined

Hinduism, Confucianism, Buddhism and Judaism, in addition to his famous studies of Protestantism. He had also sketched out an ambitious study of Islam. In his engagement with Marxism, he sought to develop a holistic sociology that added to the issue of class identities, questions of status, political power and values, which together would define the opportunity structure available to people.

1959 **Mysore Narasimhachar Srinivas** (1916–99) was invited to Delhi University to establish and head the Department of Sociology at the Delhi School of Economics, founded in emulation of the London School of Economics. In his *Religion and Society among the Coorgs of South India* (1952), Srinivas showed that the caste system was more porous than Western scholars had assumed. Social mobility was facilitated by the adoption of the language and social habits of higher castes by lower castes – a process Srinivas described as 'sanskritization'. Although sociology is still a poor cousin to economics at the Delhi School, Srinivas made an important start in establishing and promoting the discipline in the world's second most populated country.

1979 The foundation of the Chinese Sociological Association in the largest country in the world after years when the Communist Party of China (CPC) was suspicious of the discipline. Professor **Fei Xiaotong** was elected as its first and second chairperson. The association still defers to political orthodoxy, though it has wisely appropriated Mao Zedong's 'one hundred flowers' speech. According to its website (http://www. sociology.cass.cn/english/Associations/CSA/default.htm), the association aims to:

> implement the guideline of 'Let one hundred flowers bloom, and one hundred schools of thought contend' under the CPC leadership and under the direction of Marxism–Leninism, Mao Zedong Thought and Deng Xiaoping Theory; undertake sociological research in light of China's practices in a view to develop the academic cause of sociology and serve the socialism-building of a wealthy, democratic, civilized and modernized China.

1994 The year that the sociologist **Fernando Henrique Cardoso** was elected in a landslide victory to the presidency of Brazil. (Cardoso was previously the president of the International Sociological Association.) Although re-elected to a historic second term, he lost to Luiz Inacio Lula da Silva (the left-wing candidate) in 2004.

1999 The well-known British sociologist, then director of the London School of Economics, **Anthony Giddens**, took 'The Runaway World' (what is commonly called globalization) as the theme of his Reith lectures, the BBC's prestigious annual series of lectures.

2001 The year in which the number of current serving UK vice-chancellors (equivalent to presidents of US universities) comprised seven established sociologists.

2006 The first time that the International Sociological Association (ISA) had ever held its periodic conference on the continent of Africa. The theme of the first ISA World Congress of Sociology in Africa was 'The Quality of Social Existence in a Globalising World'.

Figure 1.1 **Ari Sitas (1952–)** A Lebanese South African who is a poet and dramatist as well as a professor of industrial sociology at the University of KwaZulu-Natal and one of the organizers of the first ever International Sociological Association congress in Africa.

Figure 1.2 **Fernando Henrique Cardoso (1931–)** Former president of Brazil and earlier of the International Sociological Association. He undertook major research on Brazil's poorer regions and on dependency theory. He speaks English, French, Portuguese and Spanish fluently.

Figure 1.3 **Mysore Narasimhachar Srinivas (1916–99)** One of India's most distinguished sociologists. His work on how lower castes emulated higher castes and on village life in India has helped to explain this complex society to non-Indians and Indians alike.

THE CHANGING CONTEXT OF SOCIOLOGY

In this book we are concerned with the way in which the subject of sociology illuminates our present world and will have to respond to the future reshaping of all societies. In common with other disciplines, sociology is required to expand dramatically its geographical and intellectual horizons – recognizing that the natures of local communities and national societies are being challenged by profound changes at the global level. This book is concerned with showing how these global changes can best be understood.

We know that the relationships between time, place and culture yield different social outcomes and these require different forms of sociological investigation. Even the topics that attract the attention of sociologists change as the context changes. Sociologists have to be responsive to important historical events while being aware that international, regional, national and local settings influence the character of the discipline. That context influences content is, by the way, true of other disciplines too, including natural science, engineering and medicine. However, it is particularly true of sociology, given that the discipline links the observer to the subject of the observation so directly and it has become such an important means of interpreting contemporary social life in an imaginative and critical way.

One important limitation of the discipline of sociology is that, despite the universalizing ambitions of a number of the founding figures, it has taken a long while for the discipline to expand beyond its heartland in Western industrial societies. The study of non-Western societies was, at first, left to anthropologists who found it difficult to develop general laws applicable to all humanity. They found difference rather than commonality. Looking back at the period of colonialism, one could make out a strong ethical case for preserving difference. Liberal anthropologists defended the integrity of 'their tribe' against what they considered the corrupting influences of colonial administrators, traders and missionaries. Canadian fur traders bribing Hurons with whisky, the forcible adoption of Aboriginal children by white Australians or the spreading of fatal venereal disease to the Polynesians are hardly edifying moments in the history of encounters between European and non-European peoples.

However, as we show in subsequent chapters, it is now too late to wrap people in cellophane and freeze them in a time warp. Our increasing interconnectedness and interdependency have meant that we cannot preserve tribal iceboxes or human zoos. We live in an interdependent globalizing world, in the wake of the Universal Declaration of Human Rights proclaimed in 1948. There are now insurmountable practical and ethical difficulties in defending the practice of cultural separateness. Nor can the differences between peoples be explained simply by giving each of them a different voice. We may not yet be able to develop a universal positive science, as Comte wanted. Yet we need to find ways of comprehending and comparing societies and peoples that apply from Afghanistan to Zimbabwe, from the Aborigines to the Zulus. We require, in Albrow's (1987) telling phrase, 'a sociology for one world'.

ONE STEP BACK: THE REVERSION TO NATIONAL SOCIOLOGY

How are we to reach the goal of a sociology for one world? Can we find anything of value in returning to the history of the discipline? As we have seen, some of the trailblazers of sociology – particularly Auguste Comte, Herbert Spencer, Karl Marx, Max Weber and Emile Durkheim – were in fact very interested in countries outside their own. But, despite this promising beginning, from about 1914 to the end of the Second World War, comparative and holistic sociology went into decline in Europe and North America. This probably had something to do with the growth of intense nationalist feelings and the attempt to fabricate exclusive, powerful, modern nation-states.

As the First World War approached, imperialist and nationalist sentiments were easily inflamed while inter-European rivalry was raging remorselessly. These big events and large-scale forces can often be tellingly illustrated by small examples. Witness the case of the humble dachshund, the German 'sausage dog'. The British are world renowned for their love of animals – the Royal Society for the Protection of Cruelty to Animals was founded as early as 1824. Yet in 1914, as war approached, dachshunds were stoned in the streets of London as a living symbol of the hated 'Hun'. George V, the British monarch, dropped all his German titles and adopted the appellation 'Windsor', the name of one of his

Xenophobia The hatred and fear of foreigners.

The **Great Depression** (1929–39) was the most severe capitalist downturn ever known. By late 1932, in the USA alone, around 15 million workers were unemployed. The crisis began in October 1929 when company share values on New York's Wall Street stock exchange crashed. A number of stockbrokers and investors jumped to their deaths from their skyscraper offices. A series of escalating bank and currency collapses soon turned the crisis into a global one. German Nazism and Japanese Fascism were partly caused by the world economic collapse.

castles. The Battenbergs or 'Mountbattens' said 'call me Windsor'. German Knights of the Garter were struck off the roll, while grocers with German names were accused of poisoning the public. In this frantic atmosphere, those espousing international causes were derided. Even the international labour movement found itself at the mercy of **xenophobic** passions. Instead of accepting the Marxist message that 'workers have no country', young men lined up to fight for their emperors, tsars, kings and kaisers. Many perished in the withering shellfire and churning mud of the killing fields in France.

Sociologists were inevitably caught up or caught out by this nationalist fervour. Like other academics in that country, in Russia they became little more than servants of the state. Others, who were dissenters or members of victimized minority groups, left their countries of birth. Prominent Italian, Austrian and German scholars had to flee from Fascism and Nazism to other European countries or the USA. After the Second World War, these scholars were to play an important role in internationalizing the discipline and made major contributions to the intellectual life of their adopted countries.

In the period up to 1945, sociologists in the USA and the UK remained intelligent observers and critics of their own societies, but they rarely lifted their heads above the concerns immediately around them. In front of their eyes were the mass unemployment caused by the **Great Depression**, the mobilization of men for the front and the deployment of women on the 'home front'. Discussions of social problems and social realities were focused almost entirely on local community, urban or national contexts.

TWO STEPS FORWARD: THE BEGINNING OF GLOBAL SOCIOLOGY

The end of the Second World War heralded a new balance of international forces. Japan was one of the defeated countries, yet it had given the European powers a bloody nose and had brought the USA into the war. Without Uncle Sam and the devastating atomic bombs that the US air force dropped on two Japanese cities, it is doubtful that the Japanese armies could have been contained. The Second World War also shifted the locus of political power from Europe to the USA (which had already asserted its industrial strength) and also to the Soviet Union; though it was clear even in 1945 that Moscow was punching above its economic weight. The USA (itself a former colony) had no stake in protecting the European empires, which rapidly began to unravel under the impact of nationalist pressures. This shifting balance of power prompted four sets of questions and preoccupations for sociologists and other social scientists:

1. Like other observers, sociologists asked what accounted for Japan's sudden rise to power. Were there certain elements in Japanese culture that generated forms of work and military discipline that had propelled the country into the first rank of industrial powers? Was there some connection between the revival of Shintoism and Japan's interest in European science, akin perhaps to the

Enlightenment or even to Max Weber's idea that particular kinds of religion were linked to the development of capitalism? Was the restoration of the emperor the crucial historical event, or the end of feudalism in 1869? Much of the history and basic dynamics of the Japanese spurt to industrial, political and military prominence was simply inexplicable to all but a few non-Japanese social scientists, the sociologist Ronald Dore (see Box 1.2 below) being an honourable exception.

2. Was the USA able to stabilize the world through a mutual threat of annihilation with the Soviet Union? The very acronym MAD (mutually assured destruction) suggested a sort of crazy logic, depicted brilliantly in the classic movie, *Dr Strangelove*. The 'iron curtain' separated East from West, but there were intense and often dangerous rivalries in the space race and even in sporting contests. The East German government is now known to have authorized the doping of many of its athletes to show the superior glories of state socialism. (They did win an amazing clutch of medals.) Passionate debates arise over the virtues and drawbacks of planning or the market, an assured basic standard of living or individual freedom. These debates were played out in the countries in what was then called 'the Third World', whose allegiance was eagerly sought by the rival superpowers.

3. The old empires were clearly on the way out. Not without bloodshed and mayhem, the British were persuaded to leave India, which became independent in 1947. This was the prelude to the decolonization of the rest of Asia, Africa, the Middle East and the Caribbean. The Dutch left Indonesia in 1949, though the French and Portuguese slugged it out against the tide of history. Eventually they too were forced to abandon their colonial possessions in Asia and Africa, often retreating in the face of armed rebellion. The French left Algeria in 1962, while former Portuguese Mozambique became independent in 1975.

4. There were new actors on the world stage. People of all colours and backgrounds, not just white people, were 'making history'. It had been arrogant and even absurd for white people to believe that they were the only ones who counted. But given the extent of their empires, the superiority of their arms and the dominance of their technology and manufacturing products, that is exactly what many Europeans and US citizens did believe. All these fanciful convictions of racial superiority were shaken to the roots after 1945.

As you might expect, some people continued to live in the past. However, far-sighted thinkers and politicians realized that the post-1945 period required a change in public consciousness. One example of the new openness was the foundation in Paris of the United Nations Educational, Scientific and Cultural Organization (UNESCO) in 1946. The preamble to its constitution set the tone. This declared that:

> the great and terrible war which has now ended was a war made possible by the denial of the democratic principles of the dignity, equality and mutual respect of men and by the propagation in their place, through ignorance and prejudice, of the doctrine of the inequality of men and races.

These days we would of course add 'women' to such a statement, though no doubt the drafters intended to be inclusive. The members of UNESCO's governing committees set themselves the task of studying the basis of racial discrimination and over a period of 30 years provided a number of authoritative statements that were agreed by panels of eminent geneticists, biologists, anthropologists and sociologists. Article 1 of the General Conference of 1978 proclaimed that 'All human beings belong to a single species and are descended from a common stock. They are born equal in dignity and rights and all form part of humanity' (Banton 1994: 336–7).

Not only was there a shift in mood towards universalism but there was also a legion of societies 'out there' whose conditions of life, fates and fortunes were largely unknown to Western scholars. Led by the USA, but soon followed by Japan and the European countries, 'area studies' programmes were announced or augmented. Scholars were encouraged to find out anything and everything about the formerly colonized countries as well as about the communist countries behind the Iron Curtain. Moreover, significant bodies of writers and academics, sociologists included, from outside Europe and North America began to make their mark.

Latin America had been decolonized in the nineteenth century, so it was perhaps not surprising that Chilean, Brazilian and Mexican sociologists had time to develop sophisticated theories to explain why their societies remained economically and culturally dependent, despite being politically autonomous for decades. One important Latin American sociologist addressing this issue was Fernando Henrique Cardoso (see Cardoso and Falleto 1969), later the president of Brazil. Other influential contributions came from the Egyptian political economist Samir Amin (1974), the Martinican psychiatrist and political activist Frantz Fanon (1967) and sociologists like the Pakistani Hamza Alavi (1972) and the Jamaican-born Orlando Patterson (1982) who wrote key works on the evolution of slavery and freedom.

Gradually, sociologists working in Europe and North America began to appreciate that they needed to widen their comparative perspectives. In so doing, they found themselves returning to some of the concerns of the pioneer sociologists, finding fresh possibilities of understanding other societies and helping to illuminate their own cultures and contexts. Their theories were many and diverse and we can share only a little of this new ferment of ideas in a few examples (see Box 1.2).

Box 1.2

Post-1945 Western sociologists and the non-Western world

- **Barrington Moore** (1967, 1972) thought that a comparative historical sociology was needed to understand why some societies prospered while others languished, why some turned into democracies and others dictatorships.

- **Clark Kerr** (1983) maintained that the varying paths taken by different societies were ultimately to be joined by the unifying logic of industrialization. Thus, whatever the political differences between regimes, 'convergence' arose because economic goals provoked certain common responses.

- Other US sociologists like **Talcott Parsons** (1971) tended to talk in terms of a wider notion of 'modernization', which involved the 'non-Western' world 'catching up' with the achievements of the 'Western' world and Japan.

- Some European sociologists (discussed in Taylor 1979) returned to Marxist ideas of the successive stages of what Marx called 'modes of production' (slavery, feudalism and capitalism are examples of modes of production). Many of the poor countries, they suggested, were locked in an uneasy middle ground between the capitalist and non-capitalist modes of production.

- The German scholar **André Gunder Frank** (1967, 1969), who worked in Chile for a number of years, was very influenced by the theories of 'dependency' and 'underdevelopment' current in Latin American circles. He both popularized their work by writing in English and extended it in new directions.

- Although the term originated with a French journalist, the English sociologist **Peter Worsley** (1967) also drew on writings by Latin Americans, Asians and Africans to define the distinctive characteristics of the 'Third World', one that was relatively poor, neither capitalist nor communist, Western or non-Western.

- **Ronald Dore** learned his Japanese during the Second World War and is one of a handful of Western sociologists who has been acclaimed in Japan for his understanding of Japanese society. His major books in the 1950s and 60s were *City Life in Japan* (1958), *Land Reform in Japan* (1959) and *Education in Tokugawa Japan* (1965), when he was largely concerned with describing and analysing the remarkable process of Japanese industrialization and modernization. He has been working on Japan for about 60 years and was elected to the Japan Academy in 1986 as an honorary foreign member.

- **Ulrich Beck** updated *The Risk Society* (1992) with *World Risk Society* (1999a), now arguing that we are increasingly intermeshed with other societies by virtue of 'manufactured risks' that cross boundaries. Unlike the earthquakes and floods of old, our risks, which operate on a global level, might arise from nuclear energy, carbon consumption, genetic engineering and the cutting down of the tropical rainforests.

What emerged from the disparate contributions of Western sociologists was that the paths of development or underdevelopment of individual countries could not easily be predicted. As Crow (1997: 130–57) argued, in some respects this still holds true. The rich countries usually become richer and some poor countries collapse into stagnation, poverty and disorder. However, what was less predictable was that *the pattern of polarization is unstable and inconsistent.* Within what used to be called the 'Third World', some countries 'took off' and succeeded in economic terms while others bumped along at the bottom. We can contrast, for example, the case of Ghana (not, by the way, the poorest country in West Africa) with South Korea. Crow (1997: 130) cites data showing that whereas the two countries shared a similar **gross national product** (GNP) per capita in the 1960s (about US$230), three decades later South Korea was ten to twelve times more prosperous.

Again, there were strong social and cultural contrasts between countries. Some, like Singapore and Japan, appeared seamlessly to adapt the values of Western countries in their own settings, or to develop a novel and creative synthesis between local and imported cultures. Others, including some societies in the

Gross national product is a common measurement used by economists to assess a country's wealth.

Middle East, found that the religious convictions of their populations jarred with the largely secular, consumerist culture of the West. Many societies that had historically been characterized by large rural populations and agrarian pursuits now suddenly had bloated urban concentrations with massive levels of unemployment. Some suggested that they became 'dual societies' – Westernized in urban, industrialized areas, yet retaining a strong local identity in the countryside.

If we take into account the diversity of the societies previously classified under the rubric **THIRD WORLD** and the historical rhythms of fortune and misfortune for all countries, it becomes apparent that classifying countries into different subsections of the globe is a perilous and inexact business. Moreover, as we see later in this book, there is a high level of interpenetration between countries (through travel, migration, financial flows and cultural borrowings, to name but a few factors). Sociologists found that it was increasingly difficult to isolate a country and declare that all people living there comprised a single society. In effect, they could not be sure of the difference between the 'internal' and the 'external'.

key
concept

THIRD WORLD This expression was used mainly during the Cold War period to distinguish the non-aligned poor countries from the First World (the rich capitalist democracies of the West) and also from the Second World (the communist-led countries of the Soviet bloc). Increased differentiation between the rich and poor countries of Asia, Africa, Latin America and the Middle East, together with the political collapse of nearly all the communist countries, has meant that the term is of less and less use. Although countries are still highly unequal in their wealth and power, they do not fit neatly into three groups.

Wallerstein (1974: 51) made perhaps the most daring and important response to this problem (see Global Thinkers 1). In the opening book of a series of works, he advanced the notion of 'the modern world system'. Having considered the difficulties of arranging the world into neat hierarchies and isolating the nation-state as the primary unit of sociological analysis, Wallerstein decided he would

> abandon the idea altogether of taking either the sovereign state or that vaguer concept, the national society, as the unit of analysis. I decided that neither one was a social system and that one could only speak of social change in social systems. The only social system in this scheme was the world system.

This declaration symbolizes what an increasing number of sociologists have come to realize. We have to try to think globally, recognizing that while social changes may vary considerably in each setting, there are overarching processes and transformations that operate at a global level and impact to one degree or another on everybody.

Global Thinkers 1   **IMMANUEL WALLERSTEIN (1930–)**

Immanuel Wallerstein pioneered 'world system theory', one of the most important accounts of large-scale social change since the 1970s. At the beginning of The Modern World System *(1974: 15), Wallerstein boldly announced that 'in the late fifteenth and early sixteenth century, there came into existence what we may call a European trade economy … it was different, and new. It was a kind of social system the world has not really known before and which is the distinctive feature of the modern world system.' The book was the opening salvo in a stream of publications on the modern world system, written by Wallerstein himself, and his colleagues and associates at the Fernand Braudel Center at Binghamton (upstate New York). The Braudel Center's journal, simply titled* Review, *also carries the debate forward. What was hidden behind Wallerstein's apparently simple declaration was a challenge to a number of conventional understandings of the world:*

■ *For Wallerstein, political structures (like empires and states) were given undue importance, and instead he laid emphasis on interpenetrating trade networks that crossed state boundaries. Transnational competition for labour, market share and raw materials were what drove the world system forward and linked it together. This emphasis on trade led many scholars to accuse Wallerstein of being 'an economic determinist'. Despite writing extensively on culture, social movements and politics, he has never entirely shaken off this charge.*

■ *In line with his demotion of formal political ideologies, he was not taken with the division of the world into 'First' (rich capitalist), 'Second' (communist state-planned) and 'Third' (poor Southern) worlds. Instead he proposed an alternative trichotomy – core, semi-peripheral and peripheral. Of course there is a resemblance to the '3 worlds' theory, but there are important differences too. The core societies draw profit from the peripheral societies, while the peripheral societies are underdeveloped because they are locked in a subordinate relationship to the core. However, ascending peripheral and declining core societies can move to the semi-periphery. The great virtues of this model were to insist that all societies were locked into* one *world system and that there could be movement within the system. (The rise of China and India is better explained by world system theory than by 3 worlds theory.)*

■ *Wallerstein was able to locate and integrate many units of social scientific analysis – states, nations, regions, classes, ethnic groups – into a whole. Their particular structure, function and trajectories could be understood by situating them with the world system and observing their relationship one to another. This notion of evolution and causality depends greatly on accepting the metaphor of 'a system', whereby components are, by definition, interrelated, interacting and interdependent. While this is a possibility, it may be that the units are somewhat more anarchic, more sporadically connected to the whole and more autarkic than Wallerstein allows.*

We have hinted at some problems with Wallerstein's commanding synthesis. More explicit attacks were mounted by Abu-Lughod (1989), who suggested that Wallerstein had totally missed prior non-European world systems. Others argued that world systems alone could not explain the collapse of state communism in 1989. Again, a number of commentators have maintained that Wallerstein does not allow a sufficient place for politics and cultural analysis in his arguments, a charge Wallerstein (1989, 1991) denied. Despite such criticisms, his theory remains an influential and powerful current in global sociology.

SOURCES: Wallerstein (1974, 1989, 1991); Abu-Lughod (1989); Hall (1996)

REVIEW

Sociology has its 'grand traditions' that constitute the mainstream of the discipline. It also has many tributaries, streams and no doubt stagnant pools where some of us have wandered. Because the discipline is diverse and plural, we needed to identify some key starting points. We argued that:

■ The discipline draws on its origins in Enlightenment thought and has a powerful current of scientific, *positivist* thought.
■ Because we are dealing with human nature and social conduct, we need to identify commonalities but also differences, as societies evolve and take different paths to development. Sociology therefore necessarily needs a *historical* and *comparative* perspective.
■ To penetrate between surface appearances and motivations, we need to include a *subjective* or *interpretative* element in the discipline.
■ While interpretative sociology might involve consideration of irrational or unintended elements in human behaviour and face-to-face methods of gathering hidden or intimate data, our *search for knowledge* must remain robust and free of ideological claims.
■ Despite our professional methods and claims, sociologists can and do intervene in important areas to provide alternative policies, self-criticism of our own theories and critiques of the existing political, social, economic and moral order. These four types of sociological practice are usefully labelled *professional sociology, critical sociology, policy sociology* and *public sociology*.

In this book, we are particularly concerned to show how these starting points can be used to develop a *global sociology*. Classical sociologists such as Marx, Weber and Durkheim undertook fundamental and important work in comparing different societies, though they never undertook systematic observations in other countries. Unfortunately, their pioneering work on international issues was displaced over the period 1914–45, when sociologists in Europe and the USA were preoccupied with the problems of their own societies. In the wake of the Second World War, a new balance of political forces led to a reawakening of comparative and international themes in sociology. This was aided by the new voices of sociologists from Asia, Africa and Latin America, while to these voices were added the insights of sociologists from the countries where the discipline had been firmly established.

Sociology has to adapt to the changing world even as it seeks to explain it. Global changes demand that we extend our state-centric theories, define new research agendas and develop an agreed comparative method. In short, the interdependence of the local, national and global demands a global outlook. This book is thus published at a particular moment in time. It is an introductory textbook, yet it is not only that, for it seeks to mark the shift in the moorings of the discipline itself. Of course, this is an ambitious claim and we do not want to be seen as unrealistic, pretentious or arrogant. Ultimately, the discipline will be transformed by the work of hundreds of theorists and thousands of those engaged in more factually based studies. Work by other social scientists in related fields will also be essential. Following in the footsteps of a few innovative sociologists before us, we have sought always to move alongside and beyond a state-centric analysis by showing how some aspects of global social change impact on and are influenced by changes at local, national or regional levels.

FURTHER READING

- If you would like to get into the theory and concepts that inform the discipline (on which we have little space to expand), a reliable account is J. Scott's *Social Theory: Central Issues in Sociology* (2004), in which there are 'focus boxes' to aid comprehension.

- Graham Crow's book *Comparative Sociology and Social Theory* (1997) gives a good account of how sociologists of development came to understand societies other than their own. Chapters 6 and 7 are particularly helpful.

- Leslie Sklair's *Sociology of the Global System* (2nd edn 1995) has been a pioneering introductory text. Despite the title, he particularly stresses the economic aspects of globalization. Another good text, with a global orientation, is John J. Macionis and Ken Plummer's *Sociology: a Global Introduction* (2005).

GROUP WORK

1. Split into three groups. Group A will revise what Auguste Comte meant by positivist sociology. Group B will find a work on social stratification in the Comtean positivist tradition. Group C will similarly find a work on patterns of crime in the Comtean mode. Nominate spokespersons and report to the class.

2. Three groups will take one of three pioneer sociologists – Karl Marx, Max Weber and Emile Durkheim – to read. What were their principal contributions to the sociological study of non-European societies?

3. Split into two groups, one concerned with 'the subordination of women in a chosen society', the other with 'world poverty'. Both will plan an intervention in public sociology. Without actually doing the research, each group will report to the class on (a) how they would research the topic, (b) how they would diffuse their results and (c) how they would seek to move people to action to ameliorate the conditions they describe.

1. Is Burawoy's distinction between professional, critical, policy and public sociology an adequate characterization of the discipline?

2. Why did sociology take a 'national turn' in the period 1914–45 and is the discipline still marked by national preoccupations?

3. Provide a sociological account of why Japan has been so successful in the post-1945 period.

4. Find through a web search or through following up on the names provided in this chapter, the principal work of an African, Asian, Latin American or Caribbean sociologist. Summarize her or his book with the particular task of finding out what you did not know before and what helps you to understand the human condition.

**WHAT'S ON
THE WEB**

- http://bitbucket.icaap.org/ Although it contains social science terms and concepts more generally, this is an online service by Athabasca University that helps to define 1,000 terms. Check our Glossary on the companion website first, then turn to this site. The same university, Canada's Open University, brings out an online journal published three times a year. See www.sociology.org. Pay particular attention to 'Tier 1' articles, ones that have been externally refereed.

- http://www2.fmg.uva.nl/sociosite/index.html This is a site, run by the University of Amsterdam, with lots of branches, including short summaries of the ideas of many prominent sociologists.

- www.soc.surrey.ac.uk/socresonline The British Sociological Association has started a highly regarded web-based journal, which carries full-text refereed articles. Called *Sociological Research Online*, it can be accessed at this site. Remember to visit the 'archive' – the button is on the strip at the top and could be made more visible.

- http://www.intute.ac.uk/socialsciences/lost.html A rich site funded by the UK Joint Information Systems Committee (linking UK universities) and the Economic and Social Research Council (ESRC), the country's main funder of sociological research.

- http://www.ifg.org/index.htm The International Forum on Globalization is an alliance of 60 scholars and a similar number of organizations designed to promote new thinking on global issues. Remember these are sociologists doing 'public sociology'.

CHAPTER 2

Thinking Globally

CONTENTS

Sociologists have always studied societies other than their own. The discipline contains a rich comparative tradition clearly traceable through the work of leading figures like Auguste Comte, Karl Marx, Emile Durkheim, Max Weber and Talcott Parsons. Nevertheless, these pioneers and many subsequent sociologists often regarded societies as if they were separate entities, each with its own clear boundaries. The focal point was to acquire an understanding of a society's *internal* dynamics and structures, its distinctive historical and cultural traditions, its unique patterns of inequality and its particular directions of social change. Until recently, this was perfectly valid and generated many useful insights. The growing significance of global changes for all societies, however, has rendered this approach and the national traditions it generated less meaningful.

In this chapter, we explore the meaning of 'globalization' and 'globality' and ask what is distinctive about the processes so described. Sociologists are notorious for coining new words and concepts. Do we require yet further additions to our terminology? Are globalization and globality new phenomena in the world and, if so, to what extent and in what senses? It will become clear that globalization has developed from immanent forces like modernity and capitalist industrialization. Nevertheless, we are not suggesting that globalization is beyond the control of human agencies. On the contrary, human actors and social organizations have been intimately involved in shaping the nature and direction of global forces in the past and there is both a need and an opportunity to take up the challenge of doing so in the future. Never before has there been a greater urgency to make decisions or resolve conflicts to secure humanity's future.

WHAT IS GLOBALIZATION?

According to Albrow (1990: 9), globalization refers 'to all those processes by which the peoples of the world are incorporated into a single society, global society'. These changes are incomplete. They are long in the making and impact on different locations, countries and individuals in a highly uneven manner. They have nevertheless increased in scope and intensity and this has been happening at an accelerating rate. We suggest that globalization is best understood as a set of mutually reinforcing transformations that occur more or less simultaneously. No single one of these is necessarily more significant than the others. One way of thinking about this is to imagine a number of threads being woven into a length of multicoloured fabric. Once woven together it would be impossible to assign a special role to each thread – each only has value or significance as part of the whole.

However, *before* our cloth of globalization has been woven, we identify at least six component strands, each of which will be explained in greater detail below:

- changing concepts of space and time
- an increasing volume of cultural interactions

- the commonality of problems facing all the world's inhabitants
- growing interconnections and interdependencies
- a network of increasingly powerful transnational actors and organizations
- the synchronization of all the dimensions involved in globalization.

CHANGING CONCEPTS OF SPACE AND TIME

Robertson (1992: 8, 27), a leading globalization theorist, shows how cultures and societies – along with their members and participants – are being squeezed together, increasing their mutual interaction. He describes this as 'the compression of the world'. As shared forces and exchanges powerfully structure our lives, so the world is becoming one place and one system. With all this comes a radical shift in our understanding of space and time. Here, Harvey's work (1989: 240–54) is especially relevant. He argues that in premodern societies, space was understood in terms of concrete localities. Movement was dangerous and difficult while war, pestilence and famine often made social life unpredictable. For most individuals it was safer to remain in those places where they and their families enjoyed fixed and unchanging rights and obligations. Similarly, the memory of past disasters, the passing of the seasons and the cycle of agricultural work determined understandings of time. However, a number of important changes, including the following, gradually altered how people understood space and time:

1. The beginnings of Arab, Chinese, Pacific Islander and European exploration and navigation of the world.
2. Copernicus's theory, published in 1543, which established that the sun, not the earth, was the centre of our planetary system.
3. The discovery of the rules of perspective in visual art.
4. The rise of humanist, people-centred ways of thinking about human life during the **Renaissance**, which tried to escape from a solely religious preoccupation with the divine as the source of all meaning and truth.
5. The increasing use of the mechanical printing press.
6. The advent of the mechanical clock.
7. The unfolding revolution in transport technology associated with industrialization.

Let us consider transport technology in more detail. Until the advent and increasingly widespread use of the steamship from the 1850s, the movement of all goods was slow, expensive and unreliable. But by the mid-twentieth century, commercial aircraft and large ocean-going vessels (superfreighters) were rapidly shrinking 'real' distances and vastly accelerating – and cheapening – the movement of people and goods.

Renaissance
The word derives from the French for 'rebirth' and refers to the revival of classical philosophy, literature and art in early modern and modern Europe. Over a period of 800 years, starting in the eighth century, artistic and scientific thinking flowered in Europe. This was accompanied by the rise of intellectual life (including the founding of universities), secular states and rational values.

TABLE 2.1	Changes in the speed of transport, 1500–1960s (kilometres per hour)			
1500–1840	1850–1930	1950s	1960s
Horse-drawn coaches/sail ships	Steamships and locomotives	Propeller air	Jet air
16 kph	56–104 kph	480–640 kph	800–1120 kph

SOURCE: Reprinted by permission of Sage Publications Ltd from Dicken (1992: 104)

Step by step, often through quite sudden bursts in technical knowledge, it became possible to measure, divide and so map the physical and temporal dimensions of the world into universal, standardized and predictable units. For example, without the geographical coordinates of longitude and latitude, travel by ship or aeroplane would be considerably more difficult. Harvey (1989: 240) calls the outcome of these ideas and discoveries 'time–space compression'.

What are the implications of this shift? Time and distance have dwindled in significance in shaping human actions. Less bound by ties to specific places and events, both space and time have become freely available for us to manipulate and control. We can accomplish far more things in any given unit of time and events crowd in on us at an ever greater speed; but with life becoming faster, so distance is conquered. Not just in metaphorical terms but in relation to our experiences, the world not only *appears* to be contracting, but in a sense *really is* shrinking. Increasingly, we judge distance in terms of the time required to complete a journey rather than by the number of kilometres between two points. Also, territory has lost its salience now that mass travel enables many to experience other cultures. Another implication of the idea of space–time compression is that our social horizons are indefinitely extended. We are less dependent on particular people and fixed social relationships. Moreover, since the 1950s, mass television ownership, coupled more recently with satellite communications, 'makes it possible to experience a rush of images from different spaces almost simultaneously, collapsing the world's spaces into a series of images on a television screen' (Harvey 1989: 293).

Thus, time–space compression, facilitated by the electronic media, has put many of the world's inhabitants on the same stage and has brought their lives together for the first time. There is scope, even for people who do not know one another personally, to interact meaningfully through internet chat rooms, blogging and other forms of virtual relations in cyberspace. For example, the various worldwide Manchester United fanzines or followers of punk rock groups are globally linked (O'Connor 2002). Those who share radical political opinions have used the internet to expose the sweatshop conditions experienced by many workers in newly industrializing countries (NICs) or to fight for fair rather than simply free trade (Klein: 2001). Yet others hatch business deals or participate in world media events via satellite television – all at the same moment in time and across vast distances.

We must remember that the world's inhabitants do not experience these changes equally. Imagine, for example, people living in two villages located 30 kilometres apart in a particularly poor region of West Africa. Here, the only telephone does not work, the roads are neglected (perhaps they are even impassable during the rainy season) and no one can afford batteries to keep the few radios working. Such people remain almost as far apart in terms of their ability to interact effectively as they were 100 years ago. In a sense, they are *more* distant from each other than people living in, say, Sydney and Paris.

INCREASING CULTURAL INTERACTIONS AND FLOWS

A second component thread of globalization concerns the increase in cultural flows propelled around the world in unprecedented quantities and with great speed and intensity. The term **CULTURE** has a multiplicity of meanings.

CULTURE Most sociologists see culture as the repertoire of learned ideas, values, knowledge, aesthetic preferences, rules and customs shared by a particular collectivity of social actors. Drawing on this common stock of meanings enables them to participate in a unique way of life. In this usage, the human world consists of a plurality of valuable cultures. Each can only be fully interpreted by its participants.

For many sociologists, culture is used very broadly to depict all the modes of thought, behaviour and artefacts that are transmitted from generation to generation by example, education or the public record. In an everyday context, however, it refers to specific intellectual, artistic and aesthetic attainments in music, painting, literature, film and other forms of expression. Culture in this sense is particularly rich in imagery, metaphors, signs and symbols. The magnificent stone sculptures (called *moais*) executed by the Neolithic peoples of Easter Island are just one illustration (Figure 2.1). With respect to this second depiction of culture, in Western societies, earlier distinctions between 'highbrow' and 'lowbrow' (popular) culture enjoyed by ordinary people are eroding. Nevertheless, it is clear that the great majority of such cultural experiences, from art galleries to pop music and blockbuster films, are now thoroughly commercialized – only available by paying money. Contemporary commercialized culture is linked especially to the rise of the mass media and the widespread dissemination of consumerist lifestyles.

Closely linked to culture, we also need to consider the growing importance of knowledge pertaining to abstract systems of understanding. Unlike culture as a way of life or as expressed in artistic forms – where meanings are rooted in particular societies or social groups – knowledge remains applicable in any context. This is because it refers to impersonal, largely autonomous and universal (scientific) truths. The elaboration of the binary codes that drive the language of computers provides a good example.

Throughout most of human history, culture and knowledge were acquired and reinforced mainly in informal, everyday learning situations associated with close relationships in family, church and community life. Their diffusion to other

Figure 2.1 *Moais* **at Ahu Akivi ceremonial site, Easter Island, *c*.1999**
The sculptures were moved about 20 kilometres and averaged 14 tonnes in weight. They were pushed along tree logs lubricated by oil from palm trees. So devoted were the islanders to appeasing the gods by making massive sculptures that they cut down all the trees and then died out because they had destroyed their environment. This experience may tell us something about the depths of unchecked human folly.

Columbus 'discovered' the 'New World' in 1492. (Of course those who were 'discovered' already knew they were there.) This opened the way for Portugal and Spain to begin colonizing the ancient Inca and other civilizations of South America. It also gave momentum to the circumnavigation of the oceans, encouraged other European powers to establish plantation economies based on African slave labour in the Americas and led to the establishment of the USA.

social contexts took place slowly and in a fragmentary way, for example through sea voyages, trade, conquest and religious proselytization. Perhaps the most far-reaching of such voyages was that undertaken by Christopher **Columbus** who, with the support of the King and Queen of Spain, set sail in 1492 across the Atlantic to get to India. Instead, he reached the Bahamas, the Caribbean and South America.

The cultural interactions arising from increased contact between peoples have transformed our experience of cultural meanings and knowledge. Ultimately, this led to an immense expansion in the scope and spread of abstract knowledge linked to science and the growing availability of mass, formal education. Moreover, the humble letter has been augmented by the telephone, the fax and electronic networks, rendering communication ever more swift and telling. The electronic mass media enable even those who lack education to encounter new ideas and experiences. Seven important consequences have followed:

1. It has become increasingly possible to lift cultural meanings out of their original societal contexts and transplant them to other societies.
2. Although cultural experiences from outside society often reach us as fragments, we now have the means to access rapidly far greater quantities of such fragmentary meaning than ever before and from a multiplicity of sources.
3. We can obtain full pictures of other lifestyles, especially through the power of visual images conveyed in television and film.

4. It is increasingly possible (and necessary to our very survival) to know about other people's cultures. If we do not, we run the risk of being excluded from many potential benefits.

5. The electronic mass media of communication, along with fast transport, have the capacity to affect all those who are exposed to them and to incorporate them into a single experience. Accordingly, we live in what McLuhan (1962: 102) called a 'global village'. This is especially evident in the case of global mega-events such as the Olympic Games of 2004.

6. We are made conscious that we live in a pluralist, multicultural world and are invited to participate in its many different possibilities embodied, for example, in cuisine, music, religious practices and marriage customs.

7. Notwithstanding the last point, Western and especially US influences appear at present to dominate the volume and character of cultural and knowledge flows. However, this is about to change, with the rise of Brazil, China, India and other powerful emerging societies adding their unique contributions to global cultural flows.

THE COMMONALITY OF PROBLEMS

Interlaced in the fabric of globalization is the growing commonality of problems facing all nations and peoples. One way of thinking about this is to use Beck's idea (1992, 1999a and 2000a) that we all now share the problems of living in a world risk society, which we discuss later in this chapter and in Global Thinkers 20. We can be sceptical about how widely such perceptions are shared, for the lives of many people are still governed by long-held social customs, deep religious beliefs and unquestioned national identities. However, it is a common perception that the world is constantly under assault. The media have long brought the events and crises taking place in near and distant locations into our living rooms on a daily and hourly basis. At the beginning of the twenty-first century people everywhere can recall at least these events:

- the destruction of the twin towers in New York on 11 September 2001
- the second invasion of Iraq in March 2003 – preceded on 15 February by at least 300 anti-Iraq War marches taking place in more than 60 cities across the world
- the plight of the people of Darfur, who were hounded out of their homes and often murdered by forces aligned to the Sudanese government in 2004
- the tsunami on 26 December 2004 when the ocean floor was ripped apart leading to the loss of 200,000 lives in 13 countries
- hurricane Katrina, which flooded New Orleans on 29 August 2004, killing hundreds and exposing the incapacity of the US authorities to bring aid to its poorest citizens.

Such events graphically remind us of our common humanity – our vulnerability to accidents and misfortunes – and the existential truth that we all inhabit the same small planet.

While startling visual images are experienced as collective shocks, there are more material reasons for our sense of empathy with other human beings. In our compressed and integrated globe, our choices not only rebound on our own lives, but also directly affect the lives of others far away. Often, we are unaware of this and do not intend our actions directly to harm distant strangers. For example, in the closing years of the last century, the most prosperous fifth of the world's population, mostly living in the advanced economies, consumed around 86 per cent of global income (McMichael 2000: xxvii). Because their global economic clout is so great, their decisions about what to produce and consume, how to invest their money, their lifestyle preferences and leisure pursuits may cause unemployment, falling export prices and loss of livelihood for workers and peasants in distant lands.

■ ■

Global Thinkers 2   **ROLAND ROBERTSON (1938–)**

Robertson's contribution to globalization studies has been extremely significant and goes back to the late 1960s. His central interest in culture, particularly religion, provided one entry point through which he gradually developed his theoretical work on globalization. We draw heavily on some of his ideas throughout the book, so here we elaborate themes not discussed fully or at all in the main text.

Thematization of the world as a single space

Robertson argues that, even though most individuals retain strong affiliations to localities, nations and peoples, it is vital to place the world as a whole and the global human condition at the centre of our thinking. Thus, despite continuing conflicts and divisions within and between societies, the world exists in its own right as an increasingly autonomous and integrated entity, with its own unfolding and inescapable logic, dynamics and integrity. Analysing it requires new conceptual tools.

Directions for global study

He suggests that there are four directions from which we can approach the study of an emergent global society and around which the world has assumed a particular overall shape. Each of these relates to a relatively autonomous but also overlapping social sphere:

- *national societies, each with its own invented traditions, territory, boundaries and state*
- *the world system of international relations between nation-states*
- *individual selves ('globalization is as much about* people *as anything else')*
- *humankind as a whole.*

The history of globalization

He suggests that globalization has continued for a long time and is not simply a product of modernity. He identifies five phases. For example, the first began in the late medieval period from around 1400 and the most recent commenced in the late 1960s (the 'uncertainty phase'). The latter has been characterized not only by accelerating technological change, increasingly numerous global actors and social movements and a heightened sense of global consciousness, but also by growing crises associated with, for example, environmental problems, growing multiculturalism and the rise of groups resistant to globalization, such as religious fundamentalists.

Wilful nostalgia

Robertson explores how modernization processes involve national elites in struggling to invent traditions, codify identity and encourage patriotism, for example by 'discovering' ancient crafts and folklore or establishing majestic state ceremonies. Although partly meant to counter the supposed collapse of traditional communities and the social and moral order they had provided, they were also being undermined by an urban, industrial society driven by market forces and contractual relations.

The local and the global

Robertson often reminds us that globalization does not mean the destruction of localities and their identities. Rather, exposure to the former compels the local to reinvent itself in the light of the incoming global by selecting and absorbing those elements it finds conducive. This is precisely what modernizing countries like Japan did in the nineteenth century; it reinvented its unique national particularity in relation to the universal models and pressures flowing in from other modernizing nations by drawing on, imitating and then rendering them 'Japanese'. Indeed, the very existence of the local or the particular has always presupposed a framework of self-understanding that involves knowledge of the universal – other peoples, countries or cultures. As with individuals or societal collectivities, identity construction always requires an 'other' or 'others' against which difference can be measured.

SOURCES: Robertson (1992, 1995, 2001); Robertson and Inglis (2004)

▪▪

Another reason for sharing concerns is that certain global problems require global solutions. Acting alone, governments cannot protect their borders, territories or the lives and well-being of their citizens from a number of situations. The cross-border fallout of radioactive material following the 1986 nuclear accident at Chernobyl, the threats to national currencies from speculation on the world's financial markets, international drug trafficking and global terrorism are all examples of relative national impotence. Only collaboration between governments and regulations at the global level can provide genuine solutions. Whether or not this will be forthcoming is open to doubt. We are uncertain how far citizens will exercise pressure on governments and agencies at both national and transnational levels.

The **biosphere** consists of the atmosphere, the oceans, lakes and rivers, and the varied and complex systems of plant life and living organisms, from bacteria to fish, animals and humans.

The impact of global industrialization on the planet's **_biosphere_** perhaps provides the most obvious and compelling example of the shared, global nature of many problems. According to Yearley (1996a: 28): 'the world's growing environmental problems are connecting the lives of people in very different societies … it is ultimately impossible to hide oneself away from these phenomena altogether'.

It is not solely the materialistic lifestyles of the world's rich minority that are responsible for global environmental devastation. In many developing countries, even the poorest and most marginalized people have been driven to abuse their own environments. This arises from rapid population growth and the pressure on poor people to cultivate steep hillsides and semi-desert. The less fortunate also often overgraze pastures already crowded with livestock and tend to strip dryland zones of their tree covering for fuel. By contributing unwittingly to soil erosion, rainfall depletion and deforestation, the world's poorest people also play a role in global climate change that affects us all.

INTERCONNECTIONS AND INTERDEPENDENCIES

Fast expanding interconnections and interdependencies bind localities, countries, companies, social movements, professional and other groups, as well as individual citizens, into an ever denser network of transnational exchanges and affiliations. Increasingly, sociologists have argued that these multiple networks, vastly empowered by the worldwide web, now provide the dominant form of social life. Thus, we live in a 'network society' (Castells 1996) and social relations are driven by a network rather than a society logic. Indeed, Urry (2000, 2003) suggests that words like networks, fluids, flows, 'scapes' and mobilities provide far more revealing metaphors for understanding the spreading, less predictable and decentralized character of contemporary life than words like society, structures and institutions, which conjure up images of territorial fixity and the detailed regulation of life within social containers (see Global Thinkers 12). These networks have burst across territorial borders, rupturing the cultural and economic self-sufficiency once experienced by nations. What drives these networks and empowers those participating in them is knowledge and information. As Castells (1996: 469) suggests, the power of knowledge flows 'takes precedence over the flows of power'. The overall cumulative impact of these interconnections has meant that societies, and their cities and regions, have tended to spread outwards so as to merge and become coextensive with other societies (see our discussion on global cities in Chapter 17). At the same time, the once clear-cut separation between the sphere of national life and the international sphere has largely broken down.

Until quite recently, most social scientists, especially political theorists, thought about interactions at the world level almost entirely in terms of interstate dealings and exchanges. Thus, nation-states were considered to be far the most dominant, if not the only, players in world affairs. Burton (1972), for example, argued that well into the twentieth century, the power each government and state enjoyed as it sought to interact with and influence other states mostly determined international relations. Such interactions might involve trade pacts, arms agreements or the pursuit of diplomatic alliances to avert wars by winning allies or isolating countries considered likely to pose a threat. Yet, Burton foresaw that because a swelling number of powerful *non-state actors* were forming relationships and pursuing their own interests, their networks of ties and connections would parallel purely interstate relations. Ultimately, as Waters (1995: 28) observed, we can expect a situation in which 'the entire world is linked together by networks that are as dense as the ones which are available in local contexts'.

TRANSNATIONAL ACTORS AND ORGANIZATIONS

Who or what are these leading non-state transnational agents whose actions have done so much to extend and intensify the interconnections across national borders since the Second World War?

Transnational corporations (TNCs)

In many ways these are the most powerful of such agents. We have a much longer discussion of TNCs in Chapter 7, but here we record three of their most important features:

- their global power and reach – half the largest economies in the world are TNCs not countries
- their key role in creating an interdependent world economy, as each TNC superimposes its own global grid of integrated production lines and investment activities across countries and continents dictated by its own, not national, needs
- their connections to the world financial system, including the instantaneous, computerized markets for foreign currencies where the equivalent of US$1.2 trillion (a million, million plus) of stateless money is bought and sold every single day.

International governmental organizations (IGOs)

Like TNCs, IGOs constitute an important case of a wider phenomenon – the rising ability of supra-state actors to shape world affairs. Indeed, it is precisely because states cannot solve global problems alone that they have established a large number of IGOs to function at their bidding. However, sometimes, as you might expect, these organizations take on lives of their own. Such bodies first began to be effective in the nineteenth century, with the growing need for rules and procedures to standardize cross-border transactions. Probably the best known IGOs are the League of Nations, established in the wake of the First World War, and the United Nations (UN) founded after the Second. While in 1900 there were 37 IGOs, by 2000 the number had risen to 6,743 (Held and McGrew 2002: 18–19).

International non-governmental organizations (INGOs)

Like their national counterparts, INGOs are autonomous organizations not accountable to governments, though they may work with them at times. Particular INGOs have often been powerful forces in world affairs. For example, peace, anti-slavery and labour organizations collaborated extensively across national borders in the nineteenth century. The numbers of INGOs have grown at a remarkable rate, especially since the 1950s. Today, their range of activities is vast, encompassing religious, business, professional, labour, political, green, women's, sporting and leisure interests among many others. You have probably heard of some of the most famous INGOs, such as Greenpeace, the Red Cross, Oxfam and Amnesty International. But there are literally thousands of others operating transnationally, and many more that mainly confine their operations within nation-states. According to Held and McGrew (2002: 18), there were more than 47,000 INGOs by 2000, though not all were equally global in scope.

Global social movements (GSMs)

Although there is a great deal of overlap between these two descriptions, we can consider that particular INGOs are nested within more general global **SOCIAL MOVEMENTS**.

key concept	**SOCIAL MOVEMENTS** are informal organizations working for change but galvanized around a single unifying issue. Examples of global social movements include the human rights, peace, environmental and women's movements (see Chapter 18).

Because the more activist INGOs mobilize world opinion on political and moral issues, their campaigns sometimes mesh with the activities of GSMs. An example of this convergence was demonstrated at the UN's 'Earth Summit' held at Rio, Brazil, in the summer of 1992. Then, an estimated 20,000 representatives from environmental and other INGOs held an alternative 'green festival' in alliance with people associated with the world's stateless and Aboriginal peoples. The global media generally found this unofficial festival more compelling than the official forum attended by governments and experts.

Diasporas and stateless people

A number of **DIASPORAS** (like the Greek, Jewish and Parsi ones) predate the nation-state. However, other diasporas arose because of religious, ethnic or political disputes with governments over the demand for full citizen rights, the recognition of semi-autonomy or the granting of independent national status. Their experience of persecution or neglect compelled some to leave voluntarily or seek asylum in other countries, thereby forming global diasporas of linked, displaced peoples (Cohen 1997). Among such groups are Africans, Kashmiris, Tamils, Sikhs, Armenians and Palestinians.

<table>
<tr><td>

key

concept

</td><td>

DIASPORAS are formed by the forcible or voluntary dispersion of peoples to a number of countries. They constitute a diaspora if they continue to evince a common concern for their 'homeland' (sometimes an imagined homeland) and come to share a common fate with their own people, wherever they happen to be.

</td></tr>
</table>

Distinct from diasporas because they have not been dispersed internationally, there are said to be around 5,000 Aboriginal 'nations' (Friburg and Hettne 1988; Robertson 1992: 171) that lack state structures and demand the return of their tribal homelands and proper recognition of their cultural identities. These Aboriginal groups, stretching across Canada, the USA, Australasia and South America, have recently formed a World Council of Indigenous Peoples. They have worked with the UN Centre for Human Rights (UNCHR) in the attempt to establish a universal declaration of rights for non-state peoples worldwide.

Like the INGOs, such groups need no convincing that in today's world the expression of local identities is only viable in a global forum and context. To this end they coordinate their struggles at the global level and try to harness media opportunities to bring attention to their plight. According to Friburg and Hettne (1988), their political activities and intentions are captured exactly in the catch phrase, 'act locally but think globally'.

Box 2.1.

Acting locally and thinking globally: the runners of Tarahumara

The Tarahumara Indians live in Chihuahua State, a remote region, high up in the mountains of northern Mexico. Here, they have earned a reputation for extra-ordinary feats of endurance, with their champion runners sometimes racing continuously for two days and nights at very high altitudes. Life for the approx-imately 60,000 Tarahumara people is arduous. Over time they have been forced to move from their original homelands by the pressures of commercial develop-ment dominated by white Mexicans, and have been pushed on to higher lands where cultivation is unrewarding. Temperatures often fall to −20°C in winter.

In the early 1990s, several years of drought – probably linked to heavy defor-estation in the area – meant that their 'normal' condition of hunger turned to famine. Most children suffer from malnutrition to some extent and among the poorest communities infant mortality may exceed 50 per cent. Sadly, these pres-sures have compelled more and more Tarahumara people to migrate in search of temporary or permanent settlement in Mexico's largest cities.

In a bid to gain the world's attention, the leaders of an organization dedicated to alleviating the Tarahumara's conditions – Wilderness Research Expeditions – encouraged their best runners to visit the USA and participate in important athletic events. Running to win international publicity and raise money for food aid began in 1993.

In late September 1996, six Tarahumara champions spent a weekend running the equivalent of four 26-mile marathon races through the Angeles National Forest in California, much of it above the snow line. In doing so they were not equipped with the high-tech, designer sports gear deemed essential by Western athletic personalities. Instead, they wore leather sandals made at home. They are said to be rather bemused by all the fuss Westerners make about the rules of competition, timetabling and accurate measurements of fixed racing distances. Moreover, they find the experience of running in major US events rather boring, since back home their races combine long-distance racing with kicking a ball up and down the mountains. Nevertheless, and with the help of Wilderness Research Expeditions, the willingness of these runners to 'go global' generated the funds to distribute 60 tons of food to the Tarahumara people between 1993 and 1996.

SOURCE: Gunson (1996)

Other transnational actors

Daily, huge numbers of ordinary citizens are engaged in forging transnational connections as they travel, alone or in small informal groups, across national boundaries. At their destinations, they may reside as temporary visitors or seek long-term settlement. Whatever their circumstances and motives, they transport their cultures and lifestyles with them while becoming exposed, to various degrees, to the host societies' cultures. Thus, global cultures are juxtaposed and sometimes merged. Among the many categories of individual or small group travellers, we can identify the following six types:

1. Migrants in search of income opportunities in the growth poles of the world economy, such as Chinese family tycoons stretching their business interests from Hong Kong to Toronto or Los Angeles (Mitchell 1995; Zhou and Tseng 2001) or poor Mexicans (Smith 1998) constructing family, religious, political and entrepreneurial linkages between their new homes in New York City and their home villages.
2. International tourists whose numbers reached over 703 million in 2002 – despite the decline of tourism in the Americas following the events of September 2001 – compared with 159 million in 1970 (www. world-tourism. org/facts/menu.htm).
3. Professionals such as lawyers, journalists, architects and scientists, many of whom, according to Hannerz (1990: 237–51), evince a cosmopolitanism that enables them to feel 'at home' anywhere in the world so that they contribute to the formation of a transnational culture and, in some situations, whose shared experience of being strangers working together on the same project away from their countries of origin may bind them together into enduring multinational friendship networks (Kennedy 2004).
4. Media, rock/pop and sports personalities such as Bono and Bob Geldorf.
5. Corporation personnel, business consultants and private entrepreneurs whose multifarious activities knit together the strands of the global economy and who increasingly share a common outlook as world economic elites (Sklair 2001; Carroll and Carson 2003).
6. A miscellaneous group including students, airline pilots, drug dealers, diplomats, au pairs and many more besides.

SYNCHRONIZATION OF ALL DIMENSIONS

We can point to a final thread in our garment of globalization. All the dimensions of globalization – economic, technological, political, social and cultural – appear to be coming together at the same time, each reinforcing and magnifying the impact of the others.

In the economic sphere, governments have lost some of their power to regulate their economies as a host of largely autonomous agents like international banks, TNCs and currency markets have flourished in the ever more integrated world economy. Although they are formed through intergovernmental agreement, bodies like the World Trade Organization (WTO) have taken on a life of their own and often compel recalcitrant governments to adopt trade policies they see acting against their particular national interest. Meanwhile, the lure of the free market has drawn many more countries into its orbit. This has allowed money values to penetrate every corner of the globe and most facets of social and cultural life.

In political life, citizens in many countries have become alienated from conventional party politics, a trend seen in the drop in voting participation in recent Western elections. This does not mean that people are detached from all forms of politics. Instead, many participate in political and social movements. These social movements may operate on a national or global level (see Chapters 18, 19 and 20). Participants in global social movements are concerned with questions such as how governments can best cooperate to counter global environmental degradation or deal with the economic insecurities resulting from the progressive worldwide deregulation of trade, capital and money markets since 1980. The anti-globalization movement (or the more appropriately named global justice movement), which first came to international public attention in December 1999 during the WTO conference at Seattle, is probably the most notable example of such a move to expand the agenda of governments away from a primary concern with military security.

There is growing mass participation in the market economy by workers, consumers, tourists, listeners and, above all, viewers. This, together with the revolutions in electronic media and information technology, has generated the basis for the enormous expansion of cultural flows across the world. Culture in all its forms – as consumer aspirations, pop or rock music, religious, moral and ethnic values or the political ideologies of democracy and socialism – has become the most recent and perhaps most potent addition to globalization. Transmission takes place through different means – through visual images in the mass media, abstract knowledge or the social milieux created by more varied interpersonal relationships. The explosive potential for enfeebling national cultures and affiliations and providing new foci of identity and collaboration between citizens of distant countries has only begun to work its way through the world order.

■ ■ ■ ■ ■ ■ ■ ■ ■ GLOBALITY: A NEW PHENOMENON

In Chapter 3 we will be reminded that some of the processes involved in globalization have long historical roots, though, as we show later in this book, a quantitative acceleration of them has recently become evident. What is distinctive and new in the world today is the emergence of 'globality'. In the 2000 edition of this book, we referred to this phenomenon as 'globalism'. However, the latter has since generally come to be equated with the neoliberal 'ideology of rule by the world market … reducing the multidimensionality of globalization to a single, economic dimension' (Beck 2000b). Accordingly, by globality we now mean the same as Robertson (1992: 132), when he defines it as the 'consciousness of the (problem of) the world as a single space'. In similar vein, Albrow (1990: 8) refers to those 'values which take the real world of 5 billion people as the object of concern … everyone living as world citizens … with a common interest in collective action to solve global problems'. In short, whereas globalization refers mainly to a series of objective changes in the world that are partly outside us, globality refers to the subjective realm. How have we internalized the changes associated with globalization so that they are now incorporated into our emotions and our ways of thinking about everyday life? There are four major aspects of globality:

■ thinking about ourselves collectively while identifying with all humanity
■ the end to one-way flows and the growth of multicultural awareness
■ the empowerment of self-aware social actors
■ the broadening of identities.

THINKING ABOUT OURSELVES COLLECTIVELY

Humankind, and not just a small coterie of intellectuals, has begun to be capable of thinking about itself collectively as one entity. For some of the time at least, our shared concern with the category 'humanity' is beginning to extend beyond our affiliation solely to people of the same ethnic, national or religious identities as ourselves. Applying this idea, Robertson (1992: 183) argues that while we are still a long way from the world being capable of acting 'for itself', the idea of this is becoming more and more significant and pressing. For example, many people, particularly young and educated people, articulate a strong conviction that everyone has certain rights as a human being. They express moral outrage when it transpires that these rights are being violated and demand that human rights are universally protected and enshrined in international conventions and laws.

This involves a clear break with even the recent past. A poignant illustration of this capacity to empathize across old divides was the successful worldwide campaign demanding the release of Nelson Mandela, who had come to symbolize the fight against **APARTHEID** and the denial of human rights in South Africa (Figure 2.2).

APARTHEID was not simply the informal practice of racial discrimination, but an elaborated ideology of state-sanctioned and legalized 'separateness', based on racial groups. The whole population was classified into four main groups – Whites, Bantu (Africans), Coloureds (people of mixed heritage) and Asians – who were provided with separate schools, universities, social facilities (even down to park benches) and housing. In practice, whites got the best deal.

key concept

GROWTH OF MULTICULTURAL AND TRANSNATIONAL AWARENESS

Perlmutter (1991: 898) argues that previous attempts by imperialistic powers to impose 'civilization' on the rest of humanity were based on what he calls a 'dominance–dependence' mode of interrelationship. Here, incorporating other groups and societies normally involved conquest. Similarly, access to the 'benefits' of the victor's civilizing values required a willingness to submit to its 'superior' laws and institutions. Now, however, for the first time in history, 'we have in our possession the technology to support the choice of sharing the governance of our planet rather than fighting with one another to see who will be in charge' (Perlmutter 1991: 901). In this view, the long era of one-sided cultural

Figure 2.2 **Nelson Mandela in March 1990 on his release from 25 years in prison**
He went on to lead the African National Congress (ANC) to victory four years later, when he became state president of South Africa. Apartheid was formally ended and full citizenship granted to all South Africans. His extraordinary dignity, wisdom and other human qualities crossed many barriers of caste, class, ethnicity, nationality and religion.

and political flows is over. At last, nations and cultures are more willing to recognize and accept cultural diversity. Increasingly, too, they regard cooperation around a set of shared values and structures as possible, necessary and desirable.

Giddens (1990: 51–7) makes a similar point when he observes that although most of the features we associate with **MODERNITY** originated in the West, these forces have now spread and flourish autonomously across the world. Each country is capable of determining its own version of modernity and projecting this onto the global order, as Japan has done during the last half-century. By dissolving the West's former distinctiveness and ability to monopolize modern forms of power, the globalization of modernity is simultaneously bringing the period of Western dominance to an end (see Chapter 3).

MODERNITY The year 1492, when Columbus reached the Americas, can be taken as a convenient symbolic marker opening the modern era. However, the orientations towards modernity only began to crystallize from the seventeenth century onwards. They involved the growth of a questing spirit, a powerful leaning towards rationality – the search for valid, verifiable knowledge – and a belief in the possibility of transforming the material world in the pursuit of social 'progress'. The project of modernity eventually boosted science and culminated in industrialization and urbanization.

REFLEXIVE SOCIAL ACTORS AND MODERNITY

Globality contains a further important subjective component. Several writers (Giddens 1990, 1991; Beck 1992; Beck et al. 1994) have pointed to the growing number of social actors who are empowered to exercise **REFLEXIVITY** in their daily lives.

REFLEXIVITY All humans reflect on the consequences of their own and others' actions and perhaps alter their behaviour in response to new information. This quality of self-awareness, self-knowledge and contemplation is of great interest to sociologists because it speaks to the motives, understandings and intentions of social actors. In contemporary societies, reflexivity is said to intensify as every aspect of social life becomes subject to endless revision in the face of constantly accumulating knowledge (see also Global Thinkers 5 and 20).

Reflexive individuals tend to be self-conscious and knowledgeable. They seek to shape their own lives while redefining the world around them. In many contemporary societies, the growing number of such individuals has begun to form a critical mass of those willing and able to activate and seize control of the dough of social life through the yeast generated by their own capacities for critical self-determination.

This widening exercise of reflexivity is partly linked to the development of mass education and the wide dissemination not just of scientific knowledge but of the principle of doubt on which scientific method is built. These have provided keys to citizen empowerment such as access to specialized systems of expertise, professional training and the means to acquire various kinds of lay expertise. Suitably armed, reflexive citizens may challenge the truth of claims put forward by governments, corporations and the scientific community itself.

Beck (1992, 1999b, 2000b) and Beck and Beck-Gernsheim (2002) articulate this idea with particular force. They argue that modernity and its consequences – relentless economic growth, the unchecked powers of military, technological and scientific institutions – now seem to threaten the viability of the planetary biosphere. Having been liberated from the risks once endemic to an era of economic scarcity (at least in the rich countries), we are now surrounded with vast, new, all-pervasive and possibly uncontainable risks. These are directly caused by the very institutions of science and industry that modernity itself engendered. At the same time, Beck argues, the once powerful identities provided by class, family, patriarchal gender relations, community or church have largely been destroyed. This, he continues, is mainly beneficial, for it has helped to enlarge the scope for exercising individual freedom, especially for women.

However, such gains come with costs. Greater personal freedom to define who we are and how we wish to live also compels us to assume full responsibility for determining our own life paths, including any mistakes we may make. Thus, we are on our own; our lives have become more insecure. We have greater freedom and more personal responsibility for managing our own lives. In a sense we have no choice now but to engage in harsh reflexive activities involving 'self-confrontation' (Beck et al. 1994: 5), while engaging in the critical appraisal of established institutions because our survival and that of the planet depend on this. The discipline of sociology is itself both a product and an outcome of our greater capacity for reflexivity.

However, one does not have to confine such insights to the sociologically trained, for the sphere of the global is no longer remote to most humans; it has become 'in here', rooted in our consciousness (Giddens 1994: 95). Because globalization has brought knowledge of other cultures into the heart of our daily lives, it has become yet another major force that fosters increasing reflexivity and individualization. According to Rosenau, the capacity for reflexivity has also increased among the most disadvantaged citizens in many developing countries. As he explains, 'today's persons-in-the-street are no longer as uninvolved, ignorant, and manipulable with respect to world affairs as were their forbears' (Rosenau 1990: 13). They have also widened their emotional loyalties far beyond immediate family and community.

A burgeoning, transnational power base of non-state organizations and increasingly connected global citizens' networks is taking shape. Many of those involved are also highly critical of the established order. This offers a potential for the formation of effective global alliances from below, as four world social forums (WSFs) comprising worldwide representatives from a kaleidoscope of people's associations and INGOs held between 2001 and 2004 have demonstrated. For example, among the many other groups represented at WSF4 at Mumbai, India in January 2004 were trade unionists from 40 different worldwide international and national labour organizations, which, among other events, held a rally, two conferences and eight workshops. Included in the trade union section of WSF4 were representatives of the Dalit Handloom Weavers Welfare Group – an Indian labour rights association that especially protects the interests of workers from the untouchable castes (Waterman and Timms 2005).

THE BROADENING OF IDENTITIES

A final subjective component of globality that is helping to change the way we construct our identities and orient ourselves towards life in the world concerns what Robertson (1992: 29) calls 'relativization' and we will call 'broadening'. Today, no person or institution can avoid contact with, and some knowledge of, other cultures. But our allegiance to the particular local cultures in which most of us remain rooted at any one point in time are altered by our comparisons with and understandings of other cultures – the local or particular ceases to provide sufficient resources to enable us to make decisions about our lives and where we belong.

However, the reverse process also becomes important to us; we need to judge and reach some decision on how we feel about other cultures in the light of our participation in the particular and the local. As Robertson (1992: 100) suggests, there is a steady increase in the interpenetration of the local and the global by each other. We can respond to the reality by selection, adaptation or resistance, as we explain below:

- *Selection:* We may select from the global only that which pleases us and then alter it so that it becomes embedded in and accommodating to local conditions and needs. Borrowing from a marketing term employed by Japanese companies that modify their global products to match and blend with each country's cultural requirements, Robertson (1992: 173–4 and 1995) describes this process as **GLOCALIZATION**. Here, the global is modified by its contact with the local. Thus, there is no homogenizing force at work here but rather various possibilities of fusion and creativity.

key **concept**	**GLOCALIZATION** A term used to describe how global pressures and demands are made to conform to local conditions. Whereas powerful companies might 'customize' their product to local markets, glocalization operates in the opposite direction. Local actors select and modify elements from an array of global possibilities, thereby initiating some democratic and creative engagement between the local and the global.

- *Adaptation:* Whether we feel moved to reject or embrace the global, our growing knowledge of the latter almost certainly heightens our awareness of the local and may serve to intensify rather than weaken our feelings of loyalty to it. Thus, it is perfectly possible to participate in the global and the local simultaneously. The British, for example, need not feel any less so because their country has become deeply immersed in the European Union (EU). Rather, their greater exposure to and increased enjoyment of continental cultures might serve to sharpen and enhance, or even help to define, a sense of Britishness.

■ *Resistance:* Another possibility is resistance. Thus, some religious, ethnic or national groups are deeply antipathetic to other cultures and try to resist incorporation in the global sphere. The mentality of 'fortress Europe' in the face of immigration and other outside influences can be observed in many EU countries, along with the rise of political parties like the Front National in France. Neo-orthodox Islamic movements in countries such as Algeria and Iran represent another example of this phenomenon, though globalization is by no means the only reason for the current strength of militant Islam (Ahmed 1992; Turner 1994: Chapter 6). Such fundamentalist religious movements are partly generated by the very knowledge of Western and other cultures – a knowledge that feeds a suspicion that the latter threaten the purity of an all-encompassing life path and truth (Giddens 2002). However, what we see here is that wherever these feelings occur, even rejections of the global are driven largely by knowledge of it. The juxtaposition of the local and global has become an important force in world politics and its impact is likely to increase.

REVIEW

In this chapter we have made a crucial distinction between the process of globalization, comprising a series of objective, external elements that are profoundly changing our world, and globality as a subjective and reflexive awareness of these changes. We have argued that our six processes of globalization are inseparable and synchronous. In identifying the four aspects relating to globality, we have suggested that the dough of social life can be manipulated when people use the yeast generated by their own capacities for critical self-examination. This emphasis is in marked contrast with much of the literature you will read, where individuals are often represented as helpless chaff, victims of the tornado of globalization. We are much more excited by the possibilities that individuals, groups and movements can use the opportunities provided by these changes to advance the common cause of humanity.

Even if the writers we cite are only partly correct in their analyses, it would seem that a challenging future beckons us, albeit a rather dangerous one. Ordinary people everywhere have an unprecedented potential to grasp the levers of change. Moreover, much of this is given added tension by our growing capacity to wonder whether certain physical and social limits may now have been reached in humanity's long scramble for material progress. If so, then the project of modernity centred on the nation-state may now need to be drastically rethought and renegotiated. Globality – as both cause and consequence of such ideas – is at the centre of an alternative vision.

FURTHER READING

- Roland Robertson is a leading sociologist of globalization who blazed the trail that others now follow. Although his book, *Globalization: Social Theory and Global Culture* (1992), is quite advanced, you should sample some chapters, especially 1, 3, 5, 6 and 12.

- David Harvey's *The Condition of Postmodernity* (1989) is wide ranging and raises many issues we discuss later on. Parts II and III are particularly relevant.

- John Urry's *Sociology Beyond Societies* (2000) is a quite difficult but useful book that expands and builds on many themes relating to the sociology of globalization developed by earlier writers.

- For a light-hearted and delightfully contrasting book that explores the exciting, exhausting and whirling nature of life under global conditions, you could try Pico Iyer's *The Global Soul: Jet-lag, Shopping Malls and the Search for Home* (2001).

GROUP WORK

1. Working in small groups and drawing on your own pooled experiences, consider all those ways in which globalization has already affected *your* personal life. Organize this list around some key themes, such as holidays, leisure, preferences in cuisine, changing loyalties to sporting teams and future career prospects.

2. List the key threads that make up the warp and weft of globalization. Do you think that one or more of these have greater significance? If so, why? Have we left out any important components in our account? Prepare a comment on the key components of globalization for your class tutor/instructor.

3. Among your close friends and family who have not studied sociology, how many would (a) readily understand what is meant by globality if it were explained to them and (b) would feel a close affinity towards its ideas? Can you explain these different propensities in terms of the particular biographies of the individuals involved?

QUESTIONS TO THINK ABOUT

?

1. To what extent does the distinction made between globalization as a set of objective processes and globality as subjective awareness hold true?

2. What is 'time–space compression'? What implications arise from this concept?

3. Identify the main forms of transnational activity in which non-state organizations, movements and individuals engage and evaluate the different ways they may contribute to globalization and globality.

4. Why is 'reflexivity' necessary to the appreciation of globalization?

WHAT'S ON THE WEB

- http://www.sociology.emory.edu/globalization/index.html This is a site directed by the sociologist Frank J. Lechner, who is one of the editors of a student reader, *The Globalization Reader*. (A 'reader' is a collection of previously published articles, usually in the form of short extracts.) To a degree, the site is built around extending the use of the book, but there is plenty of other useful material. Follow, for example, the arrows to 'Theories' and 'Debates'.

- http://www.ifg.org/news.htm The site for the International Forum on Globalization, the leading left-leaning web source for scholars and activists. Be careful to separate scholarship from advocacy. That said, there is material here that reflects research and writing from many countries and a variety of scholars not easily available elsewhere.

■ http://news.bbc.co.uk/hi/english/static/events/reith_99/default.htm This is the site for the 1999 BBC Reith lectures on the theme of 'The Runaway World', delivered by Anthony Giddens (former professor of sociology at the University of Cambridge and former director of the London School of Economics). You can read the text of and the email debate on the six lectures and, if you have the facilities on your computer, you can also hear and see the lectures as they were delivered. This is an entertaining and instructive way to get into the field of global sociology.

CHAPTER 3

Modernity and the Evolution of World Society

CONTENTS

When did humankind first become capable of understanding itself collectively? All early societies fabricated mythologies to explain their origins and separate themselves from others. For the Sioux, the creator was the 'Great Spirit', for the Yoruba 'Olodumare', for the Jews 'Yahweh' and for the Polynesians 'Maui'. Their human followers would gain protection by the fervour and constancy of their devotion. It was but a short step for scattered peoples to understand themselves as distinct 'humans' protected by their own god(s). Other people with whom they came into contact were thought of as potentially dangerous 'barbarians' or 'subhuman'. Through trade, travel and conquest, diverse and separated societies across the globe slowly began to relate to each other – though past fears were often not far from the surface.

From about the seventeenth century, the European powers began to outstrip the rest of the world in the sophistication of their ideas, the devastating force of their military technology, the strength of their navies and the organization of economic production. This astonishing transformation in Europe's fortunes eventually enabled it to spread its new institutions all over the globe and triggered the phenomenon we call 'modernity', the logical precursor to the current era of globalization.

In this chapter we examine four successive phases of modernity and global integration:

- the development of forms of proto-globalization among a number of civilizations before the modern era commenced
- the emergence of capitalist modernity in Europe and the region's rise to global dominance
- the colonial and racial domination effected by European powers in various parts of the world
- the transformations that have taken place in the world economy since the Second World War and especially the rise of the USA.

PROTO-GLOBALIZATION

Proto-globalization Early aspirations to universalism that nonetheless failed to embrace all humanity or attain global reach.

A number of the threads making up the garment of globalization described in Chapter 2 were already manifest in the world long before the rise of modern nation-states. As empires evolved and religious domains spread, forms of **proto-globalization** developed. Historians of the premodern world (Needham 1969; McNeill 1971; Roberts 1992) show how many ancient societies were connected in important ways and how cultural legacies were bequeathed by declining or conquered civilizations.

The ancient civilizations of the Middle East, China, Greece and Rome unified large areas. Even from the ninth to the thirteenth century, when Europe consisted of a patchwork of separate, fragile kingdoms and aristocratic fiefdoms, it was held together in relative tranquillity by the overarching framework of Christianity. Christianity provided the following features:

1. The cultural universalism of shared religious belief and ritual.
2. The use of Latin as a common language of interstate communication in addition to its use in church liturgy.
3. The power and status of the papacy as a mediator between states and a restraining influence on political rulers at many levels.
4. The organizational structure of the Latin Church itself, built around various monastic orders and straddling territorial boundaries.

In short, the Church functioned as a powerful and unifying trans-European body for centuries (Wight 1977: 26–9, 130–4). It was assisted by other structures, especially interstate links based on dynastic marriages, the alliances between Christian royal houses and the system of diplomacy involving rules of mutual recognition concerning emissaries and ambassadors (Bergeson 1990: 67–81).

Europe was also involved in multiple relations with other civilizations during this period. The rise and expansion of Islamic states in the seventh century eventually extended Muslim influence to North Africa and over much of Southern Europe. Muslim rulers were finally expelled from their last stronghold in Grenada, southern Spain, in 1492. The long struggle to push back the frontiers of Islam helps to account for the earlier emergence of powerful monarchies in Portugal and Spain compared with the rest of Europe. The formation of the Holy Roman Empire in AD 962 – an alliance between Christian states – was also linked to the desire to protect Christendom from external attack (Smith 1991: 59, 62).

During this period, Islamic authority, especially in southern Europe, was considerable. Islam made important contributions to the arts and sciences, the establishment of centralized forms of government and innovations in agriculture – especially the introduction of irrigation systems. These agricultural reforms later proved highly beneficial to the semi-arid countries of Spain and Portugal. The long saga of Islamic–Christian conflict, including the Crusades – designed to liberate the 'Holy Land' from Islamic control – created a legacy of mutual mistrust and misunderstanding of each other's cultures and intentions that still endures and has dangerously escalated recently.

Europe's economy and trading relations also depended on links with other civilizations. Gold, brought across the Sahara by Arab camel caravans from the mines of West Africa, was Europe's most important source of bullion from Roman times until the sixteenth century. The Spanish conquest of South America opened up silver imports (Hopkins 1973: 46). With European traders tending to run a more or less permanent trade deficit with the Orient, bullion flowed East to pay for items such as Indian textiles of unrivalled quality, silk, indigo and spices. Indeed, this trade provided the principal motivation for the first explorations of the globe by Portugal and Spain in the fifteenth century. Colonial conquests followed (Smith 1991: 70).

However, it was by no means clear that Christianized Europe would take the lead. Not only had the Islamicized countries provided important sources of knowledge, for example in mathematics, so too had India and Persia. Indeed, other civilizations had long been far ahead of Europe in many spheres. This is especially true of China from where many inventions, ideas and much technological knowledge flowed to Europe during the fourteenth and fifteenth centuries. According to Jones (1988: 73–84), even before this time the Sung dynasty in China had attained hitherto unsurpassed levels of economic development. China had developed irrigation, terracing and manuring in agriculture; the techniques involved in manufacturing iron, especially the use of coke in blast furnaces; the harnessing of water power for spinning cloth; the growth of specialized regional markets; and state investment in canals and other public assets. Some of these innovations were not widely adopted in Europe until the early eighteenth century.

Despite the significance of these early exchanges between civilizations and the expansionist ambitions of ancient empires like Rome, there are important differences between such forms of proto-globalization and the contemporary situation. This also holds for the universalizing religions of former times, including Islam and Christianity. These were universalizing in the sense that they *aspired* to reach all people. However, they never *attained* the influence that globalization and globality have achieved in today's world. There are several reasons for this:

1. The globalizing missions of ancient empires and religions did not incorporate more than a minority of people outside their heartlands.
2. People everywhere lacked detailed knowledge of other cultures. What knowledge the tiny educated minorities possessed was fragmentary and often distorted by bigotry and reliance on the hearsay of a few travellers.
3. Most of these ancient empires and religions viewed the world in terms of a clear division between the 'civilized' and the 'barbarian', between those who had been converted and those who lived without the benefits of a 'true' religion.
4. Thus, their mission was to *civilize* non-believers or foreign barbarians, which involved a one-way transmission of 'culture' from the superior to the subordinate group. The possibility of mutual acceptance and interaction on equal terms was either inconceivable or highly unusual.

■ ■ ■ ■ ■ ■ ■ ■ CAPITALIST MODERNITY: EUROPEAN FOUNDATIONS

A number of significant changes took place in Western Europe between the sixteenth and eighteenth centuries. 'Modernity' is the term used to describe this 'nexus of features'. As Albrow (1996: 55) maintains, modernity 'included the combination of rationality, territoriality, expansion, innovation, applied science, the state, citizenship, bureaucratic organization and many other elements'. Here, we want to concentrate on three of these elements. The emergence of the nation-state, the rise of the Enlightenment (see below) and the development of science were mutually reinforcing.

Each helped to create an environment hospitable to the eventual emergence of industrial **CAPITALISM** and the process of modernity. Drawing on important contributions to historical sociology by writers such as Tilly (1975) and Skocpol (1979), Giddens (1985) argues that the emergence of the European nation-state was probably the single most crucial force accounting for the rise of successful capitalism in Western Europe.

> **key**
> **concept**
>
> **CAPITALISM** In capitalist economies, wealth-producing resources are largely privately owned rather than being subject to family, customary, community or national control. Most producers depend on wage employment for their livelihoods instead of self-provisioning, while the goods they produce are commodities sold in markets. Moreover, production is organized almost entirely for profit, which is earmarked for reinvestment and further wealth accumulation.

THE NATION-STATE SYSTEM

Unlike other world civilizations, Europe consisted of a number of autonomous countries in close proximity to one another, each of more or less equal power. Their survival as independent entities in a climate of nearly continuous war required a long process of internal state-building. This culminated in the rise of a succession of powerful rulers. The state's bureaucratic reach and control over its population was progressively strengthened and deepened through measures such as:

■ increasing tax revenues
■ improving communications
■ partially taming the nobility by making it more dependent on the perks derived from state office
■ centralizing the nation by suppressing regional identities
■ monopolizing the most efficient means of violence for conducting wars
■ encouraging and subsidizing technological and craft development
■ investing in naval and army strength
■ nurturing local trading classes whose wealth could be taxed or borrowed to help finance state expansion.

Alongside all this, many governments pursued a policy of national economic aggrandizement, called **MERCANTILISM**. European states engaged in naval warfare, amassed gold and silver, gave preference to domestic business and, wherever possible, insisted that goods be carried in nationally owned ships.

> **key**
> **concept**
>
> **MERCANTILISM** describes an economic theory and practice prevalent in the seventeenth to early nineteenth centuries. The theory was based on the idea that the nation's stock of gold and silver signified its wealth. Those countries that did not have their own mines had to engage in aggressive forms of foreign trade to acquire bullion. A country's currency was guaranteed by the amount of gold in the national vaults.

The key role of actual and potential interstate violence and competition in stimulating these changes seems clear. What resulted was a fragile balance of power between the various European states and an elaborate system of alliances. No state was sufficiently ascendant to crush its rivals permanently and create an empire. Had one giant European empire emerged, similar to the Russian or Ottoman Empires, internal reform would probably have been stifled, as there would have been little external pressure on rulers to tolerate such things as the growth of a vibrant **CIVIL SOCIETY** of independent entrepreneurs, craftsmen, scientists and intellectuals. Again, in a large empire, high-ranking officials would have been recruited on the basis of aristocratic privilege rather than merit.

key concept	**CIVIL SOCIETY** consists of the networks of political groups and voluntary associations emerging in the social space between the individual and the state. These bodies are engaged in expressing their members' interests and trying to shape national political culture – its values, goals and type of decision-making practices. A flourishing civil society is a sign of social health and is likely to foster compromise, innovation, vigorous public debate and the reduction of state interference in social life.

By around the end of the eighteenth century, the much-strengthened European states were much better equipped than states elsewhere to impose institutional reforms from above. They abolished feudalism, imported and/or encouraged advanced technologies and science or removed the obstacles to market freedom – necessary measures for a leap into large-scale production and a turning away from crafts and farming. Of course, the absolutist monarchs and governmental elites who took steps to strengthen the state did not intend that this would pave the way for a subsequent drive to industrialization and modernity. As Elias (1994) argued (see Global Thinkers 15), the complex networks of interdependent social interactions in which humans constantly and consciously engage often lead to unanticipated consequences.

Moves towards industrialization were not solely the result of actions imposed by state elites anxious to protect the nation from the threats posed by rival and more technically advanced nations. Industrialization was also driven by the rise of populist nationalism based on the notion of equal citizenship (an idea we will return to in Chapter 5) generated by the 1789 French Revolution. Other factors were the spontaneous emergence of an industrial bourgeoisie in Britain and the unplanned, non-state directed and very slow onset of the world's first major Industrial Revolution beginning around 1780. From this date we can notice the increasingly widespread deployment of machinery – driven by non-animal sources of power – and full-time wage workers in permanent factories. It took about another 70 years for factory production to spread from cotton textiles to most other industries.

The technological and economic lead provided by the Industrial Revolution also gave Britain military opportunities not available to other nations. Not surprisingly, the British example was eventually followed by other imitative, modernizing governments in Europe and the newly independent American states in the following decades, largely driven by the interstate tensions and rivalries we have described.

EUROPEAN ENLIGHTENMENT THOUGHT

We have already referred to the Enlightenment (see Box 3.1 for more). This was a body of influential ideas that gradually spread across Europe during the eighteenth century. Its optimistic view of the potential for human progress through the power of reason was considerably assisted by the scientific discoveries and advances achieved in the previous century by people such as Copernicus (Figure 3.1), Bacon and Newton (Badham 1986: 10–20). Their ideas, in turn, contributed to the continuing development of science while boosting the orientations towards modernity. Enlightenment thinkers included philosophers and writers such as Hume, Diderot, Montesquieu, Condorcet, Voltaire, Kant and Goethe.

Figure 3.1 **The cleric and philosopher Nicolas Copernicus (1473–1543)** (after a painting in the Historical Museum, Krakow)
He made the bold claim that the earth rotated on its axis every 24 hours and that it went round the sun once a year. The German philosopher Goethe maintained:

Of all discoveries and opinions, none may have exerted a greater effect on the human spirit than the doctrine of Copernicus. The world had scarcely become known as round and complete in itself when it was asked to waive the tremendous privilege of being the centre of the universe. Never, perhaps, was a greater demand made on mankind – for by this admission so many things vanished in mist and smoke! What became of our Eden, our world of innocence, piety and poetry; the testimony of the senses; the conviction of a poetic religious faith? No wonder his contemporaries did not wish to let all this go and offered every possible resistance to a doctrine which in its converts authorized and demanded a freedom of view and greatness of thought so far unknown, indeed not even dreamed of.

SOURCE: http://www.blupete.com/Literature/Biographies/Science/Copernicus.htm

Box 3.1

The central ideas of the Enlightenment

- The notion that humans are social animals whose cultures and individual capacities for good or evil are not innate or fixed but originate in social relationships and so can be modified and improved.

- A belief in the importance of critical reason, scepticism and doubt.

- The human capacity to utilize these resources through observation, empirical testing and the acceptance of the fallibility of all knowledge.

- A consequent rejection of the intolerant, closed ways of thinking associated with blind religious faith and metaphysical speculation.

- The notion that all human beings have a right to self-direction and development – best achieved where governments became constitutional or accountable.

- The possibility of attaining self-realization through practical involvement in, and attempts to transform, the material world.

SOURCE: Seidman (1983: Chapter 1)

Together, the arguments of Enlightenment thinkers added up to a virtual revolution. The ideal modern person was seen as a unique individual with enormous potential for learning and improvement and deserving of the inalienable right to freedom. Implicit in these ideas was the promise of a tolerant, multicultural and secular society engaged in the pursuit of human progress through scientific endeavour and free from unaccountable government, religious bigotry and superstition.

American Revolution
Following a war with the British starting in 1775, the USA became the first modern country to win independence from colonial rule. Representatives of the individual states finally agreed at the Philadelphia Convention in 1787 to establish a federal government with limited powers enshrined in a written constitution.

Those who wrote the US Constitution of 1787 in the wake of the **American Revolution** perhaps best exemplified the practical possibilities of the Enlightenment ideals. The Declaration of Independence began with the famous preamble: 'We hold these truths to be self-evident, that all men are created equal, that they are endowed by their Creator with certain inalienable Rights, that among these are Life, Liberty, and the pursuit of Happiness.' At the time, it barely entered the heads of the founders of the US state that these rights should also be granted to women, or to Native Americans and African-Americans, as these groups' representatives now often angrily point out. We fully concur in their criticisms, but the argument has to be taken one stage further. That the Constitution was proclaimed in universal terms *at all* meant that representatives of the excluded 'others' could eventually use its provisions in their struggles to join the 'self' and the included. This eventually allowed them to mitigate some of the many injustices perpetrated against them.

MARX'S ANALYSIS OF CAPITALISM

The Enlightenment provided a powerful intellectual critique of the highly regulated forms of feudal life but, as Marx understood more clearly than his contemporaries did, feudalism was also a spent force in economic terms. Industrial

A **mode of production** was used by Marx to describe the characteristic social relations that marked particular ways of organizing production. Slavery, feudalism and capitalism are all modes of production in this sense.

capitalism, its successor **mode of production**, was a highly dynamic and indeed unstoppable force for generating social transformation. Many preceding changes had paved the way for the emergence of capitalism, but especially significant were:

■ the creation of a fully commoditized economy in which everything, including land and labour, had a price and so could be bought and sold in a market
■ the exercise of, often violent, measures to dislodge self-sufficient peasants and craft producers from their farms and workshops – so forcing them in ever greater numbers to live by selling their labour to capitalist entrepreneurs as wage workers.

This separation of direct producers from their *means* of production (from their land, animals and tools) was a crucial precondition for the rise of industrial capitalism. Once self-sufficient producers were brought under the domination of capital, the way was open for three crucial changes to take place in the productive system, changes that had never before been realized on such a scale:

1. Labourers could be organized more efficiently alongside the plant, tools and machinery, for they had in effect contracted to sell their labour for an agreed price to the entrepreneur concerned. The employer, who owned the means of production, was therefore free to decide how both equipment and workers should be utilized.
2. Incorporating producers into the system as dependent wage workers made them unable to supply their own means of daily subsistence from self-employment. This simultaneously transformed them into consumers who would spend their incomes in the very same markets that were being created by the growing capitalist system.
3. Once in existence, capitalism contained certain internal motors that drove it relentlessly onwards to subjugate the remnants of pre-capitalist craft and peasant production, by outcompeting them wherever these were encountered and constantly transforming its own system of business organization and technological capacities.

These built-in mechanisms for restless, perpetual change included the drive for profit and business expansion, competition between individual capitalists and firms and the inevitability of class conflict between wage labourers and entrepreneurs over working conditions and the distribution of profits. Together, these factors impelled capitalists constantly to find ways to cheapen and improve their products so as to capture new markets or displace their rivals. As the labour force gained in maturity and organizational strength, employers were compelled to raise the productivity of labour by investing in more advanced plant and machinery and adopting more streamlined systems of business organization and marketing.

An important consequence was the tendency for capitalism to expand the productive forces by developing ever more advanced technology, harnessing the power of science, increasing the scale of production and developing business arrangements to facilitate greater capital pooling. Thus, as Marx observed, nothing under capitalism ever remains static for long. Rather, constant change, not only in the productive process but at all levels of society, is inevitable. Another consequence, again apparent to Marx, was capitalism's drive to expand globally (see Box 3.2).

Box 3.2

Marx and Engels argue that capitalism must expand globally

In the passages below, Marx and Engels vividly anticipate most of the globalizing consequences we have since come to associate with capitalism. These are:

- the Western drive to incorporate the non-Western world into the global economy through imperialist conquest
- the necessity for independent but backward countries to adopt their own local capitalist projects
- the potentially universalizing power of materialism and rising consumerist aspirations in fostering the desire for change
- the tendency for capitalism to transform societies in rather similar ways wherever it takes root.

> The need for a constantly expanding market for its products chases the bourgeoisie over the whole surface of the globe. It must nestle everywhere, settle everywhere, establish connections everywhere.

> The bourgeoisie has through its exploitation of the world-market given a cosmopolitan character to production and consumption in every country ... All old-established industries have been destroyed or are daily being destroyed. They are dislodged by new industries, whose introduction becomes a life and death question for all civilized nations, by industries that no longer work up indigenous raw material, but raw material drawn from the remotest zones; industries whose products are consumed, not only at home, but in every quarter of the globe. In place of the old wants, satisfied by the products of the country, we find new wants, requiring for their satisfaction the products of distant lands and climes. In place of the old local and national seclusion and self-sufficiency, we have intercourse in every direction, universal interdependence of nations. And as in material, so also in intellectual production ... National one-sidedness and narrow-mindedness become more and more impossible.

> The bourgeoisie, by the rapid development of all instruments of production, by the immensely facilitated means of communications, draws all, even the most barbarian, nations into civilization. The cheap prices of its commodities are the heavy artillery with which it batters down all Chinese walls, with which it forces the barbarians' intensely obstinate hatred to foreigners to capitulate. It compels all nations, on pain of extinction, to adopt the bourgeois mode of production; it compels them to intro-duce what it calls civilization in their midst, that is to become bourgeois themselves. In one word, it creates a world after its own image.

SOURCE: Marx and Engels (1967: 83–4)

THE GROWTH OF RATIONALITY

In looking at the spread of modernity, contemporary sociologists lay more emphasis on cultural and intellectual changes than on Marx's economic argu-ment. In this view, the belief in progress through rationality was a major factor in transforming societies. This idea lies deep in European cultural and political history, but was particularly associated with the gradual extension of literacy, the development of science, the pressures for more democracy and the heritage of the Enlightenment. Also, once established, capitalist rationality and modernity were mutually supportive, each creating scope for the other.

Another extremely influential line of thought concerning the historical development of rationalization comes from Weber, whose ideas we summarize in Global Thinkers 3 below. Although Weber believed that all humans reflect on their actions and actively interpret and explore the implicit 'logic' attached to the cultural meanings occurring in their societies, he also thought that over time a particularly powerful kind of rationality had emerged uniquely in Europe. He called this 'formal rationality' and he believed that ultimately this had overshadowed other kinds (Weber 1978; Brubaker 1991). Its rise had been fed by several causal processes. Among these were the quasi-equalitarian and cross-ethnic civil society that had emerged in the medieval city, the legacies of Roman law and the fact that in Christianity, kinship relations (as opposed to the worshipping individual) have no special ritual significance. Europe also drew on the resources provided by colonial exploitation and saw the gradual emergence of free labour – no longer bound by social, locational or religious obligations to serve particular interests. Weber further argued that, from the sixteenth century, Protestantism also played a key role in helping to transform the character of Western rationality since it emphasized the importance of a lifelong, disciplined, self-denying, not to say perfectionist, approach to whatever vocation or position God had called one as a necessary path to achieving salvation in the next world (see Chapter 16).

As these rationalization processes gradually merged, Weber believed that something very crucial took place. The pull of tradition, affective bonds to friends or family and non-self-serving goals, such as duty to God or the desire for justice, equity or fraternity, became partly smothered by the rise of formal rationality. Increasingly, individuals, groups or institutions constantly seek the most efficacious and least costly means of attainment by matching means to ends in a systematic, calculative way by applying scientific and empirical knowledge. This deliberate process could, in principle, be applied to most kinds of activities. However, it is in the modern governmental, professional and organizational bureaucracies (where officials are engaged in achieving consistent, standardized and coherent rules and systems of administration) and in the ruthless competitive and profit-driven struggles among capitalist businesses that formal rationality becomes both most appropriate and most dominant.

As we show in Global Thinkers 3, Weber became pessimistic about the prognosis for modernizing societies, since he believed that the dominance of formal rationality might lead to ruthless market competition and one-sided materialism along with an 'iron cage' of powerful, super-efficient but secretive and unaccountable bureaucracies. Moreover, it was not clear whether or how we might escape from these all-pervasive influences, with their narrow and probably unethical preoccupations.

Turning to a more recent and optimistic view of the links between rationality and modernity, Giddens (1990) sees the latter as consisting of three kinds of mutually reinforcing orientations. Together, their power to underpin and shape our world has slowly grown and spread along with rationality. He oversimplifies the complexity of 'tradition' in arguing that premodern people were mostly rooted in specific and bounded locations – village communities – where they spent their lives working, worshipping, raising families and socializing with the same few people. However, there is no doubt that with vastly improved, cheaper and safer means of travel and communication and the ever more precise measurement of space and time, people experienced 'time–space compression'. It became possible for social exchanges to flourish independently of place and time, across vast distances and time zones. Thrift (2004: 583) adds that new forms of spatial awareness can generate new qualities of existence. Boundaries are subverted by 'fluid forces which have no beginning or end and which are generating new cultural conventions, techniques, forms, genres, concepts, even … senses'.

Similarly, there was a diminishing dependence on face-to-face ties to particular people and specific social contexts. These changes, or 'disembedding' processes, meant that social life became more dependent on abstract systems of knowledge and impersonal forms of communication. Critical here was the wide dissemination of education and literacy and a generalized use of symbolic tokens such as money and credit. But also essential was the proliferation of expert systems, or professional services, in which clients could safely place their trust. As we saw in Chapter 2, Giddens (1990: 36–45) also sees self-monitoring or 'reflexivity' as fundamental to modernity. He claims that whereas 'all forms of social life are partly constituted by actors' knowledge of them', what is 'characteristic of modernity is … the presumption of wholesale reflexivity – which of course includes reflection upon the nature of reflection itself' (Giddens 1990: 38, 39). In modern societies, self-monitoring is applied to all aspects of life; it takes place constantly and is undertaken as much by organizations and governments as by individuals. Indeed, the discipline of sociology itself, in collecting and interpreting knowledge about social action, has become heavily implicated in the process of reflexivity at many societal levels. Not only do governments and other agents draw on sociological knowledge to assist them in modifying such things as laws and social policies, but the changes brought about in social life as a result of such actions in turn require sociologists to respond by rethinking their concepts.

Giddens further argues that these three orientations facilitate the reordering or 'stretching' of social relationships across the world and sustain complex interactions between people situated far apart. Indeed, he explicitly states that modernity is an 'inherently globalizing' force (Giddens 1990: 63, 177). It also helps to create what he calls a 'runaway world', where nothing is certain and every aspect of life seems to be in constant flux (Giddens 2002). Nevertheless, important though his argument concerning the three orientations is, it implies that globalization is simply modernity (plus capitalism and the nation-state) writ large. This seems rather a limited view because, as we show in Chapter 2, globalization can be said to have generated certain unique properties, especially the emergence of a global consciousness that we have called 'globality'. This and other features could not necessarily have been inferred solely from a familiarity with the struc-

tures and orientations of modernity. As Robertson (1992: 60) insists, globalization has acquired a 'general autonomy' and 'logic' of its own.

RACE AND COLONIALISM

European countries were able to spread out of their continent precisely because
of their economic, military and intellectual lead, often borrowed from other
civilizations. The decisive advances were in seafaring and navigational techniques – improvements in the compass, navigational charts, astrolabe and
rudder – and the use of gunpowder and firearms, cannons and guns (Smith
1991: 56). The Portuguese, who led the field in navigational exploration, reached
the tip of southern Africa in 1489. Vasco da Gama finally entered the Indian
Ocean in 1497. Brazen exploits, including the defeat of the Muslim fleet in the
Indian Ocean in 1509 and the creation of a whole series of forts and trading
stations across Asia, soon followed. Thus began the long period of European
trading domination over much of the non-Western world and the extension of
colonial rule that was eventually to follow (Smith 1991: 77–8).

The European explorers met small, scattered societies (like the Khoi and San
in South Africa) as well as large empires like China. There the emperor and his
court believed that theirs was the 'central kingdom' around which all others were
scattered. Strange stories abounded. As late as the Opium War (1839–42) –
waged by the European powers to control the profitable drugs trade – many
Chinese thought that Europeans would die spectacularly of the explosive consequences of constipation if deprived of rhubarb (used then as a purgative). English
sailors were depicted in drawings with tails behind their legs.

Such depictions were the mirror images of the racial bigotry that was eventually to characterize much of the European colonial expansion. We examine race
and racism in more detail in Chapter 6. Here we merely note that the disdainful
manifestations of nineteenth-century European power contrasted markedly with
earlier European travellers' awed wonder and astonishment at seeing the Taj
Mahal, the delicacy of the Benin bronzes (Figure 3.2), the palaces of Iztapalapa
and the massive pyramids of Egypt. At the time of the encounter with Europe,
these buildings and artefacts showed that other advanced civilizations had often
surpassed any equivalent achievements in Europe.

A generous universal spirit was often displayed by the Enlightenment thinkers,
who regarded humanity as a single species on a gradual path to self-
improvement, whatever the dissimilarities and lags between peoples and regions.
All were capable of reaching the end state of 'civilization'. There was an undoubted
arrogance in such views, which implied that what obtained in eighteenth-century
France and Germany was the preferred destination of all humanity. However, this
ethnocentrism was ameliorated by a frequent recognition that humanity had
forfeited as well as gained something through 'civilization'. For example, Milton's
famous poem *Paradise Lost* and Rousseau's celebration of the 'noble savage' both
celebrated an Arcadian innocence, where minds, bodies and emotions united with
the natural world in a symbiotic and healthy innocence.

Ethnocentrism derives from
the Greek word for people,
ethnos. Ethnocentrists see
their ethnic group or nation
as the model against which
all others have to be judged.

Figure 3.2 **Benin bronze, representing an Oba, a Yoruba king (late sixteenth century, Nigeria)**
The casting uses complex and delicate processes involving wax, clay and brass (more common than bronze, though the latter description stuck). So unexpected was the technological sophistication shown that some Europeans surmised (wrongly) that the Portuguese, the Egyptians or a 'lost tribe of Israel' must have passed on the skill.

Most European imperialists and colonialists of the late nineteenth century were not troubled by such reflections. The 'lords of humankind' strutted around, annexing territories in the name of their monarchs, sending out governors in plumed hats and announcing that they had assumed 'the white man's burden' in civilizing the rest of earth. At the Berlin Conference in 1885, the European powers drew lines on maps and parcelled out great chunks of the world to each other. Enlightenment and Arcadian notions were swept aside as imperialists realized that there were massive fortunes to be made by subordinating the rest of humanity. Rubber trees were stolen from Brazil, gold and diamonds mined in South Africa, lumber logged from the equatorial forests and opium extracted from China. Sugar, cocoa, tobacco and sisal plantations were established, using cheap or coerced labour and speculative capital. These imperialist adventurers, the plantations they started and the financiers who propped them up were the early precursors of the TNCs discussed in Chapter 7.

The cruelty that attached to many colonial occupying forces was legendary. Take the case of South West Africa, now Namibia. After declaring that an immense African landmass now belonged to Germany, in October 1904 General van Trotha, the military head of the occupying forces, issued an extermination order directed at the local population, declaring that

inside German territory every Herero tribesman, armed or unarmed, with or without cattle, will be shot. No women or children will be allowed in the territory: they will be driven back to their people or fired upon … I believe that the Herero must be destroyed as a nation.

Within a year that is virtually what happened. The Herero population dwindled from 60,000–80,000 people to 16,000 – a loss of some 75–80 per cent.

Although many peoples put up spirited fights for their independence, the superiority of European guns and military tactics usually won through. The very ease of these brutal victories promoted ideas of **Social Darwinism**, which European imperialists supposed lent support to the idea that they were inherently superior to the people they colonized. With the legacy of the Atlantic slave trade and the colonial subjugation of all sub-Saharan Africa other than Ethiopia, it is difficult, even now, for Africans to escape discrimination and prejudice.

Social Darwinism applied, or more often misapplied, to human situations the role assigned by Darwin to the process of natural selection in the evolution of species.

■ ■

Global Thinkers 3

MAX WEBER (1854–1920)

Max Weber's groundbreaking contributions to sociology included the following interventions:

1. *Defining social action. The idea that 'society' is constructed around the meanings interpreted by and shared between individuals, whose actions then partly express these meanings and are motivated by them. Sociologists can also use this same empathizing capacity and process as a pathway towards 'understanding' social actions – a methodological approach Weber called 'Verstehen', perhaps usefully translated as 'empathy'.*
2. *Power versus authority. Power can only endure if it is incorporated into our everyday beliefs, thereby becoming accepted as legitimate (modernists believe that rule-making processes are based on abstract principles of equity and impersonality that they can help to determine through democracy).*
3. *Rationalization. The realization that while rationalization processes (see below) have always been present, modernity intensified massively in Western Europe – encompassing law, politics, science, capitalism, professionalism and administration/bureaucracy – and penetrated deeply into every crevice of social life leading to an irreversible break with the past.*

Formal rationality
With modernity, the life of societies becomes dominated by 'formal rationality', where:

■ *actions are oriented towards greater* **calculability** *– we purposively and self-consciously reflect on how to link more logically and effectively our actions to our goals; we seek desired and planned consequences*
■ *actions become more* **systematic** *(streamlined, consistent, regularized and standardized) and so applicable to all situations and people*
■ *all humans reflect on the consequences of their actions and rely on incoming information as well as technically specialized/scientific* **knowledge** *that can be empirically validated.*

Formal rationality brings greater impersonality, predictability and control to factory, office, army, hospital or law court. This leads to greater efficiency, economic growth and control of nature. However, Weber was also worried by three other consequences that he found disturbing:

- ■ *World disenchantment: Science, technology and material improvement lead to a 'disenchantment of the world' – religion and magic become less believable. Religion provides ethics – concerning how we should live – but formal rationality undermines meaning and ethics and is spiritually barren. It is only concerned with facts and the most efficient means for achieving goals. The individual is left alone to find his or her own values and direction.*
- ■ *The iron cage: Once established, the logic of formal rationality – whether through the capitalist market or bureaucratization processes – remorselessly dominates modern life; it spares no one. Rationalized bureaucracy stifles us in red tape.*
- ■ *Substantive rationality withers: Historically people have attached the highest value not to self-satisfaction or economic gain but to goals such as serving God, fraternity, equality, justice and moral duty; doing what is 'right'. But formal rationality undermines and replaces these with a narrow materialism.*

Weber and globalization today?

Because of deregulatory, neoliberal policies and the technologies of time–space compression, capitalism is now clearly global; the iron cage of market compulsion encompasses consumers and workers worldwide. It also compels pharmaceutical companies to invest in drugs that will sell rather than those that are needed by the world's poor who lack purchasing power (see Chapter 11). Yet, simultaneously, we also see global social movements such as Jubilee 2000 and the global justice movement (see Chapter 18) struggling to reform world capitalism so as to make it fairer, less unequal, that is, to replace formal with substantive rationality on a global level.

SOURCES: Gerth and Mills (1946); Weber (1978); Brubaker (1991)

After the Second World War, there was a new balance of international forces, which was to threaten notions of racial superiority. Japan had given the British a bloody nose in the Far East. Through the force of mass protest and led by a remarkable leader Mahatma Gandhi, the British were persuaded to leave India, which became independent in 1947. This was the prelude to the decolonization of the rest of Asia, Africa, the Middle East and the Caribbean. European expansion and colonialism had fulfilled its historic mission. It had drawn far-flung parts of the world into a relationship with the global economy. However, it had often done so with great cruelty and without the consent of the colonized peoples who, after 1945, were ready to enter a new era.

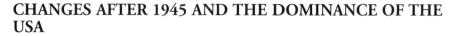

CHANGES AFTER 1945 AND THE DOMINANCE OF THE USA

To decolonization were added a number of other important changes over the period 1945–73, which we shall discuss in turn. Each served to enlarge and deepen the extent to which a world society was evolving. They were:

- a long period of sustained economic growth
- the establishment of the Bretton Woods financial system
- the rise of US global economic power and political leadership
- the widespread adoption of Keynesian national economic management
- the rise of mass consumption and changes in lifestyles.

ECONOMIC GROWTH

Although estimates vary, during the long boom from 1950 to 1975, the world's economic output is said to have expanded by an unprecedented two-and-a-quarter times (Harris 1983: 30). Using slightly different dates, Hobsbawm (1994: 288) claimed that the 'golden years' of economic growth and technological development from 1950 to 1973 meant that for '80 per cent of humanity the Middle Ages ended suddenly in the 1950s'. Although most remained very poor by Western standards, even people living in the colonial and ex-colonial countries were caught up in this economic transformation.

By the mid-1950s, Europe and Japan had recovered from the devastation of war and were achieving new levels of prosperity. In 1959, Harold Macmillan was re-elected as the British prime minister with the famous slogan attributed to him, 'You've never had it so good.' Even the poor developing countries had a good decade, with commodity prices for their agricultural produce and minerals attaining heights never achieved before or since. During the 1960s, Japanese might and the rising power of the newly industralizing countries (NICs) became evident, along with rapid rates of industrialization and urbanization in countries like Brazil and Taiwan.

THE BRETTON WOODS FINANCIAL SYSTEM

Bretton Woods is the name of a small town in New Hampshire where 44 countries, mainly allies of the USA, met in July 1944 to formulate policies for global economic cooperation. The conference played a major role in stabilizing the postwar financial situation (Brett 1985: 62–79). Here, it was agreed that Western countries would operate a system of semi-fixed exchange rates in managing the value of their currencies, while minimizing as far as possible their use of trade-inhibiting policies such as currency **devaluation**, tariffs and import controls. Meanwhile, the USA agreed to stabilize the dollar – already by far the world's

Devaluation Lowering the value of your currency against that of your competitor countries to cheapen the price of your exports and make their imports more expensive.

strongest currency – tying its value to gold reserves and permitting its currency to be used freely as world money.

The Bretton Woods system also involved establishing several key economic international governmental organizations (IGOs). Of these, the most important were:

- the World Bank, designed to help individual countries finance long-term infrastructural projects through providing loans at favourable rates
- the International Monetary Fund (IMF), which provided short-term financial assistance
- the General Agreement on Trade and Tariffs (GATT), a world forum to facilitate regular discussions between member countries on these issues.

US GLOBAL ECONOMIC POWER AND POLITICAL LEADERSHIP

The Cold War
Led by the Soviet Union and the USA, the world was split into two antagonistic camps over the period 1947–89. This involved an ideological battle between capitalist democracy versus socialist planning, a massive build-up of arms and the twin races to achieve supremacy in nuclear and space age technology. Despite several flash points, for example in 1948 and 1962 (see timeline in Box 3.3), the superpowers themselves never engaged in head-on aggression. Rather, conflict was deflected into regional or minor wars involving the developing countries – as in the Korean and Vietnam Wars.

The USA was very powerful economically at the close of the First World War, but periods of isolation and economic protectionism restricted its global role. After the Second World War, its economy emerged undamaged with stronger, re-equipped industries. This time it assumed the burden of managing world capitalism, including its central role in the Bretton Woods system. Generously, it kept its own huge economy open to imports while tolerating some protectionist measures by weaker countries as they recovered from war. It also freely permitted the purchase of its technology. The USA became the world's leading creditor nation, supplying grants to Europe (through the Marshall Aid Plan) and Japan. It supplied loans on favourable terms to other countries, though this was something of a Trojan horse, allowing US-located TNCs to penetrate new markets.

The East–West **Cold War** confrontation dominated global politics from 1947 to 1989. It created a bipolar system with each side managed and ruled by its dominant power – the communist bloc by the Soviet Union and the capitalist democracies by the USA. Each side tried to gain the technical lead in a race to acquire supremacy in nuclear arms and space age technology. President Truman persuaded the US Congress to pour dollars into the national and world economy via arms expenditure and military aid. There were large deployments of troops in Europe and Asia, while the onset of the Korean War helped to encourage the long postwar boom (Arrighi 1994: 273–98).

Successive US administrations encouraged further decolonization by France, Britain and the Netherlands. There were political and economic motives for doing so. The USA wished to prevent the spread of communist movements and regimes, especially in the war-torn Asian countries (though it failed to do so in North Korea, China and Vietnam). It also wanted to penetrate the previously closed colonial markets. The European powers had used these markets as captive outlets for their home industries and as key sources of raw materials for metropolitan industries. The USA now wanted 'a share of the action'.

Box 3.3

Global peace and war

1945   End of Second World War but the onset of the nuclear age when, in August, the USA exploded two atomic bombs in Japan. The UN was established and in December it issued the Universal Declaration of Human Rights.

1947   Cold War 'officially' began with President Truman's declaration that the USA would protect democracies from the threat presented by totalitarian (communist) regimes. In Europe, the Iron Curtain – an expression coined earlier by Winston Churchill, the British wartime prime minister – divided the communist Warsaw Pact countries from the Western NATO (North Atlantic Treaty Organization) allies.

1948   From June (until May 1949), the USSR blockaded West Berlin. This triggered extensive air lifts to provide food and fuel to the citizens of West Berlin.

1949   China went communist under the leadership of Mao Zedong and drove the nationalist and pro-capitalist forces into exile in Taiwan. The USSR exploded an atomic bomb.

1950–53   The Korean War began in 1950 when the communist North invaded the South with Chinese support. The USA promised military protection for East Asia.

1957   The USSR launched Sputnik, the first human-piloted space craft. The space race began in earnest.

1962   Cuban missile crisis: Soviet nuclear missiles placed in communist Cuba led to a confrontation with the USA. The world was poised for nuclear war but this was narrowly averted when Soviet Premier Khrushchev agreed to remove the missiles.

1963–75   American military involvement against North Vietnam's largely peasant army. After years of heavy US bombing and escalating conflict, US forces were pushed into a stalemate and withdrew.

1969   Moon landing by US team: the majesty of planet earth became fully apparent to everyone with media access.

1972   Rapprochement between the USA and China following President Nixon's visit.

1980s   President Reagan initiated his 'Star Wars' nuclear 'defence' programme. The sheer expense involved highlighted Soviet deficiencies, especially in computerization, and declining ability to fund the arms race. But it also shackled the USA with colossal national debts ($3 trillion by the early 1990s).

1989   Soviet Premier Gorbachev relinquished further claims to 'defend' Warsaw Pact countries; collapse of Eastern Europe communist regimes as popular revolutions broke out. Cold War ended.

1992   End of communism in Soviet Union and ancient Russian empire began to dissolve into independent republics. First Gulf War to reverse Iraqi invasion of Kuwait and 'safeguard' world oil reserves. Sanctioned by UN, but demonstrated US leadership and power was now unrivalled.

1992–99   In many regions, years of bloody civil wars, episodes of ethnic-cleansing, mass genocide and sometimes disintegration into

	warlordism, partly as the aftermath of the Cold War, and requiring a huge increase in UN peacekeeping operations and/or NATO or US interventions legitimized by the UN, for example Bosnia (1992–96), Kosovo (1999), Somalia (1993), Rwanda (1993–94), Democratic Republic of Congo (1999/2000) and East Timor (1999).
2000	George Bush became US president and soon blocked or revoked several weapons treaties such as the Comprehensive Test Ban Treaty, refused to sign up for the Kyoto protocol in 2002, saying that the US economy would be harmed by measures to reduce its emissions of greenhouse gases and refused to recognize the International Criminal Court, designed to deter political leaders from permitting extreme human rights abuses in their countries.
2001	An Islamic terrorist group, reputed to be closely linked to Osama bin Laden's al-Qaeda group, destroyed the twin World Trade Centre towers in New York, killing 3,000 people and provoking mass world revulsion. Bush declared a 'war against terrorism'.
2001–02	US bombing campaign and then invasion of Afghanistan as part of a concerted strategy to eliminate global terrorism.
2003	After much opposition within the UN, the EU and from worldwide anti-war movements, coalition forces (mostly US and UK) invaded Iraq, ostensibly to rid the world of Saddam Hussein's weapons of mass destruction.

SOURCES: Castells (1998); Pugh (2002); Chomsky (2004)

In Chapter 4 we explain how during the 1970s, America's willingness and capacity to continue carrying the postwar role of providing economic leadership to its non-communist allies declined sharply (Box 4.2). Moreover, during the Reagan years from 1981 to 1988, the neoconservatives who came to the fore encouraged the US government to pursue two major policies that massively transformed or reversed these earlier tendencies. One was to pursue a relentless and expensive weapons strategy designed to end the supposed military and weapons threat from the Soviet Union; this helped to bankrupt the USSR and end the Cold War. The huge costs incurred in this venture also severely crippled the USA, but it was able to weather this financial crisis by achieving a burst of economic growth during the 1990s, which was linked to strong government support for high-tech industries, including information technology, the peace dividend brought by the end of the Cold War and an era of falling real wages until 1997 unprecedented since the 1940s. America's ability from the 1980s to impose a financial system on the world that was especially beneficial to US banks, stock market brokers, insurance and other financial interests also aided this economic recovery. This, in turn, was linked to the second major policy change set in motion during the 1980s, namely the development of the 'Washington Consensus' (Bello 1994, 2001).

While claiming to help poor countries solve the huge debt problems they had built up between 1970 and 1982 and encouraging them to adopt more sensible market-oriented development policies, the USA used its control of the IMF and

World Bank and its influence over the G7 governments to compel many weak states to accept economic reforms called 'structural adjustment programmes'. In exchange for debt relief and continued access to US and G7 markets, these neoliberal policies required governments to open their economies to overseas trade (led by Western corporations) and capital flows (almost entirely G7 investment, often involving short-term 'hot' money inflows), while demanding the privatization of state assets and the abolition of subsidies and price controls designed to foster local businesses and protect poorer citizens. We enlarge on this theme in Global Thinkers 8. By the later 1990s, even the highly conservative IMF conceded that these policies may actually have increased poverty in the poorest countries and inequality over the world as a whole. Many commentators (for example Bello 2001; Stiglitz 2002; Harvey 2003) have criticized these policies and their worldwide imposition. They claim that they can be seen as a thinly disguised attempt by conservative US interests to reverse some of America's relative economic and industrial decline in the face of the greater economic unity of the EU, the rise of the Asia Pacific region, especially China, and the prospect of yet further countries, for example India, increasingly 'capturing' US industries and competing for the world's raw material supplies, especially oil.

KEYNESIAN NATIONAL ECONOMIC MANAGEMENT

John Maynard Keynes was a major twentieth-century economist. In the 1930s, when unemployment brought on by the Great Depression was causing widespread distress, his theories challenged orthodox views on how best to explain and deal with the booms and slumps characteristic of capitalism. They also had important political and social implications. The uncertainties and diverging expectations of consumers, savers and investors often worked against each other and made rational economic decision-making difficult. He saw that, left unregulated, market forces tended to generate widening inequalities of income and wealth, making it impossible for mass demand to reach levels sufficient to keep consumption, investment and therefore employment at politically acceptable levels. He suggested that governments play a more proactive role in spending on public investment and stimulating demand – so creating jobs and investment.

Although far from being a socialist, Keynes thought that governments should use the tax system to redistribute income from rich to poor (called 'progressive taxation'). He reasoned that the poor would normally spend (rather than save) any increased income and that this would expand the economy by fuelling demand. At the time, such deliberate 'interference' in the working of free markets was regarded as heresy, but his arguments became widely accepted by Western governments in the 1940s. With widespread unemployment in the 1930s and political ferment after the Second World War, it is only a slight exaggeration to say that Keynesian policies gave capitalism a new lease of life. They also strengthened the long boom and so contributed to globalization.

MASS CONSUMPTION AND CHANGES IN LIFESTYLES

The long boom after the Second World War was triggered by an increasing demand for goods and services. These were produced with corresponding efficiency – using mass production methods based on those pioneered by Henry Ford in his car assembly plants in Detroit (see Chapter 4 for a full discussion). Prosperity helped to fuel important changes in social life, especially in the advanced countries. Life expectancy rose and many people were better educated than ever before, even in the developing countries. The consequences of such changes first became widely evident in the 1950s. However, they almost certainly generated cumulative effects, which by the late 1960s were giving rise to the demand for, and higher expectation of, greater personal freedom of choice in all spheres of life. Meanwhile, globalization meant that such powerful influences could not be contained within the rich countries but spread to the communist and developing world through education, the mass media, tourism and TNCs. Box 3.4 provides a timeline of these changes.

Box 3.4	**The desire for more personal freedom**

Private leisure and consumption

1954	Dawn of the TV age. Thirty per cent of households in the UK had TV. (This rose to 89 per cent by 1963.)
1950s	The invention of the 'teenager'. Youth cultures became ever more evident and generated their own markets, musical and other cultural concerns.
1956	The new genre of 'rock music' emerged. Elvis Presley achieved international fame with 'Heartbreak Hotel' and the film, *Jailhouse Rock*. Adolescent rebellion became fashionable. Popular culture became big business.
1960s	Age of mass ownership of the motorcar got underway. Suburbanization increased while inner-city zones declined. Spread of supermarket shopping.
1960s	The rapid expansion of systems of higher education across the world.
1960s	International tourist travel took off.
1970s	The sexual revolution characterized by greater freedom to experiment and have multiple partners became stronger and was allied to the feminist and gay rights movements. In the West, rising divorce rates and fewer children suggested the retreat of the family.
1980s	Pop rock, with its emphasis on electric technologies, loud, continuous rhythms and self-expression, was absorbed into and hybridized by non-Western musical forms, everywhere helped by the spreading use of cassettes, videos and TVs across the world (see Chapter 13).

Action for greater personal freedom and justice

1954	Beginning of the civil rights movement in the USA by African-Americans. Reached its heyday in the mid-1960s.

Mid-1960s	Anti-war movement in the USA against involvement in Vietnam began and spread to Europe. Coalesced with drug culture and the 'hippie' revolt against continuing bureaucratic restraints on sexual/personal freedom.
1968	May 'revolution' by workers and students in France against the materialist pressures of capitalism.
Late 1960s	Feminist movement for gender equality took off in the USA and soon spread.
1969	Birth of the gay rights movement in the USA.

THE SPREAD OF ENGLISH AS AN INTERNATIONAL LANGUAGE

The use of English as a world language (ironically called a lingua franca) has fostered the emergence of a world society. Historically, spoken English came to occupy this role when Britain emerged as the world's first industrial nation. It controlled the largest empire until well after the Second World War and, until the First World War, was the leading world supplier of investment capital, banking services and commercial shipping networks. When the USA assumed this leading role after 1945, by an accident of history, it also happened to be an English-speaking country. Moreover, the USA continues to dominate the various mass media and advertising, which are so influential in shaping global consumer and lifestyle aspirations. As the world economy has grown, so too has its reliance on English as a world language. English also remains dominant as a scientific language (over 90 per cent of academic papers are in English) and as a language of the internet. However, population growth in non-English-speaking countries has been high and projections accepted by the British Council have pointed to the much larger expected numbers of Chinese speakers and very strong growth of Hindi/Urdu, Spanish and Arabic speakers (Table 3.1).

TABLE 3.1	English language speakers: past, present and future		
Index	1990	2004	2050 (projected)
Number of countries where English is dominant	75 (out of 170)	76 (out of 191)	n.d.
Number who speak English as a first language	377 million	400 million	508 million*
Number who speak English as a second language	140 million	600 million	1.2 billion

NOTE: *Compared with a projected 1,384 million Chinese speakers, 556 million Hindu/Urdu speakers, 486 million Spa nish speakers and 482 million Arabic speakers
SOURCES: Crystal (1995); www.britishcouncil.org/learning-elt-future.pdf

The likelihood is that English will remain crucial in business, science and the knowledge industries, where non-English speakers will have to acquire competence, but that it will slip back in vernacular settings from about 9 per cent to 5 per cent of the world's mother-tongue speakers. A cluster of powerful languages will emerge, while small language groups will disappear. Early in the twenty-first century, linguists recorded 6,700 languages, but they were being lost at the rate of one every two weeks (Nettle and Romaine 2000).

REVIEW

A world society does not drop from the sky like an alien invasion. It has been emerging in a halting way ever since the inhibitions induced by local beliefs and mythology were first questioned by the world religions, particularly through the spread of Buddhism, Islam and Christianity. However, a narrow ethnocentric outlook was challenged more fundamentally by the rise of modernity in Europe.

The formation of powerful, well-armed nation-states provided a basis for capitalist industrialization. Meanwhile, the Enlightenment led to new cultural and scientific outlooks that fed into modernizing impulses. Eventually, the momentum for change created by the fusion of capitalism and modernity proved to be unchallengeable. Empowered by new wealth and technology and energized by capitalist competition for markets and raw materials as well as by national rivalry, the European powers subjected other peoples to their rule. This served to widen markets and spread European languages and social and political institutions.

During the first three-quarters of the twentieth century, globalization was given another massive boost by the emergence of the USA as a giant economic engine and then as a superpower. From the end of the Second World War and at least up to the 1970s, its economic, ideological and military leadership of the West went largely unquestioned. Although the Soviet Union occasionally confronted the USA, state communism was a hollow shell. By 1989 it was failing and soon collapsed.

In recent decades, other trends have become apparent in the moves towards a world society. Globalizing forces have become largely autonomous and self-sustaining. Less and less does their survival or expansion depend on the actions of particular nations, even very powerful ones such as the USA. Thus, on the one hand, it is likely that the continuing poverty of the poorest countries and people have probably been caused partly by G7 economic policies since the 1980s. (Russia became a full member in 2006, making the organization the G8.) On the other hand, it is not difficult to produce evidence suggesting that America's ability to shape world affairs is less effective than it sometimes appears. For example, despite its continuing military superiority and the economic strategies that conservative groups in America have adopted since the 1970s, these have been unable to prevent the continuing rapid industrialization of China and India. US policies designed to contain global terrorism have also proved conspicuously unsuccessful so far and, indeed, its 2003 invasion of Iraq seems to have increased the incidence and likelihood of terrorism.

There are other indicators of the relative decline of the power of the USA. For example, only 27 of the world's top 100 TNCs in 2000 were wholly or partly American owned (Dicken 2003: 222–4). In short, no one country, not even the mighty USA, can any longer shape global change more or less as it pleases, and though it can and does exercise a very considerable influence, other countries and agents that can influence globalization are growing in importance. Meanwhile, the ability of nations and states to cope with the problems presented by globalization, for example worldwide pollution, is likely to depend on the active support they receive from a whole gamut of transnational groups, interests and experts.

A paradox has become apparent at the heart of globalization. On the one hand, we see the virtual worldwide spread of certain very powerful universalizing trends. Capitalist modernity generates both similar experiences, for example in education, health, industry, market exchange, urban life, and common aspirations for greater personal freedom. (Of course, as we shall see later in this book, not all these are beneficial.) On the other hand, a more complex, polycentric world of competing powers, each with its own version of modernity and particular cultural legacy on offer, has replaced the bipolar one of the superpowers. We live in a world of many robust players, transnational and national, state and non-state, and each is determined to influence local and global events. We will encounter these two themes many times in the chapters that follow.

FURTHER READING

- *Formations of Modernity*, edited by Stuart Hall and Bram Gieben (1992), offers a highly accessible discussion of the nature and causes of modernity. You may find Chapters 1, 2 and 6 especially helpful.

- Anthony Giddens' *The Nation State and Violence* (1985) provides a readable account of the rise of the European absolutist states.

- K. Marx and F. Engels' (1967) short pamphlet, *The Communist Manifesto*, first published in 1848, the year of revolutions across Europe, offers a passionate and clear introduction to their theory of capitalism.

- E. A. Brett's, *The World Economy Since the War: The Politics of Uneven Development* (1985) contains an excellent analysis of the postwar world economy.

GROUP WORK

- List and briefly outline the early historical phases of the emergence of world society that we have discussed. What might be added to this list that we have omitted or neglected, and why?

- Pair off. Each pair will look up the history of the European occupation of one non-European country (Kenya, India, Nigeria, Senegal, South Africa, for example). How would you characterize the racial attitudes of the colonizing force?

- Draw up a list of all the economics words and phrases we have used in this chapter. Start with 'devaluation', 'exchange rates', 'protectionism' and 'mercantilism'. Can you spot any others? Find their meanings in a dictionary and write them down.

QUESTIONS TO THINK ABOUT

?

1. What were the main historical antecedents to the evolution of a world society and why were they limited in their effects?

2. Which one or more of the historical causes discussed do you think exercised the strongest influence in intensifying the process of globalization? Give your reasons.

3. Outline the main ways in which the USA played a leading role in reshaping the postwar world.

4. Why were there such dramatic changes in people's lifestyles, at least in the rich countries, in the 1950s and 1960s?

WHAT'S ON THE WEB

■ http://yaleglobal.yale.edu/display.article?id=702 Run by the Yale University Center for the Study of Globalization, this site has some useful short articles with a bias towards history. Look out particularly for the ones by Bruce Mazlish, a historian who has been a pioneer in global studies.

■ http://www.polity.co.uk/global/ This site has been developed to sustain a text-book called *Global Transformations* and other related publications (Held et al. 1999). We wish to be generous about a good book that in some respects rivals this one and think this site is very helpful. Notice, however, that the disciplinary perspectives are politics and political economy, not sociology.

■ www.britishcouncil.org/learning-elt-future.pdf A 66-page report sponsored by the British Council on the future of English in relation to other world languages.

CHAPTER 4

The Changing World of Work

CONTENTS

How people experience and cope with work is a central and enduring theme in sociology, though much recent work in the discipline has also been concerned with consumerism, leisure and personal lifestyles, popular culture and the media. Despite this new emphasis, for most of us the passport that gives access to the pleasures of contemporary non-work life continues to be the money we earn from paid employment in the production of goods and services. What is the changing nature of work in the global age and in what ways do these transformations impact on us?

In this chapter we look first at the so-called 'golden age' of mid-twentieth-century 'Fordist' prosperity and examine its rise, its main structural features, the national and global basis for its success and its impact on work and social life. Then we examine the explanations for its partial decline, which accelerated during the economic crisis of the 1970s. Here, we outline some of the coincidental transformations that were gathering pace at the same time such as the growth of IT and computerization, the quickening pace of the switch of jobs into services rather than industry, the rise of industrial competition from NICs and the huge flow of women into part- and full-time employment. Finally, we consider the growing worldwide realities of job insecurity and the casualization of employment, which have become increasingly evident since the late 1970s and which some observers have labelled as the era of 'post-Fordism'. Despite these vast changes, it is important to remember that the realities of capitalist competition, market pressures and the unequal exercise of economic power by big corporations and wealthy elites have provided an underlying continuity throughout this period.

ACCUMULATION AND REPRODUCTION: OVERVIEW

The issues of capitalist accumulation and reproduction have long preoccupied sociologists and others. You will recall that in Chapter 3 we considered Marx's argument that the rise of industrial capitalism in the West required a preceding period of often-violent 'primitive capital accumulation'. State power was used to separate peasants and craftsmen from their independent sources of livelihood and create private property. Somewhat later, Weber, in his famous book *The Protestant Ethic and the Spirit of Capitalism* (1977), also speculated about the possible cultural and political origins of early capitalism and the rationalization process, which he saw partly in terms of the unique, cumulative legacy of European tradition. This included the powerful tensions evoked by Protestantism and the drive towards a life of ceaseless work and rational striving in the hope of earning religious salvation.

Not only does capitalism first need to be carved, often brutally, out of traditional cultures, but once set on a course for industrialization it cannot operate alone and unaided. Capitalist economies continue to require various kinds of supports. From the state, among other things, domestic capital needs taxation policies that encourage investment, some protection in the early stages of industrialization from overseas competition and a willingness to finance public assets that enhance international competitiveness – especially infrastructure and rising educational attainment. For their part, society's members must be willing, for example, to pay taxes, tolerate a degree of inequality, respond to material incentives and be able to cope with constant changes in technology along with the adjustments these dictate in private lifestyles.

'Regulation' theorists such as Aglietta (1979) and Lipietz (1987) added to our understanding of the issue of capitalist reproduction. They argue that despite its proneness to periodic crises, capitalism often passes through long periods of relatively uninterrupted economic growth. However, these eras of stability require the conjunction of two sets of conditions, a 'regime of accumulation' and a 'mode of regulation':

- *A regime of accumulation:* This refers to the way production is actually organized in factories, mines, offices and other workplaces. Employers seek to maximize profits by both paying their employees less than the value of what they have helped to produce and ensuring the efficient control and disposition of labour and machinery at the workplace. Profits are then 'realized' by selling commodities on the market. Both capitalists and society also need to strike some sort of balance between the proportion of profit invested in expansion and the share that is consumed by individuals (as wages) and by governments (through taxation) on public goods such as health and education.
- *A mode of regulation:* This involves common acceptance of a cluster of rules (for example in relation to negotiation procedures), norms, institutions, cultural expectations about 'proper' consumption levels and supportive political policies. By guaranteeing social stability and appropriate government, these ensure the reproduction of capitalism over time.

When one or both of these sets of conditions ceases to be effective, a period of crisis is likely to erupt. Profits fall, economic growth slows down and signs of social conflict and distress become evident. Radical restructuring of the production process and a new mode of regulation may become necessary before a new era of stable accumulation can emerge. Similarly, an enduring period of capitalist accumulation is probably more likely when a suitable regulatory climate is also in place in the ordering of world as well as national politics. Indeed, this seems to have been the case between 1948 and the early 1970s.

THE FORDIST REGIME OF ACCUMULATION

As a regime of accumulation, **FORDISM** is said to have slowly increased its domination of the world economy from the end of the nineteenth century until the early 1970s. It was accompanied by a highly effective mode of regulation at both the national and world levels. Henry Ford developed 'Fordism' in his manufacture of the model T car at his Highland Park and Rouge plants in Detroit between 1908 and 1916 (see Figure 4.1 later in this chapter). He is generally credited with pioneering the mass production techniques imitated in many countries, industries and packing processes, even in agriculture (see Figure 4.2). You will gain some idea of what it was like to work under Fordist conditions from Box 4.1.

FORDISM Named after its pioneer, the car maker Henry Ford, this industrial system involved the mass production of standardized goods by large, integrated companies. Each company was composed of many different, specialized departments, each producing components and parts that were eventually channelled towards the moving line for final assembly.

Box 4.1

Work experience in a Ford motor plant in the 1960s

Huw Beynon's (1973) classic study of the Ford motor plant at Halewood in Liverpool offers a fascinating account of working life at a fairly typical mass production plant in the late 1960s. Here, we briefly glimpse some of the experiences involved. Ford established its three Halewood plants between 1958 and 1963, though its largest UK investment remained at Dagenham. At Halewood, the moving assembly line – which came to symbolize the essentially disempowering nature of twentieth-century, machine-dominated 'Fordist' manufacturing – was situated in the same factory where the car bodies were painted and fitted with their final trimmings (lights, seats and so on). Over 80 per cent of the manual workers employed in a car assembly plant supplied back-up support for those working on the line.

About 16,000 different components had to be 'screwed, stuck or spot-welded' (Beynon 1973: 105) to the moving car bodies as they slipped down the line. Each worker was tied to his station and endlessly repeated the same fixed tasks. On average, the line workers were allocated two minutes to complete each job, depending on the exact 'timing' that management judged was sufficient for its completion. When market demand was expanding, the management might decide to speed up the line or reduce the manning levels. This meant frequent changes to work schedules and a need for intensified output. Six minutes out of the 480-minute working day were allowed for visits to the toilet and other natural functions. Unlike workers making or supplying components, those on the moving assembly line were rarely able to increase their output by a burst of effort to create a brief space for smoking or chatting with workmates. Moreover, the noise levels made talking virtually impossible (workers resorted to hand signals). Workers could not disrupt the smooth sequence of operations by leaving the line or failing to complete a task in the allocated time, which made it difficult to seek temporary relief from work by socializing with workmates.

The loneliness, mind-blowing tedium and relentless pressures occasioned by working on the line generated considerable frustration. Not surprisingly, the changes to manning levels and speed-ups compounded these problems and were all-too-frequent bones of contention between workers and management. They often generated tensions, disputes and work stoppages. How did the employees, especially those working on the line, cope with their jobs? They blanked out their minds, thought about the relatively high wages they would spend at the weekends (better money than could be obtained by semi-skilled workers elsewhere in Liverpool), joked with their workmates or played tricks on the foremen. Some dreamed of moving to a more 'worthwhile' job.

SOURCE: Beynon (1973)

From the perspective of the employees, the Fordist production regime involved a number of difficult and **ALIENATING** experiences. Work was fragmented into many different activities, for example welding a particular bolt onto the corner of a toy or operating a specialized machine for pressing out one of the metal pieces used to assemble a refrigerator door. Each worker carried out one of these highly specialized tasks repeatedly, often remaining on the same job for long periods of time. This made work tedious and unsatisfying, but it simultaneously made for overall speed and efficiency.

key concept	
	ALIENATION Marx believed that it is mainly through creative, self-directed work in the satisfaction of our own needs that we fully realize our inner selves and potential. However, under capitalism, workers become estranged or alienated from their skills and their potential, since now they are driven to work for capitalists in order to survive, and the product of their labour no longer belongs to them. Sociologists have employed this term more generally to describe the powerlessness and lack of creativity believed to be endemic to many aspects of contemporary life.

■ ■

Global Thinkers 4 KARL MARX (1818–83)

Karl Marx was a social scientist as well as a revolutionary, the two roles being fused in his famous statement: 'The philosophers have only interpreted the world differently; the point is, to change it.' Marx tried to do both. His social theory generated a rich vein of ideas, propositions and historical arguments that have preoccupied scholars for 150 years. His political interventions gave rise to 'Marxism', an ideology that informed radical social thinkers, movements for international labour solidarity and revolutionary parties in many parts of the world. The great revolutions in Russia and China were underpinned by his thinking, while the remaining communist regimes, in North Korea and China, still evoke his name. It is probably the case that Marx would have been shocked by repressive state-centred forms of communism. Here we evoke his key starting points and ideas.

1. *Marx was a **materialist**. He drew on previous German philosophers like Hegel who saw the world moving forward through a relentless competition of ideas – as one idea emerged, another contradicted it. The resulting thesis in turn generated opposition. This* dialectic *attracted Marx but he rejected Hegel's* idealism *(in the sense of spirit, ideas and consciousness) in favour of* materialism. *What people ate, how they lived and how they produced goods and commodities needed to be placed at the centre of any analysis, thereby extracting, as he put it, 'the rational kernel from its mystical shell'.*
2. *Marx was a **historian**. He placed the movement of the dialectic within successive historical 'modes of production'. Primitive communism* was replaced by *slavery. The dialectic conflict between masters and slaves led to* feudalism, *the internal*

contradictions of which led in turn to capitalism. *There the workers and capitalists (Marx called them the 'proletariat' and 'bourgeoisie') would engage in a massive social conflict leading to* socialism *and thence (in its higher stage) to* communism. *Only then would human conflict end.*

3. *Marx was a* **political economist**. *The two subject matters of political science and economics have now generally separated, but in the nineteenth century they were usefully united in the work of scholars like Adam Smith and David Ricardo. Marx drew selectively and critically from this corpus, emerging particularly with a theory of surplus value. This showed how in their labour workers first paid for themselves, next paid for their reproduction (enough for the family and other social provision), then left enough 'value' for the capitalists to cream off in the form of profits and dividends. This crucial insight, elaborated in three volumes of* Das Kapital, *provided the core for Marx's scientific claims.*

4. *Marx was a* **sociologist**. *He had many insights into how the 'forces of production' linked to the 'relations of production'. This is sometimes called the 'base-superstructure' question in Marx and we can recognize it as similar to the 'structure–agency' question in contemporary sociology. For Marx, forms of consciousness derived from a particular relationship to the means of production. Thus, when 'great masses of men are suddenly and forcibly torn from their means of subsistence and hurled onto the labour market' (Marx 1976: 876), they become conscious as a class. Working together in difficult factory conditions led to trade unionism and, Marx supposed, a commitment ultimately to overthrow capitalism by revolutionary means. In this prediction, Marx was clearly wrong, though why he was wrong still provokes passionate debate.*

SOURCES: Avineri (1968); Marx (1976); Cohen (1978).

A precondition for efficient production was the adoption of the principles of 'scientific management', or **TAYLORIZATION**, a term derived from the American engineer Frederick Taylor. From the 1890s, he played a leading role in encouraging US industrialists to measure work activity precisely while establishing the optimum time required for each task. It has been widely argued that Taylorist techniques were ultimately designed to capture the shop-floor knowledge and skills once possessed by workers and to incorporate these into machinery and management practices. This progressively deskilled the workforce and increased management's ability to control the labour process.

key concept	**TAYLORIZATION** is the name given to the process accompanying Fordism, whereby most work processes were scientifically studied by managers so as to find ways to break them down into highly specialized and efficient tasks while removing most of the skill and responsibility formerly exercised by the workers.

At the plant level, a techno-structure of scientists, engineers and others became necessary, supported by a hierarchy of managers striving to coordinate the levels of multiple activities. The result was that both the creative design processes involved in production and the actual control of the latter shifted decisively from workbench to laboratory and office. These changes in work organization normally enabled management to obtain much higher and perhaps continuously rising levels of worker productivity for each given level of investment in plant and machinery.

Not surprisingly, Fordist plants required heavy and long-term investment in plant, capital-intensive equipment and research facilities. Thus, plants contained numerous departments each specializing in a different activity from processing incoming raw materials such as rolled steel to manufacturing most of the remaining engine and transmission components as well as body parts needed to produce the finished product and then all the way up to the finishing touches such as lighting, paintwork and upholstery. The outputs of all these departments were then brought together for final assembly. This meant that large complex corporations became the dominant forms of business enterprise. In the late 1960s, for example, the Ford factory in Detroit employed 40,000 workers on one site, while Ford factories at Birmingham and Oxford in the UK each had more than 25,000 workers (Webster 2002: 64). Indeed, in 1963, one-third of the British labour force employed in private industry worked in companies of 10,000 or more (Webster 2002: 64).

Despite its negative features, mass production also led to increased productivity, the possibility of higher wages and gradually improving work conditions. Ford introduced the US$5 daily wage and considerably reduced working hours as early as 1914, though this was partly an attempt to reduce the high rates of absenteeism and labour turnover generated by the intensity and speed of work required at his plants. But these gains did not necessarily mean that unions gained full recognition from Fordist employers. Most of the large US corporations only acceded to worker and public demand for unionization as a result of intense plant struggles and political pressure during the New Deal era in the late 1930s or – in Ford's case – in 1941.

Two additional features of the Fordist era need to be carefully noted. First, Fordism was constructed very definitely on the assumption that the labour force would be predominantly male. Along with this went the, then, widely accepted social convention that the husband was the main breadwinner and this pattern guaranteed the social and biological reproduction of the nation based on a 'stable' mother-centred family life. Of course, since the beginning of the industrial era, the majority of women had always worked before marriage and often returned once their children were older. However, only a minority had worked full time. For example, the proportion of UK women who did this between the 1950s and the 1980s remained more or less constant at one-third (Edgell 2005: Chapter 4). The second feature to note is that in all countries the Fordist economy rested mostly on national foundations. Again, this is demonstrated by the British case in which even by the late 1960s UK firms supplied nearly 90 per cent of the domestic market for manufactured goods (Webster 2002: 67).

Figure 4.1 Ford's Highland Park plant in 1913
History was made as the flywheel magneto was the first manufactured part to be built on a moving assembly line. Mass production was born. By breaking up jobs into simple repetitive tasks, the power of craftsmen was broken.

Figure 4.2 Chiquita Banana Plantation, Cahuita, Costa Rica, 1996
Central American bananas are generally cut and packed on Fordist principles. The idea of a moving assembly line was copied from Chicago meat packers, who in the 1900s adopted the practice of hanging hog carcasses from a moving overhead rail, a technique used now in banana packing and many industrial processes.

THE RISE OF MASS CONSUMPTION SOCIETY

Not only did Fordist production often lead to rising wages but the sheer scale and relatively standardized nature of the output drastically reduced the costs of producing each item. For example, the average price of Ford's model T car fell from US$950 to US$360 between 1909 and 1917 (Edgell 2005: Chapter 4). Gradually, therefore, the increased flow of cheaper, standardized commodities meant that mass production slowly generated the basis – and the necessity – for the era of mass consumption. This was accompanied by the expansion of the advertising industry, the extension of credit facilities for average income earners and the increased importance of sales and marketing. An expanding public sector and the growth of science and administration also boosted the growth of the services sector in Fordist economies. At the same time a leisure society gradually evolved, where workers spent their rising wages and growing non-work hours on enjoying the private pleasures of participation in car ownership, holidays, consuming radio, film and television, and the improvement of their homes. In short, Fordism enabled capitalism to solve one of the recurring problems that had slowed economic growth and generated endless conflicts over low wages and unemployment during much of the nineteenth century, namely a tendency towards underconsumption or narrow markets.

AN EFFECTIVE MODE OF REGULATION AT GLOBAL AND NATIONAL LEVELS

In the USA, much of this prosperity generated by Fordism began in the 1920s but was delayed by the Great Depression and the Second World War. Elsewhere, the era of mass consumption only really arrived when the long boom got underway in the 1950s, along with the widespread diffusion of US management techniques and the re-equipping of postwar industries. Fordism helped to lay the foundations for postwar prosperity in the factories. But the successful Fordist formula also lay in the highly favourable mode of regulation created by government policies such as Keynesianism in the period after 1945.

In Chapter 3 we outlined the main ways in which global forces boosted prosperity after the Second World War. At the national level, too, we can identify a cluster of policies that provided a good environment for Fordist expansion. In good part these measures were influenced by the Western democracies' fear of communism and the spectres of the Great Depression and Fascism. The key plank of these measures was an accommodation between labour and capital, including full union recognition, accepting skill demarcations demanded by workers, linking wages to productivity gains and improving wages, working conditions and pensions. In some companies, jobs were traded in exchange for workers' acceptance of Fordist production methods, while other firms, especially in Germany and Scandinavia, adopted more conciliatory worker–manager consultation schemes.

Issues of social cohesion and social justice were also given much more attention by the state, in an effort to establish a consensus with its citizenry similar to that being pursued by employers in the work sphere. State intervention was designed to achieve a social democratic accord. This implied that everyone had a right to a minimum of lifetime protection and security. In the European countries – less so in Japan and the USA – governments improved the welfare state. Keynesian spending policies were widely adopted to stimulate growth through increased investment in publicly owned services and enterprises. Full employment policies became the top priority, while some attempt was made to achieve income redistribution through progressive taxation.

EXPLAINING THE DECLINE OF THE 'GOLDEN AGE'

The 'golden age' of high production, high consumption and secure employment slowly began to disintegrate in the late 1960s, a tendency that gathered pace during the 1970s. At the same time, other powerful economic, technological but also social changes increasingly intervened in ways that undermined the previous economic foundations. We now examine these forces that together led to a decline in the Fordist system.

THE CRISIS OF FORDISM AS A PRODUCTION REGIME

We begin by examining five contradictions that developed within the Fordist production regime itself:

1. In a sense its very success in helping to create a long period of full employment and rising prosperity was its own undoing. Thus, union power was enhanced

by increased prosperity but, while consumer demand continued to expand, many employers were reluctant to risk losing their market share through prolonged industrial conflict. Accordingly, it was hard for employers to resist wage demands and this contributed to the build-up of inflationary pressures. This meant that some firms became uncompetitive.

2. It became more difficult to achieve continuous increases in worker productivity while keeping ahead of wage rises and maintaining profitability. This was linked to the inherent inflexibility of large plants relying on overspecialized equipment in the face of rising consumer sophistication. Union resistance towards increasing work fragmentation and attempts to intensify the pace and machine-driven nature of work also challenged managerial authority. This resistance was widely signalled in 1968, when across Europe, but especially in France and Italy, workers and students demonstrated their antipathy to the 'Fordist bargain', whereby workers agreed to exchange disempowerment at work for greater material prosperity.

3. Profits began to fall in the late 1960s and economic growth slowed. This was exacerbated by wider factors such as the oil price rises of the 1970s and increasing worldwide competition especially from Japan (see below) and some NICs such as Brazil and South Korea. Indeed, the 1970s saw a major profits crisis for Western capitalism and was associated with several years of economic recession.

4. By the 1950s, a consumer youth culture had emerged with no memory of prewar poverty. For the next decade or two the main priority of most consumers was simply to acquire the new commodities and the social status bestowed by ownership. They bought their first washing machine or second-hand family car and tried to 'keep up with the Joneses' (Murray 1989). This contrasts markedly with the period from the 1970s, when **POSTMODERN** sensibilities were aroused and consumers became interested in the creation of personal identity and individual lifestyles through the possession of fashion and designer goods (Featherstone 1992).

5. The growing market pressures for more customized goods – designed to meet the individual's personal requirements – helped to cut a giant swathe through the rather rigid Fordist mass production system. In its place, a more adaptable system gradually emerged, based, among other things, on smaller enterprises, a greater ability to cope with rapid changes in demand and more immediate contacts between producers and their market outlets.

key concept	**POSTMODERNISM** According to postmodernists, unlike the earlier era of modernity, our lives are now said to be less and less determined by family, class, community and national loyalties or by social expectations linked to such things as gender or race. Instead, these structures, along with the moral and political certainties about the nature of truth and destiny with which they were associated, have largely disintegrated. Simultaneously, our increasing exposure to huge amounts of information, often associated through the mass media and advertising with a battery of swirling signs and images, caused a communication overload. We no longer know what

'realities' are being represented by signs so everything becomes a simulation. Like truth and morality, reality and authenticity become less believable. All this leaves us free to forge our own identities out of an increasingly diverse cultural repertoire of fragments, although this may also cause us some anxiety.

A COLLAPSING MODE OF NATIONAL AND GLOBAL REGULATION

Another set of explanations for the demise of Fordism concerns the piece by piece disintegration of all the national and global elements that had previously appeared to sustain a favourable mode of regulation. While it may have been no more than coincidence, from the early 1970s all these wider forces supporting the Fordist production system seemed to lose something of their former momentum more or less concurrently. As this happened, the Fordist era gradually waned. Depending on which interpretation is utilized, it changed either towards the new era of greater flexibility or to the disorder and uncertainty characteristic of global capitalism today. In the latter interpretation, we seem to be left with a system in need of a viable regulatory regime capable of restoring some semblance of the lost golden years. We alluded to some of these issues in Chapter 3. However, Box 4.2 provides a refinement of that earlier discussion along with some further details.

Box 4.2

The collapse of the Fordist mode of regulation

At the national level

The relations between labour and capital deteriorated. Organized labour was increasingly blamed for inflationary wage demands, resisting technological change and wresting control from capital, thereby hitting profits. Consequently, governments:

1. Reduced or abolished minimum wage laws and employment protection.

2. Weakened trade unions with restrictive legislation and discouraged national pay bargaining.

3. Reduced or ended universal welfare benefits and attacked public spending.

4. Moved towards indirect taxation levied on consumption and cut income taxes on the rich.

5. Abandoned full employment policies.

The social democratic consensus ended

At the global level

Bretton Woods collapsed in the early 1970s and international finance became more disordered:

1. The USA devalued the dollar in 1971 and exchange rates began to float, causing currency uncertainty.

2. Banks were allowed to deregulate their international operations. These banks gradually formed a privatized global credit system outside governments' control and absorbed surplus dollars around the world. This undermined domestic economic policy.

3. From the mid-1970s the IMF and World Bank relaxed their responsibility for monitoring world borrowing. Thus, the vast funds in the global credit system were lent to developing countries, often for wasteful purposes.

and Keynesianism was rejected (especially in the USA and the UK):

1. The free-market agenda became pre-eminent, leading to privatization, the deregulation of markets and the creation of more incentives for private business.

2. Keynesian policies became discredited. Thus, government spending to stimulate the economy was now regarded as inflationary and obstructing free markets and the efficient allocation of resources. Accordingly, public spending on public utilities and welfare was reduced.

3. Monetarist policies – a shift to the control of interest rates and the money supply – became pre-eminent.

4. The control of inflation became the priority.

5. Transnational controls on money and capital flows were abolished. This accelerated the globalization of money, bank lending and stocks and shares.

4. Inflationary pressures built up in the world economy driven by 1, 2 and 3 plus extravagant Western spending policies carried out to win elections. (However, Keynesian domestic policies and 'strong' trade unions got most of the blame for global inflation).

The USA's capacity for world economic leadership declined:

1. Growing import penetration began to cause deindustrialization in some of the USA's once vibrant regions ('rust-belts'). Rising military spending aggravated inflation and further worsened the balance of payments deficit.

2. Domestic crises and foreign humiliations (growing defeat in Vietnam) rocked the presidency (for example Nixon's impeachment in 1976) and domestic political stability.

3. Reagan's policy in the 1980s of further military expansion required a huge rise in interest rates to encourage more lending to the US government via purchases of treasury Bills.

4. This precipitated a severe world recession and caused an international debt crisis because raw material prices and earnings fell while the cost of debt servicing soared. The USA was also saddled with a crippling debt burden.

5. The US military invasions of Afghanistan and Iraq after the events of 11 September 2001 also raised the prospect of 'imperial overreach' and started a decline in the value of the US dollar.

Fordism was also placed at risk by its very success in contributing to the spread of worldwide industrialization, so intensifying international competition. Thus, by the 1960s, the war-torn economies of Europe and Japan had recovered. Soon they began to export to the US economy. These exports enabled them to generate the dollars required to repay US loans and purchase American machinery. During the 1960s, US TNCs increasingly tried to capture a share of the growing European markets by engaging in foreign direct investment (FDI) as the economic recovery gathered pace. But, quite soon this accelerated 'Americanization' of European economic life was also matched by a parallel drive on the part of the Europeans to invest directly in the US market.

Meanwhile, Japan had been pursuing a highly successful policy of export-led growth since the mid-1950s with US approval. By the 1970s, technological advance, its investment in overseas trade networks and its keen responsiveness to changing consumer requirements enabled Japan to make massive inroads into the home markets of all its competitors, while keeping its own domestic economy relatively closed. At the same time, growing manufactured exports from the NICs, initially of fairly standard, low-value goods, also resulted in rising import penetration into the North American and European markets.

The net effect of this rapid increase in international competition – with major cities everywhere displaying all the offices, sales networks, adverts and neon signs of the leading TNCs – was to place further pressure on companies to increase the distinctiveness of their own products. Cut-throat competition also underlined the importance of price as a factor in competitiveness and highlighted the problem of rising domestic wage levels relative to those in other countries. Higher wages were no longer seen as a boon but an obstacle to Fordist success.

JAPANIZATION AND THE RISE OF FLEXIBLE LABOUR

So successful was foreign, especially Japanese, competition by the 1970s that many European and US companies began to imitate Japanese management practices, a process known as **JAPANIZATION**. We can see why from the following data. In automobile production – a core part of the structure of developed economies – Japanese output rose rapidly, reaching 11 million vehicles in 1980 compared with 8 million in the USA in the same year (Dohse et al. 1985: 117). Also in 1980, Japanese home production accounted for 28 per cent of total world output and captured 25 per cent of the US market. By 2006, Toyota was set to outstrip General Motors as the world's number one car maker.

key concept	**JAPANIZATION** refers to the conscious attempt, especially in the 1980s, to imitate the organizational culture developed by Japan's huge companies, such as Toyota, and especially their highly effective strategies with regard to managing labour relations in factories (see also Box 4.3). Such attempts at transplanting Japan's methods to other countries have not always been completely successful.

From the mid-1980s Japanization was helped by the fact that a growing number of Japan's TNCs established branch plants in Europe and North America – especially in vehicles and electrical consumer goods. This created yet more opportunities for direct comparisons with Japanese business techniques while exposing workers to unfamiliar labour relations at first hand. These moves by Japanese companies occurred because they were anxious to escape the possibility that their export success would invite protectionist retaliation. Also, the USA persuaded Japan's government to revalue the yen in 1985 in an attempt to make Japanese goods more expensive and so reduce the US trade deficit.

Two contending arguments in the literature attempt to throw light on the nature of post-Fordism and whether the forms of production developed in Japan caused a fundamental rupture in work methods (Box 4.3).

Box 4.3

Japanese production and the changing nature of global work

Dore (1986), Kenny and Florida (1988) and Womack et al. (1990) claim that although Japan was influenced by Fordist techniques after 1945, certain unique social and cultural arrangements have always been built into its very system of factory, work and business organization. These have helped to make its workers highly productive and capable of absorbing continuous technical improvements, while enabling its factories to adapt quickly to market changes. Thus, flexibility – the hallmark of post-Fordism – has always been present. Its roots are said to lie in the following arrangements.

The supporting culture of Japanese production systems:

■ For workers employed in the largest companies (perhaps one-third of the workforce), employment is guaranteed over a lifetime and the pay system is based on a mixture of reward according to individual performance and seniority.

■ Labour markets are segmented such that workers in progressively smaller companies – right down to tiny rural enterprises – enjoy fewer and fewer benefits.

■ Specialized support organizations for manufacturers (called *keiretsu*) operate across enterprises and industries. They provide all member firms with guaranteed contracts, access to new knowledge and perhaps credit on preferential terms. The *keiretsu* also create chains of subcontracting arrangements, permitting companies to minimize their investments and risks while retaining the advantages of specialization.

■ Workshop organization encourages employees to seek constant technical improvements and accept job and skill rotation as production needs change. A hands-on managerial approach to production and a willingness to value worker experience boost this flexibility.

What results from all this is *just-in-time* and *lean* production. Close proximity to suppliers minimizes the need for companies to carry vast stocks of materials and components. Meanwhile, a highly motivated workforce, empowered by its approach to management and favourable terms of employment, seeks constant improvements.

Mean production? However, other writers (Dohse et al. 1985; Williams et al. 1992; Elger and Smith 1994) see a very different picture. They explain Japanese production efficiency in terms of mean rather than lean production. This is an intensive kind of Fordism, based on unlimited managerial control over a super-exploited workforce made possible by the defeat of Japan's organized workers in the early 1950s.

Understanding Japan's way of organizing production is important for a couple of reasons. First, it meant that, perhaps for the first time during the era of spreading modernization, the flow of ideas and models from the West outwards to the rest of the world had been significantly reversed. Japan had become the teacher not the learner. Second, the Japanization of work and business organization – and not simply the increased competition it generated – has been seen by many scholars as another highly significant factor in the worldwide shift towards an era of much greater flexibility and insecurity in work conditions that some, though not all, observers think is sufficiently different to be called **POST-FORDISM**.

---

key concept

POST-FORDISM This condition exists where most workers are employed on a temporary or casual basis, enjoy few if any pension or other rights and where labour has limited power to organize in order to resist employer demands. Capitalists therefore enjoy more direct control over their employees than was possible under Fordism, including the ability to maintain a highly flexible and adaptable labour force. Other writers are less convinced and see more underlying continuities than discontinuities between the eras preceding and following the 1970s, though they concede this was a watershed in many respects. They therefore prefer to use the label neo-Fordist rather than post-Fordist.

■■■■■■■■■ TRANSFORMATIONS ACCOMPANYING THE DECLINE OF FORDISM

The weakening of Fordism as a regime of accumulation and a mode of regulation at national and global levels rocked its once apparently secure foundations. Even more destabilizing was the fact that, by the 1970s, Fordism had also been beset by several additional transformations that were working their way through the world economy. These were the increased importance of the service industries, the revolution in ICTs, the growing role of women in the workforce and the more competitive world market pressures resulting from economic globalization.

THE SHIFT TO SERVICE JOBS

In the 1960s, the shift of employment towards the service industries that characterized all modernizing societies became more important. Just after the Second World War, services accounted for 49 per cent of jobs in the USA (Bell 1973: 132), but by the 1990s this proportion had risen to between 70 (Webster 2002: 45) and 75 per cent (Dicken 2003: 525), not only in the USA but in practically all the advanced countries. The associated decline in manufacturing jobs was particularly acute in the UK from the mid-1960s, but accelerated during the 1970s across most European countries (Dicken 2003: 525). According to Castells (1996: 226), manufacturing employment in the USA was expected to fall from 17.5 per cent of the labour force in 1990 to 14 per cent by 2005. Included in this large services category are the professions. By around 1990, people in these jobs (which included those engaged in medicine, research, science, law, engineering, the 'caring' occupations and, among others, those working in ICTs, the media and education) made up nearly one-third of the workforce of the advanced countries.

The many less well-paid, secure or fulfilling jobs in the leisure and entertainment sectors are also, of course, included in the general category of 'services'. One of the most obvious inclusions here is the fast-food industry, associated, above all, with McDonald's, though numerous additional restaurant chains like Pizza Hut, Taco Bell and Starbucks have spread across the world since McDonald's first opened in the USA in 1955. Although under some threat through overexpansion, by 2003 McDonald's had 31,172 restaurants across the world – over half of which were outside the USA – with total sales of US$41 billion in 2002 (Ritzer 2004a: 2–3). What is interesting about the fast-food industry is that it has developed some key organizational features that are generally acknowledged to be strongly Fordist in character. In addition, a number of other service industries, which include not only businesses like The Body Shop, IKEA, Wal-Mart, H&M Clothing and Gap but also private health-care, certain aspects of private and public education, tourism and sports facilities, have also, at least partly, moulded their organizational arrangements along the lines of the Fordist-leaning fast-food industry.

In various publications, Ritzer (1993, 1998, 2004a, 2004b) has applied Weber's insight into the dominant tendency towards formal rationality in modern capitalist economies (see Global Thinkers 3) to the fast-food and other service sectors. He argues that these sectors have achieved great success because they have maximized the market and profitable potential provided by four operating principles: efficiency, calculability, predictability and control through technology. While the first offers customers a cheap, convenient and accessible way of satisfying their various needs – such as feeding hungry children who are easily seduced by fatty, bland yet tasty foods supplied in cheerful surroundings – the second guarantees solidly reliable products in terms of their size, dimensions, content (for example the Big Mac in various sizes) and the time required to provide them. Here, quantifying costs and profits for the business and price and quality for the customer is paramount. Predictability involves the assurance 'that products and services will be the same over time and in all locales' (Ritzer 2004a: 14), as well as the need for employees to adopt certain 'scripted' behaviours when dealing with customers, including ritualized 'pseudo interactions' such as wishing everyone a 'nice day' and being dressed in familiar company uniforms (Ritzer 2004a: 91). Finally, business and work arrangements (limited menus, timed and programmed operations, technologies that standardize food mixtures and an assembly-line system), coupled with time-saving equipment like microwave ovens and automatic drink dispensers, all combine to deskill the workers and fragment their work experience (Ritzer 2004a: 15, 189).

Accordingly, emotion, spontaneity and any room for autonomy on the part of workers and even customers are minimized so that standardized products are mass produced by homogenized and interchangeable employees for highly ratio-nalized and profitable companies. To a greater or lesser extent Ritzer claims that similar processes can be observed in many other service industries, though the scope for such intense rationalization is obviously somewhat limited in organiz-ations like schools, nursing homes or health centres, while some contemporary restaurant chains have tried to be less instrumental. We might categorize the latter as neo-Fordist, therefore, rather than Fordist (Edgell 2005: Chapter 4).

THE REVOLUTION IN ICTs AND THE RISE OF SYMBOLIC ECONOMY

Another impact on work and leisure has been the revolution taking place in information and communication technologies (ICTs) – much of it emanating from the innovative mix of young and experimental technologists working in numerous tiny firms and/or linked to universities, many based in and around California's Silicon Valley (Castells 1996: 53–60). This revolution, which gathered pace during the 1970s, was boosted in 1971 by the invention of the microprocessor or chip, which hugely increased the amount of information that could be stored. This heralded an 'information society', whereby knowledge – whether in the form of scientific research, design, the media, creating new products, formulas or symbols – became the key component in wealth creation, reducing the significance of other inputs like manual labour, raw materials or energy. The emergence of the knowledge or symbolic economy, in turn, has made possible the rise of what Castells and other writers (Webster 2002; Urry 2003) call the 'network society'. Here, business enterprises and other organizations can now spread more easily across borders, may become less centralized and hierarchical while transferring power more into the hands of the knowledge-makers and disseminators. Castells also avers that the ability of capital to undertake this worldwide reorganization was massively enhanced by ICTs, because businesses could utilize the possibilities these presented for coordinating complex operations across vast distances and linking consumers more closely to production processes. Thus, the transition to post-Fordism was partly rooted in technological change (Castells 1996: 240). We say more about the reverberating implications of ICTs in Chapter 14.

THE DRAMATIC MOVEMENT OF WOMEN INTO THE WORKFORCE

The proportion of women in paid work in the USA increased from 49 to 69 per cent between 1970 and 1990 (Beck 2000a) and reached 70.5 per cent by 1994 (Castells 1997: 159). Similar rises have been recorded for other countries over the same period from 1970 to 1990, from 33.5 to 43.3 per cent in Italy, 47.4 to 59 per cent in France and 48.1 to 65.3 per cent in Germany (Castells 1996: 253). The scale of this increase is not confined to the developed countries but also occurred in countries such as Egypt and Brazil. Overall, more than 850 million women were economically active – most outside their homes – across the world in 1990, nearly one-third of the global labour force or 41 per cent if we only include those over the age of 15.

Linked to this massive and more or less worldwide increase in female paid employment has been not only the improved educational participation rate for girls but also greater economic independence from kin and husbands. Beck and Beck-Gernsheim (2002: 23) regard this overall transformation as little short of a 'global gender revolution', since it has paved the way, albeit unequally across countries, for women to exercise more choice over whether or who to marry (or divorce), when and whether to have children and how to balance career and family identities. Whereas for nineteenth-century middle-class women 'everyday life was nearly always a fenced-off preserve of family and neighbours' (Beck and Beck-Gernsheim 2002: 64), now women can 'display expectations and wishes that extend beyond the family' (Beck and Beck-Gernsheim 2002: 56) and begin to 'make a life of their own'. Similarly, Castells (1997: 135) talks of the 'challenge' to the patriarchal family and the 'transformation of women's consciousness' that have occurred during recent decades and relates these partly to the increase in women's paid employment. We discuss these changes and their implications more thoroughly in Chapter 19.

GROWING COMPETITION FROM NICs

As we saw above, Japan's successful incursions into European and North American home and overseas markets intensified the crisis of Fordist businesses – rising inflation, falling profits, contracting markets and rising unemployment. However, since the 1950s, a growing number of NICs had also been starting to manufacture and export a widening range of products. Between 1953 and the late 1990s, the share of world manufacturing output coming from NICs rose sharply from around 5 to 23 per cent, while that of the developed countries correspondingly shrank from 95 to 77 per cent (Dicken 2003: 37). Since the late 1950s, Southeast Asia's four 'tiger' economies of South Korea, Taiwan, Singapore and Hong Kong had been playing an early role in spearheading this competition, but other countries, including Brazil, India, Malaysia, Thailand and Mexico, also became increasingly important players. Moreover, by 2000, Hong Kong, South Korea, Mexico, Taiwan and Singapore ranked tenth, twelfth, thirteenth, fourteenth and fifteenth respectively in terms of the leading world exporters of manufactured goods, with between a 3.2 and 2.2 per cent share compared, for example, with Canada's 4.3 per cent, Italy's 3.7 per cent or France's 4.7 per cent share, also in 2000 (Dicken 2003: 40).

By the turn of the century, two slumbering giants, China and India, had joined the cluster of Southern industrial powers. By 2005, China had moved into third place (behind the USA and Germany, but ahead of Japan) in the export of manufactured goods – it has 5.8 per cent of the world's total compared with the USA's 9.8 per cent. China's industrial output has been growing at such an astonishing rate that it is increasingly being labelled as the 'workshop of the world', while its GDP overtook the UK's in 2005. Since its admission to the WTO, China's dominance in textiles, shoes and computer parts has been steadily growing. In the first four months of 2005, Chinese shoes exported to the EU rose by 700 per cent, threatening shoe manufacturing in Spain and Italy. Likewise, 237 million T-shirts were imported into the EU. Manufacturers in China have perfected the art of the niche market. Look down at your fly on your trousers or the zipper on your skirt. It is 80 per cent certain that it was produced in a dusty town called Qiaotou in Zhejiang province. There, 25 years ago, three Chinese brothers started a button and zip factory by picking up buttons on the street. Now the town exports two million zips a day (*Guardian*, 25 May 2005). In

1991, India further opened its economy to overseas investment and competition and has expanded its already substantial industrial base. Given the huge populations of these manufacturing giants and their continuing high rates of economic expansion, it seems likely that competition from the South will continue to create both new market opportunities and continuing uncertainties and tensions in the global economy for everyone, including the advanced countries. Not least of these will be the threat of high and rising oil prices as China's and India's energy requirements intensify.

THE AGE OF 'FLEXIBLE' LABOUR AND ECONOMIC INSECURITY

In the advanced countries until the mid-1970s, relatively safe jobs were easily found, while welfare standards were rising. People believed they could look forward to a constantly improving future. Now, hardly a day goes by without someone reminding us that we live in an age of 'hard times', one supposedly dominated by unprecedented technological and economic pressures. Change is said to be rushing across the entire globe and sweeping virtually everyone into its harsh embrace. This is especially threatening for the poor and unskilled, but even educated people with marketable credentials face an insecure future of frequent career changes and unreliable incomes.

While we are probably viewing the golden postwar years through rose-tinted spectacles, and seeing the supposed sharp contrast with the present, it does seem certain that a major shift has taken place in the nature of work and production. This era of insecurity has been variously described as the era of 'post-Fordism' (Lipietz 1987), 'disorganized capitalism' (Lash and Urry 1987), 'flexible specialization' (Piore and Sable 1984), 'flexible accumulation' (Harvey 1989), neo-Fordism (Webster 2002) or simply as the age of flexible labour and casualization. Employing the terms 'post-Fordist' and 'flexible labour', we now explore their implications.

POST-FORDISM AND BUSINESS ORGANIZATION

Three pressures are increasingly driving capital. Although none of them is new, they have all increased in intensity, thereby creating growing uncertainty:

1. Contemporary consumers have become much more demanding, giving rise to the 'globalization of style'.
2. The globalization of capitalist production has intensified competition between firms and countries particularly with respect to consumer goods such as clothing, shoes, electronic products and other consumer goods.
3. Rapid technological change, especially the application of computers and other electronic refinements to production and marketing, the increased use of adaptable machinery and the switch in some industries to advanced auto-

mation and robotization (replacing workers with robots) have heightened the role of knowledge in production. This has also created new opportunities for small businesses to carve out viable and specialized market niches.

NEOLIBERAL policies – involving the deregulation of economic life, reducing the role of states and opening up capital and trade to global market flows – pushed by the USA and G7 nations onto both their own and weaker economies have increased the openness of countries to global economic pressures and competitive forces that are difficult to resist or control.

---

key concept

NEOLIBERALISM is an economic ideology that celebrates the free market, the minimalist state and individual enterprise. British Prime Minister Margaret Thatcher and US President Ronald Reagan embraced it so readily that 'Thatcherism' and 'Reaganism' are now seen as synonyms for or variants of neoliberalism. The doctrine was dominant in the period when failing and unattractive forms of communism prevailed as the major ideological contrast. However, with visible social inequalities and the incapacity of the state to act effectively in situations like the flooding following hurricane Katrina, there is increasing concern that neoliberalism has 'gone too far'.

Together, these pressures have compelled businesses to make drastic changes. The premium is on creating an *adaptable or flexible workforce* so that companies can respond quickly to changes in market demand and fashion. Employers want job rotation and multiskilling to be accepted as a matter of course by their employees. Managements have been encouraged to overcome any worker resistance there may be to technological changes that threaten jobs or organizational arrangements that reduce employees' sense of personal control at the workplace. Accordingly, businesses are likely to regard strong trade unions and tough laws protecting workers from unemployment as obstacles to market success.

Employers also want to *cheapen labour costs* whenever possible and this has encouraged them to develop the following main strategies:

1. The relocation of the more labour-intensive aspects of business to 'safe labour havens' with low wages, unorganized workers and repressive governments. This is exactly what many TNCs did from the late 1960s when they either moved plants to relatively non-industrialized 'sunbelt zones' within their own countries – such as Texas in the USA – or invested in export-processing zones (EPZs) conveniently set up by the governments of many developing countries (see Chapter 7).
2. TNCs have also striven to match their varying labour and technical requirements to the skills found in different parts of the world, while taking into account different cost levels and the quality of available infrastructure. This process of spatially optimizing a company's activities involves seeking rationally to fragment overall operations on a worldwide basis. The world becomes one vast arena onto which companies superimpose their changing grids of multifaceted activities regardless of national borders.

3. Lower labour costs can also be achieved by reducing the proportion of the workforce who are eligible for regular wage increases by virtue of their long period of service or who are entitled to enjoy other advantages like a pension, sickness and unemployment benefits. As this core of permanent employees shrinks, they are replaced by a growing army of casualized workers made up of part-time, temporary, seasonal or homeworkers.

During the 1980s and 90s, part-time work as a proportion of total employment in the advanced countries increased rapidly to between 30 and 40 per cent (cited in Beck 2000a: 56). Beck refers to this process as the 'individualization of work', in which everyone is compelled to take responsibility for his or her own economic future and can no longer rely on protection from employers, governments or trade unions. In effect, labour has become segmented – or bifurcated (McMichael 2000: 191) – between a permanent core and a casualized majority. The latter normally enjoys few if any rights and is exposed to the constant risk of unemployment because firms are free to disclaim any responsibility for these workers when the market contracts.

Businesses also seek to minimize their costs and risks by *downsizing*. Basically, this involves shrinking their operations to a core of activities where they enjoy a special expertise, a technological advantage or an established market niche. Simultaneously, they subcontract more and more of their manufacturing processes to a multitude of other specialized firms, often on a worldwide basis. This process of 'outsourcing' may also extend to leasing certain operations – including marketing, advertising, design, transportation and so on – to small agencies. Franchising represents yet another such activity where large firms patent their product to smaller companies on a profit-sharing basis. Increasingly, too, many companies are forming networks with other small businesses to pool ideas and skills, share design, research and other costs or simply to divide up large contracts.

There are numerous examples of companies engaging in outsourcing. For example, in the 1980s, Benetton, the Italian clothes manufacturer, reduced its core labour force to around 1,500 by franchising most of its production to more than 3,000 operators in 57 countries (Webster 2002: 76–77). Moreover, since the mid-1980s, many companies producing goods such as textiles, shoes and other light manufactures have increasingly shrunk their previous manufacturing activities to a tiny or non-existent level and, instead, have outsourced production to numerous countries, while concentrating on cultivating their company brand image as their primary source of profit through design, advertising and marketing activities (Klein 2001). Not only the branded companies but also supermarkets, big retailing chains and department stores have used outsourcing to obtain clothing and other manufactured products, as well as year-round fresh foods, flowers or exotic food products previously unavailable to most people in the West. To take just one example, Wal-Mart – the world's largest supermarket/retailer by far, with worldwide sales of US$245 billion in 2002 – bought its products from 65,000 suppliers across many countries and also operated 1,300 stores in these countries (Oxfam International 2004: 33).

The need to gauge *rapid and subtle fluctuations in fashion* has compelled many businesses to do two things. One involves using more adaptable, multipurpose equipment while arranging plant and work organization so that they can produce a wide range of non-standardized products in small batches. The other is to establish much closer contact either with retailers, designers and advertisers or directly with consumers. Here, instant communication made possible by electronic links has proved invaluable. Indeed, increasingly, the distinction between the service and manufacturing sectors appears to be breaking down.

▪▪▪▪▪▪▪▪▪ WORKERS IN THE POST-FORDIST PERIOD

How have all these changes affected workers? Those who earn sufficiently high wages have probably gained as consumers, providing all these attempts to cut costs and increase efficiency are in fact being handed on to us in terms of lower prices – something that is not easy to establish beyond doubt. Perhaps, too, our cravings for variety and individuality are being satisfied. These advantages, it is hoped, also compensate for any losses we may experience as insecure wage earners.

However, for a large and perhaps growing proportion of people, living in the North, the South and the former communist world, and including many who are skilled and educated, these compensations may be much less certain. We now offer a selection of key examples illustrating the range of insecure post-Fordist work experiences found in the global economy – in homeworking, in the deindustrializing areas of the rich countries, in Russia and among those who are unable to find even casual work.

WOMEN AND THE NEW CASUALIZED EMPLOYMENT

Previously, we saw that since the 1970s there has been a huge increase in female participation in the labour force. Although this has brought advantages to many women, there has also been a downside. Thus, in the developed countries, it is women who have mostly moved into the fast-expanding service industries but a rising proportion of the jobs created here have been termed 'McJobs' – a term adopted because the conditions it describes are especially typical of the fast-food industry dominated by McDonaldization processes. As such, they offer little security, low wages, limited training or long-term career opportunities and are more often than not part time, seasonal and temporary. Although the part-time, temporary nature of so many service jobs has often benefited women because they provide enough flexibility to enable them to juggle work with looking after children (Dicken 2003: 526), all too often the limited opportunities associated with such work prove to be a permanent feature of many women's work experience.

Women supply much of the labour that has fuelled the vast expansion in manufacturing jobs in the NICs, especially in the garment sector, electronics and basic assembly work; they also do much of the agricultural work for the numerous growers who supply supermarkets with fresh produce. In Honduras, women make up 65 per cent of the workforce in the garment and fresh food sectors, while the proportion is 85 and 90 per cent in Bangladesh and Cambodia respectively (Oxfam International 2004: 17). However, employment conditions for women in these and other countries are often precarious. Ever increasing pressures to work longer hours without overtime pay, being paid the bare national minimum wage (often set at levels dating back several years but long since eroded by inflation), no job security, and the risk of bullying, intimidation and sexual harassment are sadly widespread.

Tesco, the leading British supermarket, outsources its groceries, including fresh produce, to suppliers based in more than 100 countries. This is beneficial because it brings much needed employment to millions of women – and some men – across the world. But Tesco can be an exacting taskmaster. It recently demanded that in future its grape suppliers in South Africa place all fruit in sealed plastic bags in an attempt to reduce the likelihood that its customers would slip on crushed grapes when shopping or at home. Complying with this request increased the time needed to package the fruit by up to 30 per cent, while plastic bags are much more expensive than paper ones. Tesco made no allowance for these extra costs. Other supermarkets soon followed suit. In effect, therefore, the outsourced workers' profits and wages fell substantially, for their weak bargaining position in relation to the market dominance of these huge supermarkets left the women involved and their local employers with little or no room for manoeuvre. Like most other women workers in low-wage countries, they are forced to accept casualization and inequality, irrespective of their needs or the size of their contribution to the global economy (Oxfam International 2004: 74).

DEINDUSTRIALIZATION AND 'RUSTBELT' ZONES

The globalization of industrial production, the widespread adoption of free-market economics and the trend towards post-Fordism have together led to the deindustrialization of many once established and prosperous regions in the advanced countries. As we show in Chapters 8 and 9, the main casualties of these rustbelt zones have been blue-collar manual workers. To take one example of rising labour redundancy linked partly to deindustrialization, in the period 1973–1993, France's GNP grew by 80 per cent, but unemployment increased by around twelve times, reaching over five million in 1993 (McMichael 2000: 191). Massive declines in traditional factory employment have often subjected whole communities to poverty, mental illness, rising crime and other problems because of the downward spiral created by a huge diminution in worker spending power on local taxes, leisure facilities and the social fabric. In addition to blue-collar unemployment, deindustrialization has also brought about a decline in unionized labour and falling real wages especially, though not only, for the remaining manual workers in most of the advanced countries. Thus, in the USA, real average wages fell by nearly 20 per cent from 1975 to 1995, but this decline seems to have been reversed since the late 1990s (McMichael 2000: 191).

The wholesale adoption of post-Fordist, free-market solutions in the wake of the collapse of communism has had variable results in the former Eastern bloc countries, with some economies – notably the Czech Republic, Hungary and Poland – showing notable advances. However, in other countries like Russia, the experience seems to be wholly deleterious, as least in the first decade of free-market capitalism. One Russian worker in four, more than 20 million people, is not paid regularly and delays can be as long as six or even twelve months. According to 1998 figures, Russia's wage debt amounted to US$10 billion. In Moscow 400 enterprises had wage debts. Trade union officials claimed that there were strikes at 1,283 enterprises and organizations in Russia during the first four months of 1998, most concerning the non-payment of wages (Box 4.4).

Box 4.4

Surviving without wages in Russia

How do people manage to survive for months without receiving any wages? The editors of a trade union-supported newsletter interviewed Larisa Seliverstova in mid-1997 to supply the answer to this question. (She is the chairperson of the trade union committee of School Number 10 in Prokop'evsk, Kemerovo administrative division.)

'My salary is now 620,000 roubles (US$108) per month. I work one shift, which amounts to 23 hours a week, although almost everyone in our school works a double shift. I have been paid for October 1996, 60 per cent of my pay for January 1997 and 27 per cent of my pay for the summer vacation. I have not received any child benefit (that would add about 70,000 roubles a month to the family budget) since April 1996. We have one child, a nine-year-old son. My husband works in the special department for preventive maintenance for the suppression of underground fires. He earns 1.2 million roubles, but he was last paid in September 1996.'

If you hardly ever receive any money from your main job, do you or your husband have any chance to earn something on the side?

'We don't have any additional earnings. Basically we work on our garden plot.'

Why does your husband not go somewhere else, if he has not been paid for so long?

'He still has two and a half years to work to qualify for a special pension. Then, certainly, if it goes on he will look for work with pay.'

How do you survive? Does someone help you?

'Our parents help: my husband has two and I have one. My father gives us all of his pension – he is still working. My husband's mother helps with food. Grandpa and grandma completely support our child. They live in a private house, which has a garden, and they also have an allotment. In July, on the eve of [a] day of action, my husband received his wage for last September. His director has gone on vacation so he cannot expect to get any more money before October.'

SOURCE: Extracts from Newsletter 2 (September 1997) of the campaign on the Non-Payment of Wages in Russia – www.icftu.org

Where new jobs have emerged to replace the permanent well-paid ones that have been lost, the former normally involve non-contractual, insecure forms of casualized work or McJobs – part-time, temporary or seasonal – lacking prospects or social benefits. Moreover, many such workers, especially those who belong to migrant communities, can only support their families by undertaking several casualized jobs at the same time. Thus, Beck (2000a) shows how, by the end of the 1990s, 45 per cent of the economically active US population was working in these insecure, poorly paid jobs, while in Germany the ratio of people in regular or standard employment – full time, permanent and secure – had fallen from 5:1 in the early 1970s to 2:1 by the mid-1990s (Edgell 2005: Chapter 4).

Overall, between one-quarter and one-third of the population forms a marginalized group dependent on state support – where it is available. These people take on multiple, low-paid and fluctuating forms of employment, rely on community or family support and engage in semi-criminal activities. This has been particularly noticeable in the cities of countries like Brazil, Colombia, India and the Philippines. Given that such trends have also spread to many of the cities and older industrial zones of advanced countries over the last 30 years, many commentators have argued that we are now seeing the peripheralization (Hoogvelt 1997) or 'Brazilianization' of the North (Beck 2000a). Ethnic and racial minorities, often recent migrants with a history of exposure to discrimination, are especially likely to be found among these marginal groups. However, a large and increasing proportion, whether from native or immigrant backgrounds, also have little or no education and few marketable skills.

REVIEW

The era of high productivity, high consumption and employment security is now over. Instead, we have moved into a period of economic globalization, rapid technological change, post-Fordism and the widespread adoption of free-market policies. Their combined effect has been to weaken labour's bargaining power and expose a growing proportion of employees everywhere to the risk of unemployment or conditions of work and pay that reduce workplace autonomy and increase lifestyle insecurity. At the same time, a growing proportion of the global population has been sucked into, and become dependent on, the capitalist, profit-oriented market system for their livelihoods.

The label 'globalization' tends to be blamed for these and other problems. But increased globalization also needs to be seen partly as a consequence of the widespread adoption of free-market economic policies. These have removed earlier constraints on capital flows and torn down the remaining barriers to the spread of capitalist production. At the same time, the work insecurities we have discussed owe as much to the deliberate shift, since the late 1970s, towards deregulated markets, greater inequality and policies designed to undermine workers' rights and reduce public spending, as they do to economic globalization per se.

Meanwhile, as one commentator complains, many governments have allowed themselves to 'become convinced' that only private markets and those who juggle money between them should be permitted to determine the world's shape and direction – not states, political leaders or, presumably, the citizens who elect them (Hutton 1998: 13). As world capitalism becomes more complex and extensive, its dependence on a supportive mode of regulation at global (and national) levels, forged by far-seeing and cooperative governments, would seem to be more relevant now than ever before. Even George Soros (1998), one of the most prominent financial speculators who profited from the deregulation of the global economy, has complained about the present generation of world leaders. He suggests that they seem to lack the imagination and be unwilling to provide the leadership to challenge orthodox views of how the world's economy might better be organized and managed.

FURTHER READING

- S. Edgell's book, *Sociological Analysis of Work: Change and Continuity in Paid and Unpaid Work* (2005) offers an up-to-date, thorough and very accessible examination of most themes relating to work, including Fordism and post-Fordism. Chapter 4 is especially relevant.

- F. Webster's analysis in *Theories of the Information Society* (2002) explores many issues and debates pertaining to the ways in which ICTs are changing our experience of work and leisure.

- The two readers by A. Amin (ed.) *Post-Fordism* (1994), and T. Elger and C. Smith (eds) *Global Japanization?* (1994) contain up-to-date summaries of the main debates in these areas. They are really aimed at advanced students and academic specialists, but most of the readings are nevertheless reasonably accessible and will amply reward those who persevere.

- Written in simple but lively prose, the book edited by A. Ross, *No Sweat* (1997), offers a wide range of up-to-date material on the various and recent worldwide experiences of casualized workers and their struggles to bring about change.

GROUP WORK

- The class will divide into two groups. Using the text and Box 4.1, one group will draw up a list showing the advantages and disadvantages of (a) being a worker and (b) a consumer during the Fordist era. The second group will follow the same procedure for the current era of post-Fordism. After hearing the two accounts, each student will briefly give reasons why they might prefer to live under Fordism rather than post-Fordism or vice versa.

- Working in small groups, students will study the section 'The crisis of Fordism as a production regime'. Now draw up a list of possible explanations for the decline of Fordism in their order of relative importance. Write down the reasons for your prioritization. Once every group has given their report, the class as a whole might consider two issues: (a) the degree of consensus, if any, concerning the weighting given to global as against other explanations; and (b) the problems involved in engaging in exercises of this kind.

- Arrange a class discussion/debate around the following topic: 'The world has become too complex for us ever to return to the postwar golden years. What can or should the world's leading figures and organizations (states,

IGOs, companies, political leaders and so on) do to construct a global mode of regulation capable of supporting a more stable and prosperous world capitalism?'

QUESTIONS TO THINK ABOUT

?

1. Summarize the main differences between Fordist and post-Fordist production either (a) as systems for organizing production and dealing with market demand or (b) in terms of their effects on employees' work experiences and styles of life.

2. How did changing global factors contribute to the decline of Fordism?

3. Evaluate the contradictions of Fordism as a production regime.

4. Is Marxism still relevant to contemporary social theory?

5. How and to what extent did Japanization contribute to the rise of post-Fordist casualization?

WHAT'S ON THE WEB

■ http://www.intute.ac.uk/socialsciences/cgi-bin/browse.pl?id=120793&gateway=% This is the main UK gateway to research on the sociology of work. It's managed by the University of Surrey and has excellent links. Particularly helpful are the short accurate descriptions of each link, which allows you to make the decision whether to open it. Why waste your time on a futile link? The individual papers are of high quality but rather diverse in theme.

■ http://www.ilo.org/public/english/bureau/inst/papers/index.htm This is the site for the International Institute for Labour Studies, part of the International Labour Organization (ILO) (an international body linking employers, worker organizations and governments, now part of the UN system). The discussion papers are particularly helpful.

■ http://www.warwick.ac.uk/fac/soc/complabstuds/russia/index.html A specialized, but interesting site on labour issues in post-Soviet Russia, with some new comparative research reaching out to Vietnam and China.

■ http://oohara.mt.tama.hosei.ac.jp/posengl/index.html Again a specialized and unusual site hosted by the Oohara Institute of Social Research, showing digital images of posters of the Japanese labour movement. The slide show starts automatically. It will not be of use to you in writing essays or answering examination questions, but the images are revealing.

CHAPTER 5

Nationhood and Nation-states

CONTENTS

In the nineteenth and early twentieth centuries, modernizing governments were largely successful in persuading individual citizens to submerge their personal passions and identities into those of the **NATION-STATE**. Three entities, society–people–country, came to be regarded as virtually coterminous with, even subordinated to, the idea of the nation. In this chapter we look at sociology's contribution to the study of nationalism, the nation-state and the idea of citizenship, and how this is changing in the face of globalization.

key concept	**NATION-STATES** are constituted by governments assuming a legal and moral right to exercise sole jurisdiction, supported by force in the last resort, over a particular territory and its citizens. This involves institutions for managing domestic and foreign affairs. From the late eighteenth century, ordinary citizens in most Western countries began to feel strong loyalties to their nation-states, while local and regional identities were suppressed. Popular nationalism has been more difficult to achieve in some developing countries.

We also assess the power and role of nation-states in a global era. Many observers have suggested that in a globalizing world, the capacity of nation-states to shape domestic and world change has already declined and may do so further. This has given rise to such concepts as the 'hollow state' (Hoggart 1996) or the 'borderless world' (Ohmae 1994). Some commentators go much further than this, suggesting that the era of the nation-state may be ending. Most submit that this conclusion is too premature and that the functions of the nation-state are merely changing in the face of globalizing forces. We assess this debate and argue that, despite the global changes undermining the exclusive primacy of the nation-state system as a focus for political and social action, securing recognition as a nation-state is still an urgent goal for many currently stateless people.

SOCIOLOGY, NATION-STATES AND THE INTERNATIONAL SYSTEM

We argued in Chapter 3 that the nation-state, particularly in Europe, predated the rise of modernity and industrial capitalism. It acted as a centralizing agency, steadily acquiring control over traders, aristocrats, towns and religious bodies. Driving this process of state building was military and economic rivalry between several European nations.

Both the French and Industrial Revolutions gave a new and forceful momentum to the processes of state- and nation-building in the context of international rivalry. The first of these revolutions proclaimed the universal rights of humanity, further centralized the French state and, by unleashing citizen armies, propelled nationalist fervour across Europe's territories. This galvanized the birth and spread of modern popular nationalism. Britain's Industrial Revolution compelled other countries to recognize the potential military threat to their national security posed by a more technologically advanced economy.

One by one the nineteenth-century nation-states – in Europe, America and, later, Japan – began to push towards the goal of state-led industrialization. They strengthened the structures of the state and imposed reforms designed to remove any remaining obstacles that might impede the release of enterprise, market incentives or scientific and technological learning. More recently, many other states have followed a similar course. Indeed, those faced with even greater external military threats to national survival after 1945, including several Southeast Asian states such as South Korea, responded in even more determined ways to the challenge of state-led industrialization as the main path to national survival.

In short, the forces most responsible for promoting modernization came not just from social pressures created by civil society, they originated within and among the elite who controlled the nation-state itself. Thus, as Albrow (1996: 7) succinctly explains 'the story of modernity was of a project to extend human control over space, time, nature and society. The main agent of the project was the nation-state working with and through capitalist and military organization.'

| Box 5.1 | European nation-states in the twenty-first century: towards the past? |

Medieval Europe consisted of an assortment of political units with local identities that were often far stronger than any national loyalties. They were also involved in multiple affiliations to cities, the Catholic Church based in Rome and various monastic orders. Today, economic integration among the member states of the European Union (EU) continues to deepen. In May 2004, the number of member states rose from 15 to 25, though there is concern that this may slow down future integration, because it becomes more difficult to reach policy consensus with such a growing diversity of needs and interests. In spring 2005, both the French and Dutch electorates voted decisively against ratifying the EU constitution, which was designed to intensify and streamline EU integration. Meanwhile, the EU states are subject to the same kinds of global forces as those affecting nation-states everywhere. In view of all this, is Europe returning to its medieval past? Perhaps, yes, if the German situation is any indication.

German politics today

Like many countries, for example the USA, Australia and India, Germany forms a federation with 16 units of provincial government, called *Länder*, each enjoying considerable political autonomy from central government. It appears that the *Länder* are trying to extend their 'independence' even further. Thus:

■ Each *Länder* has established its own offices at, and relationships with, the EU in Brussels in an attempt to obtain resources.

■ The *Länder* have altered the federal constitution so that they can resist any further ties developing between central government and the EU of which they might disapprove.

■ Some *Länder* are trying to establish their own special trading relations with nation-states outside the EU such as China.

The wider European picture

The German *Länder* are not especially unusual. For example:

■ Much of the above is equally applicable to other EU countries, where strong regional loyalties and even antipathy to central governments have long been obvious. Catalonia in Spain is one notable example but Belgium, Italy and

France also have regional governments and deep local identities.

- In 1999, even centralized Britain devolved power to newly elected govern-ments in the 'Celtic' regions of Scotland, Wales and Northern Ireland and later re-established London as a city-region with substantial autonomy. In 2004 the government tried to extend a weaker version of regional govern-ment to the English regions, though initial responses, for example in the northeast, suggest that there is currently little enthusiasm for this among the mass of citizens.

- Across Europe, cities as different as Barcelona, Manchester and Lyons are establishing special ties to the EU and cities in other European countries (and outside the EU) to obtain grant aid, attract investment and encourage cooperation in sport and education as well as cultural and other exchanges.

- Universities, schools, town councils and professional associations are also making cross-boundary links, therefore bypassing the national government.

SOURCE: Freedland (1999)

CLASSICAL SOCIOLOGY AND SOCIAL CHANGE

By the middle decades of the nineteenth century, many observers were becoming increasingly alarmed by the multiple consequences brought about by industrial capitalism. Not surprisingly, early European sociologists struggled to understand these changes and their dangers and possibilities. At the core of much of their thinking was the attempt to conceptualize the essential features of *traditional* compared with *modernizing* societies and, in part, to come to terms with the assault that the latter was having on the imagined virtues of the former. Here we give just three examples of such thinking:

- *The loss of community:* The German sociologist Tönnies (1971) mourned the demise of the warm, all-embracing *Gemeinschaft*-type communities of medieval times, based on unquestioned friendship and shared beliefs, and their replacement by the impersonality, even anonymity, found in modern, urban *Gesellschaft* societies. The latter are built primarily around loose, often impermanent, essentially contrived and non-overlapping associations. The relationships they contain are driven primarily by the demand for achievement and legitimized by contract and mutual interests.
- *Declining social cohesion and moral order:* Another concern theorized by sociol-ogists was the impact that industrialism, urbanism and **SECULARIZATION** were having on societal cohesion and the tendency for individual citizens to exper-ience moral and social isolation. Modern societies seemed to be marked by growing materialism, class conflict, egotism and individualism compared with earlier societies. These changes, combined with the declining hold of Chris-tianity, threatened to push individuals either into social isolation – due to changes such as rapid urbanization or economic crises – or moral confusion.
- *The conscience collective:* To avoid these problems, Durkheim thought that modern societies must evolve a crucial bulwark alongside the integration

produced by the division of labour, namely the emergence of a more flexible and abstract value system. This would be based on the *conscience collective*, 'a new set of universally significant moral bonds' (Turner 1994: 135) that championed mutual respect for human rights and the sanctity of the individual. Although still at a national level, this resembles the idea of globality – whereby humans share an intensifying consciousness of themselves as forming one single collectivity – discussed in Chapter 2.

SECULARIZATION refers to the declining hold of religious belief and practice over most people's lives during the industrialization process. Growing exposure to scientific knowledge and new ideas, combined with a more materially secure environment, render most individuals less reliant on the moral and spiritual certainties provided by religion in preindustrial societies (see Chapter 16).

UNIVERSALISM AND NATIONALISM

Interest in universal themes and the progress of all humanity can be traced back to the 1830s via the social theory of Saint-Simon, the founder of French socialism (Turner 1994: 133–5). Durkheim was very influenced by Saint-Simon, especially on the question of how to find a 'new set of universally significant moral bonds' to replace the religious convictions threatened by secularization, while cementing together the more complex national and world orders created by industrialism. However, Durkheim was also strongly counter-pressured by the force of political events. One especially salient experience for him was France's humiliating defeat in the short war with Prussia in 1871, and the powerful patriotic sentiments this generated.

Durkheim began to think that the heady unifying passions generated by French nationalism might provide a substitute for declining moral certainties and societal incoherence. In short, more universalist themes and concerns were largely, though not entirely, displaced from Durkheim's thinking. The urgency with which modern nation-states sought to deepen their control over industrial societies in the last decades of the nineteenth century was accentuated by the spectre of socialism. Marx had predicted that capitalist exploitation would ultimately create the conditions for an increasingly organized and militant working class to foster a revolution and introduce socialism. This, coupled with abundant actual evidence of working-class strength and the internationalist aspirations of socialism, 'sent shudders through nation-state society', pushing it 'into overdrive to find an alternative and better theories' (Albrow 1996: 45). Another crucial event that reinforced the national leanings of many intellectuals, at least initially, was the outbreak of the First World War in August 1914. Much to the astonishment and deep regret of many, especially those on the Left, this was met by surges of patriotic sentiment right across Europe.

As with other kinds of experts, sociologists were increasingly drawn into the processes with which states tried to head off social conflict. They conducted research into poverty and similar problems, often with state funding, established specialized teaching programmes linked to these issues and generally contributed to the formation of policies designed to ameliorate adverse social conditions. In all these ways, their thinking was also increasingly built around the nation-state and its needs. Many governments also began to create a welfare state. This was designed to offer some degree of economic security for ordinary people from the inherent uncertainties of market economies in the form of unemployment, old age, sickness and other benefits. The extension of the state into everyday life created a new form of social bond, **CITIZENSHIP**. Indeed, it can be argued that state/political elites deliberately used citizenship as a nation-building strategy (O'Byrne 2003: 64). However, this, in turn, powerfully linked the idea of citizenship with territorial affiliations, legal/administrative institutions and a state-centred discourse. Many have argued that these biases, in turn, have led to adverse consequences for many, while making it difficult to adapt citizenship to the changing circumstances of a globalizing world. We examine these issues below.

key concept	**CITIZENSHIP** alludes to membership of and inclusion in a national community. Citizenship confers a set of entitlements – to legal equality and justice, the right to be consulted on political matters and access to a minimum of protection against economic insecurity – but simultaneously requires the fulfilment of certain obligations to state and society.

CITIZENSHIP: ENTITLEMENTS AND OBLIGATIONS

Citizenship is basically a modern and a Western invention. It is underpinned by two principles. One involves the idea that there should be a bundle of *uniform* rights to which everyone is equally entitled. This would have been unthinkable in premodern societies. The second principle concerns an implicit *bargain* or *contract*, where, in return for a set of rights or entitlements, citizens are expected to demonstrate loyalty to the nation-state and its objectives, while accepting certain obligations or duties. These include the willingness to accept military conscription, pay taxes, seek employment and obey the law. Thus, historically, rulers were able to bring about widespread change successfully by providing citizens with a stake in nationhood and industrialization. This also meant democratization by providing 'an equality of membership status and [an] ability to participate in a society' (Roche 1992: 19).

T. H. Marshall's (1950) ideas about citizenship influenced a generation of thinkers. He observed that citizenship involved three sets of rights, which, he claimed, had emerged in a sequence as a result of events taking place approximately in the eighteenth, nineteenth and twentieth centuries. These rights were as follows:

■ *Civil rights* were attained first. They include the right to own property and arrange contracts, to free assembly, speech and thought and the right to expect justice from an impartial legal system based on laws that apply equally to everyone. Where civil rights do not exist, neither personal freedom nor market enterprise is fully realizable.

■ *Political rights* confer the ability to participate in national decision-making through voting for the political party of your choice at elections. However, political citizenship also implies the right to establish your own movement or seek direct access to positions of leadership in party, government or some other power-exercising forum.

■ *Social rights* involve access to welfare provisions that provide a protective floor below which individual and family incomes are not supposed to fall. Normally, social rights include old age, disability, family and unemployment benefits and the right to decent housing, education and health. It is hoped that such minimum security gives everyone an equal chance to enjoy personal autonomy and the benefits of economic growth. Underlying the idea of social rights is the assumption that, without them, the inequalities and insecurities inevitably generated by capitalism might push some people to levels of permanent poverty where they are too weak to exercise their civil or political rights.

Over the past 20 or so years, interest in citizenship has revived strongly but this has been accompanied by both a critical reappraisal of Marshall's ideas and a growing parallel interest in other related issues such as universal human rights. Here we mention just a few of these newer arguments.

First, Marshall's analysis was based far too closely on Britain's history (Mann 1996). Other countries have often had different experiences. For example, Germany began to establish a rudimentary welfare state somewhat earlier than Britain – during the 1880s – and 30 years before universal voting rights were finally established in 1919.

Second, citizenship is based on membership of and inclusion in a particular national community and territory. But the process of deepening the commitment of the 'natives' to the state simultaneously raises the possibility of exclusion (Lister 1997: Chapter 2). This exclusion can and frequently has applied to internal groups, especially the disabled, women and children. Here, the very state-centredness of civil and political rights, their dependence on 'the legal or political spheres … has drawn attention away from non-state violations which occur within the social or cultural realms' (O'Byrne 2003: 64). At the same time, women were 'banished to the private realm of the household and family' (Lister 1997: 71) because of employment and welfare policies. We say more about women, nationalism and the state later on. Of course, 'external' groups have also experienced exclusion. In a globalizing world, where disadvantaged migrants increasingly seek work or political asylum in the prosperous countries, many will encounter racism and discrimination from officials or host members and will become 'non or partial citizens' (Lister 1997: 42, 45), irrespective of their societal contributions.

Third, there is a further complication regarding many migrants moving to North America, Japan and Western Europe, as, unlike their nineteenth-century counterparts, they seek only partial assimilation into their host societies, while retaining strong and enduring transnational family, cultural, political and business connections with their home country (see, for example, Faist 2000;

Jordan and Duvell 2003). The existence of ethnic groups in multicultural societies, with limited loyalties to each other and dual or overlapping affiliations to their host and home societies, raises complicated ethical, political and practical issues over whether, acting mutually, states need to make access to citizenship more flexible. One case might involve allowing many more individuals to hold dual citizenship. Alternatively, under certain circumstances, like marrying a national or paying full tax over a period of time, states might recognize at least some of the citizenship rights that individuals have acquired elsewhere and allow them access to certain native privileges. Again, in their turn, citizens living in a global world of constant mobility will also need to accept changes and this may include learning to become cosmopolitan citizens (Delanty 2000; Held and McGrew 2002). Among other things this involves the willingness to assume 'a role which encompasses dialogue with the traditions and discourses of others with the aim of expanding the horizons of one's own framework of meaning and prejudice' (Held and McGrew 2002: 107).

Figure 5.1 **A statue in the main square of Jayapura glorifies the military occupation of West Papua by the Indonesian military** The nationalist struggle in West Papua has been firmly suppressed by force, while the sponsored transmigration of Indonesian farmers has been used to provide a pro-government population.

Finally, for the past 20 years or so, right-wing thinkers and politicians have also been challenging earlier ideas about citizenship. They argue that citizen rights have been stressed far too much, while the corresponding duties of citizens to seek paid employment and assume proper responsibility for family and community commitments have been neglected. Accordingly, many on the Right have criticized welfare rights. Partly, this is because of the increasingly heavy burdens they place on public spending, especially at a time of high unemployment and the rising costs of healthcare and old age provision. But they have also attacked the 'dependency culture' supposedly generated by the welfare state, which is said to undermine individual autonomy and moral responsibility.

Clearly, the sociology of citizenship is being radically rethought. One of the biggest challenges it now faces, as we have seen, is the idea of *global citizenship*, as national economies become increasingly integrated, governments are compelled to cooperate and numerous transnational agents collaborate across national borders (Delanty 2000).

■ ■ ■ ■ ■ ■ POLITICAL THEORY AND INTERSTATE RELATIONS

As we have seen, during most of its history, sociology can be said to have prioritized the study of single societies and rather taken the nation-state for granted. Even Marxist sociologists showed little interest in the emerging relationships and connections forming between societies or states until the 1960s. On the Left, this task was left to revolutionary intellectuals like Vladimir Lenin (the leader of the communist revolution in Russia in 1917) and Rosa Luxemburg (a German revolutionary murdered in Berlin during an unsuccessful communist insurrection in 1919). Both wrote extensively on the theory and practice of imperialism.

TABLE 5.1	The age of the nation-state system		
Date	Number of new states	Cumulative totals	Comments
Before 1800	14	14	Not including the Ottoman, Russian, Chinese and Austro-Hungarian Empires
1800–1914	37	51	South American countries gained independence from Spain and Portugal plus UK dominions
1915–39	11	62	For example, Ireland, Poland, Finland
1940–59	22	84	Surge of independence for former colonies especially in Asia and Middle East
1960–89	72	156	Veritable flood of developing countries gaining independence in Africa (41), the Caribbean (11), Asia (14) and elsewhere
1990–2003	52	208	Dissolution of USSR and Yugoslavia (22 new states) plus Namibia, Eritrea (following war with Ethiopia), Yemen, East Timor (2003) and others

NOTES:
1 Not all sovereign states automatically choose to join the UN or are recognized by that body. In 2005, 191 states were UN members
2 A number of countries are caught in anomalous situations: Taiwan (not recognized because of dispute with China); Palestine (still in the process of achieving formal autonomy from Israel); North and South Korea may eventually unite; many countries and territories are still dependencies of some kind. Civil wars and disputes in some countries (such as Sudan, Sri Lanka and perhaps Iraq) mean that the founding of new states – certainly Montenegro, perhaps Kurdistan – cannot be discounted. Others see a future where vastly populous city-regions become, in effect, more powerful than states
3 Some states recognized as sovereign and independent have very small populations. If those with fewer than 100,000 were to be excluded, the number of states would fall from 208 to around 165
SOURCES: Kidron and Segal (1995); Anheier et al. (2001); Kegley and Wittkopf (2004)

A more academic perspective on international affairs came from political science, through a subdiscipline called international relations theory. We now discuss this briefly.

THE REALIST PERSPECTIVE EXPLAINED

For a long time international relations theory relied on a particular model of interstate relations called 'the realist perspective'. Like the everyday meaning of the term, the 'realist' label is employed to suggest that abstract or idealist considerations are rarely significant in human affairs and certainly not in the sphere of nation-state relations. Rather, naked interests and power-seeking are normally paramount. Adherents of the realist perspective argue that international politics has certain inherent characteristics. The 'classic' statement of this position is found in the work of its leading early exponent Morgenthau (1948), who advanced four main positions:

> The **sovereignty** of a state lies in its ability to make and enforce its own policies and laws in its own territory and over the people living within its borders.

1. World society, if such can be said to exist, is largely synonymous with the relationships between states.
2. A world of **_sovereign_** nation-states contains an inherent risk of conflicts erupting. This is because states are driven by their very nature to engage in power-maximizing activity – they seek to enlarge their autonomy and spheres of interest at the expense of others – and because the nation-state system is anarchical – by definition it lacks a recognized supranational authority.
3. Accordingly, relations between states are mostly dominated by questions of military security and the need to pursue appropriate foreign policies designed to safeguard national security and maximize international status.
4. The world polity is characteristically hierarchical. States are not equal in their capacity to shape events. The more militarily powerful tend to either dominate weaker states through various kinds of coercion or take a lead in managing world affairs by forming alliances and trying to achieve a balance of power.

THE REALIST PERSPECTIVE ASSESSED

Different versions of the realist perspective have remained quite influential among international relations theorists. Nevertheless, this view has been increasingly subject to criticism. The insistence of realist theorists that states are primarily preoccupied with national security issues and therefore with military matters and defence is increasingly dubious. State agendas have always been much broader than this. Moreover, they have certainly widened rapidly in the late twentieth century to include such compelling issues as how to manage information flows through the internet, the global spread of diseases such as AIDS and tuberculosis and the need to deal with environmental issues.

Since the late 1960s, economists and sociologists have been struck by the rapid growth of powerful non-state, transnational bodies, especially TNCs. The realist perspective was seen to place too much emphasis on a state-centric view of world politics, while neglecting the growing importance of transnational exchanges in the world economy. Indeed, the latter were rapidly calling into question the very meaning of national sovereignty and territorial autonomy. Increased interdependence between states required more cooperation between the leading industrial countries and IGOs, such as the World Bank and the IMF, in order to manage the global economy more responsibly. Unilateral actions by even the most powerful states were therefore less possible.

PUTTING 'SOCIETY' BACK INTO NATIONAL AND GLOBAL POLITICS

Since the 1960s, sociologists' interest in global matters has begun to flourish. Thus, a considerable number of non-Marxist sociologists have joined scholars such as Wallerstein (1974) in the rediscovery of transnational exchanges and relations. At the same time, sociology has offered a much sharper analysis of the shortcomings of international relations theory. In this section, we first explore one such recent critique and then discuss two important sociological approaches – deriving from historical sociology and feminism – to the study of nationalism and global relations.

■ ■

Global Thinkers 5 **ANTHONY GIDDENS (1938–)**

Globalization and modernity

Giddens' work has been centrally concerned with globalization. In Chapter 3, for example, we outlined his concepts of time–space compression, disembedding and reflexivity. In the practice of social life these enable relations to spread across the world, making modernity an inherently globalizing force. His argument goes as follows.

In premodern *societies, social action ran along familiar grooves. Past actions authenticated the present, while sacred beliefs and customs, channelled through guardians of tradition, provided habitual certainties.* Modernity *brings an entirely new kind of society, one that is inherently transforming; nothing can remain certain for long. A major reason for this is that human reflexivity changes; the self-monitoring of conduct through perpetually incoming knowledge encourages redefining the content of actions rather than accepting traditional guidelines.*

But globalizing processes further heighten this transformational tendency. We therefore live in a 'runaway world' where everything 'seems out of our control', including influences such as scientific and technological developments that were supposed to make life more predictable and secure. Globalization is also 'in here', part of our subjectivity, so that our personal lives – family, everyday relationships – are also being revolutionized and reinvented. Some of the core characteristics resulting from late modern globalizing conditions are as follows:

1. *Tradition:* As the routines provided by tradition slowly wither, once powerful solidarities such as class, locality and kinship no longer provide clear social directions. 'Moderns' are therefore compelled to take charge of constructing their own self-identities and life biographies.

2. *Lifestyle:* The life plan that moderns must create is significantly focused around lifestyle. This is more than a 'superficial consumerism' but requires the selection of a fairly integrated set of practices that enables the individual to achieve self-actualization through a coherent life narrative and personal identity.

3. *Risk:* Dangers manufactured by past and present human actions – especially those unleashed by modern industrial and scientific activities – rather than those resulting from nature become central to modern life and are also globalized (for example chemical spills, global warming and climate change).

4. *Intimacy:* Modernity also leads to a 'democracy of the emotions'. Family relationships and friendships are built on openness, trust, equality and mutual respect. These provide the basis for intimacy and this compensates for the anxieties and personal risks associated with declining tradition, though therapists, counsellors and self-help manuals also appear to be necessary supplements for managing modern intimacy.

5. *Family:* Modern birth control and education also separate sexuality and love from reproduction. Thus, women across the world now either enjoy, or increasingly demand, more choice regarding marriage. Indeed, the potential liberation from kinship pressures and constant childbirth is leading to 'coupledom' rather than lifelong marriage in many societies. Children, too, are more likely to be treated as individuals.

6. *Rising fundamentalisms:* Much of this is increasingly feared and resisted by various religious, national and ethnic fundamentalisms. Adherents to these fundamentalisms try to restore the rule of one all-encompassing truth and life path that believers are duty bound to obey on pain of divine or secular punishment. Here, the changes promised to family life and women by the globalization of modernity are seen as especially dangerous.

Thus, Giddens sees a global struggle not between civilizations but between those who desire cosmopolitan openness in a world of cultural complexity versus those who seek refuge in 'renewed and purified tradition'.

SOURCES: Giddens (1990, 1991, 1992; 2002); O'Brien et al. (1999)

SOCIETY AND INTERNATIONAL RELATIONS

Here, Shaw's (1994) work is especially illuminating. He makes several criticisms of international relations theory. First, he suggests, international relations theory has largely ignored the state's embeddedness in the many dense networks of class and other interests and identities that make up society. These aggregates of complex social relationships that constitute 'society' are often locked into conflict over questions of ethnic, regional, religious, gender and class affiliation. Accordingly, the emergence of a strong populist sense of national community and identity – during the nineteenth century in many Western countries – was all the more remarkable and requires explanation (Shaw 1994: 89, 92).

Second, during the early modernization process, intellectuals, artists, political leaders and others both created the very idea of nationhood (or national community) and brought it more sharply into focus. To describe this process, Anderson (1983) employed the term **IMAGINED COMMUNITIES**. Similar tendencies have appeared more recently in some developing countries. In other words, nationhood does not spring into life of its own accord and it is not purely an extension of state power as realists appear to suggest.

key concept

The nation is an **IMAGINED COMMUNITY** in four senses. It is imagined because a member of even the smallest nation will never know most of its members. The nation is imagined as limited because even the largest of nations has a finite boundary beyond which there are other nations. It is imagined as sovereign in that it displaces or undermines the legitimacy of organized religion or the monarchy. Finally, it is imagined as community because regardless of actual inequality, the nation is conceived of as a deep, horizontal comradeship (see Anderson 1983: 15–16).

Third, the notion of a civil society – social groups with shared interests operating in the political arena – existing between the individual and the state has not only been revived and developed but has been increasingly applied to the global sphere (Anheier et al. 2001, 2002; Keane 2003). We discuss the idea of global civil society much more in Chapter 18. Societies have never been simple appendages of states and nations and cannot be regarded as coterminous with them. In most Western nations, and in many others, society preceded the state and the nation, as did individual loyalties to social groups (Shaw 1994: 94).

HISTORICAL SOCIOLOGY

A revived interest in comparative historical studies of modernization has also helped to reground the sociological interest in nation-states, international life and global exchanges. For example, writers like Gerschenkron (1966), Moore (1967), Skocpol (1979) and Mann (1988) have explored the circumstances surrounding the successful transitions to industrialization in countries such as Britain, America, Germany and Japan, compared with the failure or delayed nature of such transitions in tsarist Russia and China. We have already emphasized how these state-led transitions were motivated at least partly by external threats and nation-state rivalries. For example, the Napoleonic invasions of Prussia, Austria and Russia between 1805 and 1812 spurred the elites in these countries to embark on the process of modernization, though they were not all equally successful. Between the mid-1850s and 1870s, both Japan and Italy also tried to head off the perceived risk of future external domination by embarking on extensive industrialization programmes.

However, it is important not to ignore the role of three other factors changing state structures:

- Internal pressures from domestic groups were influential. In addition to intellectuals and artists, an assortment of educated, middle-class and business groups clamoured for more accountable and predictable systems of administration, greater recognition of merit rather than privilege in the allocation of state resources and measures designed to increase economic opportunity.
- The political ferment and economic transformations generated within one country sometimes spilled over and influenced the middle classes in neighbouring or distant ones, stimulating demands on state elites to hasten similar change at home, for example during the revolutionary unrest across Europe in 1848.
- The need to catch up with more advanced national rivals often generated a 'late development effect' (Gershenkron 1966). Thus, government officials, intellectuals, technicians, businessmen and others were sent abroad and instructed to decide which institutional innovations, for example legal codes, mass education systems or forms of business organization, should be imitated by the home country. The Japanese propensity to borrow extensively from Western countries during its late nineteenth-century period of rapid modernization has often been noted. It helped that the traditional Japanese religion (Shintoism) had always tolerated and absorbed new and multiple religious identities (Robertson 1992: 92–6).

THE FEMINIST REASSESSMENT

In Chapter 6 we will examine feminist theory and its considerable importance in compelling all academic disciplines to rethink many of their theories and assumptions about gender relations. However, some feminist theory has also been central in contributing to sociologists' interest in nation-states and global affairs since the 1960s. We now summarize three examples of such contributions, all of which concern not only women, society and the nation-state but also war and violence.

WOMEN AND THE STATE

Far from being gender neutral the state not only 'treats women unequally in relation to men … it [also] constructs men and women differently' (Yuval-Davis and Anthias 1989: 6). State power has been used to enforce control over women in many ways. A key example is shown by government policies during the two world wars. At first, women were pressed into factories, offices and other forms of war work as men were mobilized for military service. Later, governments conducted campaigns to persuade women to return to domestic life when the men were demobilized for fear of social unrest caused by male unemployment.

Welfare policy is also important, especially the decision to withhold certain child benefits from single mothers. Thus, governments wishing to discourage such families could decide to make such rights conditional on women responding to certain compulsory training or work schemes.

WOMEN AND NATIONALISM

The very way in which women's contribution to nationhood is envisaged and understood – whether by established traditions or state officials – reveals the hold of certain deep-rooted assumptions about the 'proper' role of women in national life (Halliday 1994: 160–4). In particular, in most countries women have been regarded as the main carriers of their country's unique cultural heritage, which it is their duty to transfer to the nation's children through their role as mothers (Yuval-Davis and Anthias: 1989). This is also linked to their child-bearing capability, enabling them to produce the next generation of male warriors for future wars. Here, population policies – what Foucault (1977) referred to as the exercise of 'biopower' by states – have often been crucial in either encouraging women to have more children, as in nineteenth-century France and the Soviet Union after the 1917 revolution, or in discouraging certain 'undesirable' minorities from doing so.

WOMEN, VIOLENCE AND CONTEMPORARY WARFARE

Until recently, in wartime women were usually either kept away from the main zones of conflict or they served in some way (for example in field hospitals or as drivers) but usually in an auxiliary capacity. However, much of this appears to have changed since the end of the Cold War and with the resurgence of recent nationalisms, genocidal wars and the collapse of many states, especially in Africa. First, there has been a 'wide-scale retreat from even a qualified observance of those historic rules of war which had offered protection to noncombatants' (Jacobson et al. 2000: 4), so that civilian women and even children have often been deliberately targeted as war victims. Second, in certain recent wars, for example following the collapse of Yugoslavia and in Liberia and Sierra Leone during the 1990s, we have seen 'the use of rape as a war strategy' (Jacobson et al. 2000: 12) and the systematic sexualization of violence. Finally, in countries like China and the USA, increasing numbers of women have actively sought to become frontline warriors. In the USA, for example, women comprised 14 per cent of the total armed forces in 2002 (Smith and Bræin 2003: 76).

▪▪▪▪▪▪▪▪▪ DOES GLOBALIZATION MEAN THE DECLINE OF THE NATION-STATE?

It is useful to set the scene for this discussion by heeding Shaw's (1997: 497) warning 'that it is erroneous to counterpoise globalization to the state', since this can only lead to a 'sterile debate'. Thus, he suggests that instead of saying states' powers are declining, it makes more sense to say they are undergoing a transformation in their structures and processes. Such changes are a precondition for further globalization and a consequence of it. Shaw also reminds us that this debate has not been helped by confusion over what exactly we mean by the 'nation-state'. Normally, people are referring to its 'classic' nineteenth- and early twentieth-century form. Then, there were far fewer autonomous states than now (see Table 5.1 above). Moreover, most really did rely on their own independent military capacity to protect their sovereign territories and monopolized the legal control of the right to use violence over their territories and citizens – which was how Max Weber defined the modern state.

But does this situation exist any longer? Shaw argues that it does not. Only the USA and USSR (until its demise in 1992) have actually enjoyed the 'real' sovereignty possessed by most states before 1945 and this includes the vast majority of the new nations formed since decolonization. Why is this? Since the Second World War, the dangers and costs involved in maintaining a nuclear and conventional military capability have meant that 'many even of the strongest nation-states have lost or given up the capacity to mobilize violence independently of their allies' (Shaw 1997: 500). Here, NATO (North Atlantic Treaty Organization) is the obvious example of allies sharing military power across borders. On the other hand, although total world military spending in 2001 (at US$800 billion) was roughly two-thirds of what it had been in the mid-1980s at the height of the Cold War, America's world share of military capacity at US$322 billion (2001) remained formidable and was equivalent to the combined capacity of the next ten highest world military spenders (Smith and Bræin 2003: 75). In addition, the conservative Republican government of President Bush has been prepared to exercise US military power either unilaterally or in coalition with a few other nations and without the majority agreement of the UN, much to the consternation of millions of people worldwide. Such actions, along with others such as the US's repudiation of the 1999 Kyoto agreement on greenhouse gas emissions, have prompted a number of observers to suggest that we are moving into a dangerous new era, in which the world's single superpower is seeking to exercise not just unilateralist but, indeed, wanton and reckless imperialist power in order to maintain its current hegemonic domination of world resources, in the face of rivals like the EU, China and India, far into the future (Bello 2001; Brenner 2002; Harvey 2003).

Clearly, there are deep contradictions at work here. Bearing this in mind, we now consider the case for arguing that despite the above comments, the power of most nation-states has dwindled. We begin by employing Held's (1989) useful distinction between sovereignty (a state's ability to make and enforce its own policies and laws) and autonomy (a state's capacity to achieve its policy goals). A loss of sovereignty has happened (as we saw earlier) but only to a limited extent. It is most noticeable in those states prepared to recognize international law or those that belong to powerful regional blocs such as the EU. The latter requires member states to devolve some decision-making to the Brussels-based European

Commission and the Council of Ministers and to accept certain common directives and regulations.

What is clearer, however, is the extent to which states have lost a good deal of their former autonomy, though the nation-state system and capitalism's global character have always limited state autonomy to some degree. Held (1989) identifies five areas in which most states have progressively lost some of their national autonomy in recent decades:

1. States have to adhere to the demands of IGOs such as the IMF and World Bank when requiring external financial assistance.
2. The majority of states have a declining capacity to determine their own military strategies and foreign policies. This is because security arrangements, weaponry and national defence organizations have become integral to joint alliances and power blocs are controlled by unified command structures such as NATO.
3. Following the disintegration of the former Soviet Union with its vast arsenal of weaponry, it is now relatively easy for terrorists, secessionists and criminals to obtain lethal arms, small explosives and even certain types of nuclear weaponry. This privatization and democratization of the means of destruction represents a further dimension of declining state control (Hobsbawm 1994: Chapter 19).
4. A growing body of international law is increasingly infringing on state autonomy. In general, compliance rests on the interests and goodwill of the states themselves. However, there are significant exceptions to this, including several rulings of the European Court of Human Rights (ECHR) on the questions of equal pay and sexual discrimination in the workplace, which have forced member states to alter their national laws (Held 1989: 199–200). In addition, a permanent world criminal court, the International Criminal Court (ICC) at The Hague in the Netherlands, finally obtained the capacity to charge heads of states and other leading figures with genocidal crimes against humanity in 1997. (The USA withdrew from this agreement in 2002.) Several world leaders have since been indicted for crimes against humanity, including Milosovic of Serbia and Pinochet from Chile (Kegley and Wittkopf 2004: 584).
5. The ability of states to determine effective national economic policies is declining in the face of globalization. We now discuss this aspect in more detail.

ECONOMIC AUTONOMY

Excluding the special restrictions on members of regional economic groupings, such as the EU and NAFTA (North American Free Trade Agreement), and the rules governing membership of IGOs such as the IMF and GATT (now the WTO), there are several aspects to a loss of economic autonomy:

1. The key role played by TNCs has made some capital far more mobile, even footloose. TNCs can decide where to deploy their various plants across the

globe in the most profitable way, what forms of employment policy they prefer and where to deposit their liquid assets.

2. Linked to the rise of global corporate power through the TNCs, Sklair (2001) sees the formation of a transnational capitalist class. Its members share several things in common: they seek to exercise control over the workplace, over domestic and international politics and over the effects of the consumer culture on everyday life. They also share global rather than local perspectives, come from many countries, think of themselves as citizens of the world and often share similar luxury lifestyles (Calhoun 2002).

3. The value of a country's currency and its government's ability to determine interest rates were once important economic weapons. Now, with deregulation of the banks, the growth of 24-hour currency markets and developments in communications technology, the transnational economy is dominated by often uncontrollable money flows (Drucker 1989). Moreover, their endlessly speculative and uncertain nature has given rise to a kind of 'casino capitalism' (Strange 1986). All this renders the key tools of government economic management decreasingly effective.

4. Governments confront a 'borderless world' but not only with respect to flows of technology, investment and money. According to Ohmae (1994: 18–19), of 'all the forces eating them [territorial boundaries] away, perhaps the most persistent is the flow of information'. Once governments could monopolize information 'cooking it up as they saw fit' and this enabled them to 'fool, or control the people'.

However, the flows of ideas, images and information made possible by IT are not amenable to the traditional controls that governments have always exercised over the movements of goods and people. The implications for state autonomy are not purely economic. Thus, local citizens' consumer and lifestyle preferences – and perhaps their rising sense of unsatisfied economic expectations – are increasingly shaped by external influences outside government control. This further undermines government policy-making.

THE ANTIPATHY TO MODERNITY

In addition to losing power to supranational and transnational agents, governments are increasingly being questioned and confronted from below by one or more of the following:

- highly informed reflexive citizen networks
- disgruntled ethnic and regional minorities demanding the devolution of some or most central powers to local levels
- widespread public disillusionment with the rhetoric of conventional party politics.

Camilleri and Falk (1992) believe that this discontentment with the nation-state, especially in advanced countries, is linked to a rising antipathy towards modernity. Many citizens regard the once unquestioned belief in scientific and material progress as naive and possibly dangerous. The continued preoccupation of governments with these goals strikes many people as absurd, further undermining state power.

This is complicated by the rise of postmodern sensibilities to which we referred in Chapter 4. Many sociologists claim that the changes associated with postmodernity are transforming all social and cultural experiences in a number of ways:

1. Former certainties about what constitutes 'truth' are disappearing, along with the downgrading of such **META-NARRATIVES** as liberalism, nationalism and socialism as significant factors in our lives.

META-NARRATIVES are more than simply 'grand' theories claiming to possess demonstrably valid explanations for all societal evolution and change. Rather, they also offer ultimate, epic stories about the truth of human experience. Socialism, for example, insists that history is dominated by the oppression of different classes – from slaves through to workers – and these groups' perpetual struggles against economic exploitation.

2. All boundaries and status hierarchies are breaking down: between social groups, between artistic forms and styles and between the once clearly demarcated spheres of social life, especially work and leisure, production and consumption and home life and employment.
3. Every aspect and area of cultural and social life is acquiring a money value.
4. The pursuit of individual self-realization, narcissistic enjoyment of the body and the construction of private and distinctive lifestyles are becoming predominant orientations for most people, thus highlighting the key role of consumption in contemporary life.
5. Citizens are being swamped with an ever rising volume of information, images and messages. Their sheer quantity and inherently fragmented nature give life a shallow, unreal quality.

Camilleri and Falk (1992) believe that these postmodern sensibilities have created an interpretative crisis not only in social relations and culture but also in national politics. Thus, they leave us exposed to a confusing multiplicity of values and meanings and more liable to criticize the pretensions and ambitions of modernity. They encourage us to challenge and deconstruct the meta-narratives of nationalism and democracy. These now appear parochial and irrelevant. We may, for example, see current forms of democracy as largely vacuous, incapable of reaching the needs or tapping the energies of contemporary citizens.

Cultural pluralism – intensified by globalization – undermines national politics. This is because the historical building blocks of the nation-state are an imagined community, territoriality and sovereignty. But these are threatened by the deconstructionist tendencies implied by postmodernity. Thus, numerous forces in our lives mean that it is becoming more difficult to think in terms of the 'anchoring' (Camilleri and Falk 1992: 250) of particular societies to specific places or territories. Thus, it is more difficult to decide what we mean when we talk about a 'British', a 'Canadian' or almost any other 'national' identity and culture.

THE CONTINUING NEED FOR EFFECTIVE NATION-STATES

Can the nation-state really be in a situation of terminal decline when its long-standing preoccupation with military security, autonomy and national identity continues to shape world politics? Certainly, recent crises remind us of the continuing saliency of unresolved or new military, nationalist, interstate or ethnic conflicts in many parts of the world and their capacity to ignite tensions. According to Smith and Bræin (2003: 70–1), there were more than 125 wars across the world between late 1989 and early 2003 and the great majority – around 90 per cent – involved civil wars rather than interstate wars. Together these wars killed around seven million people, most of them civilians. The ending of the Cold War and the collapse of the Soviet Union have given impetus to the resurgence of national and ethnic demands and rivalries. Here are some examples:

1. The crisis in the Balkans, which began after the dissolution of Yugoslavia in 1989, was followed by the eruption of genocide and civil war in Bosnia until 1995, and was then rekindled in Kosovo, leading to NATO's bombing attacks against Serbia that began in March 1999.
2. The first Iraqi invasion of Kuwait in 1990, followed by the Gulf War of 1991, and then the second Iraq War led by US forces in 2003.
3. The continuing dispute between China and Taiwan, which briefly escalated into armed conflict in 1995, perhaps a foretaste of future conflicts in the Asia Pacific region.
4. The uncertainties over long-established ethnic, linguistic, religious or regional demands for autonomy in Northern Ireland, Canada, Spain, Palestine and several African countries.
5. The uncertainties surrounding the UN's interventions, especially its ability to undertake effective global peacekeeping responsibilities in the light of its failures in Somalia, Bosnia, Rwanda and the multistate involvement in the war emanating from the Democratic Republic of Congo.
6. The proliferation of chemical and nuclear weaponry as a rising number of countries (India, Pakistan, Israel and South Africa) have acquired the capability to produce their own weaponry or seem likely to do so in the near future (Iraq, Brazil, Iran and Argentina).

Some of these conflicts are the legacy of a previous government's failure to provide the conditions for successful economic growth or correct regional and ethnic imbalances in the distribution of economic gains. Others need to be seen within the wider context of globalizing influences. For example, Held (1995: 94) observed that the globalization of information, 'far from creating a sense of common human purpose ... has arguably served to reinforce the sense of the significance of identity and difference'. This encourages peoples without states to demand their own. There is also a relationship between globalization and nationalism in respect of arms proliferation. New nations buy arms to acquire the symbols of international prestige and independence, while arms-manufacturing countries are reluctant to regulate the arms trade because of its contribution to export earnings.

The conflicts fuelled by new nation formation, ethnic hatred, international terrorism and the arms trade have created enormous difficulties for the UN. Recalling the circumstances surrounding its foundations in 1945 highlights its current predicament. Then, there were far fewer nation-states and reaching international agreement was correspondingly easier. The UN's remit was primarily designed to prevent future conflicts between nations. This left the UN ill-equipped to deal with the disputes and civil wars that have been erupting within states in recent years, and it is these that have often dominated the global agenda. Nevertheless, despite these forces undermining the nation-state system, becoming a recognized nation-state is still a popular goal for political movements. As we have seen, following the demise of colonialism after the Second World War, the nation-state system was vastly extended and the UN played a pivotal, supervising role in this process (Giddens 1985: 283).

In other words, states are not disappearing; there are more of them and they are starting to exercise different sorts of power. This is evident, for example, in the rise of the 'competition state' (Teschke and Heine 2002: 176) in place of the welfare state. Robinson (2002: 215) interestingly argues that because of globalization, a transnational state apparatus is emerging 'from within the system of nation-states'. Thus, as capitalism is transformed and breaks free of the nation, so too do the political institutions of the state change and become increasingly internationalized to serve the interests of transnational capitalism. Together they form what Robinson calls a 'transnational state'. This includes a transnational network of politicians and officials who are sympathetic to global capitalism together with elites linked to various supranational economic and political forums. These 'transnational state cadres act as midwives of capitalist globalization' (Robinson 2002: 216).

Meanwhile, in an attempt to force down wages, politicians across the world have used globalization as a pretext to cut welfare expenditure, remove trade union rights and deregulate labour markets. Between 1979 and 1990, the Thatcher government in Britain was largely successful in centralizing the state apparatus. This went against all the supposed trends towards the diminution of state power. Indeed, some observers have argued convincingly that it is mythical to suppose that contemporary states are unable to govern their economy's economic direction in the face of globalization (Weiss 1998), though this may be more difficult for the weaker countries. Where governments have lost some economic control, they may have been under strong pressure from particular foreign powers to dismantle the controls over the inward and outward movement of money and investments, as in South Korea during the early 1990s (Gowan 1999). At the same time, political power and strong policy preferences in the hands of determined governments remain highly significant.

■ REVIEW

We have examined sociology's contribution to our understanding of the links between society and the nation-state, accepting that its study of global relations has hitherto been limited. Then we explored both sides of the debate concerning the supposed decline of the nation-state in the face of globalizing tendencies and have suggested the need to exercise caution when considering such arguments. Here, it might be useful to end by drawing upon the recent case put forward by Held and Archibugi (1995). They argue that the world needs something they call 'cosmopolitan democracy'.

This would mean ensuring 'citizens, wherever they are located in the world, have a voice, input and political representation in international affairs, in parallel with and independently of their own governments' (Held and Archibugi 1995: 13). It also 'requires the creation of authoritative global institutions able to monitor the political regimes of member countries and to influence the domestic affairs of states where necessary' (Held and Archibugi 1995: 14). Among the many institutional changes this might require are the following: creating regional parliaments; adopting cross-national referenda on such issues as regional transport; strengthening people's rights partly by increasing the power and influence enjoyed by international courts; and reforming the UN to strengthen its effectiveness and legitimacy, for example by ensuring that all regional interests are more genuinely represented and reducing the UN's current exposure to US influence (Held 1995: 106–9).

Such ideas and institutions are a long way from being implemented at the present time. However, set against the daring, innovative nature of such thinking and the fast-changing realities of the 'global political order', it does seem as if the debate about the nation-state versus globalization is rather dated and simplistic. At the same time, nation-state power in the emerging global order seems full of contradictions. On one hand, for example, NATO's attacks on Serbia in 1999 raised yet again the crucial issue of whether, how and under what circumstances the world community is justified in intervening in the internal affairs of other nations, even where vicious governments are blatantly abusing universal humanitarian principles and/or threatening the security of surrounding areas. On the other hand, the intervention of American-led coalition forces in Iraq during 2003, and the resulting rise of insurgency, multiple killings of civilians and soldiers and the declining popularity of the US government both at home and abroad in the face of all this, suggests that even a mighty military superpower's room for manoeuvre is less than it might appear at first sight. Everything is changing but exactly how far and in what direction is uncertain.

Finally, as we have stressed, the role of states in overcoming economic backwardness has historically been paramount everywhere. Thus, during the early stages of industrialization, most governments invested in infrastructure and education, fostered local capitalists and protected infant industries from foreign competition. Many Asian states have gone much further than this role. It is difficult to see how the remaining poor countries could escape their current situation without adopting similar state-led strategies.

FURTHER READING

- C. W. Kegley Jr and E. R. Wittkopf's book *World Politics: Trend and Transformation* (2004) provides a wide-ranging discussion of both changing approaches to the study of international relations and the volatile nature of world politics in an age of rapid globalization. It is regularly revised and includes pictures, maps, tables and other accessible material.

- D. Held and A. McGrew have written a number of leading works on politics and globalization. Their short book *Globalization/Anti-Globalization* (2002) includes an immense amount of relevant information and many carefully summarized assessments of the debates on the changing nature of power.

- G. Delanty's book *Citizenship in a Global Age: Society, Culture, Politics* (2000) offers a comprehensive review of theories of citizenship and shows how it needs to change with globalization.

- R. A. Nisbet's *The Sociological Tradition* (1970) still offers a highly readable account of sociology's early development as a discipline. Try Chapters 3 and 4.

- The chapters on democracy by P. Lewis (1992: Chapter 1) and citizenship and welfare by D. Riley (1992: Chapter 4) in *Political and Economic Forms of Modernity*, edited by John Allen, Peter Braham and Paul Lewis (1992) would be useful accompaniments to the first part of this chapter.

GROUP WORK

- Students should consider how they feel about their own sense of national identity. How strong is it and why? Does globalization or regionalization threaten national identities? Do students have other, stronger, loyalties? Everyone will report to the class. How far do individual positions differ and how can this be explained?

- Working in small groups, students will collect cuttings from quality newspapers/magazines over several weeks demonstrating: (a) what is happening at the UN; (b) how globalizing forces, for example Western TV programmes, are undermining some governments' domestic policies; (c) the tensions arising between states during this period and why. Groups will compile a brief report on their issue to be presented to the class.

QUESTIONS TO THINK ABOUT

1. Explain how and why mainstream sociology paid little attention to states and global relations until relatively recently.

2. Critically assess the contribution of the realist perspective to our understanding of the world order.

3. Are Marshall's three kinds of 'rights' adequate for an understanding of contemporary forms of citizenship?

4. 'The nation-state is in terminal decline, but there is no alternative structure capable of picking up its former functions.' Discuss.

5. What are the chief difficulties involved in considering the debate about globalization and the nation-state?

■ http://web.inter.nl.net/users/Paul.Treanor/plana.html A site maintained by Paul Treanor and developed around a journal article in *Sociological Research Online* on nationalism that just grew and grew. We find the site rather chaotic visually, but persistence pays off and you can find some useful gems.

■ http://www.intute.ac.uk/socialsciences/cgi-bin/search.pl?term1=nationalism&gateway =Sociology&limit=0 The Intute gateway on nationalism offers a fair amount of downloadable material even if you don't follow the invitation to register. A strong orientation to politics.

■ http://www2.ids.ac.uk/drccitizen/ An unusual alliance between scholars, civil society organizations in seven countries, government (in the form of the UK Department for International Development) and the Rockefeller Foundation. Called the Development Research Centre on Citizenship, Participation and Accountability, it focuses on widening citizenship and participation. This group seeks to document and explain the new ways in which citizenship has changed from the original models inherited from the French Revolution or described by Marshall.

PART TWO

Divisions

CHAPTER 6

Social Inequalities: Gender, Race and Class

CONTENTS

Sociologists have always sought to conceptualize and explain the forms of social inequality found in all societies and the ways in which these vary both between societies and over time. The unequal distribution of power, wealth, income, opportunity and social status between individuals and groups is not randomly distributed, but is patterned and structured. Particular social groups find themselves persistently denied the same degree of access to social rewards and resources as other groups. Disadvantaged groups are also exposed to forms of discrimination as well as ideologies, culturally dominant values and learning roles that induce them to accept their 'proper' social place, a process known as **SOCIAL-IZATION**. Customary beliefs, political ideologies and organized religion have often played central roles in instilling convictions that a given social order is normal, necessary or divinely sanctioned.

key **concept**	**SOCIALIZATION** The processes through which we learn to understand, assimilate and reproduce the rules, values and meanings shared by members of our society and which are constantly enacted and negotiated in everyday life. The child's relationships within the family are normally crucial to this learning process – along with school and peer groups – but socialization continues throughout life as we are continuously exposed to different social experiences, including the media.

In general, we can say that structured forms of inequality often operate along three main axes. These are related to social actors' gender, race/ethnicity or class. So frequently are these three factors mentioned in discussions of social inequality that some irreverent sociologists know them as the 'holy trinity'. Each of these in turn generates its own structure of unequal practices giving rise to institutionalized sexism, racism or class divisions/conflict. Gender, race and class also crosscut each other in various complex ways, sometimes reinforcing and at other times weakening the impact of existing inequalities. In this chapter we explore the ways sociologists, past and present, have grappled with various schemes and arguments to understand how the 'holy trinity' shapes our lives. In doing so, we will also need to remember that the relative significance of different kinds of inequality can change. The particular manifestation of these axes of disadvantage has varied quite markedly between different societies and over time, while other sources of inequality such as religious affiliation, disability, civic status or age have also operated to create social inequalities. We say something about these other factors below. We also need to emphasize that inequality is a global phenomenon not simply in the sense that in its varying forms it is found in virtually all societies, but also because wide and growing inequalities are clearly manifest at the regional and world levels (see also Chapter 8).

▪▪▪▪▪▪▪▪▪ SOME UNDEREXPOSED FORMS OF SOCIAL INEQUALITY

Before dealing with gender, race/ethnicity and class in detail, we want to give at least some brief consideration to four other sources of discrimination and social inequality.

RELIGIOUS AFFILIATION

Many of the world's 191 UN-recognized nation-states have constitutions that protect the rights of their citizens to worship freely and choose their own religious affiliation. However, there are notable exceptions. Here are just two. The Bahai (sometimes written as Baha'i) faith, founded in the mid-nineteenth century, has experienced continuous persecution in Iran, where many thousands of its adherents have been martyred and executed. Bahais are accused of apostasy, which makes them liable to death, lifetime imprisonment and persecution. Their houses are plundered, their property confiscated and they are denied legal and employment rights (Cooper 1985). In China, the Communist Party (CPC) still declares the country to be atheist and discriminates against openly practising members of the five religious faiths it recognizes – Buddhism, Taoism, Islam, Catholicism and Protestantism. However, the CPC has been especially intolerant of the Falun Gong, founded in 1992, which it denounces as 'an evil cult'. Its followers may number as many as 70 million, which rivals the membership of the CPC itself. There are reports of 2,786 deaths of Falun Gong members in police custody and over 100,000 have been sent to labour camps (Schechter 2000).

DISABILITY AND 'MOBILITY RIGHTS'

Discrimination on the grounds of impaired mobility (for example people who are wheelchair users) has been brought to many people's attention where disabled groups are well-organized and lifts, ramps, parking spaces and toilets have been adapted and designated for their use. The category 'disabled' has been notably expanded by lobby groups like the US Disability Rights Education and Defense Fund (www.dredf.org), who include in their membership those suffering from cancer, epilepsy and diabetes as well as those experiencing impaired mobility. Some 49 million people in the USA are therefore grouped into the 'disabled' category and they constitute a powerful constituency. In most of the poorer countries, there is little self-organization among disabled groups and their protection and welfare tends to be left to episodic acts of charity.

Cass et al. (2005) advocate adding spatial or *mobility rights* to the normally accepted categories of civil, political and social rights. They argue that disabled persons are not the only people affected. Restricted physical access to goods, values and commodities is, they insist, a more general phenomenon. As social networks in work, family life and leisure become more extensive, geographical isolation, the cost of transport and information deficiencies lead to isolation and social exclusion. Mobility in terms of the availability and price of transport, and access to information, goods and services, shows wide global and regional discrepancies and a basic difference between rural and urban people, and poor and rich. (Think of the poor, mostly black, residents of New Orleans without their own transport trying to evacuate the city as hurricane Katrina approached.)

CIVIC STATUS

In ancient Greece, the Spartans relied on a subordinated foreign labour force, the Messenian helots, who had to give part of their produce to their masters, could not serve in the army and had no legal or civic rights. Many contemporary societies also show an increasing tendency to create new helots – people who are tolerated because they work or provide services, but for whom the longstanding population has little sympathy and does not wish to include in the body of citizens. The question of who should have access to the vote, a passport, free or subsidized healthcare, free or subsidized education, unemployment and disability benefits, a pension and a host of other entitlements is increasingly becoming contested as host populations confront newcomers in their midst. The proliferation of temporary statuses that governments have invented to assign to new helots is illustrative. Newcomers are given 'exceptional leave to remain'. They are 'temporary workers', 'guestworkers', 'resident aliens', 'protected persons' or 'undocumented persons', anything short, that is, of full citizens with a complete set of benefits and entitlements.

AGE

There are many wealthy senior citizens, nonetheless, age will become an increasingly important axis of social inequality in all societies, but particularly in rich Western societies and Japan, as the demographic profile changes (Table 6.1). Poverty is often concentrated in the elderly, though social intervention can help. For example, in the UK, the number of elderly people needing social assistance fell from 1.8 million in 1974 to 1.4 million 17 years later. With longer life spans, more pressure on the health services, more elderly people and fewer people of working age being taxed to sustain increases in pension payments, these gains are easily reversed. In addition to poverty, the elderly are more prone to sickness, more likely to be disabled and more likely to experience mental health problems. Mental health problems may arise because of dementia (affecting about 5 per cent of the UK population), isolation (as friends and families die or move away), bereavement (when spouses and family die) and overreliance on other elderly carers, who are themselves vulnerable to the trials and tribulations of increasing age (Spicker 2005).

TABLE 6.1	**Percentage of 60+ people in the population**	
Year	2000	2050 (projected)
More developed regions	19	32
Less developed regions	8	20
World	13.5	26

SOURCE: UN (2004)

The higher likelihood of older people being marginalized and excluded demonstrates how the different axes of social inequality can become additive and mutually reinforcing. To illustrate: an older person in insecure, low-paid employment (the class axis), is more likely to retire to a poorly ventilated or heated home, more likely to experience health problems and more likely to have an inadequate retirement income (the age axis). Again, women generally outlive men (the age axis), but because they were more likely to be in poorer paid jobs, often took time out for child-bearing and child-raising, and were less likely to be paying into an occupational or state insurance fund (the gender axis), they are more likely to spend long years of their advancing age in poverty.

In the case of poorer countries and rural populations, the greater durability of the extended family system has been thought to protect the elderly, who are often treated with great respect and affection. However, many countries of the South are becoming urbanized and the nuclear family is rapidly becoming the norm. Although this was virtually unknown in Africa, say 50 years ago, older people are sometimes now discarded by their families. Even more frighteningly, many are having to become parents again. In 2001, the International Federation of Red Cross and Red Crescent Societies announced that at least five million grandparents were looking after children who had lost their parents to HIV/AIDS. The statement continued:

> The psychological strain of caring for terminally ill children and coping with their death can be devastating. The stress of taking on the burden of responsibility for orphaned grandchildren is also huge. It is not unusual for grandmothers to be caring for 20 children. (Medilink 2005)

FEMINISM: CONFRONTING GENDER INEQUALITY

Throughout most of this century, and especially from the late 1960s, there has been a growing awareness of the multiple sorts of oppression to which women in most societies have been historically subjected. Numerous scholars, often women scholars, have undertaken a fundamental re-evaluation of most existing theories in the humanities and social sciences, on the grounds that these mostly ignored, or misunderstood, women's historical and contemporary roles (see Box 6.1 later in the chapter). Consequently, and especially in sociology, an influential and distinctive perspective has emerged.

Despite their greater visibility arising from this new interest, women's struggles have a long history. During the nineteenth century, mainly middle-class or aristocratic women joined campaigns such as the anti-slavery movement and the demand for prison reform. They also began to organize in favour of the extension of voting rights to women, especially in the USA (Stienstra 1994: 44–9). In the twenty years or so before the First World War, the **suffragette movement** became a highly significant form of mass collective protest in many advanced countries. The demand for voting rights normally went hand in hand with demands that women should enjoy the same educational and job opportunities as men and the same freedom of access to social and public life.

The **suffragette movement** demanded votes for women as a first principle of equality and liberation. The movement was at its height in the USA and the UK in the late nineteenth and early twentieth century, but it was not until women were used 'on the home front' in factories during the First World War that their cause was won. Even then, when the vote was conceded in the UK in 1918, only women over 30 were eligible. In the USA, women's suffrage was granted two years later.

Figure 6.1 **A suffragette poster in favour of votes for women distances the intelligent woman graduate from a convict or a lunatic**
Although the moral inferiority of the convict is taken for granted here, there is an arguable case for prisoners not to lose the franchise.

We can distinguish two waves of feminism:

- *First-wave feminism:* This liberal feminist concern for the attainment of what were essentially individual freedoms formed the first wave of the women's movement. It involved what Zalewski (1993: 116) called the 'add women and stir' variety of feminist thought. This is the idea that first and foremost women's liberation required the extension of the Enlightenment principles of equal dignity, respect and rights for all citizens. Everyone, including men, would benefit from the new energies and abilities unleashed once women – the other half of humanity – were free to seek personal fulfilment. Liberal feminism remains influential today, but it has also continued to be largely the preserve of white, middle-class, Western women.
- *Second-wave feminism:* A second wave of feminism, which burst onto the world scene from the late 1960s, spread outwards from the USA. A common idea was that women possessed certain distinctive characteristics such as a greater capacity for nurturing than men and a stronger inclination to seek harmonious relationships. It followed that if women could stamp their own, more highly developed moral preferences and priorities onto political and public life through the attainment of political power, the world might be more peaceful (Stienstra 1994: 52).

Four central propositions emerged from the post-1960s second wave of feminist thinking. After outlining these, we proceed to explore them in more detail:

- male and female roles and characteristics are mostly learned and/or imposed on individuals and this results in a process of societal engendering
- women's contributions to social life are invariably regarded as less significant than those of men and give rise to a condition of gender inequality
- relationships in virtually all societies have been characterized by a long-held cultural acceptance of gender inequalities
- forms of oppression of women have moved from the private to the public sphere as they have escaped or augmented their domestic roles.

THE ENGENDERING OF FEMININITY AND MASCULINITY

In virtually all societies it has been assumed that maleness and femaleness are natural states that cannot be changed. Men supposedly find it easy to be brave warriors, technical experts and clear-headed, rational thinkers free from cloying emotions. Women, we are told, naturally lean towards caring roles and home-making activities. A clear division of labour in the allocation of economic tasks between men and women has always been partly justified in terms of these supposedly natural, biological differences.

Second-wave feminists disagreed profoundly with these characterizations. Instead, they argued that unlike those *biological* differences that are anatomical and genetic in character, *gender* is an acquired identity. As Peterson and Runyan (1993: 5) bluntly put it: 'We *learn*, through culturally specific socialization, how to be masculine and feminine and to assume the identities of men and women.' In this view, it is not biology but differing cultural expectations and social treatment that makes us into 'males' or 'females'. Similarly, it is mostly cultural processes that determine whether a person is allocated child-rearing and home-making roles along with economic activities linked to domesticity (cooking, cleaning or caring for others), rather than occupations such as hunting, herding animals, working with machines or exercising political leadership.

THE GENDER HIERARCHY AND FEMALE SUBORDINATION

In most societies, gendered identities are not only regarded as completely distinctive, forming opposites in a binary system, but they are also evaluated differently. Masculine characteristics are generally assumed to be more socially 'useful', technically 'difficult' and generally more 'important' than feminine ones. Feminists argue that in most societies this results in a hierarchically structured system in which gender relations are highly unequal. Consequently, fewer rewards accrue to them and they enjoy less power to shape social relations. Even the attainment of civil or political rights alongside men is unlikely to remove all the sources of oppression women face, since these rights usually refer to public life, not to the private realms of household and family. There, women may remain subject to forms of domination from husbands, sons and male kinsmen that may be legitimized by cultural values and/or underpinned by economic dependency.

PATRIARCHAL SOCIETIES AND PATRIARCHAL RELATIONS

Can female subordination only be fully understood within the context of generalized male domination or **PATRIARCHY**? Discussion among feminists regarding the nature, extent and causes of patriarchy has generated an important debate and not a little disagreement. In Box 6.1, we outline the main divisions within recent feminist thinking with regard to the nature, causes and significance of patriarchal relations for women.

key concept	**PATRIARCHY** is a form of oppression that elevates men to positions of power and authority. Feminist writers argue that patriarchy is so deeply embedded that it appears in early societies as well as in feudal, capitalist and self-proclaimed socialist societies. Those feminists who are influenced by Marxism stress that sexual divisions of labour are functional and related to the evolving class structure. Other writers have pointed to the role of religion or the structuring and labelling of female and male roles. Whatever the origin of this role differentiation (most feminists discount, but some include, the different biological functions of men and women), it has now become culturally and even psychoanalytically inscribed. This makes patriarchy difficult to dislodge.

Early sociologists such as Maine, Engels and Weber defined patriarchy as a system of social organization in which the eldest males in a family exercised more or less unconstrained power both over younger males and women and where production was based almost entirely in the household. They regarded patriarchy as a social form specific to certain historical (preindustrial) eras and societies. For Weber, the classic form of patriarchy existed several thousand years ago in many Middle Eastern societies where direct personal rule was exercised by the elders; social bonds were defined by blood or kinship links and economic activity was nomadic. Extensive twentieth-century anthropological research has largely confirmed Weber's observations that rule by the oldest males is the most striking and dominant aspect of social organization in pastoral and stateless societies. Social life is mainly organized around allegiance to extended systems of kinship (or lineage) based on descent from a common blood ancestor.

Women normally bear all the direct responsibility for childcare and domestic life – including fetching water and fuel. However, their burden of biological and social reproduction also encompasses playing a key role in food production through agriculture. Such women feed their husbands, children and perhaps some of their extended kin not simply through preparing food but by growing a large part of it themselves. This primary role of women in food production has often been ignored or misunderstood, whether by colonial states, agricultural experts seeking to 'improve' the productivity of traditional farming practices, or by the elite of modernizing governments who have ruled such societies since independence.

In contrast to the African case, the peoples living in most parts of Asia and some of the Middle East practised a more intensive and efficient form of agriculture. This involved permanent settlements, customary land rights and the need for frequent manuring, irrigation and deep ploughing, which was reliant on access to heavy animals such as oxen. These societies were also more hierarchical. According to Boserup (1970), intensive, plough-based agriculture created a sexual division of labour in which men played a more central role in crop cultivation than their counterparts in pastoral and stateless societies. In particular, men assumed the main responsibility for the heavy physical work associated with harnessing animal power to field management and staple cereal production. Women undertook lighter agricultural tasks such as weeding and winnowing grain, assumed responsibility for dairy production and reared smaller animals.

Purdah The practice of secluding women by covering their bodies from the male gaze and virtually excluding them, behind screens, from all forms of public life.

Superimposed on this division of labour were religious beliefs and customary arrangements that largely confined women to the home or domestic sphere, while assigning them to the responsibility and control of husbands and male kinsmen. One extreme form of this was the demand for **purdah** in Islamic societies, though the degree to which such practices were strictly enforced varied a good deal. For example, they were invariably less evident – and less possible – in poorer households. In the more prosperous families of traders, government officials or larger landowners, it was a mark of social status that their women could more or less withdraw from undertaking all but the least onerous economic tasks, while their exclusion from public life might be quite strictly enforced.

Kandiyoti (1997: 91) argued that women living in such societies could negotiate with husbands and male kinsmen over the 'patriarchal bargain – protection (from males) in exchange for submissiveness and propriety'. They could also resist changes introduced by men when these threatened female security. Thus, women in patriarchal societies should not be regarded as passive victims. For example, in many parts of sub-Saharan Africa, the spread of market opportunities has often led men to impose heavier demands for farm labour on their wives or to renege on their customary obligations to supply wives with their own plots of land. This is to assist them in the cultivation of more commercial crops. Women often responded to such pressures by deserting their husbands, demanding the payment of wages in return for labour on commercial farms or devoting more time to their own trading activities. At times, women have also engaged in open dispute with local males.

Box 6.1

Recent feminist debates on patriarchal relations

Radical feminists

Many feminists argued that patriarchy exercises a totalizing influence over women in modern societies. Thus, Millet (1977: 25) defined patriarchy as the 'institution whereby that half of the populace which is female is controlled by that half which is male'. For radical feminists, male supremacy derives from men's ability to control women's bodies, for example in sexual relations, through women's role in childbirth and in the tendency for modern health practices and technology to be dominated by a predominantly male expertise. The latter has systematically stigmatized and excluded the knowledge accumulated by women herbalists and health practitioners in the preindustrial era. Male dominance is also reinforced by the prevailing ethos of heterosexuality as the supposedly 'normal' form of sexual relations. It is also made possible by widespread male violence especially in domestic life – a situation that has generally been tolerated or ignored by the authorities. Despite some faults (see below), radical feminism has been enormously influential.

The critique of radical feminism

In addition to the emergence of other streams of feminist thought, radical interpretations were increasingly contested, especially from the late 1970s, partly on the following grounds:

Because the roots of male domination appeared to lie primarily in women's sexuality and their child-bearing/rearing roles, such conceptualizations of patriarchal relations might compel feminist aspirations to lean on those very assumptions from which they had been trying to escape, namely the conventional view that women's subordination is biologically determined.

These views of patriarchy are employed indiscriminately and without regard for its distinctive relevance as a total way of life to specific historical periods and cultures (see above and Kandiyoti 1997).

It is unclear what is systematic about patriarchy within and across different societies and why it takes many varying forms, and how exactly it is grounded in concrete social relations so as to make possible persistent and totalizing male oppression.

Marxist feminists

Marxist feminists argue that the primary source of women's oppression derives from the logic of capital accumulation and profit. Capitalists need to cheapen the cost of producing each generation of workers. The unpaid family domestic labour and child-rearing provided by women enables capital to achieve this aim, though helped by the social welfare and educational provisions supplied by the state. In addition, capital can exploit the reality of women's domestic responsibilities by using this as an excuse to pay women lower wages. For similar reasons they can also conveniently slot women workers into part-time and temporary employment as and when the market demands, without the necessity to pay social benefits or provide job security. However, many Marxist feminists have increasingly recognized that certain aspects of patriarchal relations, for example the widespread resort to male violence, are not always reducible to the needs of capital. Patriarchy often has its own logic, which interacts with capitalist oppression.

The ethnic/race critique of white feminists

Feminists living in the South have argued that the chief sites of female oppression for them may be quite different from their white, Western counterparts. Thus, colonial exploitation, the need for male–female unity in the struggle to overcome Western imperialism and the repression exercised over women by newly independent states have often been more significant for Southern women than the issues of family life and control over sexuality. Similarly, non-white women living in Western countries often encounter many forms of discrimination that shape their lives more dramatically than any tensions that may emanate from 'traditional' cultural family values. Even the labour market problems experienced by women from ethnic/racial minorities may be unique to them. Thus, Afro-Caribbean women in Britain are more likely than white women to take full economic responsibility for family life (Bruegel 1988). They are more successful than male Afro-Caribbeans in obtaining educational qualifications. Despite this relative success, poverty compels many to seek full-time jobs but ones that are often low paid. White women, with more secure family lives and husbands who are better paid, are more likely to see the 'problem' of employment in terms of the difficulty of escaping from part-time work.

Postmodern feminism

Postmodernists emphasize the multiple and ever shifting discourses that permeate social life – so that there can be no 'fixed' structures shaping human behaviour or absolute values. They also celebrate cultural differences and insist on the individual's increasing capacity to construct (or deconstruct) lifestyles and their social personæ. Postmodernists have been highly sceptical of other feminist views. Thus, the argument that we can clearly delineate the social category of 'women' and that all women share a common unity of interests, one that clearly divides them from men, smacks of essentialism (a belief in the innate and irreducible nature of things or social entities). From a study of women's magazines, Coward (1978) argued that whereas the magazine *Good Housekeeping* expressed femininity in terms of family and household roles, *Cosmopolitan* encouraged women to seek sexual expression through a concern with glamour and bodily beauty. Its articles also assumed that readers had little interest in conventional ideas of domesticity but desired freedom of sexual choice, economic independence and careers.

FROM PRIVATE TO PUBLIC FORMS OF PATRIARCHY

It seems clear from the debate outlined in Box 6.1 that any consensus on the nature, causes and direction of change associated with patriarchy that may once have existed among feminists has gradually broken down since the late 1970s. Walby's (1990) work is especially useful in enabling us to sift out the most valid claims and take stock of recent changes. Overall, she believes that a major shift has taken place in the forms of patriarchal domination characteristic of industrial societies from the private to the public sphere.

Various structures operating outside the household have worked to underpin private patriarchal domination. Over the past 150 years or so the public sphere has become more accessible to women. Yet, women are still exploited and remain subject to new patriarchal forms because, within public life, they continue to face certain disadvantages compared with men and tend to experience segregation. This new gender dynamic is discussed at length by Walby (1990) and is summarized below:

- *Working but still low paid:* Not only are women no longer excluded from formal paid employment but by the late 1980s they made up virtually half the official labour force in most Western countries. However, nearly half are employed part time. Despite legislation designed to ensure wage equality, they continue to earn roughly three-quarters of male wages for the same work. Moreover, they tend to be segregated within certain female-designated employment enclaves such as the caring professions (in health, social work and education) or low-paid industries and services.
- *More choice, but still the child carers:* Access to paid employment, the attainment by girls of educational levels similar if not increasingly superior to those obtained by boys, the right to divorce and to birth control, and the assignment

of formally equal citizen rights have all helped to give women much greater freedom of personal choice and more control over their bodies. Yet, while they can break free from unhappy marriages and even rear children as single mothers, such options leave them dependent on state welfare and legislation, highly susceptible to a life of poverty, for example after divorce, and still faced with the primary responsibility for childcare.

■ *Sexually free but still in danger:* Women still face the very real possibility of male violence in domestic and public life and are exposed to a double standard of personal morality that tends to label them as 'slags' if they choose multiple sexual partners, even though such freedoms clearly benefit men as well while not exposing them to the same stigma. At the same time, pornography has now become a vast industry and most of this trade degrades women and exposes them to increased risks of personal exploitation and physical danger.

■ *New models, old realities:* The representations of women in the media appear to offer new models of femininity, promising society's respect for the goals of independence, freedom and equal opportunity. Yet, scratch beneath the surface generated by the glossy images and the message points in a very different direction. Personal fulfilment is still thought to depend on motherhood, heterosexual love and marriage based on lasting relationships. The divorced woman is usually portrayed as returning to the safe fold of male protection through a 'happier' second marriage. Meanwhile, the need to cultivate sexual attractiveness as the key to winning male approval continues to be strongly emphasized in popular culture.

Global Thinkers 6 **SHEILA ROWBOTHAM (1943–)**

A central theme in Rowbotham's work has been her explorations into why women have been oppressed but also their worldwide struggles to counter patriarchy and economic and political inequality. Below, we sample a few of her contributions to this field.

British women's experiences
Her intellectual focus became evident in Hidden from History *(1973), a historical analysis of women's conditions and struggles in Britain as the first country to pass through a capitalist industrial revolution. She argued that:*

1. *Many of the eighteenth- and nineteenth-century radical thinkers who attacked the idea of a religiously sanctioned hierarchical social order nevertheless continued to identify humanity with men and believed that males should continue to dominate society, science and the emerging political order.*
2. *As enterprises grew in size, the factory system in the nineteenth century destroyed the competitiveness of family businesses, driving people into wage work. This undermined women's economic activities at home. It was also difficult for*

women to take up factory employment without childcare facilities. This often made them more dependent upon men.

3. *Yet, factory and other employment in a market economy increasingly opened the possibility that women might one day be able to lead an independent economic existence perhaps for the first time in history.*

4. *The prospect of women's eventual freedom to choose left many thinkers hesitant to advocate more than minimum reforms. Male working-class discontent with factory employment and their demand for a living wage was aimed not just at the injustices of capitalist exploitation but also reflected their desire to earn enough to live comfortably without the need for their wives to work. This would enable them to remain 'masters in their own home', while protecting women from the evils of factory work.*

Women, technology and feminism

In a wide-ranging review of issues surrounding women and technology, Rowbotham criticized the feminist view that women could bring a more caring, socially responsible approach to science and technology. This would counter the dangers of the dominant 'masculine' view that had produced a detached belief in progress and objectivity, while ignoring the destructive consequences of technological development on warfare, the environment and work experience. She argued that if 'female' values are placed in opposition, there was a danger of taking the feminist movement back to the position it had struggled against for so long; namely, one that equated women with 'nature' as against the rationality of dominant maleness.

In the same work, she also reviewed the worldwide historical evidence for modifying the usual view that women have always been excluded from scientific and technological development. Thus, in ancient societies as diverse as China, Egypt and Islamic Arabia, a few women from wealthy families studied at medical schools, wrote about military technology and contributed to engineering projects, among other things.

A contemporary focus

More recently, women's relative historical exclusion from scientific advances has been reversed with their involvement in computers and information systems. The need for the newly industrializing countries to adapt to the new as well as the older industrial technologies has provided a central role for women workers in many industrial sectors. Feminists in these countries have sought to link women workers and community groups. In contrast, some Western feminists have become preoccupied with the difficulties women face in winning the top jobs.

SOURCES: Rowbotham (1973, 1993, 1995a, 1995b); Rowbotham and Mitter (1994)

RACE AND ETHNICITY

The second major axis of inequality we consider is race, and its related phenomenon, ethnicity. The word 'race' is now inextricably associated with the idea and expression of 'racism' – discrimination on the grounds of observable difference. This was not always the case. The expression 'the human race' was meant once as a unifying notion, suggesting more commonality than difference. It laid emphasis on a single species, the implication being that we share more common features – physical, biological and social – than the characteristics that divide us. To avoid the confusion of using race in the sense of the total human race, it is probably sensible nowadays to talk of 'humanity' or 'humankind'.

Race was also used to refer to a group of persons connected by a common origin and sharing common features because of their supposedly common descent. Often such a depiction also included social and historical features such as the evolution of a shared language, a single place of settlement and the development of a political community, what we would nowadays see as a 'nation'. Before the Second World War, it was common for people to talk of 'the French race', 'the German race' or the 'British race' in this way, though such notions now seem either quaint or perhaps somewhat sinister.

In general, the expression 'race' continues to be used in two senses. First, in a supposedly scientific sense by some biologists and physical anthropologists and, second, as a sociological means of understanding how popular forms of heterophobia (fear of difference) are expressed, diffused and acted on.

EVALUATING BIOLOGICAL NOTIONS OF 'RACE'

Apartheid is the Afrikaans word for 'separateness', the system of systematic, legalized discrimination that existed in South Africa between 1948 and 1994. Under the Population Registration Act 1950, the population was classified in different racial categories, with education, residence and marriage only permitted within each category. Although the system technically supported difference rather than hierarchy, in practice, the good jobs, the best housing, the vote and other favourable opportunities and resources were reserved for the whites. With the election of Nelson Mandela as president in 1994, the system was legally dismantled, though some apartheid-like practices still continue informally.

The idea of classifying people into racial categories started in the sixteenth century and remained an important concern for biologists and physical anthropologists until the 1950s. As Stephan (1982: 171) argues:

For more than a hundred years the division of the human species into biological races had seemed of cardinal significance to scientists. Race explained individual character and temperament, the structure of social communities, and the fate of human societies ... At times this commitment to race subtly modified the reception and interpretation put upon new biological theories. At the very least, belief in the fixity, reality and hierarchy of human races – in the chain of superior and inferior human types – had shaped the activities of scientists for decades.

The scientific credibility of the idea of a racial hierarchy within humankind was fundamentally questioned in the wake of the Second World War. Nazi racism and anti-Semitism had been defeated on the battlefield and their horrific consequences had been witnessed as the starving remnants of the *Undermenschen* (the word used by the Nazis for 'subhumans') stumbled from the concentration camps. Although their intentions were not genocidal, the ideologists of the *apartheid* regime in South Africa also used racial categories for discriminatory social practices, suggesting, for example, that only certain races were fit for certain tasks.

The association between 'racial science' and political repression all but eliminated the word 'race' from polite scientific discourse. However, a small but determined group of biologists and physical anthropologists still insists that it is important to study subspecies (of the human species) that have developed distinguishing characteristics through segregation or relative isolation. Generally, such biologists do not stress *phenotypes* (appearance) but rather more complex and less visible biological characteristics (called *genotypes*). For example, biologists will refer to blood types and their distribution, to particularities of 'gene pools', to differences found by the human genome project and to the chromosomes of different populations.

Figure 6.2 **Memphis, Tennessee, USA, 1968**
Black civil rights activists trying to stage a protest against racial discrimination are hemmed in by National Guardsmen brandishing bayonets and a line of tanks.

Some of this is valid science, but it can have dangerous social and political implications. Occasionally, it has to be conceded, such studies can be used for socially responsible ends, for example in the testing and treatment of diseases such as sickle-cell anaemia, more common in those of African descent. However, discussions of genotype have also been more dubiously linked to the distribution of intelligence across populations (see Box 6.2). Steve Jones (1993), a leading geneticist, has warned against the tendency to dress up prejudices as science and points out that human beings are the products of about 50,000 genes (only about ten of which are concerned with skin colour), which act in complex and unexplored ways. Much of the existing material on heredity and race is simply bad science. The most damaging refutation of biological notions of race lies in the extensive history of the migration and mixing of peoples, and the breakdown of all reputed 'pure' types.

Box 6.2

Race and intelligence: US experiences

Elementary intelligence quotient (IQ) tests were first applied on Ellis Island, near New York, where 12 million immigrants entering the USA were processed. The fear of allowing simple-minded 'inferior' immigrants from Eastern and Southern Europe prompted this development. In the First World War, IQ tests were given to army recruits and school pupils. The lower scores of African-Americans and Americans of Eastern and Southern European descent were held to be attributable to their inferiority, but served only to indicate the cultural and linguistic biases of the tests. In these tests, Jews were held to be inferior, which is difficult to square with the fact that 37 per cent of US Nobel laureates are Jewish, some 19 times their percentage in the population.

In the 1960s, the controversy erupted again around the work of the Harvard educational psychologist Arthur Jenson (1969), who argued that 80 per cent of variance in IQ performance was attributable to heredity and that African-Americans were inherently inferior in certain intellectual abilities. These 'findings' were explosive, in that conservative and reactionary politicians used them to block remedial educational and social programmes, like 'Operation Head-start', designed to provide early educational support to deprived communities. If, these politicians reasoned, African-Americans were incapable through their genetic inheritance of changing their situation, why waste taxpayers' money? There are many problems with this analysis, not least that other groups, unrelated to African-Americans, showed a similar gap of 10–15 points in IQ tests, that other African origin groups (like those from the West Indies) did not manifest a gap and that in any case 'to make statements of heritability concerning such a polygenic trait [as intelligence] goes well beyond the scope of modern genetics' (van den Berghe 1994: 151).

Like a bad tune that will not go away but floats back in a slightly different key, Herrnstein and Murray (1994) argued in their 845-page tome, *The Bell Curve*, that inequality is at the heart of the human condition and that difference is in the nature of things. Their racial thinking is only thinly disguised. Instead of 'races', their world is made up of 'clans' (a complete violation of the meaning of this word), each possessing different qualities – all of which, we are told, we should value. Rather than bemoaning the fact that blacks are intellectually inferior to whites (a claim they virtually take for granted), the authors suggest we should celebrate their values of spirituality, movement, dance, rhythm and music. By including a discussion of the low IQ of the *white* 'underclass' (see below and Chapter 17), they hoped to dilute the exclusive concentration on black failures in other similar literature. Yet these devices are by way of a mask beneath which are still visible the old, discredited claims of biological inferiority and superiority.

SOURCES: van den Berghe (1994); Malik (1996: 205–9); http://en.wikipedia.org/wiki/Jewish_American

SOCIOLOGICAL NOTIONS OF RACE

Sociologists fully accept that race categories are commonly, but normally ignorantly, used in popular discourse and in social and political life. However, they point out that these common categories are imperfectly related to physical attributes like skin, hair or eye colour. For sociologists, phenotype (appearance) is important, but only as one social marker – one among many – that serves to generate the categories that regulate the distribution of advantage and disadvantage. The loose use of the expressions 'black', 'Asian' or 'white' provides a good example of how contingent, and temporary, are these popular racial expressions and labels (Box 6.3).

Box 6.3   **The strange story of race labels**

1. In apartheid South Africa, 'black' meant the totality of non-whites, including Indians, Coloured (people of mixed heritage), San and Khoi-khoi as well as those of dark-skinned African descent.

2. 'Black' in Australia means of Aboriginal descent. (Incidentally, native Australians have only a remote genetic connection to Africans.)

3. 'Black' in Brazil means somebody who is self-evidently thought to be of African descent. (Many Africans were brought to Brazil as a result of the slave trade.) Indigenous people and those who have mixed ancestry are excluded. According to popular Brazilian folk wisdom, 'money whitens the skin', so rich black Brazilians are 'white'.

4. In the USA, by contrast, people who are only barely discernibly of African descent will be considered 'black' (often legally so in the Southern states before the 1960s and now socially). They also may well describe themselves as 'black', though this label has been discarded in favour of 'African-American'.

5. If we turn to Britain after the 1950s, the category 'black' was used by some of the immigrants from the Caribbean and the Indian subcontinent (together with the radical intelligentsia) to suggest that they were being met with similar hostility or indifference. They saw themselves as forming an underclass or poor section of the working class and being denied access to the most favoured goods and resources.

6. Later in the UK, those of Indian, Pakistani and Bangladeshi background became more generally known as, and used the self-description, 'Asian'. However, 'Asian' excluded Chinese, Japanese and Malaysian people.

7. These last exclusions are received with particular puzzlement in the USA, where the category 'Asian American' definitely includes Chinese and Japanese.

8. Finally, by way of a final absurdity, we might note that in apartheid South Africa, because the Japanese did not fit the local categories and the government was anxious not to offend such a powerful investing and manufacturing nation, the Japanese were regarded as 'honorary whites' by the regime. They were, for example, allowed to stay in 'white' areas and hotels.

One after another, racial labels are found to be socially and politically constructed and reconstructed in particular settings. This has led some sociologists to argue that the category 'race' is too insubstantial to consider in a sociological sense. Some, like Miles (1989), would like to abolish 'race' (or always keep it in inverted commas), though they are certain there is a phenomenon called 'racism'. This position is not as bizarre as it may seem. The fact that 'races' are socially constructed does not mean that they are fictional or unimportant. Sociologists often remark that 'what's real in the mind is real in its consequences'. In other words, people think in racial terms, therefore their conduct and behaviour and the wider structure of social action will reflect those beliefs.

John Rex (1986), another prominent race relations theorist, suggests that we can delineate what he calls 'race relations situations'. If, he argues, inter-group interaction is marked by severe conflict, hostility, oppression and discrimination (all these going beyond in degree what the competition of a free labour market permits), we have a 'race relations situation'. There are clear practical advantages to this idea. It is both sociological and contextual. It can be used to account for the variety of labels and situations that apply to different groups. For example, the Jews in the context of Nazi Germany were a 'race', while in the context of, say, contemporary USA they are 'only' an ethnic group. Again, because there is often an element of biological determination in the justifications proffered for discrimination, it may be valid to consider that all inter-group hostility of the severity described can be considered a 'race relations situation'.

ETHNICITY

As the extent of inter-group conflict has proliferated – in Lebanon, Northern Ireland, Sri Lanka, the former Soviet Union, the former Yugoslavia and many African countries - it has become difficult to contain all cases of conflict-ridden interaction between similar-looking groups under the heading 'racial'. This leads to a suggestion that we might distinguish between race and ethnicity in one simple and obvious way. In the case of 'race', social construction is based on physical difference, while the social construction of ethnicity is based on less obvious differences, or social markers, for example those of culture, nationality, language or religion.

However, the contemporary use of the notion of ethnicity, or what some writers like Hall (1992) call 'new ethnicity', goes well beyond a further move-ment away from biological categorization. Sociologists have sought to find out how 'otherness' and 'difference' are constructed through discourse, imagery, representation and language, as well as through behaviour. Despite their allusive, metaphorical and literary quality, discussions of otherness in this mould are inherently more subtle and often more optimistic than many discussions of racism. They easily admit more liberating possibilities of self-examination and auto-critique, while an appeal to conscience, common humanity or self-interest can, Sampson (1993) suggests, be used to reduce perceived difference.

This more open view of identity construction starts from the assumption that, in our postmodern world, identity is more fragmented and the phenom-enon of multiple social identities is more common than previously had been assumed. Individuals may attach themselves to, or withdraw from, any one identity or category in a more fluid way, depending on the context. This is what is called **SITUATIONAL IDENTITY**.

key concept

SITUATIONAL IDENTITY arises when an individual constructs and presents any one of a number of possible social identities, depending on the situation. In the most individualistic versions of this phenomenon, an actor deploys an aspect of their identity – a religion, an ethnicity or lifestyle – as the context deems a particular choice desirable or appropriate.

There are obvious limits to the manipulative use of situational identity. It is relatively easy to change a religion or one's clothes. It is very difficult to alter one's physical appearance, though the large sales of skin and hair-altering products signify a successful strategy of 'passing', even in such racially divided societies as the USA and South Africa. The idea of 'new ethnicities' has proved liberating for many sociologists, despite its real-world limitations. Diversity and difference can be celebrated, while those who have been traditionally regarded as enduring victims can be more positively seen as evincing but one flexible cultural possibility and social persona among many.

CLASS

Although his fortune was halved to under US$50 billion in 2005, at its height, on 1 April 1999, a surge in the stock market price for his company, Microsoft, meant that Bill Gates was worth US$100 billion. His personal fortune was greater than the GNP of all but the richest 18 nations, and was worth more than twice all the US dollar bills in circulation. If Gates stacked the bills on top of each other, he would have had to climb 16 miles to get to the top (*Daily Telegraph*, 8 April 1999). On the same night, 1 April 1999, there were three million people in the USA sleeping in hostels, shelters or on the streets.

This massive discrepancy of fortune within one country is paralleled by large discrepancies between countries. Sociologists discuss these and similar differences under the terms 'social stratification' or 'class'. Strictly speaking, class differences are but one form of stratification. Others include:

- *Slavery:* In many ancient societies, slavery was practised and those with this status were worked to death in mining and constructing the pyramids, religious monuments, irrigation systems and public works. In some settings, like northern Nigeria, household slaves were treated more benignly, sometimes as favoured servants. But the plantation slaves of the New World were firmly put in their place, and until emancipation (1834 in the British Caribbean, 1865 in the USA) were treated as goods and chattels that could be owned, bequeathed or inherited. Sadly, there are still many slaves in the world.
- *Caste:* Associated principally with Hindu India, a caste system involves an inherited status in which occupations are assigned to one of four theoretically impermeable groups. The priests (Brahmins) claim the highest status, as they are regarded as closer to religious purity. Then follow the warriors, merchants and labourers. The 'untouchables' fall below this hierarchy and historically had to undertake 'unclean' tasks like collecting human excrement from cesspools. (Mahatma Gandhi, the great Indian leader, sought to liberate the 'untouchables' by renaming them *Harijan* – people of God – and insisted on them having the full rights of social citizenship.)

Slavery and caste are systems of social closure, though some limited social mobility is sometimes possible (see Srinivas 1952). A system of class stratification allows somewhat more, or very much more, movement between classes, though it always must be remembered that movement can be 'downward' as well as 'upward'. There are several ways of understanding how class is defined, how classes are formed and how their power is perpetuated or undermined. Again (as in gender or racial inequality) pre-Enlightenment thinkers tended to assume that class differences were natural or divinely sanctioned. However, sociologists have tended to position themselves around three major perspectives, which overlap to some degree. These are Marxist and neo-Marxist notions of class, Weberian views of class and applied definitions of class.

MARXIST AND NEO-MARXIST NOTIONS OF CLASS

Marx's considerable body of writing included intermittent and sometimes inconsistent attention to the issue of class. When he was writing for a popular audience, as he and Engels did in the 1848 *Communist Manifesto*, he tended to simplify his scheme into two 'great' classes, the *bourgeoisie* and the *proletariat*. On other occasions he talked of six different classes in Germany and seven in Britain, and also wrote about the peasantry and the *lumpenproletariat* (the urban poor, without regular employment) in considerable detail. Discussions of the intermediate and adjunct classes surrounding his two 'great' classes were later revived by neo-Marxists.

The basic schema rested on a distinction between 'a class *in* itself' and a 'class *for* itself'. The first was drawn from an observer's (like Marx himself) external and objective description. Marx thought that classes could be defined by the particular relationship they held to the means of production, distribution and exchange. Did they own property, capital or factory premises? Had they inherited money? Did they buy or sell goods or their labour, and at what level? Marx defined the proletariat principally by arguing that they had nothing to sell other than their **labour power** and nothing to lose other than the 'chains' that oppressed them.

> **Labour power** The *capacity* to work for a given time, at a given rate of pay and a particular level of skill and effort.

Marx was clear that it was a necessary but insufficient definition of class for a common objective situation to be present. Members of a particular class also had to subjectively feel part of that class and seek to defend, advance or maintain their class interests. He described peasants in France as a 'sack of potatoes', artificially bundled together but unable to act on their own behalf. They could not represent themselves, they had to be represented, he averred. Because of the absence of class consciousness, peasants were not a class.

Marx's model has been criticized on a number of levels. Nowadays, with a family car, a house and a share of capital represented (typically) by a pension, many workers have a lot more to lose than their chains. A significant number of middle-class occupations (clerical, professional, service and information-related) have also developed, which make the idea of a bipolarized class structure too simple. Managers, small employers and the self-employed also have contradictory class positions, which make them neither workers nor owners of capital. A number of neo-Marxist sociologists, like Wright (1985), have sought to accommodate these changes in revised versions of Marx's class structure. Again, Braverman (1974) has shown how office work – hitherto regarded as an escape from a proletarian blue-collar status – was itself becoming proletarianized by forcing workers in such settings to lose their autonomy.

WEBERIAN VIEWS OF CLASS

Max Weber thought that Marx's views on stratification were too narrowly structured around economic factors and he insisted that social and political aspects had to be added to round out the picture. Consequently, Weber developed three intersecting aspects of stratification:

- *class*, which at a descriptive level, is not that dissimilar to Marx's scheme
- *status groups*, which defined the 'social honour' accorded to a particular group or occupation
- *political power* (Weber confusingly calls this 'party'), which analysed how people are mobilized to secure their advantage in competitive settings.

Weber's scheme is quite complex but it has generated some important new lines of sociological reflection and enquiry. Following Weber, we need to accept that a multiplicity of class positions arise when his three aspects of stratification – economic class, social status and political power – do not coincide. Thus a ruthless, wealthy capitalist with little sense of etiquette and undiscriminating cultural taste might be denounced as nouveau riche, shunned as a marriage partner by an aristocratic family, excluded from political office and ostracized when trying to join a fashionable club. By contrast, a parson, colonial officer, nurse or poet might have little in the way of income, savings or property, yet be a respected and valued member of the community. In effect, a stock of **CULTURAL CAPITAL** may offset their meagre financial capital. Finally, a trade union leader or tough mayor of a US city may routinely exercise considerable influence, yet have neither money nor a high status.

 **key concept**

CULTURAL CAPITAL Despite the marked tendencies towards social levelling associated with mass education, affluence, consumerism and highly accessible forms of popular culture, Bourdieu (1984) argues that a dominant 'high' culture continues to flourish. Those whose education or other experiences have enabled them to acquire taste and distinction by investing in various kinds of discerning, detailed, cultural knowledge may be able to gain advantage in the competitive struggle for wealth and power by using their cultural capital.

APPLYING CLASS MODELS

The development of schema and typologies of class has proved to be of considerable practical importance in such diverse areas as developing social and employment policy, conducting censuses, marketing goods and services and predicting social and demographic trends. The most commonly applied models of class are based on occupational stratification. It is an immediately compelling argument that the reward system (how much you get paid), the status system (how much you are valued) and the conditions you encounter at work, follow occupational lines. Three such models are compared in Table 6.2.

TABLE 6.2 Class schema in the UK		
UK Registrar-General's scale	Goldthorpe's scheme (simplified)	Runciman's classes (percentages in 1990)
Professional occupations	Professionals/administrators/managers	Upper class (<1%)
Intermediate occupations		Upper middle class (<10%)
Skilled occupations	Non-manual employees/sales personnel	Middle middle class (15%)
Partly skilled occupations	Small proprietors/self-employed artisans	Lower middle class (20%)
Unskilled occupations	Farmers/smallholders	Skilled working class (20%)
	Technicians/supervisors/skilled manual workers	Unskilled working class (30%)
	Semi-skilled/unskilled	Underclass (5%)
	Agricultural workers	

NOTE: The Registrar-General is responsible for the conduct of the decennial census in the UK. Goldthorpe and Runciman are well-known UK sociologists.

SOURCE: Marsh et al. (1996: 237–9), citing the work of Runciman (1990) and Goldthorpe et al. (1980)

While there is by no means a perfect match between the three schemata provided in Table 6.2, there was nonetheless a broad consensus that the class hierarchy matches an occupational scale. This sort of neo-Weberian view of class was virtually unassailable until the early 1990s, when it was questioned on a number of grounds. Feminist scholars were concerned that occupational scales tended to favour those in formal employment and miss those in part-time and domestic household work. Women's class position was also rather too simply inferred from their husband's or father's occupation. Also, as we have argued in Chapter 4, the nature of work has itself changed and it is more and more likely that individuals will have multiple occupations, at different points of the scale, over their life spans – as well as periods of unemployment. Many become small entrepreneurs, but only for limited periods. Applied models of the class structure will have to be adjusted to take account of these developments.

THE EMERGENCE OF A TRANSNATIONAL CLASS

Another key limitation of the applied model of social class analysis is that none of the practitioners has moved beyond the national level, although there are occasional binational comparisons. At the top level of the class structure, elites have always been transnational. The European royal houses intermarried and held land and political titles in several countries, while aristocrats were frequently multilingual, with dispersed residences and a cosmopolitan consciousness. It was the power won from such elites in transformations like the French Revolution that concentrated power in the hands of national bourgeoisies, who used national state power to consolidate their grip on wealth and social position. Sklair (2001: 2) argues that the role of the state has now diminished and

> transnational forces, processes and institutions, not based on the state, might be taking its place. The prime candidates for this role as we enter the twenty-first century are the transnational corporations … The power and authority of the transnational capitalist class derives from the corporations they own and control.

This position is also held by Robinson and Harris who concur that transnational corporations and financial institutions now drive contemporary capitalism. As they put it: 'Organic class formation is no longer tied to territory and to the political jurisdiction of nation-states' (Robinson and Harris 2000: 12).

In Chapter 7 we address the question of the respective power of TNCs and nation-states in more detail. In the meantime, we can indicate that the idea that a new global ruling class has emerged can be supported by a host of aggregate economic data, especially the increasing relocation of production to multiple sites, the growth and increasing mobility of financial capital, the global marketing of key brands, the globalization of legal, architectural and accounting firms, the enormous rise of cross-border mergers and acquisitions, and the equally spectacular growth of foreign direct investment (FDI) flows. Such data would satisfy some Marxist sociologists who are prone to the argument that economic forces determine social relations. However, Robinson and Harris (2000) are careful to add that members of the transnational capitalist class tend to:

- occupy key positions in government ministries and the central banks
- staff organizations that support globalization like the WTO
- attend certain prestigious universities and business schools
- sit on the boards of key foundations (for example Ford and Carnegie)
- dominate bodies like the World Economic Forum, business round tables and chambers of commerce.

Although this adds something to the debate, the numbers and percentages need further work and the argument is still inferential rather than conclusive. What a sociologist would, ideally, need to establish that a transnational capitalist class exists, both in and for itself, would be much 'thicker' evidence, like the number of marriages across nationalities but within the putative class, the development of friendship networks among their children, the proportion attending international schools, the extent of multilingualism, the spread and sequencing of jobs in different countries and the loss of national identities in favour of cosmopolitan ones. While the emergence of a new transnational capitalist class is a useful hypothesis, we would need to see further evidence that it has the capacity to reproduce itself and advance its class interests.

GENDER/RACE/CLASS INTERACTIONS

We have seen how difficult it is to move to a consensual view of how each axis of social inequality should be analysed. However, it is also apparent that social reality does not allow the complete separation of these axes. In practice, they all work simultaneously and interact with one another. This complexity serves as a useful warning to those who would wish to truncate reality, or order it ideologically. Although we are often enjoined to do this, sociologists cannot decide in advance of their research that the social order is best understood only through one axis – be that gender, race or class.

Many feminists demand that we subordinate class and race categories to the overall determinacy of patriarchy. By contrast, Marxists often dismiss race as an epiphenomenon – a symptom of something else. Sometimes this is presented in a sophisticated way, suggesting that in a complex manner, 'race' becomes the mechanism through which class conflicts are refracted and reflected. Sometimes, the notion is more crudely articulated, for example in the argument that the capitalist class wants to divide worker from worker so they conspire to separate sections of the working class into hostile warring elements. Orthodox Marxists, who think that the key issue about gender equality is to encourage women to join the labour force, also often treat the liberation of women rather narrowly. Just as ideological are those who start from the assumption that everything can be understood through the prism of race. Race is held to be 'primordial', fundamental and logically prior to other forms of inequality.

The attempt to privilege one index of social inequality over another can be considered a kind of ideological overclaiming. Although there is no full agreement on this, many sociologists advocate an interactive and complementary model. While undoubtedly a massive improvement on the monocausal explanations proffered by each camp, we have also to note some problems in the interactionist model:

1. The answer to which axis is predominant may be context-driven (situational). Alternatively or additionally it may vary over time (that is, be historically driven).
2. We cannot assume an equal salience for each axis and may have to weight different forms of social differentiation either through further theoretical argument or through sophisticated statistical analysis. (This is no place to blind you with statistics, but it might be helpful to know that a technique called

'multivariate analysis' allows a researcher to hold one factor constant, while varying the others, thus giving a hierarchy of likely causality.)

3. Two or three of the axes may act together, indeed so closely together that it may be difficult to separate them out. Thus someone who is poor, female and black may experience discrimination on all three grounds and in a composite manner. The effects of this composite mode of discrimination are likely to be cumulative and additive and therefore exceptionally difficult to separate, root out or oppose.

REVIEW

We have taken a little space to show that beside the holy trinity of class, race and gender, other axes of social inequality, like religious affiliation, civic status, restricted mobility and age, can also be extremely important. There are others, like nationality or even lifestyle, too. Different forms of interest and association appear to be upheld simultaneously, successively or separately to the three main axes and with different degrees of force, conviction and enthusiasm. When we considered gender, race/ethnicity and class, we were able to draw on an impressive body of theory and research that has developed along each principle. However, the complexity of social reality demands that we pull all these differentiating principles together, however difficult this is theoretically and analytically.

We can also note two interesting confluences. First, along each line of differentiation, there appears to be a naturalist assumption, followed by a sociological critique. 'Women are the weaker sex', 'whites are a superior race' and 'the poor will always be with us' are three typical, popular (however wrongheaded) beliefs; notions moreover that are often supported by pseudo-scientists. Sociologists have been adept at exposing the weak foundations of these naturalist beliefs and have presented coherent social, historical and cultural explanations for the continuation of inequalities.

Second, within each axis, bipolar models of reality are being discarded in favour of multiply located and expressed forms of identity and organization. Even in the case of the 'opposites' of male and female, the distinction between sex (as biologically defined) and gender (as socially constructed) has become blurred. This is much reinforced by discussion of gay, lesbian, bisexual and transsexual identities and the development of androgynous musical and dress styles. Ethnicity, particularly the 'new ethnicity', is also about expressing both imagined and self-constructed kinds of identity. Hybridity, cosmopolitanism and transnationalism are now important concepts in debates about race and ethnicity, though of course this does not mean that in many places crude racism and nationalism are not present (see Chapter 21 for more). Finally, contemporary models of the class structure have to consider the extent to which a transnational capitalist class (and perhaps other transnational classes) have emerged. Such models will also have to embrace fluidity, multi-positioning and contradictory class locations.

FURTHER READING

■ Sylvia Walby's book *Theorizing Patriarchy* (1990) summarizes the complex debates and evidence on this key aspect of feminist thought in a very readable and lively way.

■ Kenan Malik's *The Meaning of Race* (1996) is a lively and interesting account, while Ellis Cashmore's *Dictionary of Race and Ethnic Relations* (1994) should be available in most university libraries and contains excellent short entries by the world's leading scholars.

■ Class analysis is a little out of favour compared with the 1960s and 70s when Marxism was an influential political current that sociologists had to consider. A neo-Marxist account of class can be found in E. O. Wright's (1985) book, simply titled *Classes*. An influential non-Marxist account of Britain's class structure is Goldthorpe et al. (1980).

GROUP WORK

■ Assigning the work in advance, students will work in small groups to collect material on how women are represented in the various media. Different newspapers and magazines could be compared along with an agreed selection of TV programmes and films. How different are these representations and to what extent do they reflect or challenge the main body of feminist theory?

■ Undertake some historical and biographical research on the following figures, all of whom insisted on the importance of 'race': (a) Marcus Garvey, (b) Hendrik F. Verwoerd and (c) Adolf Hitler. An encyclopedia will give you a good start on all three, while E. Cashmore's *Dictionary of Race and Ethnic Relations* (1994) has useful entries on the first two. Present the outline of their ideas to the group and suggest a critique.

■ Examine the class schema listed in this chapter. Group A will put into the rows in any of the three columns the following occupations: computer operator, university professor, nursery schoolteacher, homeworker sewing garments, an operator in a call centre, a travel agent, an actor and a self-employed plumber. Provide reasons for your choice and let group B comment.

QUESTIONS TO THINK ABOUT

?

1. How important are forms of exclusion and inequality that are not specific to ethnicity/race, class or gender?

2. How useful are theories of patriarchy in depicting the position of women in different societies and eras?

3. What is the difference between ethnicity and race?

4. Is class analysis still important to understanding social inequality?

5. Provide examples about how gender, class and race inequalities (a) reinforce each other and (b) contradict each other.

WHAT'S ON THE WEB

■ http://www.irr.org.uk/ An online service provided by the Institute of Race Relations (IRR) in London, a left-of-centre independent research institute. It hosts a race and refugee news network containing accessible news items dating back to 1992. Although much of the material is UK-based, the IRR has a strong interest in race issues in a number of other countries.

- http://vos.ucsb.edu/browse.asp?id=2721#id154 This is a portal to 'minority studies' (a rather too US expression, for many minorities in the USA would be majorities elsewhere). The links cover Africa and African-American studies, and Asian American studies especially well. As it is a portal, not a site, the quality of the information depends on the quality of the material in the linked sites. But of the score or so we have opened, they were of good to very good quality.

- http://www.intute.ac.uk/socialsciences/cgi-bin/search.pl?term1=race+and+ethnicity &gateway=Sociology&limit=0 is the Intute gateway to sites on the sociology of race and ethnicity.

- http://www.intute.ac.uk/socialsciences/womensstudies/ This Intute gateway opens this portal to a set of links on the subject of feminism and gender.

- http://www.number10.gov.uk/files/pdf/lifechances_socialmobility.pdf Stephen Aldridge produced a briefing for the Prime Minister's Strategy Unit in the UK Cabinet Office on Life Chances and Social Mobility in 2004. The charts and statistical material are very clear, though the theory is very sparsely articulated.

- http://www.trinity.edu/~mkearl/strat.html The site for a passionate US sociologist's take on social inequality, which he does not like one bit. Full of pithy facts, like when the *Titanic* sank in 1912, 60 per cent of the first-class passengers survived, 40 per cent of the second-class made it, but only 25 per cent of the third-class passengers remained to tell their stories. We did not see that in the movie!

- http://www.as.ysu.edu/~cwcs/wclinks.html#Ideas%20about This provides a set of links from a research centre dedicated to examining working-class cultures. Although based in the USA, it has good international links.

CHAPTER 7

Corporate Power and Social Responsibility

CONTENTS

Some writers argue that the globalization of economic life has already proceeded to unprecedented levels and is set to intensify. At the heart of these claims is an assessment of the activities of the transnational corporations (TNCs). These ubiquitous entities can be seen as the Trojan horses, or perhaps the battering rams, of global capital. Such is their power and influence that they are often accused of dictating to rich and powerful states, while completely overwhelming poor states. Is this kind of characterization demonology rather than social science? What are the origins of these organizations? Have they, in fact, escaped their national origins? What is their economic role in integrating the global economy? What are the social consequences, positive and negative, of the TNCs' activities?

It is often assumed that TNCs have a wide sphere of autonomy. This is partly true and this tendency will probably grow. However, to assess their effects, we need to see their activities in the round. The advocates and detractors of TNCs can each mount good cases for suggesting that their influence is benign or malign (Table 7.1). While much of the academic literature in the past concentrated on TNCs in the manufacturing, extractive and financial sectors, we include a discussion on supermarkets and how their immense buying power affects farmers and others in the **GLOBAL SUPPLY CHAIN**.

---

key concept

GLOBAL SUPPLY CHAINS are networks of businesses linking consumers to the smallest producers at the bottom of the chain. The latter include homeworkers or employees in tiny firms to which larger companies have subcontracted some of their operations. Between these two extremes are large factories, warehouses, freight companies, wholesalers and retailers, who now mostly outsource their production to countless manufacturers. Agricultural goods are also grown, sourced, subcontracted and packaged from suppliers in many countries through distribution centres to meet the demands of customers, often in large supermarkets in far-off countries.

We will also consider the issue of corporate social responsibility (CSR). Is this a positive sign of the TNCs' commitment to think of people as well as profit, or a fig leaf designed more for PR purposes?

TABLE 7.1   TNCs and their social consequences: contested views

Process	Positive social consequences	Negative social consequences
The expansion of TNCs	Provides consumer goods, skills and new technology	Allows power to be exercised anonymously and without social responsibility
The forging of alliances between powerful nation-states and TNCs	Allows states and TNCs jointly to develop research and technology at little cost to taxpayers	Diminishes the state's sovereignty and responsibility to its citizenry
The spread of TNCs to the NICs, especially to the export processing zones	Provides jobs, raises standards of health and safety, and pays taxes	Exploits workers and places too much power in the hands of local elites

ORIGINS AND CHARACTERISTICS OF THE TNCs

Conquest and trade were at the heart of the expansion by the European powers and were often the catalyst for the formation of the TNCs. 'Trade follows the flag' was the slogan adopted by British imperialists. Often the scale of the operation was, at first, modest. Take the case of the British traders who penetrated the mouth of the Niger River in west Africa. They immediately starting trading with the local chiefs and eventually were successful in persuading the British Crown to grant them a charter legitimating their activities. Thus, the Royal Niger Company was founded. W. H. Lever, a soap manufacturer in Britain, bought the company and then amalgamated it with another trading company, the United Africa Company, and so the giant Unilever, one of the biggest UK-based TNCs, was born.

Despite what history books in European schools maintain, overseas expansion was not only a European phenomenon. Less visible, but of profound importance, were the trading networks of Chinese, Japanese and Indian merchants all over South and East Asia – networks that started on a small scale but often ultimately resulted in very large international enterprises. We can mention as an illustration one of the big international Chinese trading clans – the long-established Teochiu. In 1939, the clan decided to advance a loan to one of its penniless but ambitious kinsmen arriving in Hong Kong as a refugee. This refugee, Li Ka-shing, eventually bought the sprawling 1986 Expo site in Vancouver for a massive expansion of his international property empire. He amassed his fortune from a transnational chain of factories making plastic flowers, buckets, toys and other household items. His economic philosophy was disarmingly simple: 'Plastic flowers are better: you can wash them and they last forever', he said (Seagrave 1995).

Like many of their Chinese and British counterparts, Japanese TNCs had their origins in giant trading companies (*sogo shosha*). National orientations are perhaps more decisive for these TNCs than in the European or American cases. Although now enormous, integrated commercial, financial and industrial conglomerates, the Japanese corporations' initial and fundamental purpose was trade and the organization of trade. There are six big *sogo shosha* in Japan, all of which are household names in the West such as Hitachi, Matsushita, Honda, Nissan, Samsung and Sony. They have massive bargaining power. The six top Japanese TNCs account for 8 per cent of world trade. The *sogo shosa* provide:

- financial services (credits, loans, guarantees, venture capital)
- information services (up-to-date market profiles, national regulations, technological developments)
- risk-reduction services (insurance, buffers for exchange control regulations)
- organizational and auxiliary services (translations, legal contracts, transport, paperwork and wholesaling).

These services are for their own manufacturing plants as well as for other small companies that otherwise would not be in a position to compete effectively internationally. Although many people are aware of the great strengths of Japan as a manufacturing economy, Japanese TNCs remain prominent in trade and have extensive interests in the services sector (finance, commerce, banking and insurance).

CHARACTERISTICS

Many of the world's leading TNCs are engaged in the exploitation of petroleum – Shell, BP, Total and Chevron being the most notable and conspicuous. Even if you do not see these brand names on the forecourt of a filling station, one of these TNCs may still own the company or supply the petrol from its refineries. These companies are also moving strongly into other energy sectors as the volume of easily exploitable oil diminishes. TNCs in manufacturing are often involved in producing the ubiquitous motorcar, which despite green protests is still a healthy money-spinner. Coming up on the rails are banks, insurance companies and a number of information technology companies (see Table 7.2 below).

It is perhaps self-evident that a crucial characteristic of a TNC is that it operates in more than one, and sometimes many, countries. Branch plants and subsidiaries, sales, R&D take place on a number of sites. Why do TNCs wish to locate abroad? Where they are involved in extractive industries or agriculture, the answer is obvious. They have to be where the oil is extracted, the timber stripped, the gold mined or the pineapples grown. However, other reasons for decentralization are to secure new markets or stop their rivals getting there first. The movement of capital away from the USA and Western Europe after the 1970s was also partly to do with the difficulties of securing high profits and subordinating the better organized labour force in the industrialized countries.

By contrast, many developing countries had abundant supplies of cheap, unorganized labour. The division of labour into more minute tasks, which was discussed in Chapter 4, allowed untrained or newly trained workers to attain rapidly the levels of productivity in the countries where industry was long established. The NICs provided freedom from planning and environmental controls, cheap health and safety standards, tax holidays and other incentives. International transport and communications facilities in the form of containerized shipping, cheap air cargo, computer, telex and fax links had improved dramatically. Especially for low-bulk, high-value goods, it was no longer necessary for the site of production to be near the end market. Moreover, world market factories could be staffed by young women who were likely to remain unorganized (Fröbel et al. 1980; Cohen 1987: 220–53).

As each new market is opened up by TNCs, the stimulation of demand can massively fuel their profits. The great new frontier is China, where by the 1990s the biggest consumer and manufacturing boom in world history had begun. By 2004, China was already the seventh largest economy in the world (see Table 7.2 below). It is projected to be 'number one' by the year 2025, perhaps sooner (Shenkar 2004). One seasoned observer of the Chinese scene (Seagrave 1995: 279) described how in the 1990s residents in Beijing helped to throw off its image as the drab capital of a drab communist country:

Chinese yuppies were washing their hair in Procter & Gamble shampoo, starting their day with Nescafé instant coffee, driving to work in new Toyotas with electronic pagers clipped to their shirt pockets, then heading for the karaoke bars where they can sing along with music videos and mix Hennessey brandy in Coca-Cola. They bought new jeans and pullovers by mail from Land's End catalogues and ordered Tanga panties from Victoria's Secret ... As average earnings passed the US$1400 a year mark, the majority of people in China for the first time were able to buy such basic consumer items as refrigerators ... Given a population of over 1.2 billion, this meant that more human beings were escaping from poverty in one brief period than at any other previous time in history.

As can be inferred from the evocation of famous brands mentioned, the TNCs act as a symbolic and practical demonstration of Western affluence and 'freedom', even if that freedom is sometimes individualistic, consumer-led and often destructive of other people's opportunities (as we shall see in Chapter 13). The former communist regimes found themselves particularly vulnerable to the naive notion that political freedom equated to consumer choice. On the day after the Berlin Wall came down, East Berlin youth celebrated their release from communist tyranny by swaggering down the main streets, tins of Coca-Cola in hand.

DEFINITION

Having described the origins and some of the characteristics of TNCs, we are now in a position to give a more formal definition. In extending Dicken's argument (1992: 47), we arrive at a sixfold definition of TNCs. They

- control economic activities in two or more countries
- maximize the comparative advantage between countries, profiting from the differences in factor endowments, wage rates, market conditions and the political and fiscal regimes
- have geographical flexibility, namely an ability to shift resources and operations between different locations on a global scale
- operate with a level of financial, component and operational flows between different segments of the TNC greater than the flows within a particular country
- spread individualism and consumerism to the far corners of the world
- enjoy significant economic and social power, which can be exercised to 'good' or 'bad' effect.

TNCs AS GLOBALIZING AND INTERNATIONALIZING AGENTS

There are two contrasting views on the economic power of TNCs. The first lays emphasis on their globalizing capacities, a position we associate particularly with the work of Dicken (1992, 2003), and with which we largely concur. The second, more sceptical view developed by Hirst and Thompson (1996) suggests that while TNCs may have flourished and fostered the long-established international economy, they have not established a global economy and have not superseded the nation-state.

TNCs AS GLOBALIZING AGENTS

Dicken (1992, 2003) argues that the TNC is the single most important force in creating global shifts in economic activity. Ever since the 1950s, world trade – the sum of all the imports and exports bought and sold by all the world's countries – has grown significantly faster than world production. Dicken (1992: 16) sees this as 'a clear indicator of the increased internationalization of economic activities and of the greater interconnectedness which have come to characterize the world economy'. This, in turn, points to the role TNCs play in binding together national economies. Foreigners own an increasing share of the value of many countries' 'national' assets in part or in whole. By the same token, a growing portion of each country's productive capacity, technological knowledge and skills is an organized extension of the capacities located in other countries. The era of nationally competing and separable capitalisms has now past. Much of the world's economic system is dominated by TNC decisions about whether or not to invest in particular locations. The resulting flows of raw materials, components and finished products, technological and organizational expertise, as well as skilled personnel constitute the basic building blocks of the global economy.

INTERNATIONAL, BUT NOT GLOBAL AGENTS

Although their work is based on somewhat old data, a cogent argument that TNCs are not major threats to nation-states has been advanced by Hirst and Thompson (1996: Chapter 4). They examined data on more than 500 TNCs from five countries in 1987 and compared these data with similar material on more than 5,000 TNCs from six countries (France, Japan, the UK, the USA, Germany and the Netherlands) for the period 1992/3. The authors wanted to ascertain whether and to what extent the activities of TNCs deepened integration between national economies, while becoming largely independent of both their home and host governments.

Hirst and Thompson concluded that what stood out most clearly from all the dimensions of TNC activity – sales, assets, distribution, profits and number of overseas interests – was the extent to which TNCs 'still rely upon their "home base" as the centre of their economic activities, despite all the speculation about globalization' (Hirst and Thompson 1996: 95). These and other findings led them to argue that the world economy may have become 'international' but it certainly was not yet a 'globalized economy' (Hirst and Thompson 1996: 8–13).

They also suggested that the world's economy may indeed be hardly more 'international' than it was before the First World War.

On the basis of the above and related arguments, Hirst and Thompson (1996) also stressed the political limitations to the mobility of capital. Businesses normally prefer to operate where they feel secure and enjoy a comfortable rapport and familiarity with a supportive local culture and market situation. Similarly, the sphere of the economic often consists in large part of relatively immovable plant, equipment and infrastructure, as well as employees 'trapped' at any given time in particular locations by community and family responsibilities, job availability, skill and language capacities and the legal restrictions of citizenship. All this presumably means that we can hardly be surprised at the continuing propensity of companies, large and small, to retain strong roots in their home economies. Nor, for the same reasons, was it possible for even the largest TNCs to be completely footloose or free from any national control.

ASSESSMENT

Despite its obvious relevance and significance, there are two problems with Hirst and Thompson's analysis; one concerns the nature of the empirical evidence and the other is a theoretical issue. At the empirical level, there is room for disagreement over how to interpret the available evidence. For example, using similar data sets, Dunning (1993a: 291) observed that the largest TNCs, namely those contributing four-fifths of all global activity by TNCs and with annual sales exceeding US$1,000 million in 1989, together produced approximately one-third of their total output outside their home countries. This estimate is quite close to that provided by Hirst and Thompson (1996), but whereas they regard it as evidence only for the existence of an international economy, Dunning sees it as an indication of a global economy.

The second difficulty with Hirst and Thompson's (1996) analysis is theoretical. Adapting an insight offered by Lash and Urry (1994: 61–2), we argue that it is necessary to distinguish between two rather different aspects of economic life – the cultural, symbolic and knowledge-based component and the more material or physical one. While the first is indeed inherently mobile and capable of rapid learning and transference across and between places and organizations, the second is necessarily rooted in specific locations at any one moment in time. In short, the first is globalizing, the second is necessarily dependent on existing sociopolitical formations and institutions. It follows that the world economy demonstrates a certain paradoxical and rather skewed character; in some respects it has become highly globalized, while in others there are, and may remain, certain finite limits to this process. Accordingly, in one sense the Hirst and Thompson position is perfectly correct, but perhaps rather misleading in another.

Hirst and Thompson (1996) also mount a political case against the notion that governments have been rendered more or less powerless to act in the face of global economic forces. Such a view, they argue, plays into the hands of national politicians and others who, for ideological reasons, may wish to justify various non-interventionist, neoliberal policies or failures at the level of intergovern-mental action. Even if we doubt their more strident attempts to refute prevailing orthodoxies, their idea that states should still deploy their existing power respon-sibly is both refreshing and welcome.

Figure 7.1 **TNCs spread consumerism to the far corners of the world**
The 'Avon lady' goes up the Amazon with cosmetics

TNCs AND NATION-STATES

As mentioned earlier, TNCs are responsible for an important chunk of world employment, production and trade. This is particularly true of production, where perhaps between one-fifth and one-quarter of all production is in the domain of the TNCs. To measure trade flows is more elusive statistically, but we know that 50 per cent of the total trade of the USA and Japan is conducted within TNCs. The Ford motorcar provides a good example of cross-border, but within-firm, trade. The standard car in its range is appropriately called the 'Mondeo' – or world car. It typically contains parts from 35 countries, most of them produced in the company's own branch plants and subsidiaries. The company skilfully mixes and blends to gain maximum benefit from the costs of labour, technical inventiveness, raw materials and transport. It is therefore able to supply some or all factories with Indonesian-produced brake pads or Spanish-produced transmissions. Dual or multiple sourcing of a similar component produces healthy intra-firm competition and is a safeguard against labour protest. If country A's plant is threatened with strike action, country B's similar product can swiftly be brought on stream.

Another way of understanding the global economic importance of TNCs is to see them as equivalent units to countries. Table 7.2 provides some evidence of the relative economic power of corporations and nation-states, treating corporate revenues as equivalents to countries' GNPs. In this measurement, of the 120 most important economic units in the world today, 54 are nation-states and 66 are TNCs, though the TNCs are concentrated in the lower half of the list. As there were 191 states recognized by the UN in 2005, this means that, in that year, 137 of these states had economies smaller than any of the biggest 66 TNCs.

TABLE 7.2 The economic power of countries and corporations, 2004/5

Rank	Country/Corporation	GDP/sales ($mil)	Rank	Country/Corporation	GDP/sales ($mil)
01	United States	11,667,515	31	South Africa	212,777
02	Japan	4,623,398	32	Greece	203,401
03	Germany	2,714,418	33	General Motors	193,517
04	United Kingdom	2,140,898	34	Finland	186,597
05	France	2,002,582	35	Ireland	183,560
06	Italy	1,672,302	36	DaimlerChrysler	176,687
07	China	1,649,329	37	Toyota Motor	172,616
08	Spain	991,442	38	Ford Motor	172,233
09	Canada	979,784	39	Portugal	168,281
10	India	691,876	40	Thailand	163,491
11	Korea, Republic of	679,674	41	Hong Kong, China	163,005
12	Mexico	676,497	42	General Electric	152,866
13	Australia	631,256	43	Iran, Islamic Republic of	152,709
14	Brazil	604,855	44	Total	152,609
15	Russian Federation	582,395	45	Chevron	147,967
16	Netherlands	577,260	46	ConocoPhillips	121,663
17	Switzerland	359,465	47	AXA	121,606
18	Belgium	349,830	48	Allianz	118,937
19	Sweden	346,404	49	Malaysia	117,776
20	Turkey	346,404	50	Israel	117,548
21	Austria	290,109	51	Volkswagen	110,648
22	Wal-Mart Stores	287,989	52	Venezuela	109,322
23	BP	285,059	53	Citigroup	108,276
24	Exxon Mobil	270,772	54	Czech Republic	107,047
25	Royal Dutch/Shell Group	268,690	55	Singapore	106,818
26	Indonesia	257,641	56	ING Group	105,886
27	Saudi Arabia	250,557	57	Nippon Telegraph and Telephone	100,545
28	Norway	250,168	58	Hungary	99,712
29	Denmark	243,043	59	New Zealand	99,687
30	Poland	241,833	60	American International Group	97,987

Rank	Country/Corporation	GDP/sales ($mil)	Rank	Country/Corporation	GDP/sales ($mil)
61	Colombia	97,384	91	Peugeot	70,641
62	IBM	96,293	92	Metro	70,159
63	Pakistan	96,115	93	Nestlé	69,825
64	Chile	94,105	94	U.S. Postal Service	68,996
65	Siemens	91,493	95	BNP Paribas	68,654
66	Carrefour	90,381	96	Peru	68,395
67	Philippines	88,429	97	China National Petroleum	67,723
68	Algeria	84,649	98	Sony	66,618
69	Hitachi	83,993	99	Ukraine	65,149
70	Assicurazioni Generali	83,267	100	Cardinal Health	65,130
71	Matsushita Electric Industrial	81,077	101	Royal Ahold	64,675
72	McKesson	80,514	102	Altria Group	64,440
73	Honda Motor	80,486	103	Pemex	63,690
74	Hewlett-Packard	79,905	104	Bank of America Corp.	63,324
75	Nissan Motor	79,799	105	Vodafone	62,971
76	Fortis	75,518	106	Tesco	62,458
77	Egypt, Arab Republic of	75,148	107	Munich Re Group	60,705
78	Sinopec	75,076	108	Nippon Life Insurance	60,520
79	Berkshire Hathaway	74,382	109	Fiat	59,972
80	ENI	74,227	110	Royal Bank of Scotland	59,750
81	Romania	73,167	112	Zurich Financial Services	59,678
82	Home Depot	73,094	113	Crédit Agricole	59,053
83	Aviva	73,025	114	Credit Suisse	58,825
84	HSBC Holdings	72,550	115	State Farm Insurance Cos	58,818
85	Nigeria	72,106	116	France Télécom	58,652
86	Deutsche Telekom	71,988	117	Électricité de France	58,367
87	Verizon Communications	71,563	118	JPMorgan Chase	56,931
88	Samsung Electronics	71,555	119	UBS	56,917
89	State Grid	71,290	120	Bangladesh	54,884
90	United Arab Emirates	70,960			

SOURCES: *Fortune* (25 July 2005); World Bank (2005a), using 2004 data

The economic power of TNCs made evident in Table 7.2 may not, of course, be exercised in a negative way, but experience has suggested that, in certain circumstances, TNCs can cause serious disruption to national economic and social plans. Here are some of the ways in which this might happen:

- Local capital has difficulty competing. TNCs will usually pay more and, in order to compete, local employers have to lower wage costs, worsen employment conditions and sacrifice quality.

- TNCs have disproportional marketing power, even for an inferior product. When one of the present authors lived in the Caribbean, locally owned shacks served wonderfully succulent, spicy portions of chicken. They were then undercut by a certain US 'brand leader', which subsidized imported chickens and took losses over a two-year period until it could drive the local firms out of business. Needless to say, the prices for its inferior, unhealthy product soon went up.

- Local politicians are anxious to encourage inward investment and are often willing to accept corrupt payments in exchange for accepting the company's plans, facilitating its operations and allowing the sending of its profits out of the country with minimal tax. Often these plans conflict with national plans. The poor countries are then often sucked into a cycle of further dependence.

- TNCs are often in a position to influence tastes and consumption patterns in a negative way. We have already alluded to a fast-food outlet, but in the next section provide a case study of tobacco in which we show that some corporations use glamorous adverts to promote cigarettes in developing countries to offset their reducing profits elsewhere. In this and other cases, TNCs have the capacity to subvert and undermine the power of even quite large nation-states.

■■■

Global Thinkers 7   DAVID HARVEY (1935–)

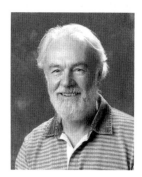

David Harvey is a social geographer, so it is not surprising that he is interested in spatial analysis. He reminds us that sociologists should be more cognizant that social relationships and human behaviour take place in particular spaces and in particular time frames. Harvey applied this perspective first to a major reinterpretation of Marxism, The Limits of Capital *(Harvey 1982). There he warned equally against the dangers of 'spatial fetishism', where the properties of space became fundamental, and against the opposite error – to see spatial patterns as an outcome of 'the processes of accumulation and class reproduction' (Harvey 1982: 374).*

While time and space provide the enabling and constraining conditions of social conduct, Harvey allows that space can, to a degree, be 'socially constructed' (Harvey 1985). In long-established societies, the impress of space and time was slowly naturalized, but the rise of industrial capitalism changed that fundamentally. The proletariat needed to be concentrated in urban centres together with 'the reserve army' (unemployed people), who were 'a necessary condition to sustained accumulation'. The crowding together of people, along with secondary forms of exploitation like rent, showed that 'the accumulation of capital and misery go hand in hand, concentrated in space' (Harvey 1982: 418).

In a condition of postmodernity, space and time were both 'compressed' and speeded up (Harvey 1989). There are a number of ways in which time–space becomes compressed: better communications, virtual contact, cheaper travel and digitalization are perhaps the most obvious factors. Harvey, however, focuses primarily on work experience and on what happens to capital. As we have explained in Chapter 4, Fordism relied on standardization, mass production and predictable supply and demand chains. The age of flexible accumulation, by contrast, induces a radical shift. At the human level, the insecurity, unpredictable quality and increased pace of life lead to changes in sensibility, even to the understanding of reality itself. He argues that 'the more flexible motion of capital emphasizes the new, the fleeting, the ephemeral, the fugitive, and the contingent' (Harvey 1989: 171). Simulacra (images or representations of reality) become reality as they are turned into commodities and increasingly occupy more and more of a person's effort and leisure. So arises one of the effects of postmodernism – life becomes mimicry or, even worse, artifice. A second effect is to drive some people into a reaffirmation of their ascribed identity (Muslim, Croatian, American or whatever) as they rush for meaning in what they experience as a meaningless world. Again, the geographical insight – they are looking for a 'place'.

A similar process occurs at the level of capital, as corporate power and the financial system, when speculation, herd behaviour, 'futures' and trading in currencies become detached from actual production. Value, money and use become disassociated and dispersed – away from the labour that has produced them. In a sense this is a consequence of the success of contemporary capitalism. As Harvey (1989: 307) argues, by putting the postmodern condition 'into its historical context, as part of a history of successive waves of time–space compression generated out of the pressures of capital accumulation with its perpetual search to annihilate space through time and reduce turnover time, we can at least pull the condition of postmodernity into the range of a condition accessible to historical materialist analysis and interpretation'.

SOURCE: Harvey (1982, 1985, 1989)

EXPORTING LIFESTYLES: THE CASE OF TOBACCO

The diffusion of Western lifestyles by certain TNCs has caused particular anxieties with respect to health problems (see also Chapter 11). We explore this by focusing on the case of the tobacco industry, but similar processes can be demonstrated for the sugar, fast-food, pharmaceutical and several other industries. Between 1900 and 1975, tobacco consumption grew in Western countries, a trend that was closely related to urbanism, modernity and the increase in leisure and consumption. Smoking among friends at work as well as at play was a way of expressing group affiliation. By the 1970s, however, there was abundant evidence that smoking hugely increases the likelihood of contracting or enhancing diseases such as lung cancer, high blood pressure and hardening of the arteries. Gradually, Western governments introduced restrictions on consumption in public places and on advertising, though companies continue to be permitted to sponsor some sport activities, pop concerts and other major events. Meanwhile, the climate of opinion hardened against smoking.

Faced with falling sales, the large cigarette TNCs turned increasingly to the consumers and workers of the South and especially to the huge Asian market. This shift in consumption meant that, by 1997, only 14 per cent of smokers were living in North America or Western Europe, while 55 per cent, 12 per cent and 9 per cent were resident in Asia, Africa/Middle East and South America respectively. By 2030, 70 per cent of deaths related to tobacco are expected to occur in the developing countries compared with 50 per cent today (www.tobaccofreekids.org/ campaign). In China, the world's most populous country, around 70 per cent of men currently smoke, compared with 35 per cent of men in the West.

Many countries manufacture their own tobacco products. Today, China's state tobacco company is the largest producer in the world. Moreover, the Chinese government raises 10 per cent of its tax from cigarette sales, though half is then spent on the health costs this incurs plus lost work time (Godrej 2004: 12). From the mid-1980s, first US manufacturers, led by market-leader Philip Morris and its famous Marlborough brand, and then the other big world companies placed pressure on China and other Asian governments to remove trade restrictions on Western tobacco products or risk incurring Western import sanctions (Godrej 2004). British American Tobacco, the second biggest tobacco TNC, evaded this blockade by establishing a secret factory in a joint partnership with the government of North Korea, one of the last remaining nominally communist countries.

Another pathway to reach smokers in all markets has been through smuggling. Smuggled products are much cheaper because they escape the duties imposed by governments for tax-raising purposes. It also allows producers to get around quota restrictions placed on imported products (Campbell 2004: 21). Whether carried out by individuals on a micro-basis or by criminal gangs on a huge scale, smuggling tobacco is illegal and is probably associated with other kinds of illegal activities such as the cocaine and heroine trade. Cigarette smuggling also offers gangs a way of laundering their earnings by buying cigarettes from the wholesalers and distributors to which tobacco TNCs sell their products (www. tobaccofreekids.org/campaign).

The entry of Western tobacco products into Asian and other markets was followed by extensive advertising offering access to an American/Western lifestyle. Adults of all income groups in the poorer countries engage in smoking, especially in urban areas. Among the poor, tobacco consumption is not just a perceived passport to a more exciting lifestyle but it also provides relief from the stresses caused by a life of relative poverty and crowded, dangerous cities (McMurray and Smith 2001). However, according to Klein (2001), since the early 1990s, this appeal – not just with cigarettes but with a whole range of products – has been especially aimed at young middle-class people.

■ ■ ■ ■ ■ ■ ■ ■ ■ WORKING FOR THE TNCs

By definition, TNCs are spatially dispersed and therefore have employees in many countries. The number of employees outside the country in which a TNC's headquarters are located can be used as a first gauge of the degree to which it has decentralized its operations. In the case of Nestlé, a spectacular 96 per cent of its 253,000 employees are employed outside its Swiss headquarters. By contrast, General Motors 'continues to employ far more people in the US than in any other single country' (Kiely 2005a: 109). The continued concentration of employment and assets in the country in which the TNC originated has been used to argue that 'the image of footloose capital dispersing investment throughout the globe is a fallacy' (Kiely 2005a: 109). This view fails, however, to recognize that *direct* employment by TNCs is only part of the story; the more common contemporary model is the use of subcontracting, both in manufacturing and agriculture, to deliver the products that TNCs wish to market and sell. Because subcontractors and farmers are often almost entirely dependent on the goodwill of a small number of TNCs – or even just one – in effect they become *indirect* employees. A mix of indirect and direct employment can be observed in two important examples – workers in the export-processing zones (EPZs), and growers and farmers supplying supermarkets.

WORKING IN THE EXPORT-PROCESSING ZONES

An **export-processing zone** is a free trade enclave in which foreign firms, or subcontracted local firms that produce goods for export, are encouraged to locate.

Since the 1960s, TNCs have been engaging in 'offshore' production through both direct employment and using subcontracting in **export-processing zones** (EPZs), mostly in developing countries. Governments offer special inducements – tax privileges, duty-free imports, the promise of cheap labour, limited or non-existent health, safety and environmental regulations and perhaps free or subsidized plant and infrastructure – to encourage foreign firms to establish their labour-intensive assembly operations in a given country. In the 1970s and 80s, most of the labourers – over 90 per cent in some EPZs – were young women, though the gender balance has been less skewed more recently. Women were said by some employers to have 'nimble fingers', making them suitable for work on electronic circuit boards. Others pointed to their industrial discipline. In these characterizations, one has to distinguish between convenient stereotypes and the reality facing many female workers in poor countries – namely, an adverse labour market and a desperate desire to escape from the powerful forms of patriarchy characteristic of many rural societies.

Locally, internationally or jointly owned industries engaged in making garments, shoes, soft furnishings, toys and other low-value consumer products are the most likely to locate in low-wage regions, including EPZs. So too are those engaged in manufacturing domestic electrical goods and in the assembly stage of the production of semiconductors. The common factor is that the goods produced are destined for export. Industrial production in such sites grew rapidly, as did its export potential. For example, between 1966 and 1972, US imports of manufactured goods from EPZs located in developing countries increased by an annual average of 60 per cent (Harris 1983: 147). EPZs now flourish widely across the developing world. They have long been prominent in Asia, including China, which established four 'special economic zones', similar to EPZs, as part of its economic reforms in the late 1970s, with Shenzhen, adjacent to Hong Kong, being the largest. Caribbean and African countries have also encouraged offshore development.

One gigantic EPZ was created by the Border Industrialization Program (BIP) in Mexico, where thousands of *maquiladoras* (labour-intensive assembly plants) have been built near the US border. This started in 1965 as the result of a deliberate government policy to create local employment in the depressed regions of northern Mexico by exporting low-value manufactured goods to the US market. The US government was also keen to mop up unemployment in the area in the wake of the collapse of an official labour migration scheme to the USA, the Bracero Program. The US authorities were hopeful that employment in Mexico would reduce the flow of undocumented migrants north of the border. However, this part of the scheme failed because the jobs mainly went to young women (not to males, who were the most numerous migrants), while unemployed people from other depressed regions of Mexico flooded into the area in a desperate attempt to find work. The attempt to create a dam to stop the migrants effectively created a 'honey pot' that attracted them (Cohen 1987). Current reports by trade union representatives continue to talk of low wages, long hours and unorganized workers in the *maquiladoras*. Despite these negative features, the BIP has officially been regarded as a success. By 1994/5, the numbers employed grew to 743,000, while the value of exports rose to US$33,000 million. By August 2005, 45 per cent of all Mexico's export earnings came from the *maquiladoras* (http://www.dallasfed.org/data/data/maq-charts.pdf).

Another EPZ on the island of Mauritius in the Indian Ocean has also been a largely unambiguous success. At its inception in 1971, 20 per cent of the population was unemployed. By 1994, unemployment was under 2 per cent and falling. The next year, the government informed the International Labour Office that the island hosted 6,205 migrant workers, brought in to offset labour shortages. Although the economic benefits of the EPZ in Mauritius are evident, the provision of employment, again mainly to women in the 16–22 age group, had another benign social consequence. In the 1950s, the period leading up to independence, British demographers were so alarmed at the rising birth rate in the country that they conjured up images of Mauritians falling off the edge of the island. As we will establish in Chapter 10, increased affluence and more reliable healthcare generally reduce the need for large families, which has indeed happened in Mauritius. The young women who worked in the EPZ were often grateful for the employment offered and extended their periods of employment, thus reducing the number of years in which they could safely bear children. The result was a massive reduction in the real and projected rise in population.

GLOBAL SUPPLY CHAINS: THE ROLE OF THE SUPERMARKETS

Four of the TNCs that make it into the top 120 are supermarkets (Table 7.2). Home Depot is mainly involved in the North American home furnishings market, while the remaining three, Wal-Mart, Tesco and Carrefour, are primarily food outlets. When you fill your shopping trolley with groceries, it is impossible not to notice the amazing variety of countries from which fresh, frozen, processed, canned and bottled food and drink arrives. The retailers are clearly responding to consumer demands for fresh, exotic, high-quality, cheap and out of season produce. Are strawberries on your Xmas menu in Northern Europe? No problem – growers in the southern hemisphere will oblige. Are you bored with beef or lamb? No problem – farmers in Australia and South Africa can place kangaroo or ostrich steaks on your dining room table.

Social scientists have undertaken some revealing research on global supply chains by carefully examining the 'trail' of particular products. Freidberg (2001), for example, followed 'the trail of the global green bean' from French and British outlets to their suppliers in Burkina Faso and Zambia. The two supplying countries had similar populations and per capita incomes (ten million and US$320 each), and continued to have close relationships with their former colonial powers, the UK and France. Thereafter, the stories diverged. The French wholesalers imported most of the African green beans to the Marché Internationale, a sprawling set of packing sheds, warehouses and loading bays near Orly airport on the outskirts of Paris. The French green bean was drawn from the country's former colony, Burkina Faso. The supply chain telescoped down to many small producers and it was in the packing shed in Ouagadougou (the capital city) where hundreds of women separated good beans from the rejects. The British also used their former colony Zambia as a source, but the suppliers were two giant farms, financed by foreign capital with expatriate managers in charge and agricultural workers paid on a piecework basis. By following the trail of the green bean, this study has revealed a significant contrast – in the first case peasant agriculture has been sustained by the global supply chain, in the second it has been undermined, perhaps destroyed, by it.

The demands of consumers, the supermarkets tell us, are for year-round produce and a wide variety of choice and price. Although irrigation and plastic sheeting can sometimes outwit nature, climate, rainfall and season still govern the supply side opportunities. For many workers in the fields, therefore, work is seasonal. As Raworth (2005: 19) maintains, this has particular effects on women, who 'are more likely than men to be hired on short-term, seasonal, casual, or homework contracts, renewed every year, every three months, or even every day. They end up working long-term but without the protection and support that comes with long-term jobs'. In South Africa, for example, 69 per cent of the temporary workers on deciduous fruit farms and vineyards are women.

TNCs: POWER WITHOUT RESPONSIBILITY

The primary social criticism of TNCs is that they exercise power without responsibility. In theory, and sometimes in practice, the power of the state is restrained by the due processes of law, regular elections and the capacity of people to organize, demonstrate, advance their views and defend their interests. Not all states have this degree of democracy. (In 2005, for example, only 19 of Africa's 53 states were commonly regarded as democracies.) However, even in the most extreme dictatorships, people have managed to bring their rulers to book through strikes, demonstrations and other forms of political mobilization. Equivalent forms of corporate power rarely have any such constraints on them. The *soga shosha* and other trading companies are often dominated by private, indeed secretive, dynastic families. Other TNCs are supposedly constrained by shareholders, but these are usually large anonymous blocks of shares bought by pension funds, insurance companies and banks, all with little interest in the company's affairs beyond the central performance indicator – profit.

The international agency UN Research Institute for Social Development (UNRISD 1995) argued that the freedoms of TNCs were significantly enhanced in the early 1990s, especially by generous GATT regimes. For example, they enjoyed new rights in international law to enforce patents, trademarks and copyrights, whereas national governments were unable to enforce demands that local labour be trained or put other strong conditions on inward investment. UNRISD argued that this corporate power should be accompanied by some social responsibility – to the environment, which is often damaged, to the local community and the workforce. There are many examples of even respectable, well-known TNCs being blind to their responsibilities in these respects. Let us cite three:

- In 1989, the oil tanker *Exxon Valdez*, owned by the then largest petroleum company in the world, struck a reef in Prince William Sound off the Alaskan coast, causing the largest oil spill in history. Nearly 42 million litres of crude oil polluted the beaches, contaminated fishing and destroyed wildlife.
- Shell in Nigeria has continued to exploit oil with a marked indifference to the local communities near which it works and whose land it has appropriated or bought for a song. Under the leadership of Ken Saro-Wiwa, an organized opposition group in the Ogoni area sought to get Shell to recognize its social responsibilities. The oil and waste from the plants had been polluting both the fishing grounds and the villages. Although a few local community projects were supported, the company's principal defence was that it paid its taxes to the federal authorities in Lagos and it was up to them to organize social programmes. Saro-Wiwa was, according to the federal authorities, implicated in the deaths of four Ogoni chiefs who were seen as pro-Shell advocates. Although it was accepted he was not there, he was convicted of conspiracy and executed, despite many calls for clemency from all over the world. On 14 December 1995, against the background of much opposition, Shell announced the continuation of a £2.5 million plant in Nigeria.
- In December 1984, a major industrial disaster took place at Bhopal in central India when the poisonous gas methyl isocyanate (MIC) leaked from a US plant owned by the Union Carbide Corporation. More than 2,800 workers, their families and others in the surrounding community died as a result of the leak. At least 20,000 were injured. Union Carbide has consistently stalled the legal proceedings instituted to gain compensation and claimed that it was not responsible for the wrongdoings of its subsidiary. (Figure 7.2 shows a graphic photograph about this event.)

Figure 7.2 **Bhopal, India, December 1984**
Following a leak in a reservoir at the Union Carbide factory producing insecticides, a cloud of poisonous gas spread over Bhopal, the capital of Madya Pradesh. The escape resulted in many deaths, injuries and genetic mutations. While the Indian directors of the local company were arrested, the US parent company largely avoided legal sanction.

TNCs: PEOPLE BITE BACK

Despite the relative quiescence of many governments and shareholders, people of many backgrounds have demonstrated that they are capable of opposing corporate social irresponsibility. When, for example, Shell proposed dismantling an oil rig at sea, which opponents claimed would result in widespread pollution, a European-wide protest began. The company backed down after continuing pressure from consumer and environmental movements in the UK, the Netherlands and Germany – including the instigation of a consumer boycott of Shell petrol, which was remarkably widely supported.

It is worth noticing that Shell was not opposed by the British or any other government. In the case of the oil rig, it was Greenpeace and other INGOs that organized transnationally to stop that particular display of corporate power. Equally, in its operations in Ogoniland, Shell was not opposed by the Nigerian government, which was deeply complicit in the company's operations. Instead, a small local protest group was supported by Amnesty International, Greenpeace, PEN (the international writers' lobby) and various other human rights groups. In later chapters, we explicitly deal with the issue of whether global social movements are now counterpoised to global corporations, making the locus of political debate and social contestation a global rather than national matter.

At one level, such protests were predictable. Led by politically active, educated students and intellectuals ('the usual suspects'), they could perhaps have been dismissed as unrepresentative of the population at large. However, Coca-Cola, one of the anti-corporate protesters' pet hates, has attracted opponents of a quite different sort. In a little village called Plachimada, in Kerala, India, local people complained that a new bottling plant established by Coca-Cola in 2001 – one of 27 in the country – was drying up its wells. The company sought to disarm its critics by distributing waste sludge, discarded after water treatment, as 'free fertilizer' to the villagers. As Rajeev (2005) remarks, this act of 'generosity' turned out to be the undoing of the company. The sludge had no value as a fertilizer and, as an independent scientific report confirmed, it was polluted with cadmium, a known carcinogen that could cause mental retardation. 'One way or another, this plant should be shut down and the management made to pay compensation for destroying our paddy fields, fooling us with fake fertilizer and drying out our wells', said Paru Amma, a village woman who lives in this once verdant area (quoted in Rajeev 2005). Finally, in August 2005, the Kerala State Pollution Control Board ordered the plant to be shut down. The company has not given up yet and 'is evaluating future steps, including a judicial review'.

Meanwhile, on the other side of the world, in a shabby part of Mexico City, a 49-year-old owner of a small corner shop took on Coca-Cola in a different way. Raquel Chavez did not like being told that if she stocked Big Cola, a rival Peruvian product, Coca-Cola would take away promotional refrigerators, awnings and free gifts and refuse to supply her. Apparently, the company was not satisfied with already securing 70 per cent of the Mexican soft drinks market. She lodged a complaint at the competition commission and meanwhile was forced to get her Coca-Cola from a more expensive wholesaler, hauling it up a hill while her husband, furious at her stance, refused to help. 'Everybody got scared and told me I was crazy and I'd be ruined. I said I'd rather die with my dignity intact than be trampled on' (quoted in Tuckman 2005). Her complaint was finally upheld and resulted in a US$13 million fine (157 million pesos) directed to the company and its distributors. Although the sum will hardly be noticed in Coca-Cola's accounts, the attendant negative publicity has been damaging to the company. In Kerala and Mexico City, things, it seems, do not always go better with Coke.

Box 7.1

Breaking the stranglehold of the big pharmaceutical companies

Under the rules governing TRIPS (Agreement on Trade-Related Aspects of Intellectual Property Rights) adopted by the WTO in 1995, countries are permitted to take action – issuing a 'compulsory licence' – in order to limit the international restrictions on patent protection in situations of a national health emergency or if they face monopoly practices by companies that push up prices abnormally. Evoking this rule has proved extremely difficult in practice.

The case of HIV/AIDs

South Africa has the highest number of HIV/AIDS victims in Africa. In 1997, it amended its legislation and ordered the issue of a fast-track compulsory licence permitting the Ministry of Health to import cheaper medicines including antiretroviral drugs.

In 1998, some 42 pharmaceutical companies instigated a law suit against South Africa's government because of the action it had taken. American companies lobbied the US government to take action against countries they saw as challenging TRIPS rules on drug products while Swiss and German companies also weighed in. (See Chapter 11 for further information on pharmaceutical companies.)

The global campaign

These moves were followed by a vigorous global campaign on behalf of South Africa's actions and against the restrictions on the export and import of cheap generic drugs and the threat of trade and other penalties against such countries. A kind of global civil society formed and mobilized around the issue of generic drugs, especially antiretroviral medicines, and was focused on the South African case. It brought together groups in South Africa, scientists in the USA and other countries, INGOs such as Médecins Sans Frontières and Oxfam and a host of activists in many countries.

The result

The campaign lobbied governments, the WTO, the UN and companies. In March 2001 demonstrations took place in 30 cities around the world. In November 2001, at the WTO conference in Doha, the system allowing countries to relax drug patenting laws in cases of extreme public health threats was simplified and extended, so making it easier to import generic drugs. By 2003, the WTO had consolidated this agreement. In addition, by 2003, President Bush had also supported moves to ensure that Africa received cheaper drugs without incurring trade penalties.

Yet, the battles may not be over. It is still unclear when the poorest countries are supposed finally to comply with TRIPS rules. Meanwhile, some poor countries have held back from issuing compulsory licences to import generics despite the WTO's concessions because they still fear trade embargoes and other retaliation from the rich countries if they do.

SOURCES: Kumaranayake and Lake (2002); Seckinelgin (2002)

REVIEW

In 1970, there were about 7,000 TNCs and there were 37,000 in 1992 and 65,000 by 2001. In 2001, TNCs had 850,000 foreign subsidiaries. As early as 1992, TNCs accounted for one-third of total global economic output (UNRISD 1995: 53). This share was considerably greater than the total value of all the goods and services entering world trade through exports by national firms selling directly from their country of origin to a market in another country. TNCs also accounted for about three-quarters of world trade (Dunning 1993b: 14). Clearly, economic power of this magnitude will have fundamental effects on the global economy, polity and society. As we have shown, there is a lively debate about whether TNCs have indeed superseded the nation-state system both in their political independence and their global economic reach. In their social role, some argue that TNCs do both good and harm, or do more good than harm. They provide employment, pay taxes that can be used to fund socially beneficial programmes, transfer technology, help to industrialize agricultural countries and sell products people want at prices they can afford. The new interest of the TNCs in CSR has also resulted in many schemes to improve the welfare of their employees and the communities in which they work.

Against this rosy view has to be set the evidence that CSR is by no means characteristic of all TNCs, because the community, consumers, the environment and the company's workers often need protection from corporate unaccountability and irresponsibility. We have cited evidence of some success in holding the TNCs to account. Sometimes the power of consumer boycotts is effective, sometimes bad publicity leads the company to mend its ways, while, in many cases, public authorities have ultimately to be involved if the protests against the TNC are to succeed.

FURTHER READING

- Easily the most accessible book on this topic is P. Dicken's *Global Shift* (1992, revised 2003), with its useful information on TNCs, changing patterns of world trade and investment and fascinating studies of key industries looked at within a global context.

- Although we have questioned P. Hirst and G. Thompson's *Globalization in Question* (1996), the authors summarize the main debates in this area and offer a controversial and thought-provoking alternative to the more usual heady views on economic globalization.

- The possibilities of internal reform of the TNC are probed in G. E. Marcus's *Corporate Futures: The Diffusion of the Culturally Sensitive Firm* (1998).

- Published by UNRISD, *States of Disarray: The Social Effects Of Globalization* (1995) contains a hard-hitting critique of corporate irresponsibility.

- J. Bové is a French farmer who gained worldwide fame or notoriety (depending on your point of view) by driving his tractor into a McDonald's food outlet. With F. Dufour and A. de Casparis, he records his strong views in *The World is Not for Sale: Farmers against Junk Food* (2001).

- M. Wolf mounts a sturdy defence of corporations, which he says are not more powerful than countries and do not dominate the world through their brands, in his *Why Globalization Works: The Case for the Global Market Economy* (2004: 220–48).

GROUP WORK

- For the purposes of debate, one group will adopt the view that TNCs are a force for global economic integration, another that they have not fundamentally moved beyond international trade patterns that have existed for a long time.

- For the purposes of debate, one group will adopt the view that the TNCs are a force for social good, another that they generate malign social effects.

- Write to the public affairs office of a large corporation requesting its annual report. (Search the web or look at adverts in the *Financial Times* or *The Economist* for addresses.) What claims, if any, does the company make to having social responsibility? Are you convinced?

- Without looking at Table 7.2, list all the TNCs you know of in the following categories – oil companies, motorcar companies, pharmaceuticals and chemicals. Compare this list with those of your classmates. Why are these companies familiar to you?

- Why would you like to work/not work for a TNC?

QUESTIONS TO THINK ABOUT

1. What reasons could be given to support the proposition that the world economy is much more internationalized and integrated than it was before the First World War?

2. Describe the major characteristics of an EPZ? Why did corporations wish to locate there?

3. Evaluate the positive and negative social effects of TNCs in developing countries.

4. Examine the origins of the TNCs, noting national differences.

5. Evaluate the power of consumers to change the conduct of TNCs.

WHAT'S ON THE WEB

- http://www.societyandbusiness.gov.uk/downloads.shtml The UK government unit to promote corporate social responsibility.

- http://www.nottingham.ac.uk/business/ICCSR/research/paperseries.html The University of Nottingham Business School has a CSR unit. This is where you can find its downloadable papers.

- http://starbucks.co.uk/en-GB/_Social+Responsibility/ Starbucks coffee struts its CSR stuff. You had better believe it or you won't enjoy another cup of coffee there.

- http://www.multinationalmonitor.org/hyper/list.html Launched by Ralph Nader and others concerned to curb the power of the TNCs, the *Multinational Monitor* reached its 25th anniversary in 2005. As the editors ruefully admit, despite their campaigns, things have not changed much.

- http://www.mtholyoke.edu/acad/intrel/mnc.htm This URL is a branch of Vincent Ferraro's home page, where you will find about 30 articles from newspapers like the *New York Times* on the activities of TNCs.

- http://www.corporatewatch.org/?lid=58 The organizers of this site claim that 'Corporations have gained a power out of all proportion to their original purpose'. They continue: 'We are a research group supporting the campaigns which are increasingly successful in forcing corporations to back down. Corporate Watch is part of the growing anti-corporate movement springing up around the world.' You should use this site and its links for your research on the many anti-corporation campaigns it covers, but remember it is overtly 'anti-corporate'.

Uneven Development: the Victims

CONTENTS

As we have noted before, globalization impacts very differently on different *regions* of the world. In this chapter, we will review how uneven development arises and concentrate on the way in which four particular *social groups* are disadvantaged. With the collapse of alternative models, market-driven economies are now 'the only show in town'. Although successful in many respects, they seem intrinsically to generate enormous discrepancies in terms of income and opportunity within and between countries. Many accept this outcome as natural or inevitable. 'The poor will always be with us' is one popular saying reflecting this sentiment. Those who have lost out in the contest for prosperity are seen as lazy, or perhaps biologically inferior. Sometimes the poor and disadvantaged even blame themselves for their condition.

Even if many people are socialized to accept a differential outcome fatefully, for sociologists the problem is more taxing and fascinating. Why do some lose and some win? Can the losers ever alter their place in the hierarchy? Is there some relationship between the fact that some win and some lose? In other words, do some win *because* some lose? Is it therefore in the interests of the rich and powerful to maintain a differential between rich and poor or does that outcome also provide a long-term threat to their continued dominance? Could it be to the ultimate benefit of the powerful that the poor achieve some social mobility and raise their standards of living? Can that social uplift be induced from the top, for example through the actions of benign politicians? Alternatively, will the only redress come from oppositional social and political movements emanating from the grassroots level?

In this chapter we will examine two theories of uneven international development – world system theory and the notion that a new international division of labour (NIDL) emerged in the 1970s. We will then look at whether globalization itself is a force contributing to powerlessness and social marginality or, as its advocates argue, a force for the generation of wealth and the lifting out of poverty of more and more people. We will come back to our overall assessment of this argument in the final chapter of this book, but concentrate here on those who are not benefiting or, to be optimistic, *not yet* benefiting from development and globalization. In our case studies, we will consider the fate and fortunes of four (these are, of course, not the only four) deprived social groups – famine victims, workers in the deindustrializing areas, peasants, and the urban poor.

▪▪▪▪▪▪▪▪ THEORIES OF UNEVEN DEVELOPMENT

In this section we consider world system theory, developed by Immanuel Wallerstein (see Global Thinkers 1 for a further discussion of his ideas) and the theory of a 'new international division of labour' articulated first by a group of German social theorists in the 1970s and 1980s.

WORLD SYSTEM THEORY

Of a number of similar theories, Wallerstein's (1974, 1979) world system theory has been especially influential. His argument is that capitalism and not nation-states have created the world order, since from its beginning capital has always disregarded national borders and was driven to spill outwards in search of profits. The world system became stabilized into a structured set of relations between three types of country belonging to the dominant *core*, the *semi-periphery* or dependent *periphery* of the overall system. The semi-periphery, characteristically neither as technically advanced or rich as the core countries nor as dependent as the peripheral countries, serves as a necessary buffer between the other two, dividing the potential opposition to continuing domination by core capital.

The designation of particular countries to a position in this hierarchy is not fixed, so some movement between them is possible – as in the case of Japan's remarkable record in rising from the periphery before the 1870s to second posit-ion in the core bloc by the 1970s. Movement from periphery to core is very difficult, because once their hold over other countries is assured, dominant players can use their control to perpetuate various unequal exchanges. Put simply, the latter involves the manipulation of control over technology and markets in order to underpay countries and producers for their goods and services and overcharge them for their purchases.

Gradually, and working on a global scale, capitalism has created an increas-ingly integrated world economy dominated by the logic of profit and the market. By the same token, it has generated excluded, marginal, dispossessed and poor people. This outcome was consequent on an often complex and ever shifting world division of labour based on two closely related processes. These are:

1. The progressive tying of more and more countries into the global market as specialized buyers and sellers of various commodities, for example, minerals, tropical raw produce, manufactured goods or advanced technology.
2. The tendency of capital to maximize whatever kinds of economic advantages were provided in a given country by the prevailing forms of labour process and class relations. If there were, for example, slaves, serfs, sharecroppers, tenant farmers or landless labourers, capitalism was able to adapt to or perpetuate these forms of social exploitation (see Cohen 1987).

Accordingly, Wallerstein's argument continues, the world capitalist system is dominated by its own logic of accumulation and it works to safeguard and expand the capitalist nature of the overall system at all times and protect the interests of the leading players in particular. At the economic level, it forms one unified system. At the political level, it is pluralistic, while socially it generates the extremes of poverty and prosperity with a variety of intermediate positions.

There have been many criticisms levelled at world system theory – mainly concerning Wallerstein's relative lack of interest in the political dimensions of power, privilege and dispossession. Bergeson (1990: 70–5), for example, argues that the role of political power was crucial in explaining the origins and spread of capitalism. He maintains that it was conquest and the introduction of state structures that enabled the colonial countries to impose various forms of forced labour and unequal trading terms on their dependencies, not their ability to slot already established local market relations into a world division of labour. Despite this bias towards the economic level, world system theory has several important advantages for those seeking to develop a global sociology, as Wallerstein:

- treats the world holistically and historically
- provides a sense of narrative and development, showing how earlier forms of what we have called proto-globalization give way to the age of globalization (see Chapter 2)
- underlines that inequality and unevenness are at the heart of the world system, but
- accepts that it is possible, within serious limits, to move up (as well as down) the hierarchy.

THE NEW INTERNATIONAL DIVISION OF LABOUR

Partly in response to the perceived deficiencies of world system theory, a team of German researchers (Fröbel et al. 1980) propounded the idea that a **NEW INTER-NATIONAL DIVISION OF LABOUR** (NIDL) had emerged. They were reacting particularly to the rapid industrialization of East Asia and the other NICs and to the partial *deindustrialization* of the old heartlands of capitalist production. As we observed in Chapter 7, from the 1960s and 70s, there was a growing tendency for some TNCs to locate the more labour-intensive parts of their overall operations in developing countries, so creating 'world market factories'.

key concept	The **NEW INTERNATIONAL DIVISION OF LABOUR** divides production into different skills and tasks that are spread across regions and countries rather than within a single company. From the 1970s onwards, hitherto agricultural countries, particularly in the Asia Pacific region, rapidly became drawn into the new international division of labour as key production functions were shifted away from the old industrial zones.

Advocates of the idea of a NIDL argued that by locating some manufacturing processes in cheap labour havens, little was done to enhance living standards and development prospects in those poor countries affected. By contrast, the export of capital contributed to the growing ranks of the unemployment in the West. The only winners, they argue, are the TNCs. While these theorists suggest that the NIDL has not fundamentally altered the core countries' ability to dominate the world capitalist system, they are alert to the existence of 'global losers' in all countries. Like world system theory theorists, they were sceptical that the periphery would overcome its condition of relative economic backwardness, despite its partial shift from dependence on raw material exports to the export of cheap manufactured goods.

Some of the criticisms levelled against world system theory can also be directed at this theory (Cohen 1987: Chapter 7). Certainly, it seems to undervalue the capacity of some states in developing countries to use political power to create conditions for a successful transition to at least semi-peripheral status in the world order. The leaders of some successful NICs like Singapore and Malaysia are very aware of the dangers of being trapped in a cheap labour, low-tech, industrial future. To counter this, Malaysia, for example, founded 11 universities and developed a 10-mile deep 'Cybercity', which, it was hoped, would supersede Silicon Valley in California (though the turbulence in the East Asian currency markets in late 1997 temporarily derailed this project). The theory also seriously undervalued the likelihood that large countries like India and China could use exported manufactures to supercharge their own economies, lifting considerable numbers of their own people out of poverty and even racking up considerable trade credits with the USA.

GLOBALIZATION AND WEALTH

Clearly, the new international division of labour, which we now recognize was an early version of globalization theory, has had complex and, to a degree, unexpected effects. Some of the strongest advocates of globalization point to the spectacular reduction of poverty over the 20-year period 1981–2001 when, measured by the number of people living on less than US$1 a day, 350 million people escaped absolute poverty. Over the same period, the percentage of the world's population in this state of poverty moved from 39.5 per cent to 21.3 per cent, a remarkable improvement of 18.2 per cent (Tables 8.1 and 8.2). The promoters of current models of globalization also point out that gross domestic product (GDP) per capita in all developing countries rose by 30 per cent over the same period. There were even more spectacular gains in the wealthy countries.

On closer examination, this image of a cornucopia of wealth cascading to the world's population soon melts away in the face of 'uneven development', the theme of this chapter. In announcing the figures just cited, the World Bank's (2004b) own press release noted that it was India and China that had delivered the reductions in poverty and that many other countries were either bumping along in much the same way or going into further relative and absolute decline. Take China out of the equation and the number of people living on less than US$1 a day actually *increases* from 845 to 888 million over the measured period (Table 8.1). Of course this does not gainsay China's and India's real achievements (GDP per capita in China alone has gone up by five times since 1981), but it does raise the question of whether we are to attribute this economic success to 'globalization' or to some special features obtaining in the high-growth countries of the former 'Third World'. In the case of China, we might think, for example, of the return of the powerhouse of Hong Kong to the mainland, the mass mobilization of labour possible in a nominally communist country, the input and importance of the Chinese diaspora, the existing relatively high levels of education and the international balance of political forces that allowed China open access to Western markets. It is clearly impossible to imagine that similar factors will obtain in Africa, Latin America and the poorer parts of Central Asia and the Middle East, whatever the political will to follow the path of the Chinese dragon.

Indeed, the World Bank (2004b) noticed that 'the number of people living on less than two US dollars a day in Eastern Europe and Central Asia rose from eight million (2 per cent) in 1981 to over 100 million (24 per cent) in 1999, dropping back to slightly more than 90 million (20 per cent) in 2001'.

Finally, as sociologists, we must remember that while these and similar statistics from the World Bank are vital general indicators of the movement of poverty and wealth, the top layers of older social structures can often adapt successfully to new sources of wealth. Let us again take the crucial case of China to make this point. Naturally, there are many examples of people who have moved from rags to riches, but there are many more instances of powerful figures from the Chinese Communist Party, the administrative cadres, the old expatriate elites or the country's armed services who have 'made it even bigger' when the Chinese economy started to roll. By the same token, even with China's breakneck growth, it is unrealistic to expect the poorest peasants in the poorest regions of the country to benefit soon.

TABLE 8.1 Number of people living on less than US$1 a day (millions)

Region	1981	1984	1987	1990	1993	1996	1999	2001
East Asia and Pacific	767	558	424	472	416	287	282	284
China	606	421	308	377	336	212	224	212
Europe and Central Asia	1	1	2	2	17	20	30	18
Latin America/Caribbean	36	46	45	49	52	52	54	50
Middle East/North Africa	9	8	7	6	4	5	8	7
South Asia	475	460	473	462	476	441	453	428
Sub-Saharan Africa	164	198	219	227	241	269	292	314
Total	1451	1272	1169	1219	1206	1075	1117	1101
Excluding China	845	850	861	841	870	863	894	888

SOURCE: World Bank (2004a)

TABLE 8.2 Share of people living on less than US$1 a day (%)

Region	1981	1984	1987	1990	1993	1996	1999	2001
East Asia and Pacific	55.6	38.6	27.9	29.6	25.0	16.6	15.7	15.6
China	61.0	40.6	28.3	33.0	28.4	17.4	17.8	16.6
Europe and Central Asia	0.3	0.3	0.4	0.5	3.7	4.2	6.2	3.7
Latin America/Caribbean	9.7	11.8	10.9	11.3	11.3	10.7	10.5	9.5
Middle East/North Africa	5.1	3.8	3.2	2.3	1.6	2.0	2.6	2.4
South Asia	51.5	46.8	45.0	41.3	40.1	35.1	34.0	31.1
Sub-Saharan Africa	41.6	46.3	46.8	44.6	43.7	45.3	45.4	46.5
Total	39.5	32.7	28.4	27.9	26.2	22.3	22.2	21.3
Excluding China	31.5	29.8	28.4	26.1	25.5	24.0	23.7	22.8

SOURCE: World Bank (2004a)

■ ■ ■ ■ ■ ■ ■ GLOBALIZATION AND POVERTY

Although both world system theory and theorists of the NIDL have made important contributions towards understanding global inequalities, some writers argue that the phenomenon of marginality was deepened by processes of globalization commencing in the 1980s. This view was evident in one of the key conclusions reached, for example, at the UN's Copenhagen Summit on Social Development in March 1995 (cited in Townsend 1996: 15–16):

> Globalization had been driven in part by high hopes of shared greater prosperity by the rapid processes of change and adjustment [but it has] been accompanied by more poverty, unemployment and social disintegration, too often residing in isolation, marginalization and violence. The insecurity that many people, especially vulnerable people, face about the future – their own and their children's – is intensifying.

It was noted at the summit that more than a billion people in the world lived in degrading poverty – with disproportionately more women, blacks, children, single parents, unemployed, disabled and elderly people. These data were supplemented by Watkins (1997), a policy analyst working for the charity Oxfam, who provides a vivid summary of the startling facts of global social inequality. In 1966, the richest fifth of the world's population enjoyed an income 30 times as great as the poorest fifth. By 1997, the average income of the rich was 78 times larger. With 12 per cent of the world's population, Africa had 1 per cent of the world's trade and investment. In Latin America, 'there were more poverty-stricken people in 1997 than in 1990, while the region's murder rate is six times the global average' (Watkins 1997: 17). Needless to say, most of the victims of violent crime are poor people.

Is there any way of characterizing 'poverty'? It is essentially a contested concept partly because, in a diverse, dynamic and changing social world, poverty may be perceived differently in different contexts, and partly because it is also a political concept, implying and requiring remedial action (Alcock 1997: 6). Sociologists have distinguished between the concepts of absolute poverty, where people live below subsistence level, and relative poverty, which is 'based on a comparison between the standard of living of other members of society who are not poor' (Alcock 1997: 89). In other words, relative poverty is defined according to social needs rather than basic material needs, but it can be devastating in its effects, impacting significantly on people's opportunities in terms of educational achievement, health and employment chances. As a loose description, if not a tight definition, the Copenhagen Summit (UN 1995: 57) proposed that we see poverty as taking the following forms:

> Lack of income and productive resources to ensure sustainable livelihoods; hunger and malnutrition; ill health; limited or lack of access to education and other basic services; increased morbidity and mortality from illness; homelessness and inadequate housing; unsafe environments and social discrimination and exclusion. It

[poverty] is also characterised by lack of participation in decision-making and in civil, social and cultural life. It occurs in all countries: as mass poverty in many developing societies, pockets of poverty amid wealth in developed countries, loss of livelihoods as a result of economic recession, sudden poverty as a result of disaster or conflict, the poverty of low-wage workers, and the utter destitution of people who fall outside family support systems, social institutions and safety nets.

Whereas in the Cold War period, mass poverty tended to be associated with the so-called 'Third World', some of the tendencies towards marginalization also appeared in the former 'Second World'. The ending of the Cold War also generated several adverse repercussions for sub-Saharan Africa. The withdrawal of former Soviet support from the communist regimes in Angola, Ethiopia and Mozambique was accompanied by the drying up of Western investment, which, after 1989, became more attracted to the established markets in Asia and the emerging markets in Eastern European countries. The ending of the East–West conflict prevented African countries from exercising their former slender bargaining power by playing off each side in the Cold War contest against the other in the scramble for aid, loans and investment.

Having described the overall character of global poverty, we now need to observe *which* particular social groups in various countries and regions are being notably affected by social fragmentation and marginalization.

■ ■

Global Thinkers 8   WALDEN BELLO (1945–)

Bello is a political economist from Thailand. He is a widely respected analyst and critic of globalization but also a campaigner for international justice.

Bello argues that neoliberal economics frees the market from its former embeddedness within society and politics. While this has produced some winners, it has generated far more losers. The winners are the already rich business elites, international banks and transnational corporations. They have been freed to relocate their capital to wherever they can earn the highest returns. They have also been empowered to maximize profits for shareholders without needing to account for the consequences of their actions in environmental or social terms. Behind this move towards economic globalization and neoliberalism, Bello sees three additional forces.

America's global power and needs
Since the end of the Cold War, the USA has been able to exercise military and economic hegemonic power, although this is now increasingly challenged. Since the early 1980s, the US government has used its power to protect the interests of its corporations and those economic sectors where it still retains a world lead. It has used its control as the single largest contributor to the IMF and World Bank and as the world's largest market to push through a neoliberal agenda that favours US companies, banks, pension fund managers, stock exchange brokers and currency dealers.

Inequality

Since the 1970s, growing inequality in both rich and poor countries has resulted in massive underconsumption or excess capacity. Thus, worldwide car output in 2002 reached 80 million but demand was barely three-quarters of this. This is just as true of countries like South Korea or Brazil, where elites resist income tax increases and other attempts to redistribute income, as it is of Europe or the USA. In the latter, wages for most workers remained static for the 20 years prior to 1997, while income and wealth distribution has become more unequal in the same period. Because the already super-rich have everything they need, their excess incomes tend to flow into speculative activities, while the vast majority have to rely on growing debts to increase their spending or continue living in poverty.

Democratic political stagnation and crisis

Governments are frightened to tackle this inequality. But the resulting underconsumption and falling profits explain why corporations require an open world economy so that they can easily move their plants in search of lower wages. Alternatively, poor returns from productive investment can be compensated by switching money into countries that have been compelled to remove their former barriers to foreign capital and offer high interest rates or opportunities for real estate speculation – as happened in many East Asian countries such as Thailand in the early 1990s, which was followed by an equally rapid capital outflow in 1997/8.

Bello's suggested reforms include:

- *reimposing controls on capital flows across borders including taxing these (the suggested 'Tobin tax')*
- *reforming the IMF, World Bank and WTO so they are more transparent and amenable to the needs of the South*
- *concentrating on regional economic management and, where sensible, deglobalizing by discouraging export growth and encouraging more nationally owned activities that create local jobs and investment*
- *exposing governments, IGOs and TNCs to much more political pressure, with a view to demanding policies that reduce inequality both nationally and globally.*

SOURCE: Bello (2001, 2002)

FAMINE VICTIMS: HOW FAMINE ARISES

Throughout the area south of the Sahara desert and north of the Zambesi River, getting adequate food from the land, then storing and distributing it has proved almost impossible. By the mid-1990s, Bush (1996: 169) observed that hunger caused 13–18 million deaths per year worldwide, or 35,000 a day. In developing countries, 60 per cent of deaths of the under-fours were caused by hunger. In Africa, he continued: 'the most vulnerable groups are agriculturalists and pastoral-

ists [and] the poor, the elderly and women are the first to suffer'. A 1994 report
for the World Bank (cited in Bush 1996: 173) depicted an equally bleak picture:

> Over the past twenty-five years agricultural production in Sub-Saharan Africa
> (SSA) rose by only 2.0 per cent a year, while aggregate population growth aver-
> aged about 2.8 per cent per year. Per capita food production has declined in most
> countries of the continent. Cereal imports increased by 3.9 per cent per year
> between 1974 and 1980, food aid by 7 per cent per year. But the 'food gap'
> (requirements minus production) is widening. In the early 1980s about 100
> million people in SSA were unable to secure sufficient food to ensure an adequate
> level of nutrition for themselves.

FOOD INSECURITY

At a global level there is a surplus of food. Why, then, are there so many starving
people in the midst of plenty? In the USA and Europe, food is often destroyed
or stored to sustain the market price. Each year thousands of tonnes of vegetables
are used as landfill or bulldozed into the sea. The process of hoarding to sustain
farm prices has yielded bizarre phrases such as 'butter mountains', 'wine lakes'
and 'meat banks'. Why not simply send surplus food to the poor countries? This
is not as easy as it might appear. Sending food abroad as aid can sometimes
distort and damage local economies. For example, the export of wheat to Nigeria,
which started as free aid during the period of that country's civil war (1967–69)
altered tastes, undermined local staple crops and ultimately resulted in the
displacement of farmers from their land. Nigeria became enmeshed in what
Andrae and Beckman (1985) called 'the wheat trap', where precious foreign
exchange was used to buy US wheat, which Nigerian consumers now demanded.
Attempts to grow wheat locally yielded only 10 per cent of the total needed.

Joining the jigsaw pieces of the world food system can, in short, result in
forcing local farmers to the wall. Many farmers in poor countries not only cannot
produce at globally competitive rates, or ward off cheap imports, they have a
struggle to keep themselves and their families alive. Is there anything that can be
done about this appalling situation? One possible solution would be to create a
self-sufficient set of societies, cut off from the rest of the world. Would this
provide an answer to the endemic crisis of production? Unfortunately, the precedents for this resolution of the problem are not particularly helpful. The path of
self-reliance was one taken by several countries in the wake of decolonization or
political revolution.

President Nyerere in Tanzania made a notable attempt to free his country from
dependency in the 1960s. He evoked a golden age of African communalism,
when people had modest resources but were thought to be happy. Politics was
decided by the consensus of the village elders, while guests would be fed for the
first night – but handed a hoe to help to produce food for the common good
thereafter. However, he found these homilies impossible to translate into real
policies for the post-independence period. With their expectations aroused by

the anti-colonial struggle, Tanzanians demanded the usual clutch of public services – clean water, roads, healthcare and Westernized education – and no amount of local agricultural production was going to pay for this. Instead, Tanzania had to rely on the export of its staple crop, sisal, which kept reducing in value as artificial fibres came on stream. Moreover, the sisal plantations taken into public ownership produced less than those in private hands. Even more disheartening was that the bureaucrats, concerned to feather their own nests, engaged in what the Tanzanian scholar Issa Shivji called 'a silent class struggle' with the government. Eventually, the country was brought to heel and provided with an IMF package effectively dictating its economic policies. Tanzania was back where it started – a poor country with a subordinate role in the global division of labour.

A more extreme example of an attempt to create self-sufficiency in food through political means arose when the Khmer Rouge, the Cambodian Communist Party, took control of the country after a civil war commencing in 1975. Under its ideologically fixated leader Pol Pot, the Khmer Rouge decided that the roots of all evil were the 'non-productive' people in the towns and cities. City dwellers were rounded up at rifle point and frogmarched into the countryside. There they were handed seeds, hoes and shovels and told to farm. Predictably, the results of this harebrained scheme were disastrous. Those who opposed the plan were ruthlessly killed, agricultural production collapsed and hundreds of thousands of Cambodians perished through starvation and disease. While neither Tanzania nor Cambodia provides a helpful model, clearly public policy, in both the rich and famine-prone countries, must have something to do with the solution to food insecurity. However, before we can address changes in policy, we need first to understand the fundamental causes of famine. Food insecurity turns into famine because of natural disasters affecting agricultural production, the lack of entitlements or access to food and policy failings.

NATURAL DISASTERS

Natural disasters, for example droughts, hurricanes, volcanic eruptions and floods, can easily disrupt a precarious agricultural system. In these cases the threat of famine occurs from a shortage in the *supply* of food arising from what is called in insurance contracts 'an act of God'. Such is the instinctive and obvious explanation for famine, one that is rarely questioned in the media or popular discussion. Yet such a view has some real limitations. Why are some societies afflicted with similar disasters able to avoid famine or recover more rapidly? Have previous agricultural policies and practices contributed to the likelihood of famine arising in the wake of a natural disaster? (For example, deforestation, burning wood as fuel and soil erosion through overgrazing might all amplify the threat of famine.) Were there sufficient roads and airstrips giving access to the sites of likely famine? Were there adequate storage facilities for grain, edible tubers or rice? Had the pipes and pumping stations for water supplies been planned or installed? Were the civil defence and emergency services organized and trained? Had a failure to promote land reform forced poor people onto marginal land where they become most vulnerable to sudden climatic or political changes?

Such questions amount to a more sociological explanation for famine – one that critically assesses commonsense assumptions and focuses on the social and political dimensions involved.

ENTITLEMENT THEORY

The most important alternative theory for famine is 'entitlement theory', developed by Sen (1981) and later extended in his joint work with Dreze. There, Dreze and Sen (1989: 9) define their concept of entitlement in the following way:

> What we can eat depends on what food we are able to acquire. The mere presence of food in the economy, or in the market, does not *entitle* a person to consume it. In each social structure, given the prevailing legal, political, and economic arrangements, a person can establish command over alternative commodity bundles (any one bundle of which he or she can choose to consume). These bundles could be extensive, or very limited, and what a person can consume will be directly dependent on what these bundles are.

Precisely what these 'commodity bundles' are is a bit cryptic, but it may be helpful to compare them, in the setting of an affluent society, with the contents of a shopping trolley. If you are well-heeled, as you walk down the supermarket aisle, you toss things into the wire trolley without much thought. The range and cost of the commodities you buy is determined by the cash you carry or, more likely, your credit card limit. However, you might notice that some people, perhaps senior citizens on a modest pension, buy the 'bargains' at the end of the line, carefully look at lists comparing prices, or examine the damaged tins in the 'give-away' rack. In short, a different entitlement is determined by a different purchasing power.

Let us now switch back to the setting of a poor society, like parts of India, Central Asia and most of Africa. Here the issue of entitlement becomes more complex. Either the rural dwellers have very modest cash incomes or they have none at all. In these circumstances other kinds of entitlements intervene. Can the rural dweller go into a local forest and trap or hunt game to supplement a family's diet? Or has that area been deemed a wilderness area, protected by armed rangers hired by the National Parks Commission or the World Wide Fund for Nature? Can the poor farmers collect fruit, berries or edible flora and fungi? Or have the big farmers destroyed all these pickings (a last remnant of a hunter-gatherer society) through the private registration of land, the use of herbicides and pesticides, and the production of (often inedible) crops for the world market? Can the peasant call on his landlord for a loan, or will this engender yet another turn of the screw of **debt peonage**? Can peasants turn to kin or clan, or are they so far down the road of private capital accumulation that they choose not to help a

Debt peonage A system whereby loans in cash or kind are made to poor peasants by rich farmers, and paid back by a share of crops or income gained by the debtor or the debtor's descendants.

relative? Can women assert their entitlement to equal treatment when historic-ally they have been victims of patriarchal family structures?

Suddenly 'entitlement' is not so obvious and the dilemmas faced by the very poor become acute. Is it better to starve to preserve one's assets, at least letting one's children have the chance to survive? Alternatively, must one throw oneself at the mercy of a local political dignitary, exchanging an oath of permanent fealty and obeisance for immediate relief (and thus, incidentally, reinventing something akin to feudalism)? Can any individual solution be successful or enduring, or does one have to organize to defend collective rights? If that is unsuccessful, finally, is there nothing else but to trudge in a pitiful line towards the feeding stations, where earnest white volunteers dole out handouts that have been flown in from all over the world?

Figure 8.2 **Amartya Sen, who developed entitlement theory**
Sen is a Nobel laureate in economics, but has made notable contributions to general social science issues. Pictured here, at a press conference on 14 October 1998, where he criticized India's social policy.

Figure 8.1 **A Dinka boy barely able to stand due to starvation at Thiet feeding camp in southern Sudan**
Hundreds of Dinka had their villages bombed and burnt by the Khartoum forces and travelled hundreds of miles to avoid hunger and death. Drawings on a wall depict the ongoing civil war dividing the Christian south from the Muslim north, which finally ended in 2005.

POLICY FAILINGS

Sen's entitlement theory has provided a radical alternative to the 'natural' explan-ation of famine and has held centre-stage for in-depth discussions of the problem of food insecurity since the early 1980s. Although they do not wish to supersede Sen's theory, other authors, for example Keen (1994) and Bush (1996), are more insistent on the political factors and failings that trigger famine. It is self-evident that adverse effects on agricultural production can result from civil war as farmers flee the land in fear of their lives. But could some political actors be using famine as a crucial part of their means of prosecuting a civil war, rather like some retreating armies pursue a 'scorched earth' policy to deny food and material to their enemies? This raises the question of whether famine is in the interests of some parties. The beneficiaries of famine might, for example, include:

- merchants, who may be hoarding staples or buying livestock at knockdown prices
- suppliers of grain from other sources
- politicians, whose desire for power and territory or hatred of other ethnic groups might incline them to be phlegmatic about famine in a particular area
- local elites, who use their access to global aid flows to feather their own nests rather than send the supplies to areas where they are needed.

Keen (1994) takes this logic even further, arguing that in the case of the famines in Sudan, there was a high level of *intentionality*. According to him, the Islamic Sudanese ruling class used famine as a massive stick with which to beat the heads of its opponents, particularly the southern Christians. This is a chilling conclusion to reach and, although it is developed in relation to only one country, it challenges some of the rival theories used to explain famine. Facing a loss of popularity with its own supporters in the north and an environmental crisis, the regime saw the creation of famine in the south as a way out of its dilemmas. Alluding to Sen's theory, Keen (1994: 13, 14) writes:

> Notwithstanding Sen's emphasis on poverty as the root of famine, it was, in a sense, precisely the wealth of victim groups that exposed them to famine. Processes of famine involved the forcible transfer of assets from victim to beneficiary groups in a context of acute political powerlessness on the part of the victims ... The 1985–89 famine was the creation of a diverse coalition of interests that were themselves under intense political and economic pressures in the context of a shrinking resource base and significant environmental crisis in the north.

In 1998, when famine in the Sudan loomed again, the country became divided into a religious front line. Christian charities poured aid into the south, while several Islamic countries supported the government in Khartoum. In short, cruel as this is, famine can be considered as an instrument of politics.

WORKERS IN THE DEINDUSTRIALIZING COUNTRIES

As we have seen in Chapter 4, the global free market has wrought great change in the lives of many people living in the old industrial heartlands of the advanced countries. According to Peet (1987: 21), between 1974 and 1983, approximately eight million relatively highly paid manufacturing jobs, representing a crucial volume of purchasing power, 'disappeared'. These losses were much greater in some countries than others, particularly in Europe, with Britain and Belgium suffering rather more than other countries such as Germany. By contrast, in Southern Europe, Latin America and Southeast Asia, this period saw a rapid creation of new manufacturing employment. In Brazil, for example, jobs in manufacturing grew by 23 per cent, in Turkey by 32 per cent, and in South Korea and Malaysia by a massive 77 per cent and 75 per cent respectively.

Not all this manufacturing expansion in the NICs simply replaced lost employment in the advanced countries. Some businesses relocated their plants elsewhere *within* the rich countries, for example in the American case to the 'sunbelt' regions of the southern states such as Texas, Florida and Arizona. Nevertheless, perhaps more than in any other decade, the 1970s was a period when a considerable haemorrhaging of manufacturing employment from the 'rustbelt' industrial zones of North America and Europe took place. The decline of regional or city manufacturing generated a falling local tax base as incomes and retail values collapsed, with a consequent deterioration in public services. The psychological and social effects of falling living standards and unemployment made their impact on the incidence of suicide, murder, mental disorder, domestic violence, divorce and admissions to prisons. Bluestone and Harrison (1987: 91) describe how the loss of 5,000 jobs in automobile plants in Michigan during the 1970s led to further job losses of around 20,000 across the USA. These redundancies occurred not just among component manufacturing suppliers but also in other car-related industries and services such as iron, steel, metal foundries, rubber, transport, car dealers, accountancy and financial services. Many of these jobs had been held by black workers attracted to the industrializing North from the agricultural South a century earlier.

Thus, deindustrialization in certain regions is linked to the rise of new industries in others. Clearly, economic globalization, both as cause and consequence, has been deeply implicated in these changes and so is partly responsible for the accompanying processes of social dislocation, increased economic insecurity and the fragmentation of communities and labour forces. It is important to recognize that globalization has been only one of the factors involved in this long and continuing process of disruptive economic change. For one thing, capitalism has always been highly uneven and unequal in its impact within and between societies and is internally driven by perpetual technological and market upheavals. Whole industries, regions and skill structures rise and fall with relentless regularity. Think, for example, about the cotton industry in northwest Britain that gave the first Industrial Revolution in the first half of the nineteenth century its leading edge. Yet, by the 1920s, its worldwide might had waned in the face of growing competition from rival textile industries in America, Europe, Japan, India and Egypt.

By the mid-1980s, well over two-thirds of the labour force in advanced countries had left manufacturing and were classified as service workers, while the wages of manual workers in America, and several other countries, have not risen in real terms for more than 20 years. The trend towards 'flexible specialization', involving, among other things, increased subcontracting to small firms and pronounced tendencies by all businesses to 'downsize' the permanent labour force and rely increasingly on temporary, casual and part-time labour, also goes some way towards explaining the apparent trend towards 'deindustrialization'. Even where job creation is successful, a large number of citizens in the industrialized countries, especially those of minority origin, are surviving only by relying on two or even three, low-paid, part-time jobs.

■ ■ ■ ■ ■ ■ PEASANTS AND LANDLESS LABOURERS

As capitalist social relations spread unevenly across the globe, one of the most notable 'losers' is the peasantry. In the nineteenth century, social theorists like Marx assumed the inevitable decline and even disappearance of the peasantry. Modernization and industrialization were thought to signal the end of rural pursuits. There are indeed indications at the beginning of the twenty-first century that urbanization is increasingly the norm (Gugler 1995; World Bank 2005b). Yet the process has been much delayed and is not as fully advanced as had earlier been expected. Large numbers of people still live in rural areas. Of course, not all are 'peasants', an ambiguous term we have used casually, though not yet defined. To do so, we need to provide some sense of the nature of rural social differentiation. The class structure of the rural world is every bit as complex as that of the urban areas, though this is often overlooked as sociologists have overwhelmingly concentrated on the latter. An elementary approximation of a typical rural class structure in Asia (where most rural dwellers live) is depicted in Table 8.3.

TABLE 8.3	**A simple rural class structure**
Landlords	Live off rented land cultivated by tenants
Rich peasants	Live off own produce and surplus produced by hired hands
Middle peasants	Live off own produce generated mainly by family labour
Poor peasants	Own or rent some land but also have to work for others for their subsistence
Landless labourers	Own no land and have to sell their labour

SOURCE: Adapted from Bagchi (1982: 149–50)

These class distinctions are overlaid with religious, gender, ethnic and (in India and some other places) caste distinctions, which were discussed in Chapter 6. For example, scavengers, butchers and night soil workers (collectors of excrement) are at the bottom of the caste hierarchy and despite the attempts by the inspirational leader Mahatma Gandhi and successive governments of India to abolish the notion of untouchability, it is often difficult for people to escape their occupationally defined and inherited castes.

THE PEASANTRY AND THE DISRUPTION OF THE RURAL WORLD

What has all this to do with uneven development? The answer is that processes of industrialization, urbanization and commercialization have disrupted the rural world in a profound way. 'The peasantry' has to be understood, therefore, not so much as a residual category (Marx's position) or an unchanging 'traditional' category, but as a differentiated group subjected to and evolving with the new international division of labour. There are now very few peasants who produce entirely for subsistence or even for consumption in the local market. Instead, most rural pursuits are now tied into the global marketplace. As we saw in Chapter 7, the global supply chains leading to cheap produce at Wal-Mart, Tesco or Carrefour often lead to a radically changed rural workforce in many countries, who could not survive without contracts to produce flowers, food and juices for the rich North.

Nor should we imagine that big corporations only operate through subcontracts. They are direct owners of land and employers of labour too. At the top of the tree are vast agricultural TNCs like Monsanto (who provide chemical fertilizers, pesticides, herbicides and genetically engineered crops) or Del Monte (whose cans of fruit are available on just about every major supermarket shelf). Such firms are correctly described as being involved in 'agribusiness'. They have bought vast areas of land in many countries, previously held as common land or owned by the middle peasantry, and turned this into a series of 'field factories' – using hired labour to plant, weed, pick and pack the produce. Small and middle farmers have been driven to the wall or can only survive by working part time for the big companies.

Green Revolution The diffusion of high-yielding varieties of seeds, particularly wheat, maize and rice. (Not to be confused with the green/environmental movement.)

Another important way in which the rural world has been integrated into the global marketplace is through the **Green Revolution**, which spread high-yielding seeds to the farmers. Governments and research workers saw the Green Revolution as a means of abolishing famine forever. At first, sociologists like Pearse (1980) argued that the unintended consequences of this innovation were highly adverse. Only the richer farmers could afford the pesticides, fertilizer and water to make the seeds most productive. The seeds also worked better on a larger scale, so the richer peasantry often bought out smaller farmers. Later social scientists reported a more benign outcome, particularly in Asia. As the cost of the technology fell, often with the help of government subsidies, poor and middle peasants were able to deploy the new seeds.

Elsewhere, the relentless globalization of the marketplace has exposed hitherto protected small producers, like the banana growers of the Caribbean, to the giant agricultural corporations. The supermarkets of the rich countries demanded a larger, more standardized banana at an even lower price than the Caribbean farmers were able to deliver. The greater bargaining and marketing power of the big international producers was thus able to drive local farmers out of business even in their own local markets. So, for example, it is an everyday sight in a coffee-growing area (say in Latin America) to find on sale a jar of Nescafé containing coffee beans (say from Ghana), processed (say in Britain) and bulk-shipped to the area. This relentless pressure on the peasantry has driven many of them into penury or landless desperation. They eke out a miserable existence on more and more marginal land, are forced to become landless labourers or drift to the slums around the big urban areas.

THE URBAN POOR

The rural areas in many poor countries are incapable of sustaining a self-sufficient life. Dim as the prospects are for obtaining permanent urban employment, the chances of gaining access to some kind of livelihood and better services are usually greater than in the countryside. The migration that ensues has been described as 'of epic, historic proportions' (Harrison 1981: 145). In 1940, the towns or cities of the poorer countries housed 185 million. By 1975, the number had swollen to 770 million, over half the increase being accounted for not by urban increases, but by migration from the rural areas (Harrison 1981: 145).

The newly arrived migrants have a wide variety of occupations and activities. Religious ascetics, the insane, the physically disabled, micro-traders (selling items like matches or nuts), touts for taxis and buses, pickpockets, thieves, prostitutes, handcart or rickshaw pullers, beggars, those seeking work, apprentices and their 'masters' – all these are part and parcel of the diverse social landscape in the cities of the poor countries.

Figure 8.3 **Garbage pickers in Bogotá, Columbia**
Many children are involved in sorting and scavenging and are often injured by glass, sharp metal and discarded chemicals.

Many of the newly arrived migrants to the urban areas seek to maintain some kind of link with the countryside, for practical as well as emotional reasons. This system is sometimes described as 'circular migration' or a 'dual system' and is succinctly described by Gugler (1995: 544):

> The 'dual-system' strategy is sustained by kinship groups that control rural resources, in particular access to the ancestral lands. The village assures a refuge in a political economy that fails to provide economic security to many of the urban population and that often threatens an uncertain political future. For many urban dwellers, the solidarity of rural kin provides their only social security, meagre but reliable. Often they look forward to coming 'home'.

Despite the resilience of this system in many areas, gradually the ties with the village are cut, the household breaks up and the migrants to the city are on their own, where many have to eke out a miserable existence in the slums. Such temporary settlements go under different names – *favelas* and *barrios*, cardboard cities and shantytowns. They are characterized by inadequate shelter, poor roads, and no sewerage, electricity or piped drinking water. Wider provisions like sports fields, libraries, schools, health centres or parks are undreamed-of luxuries.

The condition of people living in such settings is so bad that a number of post-Marxist writers have held that there is a class below that of the proletariat. As we saw in Chapter 6, Marx had noticed such a group of people in the dispossessed peasantry who flooded into nineteenth-century Paris. In *The Eighteenth Brumaire of Louis Bonaparte*, a pamphlet first published in 1852, Marx (1954) described this group as a 'lumpenproletariat', a group that could not cohere because it contained too many varied elements. He thought it impossible for them to join a revolutionary struggle because 'their conditions of life prepared them more to be "bribed tools of reactionary intrigue"'.

The most famous attack on this view came from Frantz Fanon, the Martinican psychiatrist who joined the Algerian anti-colonial struggle. Fanon argued that Marx had failed to anticipate the importance of those who had moved into the colonial towns and capitals as unemployed and underemployed job seekers. Even using the expression 'workers' for such people was inappropriate, for they were unlikely ever to find work. He uses the same expression as Marx, 'the lumpenproletariat', but has a more elevated role for them. In his famous political tract, translated as *The Wretched of the Earth* (Fanon 1967), they are assigned the role of an 'urban spearhead' to a revolution based in the countryside. In a vivid metaphor, Fanon saw this group as a 'horde of rats'. One could kick them away, but they kept coming back, tenaciously gnawing at the roots of the colonial tree.

To signify the political potential of this group, other authors have used the expression 'subproletariat' or 'peasantariat' to get away from some of the negative connotations of the expression 'lumpenproletariat'. However, despite hopes by radical writers that they may in some sense take the place of the workers (who were seen as compromised and compliant with the capitalist system), the urban poor do not in general show a revolutionary consciousness. Instead, four forms of social action seem to have emerged:

1. A conservative clinging onto peasant values, even when the conditions for sustaining a connection with the countryside have eroded.
2. A link with populist politicians who, just as Marx surmised, use the urban poor to sustain themselves in power while placating only the most troublesome.
3. A collapse into criminal activity as a way of life and the sole means of livelihood.
4. More hopefully, a reforming, self-improving zeal shown by community actions to improve the slum dwellers' environments and standards of living.

This more positive outcome is often helped by the involvement of professionals, students and NGOs, who work with the urban poor to obtain basic goods and resources. Their position seems to improve dramatically if there is a strong civil society and some reasonable degree of political democracy. Such improvements arise for an obvious reason – politicians competing for office need votes. If the urban poor can cohere for political action, gradually roads, subsidized building materials, waterborne sewerage and piped drinking water arrive. The level of public services and environmental quality will never be of the sort found in the posh suburbs, but at least some people will be able to live their lives in relative comfort and safety.

Where civil society and universal democracy are weak, the urban poor are particularly vulnerable. Take the case of China. There the dual system is still alive if not well. A 1997 survey of over 40,000 rural households in China found that 31 per cent obtained at least a proportion of their income from non-farm sources (that is, as remittances or wages). But the authorities in the southern Chinese towns are highly alarmed by the numbers of rural workers knocking at their doors. China has a rural labour force of 450 million, including 130 million who are underemployed and 70 million who have migrated outside their home province. An estimated 330,000 migrants arrive in Shanghai *each day* and about 170,000 each day in Beijing. According to newspaper accounts (*New York Times*, 9 January 1998; *South China Morning Post*, 9 January 1998), the authorities have reacted in the following ways:

1. In 1995, the Beijing authorities demolished the shantytown, Zhejiang village, which had housed 100,000 people.
2. Expulsions of migrants by the Public Security Bureau are common.
3. The Shanghai authorities have banned migrants from 23 job sectors, while Beijing has barred them from 20.
4. In the first nine months of 1997, police in 15 cities returned 190,000 migrants and beggars to their home provinces.
5. Tao Siju, the minister of public security, has said that migrants in urban areas with '3 nos' – no job, no residence permit and no identity card – should be detained and sent home.
6. Internal controls on the movements of workers have been imposed. Between 50 and 80 per cent of unregistered work seekers face criminal prosecution.

7. In China, the Communist Party actually runs compulsory work camps for displaced rural dwellers, indigents and political dissenters, subordinating workers to produce cheap goods for the international market.

Rural people have also been displaced in massive numbers as a result of dam projects in China and India. The Three Gorges project on the Yangtze River will eventually displace 1.2 million Chinese. As many as 3,000 large dams have been built in India since 1947, which have so far displaced 21.6 million people. China's 'floating population' is reckoned to be between 80 and 120 million, a significant figure when compared with the usual estimates of cross-border global immigration of 200 million. The floating population, which has appeared particularly since the modification of the *hukuo* (registration) system, is defined as the number of people who changed residence in any one year. On the same measure, the rate of change of residence may be less than in the USA, but the sheer magnitude is greater and their rate of absorption into urban employment is lower. Rural-to-urban movement also lies behind the emergence of about 30 cities in India with populations of more than a million; there are 12 million in greater Mumbai alone.

REVIEW

There have been a number of macroscopic attempts to explain why uneven development, or global inequality, arises. World system theorists, those interested in the new international division of labour and those who write about social marginality resulting from the process of economic globalization have all provided valuable insights. All three cohere on one central insight, namely, that the spread of capitalist social relations can act like the grim reaper, cutting a swathe of death through the agricultural populations and labour forces in many countries, regions and cities. This negative outcome is likely when the adoption of neoliberal economic practices is disengaged from the nature of society and the form of political governance.

In this chapter we have sought to make these general theories 'come alive' by discussing four groups – famine victims, workers in the deindustrializing countries, peasants and the urban poor. It may be difficult for those in more favoured situations to comprehend (let alone measure or theorize) the level of devastation, poverty and human degradation suffered by many in the victim groups. The basic problem that remains unresolved at a global level with regard to famine victims is that there are currently no effective ways of redistributing food surpluses from overproducing to underproducing areas. Attempts to do so through the mechanism of aid often have unintended and negative consequences. No doubt there are many partial solutions, such as extending credit, subsidizing inputs (like seed, fertilizer, water and pesticides), training farmers, freeing up markets and developing an effective price support system. However, in some countries famine has advanced too far to respond to such interventions. Besides, these solutions imply the existence of a benign government. This is hardly the case in Sudan, which might be regarded as a particularly odious example. But 'politics' and famine also seem to have been close companions in Bosnia, Rwanda and Kosovo. Lenin, in his cynical way, suggested that one way of trying to understand a puzzling political situation is to ask the question 'Who benefits?' It is stretching the argument to say that famine is 'created' by politics in all contexts, but a studious lack of vigour in combating it seems a fairly common finding. This may reflect incompetence or a sense of futility in the face of predestination. However, feeble intervention may also reflect a variation in 'entitlement' between the different victims and, more ominously, the particular political interests of some of the powerful social and political actors.

In this respect, we cannot resist mentioning the wise Greek philosopher Plato, who warned the Athenians that the income of the rich should not exceed the income of the poor by more than five times. Any more would generate economic inefficiency and risk 'the greatest social evil', civil war (cited in Watkins 1997). While we might see the wisdom of these remarks, the income inequalities indicated by the data we have quoted earlier in this chapter vastly exceed the maximum ratio suggested by Plato. Indeed, a measure of income disparity may not even be the most salient. The significant differences between the global winners and global losers may turn on such basic issues as the provision of clean water, access to shelter and healthcare and the chances of surviving infancy. Certainly, our current phase of global development is a long way from alleviating such deprivations.

FURTHER READING

- For material on peasants, look at the *Journal of Peasant Studies* if it is in your library. In addition to some high-quality, though sometimes difficult, articles, the journal carries a section called 'Peasants speak', which reproduces interviews and other material gathered at grassroots level.

- Alan Gilbert and Josef Gugler's *Cities, Poverty and Development* (1992) provides an excellent overview of urban problems. It is especially good on Latin America and Africa.

- Amartya Sen's *Poverty and Famine: An Essay on Entitlement and Deprivation* (1981) has been contested in detail, but it remains a classic work that is challenging and stimulating if you give it a little time. (You can ignore some of the more technical economics in order to get to the essence of the argument.)

- The consequences of deindustrialization in the USA, especially for black workers, are considered in Douglas S. Massey and Nancy A. Denton's book *American Apartheid* (1993).

GROUP WORK

- Access the UNHCR's site at http://www.unhcr.ch/. Summarize the main statistical changes to the data on refugees and displacees that have occurred since the data published in this chapter were recorded.

- Divide into four groups. Each group will advocate the merits of one of the strategies for social action on the part of the urban poor described in this chapter.

- Various ratios describing the income distribution between poor and rich people have been mentioned in this chapter. There are technical ways of measuring these distributions more precisely. (Just for your information, they are called the Lorenz curve and the Gini index of inequality.) Discuss how *you* would set about measuring inequalities from first principles.

- Divide the group into three. Group A will research the basic facts about poverty in the USA, group B will research Bangladesh, while group C will look at post-communist Russia. Each group will report its findings to the class as a whole.

QUESTIONS TO THINK ABOUT

1. Will the poor always be with us, as a popular saying has it?

2. How does famine start and how is it continued, deepened and ameliorated?

3. What are the respective merits of world system theory and the theory of the new international division of labour in assessing the nature of global inequality?

4. Assess the extent to which workers in industrialized countries have been victims of economic globalization.

5. Why does inequality *not* necessarily result in political turmoil?

WHAT'S ON THE WEB

- http://www.worldbank.org/data The best source for comparative indicators of poverty and development is the World Bank, particularly its World Development Indicators.

- http://www.wfp.org/english/ The site for the UN's World Food Programme gives a good account of the various episodes of famines and food shortage worldwide and what some are doing about it.

- http://www.tandf.co.uk/journals/titles/03066150.asp The *Journal of Peasant Studies* has been one of the leading academic journals in the field of agrarian change for over 30 years. Your library may well have a subscription or give you access to the electronic version. Failing that, a free copy of one issue is available online. (Of course it is pot luck what you will find.)

- http://topics.developmentgateway.org/poverty The poverty pages of the Development Gateway – a worthy attempt to inform and democratize issues of global poverty – 50 country portals and good on Latin America.

- http://www.aflcio.org/corporatewatch/stop/# Many US workers are organized by the AFL–CIO, the largest workers' organization in the USA. Here the union explains why it is against goods produced by child- and exploited-labour worldwide and how it sponsors a labelling scheme. Of course there is self-interest in this position; American workers do not want to lose their jobs to foreign workers. But there is also considerable global solidarity.

CHAPTER 9

Crime, Drugs and Terrorism: Failures of Global Control

CONTENTS

As we have shown in Chapter 5, the nation-state system has experienced serious difficulties providing suitable and sufficient responses to some of the social, economic, political and security problems that are being manifested at a global level. Whether it is trying to stop ethnic conflict in Rwanda, Kosovo, Liberia or Somalia, contain expansionist military leaders like Saddam Hussein or develop a regulatory framework to police flows of capital, bilateral agreements between nations appear to be inadequate. The development of regional blocs, military alliances like NATO and even the UN system have also not always worked effectively at the global level. While all these issues are of major concern, probably the most important failures of global control that come within our purview as sociologists are crime, drugs and terrorism. In this chapter we address these three failures.

Just as globalization and the deregulation of the economy give individual investors, tourists, banks and TNCs an increased capacity to profit from relatively open borders, so too do opportunities blossom for cross-border crime. In Chapter 12 we record that tourism is the largest *legitimate* sector of the global economy. However, the largest without the qualifying adjective is global crime, bringing in profits of around US$500 billion a year. International criminal activity can include anything from people trafficking (smuggling immigrants or illegal workers), trade in forbidden goods (for example medicines or artefacts from ancient civilizations), computer fraud, violating patent, licence or copyright agreements, illegal arms dealing or smuggling cigarettes and stolen cars.

There is some indication that a number of these activities are beginning to compete with illegal drugs as key sources of income from international crime. For example, Lyon (2005) estimated that 2.4 million people were trafficked across borders and the trade was worth US$30 billion a year. However, there is little dispute that the profits from the drugs trade are currently much greater and, moreover, highly corrosive in their effects. The turnover in the world heroin market went up more than twentyfold from 1970 to 1990, while the cocaine trade increased more than fiftyfold over the same period (Strange 1996: 114). The UN Office on Drugs and Crime (2005: 2) estimated that the global retail market in illegal drugs was worth US$320 billion in 2004. Moreover, fuelling the habits of the many people who are the clients and victims of this trade leads to vastly increased levels of domestic, often violent, crime. Those who profit from the drugs trade are primarily the 'drug barons', the smugglers and the dealers. However, it is difficult to eliminate the trade while it also forms so vital a part of the cash income gained by poor farmers in countries like Afghanistan, Bolivia, Nepal and Jamaica, and while the demand for recreational and addictive drugs in rich countries seems insatiable. In some places, growing coca, opium poppies or marijuana allows farmers to ride the tiger of the global economy without being ripped apart by it.

The challenges posed by terrorism were never more visible than on 11 September 2001, when two commercial airliners were flown into the World Trade Center in New York, while one was targeted at the Pentagon. The death toll was large – 2,889 people died in the World Trade Center and at least 189 in Washington. They included hundreds of foreigners from 60 countries and the tragedy was given particular poignancy by the loss of 343 firefighters and 78 policemen, who had rushed to help. As Alexander (2002: 1) says, these outrages were 'unprecedented in scale, coordination and timing'. That they happened in one of the world's most important cities at the heart of its financial and media districts (which, of course, was intentional) meant that the story was broadcast to the far corners of the world in graphic and explicit detail. But the very horror of these events demands that we ask difficult questions to try to explain the phenomenon of terrorism. What do we know about the origins of terrorism and can we define it? Can we learn from historical precedents? Are there some underlying patterns that would help us to explain and counter such attacks on human life and violations of our sense of security?

Crime, drugs and terrorism are not the only, but are certainly three of the most important, afflictions of global society that have eluded global control and remedy. In this chapter, we gauge their extent and effects and whether there are ways of combating them.

CRIME WATCH

'Crime' covers a multitude of activities, some extremely violent and injurious to third parties, others much less so. Those activities on the 'softer' end of the criminal spectrum include forms of conduct that many would find unobjectionable. From around the 1970s, sociologists in the USA and the UK began to use the word 'deviance' to describe 'behaviour that is banned, censured, stigmatized or penalized' (Rock 1996b: 182). While deviant conduct can include criminal behaviour, it also includes behaviour that attracts disapproval though it is not formally illegal, as well as activities that are on the fuzzy boundaries between the two. The smoking of cannabis is one example well documented by sociologists (see Global Thinkers 9).

Global Thinkers 9   **HOWARD SAUL BECKER (1928–)**

Howard Becker is an accomplished musician as well as being a sociologist working in the sociology of art. Why then are we considering him here in a chapter covering crime and drugs? This is because he wrote a much admired book called Outsiders *(1963). In this book, he established the field of 'the sociology of deviance', which looked at the way in which social rules are enforced by dominant groups, thereby creating 'outsiders', who are ready to be labelled, cast out or incarcerated. These deviants either accept that they have been justly punished (like someone who pays up without demur when caught speeding or parking illegally), or they could challenge their accusers – 'the rule-breaker might feel his judges are outsiders' (Becker 1963: 2). Good examples of this might be gay people in jurisdictions where their sexual practices are regarded as deviant or users of marijuana who might see nothing wrong with using such a drug. In both cases, attempts to legalize their conduct signal that they do not regard themselves as outsiders.*

One of the most widely read articles in sociology is Becker's 'Becoming a marihuana user', which was published first in the American Journal of Sociology *in 1953 and appeared as Chapter 3 of his* Outsiders. *Perhaps his most startling claim was that using marijuana was not automatically pleasurable. The novice user might feel dizzy, thirsty, hungry, misjudging time and distances and feel his or her scalp tingle. The sense that these sensations might be enjoyable had to be learnt from an experienced user. Getting high was, in short, socially constructed. Many students in the 1960s were transfixed by this insight and read the article like a manual. Others, who ascribed greater potency to chemistry than sociology, developed amusing graffiti like 'Howie Becker should change his dealer'. What was unchallengeable was that when Becker wrote about musicians, drugs users or those who engaged in other deviant practices, he had 'been there'.*

Becker (2005) maintains that he was doing no more than all good sociologists should do – entering empathetically the world of his subjects. This is a useful lesson for global sociologists. When an Afghan grows poppies for later use as heroin, we need to see his motivations as complex. He is growing this crop for his, his family's and his community's survival. Yet he is helping to cause harm to an end user. Does he salve his conscience by seeing the end user as a dissolute, faithless person, an outsider? Or take the case of a people smuggler. At one level, he is ruthlessly exploiting the vulnerability of poor people, exposing them to exploitation and violating national and international law. He is reviled as a 'coyote' in Mexico and a 'snakehead' in China. At another level, he is providing a service and facilitating the capacity of powerless people to oppose unjust restrictions on their mobility.

Becker's work on outsiders forces us to ask hard questions. There is undoubtedly a danger that in gaining insight into deviant behaviour, we also in some measure justify it. This is an outcome that sociologists should firmly resist, but Becker rightly asks us to enter 'the reality which engages the people we've studied, the reality they create by their interpretation of their experience and in terms of which they act' (Becker 1963: 174).

SOURCE: Becker (1963, 2005)

■■■

The very indeterminacy of the boundary between crime and deviance, which varies historically and geographically, creates difficulties in measuring crime rates. Statistics on crime are notoriously difficult to interpret: indeed, the cynical expression 'Lies, damned lies and statistics' seems almost to have been invented to cover the case of crime. In addition to the problem of definition, the other principal difficulties are:

■ There is often a large difference between the incidence of crime and the incidence of *reported* crime. For insurance purposes and other reasons, some crimes might be undeclared.

■ In many countries, crimes might be reported to a local police station, but data collection might be inefficient and statistical services might be nominal.

■ Where law enforcement is effective, reported crimes will go up before coming down. But where low, recorded rates might also indicate indifference to law enforcement, a collapse into gang rule or even warlordism.

- Victim surveys characteristically show a different incidence of crime than police figures.
- It might be in the interests of the police to show they are *more* effective than they are (where funding depends on meeting targets), or *less* effective than they are (where this can be used to leverage more resources).

MURDER, MOST FOUL

Even bearing such difficulties in mind, it is nonetheless doubtful that misreporting, statistical anomalies and definitions alone can explain the vast differences in certain recorded crime rates between countries. Take the case of the murder (or 'intentional homicide') rate in the worst 25 countries (Figure 9.1).

Country	±% per 1000 people	Amount as a bar graph
1. Colombia	0.6	
2. South Africa	0.5	
3. Jamaica	0.3	
4. Venezuela	0.3	
5. Russia	0.2	
6. Mexico	0.1	
7. Estonia	0.1	
8. Latvia	0.1	
9. Lithuania	0.1	
10. Belarus	0.1	
11. Ukraine	0.1	
12. Papua New Guinea	0.1	
13. Kyrgyzstan	0.1	
14. Thailand	0.1	
15. Moldova	0.1	
16. Zimbabwe	0.1	
17. Seychelles	0.1	
18. Zambia	0.1	
19. Costa Rica	0.1	
20. Poland	0.1	
21. Georgia	0.1	
22. Uruguay	0.05	
23. Bulgaria	0.04	
24. USA	0.04	
25. Armenia	0.04	

Figure 9.1 **Reported murder rate in worst 25 countries, 1998–2000**
SOURCE: UN Office on Drugs and Crime (2004)

Although we must be cautious because of the statistical problems mentioned, there appear to be some common patterns in the data presented. Many of the countries in Figure 9.1 have experienced rapid social change as political circumstances have altered dramatically. Before 1989, Russia, Estonia, Lithuania, Latvia, Belarus, Ukraine, Kyrgyzstan, Moldova, Poland, Georgia and Armenia were all controlled by repressive communist parties providing welfare systems. After 1989, social support was quickly stripped away to be replaced by highly competitive forms of capitalism. South Africa experienced a massive shift from rigid apartheid control on the movement of Africans to free labour mobility. Colombia and Jamaica are marked by the presence of strong drugs cartels that have seized state authority in some areas. In such circumstances, political uncertainty, social distress, a breakdown of routine policing and a loss of community cohesion may well provide the underlying conditions in which murder rates go up.

Although we must again signal a statistical health warning, the growing inequalities associated with marketization and globalization may have led to an increase in other crimes like motor theft, robbery and robbery with violence. In one account, the authors surmise that the media 'make people more and more cynical as they see that the rich take what they want, and then taunt the rest of society through the media, the movies and advertising with the "good life" of consumerism' (Burbach et al. 1997: 22). The same authors quote the conservative US foreign policy adviser Zbigniew Brzezinski, who argues that a 'permissive cornucopia' has replaced religion and moral values. People are encouraged to want goods but 'much of the world's population, unable to obtain many of these goods, grows frustrated, resentful and rebellious' (Burbach et al. 1997: 23).

Certainly, this explanation for the increases in property and violent crime has some immediate plausibility. As Burbach et al. (1997: 22) have it: 'Globalization is spawning its own barbarians who are destroying it from within.' They point to a 'culture of violence' in many cities and maintain that industrialization and modernization increase criminality – property crimes are four times higher in developed than developing countries. Such comments have to be taken seriously, but they are incomplete. Using 'globalization' as a 'cause' of crime does not always work. Take, for example, the relatively high rate of car theft in France and the very low rate in Germany. This contrast between two rather similar countries suggests that there are more proximate and particular causes of crime in France and Germany that we cannot explore here.

In the cases of Britain and the USA, however, the general argument does seem to hold up. During the Reagan and Thatcher periods, market forces were let rip and, despite the pious claims that a cascade of wealth would 'trickle down', income inequalities widened notably. Although there is some element of fake nostalgia in this, many commentators remarked on the collapse of a community spirit and the diminishing of a sense of a moral obligation to look out for wayward youth or care for the less fortunate. The respectable blue-collar working class was decimated, with massive losses of jobs in coal mines, steel mills and the 'rustbelt' areas, where Japanese imports (and later locally built cars) undermined US car production, component manufacturing and engineering. In the greater metropolitan area of Chicago, there were 616,000 jobs in the manufacturing area in the mid-1950s – three decades later they had shrunk by 63 per cent to 277,000. On 23 January 2006, Ford, the iconic US motor manufacturer, announced the closure of 10 factories and the loss of 30,000 jobs. Those who have lost jobs and those who have never had them wander the streets, often in despair. With cuts to state welfare, their plight is compounded. In Detroit, East Lansing and to a degree other cities, 'the violence, fear, alcoholism and drugs abuse that grips the underclasses … is directly linked to this despondency and hopelessness' (Burbach et al. 1997: 103).

URBAN NIGHTMARES AND RACIAL DIVISIONS

Violent crime usually involves poor people attacking other poor people. However, the massive divisions that result from urban social inequalities nonetheless create a lethal cocktail of fear among those who have money, property and employment, combined with resentment among those who are without such goods and resources. A siege mentality results, which has implications for both public and private responses to anticipated and actual crime. In California, expenditure on prisons has overtaken the education budget, while in Los Angeles alone there is an average of 35 crimes reported every hour, 10 of which are listed as violent crimes such as murder, rape or aggravated assault (Burbach et al. 1997: 28–9). US citizens spend twice as much money on private guards as the government does on police (Martin and Schuman 1997: 9). This 'internal measure' of the decay of the nation-state is every bit as telling as the argument that nation-states are losing the battle to control global capital (see Chapter 5).

Although bad enough, when social inequalities are overlaid with the prism of 'race', the cocktail becomes even more explosive. In post-apartheid South Africa, for example, property crimes involving violence reached endemic proportions for eight years following the collapse of the repressive white-dominated state, though they now seem to be abating. Rural–urban migrants, previously excluded from the cities under the notorious pass law system, have now joined immigrants from even poorer countries in the formerly 'white cities'. With little change in white economic power, massive black unemployment and the growth of shantytowns, it is hardly surprising that many have turned to crime. The long campaign of armed resistance to apartheid and the civil wars in neighbouring countries have fomented a market in weapons and a gun culture. Wealthier South African citizens, including many blacks who have 'made it', are uneasy about travelling at night and many have turned their homes into fortresses, with alarm systems, burglar-proof bars, high walls, guards, dogs and weapons. Armed response units operated by private security firms provide backup.

A similar scenario unfolds in Brazil, where one property developer has created a 'safe city', called Alphaville, west of São Paulo. He boasts that he is 'creating the conditions for heaven on earth' and knows nothing about the famous French film made by Jean-Luc Godard in the 1960s – also called *Alphaville* – that predicted a technological nightmare of total surveillance and social control (see Box 9.1). Life has truly imitated art. High walls, sensors and spotlights surround the Brazilian Alphaville. Private security officers, often policemen trying to augment their regular salaries, cruise around the periphery. Every visitor must show an identity card and must be authorized by the residents. Nannies, kitchen helps and chauffeurs have their police records checked. Even the residents are rejected if they have criminal records. Some 120,000 people live in Alphaville and there are plans for a dozen more similar cities (Martin and Schuman 1997: 171–2).

Box 9.1	### Social control in sociological theory

Social control is necessary to modern societies, in so far as sociologists believe that older forms of customary and communal authority broke down in urbanizing and industrializing societies. At the level of the workplace, the neophyte industrial labourers had to be taught the habits of punctuality, self-discipline, hard work and thrift. In the early factories, employers often complained that workers would arrive drunk, take off feast days and often not turn up at all on Monday mornings. 'Punching in' (to a time clock), penalties for lateness and other forms of surveillance were instituted to overcome these 'bad habits'.

At a more general level, systems of social welfare, prisons, asylums, children's homes as well as mass schooling and even the extension of the franchise have been seen as ways in which those with power, wealth and authority have controlled dissent and potential rebellion on the part of those without these benefits. Of course, one must be careful not to believe that there is some giant conspiracy at work. The 'exigencies of capitalism' can be used to explain too much. The professional and upper classes may be hankering for, and imagining, a nostalgic vision of a peaceful, rural community, which they seek to reproduce for the more general social good not merely their own. It is also important to remember that the poor, not the rich, are the principal targets of violence and crime. Given their greater exposure, they often favour more extreme measures of social control (like hanging, public executions and beatings).

Since the 1970s sociologists have linked the concept of social control to the study of deviant behaviour in imaginative ways. Social control is now used to refer to more general pressures to induce conformity, pressures that become more insistent from time to time. Stanley Cohen (1972), described these moments as 'moral panics', when the official agents of social control like the police and the courts swing into action against drug takers or youth gangs. Their interventions are, to some extent, conditioned by the negative labels that are used by the media, who take up the cudgels of middle-class respectability to label negatively groups that have became 'folk devils' in the public imagination. In a complicated feedback loop, some of these groups actually relish their public notoriety – so a process of 'deviancy amplification' develops as each side plays to the gallery.

Michel Foucault made other major conceptual breakthroughs. In his *Discipline and Punish* (1977), he echoes some Marxist views in seeing the 'Great Incarcerations' of the nineteenth century as part of a common design. Thieves into prisons, workers into factories, lunatics into asylums, conscripts into barracks and children into schools were all corralled in the service of capital. However, Foucault is also interested in more subtle forms of surveillance and discipline. Instead of brutal spectacles like the guillotine, the panopticon designed by Bentham (an all-seeing tower in a prison) engaged in unobtrusive but unremitting surveillance. Discipline was not merely exemplary and demonstrative, but good for you. Psychiatrists, teachers and social workers became the engineers of the deviant mind and the unwitting agents of social control.

> In wealthy contemporary societies, the capacity for surveillance has been considerably enhanced by technology. Closed circuit television sets (CCTVs) are placed in many shopping malls and busy streets, while computerized databases and the internet have generated a new set of 'footprints' that can be followed by a determined investigator. On average, adults in the developed world have their details recorded on 300 databases.
>
> SOURCES: Cohen (1972); Foucault (1977); Mayer (1983: 17–38); Cohen (1985: 25–6)

WHITE-COLLAR CRIME

White-collar crimes Those perpetrated by more respectable members of society. They often involve fraud or deception.

Globalization greatly enhances the possibilities for **white-collar crime** because of more open borders, computer linkups and enhanced means of transport and communication. One case in point is the EU, where there is no overall authority, yet there are open borders between a group of countries. Where sales tax rates differ, as they do notably in the case of alcohol and cigarettes, smuggling takes place on a massive scale. Although often carried out as a family enterprise by tourists and visitors, cigarette smuggling is also big business. In 1992, the authorities in Germany confiscated 347 million contraband cigarettes; by 1995, the figure was up to 750 million. (The annual loss of revenue was about 1.5 billion marks.) The cigarettes often arrive from the USA before being sent to the free ports in Rotterdam and Hamburg (or to the duty-free stores in Switzerland). They are then bought for export by legitimate or illegal companies – the last registered in Panama, Cyprus or Liechtenstein. The cargo sets off in customs-sealed lorries to cross EU territory for further export, but it never gets there. The traders are often known, but untouchable in that their assets have been safely stored in offshore banks (Martin and Schuman 1997: 208–9).

Smuggling in a more unlikely commodity, chlorofluorocarbons (CFCs), has also become rampant. In 1987, 24 countries signed the Montreal Protocol intended to reduce the use of CFCs, which were destroying the fragile ozone layer surrounding the earth, resulting in eye damage and skin cancer. Thoughts of these consequences did not trouble the smugglers who exported 20,000 tonnes a year from China and Russia to the USA and Europe for use in many cooling processes, including air conditioning. CFCs still work better than their safer replacements and they are the ideal product for illegal trade, being colourless and odourless. In Miami, only cocaine had a higher street value than CFCs (*The Economist*, 13 September 1998: 78).

Smuggling is often so large in volume that it threatens legitimate trade and can be used to corrupt state officials. Massive 'turf wars' result, as criminal gangs carve up exclusive territories the better to suborn bureaucrats, set up extortion rackets and gain access to illegal goods. Between 1992 and 1995, the murder rate in Moscow went up by 50 per cent, much of it explained by the attempts by 3,000 organized gangs to drive out their competitors (UNRISD 1995: 72). There is so little distinction between criminal and state activities in Russia that state arsenals of weapons are being plundered for private profits. Submachine guns are fed into terrorist organizations, while even some of Russia's nuclear arsenal is on the international market. In *Russia in the Abyss*, published in 1998 by the Nobel prizewinning writer Alexander Solzhenitsyn, Russia's post-Soviet rulers are excoriated by someone who was previously the arch enemy of the Communist Party. He claims that 'Russia is ruled by a band of selfish people who are indifferent to the fate of the people and do not even care whether they live or die' (*Daily Telegraph*, 2 June 1998).

Box 9.2

The Nigerian 'advance fee' scam

The Central Bank of Nigeria (CBN) felt compelled to publish a press statement in many of the leading magazines and newspapers worldwide. The CBN recorded that since the early 1990s, it had sought to expose the operations of fraudsters who were operating a hoax, known as 'the 419' ('419' refers to a section in the Nigerian criminal code), or the 'advance fee scam'. So far the bank had taken out adverts in 80 newspapers in 12 languages in 36 countries in an apparently vain attempt to expose the gangs. As the CBN officials noted, 'driven by fraudulent tendency, greed and the urge to make quick and easy money at the expense of Nigeria, many of the so-called victims have continued to ignore the [published] warnings'.

How did the fraud operate? Typically it would start with an email (followed by faxes or telexes) offering to transfer huge sums of money to the recipient's bank account, normally in US dollars. The money, it was hinted, came from certain 'dodgy' transactions, which the authorities were, sooner or later, going to expose. The writer offered to split the money with the addressee. If this letter was answered, it was suggested that to release the money, certain 'taxes' (namely bribes or fees) had to be paid to key bankers, corporation officials and politicians. The fraudsters lent authenticity to their 419 by sending correspondence on faked letterheads. Sometimes the 'mark' (the target of the fraud) was invited to Nigeria and given red carpet treatment by phoney bank officers, government officials or others in the scam.

Regrettably, the marks were told, 'registration fees', 'processing fees', 'unforeseen taxes', 'licence fees', 'signing fees', 'lawyers' fees', 'release fees, 'sales tax' and other inventive fabrications had to be paid upfront before anything could happen. Needless to say, once these levies had been paid, the fraudsters took off. It seems barely credible that people could be such fools as to fall for these schemes, but apparently thousands have done so and millions of US dollars are involved.

Three indignant victims (Larry Sorth and Mr and Mrs Tei) sued the CBN in a US court presided over by the appropriately named Hon. Justice Charles A. Sham. Perhaps unsurprisingly, Justice Sham concluded that the plaintiffs were not in touch with the CBN, even if they thought they were, and that 'they were, from the outset, aware that the transactions were bogus, fraudulent and too good to be true'.

The CBN described this judgement as a 'landmark case' and once again warned those who received letters or emails, like the ones described, not to fall victim to 'international criminal syndicates whose nefarious activities have been a source of embarrassment to the CBN and the Nigerian government'.

SOURCE: Central Bank of Nigeria press statement (October 1997)

Outright criminal activity has also taken hold in the respectable corridors of Wall Street and the City of London. Just two of the prominent cases were the 'junk bonds' scam – investments sold to an unsuspecting public by Michael Milken – and the 'insider trading' of Ivan Bosky. (Junk bonds offered a high yield, but had an even higher rate of default. 'Insider trading' refers to confidential information that is misused to inflate or collapse a share price.)

CORPORATE CRIME

As was indicated earlier, it is sometimes quite difficult to decide what constitutes a crime, as various jurisdictions and definitions often confuse the matter. Let us take three examples of 'corporate crime' to indicate its character and dimensions – the cases of Enron, Union Carbide and the Bank of Credit and Commerce International (BCCI). The reckless speculation in the US stock market in the 1990s inevitably led to dramatic collapse and bankruptcies. By early 2002, US$4 trillion had been lost in the value of US shares. The most dramatic example of failure was the case of the energy supplier Enron, one of the 50 biggest public companies in the USA, which recorded over US$100 billion in sales and US$1 billion in earnings in 2001. Within six months the company was bankrupt, with a loss of US$90 billion in market value. What was shocking was not so much that this massive company had collapsed, but that its managers and auditors knew about the financial position of the company and sought illegally to conceal it from investors and employees. Company executives and board members quietly unloaded shares, while Arthur Anderson, the previously respectable global accountancy firm, shredded evidence that demonstrated its awareness or complicity in these transactions. About 25,000 employees lost most of their savings.

If you are a radical critic of corporate power, you might shrug your shoulders at such evidence of corporate malfeasance, saying 'it is only to be expected'. But a powerful critique of such conduct has been mounted by a far more unlikely source. Take, for example, the views of Felix Rohatyn, a former governor of the New York Stock Exchange, managing director of the financiers Lazard Frères and Co and the US ambassador to France from 1997 to 2000. For him, 'a large proportion of the stock market was becoming a branch of show business and it was driving the economy instead of the other way around' (Rohatyn 2002: 6). Beyond the 'sordid situation of Enron itself' lay the integrity of financial markets in general. He argued that deregulation and a lack of ethical conduct could drive away domestic and foreign investors, compromise the stability of the dollar and prevent the raising of capital on the financial markets for economic development. Ultimately, he continued, capitalism itself was threatened by such ethical abuses. In May 2006, Ken Lay, Enron's founder and former chairman and Jeffrey Skilling, the company's former chief executive, were finally convicted on charges of fraud and conspiracy. Lay died of a heart attack before he could be sentenced.

Our second case concerns the horrific leak of lethal gases from the Union Carbide plant in Bhopal, India, in December 1984, discussed previously in

Chapter 7. Was this episode the result of crime or merely misfortune? Pearce and Tombs (1993: 187–211) describe the dire consequences of the event. More than 200,000 local people were exposed to fumes, 60,000 were seriously affected, more than 20,000 were injured, and about 10,000 may have died as a direct result of the leak. Babies with birth defects are still being born. The parent company in the USA denied that it had a bad safety record, claimed its Indian subsidiary was to blame and sought to deflect attention by claiming sabotage was involved. The company managed to twist the arm of the Indian government into accepting a very low settlement of US$470 million for all victims. This deal was in exchange for a guarantee that Union Carbide would escape prosecution. An attempt to try the case in the USA, where substantial damages would have probably been awarded, was deflected by the company's lawyers. They were able to override the parent company's central role in the design and installation of the plant and 'finger' the Indian government for its poor regulatory apparatus and inadequate inspectorate.

It is perhaps ambiguous whether what we witnessed in Bhopal was 'criminal' behaviour or just a gross display of corporate social irresponsibility. No such ambiguity arises in the case of the many banks deeply implicated in 'laundering' the proceeds of crime. It is rare that bank officials are innocent dupes of criminal proceeds. Offshore banking havens are situated at the crossroads of the narcotics trade. Banks in Panama and the Bahamas act to clear the profits from the cocaine trade between Latin America and the USA. Hong Kong is used for the heroin trade between Southeast Asia and the West, while Switzerland, Liechtenstein and Gibraltar shelter the proceeds of the narcotics trade from Turkey and the Middle East. In one of the biggest scandals of recent banking history, BCCI (Bank of Credit and Commerce International), with a large branch outside the super-respectable Dorchester hotel in London's Park Lane, went 'belly up' in the 1980s. Investigations by the US Senate found that it had engaged in 'illicit financial services for a very varied group of clients, including Colombian narco-traffickers, Middle East terrorists and Latin American revolutionary groups, as well as tax evaders, corrupt politicians and several multinational companies' (Strange 1996: 118).

◾◾◾◾◾◾◾◾◾◾ DRUGS: DEMAND AND SUPPLY

The trade in drugs crucially depends on a massive demand for illegal substances in Europe and the USA and a pitiful need to continue to grow drugs by farmers in a number of supplier countries. The poorest in the poor countries are linked together with the most desperate in the rich countries. Hargreaves (1992: 3) has summarized the extent of the demand in the USA in the late 1980s and early 1990s:

Americans consume more cocaine than any other industrialized country. Over 22 million say they have tried the harmless-looking white powder and between two and three million are addicted to it. In 1989, around 2,500 Americans who 'just said Yes' died of cocaine-related causes. In 1990, one in five people arrested for any crime were said to be hooked on cocaine or crack. Americans spend a staggering US$110,000 million a year on drugs (US$28,000 million on cocaine), more than double the profits of all the Fortune 500 companies put together and the equivalent of America's entire gross agricultural income.

If demand is virtually insatiable, what happens on the supply side of the transaction? Take the case of Bolivia to which, after their reverses in Colombia in 1989, the drug lords turned their attention. This poor Latin American country was already the largest producer of raw coca leaf in the world, but between 1989 and 1991 it tripled its production of refined cocaine, placing it in the number two slot worldwide. (Coca is 'refined' by mixing the leaves with sulphuric acid, paraffin and lime, before being dried for export. You are not invited to try this recipe!)

Hargreaves (1992: 34–6) recounts the story of a Bolivian coca farmer, 'Paredes'. He used to farm near the main Bolivian mining city, Oruro. He raised pigs and sheep, and grew maize. When, in 1983, drought struck, his animals died one by one. His crops failed. The ground was so hard he could not even bury the animals. He left for the coca-growing area where, after many misadventures, he managed to obtain title to five hectares of land. He worked on another farmer's plot in exchange for a promise of seeds and seedlings, but when the farmer refused to honour his promise, Paredes stole some seeds. Eighteen months later he had his first full harvest. He was in the coca-growing business. Like thousands of other farmers, he was attracted to coca growing, as virtually any other economic activity was fraught with economic insecurity. Between 1980 and 1985, Bolivia's economy had nose-dived. The GNP had dropped by 20 per cent, unemployment had increased from 6 to 20 per cent and inflation had risen to an amazing 24,000 per cent a year. It is perhaps hardly surprising that coca offered such an attractive alternative.

Given its social and economic importance to a number of countries, the drugs trade also serves to corrupt the political process. In Russia, Somalia, Jamaica, Afghanistan, Columbia and Indonesia, there is no firm distinction between illegal and legal business activity. There is often a seamless join between crime, politics and business, such that the players can barely tell the difference. Even where there have been determined efforts to crack down on the drugs trade, sometimes with the help of foreign aid, success has been limited. Let us take two examples:

1. In the 1980s, the George Bush Snr administration provided Colombia with financial aid and military personnel to crack the power of the notorious Medellín drugs cartel, which had effectively acted as a state within a state. After a year on the run, Pablo Escobar, the world's biggest cocaine boss, was finally cornered. Despite his capture, he was still influential enough to dictate the terms of his own imprisonment. He wanted, and got, a 10-acre site, with its own football field and luxurious furnishings. The authorities had effectively been turned into a free security squad protecting him against his many enemies. Meanwhile, the cartel spread its business to other Latin American countries (Hargreaves 1992: xi).

2. The 'war on terror' initiated by George Bush Jnr started with an invasion of Afghanistan and the displacement of the Taliban regime. Although indeed committed to a radical and confrontational style of Islam, this had involved at least some commitment to uprooting opium production. With the American invasion, the poppy growers were given a renewed lease of life, and the proportion of the world opium production sourced in Afghanistan, moved from 76 per cent in 2003 to 86 per cent in 2004 (Figure 9.2).

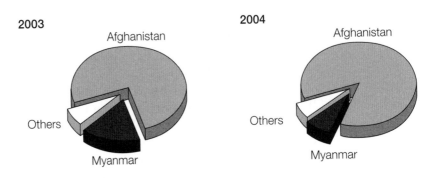

Figure 9.2 **Shares of world opium production, 2003, 2004**
SOURCE: UN Office on Drugs and Crime (2005: 45)

DRUGS IN GLOBAL SPORT

In Chapter 15, we probe some of the other dimensions of the globalization of sport. Here we concentrate on the use of drugs in sport. Most accounts suggest that the use of illicit drugs in sport rapidly accelerated after the Second World War (Waddington 2000: 114). The period coincided with two developments – the development of new performance-enhancing drugs and the escalation of political tensions arising from the Cold War. Amphetamines like Benzedrine were used by the military in the Second World War to maintain battle readiness and they crossed easily into use by sportspersons. But, in addition to such 'uppers', newly developed or newly available drugs like testosterone, steroids and growth hormones came on stream in the 1950s. As Waddington (2000: 115–34) comments, this development has led to a pharmacological or technological determinism in a number of writers' arguments. The drugs were there, so it is not surprising that they were used.

This sort of argument is inadequate for a sociologist who needs to understand the behaviour of the social actors themselves – the athletes, sports health professionals, commercial sponsors, governments – and the wider contexts in which they all operate. Probably the most important factor in driving the increased use of drugs in international sports competitions during the period 1945–1989 was the Cold War. The nuclear race resulted in mutually assured destruction (with the appropriate acronym MAD), so competition became symbolic. The supposed superior virtues of communism or socialism had to be demonstrated in sport, particularly in the Olympics. We now know that many record holders were pumped full of drugs. Perhaps the most revealing information emerged in November 2005, when former East German athletes took a drugs company to court, demanding £8 million in compensation. With the end of the East German regime, state officials are no longer there to be co-defendants indicted in the dock, but there is no doubt that they were complicit. Harding (2005) takes up the story:

> In October 2005, Germany's athletics federation announced that 22 national records set by East German athletes were suspect. The investigation came after Ines Geipel admitted she had been doped and asked for her record, set as a member of the East German women's 4 × 100 metres relay team in 1984, to be expunged.
>
> An estimated 800 athletes had developed serious illnesses, many having received Oral-Turinabol – an anabolic steroid containing testosterone made by the drugs company Jenapharm. While the 'blue bean' massively accelerated muscle build-up, its subsequent side effects included infertility among women, embarrassing hair growth, breast cancer, heart problems and testicular cancer. One well-known shot-putter, Andreas Krieger, pumped up her performance with so many male hormones she decided to have a sex change.

The drugs undoubtedly worked in the medals tables. In the 1972 Munich Olympics, East Germany came third after the USA and the Soviet Union, despite having a fraction of their populations. In 1976, East German women won 11 of the 13 swimming events. It was clear that state officials, team doctors and many (if not the youngest and most innocent) athletes were complicit in the use of these performance-enhancing drugs. Successful athletes were seen to have enhanced the image of state socialism and were given elaborate privileges.

Similar developments also occurred in the Soviet Union from the 1950s. In response to the increasing competition provided by the Soviet Union, US doctors, with the help of Ciba Pharmaceuticals, soon developed Dianabol, a steroid taken by many US athletes (Waddington 2000: 117). Sportspersons, whose self-perception and image symbolized the idea of 'health and fitness', became patients and the objects of healthcare, requiring 'routine medical supervision, irrespective of the presence or absence of any specific pathology' (Waddington 2000: 122). Coaches, trainers, doctors, physiotherapists and psychologists now routinely accompany national sides to optimize team performance. Some of these health professionals have been involved in supplying drugs.

After the end of the Cold War, the main pressure to take drugs arose from the commercialization of sport. Gold medal winners or those on top of their chosen professionalized sport (like golfers or tennis players) stand to make huge fortunes in product endorsements, appearance fees or TV commercials. Of course we do *not* make any inference whatever that he is involved in drug-taking, but just as an indication of the temptations that might attract a lesser sportsperson, the golfer Tiger Woods made US$70 million in 2004 from commercial spin-offs (http://www.forbes.com/finance/lists/). With such large rewards in the offing, it has become extremely difficult to regulate international sports.

......■ ■ ■ ■ ■ ■ UNDERSTANDING TERRORISM

Since the atrocities perpetrated by Islamic jihadists in New York, Madrid and London commencing on 11 September 2001, politicians, the media and the public alike in Europe and North America have been all too conscious of the threat posed by terrorism. However, one must not forget that Islamic extremists have been responsible for other incidents worldwide:

- 5 September 1972 when Black September killed 11 Israeli athletes attending the Munich Olympics
- 29 December 1992 when a bomb in Aden killed two tourists
- 7 August 1998 in East Africa when bombs directed at US embassies killed 224 and injured 5,000 (nearly all locals)
- 11 April 2002 in Tunisia when 20 tourists were killed
- 8 May 2002 in Karachi when 11 French naval officers and 3 Pakistanis were killed
- 14 June 2002, again in Karachi, with 12 killed and 45 injured in a car bomb directed at the US consulate
- 23 July 2005 in Sharm el-Sheikh (an Egyptian resort on the Red Sea) with 83 dead and more than 200 injured.

Chechen and Palestinian groups perpetrating atrocities are probably better considered as armed sections of national uprisings, though the Russian and Israeli governments regard them as terrorist acts.

In short, we must understand that Islamic terrorism is a worldwide phenomenon. In Chapter 16, in our discussion of global religion, we consider whether there is doctrinal support for violent jihad, why a minority of Muslims has turned to violence and what opportunities exist for peaceful coexistence and even fruitful collaboration between people of many faiths and those with none. In this chapter, by contrast, we want to gain some deeper understanding of the origins and nature of terror and terrorism and whether there are ways of understanding these phenomena beyond angry denunciation and immediate counterstrikes – understandable as these reactions are.

ORIGINS AND DEFINITIONS

According to Tilly (2004: 8–9), the word 'terror' entered the Western political vocabulary as a description of the French revolutionaries' actions against their domestic enemies. The Reign of Terror presided over by revolutionaries like Robespierre (Figure 9.3) was meant to strike fear into the hearts and minds of those who opposed the new regime. About 17,000 executions occurred legally, many of them in public using the newly invented guillotine, with another 23,000 illegal executions. The revolutionary armies also brutally repressed the counter-revolutionary uprising in the Vendée, where dissidents were flailed alive and often exhibited to strike fear into other potential opponents. Revolutionary governments have frequently used state-supported terror to eliminate their enemies and intimidate other citizens who might have some sneaking sympathy for them. Think of the purges Joseph Stalin ordered, which, together with deportations to labour camps and state-induced famines, probably resulted in the deaths of more than 10 million Soviet citizens. Think again of the madcap de-urbanization policies of Pol Pot in Kampuchea, together with his attacks on unpopular ethnic minorities and Buddhist monks, which resulted in the deaths of between 1.5 million and 2.3 million people over the period 1975–79, some one in eight of the population.

Figure 9.3 An engraved picture of the French revolutionary, Maximilien Robespierre (1758–94)

In his speech of 5 February 1794, he coupled terror and virtue, declaring:

> If the spring of popular government in time of peace is virtue, the springs of popular government in revolution are at once *virtue* and *terror*: virtue, without which terror is fatal; terror, without which virtue is powerless. Terror is nothing other than justice, prompt, severe, inflexible; it is therefore an emanation of virtue; it is not so much a special principle as it is a consequence of the general principle of democracy applied to our country's most urgent needs.

Robespierre fell victim to the terror he had helped to unleash, dying on the guillotine a few months after making this extraordinary speech.

SOURCE: http://www.fordham.edu/halsall/mod/robespierre-terror.html

The problem with seeing state-induced terror merely as a property of revolutionary fervour getting out of hand is that there are many examples of state terror perpetrated by governments that could not possibly claim any revolutionary credentials. So we can think of the Argentinean junta after 1976, when 20,000–30,000 people 'disappeared' in a 'dirty war' conducted by sections of the police and military. General Pinochet in Chile ordered the kidnapping, torture and disappearance of opponents to his right-wing regime, though he has managed to avoid trial thus far. Apartheid South Africa, Mobutu's Zaire, Idi Amin's Uganda, Stroessner's Paraguay, 'Papa Doc' Duvalier's Haiti and many other right-wing regimes show that holding on to power through terror is not a property of the political complexion of a particular government but can arise in a number of circumstances. A not uncommon pattern is for states to justify their use of terror by arguing that they need to use such means because their opponents are terrorists.

We now have the beginning of our key definitional debate, namely, is there any moral or practical difference between government and non-governmental terrorism? Is terrorism simply to be defined by its illegality, brutality, surreptitiousness and intention to humiliate, eliminate or 'terrify', whoever is the agent involved? Can governments legitimately eliminate dictators in other countries by ordering them to be killed? We know that the US government, for instance, has ordered the assassination of Fidel Castro on several occasions and former President Bill Clinton was unwise enough to disclose that he had contemplated ordering the elimination of Saddam Hussein. To press the issue, can governments legitimately order the murder of terrorists or suspected terrorists? Stephen Spielberg's movie *Munich* has brought to the public's attention the fact that Israeli Prime Minister Golda Meier ordered the assassination of Palestinians in a number of countries who were suspected of taking part in the 1972 killings of Israeli athletes at the Munich Olympics. (It later transpired that not all the victims of the Israeli intelligence agency's assassins were linked to the killings.) State officials who sanction the use of terrorism may act out of a variety of motives – to protect the public, avenge their nation's innocent dead, defend the nation or simply because the target is in their way. We may, in short, wish to distinguish between the act of state terrorism and its intention.

CHARACTERISTICS AND EXPLANATIONS OF NON-GOVERNMENTAL TERRORISM

We cannot fully understand terror or terrorism without comparing and contrasting state-directed terrorism with terrorist groups that are organized on a subnational level. Of course one must remember that there are relationships between the two forms of terrorism. In the wake of the events of 9/11, the US State Department listed what it called 'seven designated state sponsors of terrorism' – Cuba, Iran, Iraq, Libya, North Korea, Syria and Sudan. However, the USA (generally through the Central Intelligence Agency) has itself been implicated in the support of terrorist groups. Although it is hotly denied, there is, for example, some evidence that the USA supported the Taliban in the late 1990s when they were seen as a useful anti-communist force. It is unambiguously the case that Pakistan and Saudi Arabia, close allies of the USA, provided considerable assistance to the Taliban.

Despite these crossovers between state-directed, state-sponsored and non-state terrorism, contemporary concerns about terrorism are almost entirely centred on the subnational level. The US State Department, for example, *defines* terrorism as 'politically motivated violence perpetrated against non-combatant targets by subnational groups or clandestine agents, usually intended to influence an audience' (cited by Tilly 2004: 7). This is not very different from the definition of subnational/transnational terrorism provided by Bergesen and Lizardo (2004: 38), namely: 'the premeditated use of violence by a nonstate group to obtain a political, religious, or social objective through fear or intimidation directed at a large audience'. How then can we characterize and explain subnational forms of terrorism? It would perhaps be a commonly held view that such phenomena have been on the increase for many years. Surprisingly, using the definition provided by the US State Department and the data assembled by it, before 2003 the number of international terrorist attacks by non-government organizations was declining (Figure 9.4).

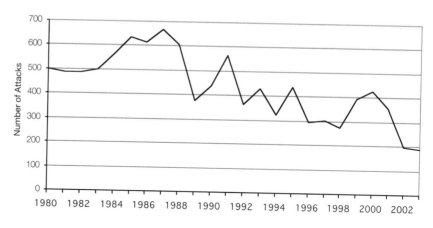

Figure 9.4 **Total international terrorist attacks, 1980–2003**
SOURCES: US State Department (2003) extending the 2001 data used in Tilly (2004: 7)

Even if the incidence of terrorist attacks had dropped from about 500 to 350 over the measured period (with a high of 660 and a low of 190), it is appropriate to say that just one episode is too much and will have devastating effects on victims and their friends, families and fellow citizens. Nonetheless, this evidence of the decline of non-governmental terrorism may explain why the horrors in New York, Madrid and London seemed to leave governmental authorities with a massive hole in their ideological and practical reactions. The event, literally in the first case, came out of the blue.

Bergesen and Lizardo (2004) fill some explanatory gaps. They suggest that the contemporary terrorist phenomenon has shifted in certain important respects and the explanations proffered have failed to capture some key structural dimensions. In terms of the shifting character of terrorism, the authors (Bergesen and Lizardo 2004: 42–3) list six contemporary features:

1. Terrorist organizations have moved to a network form. Instead of a hierarchical cell with a single command structure, the organization has become more fluid, with many centres.
2. The identity of the organization is more difficult to pinpoint. Quite often, for example, responsibility for an attack is claimed by more that one organization or by none.
3. Terrorist demands become hazier, vague or even non-existent. There were, for instance, no specific demands made at the time of 9/11.
4. There is a movement to more religious ideologies. This includes the Islamic jihadists, but also others like Aum Shinrikyo, a group that released poisonous gas in the Toyko underground (see Juergensmeyer 2003). Earlier waves of

terrorism were focused on class demands, as with the Japanese Red Army or
the German Red Army Faction.

5. Terrorist targets are globally dispersed. Rather than being centred in Europe
   and the Middle East, in recent years, transnational terrorist attacks have taken
   place in Indonesia (Bali), Argentina, Kenya, Tanzania and the USA to name
   but five countries.

6. Terrorist violence is becoming more indiscriminate, with innocent citizens,
   'non-combatants' or even passers-by being victims.

As Bergesen and Lizardo (2004: 43) go on to argue, these features of contemporary terrorism suggest that like so much else in our social, cultural, political
and economic life, terrorism has itself become globalized, making it more
difficult to control and understand. Explanations, they continue (Bergesen and
Lizardo 2004: 39–42; 46–51), have varied from the personal and psychological
(what is going on in the minds of Osama bin Laden and other terrorists?), the
group level (how do organizations frame their objectives and organize to meet
them?), the national level (why do some states sponsor non-governmental
terrorism and others become targets?) and the historical (how do contemporary
patterns of terrorism compare with earlier aetiologies?)

By drawing on the comparative and historical levels, Bergesen and Lizardo
(2004) then make their boldest suggestion. It may be that terrorism and successive phases of globalization are causally linked. Could terrorism be a defensive
reaction to the changes unleashed by hegemonic empires, now the USA, but
earlier the Ottoman, Austro-Hungarian and British Empires? The historical
precedents also suggest that terrorism arises and increases as the empire/hege-
monic power is declining. This is because the empire is no longer able to enforce
its will by economic power and consent alone. Instead, it is impelled to use military force, or the threat of military force, to maintain its position. This provokes
the terrorists, who are further encouraged when the empire shows signs of being
overstretched in military terms. There is one intriguing further observation made
by these authors, namely that the terrorists seem to be drawn from organizations
centred in autocratic, semi-peripheral states. (If you need reminding how the
semi-periphery is defined, please refer to Global Thinkers 1.)

REVIEW

Why do people commit crime? As we have seen, there are likely to be a wide
range of proximate causes, otherwise we would find it difficult to explain the
wide variety of crime rates across the world. However, there are also some global
patterns. Crime increases with prosperity. It increases as rural people are pushed
off the land into the shantytowns, where there is no work and they have to
survive by their wits. Extreme crimes like murder arise in societies that are undergoing rapid political change and fundamental social transformation.

Does crime also have something to do with social inequality or the perception of that inequality by dispossessed people or those who see themselves as

relatively deprived? One debate that has cast more heat than light concerns whether the turn to neoliberal economic policies has enhanced criminal activity. There are extreme advocates of the free-market ideology who would argue that the drugs trade (like the trade in weapons or junk bonds) is simply an example of the so-called 'law' of supply and demand. When there is an unfulfilled demand and an excessive supply of a particular commodity, dealers simply act as intermediaries, with some implication that they act in a morally neutral way as providers of services. When dealers and drug lords are interviewed, they often characterize themselves in such a benign role. In such accounts the market is 'naturalized'. It is 'invisible' and out of the hands of social actors. It is clear that if crime is to be addressed, the market has to be managed for the social good, though we are no longer certain that many states have the capacity or the willingness to address this issue.

All three issues discussed here – crime, drugs and terrorism – seem to testify to the need for a more radical break with the international, regional and bilateral agreements of the post-1945 period. The control of cross-border crime cannot be left solely to bilateral agreements, while reducing the supply of drugs cannot occur until massive transfers of resources and alternative development initiatives are provided for people whose livelihoods depend on producing drugs. Finally, the range of activities defined as terror or terrorism require a much greater understanding and a more sophisticated response than unilateral interventions – even by the world's superpower. Indeed, we have suggested that ineffective military intervention against terrorism or state-sponsored terrorism may actually signify the relative decline of a hegemonic power and provoke further acts of terrorism. Certainly, the failure to control crime, drugs and terrorism may point to the need at the very least for more effective bilateral agreements, stronger transnational agencies and, perhaps ultimately, something like a world government.

FURTHER READING

- On global crime, F. Pearce and M. Woodiwiss's edited collection (1993) *Global Crime Connections* has useful chapters on corporate crime, fraud in the EU and US policies to control the drugs trade.

- In *Snowfields*, the journalist Clare Hargreaves (1992) covers the Bolivian drugs trade, while P. Reuter has a useful book, *Disorganised Crime* (1983), on the markets the Mafia developed. Reuter has also published a number of studies on the effects of drugs interdiction.

- I. Waddington's *Sport, Health and Drugs* (2000) provides a good analysis on the use of drugs in global sport.

- M. Juergensmeyer's *Terror in the Mind of God* (2003) is an excellent account and will be helpful in Chapter 16 too, but it is, as the title indicates, concerned with terrorism driven by religion rather than the more general issues covered here.

GROUP WORK

- Study Box 9.2 on the advance fee fraud scam. What does this tell you about (a) the respective regulatory capacities of the governments of Nigeria and the advanced countries and (b) the expectations and prejudices of those falling for the scam?

■ You and a number of your friends have possibly used illegal drugs. Without talking about yourself (you may make yourself liable to criminal prosecution!), recount a story about how 'a friend' was first supplied with an illegal drug. Did your friend know of its origins?

■ Get a large piece of paper (the back of some old wallpaper will do). Half the class will draw a sketch of the habitat of a planned community of 5,000 people to be made 'safe' from violent property crime. Indicate the points of entry and exit, the defence and alarm systems and the shared public spaces. The other half of the class will concentrate on showing how the defence systems can be penetrated. Discuss later whether you would like to live in such a safe community.

■ Divide into three groups. Using the material in this chapter and extending it by reading and web research, each group will provide five examples of state-directed terrorism, state-sponsored terrorism and non-governmental terrorism. Discuss the differences and similarities.

QUESTIONS TO THINK ABOUT

?

1. How useful are official statistics to the sociological study of crime?

2. If there is so great a demand and so limitless a supply, can the trade in cocaine and heroin be stopped?

3. Show how the patterns of social control have changed in contemporary societies.

4. What are the new features of contemporary terrorism?

WHAT'S ON THE WEB

■ http://www.ojp.usdoj.gov/nij/international/global_crime.html Entering too many phrases like 'global terrorism' on your Google search can be bad for your computer's health. Look out for strange pop-ups and beeps, as intelligence agencies may be interested in why you are accessing such sites. The National Institute of Justice International Center works with the UN and, we surmise, is a kosher research institution. There are good links to pages on human trafficking, money laundering and terrorism.

■ http://www.unodc.org/unodc/index.html The official site of the UN Office on Drugs and Crime. These are lugubrious statistics, but helpfully multilingual for those who also want to access material in Spanish, French and Russian. (We know that these are first languages for some of our readers.)

CHAPTER 10

Population and Migration

CONTENTS

The number of people living on earth has increased dramatically. Although estimates vary, in about 8000 BC there were 4.5 million people. In AD 1, there were 170 million. Two thousand years later, at the end of the twentieth century, there were about 6,000 million (6 billion). Moreover, despite high infant mortality rates in poor countries, disease, poverty, famine and the spread of the HIV virus, their numbers are rising considerably or steeply, depending on certain assumptions. In this chapter, we explain how we measure population growth and whether fears of overpopulation are exaggerated. We also investigate what conditions and policies might serve to reduce population growth.

Steep rises in birth rates are normally found in agricultural societies and rural areas. The spectacular growth of urban populations is as much the result of migration to cities as increasing family sizes. High levels of internal migration are often followed by increases in international migration. Although the number of global migrants is small in relation to national migrants, their presence often provokes frenzied bursts of xenophobia in receiving countries. What new forms has international migration taken and what have been the reactions to this supposed 'threat'? Is it possible to 'manage' migration in the global interest?

▪▪▪▪▪▪▪▪▪ THE FEAR OF OVERPOPULATION

Of all global problems, fear of overpopulation is possibly the most prevalent concern of ordinary citizens. The rapid growth in the world's population has been a matter of fierce debate since at least Thomas Malthus (Figure 10.1), an English Anglican pastor, published his *Essay on the Principle of Population* anonymously in 1798, when the world's population was then less than one-ninth its current size. The book was highly influential in the nineteenth century – perhaps as important as the writings of the French revolutionaries. It strongly informed the thought of Herbert Spencer (a major early British sociologist) and also influenced Charles Darwin (Figure 10.2) and the Social Darwinists. In the twentieth century, Malthusian ideas permeated through the work of the eugenicists (who wanted to produce a better class of person through selective breeding) and eventually into contemporary discussions of overpopulation in the light of the earth's fragile ecological balance.

Malthus attracted as many enemies as he did friends and followers. Karl Marx bitterly attacked his ideas and mocked him for advocating population restraint while having an indecent number of children himself. According to Nicholls (1995: 324), Marx maliciously misrepresented Malthus while pretending merely to summarize his views. Marx wrote: 'Since [as Malthus argues] population is constantly tending to overtake the means of subsistence, charity is folly, a public encouragement of poverty. The state can therefore do nothing but leave the poor to their fate and, at the most, make death easy for them.' Nicholls' (1995) view of Malthus is more sympathetic, though he does not dispute that Malthus was part of the conservative reaction to the French Revolution and was responding to the threat to family and property that certain revolutionary ideas foretokened.

Malthus thought that a breakdown of the old social order would accelerate a natural tendency for population to grow faster than food supply. His statistical calculations were simple, his basic notion being that food supply would grow arithmetically (as in 1→2→3→4), whereas population would grow geometrically (as in 1→2→4→8). He thought that the desire for sexual intercourse and the level of human fertility were likely to be constant. We now know that considerable variations in fertility can be caused, for example, by shifts in cultural norms, patterns of disease, birth control measures and increased affluence, but Malthus had made a reasonable assumption at the end of the eighteenth century. Because of his assumption of constancy, Malthus reasoned that the only way population growth could be halted was through the painful sanction of famine.

Figure 10.1 **Thomas Robert Malthus (1766–1834), prophet of doom?**
Was famine finally going to halt a population too large for the world's resources?
Undated engraving by J. Linnell

Figure 10.2 **Charles Robert Darwin (1809–82) in his middle age**
His work on natural selection was used by the social Darwinists to justify eugenic ideas.

Nicholls shows that in several important respects, Malthus's contribution was subtler than Marx and his other detractors admitted:

- In second and subsequent editions of his Essay, Malthus accepted that moral restraint (abstinence) and later marriage would impose additional constraints on overpopulation, short of famine.
- He was not a 'zero-growth' theorist and believed that it was a religious duty to populate the world. He even lamented 'the present scanty population of the earth'.
- He thought emigration could help to match population to resources.
- He was not, as Marx said, against all forms of state intervention or the enemy

of the working class. Indeed, he supported the early socialist Robert Owen in his attempts to promote legislation to limit the use of child labour in the cotton industry.

Despite this corrective by Nicholls, there is no doubt that the expression 'Malthusian', which is now back in fashion, is being used to signify concern about the imbalance between population and resources. This discrepancy can only be resolved, so Malthusians say, by famine or other forms of severe social breakdown. Was Malthus right? In three areas, he was not:

1. His crude statistical calculations assumed the doubling of the European population every 25 years. In fact, as historical demographers have pointed out, the population doubled only after each 50 years (approximately) since 1800 and is now tapering off.
2. War and disease proved more effective means of birth control than famine. For example, the heavy losses of young men in the First World War seriously slowed down population growth in France and the UK and led to pro-natalist policies in France, while the influenza pandemic of 1918–19 killed somewhere between 20 and 40 million people.
3. The growth in European agriculture has more than kept pace with the growth in population. This is also true of much of Asia, with the partial exception of India.

Despite these major flaws in his analysis, Malthusian ideas have a nasty way of resurfacing, even in the most unlikely settings. Let us take a few examples:

1. A crude version of the Malthusian message provides ammunition to attack particular sections of the population. At various times, there have been accusations that the working classes 'breed like rabbits', or that Africans, Chinese, or other peoples or categories of people are procreating in disproportionate numbers. This form of discriminatory Malthusianism was demonstrated by the eugenics movement, which promoted procreation among a favoured few. A similar logic, in more extreme versions, justified the Aryan breeding programme of the Nazis and the policies of the apartheid regime: covert sterilization for blacks, pro-natalism for whites.
2. Following a newspaper exposé in 1997, it was revealed that in addition to Nazi Germany, the authorities in Denmark, Norway, Estonia, Finland, Sweden and one of the Swiss cantons had sanctioned the practice of enforced sterilization. Between 1934 and 1976, more than 40,000 Norwegians, 6,000 Danes and 60,000 Swedes, mainly women, were sterilized. As late as 1953, and in a country renowned for being socially progressive, the Swedish National Board of Health decided to sterilize a 16-year-old boy, 'Nils', against his wishes, on the grounds that he was 'a sexually precocious mixed type'. A 'mixed type' meant that, according to the wall charts supplied by the State Institute of Racial Biology, he was not racially pure (*Guardian*, 3 September 1997).

3. The population question is also being coupled with ecological issues. This is an important aspect of global thinking, best represented by the idea of Spaceship Earth – a vulnerable ball floating in universal space. The earth is seen as an integrated living system, with each living part interacting in a set of interlocking relationships and forms of exchange, one with another. However, this is a closed and finite system existing only in the biosphere (a thin skin of earth, water and atmosphere). It has a limited and precarious life. If overpopulation disrupts this system, so it is argued, we will plunge into a self-destructive mode. In this kind of thinking, the sanctity of human life, which is at the heart of so much religious and ethical thought, is subordinated to what is regarded as the greater good of the planet.

UNDERSTANDING POPULATION GROWTH

From our examples above, we can see that Malthusian arguments are based on a complex mixture of science (perhaps 'perverted science'), surmise and prejudice. It is difficult to oppose speculation and uninformed opinion without a systematic means of investigating the population issue. To do this fully, sociologists need to be aware of the basic toolkit of demographers (demographers deal with the size, composition, distribution of, and changes to, populations). Here we will mention just a few of the elements that go into the calculations:

■ *The crude birth rate:* This measures the number of live births per 1,000 members of a population in a given year. The US (2005) figure was 14.1 (down by 12.4 since 1947). The Kenyan rate was 53.8 in the mid-1980s. The sharp drop seen in the USA is even more evident in other advanced countries, for example the German rate is 8.3 (2005).
■ *The fertility rate:* This computes the number of live births per woman over her lifetime and is another, perhaps more intuitive, way to measure population. It takes a fertility rate of a little more than 2.0 for a population in a developed country to replace itself (because some children predecease their now infertile parents). The fertility rate has dropped from 3.8 in 1947 to 1.8 in the mid-1980s in the USA, and more dramatically in Western Europe. France and Italy (1.2) showed very low fertility rates in the 1990s. Singapore, interestingly, was also at 1.2 in the mid-1990s.
■ *The crude death rate:* This is an important way of correcting growth assumptions derived from the two calculations above. In the USA (2005), it was 8.2 per 1,000 of the population. By comparison, Chad, a poor country in West Africa, had a death rate of 44.1 per 1,000 in the late 1980s, a situation made worse by famine and civil war.
■ Closely related to the death rate is the *infant mortality rate* (IMR): This is the number of deaths among infants aged below one year per 1,000 of the infant population. Finland, Japan and Sweden have low IMRs (about 6.0), the USA has 10–11; while in the worst years of famine in Ethiopia, it was 229. The IMR and subsequent child deaths are particularly significant in determining fertility

behaviour. If there is a good chance that your child will die, it is not unreasonable that you will seek to have more children to ensure against that contingency.

Although a heavy reliance on statistical methods sometimes alarms those sociology students without quantitative backgrounds, it is important to understand the results, if not all the means, of statistical research. This is because demographers can produce powerful sociological data. The data are not powerful in the sense that they record something dramatic – a civil war, a strike, a prison riot, or a revolt against the poll tax. However, if we measure and project long-term changes in healthcare, income, social behaviour, fertility choices, personal security, levels of pollution and many other factors, we can infer complex, perhaps dangerous and, sometimes, contradictory outcomes.

To return to the issue of population, it would be foolish to deny that population growth projections provide some cause for concern. Recent data for 2002 provided by the UN Population Division – and available from the UK government Ministry of Defence (2005) – suggest that even if we take their lowest projection for overall world population growth, the latter is due to grow to at least 7,600 million by the year 2030. In stark contrast, the highest projected rate would give a world population of around 9,300 million, also by 2030. If population growth occurs at this highest rate, it is likely to have severe effects on food supply, urban management, crime, security, health and social support for the poor.

It is all too easy to forget that projections do not constitute a certainty, but rather act as a credible warning of what might happen. Present trend projections are often wrong, sometimes because people change their conduct in response to earlier plausible warnings. For example, the most crucial counter-argument to that of the neo-Malthusians is that the annual growth rate of the world's population has slowed from 2.2 per cent in 1963, to 1.5 per cent in 1992. On the basis of these trends, data supplied by the US Census Bureau for 2002, again available from the UK government Ministry of Defence (2005), suggest a projected drop to 0.4 per cent in 2050, a rapid downward trend in demographic terms.

Country studies also provide grounds for the view that population growth can be slowed, namely that the low variant of world population growth provided by the UN Population Division, and cited above, provides a perfectly possible forecast for 2030. The successful NICs (like Singapore) show a rapidly diminishing birth rate in conformity with those of the wealthy Western countries. There also seems no reason to suppose that religion interferes unduly with this pattern, as the cases of Catholic Italy and urban Latin America show.

THE WORLD'S POPULATION: CAUSE FOR CONCERN?

There are a number of principal findings by demographers and sociologists in respect of population growth:

1. A consistent result is that economic prosperity is the most powerful predictor of a reduced birth rate in all countries. With better health facilities, the IMR and child deaths decline, so there is less need for 'insurance children'. With adequate benefit systems, pensions and welfare, parents are less dependent on children for support in old age (though this will cause other problems), so they do not need to have so many of them. For individuals and families, prosperity rises with fewer children. Acquisitions of clothing, leisure, travel and holidays are enhanced and there is a cultural shift away from children towards consumption.

2. Increased prosperity is usually marked by an increased number of women entering the labour market, often in their child-bearing years. If women have careers or hold jobs, the band of years where the greatest fertility arises is reduced. The improvement of women's status, including greater opportunities in education, also reduces family size.

3. Birth control measures work less efficiently than economic prosperity. Proponents of birth control are often victims of the 'technological fallacy', the idea that people will use a technology if they are properly informed. This takes little account of the fact that they will ignore the message if they want to do something else. It also takes little account of human inventiveness. Procreation and sexual gratification are separated in the minds of all peoples; it is quite possible to have the latter without the pill, condoms, the coil and the rest of the technological package.

4. In developed countries, the main demographic problem is the low birth rate, which in the absence of high rates of immigration can have a marked effect on the social pyramid. It moves from its normal pyramid shape, through a Christmas tree shape, oak tree shape and finally to an inverted pyramid over the course of about 120 years. Young people predominate at the beginning of the period but gradually elderly people (with their greater health needs and often inadequate pensions) have to be supported by a smaller and smaller number of people of working age.

5. A number of studies in the USA have shown that within one generation, and certainly two, people who migrate from poor to rich countries rapidly conform to the birth-rate patterns of their adopted homes.

We have noted the argument that unbridled population growth could damage the earth's delicate ecology. But we have to be cautious about two aspects of this proposition. First, there have always been doomsday merchants proclaiming the end of the world. The scientific evidence of ecological fragility has to be separated from the emotional commitment to doomsday thinking by people whose fear and emotions are stronger than their reason. Second, as in many areas where science and politics overlap, there are disturbing signs of the development of a fanatical minority of pro-ecologists. In 1997 in Washington State, USA, loggers were killed with bows and arrows in an attempt to stop them cutting down trees. (This sort of conduct is sometimes described as 'ecological fascism'.)

There are also clear ethical limits to population control measures. Most people would agree that civil war, ethnic cleansing, compulsory sterilization and gas chambers are morally unacceptable. A couple of other practices that have been widely used are at the least morally dubious. Doctors used the first in the 1970s and 1980s in a number of countries (including Sweden, South Africa and the UK). They sought to persuade mothers at the vulnerable moment when they gave birth that sterilization was medically necessary or desirable. The second, used by the government of India in the 1970s but now abandoned, was to promote sterilization by bribing people with goods (like a radio) or money. Not only are these practices ethically questionable, there is considerable evidence that they do not work, or work only in a fragmentary way. Questions of population growth have to be set in the context of environmental degradation, political conflict, land reform and food security (see Chapter 8). Food producers and urban workers need adequate security (Where is my next meal coming from?), political stability (Will my family have a future?) and healthcare (Are my children likely to survive?). With these elements guaranteed, sometimes at quite low levels of income or service provision, birth rates are likely to continue to decline.

WHERE DO THEY ALL GO? URBANIZATION AND INTERNAL MIGRATION

Despite good grounds for assuming that population growth can be contained, the sheer weight of numbers in some countries creates concern. If there is little or no food for the rural populace to eat, where do they all go? The bulk of population growth is, of course, absorbed by the burgeoning cities in the developing world. Even conservative projections show that by 2010 the majority of the world's population will be urbanized. The speed of this development is unprecedented. Measuring urbanization as 'over 50 per cent of a population living in cities':

- in 1850, no country could be described as urban
- in 1900, only one could, Great Britain
- in 1970, nearly all advanced nations were urbanized
- again in 1970, 50 cities had over one million inhabitants
- in 2000, 254 cities had populations over one million people.

Crowded living quarters, tin and cardboard shantytowns (called *favelas* and *barrios* in Latin America) often disfigure many cities. At their worst, these settlements deteriorate into unhealthy, crime-ridden urban slums. Fortunately, some sociologists have observed more positive outcomes to these 'irregular settlements'. Particularly in Latin America, residents have sought to improve their dwellings and have been successful in persuading the municipal authorities to provide electricity, rubbish collections, schools and health clinics. Others of these new urbanites have continued to effect links – in their population behaviour and other social conduct – with their old villages and the countryside. We therefore witness a dual phenomenon – urbanization without industrialization and urbanization without adequate employment.

Internal migration to the urban areas was driven historically not only by population growth but by land enclosures and the need for industrial labour. While these factors still operate, nowadays we must add the demand for energy (especially hydroelectric power), the green revolution and genetically modified (GM) crops, the provision of wildlife parks and conservation areas, and the commercialization of planting, logging, cropping and packing ('field factories'). All these factors have led to the massive displacement of rural populations from the land. India and China, where one-third of the world's inhabitants are found, are the key countries involved, but others include Nigeria, Brazil, Indonesia, South Africa and Mexico.

Let us focus particularly on two cases, each with its particular dynamics, China and Mexico. In China, the commercialization of agriculture has been shifting millions off the land each year. To the casual observer, China seems to have inexhaustible supplies of rural labour, fortunately mostly absorbed by its thriving, supercharged manufacturing base in southern China. However, according to one speculative scenario (Harris 2004: 5), China might even run out of labour or expand abroad:

> [China] is now the third largest trader in the world and has overtaken Japan. This has happened in the space of twenty years, and particularly in two regions – the Pearl River Delta (PRD) and the Yangtze Delta. The PRD is already running out of labour and has a shortfall of two million workers. To compete with the Yangtze Delta region the PRD will have to look eastwards for its workers, first to other Chinese provinces and then perhaps to sub-Saharan Africa. The end of the Multi-Fibre Agreement in 2005 may encourage Chinese manufacturers to move abroad rather than pay higher wages at home.

Our second example is Mexico, where, in addition to the factors already mentioned impelling rural–urban migration, the rate of internal migration was accelerated (paradoxically) by the attempt to throttle international migration across the Rio Grande from Mexico to the USA. The idea was elegant. US and other international firms would be encouraged to locate just south of the border separating the two countries. The corporations would reduce their labour costs, the goods would be imported to the USA duty-free, Mexico would reduce its unemployment rate and, because Mexicans now had jobs, there would be less incentive for them to emigrate, usually illegally, to the USA.

At first all went well. By 1975, 800 plants had been established, hiring 67,000 workers. In 1995, 20 years later, employment had rocketed to 640,000. However, the border towns of northern Mexico became swollen with more and more Mexican migrants from central and northern states in the Mexican hinterland who were attracted by the prospects of employment in the new 'honey pot'. As Caneles (1999: 1) noted, by 1990 the previously sleepy border towns of Tijuana, Mexicali, Nogales, Ciudad Juárez, Nuevo Laredo, Reynosa and Matamoros suddenly grew, generating 'a number of serious urban problems, including a lack of drinking water, inadequate sewage services, substandard housing, insufficient garbage disposal, and air and water pollution, as well as diverse negative environmental impacts outside city boundaries'. The idea that the Border Industrialization Program (as it was called) would staunch the flow of illegal Mexican workers to the USA was also confounded. Not only did the programme attract more migrants than could possibly be employed but, until recent years, the plants also normally employed young females who were entering the labour force for the first time, thus doing nothing to mop up the demand for male employment. The temptation to cross the Rio Grande was still there and, as we shall see below, Mexicans continue to dominate both legal and illegal migration to the USA.

GLOBAL MIGRATION

It is a useful mental corrective to remember that the bulk of all migration is internal. However, some of those who have already made the step from rural to urban areas seek greener pastures in other countries. These international migrants are an important part of the phenomenon of globalization. They take advantage of the increased interdependence of the world's economies and find themselves a place, sometimes a very modest place, in the global labour market (Cohen 1987). They are also active agents of globalization, establishing a dense network of connections between their places of origin and their places of settlement. Moreover, the movement of international migrants is highly sensitive in political and sociological terms. It is true that the symbolic and real boundaries that divide societies are eroding as a result of ideas, images, money, music, electronic messages, sport, fashion and religions that can move without people. This sometimes leads to creative and fruitful forms of intercultural exchange (see Global Thinker 10). However, the movement of people is also disturbing to many longstanding residents and seems to threaten their sense of national and cultural identity at some deeply visceral level.

If international migrants are often going to be met with hostility or suspicion, why do they continue to come? Obviously, many are simply seeking to improve their material circumstances, but for others emigration is forced on them. With increased global inequalities, violent political conflict and often the complete collapse of livelihoods, attaining work and residential rights in favoured societies can be a matter of life and death for some migrants. Consequently, illegal and refugee migrants advance their claims with considerable determination. The stage is thus set for ethnic tension between the self-declared indigenes and the desperate newcomers. To be sure, the popular media exaggerate the number of undocumented and irregular migrants, which is rarely comparable with the number of tourists and other migrants who are allowed entry because of family links or common descent, or who come in on permits, visas or work programmes. However, the unpredictability of illegal migrant flows and the sense that the authorities are losing control of national borders fuel the fears of longstanding residents. To the more familiar taunts that outsiders take jobs, houses and women away are now added the charges that they bring crime, terrorism, alien cultures and contagious disease with them (see Cohen 2006).

Global migration takes many forms. Many readers are likely to be familiar with labour migration taking place after the Second World War from the South to the North – from former colonial territories to their old metropoli, or from adjacent poorer countries to their richer neighbours. Indian, West Indian and Pakistani workers went to the UK, Algerians went to France, Turks and Yugoslavs went to West Germany, while Mexicans came to the USA in even greater numbers. In the early 1970s, labour immigration for permanent settlement in the more powerful industrialized countries of Europe and North America virtually stopped. Instead, several new forms of international migration became more evident. We say 'more evident' because they are not wholly new phenomena, rather, they gain additional impetus. In the sections that follow, we will cover the following changes to global migration patterns: the growth of refugees, displaced persons and asylum seekers, the rise in undocumented workers and the rise in independent female migrants.

▪ REFUGEES AND DISPLACED PEOPLE

The ancient Greek writer Euripedes wrote in 431 BC that: 'There is no greater sorrow on earth than the loss of one's native land.' Yet, little progress has been made in protecting people from this curse. Indeed, the twentieth century can be characterized as a century of the refugee. It is, as we shall see, difficult to get an exact estimate of the scale of the global refugee population. This is partly because the word 'refugee' is used very loosely in the media and in popular conversation but very precisely in international law. 'Those seeking refuge' are, in a common-sense way, seen as 'refugees'. 'Refugees' in this loose sense refers to those who have been forced to abandon their homes because of natural disasters, wars or civil wars or are victims of religious or ethnic persecution. In short, the emphasis is on events for which the individual cannot be held responsible.

There is much to be said for the commonsense understanding of the word 'refugee'. It puts our hearts in the right place and does not seek to make any fine distinctions between people who are in acute distress. Humanitarian and pro-refugee lobbies typically have a very wide definition of the category and seek to persuade governments to offer support to all those in distress. By contrast, the legal definition of a refugee arose as a consequence of a 1950 UN Resolution, which was later incorporated in the 1951 Geneva Convention and the 1967 Bellagio protocol, both of which were signed by many countries. In paraphrase, protection was to be extended to people outside their country of nationality because of a well-founded fear of persecution by reason of race, religion, nationality and political opinion or membership of a particular social group. This definition sounded – and indeed was – very generous in spirit, but it was made clear that the determination of who was, and who was not, a refugee was very much in the hands of the receiving state. Unfortunately, this gave a virtual carte blanche to government officials and politicians, or whoever sought to narrow the grounds for admission and recognition.

The global scale of refugee flows in the twentieth century can be indicated in this quick historical overview and summarized in five points (Zolberg et al. 1989):

■ About 9.5 million refugees arose as a result of the unsettled conditions of the First World War, followed by the revolutionary upsurges in Germany and Russia.

■ The Nazi threat to the Jews and Gypsies generated another wave of refugees. The historical evidence is now convincing that Hitler's initial plan was expulsion, not annihilation. However, when it became clear that most countries were refusing entry to the refugees, Hitler moved to the final solution – eradication. (This experience provides a potent warning of what might arise in some countries today if the wealthier ones continue their highly restrictive refugee policies. Is there a danger that our attitudes invite oppressive regimes to commit genocide on their unwanted minorities?)

■ At the end of the Second World War, there were 11 million people outside their countries and in need of assistance.

■ State formation often generates large numbers of refugees. The independence of India in 1947 was followed by the creation of Pakistan. Large numbers of Hindus and Muslims crossed to their respective 'sides'. In the next year, 1948, the formation of the state of Israel produced the Palestinian refugee problem. A special agency, the UN Relief and Works Agency for Palestinian Refugees, supervised the creation of camps, especially in Gaza, where the refugees and their descendants (2.2. million people) still struggle for their dignity, independence and a decent standard of living. Their despair has driven them to commit terrorist acts against the people they blame for their condition.

■ Refugees fleeing from communist regimes during the Cold War were often welcomed in the West, as they provided useful opportunities for scoring propaganda victories. East Germans, Czechs, Hungarians, Russian dissidents and Cubans all fled to the West.

REFUGEES AFTER THE COLD WAR

Beginning in the late 1970s and early 1980s, but accelerating thereafter, the number of refugees increased dramatically. The total number recorded by the UNHCR rose from about 10 million in the 1970s to 17 million in 1991 and then to a record 27 million in 1995, before falling to just over 19 million in 2004 (Table 10.1). At the highest point, one out of every 255 people on this planet was a forced migrant. To understand Table 10.1, we need to understand that the UNHCR statistics include refugees who have been recognized as such, asylum seekers whose claims for recognition under the Geneva Convention have not yet been recognized, refugees returned to their countries of origin or third countries but who have not yet been integrated, and internally displaced persons (IDPs).

TABLE 10.1	Asylum seekers, refugees and others of concern to the UNHCR, 1997–2004						
End of year	Refugees	Asylum seekers	Returned refugees	Others of concern			Total population of concern
				IDPs	Ret'd IDPs	Various	
1997	12,015,400	776,000	926,600	4,573,100	100,300	1,404,100	19,795,400
1998	11,480,900	748,500	1,016,400	5,063,900	207,200	1,378,500	19,895,400
1999	11,687,200	833,100	1,599,100	3,968,600	1,048,400	1,491,100	20,627,600
2000	12,129,600	952,200	767,500	5,998,500	369,100	1,653,900	21,870,600
2001	12,116,800	966,000	462,400	5,096,500	241,000	1,039,500	19,922,200
2002	10,594,100	979,500	2,426,000	4,646,600	1,179,000	953,300	20,778,600
2003	9,592,800	993,300	1,098,700	4,181,700	237,800	905,000	17,009,300
2004	9,236,600	839,200	1,494,500	5,426,100	147,900	2,053,100	19,197,400

SOURCE: UNHCR (2005: 91)

Although there are considerable continuities between forms of refugee migration before and after the Cold War, there were three distinct shifts too:

1. With the collapse of the Berlin Wall, a new migratory space opened up. The switch by the former Soviet Union and its allies to a policy of open borders meant that Western countries were confronted with a large number of unwelcome migrants. Where there was a policy of welcoming co-ethnic immigrants – in Israel, Greece and Germany – no great problem arose. Elsewhere, immigration laws designed to keep people out replaced the Berlin Wall designed to keep people in. With the end of the Cold War, the political refugees of yesteryear became the economic migrants of today.
2. Whereas historically Europe was the continent that generated most refugees, after the end of the Cold War, a considerable number of the refugees and returnees were found in Africa and Asia. And, within those regions, it was the poorer countries that were most affected. War, famine and ethnic conflict commonly triggered forced migration. But, by the same token, once people returned to their country of origin, they could not easily be absorbed because of the parlous condition of their countries.
3. The collapse of the Soviet Union also generated Balkanization all over the former Eastern bloc, but particularly in the former Yugoslavia. The shocking practice of 'ethnic cleansing' was all too reminiscent of Nazi Germany. Our TV screens were filled with images of lines of pathetic people fleeing brutality and civil war in Bosnia, Croatia and Kosovo. In the early months of 1999, over half a million refugees fled from Kosovo to nearby Macedonia and Albania as NATO forces sought to halt the ethnic cleansing carried out by Serbian forces. The NATO intervention may have been morally justified, but it also served to accelerate the flight from Kosovo.

INTERNALLY DISPLACED PERSONS

Internally displaced person
Somebody who has been pushed from his or her normal place of residence by war, civil conflict or an ecological disaster, such as a fire, flood, hurricane or volcano, but who has not sought refuge in a foreign country.

While the causes of refugee flows have not gone away, the increasing restrictions on entry to stable countries have blocked many possible entry points. The result is the phenomenon of ***internally displaced persons*** (IDPs). This category has been recognized by the UNHCR, but is thought to be vastly underestimated. Hampton (1998: xv), drawing on extensive reports from all affected countries, claims that by the mid-1990s, there were 20–22 million IDPs. As one might imagine, most have been displaced by ethnic conflict or civil war – 4 million in Sudan, 1.45 million in Afghanistan and 1.2 million in Angola. In Algeria, the violent struggles between the Islamicists (comprising the Islamic Salvation Front, the Islamic Salvation Army, the Armed Islamic Group and Hezbollah) and the secular government have resulted in very large population shifts. A number of other countries exhibit similar problems.

In addition to political conflict, IDPs also arise from environmental changes (for example the rising sea level), natural disasters and ambitious development projects. We have alluded to the construction of the massive Three Gorges dam on the Yangtze River in China, which has already displaced well over a million people. Another important example is India, where the Indian Social Institute numbers those displaced by dam construction at 16.4 million. According to Mishra et al. (1998: 145):

> Studies in the northeastern state of Bihar, where millions were displaced by industries, mines and dams, have shown that many displaced families of [so-called] 'tribal' cultivators ended up as casual labourers, with lower standards of living. Uprooted from kin and their forest-based livelihood systems, traditional cultivators lose their identity and means of living.

Figure 10.3 **A woman refugee from Azerbaijan gathers fuel, 1993**
The break-up of the Soviet Union and the Warsaw Pact created a number of nation-states intent on 'cleansing' minorities from their newly formed nations.

With the end of the war in Kosovo, the UNHCR has been charged with the responsibility of resettling about half a million Kosovars. On the basis of previous experience during the 1980s, it has been shown that if refugees are dispersed far from their homelands, only about 25 per cent return. However, given that most of the Kosovars were in camps just across the border, the overwhelming majority resettled in their native province. The UNHCR and other agencies and NGOs are also involved in resettlement or feeding programmes in Sudan, Liberia, Sierra Leone and elsewhere.

■■■

Global Thinkers 10 ULF HANNERZ (1944–)

Ulf Hannerz is a Swedish anthropologist, not a sociologist, but his work has been pivotal to global sociology. In Soulside *(1969), he wrote a classic ethnography of a black community in Washington DC, showing both the abject poverty and the stoicism needed to survive in the capital of the world's richest nation. He drew on the Chicago School of sociology (see Chapter 17) for his intellectual inspiration, but also brought a distinctive discussion of 'culture' into play. The notion of culture is crucial to both anthropologists and sociologists. In this early work, Hannerz made a radical break with 'cultural relativism', the idea that there are separate cultures that are mutually unintelligible. Washington black culture was part of the wider social structure – the ghetto and American society were linked.*

He elaborated on his theme of urban culture in his next major work Exploring the City *(1980). By the time of the publication of* Cultural Complexity *(1992: 261–7), he had developed a global understanding of cultures, coming to the view that 'the autonomy and boundedness' of all cultures were a matter of degree and that cultural flows were asymmetrical and depended on prior economic and political relationships. However, he strongly opposed the notion that this would result in a global homogenization of culture. New transnational flows do not enter a 'cultural tabula rasa'. What they found was an internal market, a state, a way of life that could promote, regulate or prevent transnational flows. Moreover, each was part of a cumulative historical process – the imported and local cultures have each evolved internal dynamics.*

For Hannerz, this problematic confluence of the global and the local is best understood through the notion of 'creolization', a notion that was used mainly by linguists to describe languages of mixed origin. Hannerz (1992: 264) deploys the concept in a new and creative way, suggesting that 'creole cultures – like creole languages – are intrinsically of mixed origin, the confluence of two or more widely separate historical currents which interact in what is basically a center/periphery relationship'. He roundly criticized those who found 'hybridizing webs of meaning' artificial, inauthentic or spurious.

It was a natural development of these insights to look at how transnational flows were directed not only from centre to periphery, but in the opposite direction. The periphery could 'talk back' as fashion, music or style entered the global marketplace. In Transnational Connections *(1996), Hannerz showed how commerce, migration and tourism were turning certain cities into places where multiple cultures were 'on display'. Amsterdam and Stockholm – which Hannerz profiles – are becoming detached from their territorial states and entering into a category of global or world cities (see Chapter 17). At the same time the speed of global communications is able to connect the local and global. His graphic illustration is the 'Rushdie affair', when the book* (The Satanic Verses) *was published in the UK, banned in Iran and India and caused riots in Nigeria (Hannerz 1996: 11–12). If anything, Hannerz rather understated his case. The book was banned in a further eight countries, Rushdie's Japanese translator was killed, his Italian translator and Norwegian publisher were stabbed and 37 people were burnt to death in Sivas, Turkey, in protest at a Turkish translation. This frightening example serves to illustrate that cultural wars can be lethal.*

SOURCE: Hannerz (1969, 1980, 1992, 1996)

UNDOCUMENTED WORKERS

We use the expression 'undocumented' to include people often defined as 'illegals'. This is not a matter of being 'politically correct', but technically correct. Since the use of passports only became worldwide rather late, around 1914, illegal residence was a vague concept. In many parts of the world, particularly Africa, it remains so. That some gentlemen sat in a conference room in Berlin in 1885 drawing lines on a map of Africa does not necessarily make their boundaries a reality in the early twenty-first century. Ethnic groups were split between countries and seasonal and pastoral migratory flows continued. This is not unique to Africa. There are similarly permeable boundaries between northern Spain and France and, notably, between Mexico and the USA. Sometimes, states often simply give up the business of trying to police the border – so, in effect, tolerating undocumented migration.

Undocumented labour is now taking two predominant forms, (a) overstaying and (b) deliberate illegal entry (including that organized by intermediaries and agents, known as 'people smugglers'). The first phenomenon reflects the increasingly practical difficulties of managing the turnstiles that turn faster and faster as more and more people file through. Take London Heathrow, the biggest airport hub in the world, which serves 90 airlines and 180 destinations in over 90 countries. Some 60 million turnstiles are 'clicked' each year (of course sometimes by the same veteran travellers). There is bound to be a good deal of leakage through the system as tourists, students and family visitors pass through the gates. Some violate the terms of their entry and work when they are not supposed to (for example a student who works in a fast-food outlet). Others stay on after their entry visas have expired and enter the shadowy world of illegal work and residence.

There is increased evidence of organization behind deliberate illegal entrants. Large sums of money change hands, entry certificates and visas are forged and border guards are bribed. Often, travel and shipping agents are involved. An important dimension to illegal immigration is the frequent complicity of employers. The most obvious example here concerns Mexican labour in the USA, particularly before 1986. Up to that point it was illegal to be an undocumented worker, but not illegal to employ one. Coyotes (the local name for labour recruiters) commonly supplied gangs of workers to order. Stories of their treatment abound. For example, workers who had finished picking crops were reported to the INS (the Immigration and Naturalization Service) before they could draw their pay. There is often a contradiction between employers (who need cheap or compliant workers, or labour with particular skills and qualities) and the government, which needs to be responsive to public opinion. The unions organizing indigenous workers are also usually on the side of the state.

Mexico accounted for about one-quarter of the 7.3 million immigrants to the USA in the 1980s and almost half of the 1990 arrivals. As a result of the extension of NAFTA, returns to Mexican trade were predicted to slow emigration pressures significantly. However, using 2004 figures, Passel (2005) estimated that there were 10.3 million unauthorized foreigners in the USA in March 2004, many of them Mexicans. This was a rise of nearly two million on the 2000 figure, a net increase (that is, deducting departures and the number legalized) of nearly 500,000 a year. If the pressures to migrate are strong and the complicit employers are there to offer work, it seems that border controls are never going to be fully effective. Governments respond in at least three ways (sometimes simultaneously). They can turn a blind eye, to placate public opinion, they can pretend that borders are securely policed, and occasionally they can recognize reality by legitimating the status of illegal workers by allowing an amnesty.

WOMEN MIGRANTS

Feminists in the 1960s declared that women were 'hidden from history'. Generally, this is an accurate observation, but particularly so in the migration field. Many early studies of migration only dealt with 'the women left behind' in the rural areas. Alternatively, women were considered as dependent or family members, effectively the baggage of male workers. Some of this may have been justified in that males were often the pioneer migrants. However, even historically, we are beginning to turn up evidence that women were more independent actors than previously surmised. Being attached to a settler family, often as a family servant, gave one the air of respectability and servility, but it often involved a later escape to some kind of independence. Immigration law had the same effect. Take the case of Caribbean women coming to the USA or the UK in the postwar period. Much of the legislation during periods of restrictions forbade labour migration but permitted family reunification – on humanitarian grounds or to conform to international law. So women made opportunistic marriages and faked relationships.

Even if we can point to many examples of this sort of activity in the past, it is clear that numerically and sociologically we have entered a new phase of female migration. This is characterized by independent movements in response to a demand for women to enter the global service economy. Some of this is in the sex industry, particularly in Southeast Asia. Hostesses, sex workers and entertainers are required in significant numbers in countries like Japan and are generally supplied from China and Thailand. A more respectable version of the trade is in the 'mail order bride' trade – dominated by the Philippines. The Philippines is also the leader in the market for domestic labour, exporting tens of thousands of domestic workers each year to the Middle East and many other countries.

These markets are driven from both ends. On the supply side, the Philippine government regards labour exports much like any other export – a foreign currency earner. This is primarily because of the significant remittance income returned by Filipinas abroad. Foreign exchange is also earned on the substantial agency and recruiting fees paid from foreign sources. On the demand side, changes in gender power in Western countries have had a significant impact. Young women in the West tend to be less tolerant of 'MCPs' (male chauvinist pigs) and more reluctant to be confined to the kitchen and the home. The indigenous supply of domestic servants in Western countries has virtually dried up. As late as the 1920s, hundreds of thousands of British women were in domestic service, now there are hardly any. The gap is filled from abroad. To brides and domestic workers, add the many waitresses, casual staff in fast-food outlets, cleaners, nurses (particularly geriatric ones), secretaries, hotel reception staff and stewardesses supplied from outside the country of work. By the mid-1990s, Campani (1995) argued that women were now the majority of international migrants. Although the figures on this are unreliable, it is clear in migration studies that women are moving from being invisible dependants to independent social actors.

LABOUR-EXPORTING COUNTRIES: THE CASE OF THE PHILIPPINES

Let us look at the case of the Philippines in more detail. By 1990, the Philippines had become the largest source of permanent migrants from Asia, most of them women. Between 1980 and 1990, the net international emigration from the country was roughly 540,000, compared with 524,000 from China, 500,000 from India, and 469,000 from Pakistan. Migrants planning to settle abroad went predominantly to the traditional countries of immigration, namely the USA, Canada, Australia and New Zealand. By the early 1990s, Abella (1993) estimated that net settler emigration from the Philippines would reach another 580,000 by 2000. These estimates proved too conservative, with official estimates showing a stock in excess of 2.8 million permanent emigrants (Table 10.2).

Far larger numbers of Filipinos are engaged in other forms of migration. Beginning with the waves of contract labour migration to the Persian Gulf in the mid-1970s, the larger flows have consisted of temporary or 'circular migrants' who are not included in the 'settler' estimates. Temporary migrant departures from the Philippines greatly outnumber emigrants who leave each year to settle permanently abroad. In this 'circular flow' of temporary migrants, which has become a global phenomenon, Filipinos are also the largest national group of all the Asian countries.

TABLE 10.2	Stock estimate of overseas Filipinos by region, December 2003			
Region/country	Permanent	Temporary	Irregular	Total
Africa	318	53,706	16,955	70,979
Americas/trust territories	2,386,036	286,103	709,676	3,381,815
Asia, East and South	85,570	944,129	503,173	1,532,872
Europe	165,030	459,042	143,810	767,882
Middle East	2,290	1,361,409	108,150	1,471,849
Oceania	226,168	55,814	31,001	312,983
Region unspecified		8,767		8,767
Seabased workers		216,031		216,031
World total	2,865,412	3,385,001	1,512,765	7,763,178

DEFINITIONS: (a) Permanent: immigrants or legal permanent residents abroad whose stay does not depend on work contracts. (b) Temporary: persons whose stay overseas is employment related and who are expected to return at the end of their work contracts. (c) Irregular: those not properly documented or without valid residence or work permits, or who are overstaying in a foreign country.

SOURCE: Prepared by the Commission on Filipinos Overseas using sources covering 192 countries/territories. See www.poea.gov.ph

Pressures to emigrate are apparent across the social structure in the Philippines. In 1986, during the depths of the economic crisis, 277,000 college graduates were unemployed, together with another 284,000 who had some college education. Real wages had been deteriorating in all sectors of the Philippine economy since 1980. Average earnings of employed persons in all industries rose in nominal terms from 1,193 pesos in 1980 to 2,243 pesos in 1986, but when expressed in constant prices, wages actually declined by 27 per cent during the period. Real earnings in agriculture dropped by about one-fifth of the already low levels in 1980: the deterioration was slightly less severe in the services sector (Abella 1993).

While real family earnings declined in the Philippines, those in the more dynamic countries of East Asia rose dramatically, creating the kinds of income differentials that help to propel migration. Per capita incomes in the Asian NICs (Hong Kong, Taiwan, Korea and Singapore) rose by 6–7 per cent a year between 1965 and 1988, and by over 4 per cent a year in Malaysia and Thailand over the same period. Average wages in Japan and Taiwan are now over ten times and seven times respectively those in the Philippines. For most Filipino families, Abella (1993) continues, emigration is therefore a rational response to the state's inability to generate growth and employment within the country. The Filipino family has become 'transnational' in an effort to protect itself from declining real incomes and standards of living. Emigration is associated with the family's plans for investment in education and the acquisition of land and housing. Increased international mobility imparted a global dimension to what would otherwise be an internal reallocation of family labour to minimize risks. Since opportunities for complete relocation of a family in the more affluent countries are limited, many have opted for the only avenue possible by sending one or more family members abroad. Remittances of the migrants are evidently an important element of this adjustment mechanism, since the family is still attempting to maximize the welfare (or minimize the risk) of the core household at home through migration.

Agostinelli (1991) draws attention to another feature of migratory flows from the Philippines, namely the proliferation of contract recruitment agencies, suggesting that: 'It is the omnipresent intermediation of recruitment agencies that feeds the growing "commercialization of migration" from the Philippines and other South Asian countries to the Middle East' (Agostinelli 1991: 19). While in the early 1970s, recruiters for overseas employment were virtually unknown, the share of labour migration accounted for by recruitment agencies in the Philippines was 72.4 per cent in 1977, 82.2 per cent in 1980 and 96.6 per cent in 1985. The number of legally operating private recruitment agencies rose from 4 in 1976, to 650 in 1980 and 964 in 1985.

Family strategies and the activities of recruiters were reinforced in the Philippines by an inward-looking industrialization policy based on import substitution. As a consequence, there was a bias against exporting commodities. A host of instruments, including tariff and non-tariff barriers to trade, fiscal incentives, state rationing of subsidized credit, and an overvalued exchange rate, all served to protect inefficient domestic enterprises. It may now be too late to switch to a commodity export strategy, in that the liberalized economies of South Asia, like China and India (and other smaller countries like Vietnam), have the comparative advantage of cheaper labour and have established global dominance in many niches.

In summary, a number of complementary factors have reinforced the path of labour export:

- the government supports and promotes labour export
- remittance income continues to represent an important source of national revenue (in 2004 remittances from overseas workers amounted to US$8.5 billion)
- organized labour recruitment is a big business, with an effective lobby
- households have adopted emigration as one means of survival and risk minimization
- a 'culture of emigration' has developed, in which family members are commonly expected to go abroad either temporarily or permanently
- alternative strategies of creating labour-intensive export manufacturing are limited by competitor nations.

■ ■ ■ ■ ■ ■ ■ ■ ■ **THE MANAGEMENT OF GLOBAL MIGRATION**

In response to the perceived tensions arising from the growth of international migration, UN Secretary-General Kofi Annan established a Global Commission on International Migration (GCIM) in December 2003 to analyse the main issues and provide policy suggestions. Its final report (GCIM: 2005) is a model of restrained, careful analysis and sensible advice. The GCIM (2005: 10) observed that:

> International migration is a controversial matter because it highlights important questions about national identity, global equity, social justice and the universality of human rights. International migration policy is difficult to formulate because it involves the movement of human beings, purposeful actors who are prepared to make sacrifices and to take risks in order to fulfil their aspirations.

Policy therefore had to reconcile the differing interests, fears and ambitions of residents and migrants, countries of origins and countries of destination. The GCIM thus formulated a number of 'principles for action' that should guide global migration policy (Box 10.1).

Box 10.1	**The Global Commission for International Migration's principles for action**

I. Migrating out of choice: migration and the global economy

Women, men and children should be able to realize their potential, meet their needs, exercise their human rights and fulfil their aspirations in their country of origin, and hence migrate out of choice, rather than necessity. Those women and men who migrate and enter the global labour market should be able to do so in a safe and authorized manner, and because they and their skills are valued and needed by the states and societies that receive them.

II. Reinforcing economic and developmental impact

The role that migrants play in promoting development and poverty reduction in countries of origin, as well as the contribution they make towards the prosperity of destination countries, should be recognized and reinforced. International migration should become an integral part of national, regional and global strategies for economic growth, in both the developing and developed world.

III. Addressing irregular migration

States, exercising their sovereign right to determine who enters and remains on their territory, should fulfil their responsibility and obligation to protect the rights of migrants and to re-admit those citizens who wish or who are obliged to return to their country of origin. In stemming irregular migration, states should actively cooperate with one another, ensuring that their efforts do not jeopardize human rights, including the right of refugees to seek asylum. Governments should consult with employers' trade unions and civil society on this issue.

IV. Strengthening social cohesion through integration

Migrants and citizens of destination countries should respect their legal obligations and benefit from a mutual process of adaptation and integration that accommodates cultural diversity and fosters social cohesion. The integration process should be actively supported by local and national authorities, employers and members of civil society, and should be based on a commitment to non-discrimination and gender equity. It should also be informed by an objective public, political and media discourse on international migration.

V. Protecting the rights of migrants

The legal and normative framework affecting international migrants should be strengthened, implemented more effectively and applied in a non-discriminatory manner, so as to protect the human rights and labour standards that should be enjoyed by all migrant women and men. Respecting the provisions of this legal and normative framework, states and other stakeholders must address migration issues in a more consistent and coherent manner.

VI. Enhancing governance: Coherence, capacity and cooperation

The governance of international migration should be enhanced by improved coherence and strengthened capacity at the national level; greater consultation and cooperation between states at the regional level, and more effective dialogue and cooperation among governments and between international organizations at the global level. Such efforts must be based on a better appreciation of the close linkages that exist between international migration and development and other key policy issues, including trade, aid, state security, human security and human rights.

SOURCE: GCIM (2005)

Whether all these circles can be squared remains to be seen. Nation-states have yielded to many global pressures, but their control over immigration policy has remained zealously guarded. Many migrants need protection from traffickers and exploitative employers but, equally, many longstanding residents turn to the politicians to protect them from international migrants who generate real and imagined fears of economic competition and the dilution of distinctive national cultures. So far these countervailing pressures mean that there are few signs that the work of the GCIM will be accorded the recognition it deserves.

▪ REVIEW

To both popular opinion and concerned policy-makers, population growth is one of the most pressing problems facing the world. Since the days of Malthus, commentators and scholars have made grand pronouncements about the world's population. Politicians have sanctioned or encouraged extreme measures to control population or at least those sections of it they disliked. Precisely because of its controversial nature, it is important to distinguish evidence about population growth from prediction, projection and prejudice. We have provided you with some basic tools with which to do the job. Again, we have summarized some of the most important findings relevant to the population debate, showing, for example, that the growth rates in population are falling dramatically.

Surplus population is absorbed in the growing cities. Historically, it has been absorbed at such a rate that, in many of the developed countries, those who live in the countryside and depend on it for their livelihood are a small minority of the population (in Britain about 3 per cent). In other countries, particularly China and India and to a lesser extent Nigeria, Brazil and Mexico, a considerable proportion of the population still lives in rural areas. However, the urbanizing tendency is universal. Migrants are absorbed, usually with great difficulty, in the cities of the developing world; some – a small but sociologically sensitive group – become international migrants. We have discussed three particularly sensitive forms of migration – refugees, undocumented migrants and women migrants, showing, in each case, some of the forces impelling continued movements. The unpredictability and size of global migration flows have now been sufficient to create a global dialogue on whether there are ways and means of controlling and managing the volume and character of international migration. However, the apprehensions of resident populations have propelled more nation-states to retain – or at the very least appear to maintain – a strong grip on immigration policies, leaving little room for international cooperation.

FURTHER READING

- ■ Dorothy Stein's *People Who Count: Population and Politics, Women and Children* (1995) has useful material on India, China and Tibet and an unusually strong emphasis on children (see especially Chapter 3).

- ■ T. M. Dyson's *Population and Food* (1996) is balanced and thoughtful.

- ■ Stephen Castles and Mark Miller's *The Age of Migration: International Population Movements in the Modern World* (2003) provides an accessible introduction to many of the topics on migration covered in the second half of this chapter.

- ■ Robin Cohen's edited volume *The Cambridge Survey of World Migration* (1995) provides 95 short articles on various aspects of contemporary migration.

GROUP WORK

- ■ Using a week's supply of a quality newspaper (a broadsheet not a tabloid), cut out the articles relating to population and migration. Summarize the principal themes.

- ■ Talk to your family and friends about 'overpopulation'. How would you characterize their views?

- ■ List the ethical problems in (a) controlling population and (b) restricting emigration or immigration.

- ■ Would you like to migrate internationally? (Perhaps you have already done so.) Draw up a list of the reasons why you wish to move and why you wish to stay.

QUESTIONS TO THINK ABOUT

1. Was Malthus essentially right?

2. What reasons would lead you to the view that population growth might stabilize, without famine?

3. Are 'underpopulation' or ageing populations significant problems?

4. Why is international migration so sensitive an issue?

5. What are the most important forms of international migration since the Second World War?

WHAT'S ON THE WEB

- www.iom.ch The site of the International Organization for Migration (IOM), which started life as a body helping to repatriate migrants who had been stranded as a result of war or misfortune. However, the IOM has developed into a multifunctional organization and has considerable research capacity. This site has good links.

- http://www.unhcr.ch/ The main agency acting in support of the world's refugees is the United Nations High Commissioner for Refugees (UNHCR), which maintains this informative website.

- www.gcim.org The Global Commission for International Migration was established by the UN secretary-general to see whether it was possible to manage global migration more effectively. The site contains some important downloadable papers and its excellent final report.

- http://www.compas.ox.ac.uk/ One of the most important academic centres for the study of migration is the Centre on Migration, Policy and Society at the University of Oxford. Its site is generally informative and includes downloadable working papers.

CHAPTER 11

Health, Lifestyle and the Body

CONTENTS

Globalization affects health and disease in a number of ways. With increased mobility and time–space compression, old and new diseases are spreading more rapidly and often to regions where they had not previously existed. The diffusion of modernity and industrialization to more and more countries has meant that scientific knowledge, including that pertaining to medicine and health, has also become globalized. The chronic diseases associated with longevity, prosperity, sedentary lifestyles and increased leisure that now dominate Western life – like heart attacks and cancer – are spreading to poorer countries, even though the infectious and other diseases historically linked to poverty and inequality continue to affect many people living there. Powerful globalizing forces like international tourism and migration, combined with the marketing strategies of TNCs and the global media, bring seductive models of Western lifestyles to non-Western societies. The reverse cultural flows associated with globalization mean that many elements of Asian and other non-Western health regimes have also flowed to the rich countries. Increasingly, these are embraced by middle-class Westerners as an alternative, or an act of resistance, to what they perceive as the excessively technological character of much contemporary medical practice.

Of course, globalization is not the only factor shaping world health trends today. However, it does generate its own unique contribution to the incidence and types of diseases found within nations and worldwide. To unravel the effects of globalization on health, we explore the following themes. First, we examine the cultural influences shaping lifestyle choices that relate closely to the ways we use and abuse our bodies. Such themes have been central to the debates explored by the sociology of health and the sociology of the body (see Turner 1992, 1995; Barry and Yuill 2002; White 2002). Second, we consider the ways in which time–space compression and increased mobility create new, but also alter or bring back old, *epidemiologies* of disease.

Later in this chapter we examine continuing world inequalities in the patterns and incidence of disease by concentrating on how various globalizing influences currently affect the two-thirds of the world's population living in developing countries. Here, we encounter the paradox of the continuing, and even increasing, scourge of diseases strongly linked to poverty, alongside the rise of chronic health problems associated with advanced modernity.

The sociology of health and medicine and the sociological focus on the body have evolved more or less simultaneously over the past 15 years. We now offer a brief introduction to these areas of study by drawing on Foucault's writings and Turner's (1992, 1995) excellent work.

Epidemiology The study of the causes, consequences, patterns and distribution of disease. Sociologists of health work closely with epidemiologists to analyse the impact of well-being and ill-health on particular regions, classes, age cohorts and ethnic groups.

▪▪▪▪▪▪▪▪▪▪ THE RISE OF THE MEDICAL GAZE

Like all the modern sciences, medicine – as theory, research and professional practice – was shaped by Enlightenment thought. This emphasized the need to replace religious dogma and purely philosophical deductive thought with observation, experimentation and rationality, while applying scientific knowledge to the goal of human betterment. The needs of European governments from the late eighteenth century also propelled medicine's development, as they tried to grapple with the problems of a growing population and the expansion of over-crowded, unsanitary cities. The pursuit of war and the importance of making citizens more economically productive also made health a cause for rivalry between modernizing nation-states (see Chapter 5). In *Birth of the Clinic*, Foucault (1973) shows how French medical researchers, just before and after the revolution of 1789–94, increasingly moved in a direction we would now desig-nate as 'scientific'. Instead of classifying diseases and demonstrating their pres-ence as proof of the relevance of pre-existing theories – as if disease existed independently of actual patients – they engaged in detailed recordings of diseases and symptoms. They also used the dissection of human cadavers as an avenue for exploring the causes of diseases, while teaching, research and treatment moved from centres of abstract learning to the clinic and hospital.

Meanwhile, the French state gathered more detailed information on diseases, housing and sanitation in all regions and intensified its regulation of every aspect of national life – from abattoirs and cemeteries to mines and food production – that might spread diseases. The key medical breakthroughs came much later with changes such as the discovery of antiseptics and the advent of safer surgery in the later nineteenth and, in the twentieth century, the use of antibiotics. Neverthe-less, Foucault charts two key related changes: medicine's accelerating move towards science and linking modern medicine 'with the destinies of states' (Foucault 1973: 34). Thus, the profession – with government support – adopted a unified 'medical gaze' (Foucault 1973: 29) involving 'a new style of totalization' (Foucault 1973: 28). Here, medical professionals claimed the monopoly right to supervise every aspect of life in the name of social improvement.

MEDICALIZATION AND THE BIOMEDICAL MODEL

In Global Thinkers 11, we consider Foucault's ideas about power, knowledge and the professions in modernizing societies. Using the concept of **MEDICALIZATION**, we now discuss how sociologists have adapted Foucault's work. Until recently, the medical profession dominated discourses on health practice and illness with a biomedical model of illness. This made the following assumptions (see Barry and Yuill 2002: Chapter 2):

■ The body is a natural, physical entity subject to biological laws and processes. Its workings are quite separate from that of the mind or the social/individual person – this is the mind–body dualism basic to Western thought since Descartes.

■ The body can be regarded as working rather like a machine. Once we under-stand the biological laws that have caused its breakdown, medicine can provide suitable remedies for its recovery.

■ Each disease is best studied by developing its own scientific specialism, giving rise to a proliferation of practitioners to whom patients should be referred for specialized consultation.

■ A clear distinction exists between normal and abnormal bodily processes. Thus, dealing with disease partly involves a return to 'normalization'. This presupposes appropriating patients' bodies for analysis and cure.
■ Curing disease is the job of medical professionals based on the use of various technical or pharmacological interventions: pills, blood samples, body scans, examinations, chemotherapy and surgical operations.
■ Thus, medical technologies – forever advancing – provide the main key to overcoming disease.

<table>
<tr><td>key
concept</td><td>MEDICALIZATION is the process whereby exponents of a biomedical model transform virtually every explanation for illness into a physical or biological one that can only be solved by technology and science. The growth of large hospitals, advanced health technology, pharmaceutical companies and powerful medical and allied professional organizations are also associated with medicalization.</td></tr>
</table>

Certain consequences follow from the biomedical approach. First, curing diseases takes priority over their prevention. Second, this approach tends to play down 'how disease is produced out of social organization' (White 2002: 4), rather than simply by natural processes. This sometimes produces highly undesirable effects that are often as damaging as the illness itself. Problems that clearly have complex psychological, sociological and biological causes – such as alcoholism, depression and gambling – are turned into physical conditions treatable only by surgery or drugs. There is a danger today that the mapping of the human genome and advances in biogenetics will also transform all social and psychological 'problems' into conditions that can be normalized through the use of appropriate scientific/biological interventions.

Feminists have been particularly critical of the medicalization tendency. For example, historically, childbirth was managed by midwives whose long experience normally served them well when dealing with dangerous or normal births. Of course, until well into the nineteenth century – and still today for many poor women in poor countries – giving birth was always fraught with risks from infection and other problems. However, until the arrival of modern antiseptics and antibiotics, doctors were no better qualified to cope with childbirth than midwives and often less so, given their more limited experience. As the medical profession consolidated its grip on the management of disease, so men – few women became medical professionals until well into the twentieth century – usurped the midwife's role by supporting legislation prohibiting individuals lacking the 'appropriate' qualifications from practising.

More recently, medicalization has further invaded the experience of childbirth: an insistence on hospitalization, exposure to prenatal tests and scans, induced births to fit hospital timetables, extensive fetal monitoring during labour and dependence on surgical procedures like forceps and Caesarean deliveries. While many of these technical aids to hospitalized labour are beneficial, many women exposed to such procedures experience a loss of autonomy and dignity. A natural and social process that should involve the wider family and permit women to play the leading role is transformed into a lonely, frightening and complex medical procedure during which women become helpless objects of the medical gaze and technology. Medicalization has similarly invaded pregnancy. Lee and Jackson (2002) argue that many recent developments in reproductive technology – including oral contraception, the abortion pill, in vitro fertilization (IVF) and surrogate motherhood – have clearly benefited women by giving them more control over their fertility. However, 'the construction of the pregnant body as potentially unhealthy, and in need of extensive medical scrutiny and intervention, subject to intensive clinical surveillance' (Lee and Jackson 2002: 118–19) has also occurred.

THE SOCIOLOGY OF HEALTH, 'NEW' DISEASES AND MODERN TECHNOLOGY

More recently, the biomedical model has been challenged and medical sociology has developed into an autonomous branch of sociology that prioritizes the exploration of health and illness as sociocultural and economic topics. There are several reasons for this. First, the string of medical advances, rising standards of living, better food and healthcare, as well as marked improvements in the provision of clean water and sanitation have removed most of the causes of diseases that always plagued humanity. These, in turn, have not only given rise to increased longevity and a massive decline in child mortality, but they have also altered the character of disease over the past 100 years. Instead of dying of infectious diseases like diphtheria or polio, or respiratory diseases associated with poverty and dampness like pneumonia and tuberculosis, people now live longer and die instead from chronic or non-communicable diseases like heart attacks, arthritis, cancer, strokes and diabetes. There are several key points to note about chronic diseases:

1. Like heart transplant surgery, they are more expensive and difficult to deal with than most infectious diseases. Modern treatments often mean that patients remain alive but require continuous medication and care.
2. By definition, societies in which chronic diseases dominate also have ageing populations. In the UK, 18 per cent of the population was over 65 years of age by the last years of the twentieth century – up from 6 per cent in 1901 – and this will increase by half to 24 per cent of the population by 2025 (Tinker 1997: 167). An increasingly dependent, elderly population places a burden on the relatively declining proportion that is economically productive. (In poor countries, where up to half the population is often under 21 years of age, 'dependency' takes a different form, but the young may soon contribute to wealth creation.)
3. Many aspects of modern life contribute to health problems especially its sedentary nature, with increased car use, the decline of manual labour and the rise of the service industries. But increased stress is also linked to chronic

diseases, for example pollution, traffic congestion, crime, overcrowding and the job insecurities associated with neoliberal, post-Fordist economies.

4. Personal lifestyle choices also contribute to chronic diseases, for example a fatty and sugary diet, alcohol and cigarette consumption and how much exercise we take.

All these are difficult to change in the short term. In addition, the medical profession cannot easily influence these conditions. The lifestyle choices and identities that individuals prefer in today's consumerist society, how they spend their leisure, their choice of hobbies have all become especially interesting to sociologists. Moreover, not only do lifestyle choices have clear health implications, but Western lifestyles are being rapidly diffused to non-Western societies where they exacerbate existing or generate new health problems. We return to these themes later.

■■■

Global Thinkers 11 MICHEL FOUCAULT (1926–84)

Discourses and knowledge

Foucault argued that no one can understand the world outside a given language and the concepts and assumptions it contains. Therefore, knowledge is the product of discourses. These are systems of metaphors, narratives and unwritten and unconscious conventions about what constitutes 'knowledge' and how it is to be obtained in any one era. Thus, what we regard as disease, its causes and how we perceive it, is socially and culturally constructed – a product of the way we think. For example, fat or obese people were once seen as jolly and easy-going. Shakespeare used this notion in several plays, including Julius Caesar *and* Henry IV. *Nowadays, depending on the particular discourse we rely on to inform our interpretations of the world, we might see obesity as (a) a condition to be pitied because it may have genetic causes, (b) a manifestation of laziness and personal indulgence or (c) a condition to which those on low incomes, facing stressful lives and who are poorly educated are especially prone.*

Power, knowledge and the regulation of bodies

Foucault suggested that specialized discourses – modes of thinking and knowledge codes such as penology/criminology, psychiatry and medicine – associated with modernity increasingly confer power on those professional groups and government administrators who claim a monopoly of such knowledge. Power therefore has the following characteristics:

■ *It is synonymous with knowledge, which generates the right and means to demand obedience to various disciplines. Power also generates further access to knowledge and consolidates it.*

- ■ *It possesses a double edge because the disciplines demanded by modernity are simultaneously internalized by citizens and/or willingly accepted – they believe these serve their interests – and are externally enforced by regulations and sanctions.*
- ■ *Consequently, power diffuses everywhere in modern society, through all social relationships and wherever knowledge and professionalism are found. It is not necessarily concentrated in particular institutions or individuals.*
- ■ *In the extreme case of externally imposed regimes of control, citizens experience a high degree of panopticism, which means that aspects of their lives are subject to intense observation and regulation through the factory, the army, the system of policing including the judicial system and the prison, the hospital/clinic/asylum and the school/college.*

Biopower

The economic and military priorities of modernizing states require huge amounts of information and the need to control – biopower – the productive and reproductive, and therefore the sexual, activities of the entire domestic population. Again, this involves a combination of individual self-discipline based on acquired knowledge, for example techniques of birth control, and on external surveillance by professionals and institutions.

Power–knowledge under globalizing conditions?

Foucault was concerned with national-based societies. However, we can adapt his ideas to a globalizing world society/economy. Thus, it could be argued that global corporate capitalism today requires the exercise of control over the consuming, leisured, hedonistic body through constant advertising, media exposure and peer group pressure, but also involves the internalization of consumerist orientations so that individuals become knowledgeable, fashion-conscious and responsive spenders. Partly this involves their becoming health-conscious, self-regulating, dieting citizens encouraged to believe that they must be morally responsible for their own bodies – not the state – and this can be served by buying into the commercialized diet regimes, private health plans, food fashions, jogging kits and so forth provided by the market.

SOURCES: Foucault (1973, 1977); Sheridan (1980); Lee and Jackson (2002)

Another reason for the weakening influence of the biomedical model has been the critique from feminist thinkers. As we have seen with the debate on child-birth, feminists argued that women's health everywhere has been shaped not just by their distinctive biological characteristics but also by the unequal and cultur-ally determined relationships imposed by patriarchy – the power hierarchies of gender domination and subordination. We discuss these relationships in Chap-ters 6 and 20.

Recent technological developments, often shaped by cultural discourses on the nature of sexuality, human rights or life itself, have raised questions about the limits to and boundaries of the human body. Numerous surgical and medical interventions are already available and constantly increase. These include: IVF, surrogate motherhood and other infertility treatments; stem cell research and biogenetics, which may eventually cure or ameliorate such conditions as premature senility, diabetes or Parkinson's disease; prosthetics to replace damaged body parts; organ transplants; sex changes; and cosmetic surgery – everything from liposuction and breast transplants to the removal of tattoos. Parallel transformations are occurring in transportation and information and communication technologies (ICTs). These increase mobility and enable us to extend our bodies into space, while the virtual realities made possible by ICTs – like mobile phones, iPods, laptops and the internet – also allow us to extend our meanings into space. Indeed, the lives of many people in rich societies have perhaps now become unthinkable without these technologies. As Urry (2003) and others suggest, humans are increasingly complex hybrids – part human and part machine. This idea takes on added significance if we remember that many individuals now depend on implanted organic or non-organic parts, components and replacements for damaged organs.

These technological developments challenge our notions of what constitutes the human body and where its boundaries with nature and/or the external world lie. In an age of crystallography (long-term body freezing), life-support systems and resuscitation after death, we might enquire about the borderline between life and death. Sex change operations, accompanied by hormonal and psychological therapies to help individuals to accept a different gender identity, also question notions of male and female. Do the lifestyle choices that prompt healthy people to request cosmetic surgery really constitute health problems? Even our idea of what a healthy life is has become problematic. All this questioning and the breakdown of once familiar boundaries have a strongly postmodern ring, as does our concern with personal lifestyle orientations and our demand for diversity.

A final influence underpinning the sociology of health and medicine is a growing interest in the body as the focus of much human and social activity. The importance of embodiment or corporeality – how human flesh impinges on social life and interaction – was rather neglected by early sociologists because they wished to distinguish the sphere of the social sharply from that of nature and biology and establish that the former was significant in its own right. Several issues concerning the body have already been mentioned, including Foucault's argument that modernizing nation-states and their elites, as well as the medical and other professions, sought to enmesh the bodies of their citizens in a morass of disciplinary codes so as to render them more productive, healthy and manageable in the face of declining religion. We indicate below some additional ways in which sociological interest in the body has grown.

THE EMBODIED LIFE

The technological advances associated with modernization, coupled with the postmodern, postindustrial and consumerist character of social life today, make us increasingly aware of the role our bodies play in everyday social life. There are several interesting aspects to this, but also some contradictions. Everyone inherits a particular body with its unique DNA, shape, size and appearance. Who we are as individuals, our sense of identity, depends partly on this genetic inheritance. Moreover, the ability to identify and trace our particular genetic fingerprint is becoming a key feature of crime prevention, a means of confirming individual identities and a way of tracing mobility. Here again we encounter Foucault's ideas about knowledge regimes and their links to societal surveillance. Although science has minimized the threats to our enjoyment of life from disease, accidents, disabilities or ageing, there remains such a thing as the 'real' body containing an unavoidable biological dimension (Evans and Lee 2002: 1–12). The body must receive regular nourishment; it remains susceptible to diseases and, in the end, we can only postpone ageing and death.

Nevertheless, the body is no longer a fixed entity. Modernity has enabled us to alter it to meet our changing needs and choices, whether as societies or individuals, though there are limits to this process. Put another way, the body is largely a creation of cultural, political, economic, technological and other interests and institutions. These constantly influence ideas of what the body is, should be or might become. Turner (1992: 11) argues that in late capitalist societies, where most jobs come from services rather than manufacturing, sophisticated machines like robots and computers increasingly supplement or usurp the work once performed by humans. Accordingly, it is no longer the productive but the hedonistic body created for leisure that is most relevant. The individual whose life is driven by his or her leisure pursuits has simultaneously been socialized into the disciplines of spending money and responding to changing fashions, which include the presentation of the body. The ideal employee, therefore, is one 'who possesses the public characteristics of being an acceptable shape, size and "well dressed", and who therefore confirms the desirability of the products of a service-sector economy' (Evans and Lee 2002: 10).

Figure 11.1 **The cyborg body**
On Monday 24 August 1998, Professor Kevin Warwick of Reading University had a silicon chip transponder implanted in his forearm. Using a unique identifying signal emitted by the implanted chip, he was able to operate doors, lights, heaters and other computers without lifting a finger.

Figure 11.2 **The body beautiful**
Caroline Thomas, the photo editor for
Global Sociology, meets the Guinness
world-record holder for the most
tattooed man.

This powerful link between consumerism, commerce, leisure, self-realization and enjoyment means that the range of issues relating to the human body that is of interest to sociologists has widened substantially. This growing list of topics would certainly include sport in all its forms; sexuality and the obsession with attaining 'the body beautiful'; the making and consumption of fashion; ageing; disablement; food and dieting as self-discipline linked to knowledge and externally imposed 'standards' of an acceptable bodily shape (Evans and Lee 2002: 10); and additional modes of body enhancement such as piercing, tattoos, cosmetic surgery and dressing.

Finally, we are increasingly aware that the social construction of the body gives rise to contrasting discourses. These offer competing and compelling images that influence our choices. Perhaps the most seductive of these body discourses is the 'fantasized body' of contemporary Western culture that today's leisure, consumer, fashion and advertising industries construct and impose (Evans and Lee 2002). This leads many young women and men to become obsessed with their body appearance, size and shape as they struggle to conform to the image of physical perfection portrayed in the media and by various elite celebrities. With its built-in disciplinary requirements, the fantasy body contrasts markedly with the 'real' bodies of most people worldwide who, because of their meagre incomes, need to work, rear families and assume other responsibilities, have bodies that are several dress sizes larger, are considerably less shapely and are less intricately adorned. Moreover, the drive to adopt the fantasy body often gives rise to eating disorders like bulimia and anorexia nervosa. Thus, we see again how lifestyle choices or compulsions – often linked to commercial influences – may generate new and different health problems.

GLOBALIZATION AND HEALTH: EARLY FEATURES

For thousands of years, cultural and economic exchanges between different societies – brought by traders, explorers, conquerors or settlers – have played a key role in repeatedly spreading and altering the epidemiology of diseases.

Examples are numerous, with one case being the rise in bubonic plague in China and its spread in the fourteenth century first to the Middle East and Russia and then to Western Europe via the rats that accompanied traders overland and by sea. Repeated waves of infection probably killed about one-third of Europe's population and led to severe food and labour shortages, poverty and social chaos (Roberts 1994: 273).

Western incursions into the Americas from the late fifteenth century, Europe's growing trade with the East around the same time and the establishment of the African slave trade to the Americas in the seventeenth century all provided a 'conduit for the unintended spread of new diseases around the world' (Seckinelgin 2002: 110). Syphilis was originally thought to have been confined to New Mexico, Florida and Ecuador until the Portuguese brought it to Europe. Through growing trade links it soon spread to India, China and other parts of Asia. In contrast, smallpox was transported from central Africa to Brazil via slaves (Seckinelgin 2002: 111). Nineteenth-century colonization also led sometimes to the decimation of almost entire indigenous populations with no immunities, as in central America and parts of Oceania.

However, in the long term, globalization has brought some remarkable improvements everywhere. Thus, as we saw in Chapter 10, life expectancy has risen, infant mortality rates have fallen and populations have consequently grown in most non-Western countries, especially since 1945 and following the West's own nineteenth-century demographic transition. Between 1960 and 1996, global average life expectancy rose by 22 years, along with an associated ageing of populations in most countries. In China, life expectancy rose from 47 to 70 years between 1969 and 1988 (McMurray and Smith 2001: 8). Also, whereas 15 per cent of children worldwide died before the age of five in the 1950s, this had fallen to 4 per cent by the end of the twentieth century (*The Economist*, 22 December 2001: 12).

Of course, these improvements are unequally distributed and, in the poorest countries, some health indices have gone into reverse since the 1980s after a long period of gradual improvement. Nevertheless, the globalization of various modernizing and scientific influences and the provision of education, clean water, sanitation, better food, national immunization programmes against diseases like smallpox and diphtheria and the increased use of antibiotics have markedly improved health across the world.

GLOBALIZATION AND HEALTH: THE CONTEMPORARY PERIOD

More recently, it seems clear that growing world economic integration, coupled with the technologies that intensify time–space compression, has brought further major worldwide changes. First, diseases now spread more quickly. For example, it is claimed that there have been seven main cholera **pandemics** in human history. The last one, which began in 1963, spread much faster than the previous six. It also lasted longer, 40 years, because globalizing forces like the mass

A **pandemic** is an epidemic that covers a wide geographical area and affects large numbers of people.

mobility of people and growing inter-country trade in foodstuffs allowed the disease to keep reappearing in different parts of the world (Lee and Dodgson 2000). Second, time–space compression has created entirely new cross-national transmission belts along which old, forgotten diseases, and some that were previously unfamiliar, now migrate. By contrast, faster, cheaper, safer travel has enabled health professionals and/or patients to move transnationally more freely. While the case of the HIV/AIDS pandemic is examined in Box 11.1, we briefly discuss three other examples of these phenomena:

- *Tuberculosis* (TB): International airline travel, increased migration, tourism and transnational business have all contributed to the resurgence of TB. Its comeback is strongly linked to the HIV/AIDS epidemic because HIV/AIDS lowers the ability of the immune system to counter infections. According to the World Health Organization (WHO 2004), in Africa, where HIV/AIDS is most entrenched, 17 million individuals were infected with TB in 2000, a fourfold increase since the 1980s. The disease has also spread rapidly in the countries of the former USSR because, with the demise of communist rule, health and welfare systems collapsed, and because of a huge increase in intravenous drug use linked to an AIDS epidemic, especially among the young. Before HIV/AIDS became the leading cause of death from infectious disease, TB was already responsible for 1.9 million deaths worldwide in 1990 (*New Internationalist*, October 1995: 15).

- *West Nile fever*: A bird-borne disease, West Nile fever can spread to humans via the bites of mosquitoes and other insects. It is often fatal. Although global warming and bird migrations are the major cause of its alarming spread from Africa, where it has always been endemic, travel is also a major reason for its onward transmission, including infected mosquitoes carried on airline routes or the illegal smuggling of infected birds (McKie 2000: 26). Once established in the indigenous bird or insect population, it can recur annually. In June 2004, the WTO's website reported that mosquitoes were carrying the virus in Colorado, Ohio, Nebraska, California, Louisiana, Texas and other US states.

- *Severe acute respiratory syndrome* (SARS): This is similar to the influenza virus that killed more people worldwide in 1918–19 than were slaughtered as combatants during the entire First World War. Scientists believe that SARS probably originated among birds and then mutated and crossed the species barrier to animals (possibly pigs) and then humans. Although its flu-like symptoms and extreme breathlessness were only likely to kill the young, old and weak, SARS required hospitalization and isolation (*The Economist*, 5 April 2003: 82, 85). Infection was passed through sneezing, air conditioning or even touching door handles or lift buttons. The sale and movement of infected poultry across borders and airline travel were blamed for its astonishingly rapid dissemination.

BOX 11.1

The global spread of HIV/AIDS since 1980

Origins and nature

AIDS is now the leading cause of death among young adults and the fourth largest cause of mortality worldwide. It was first identified in the early 1980s but probably crossed the species barrier between certain African primates and humans earlier. The virus can only be transmitted through the exchange of bodily fluids involving unprotected sex, breast-feeding or blood – as in intra-venous drug use (sharing needles), transfusions or the umbilical cord. Being HIV-positive refers to the long period when there are no obvious symptoms but it is possible to infect others.

Extent

By 2002, around 20 million people had already died worldwide from AIDS and 4 million children had been infected. Today, between 34 and 46 million are infected following the huge explosion of the disease in the mid-1990s. Of these, 70 per cent live in Africa – 28 million people – and virtually all of them contracted the disease through unprotected heterosexual sex. The disease is expanding fastest in Eastern Europe and Central Asia and is now endemic in most of South and East Asia.

Globalization: transmission belts for the disease

1. Increased travel and transportation linked to an integrated world economy means that more and more people are crossing borders. Sometimes this is work-related as with professionals, artisans, entertainment, the media or prostitution. Alternatively, people travel as backpackers and international tourists, including sex tourists.

2. Then there are people whose work demands continuous travel such as airline crews, seafarers and long-distance lorry drivers. In Africa, it is suspected that lorry drivers have provided an especially strong vector along which HIV/AIDS has spread as they consort with girlfriends or prostitutes at intervals along their routes.

3. Migrants who sometimes visit their homeland may also carry the disease, especially if their meagre income opportunities limit their ability to bring a family to, or support one in, the host economy.

These groups all spread AIDS because they are most likely to seek sexual services while away from home and in doing so they link – and cross-contaminate – different localized social networks that would otherwise remain separate.

Other causes often interacting with and intensified by globalization

■ **Poverty** is especially significant among young, poorly educated women with few income opportunities and probably no independent land rights because of patriarchy and tribal customs. Low urban wages do not help. Thus, women in Thailand can earn 25 times more from prostitution than from factory work. When poverty drives women into prostitution, it may be difficult to resist demands from clients for unprotected sex, though in Kenya and other coun-tries, officials and NGOs are trying to empower women to insist that clients use condoms. Growing urbanism is a key factor because it concentrates large male populations who have left behind their wives or partners in rural areas, and may therefore seek commercial sex.

■ **Cultural influences** particularly affect women. For example, patriarchy and gender subordination often mean that wives must accept demands for unprotected sex with husbands who may be infected. To resist would be interpreted as an attack on male supremacy and would indicate a lack of trust in a relationship supposedly based on personal intimacy. Paradoxically, therefore, to some women marriage can bring the greatest risk of all.

- **Lifestyle** can also be critical, especially among teenagers and young adults. Even in the poorest countries, the desire to escape to cities away from elders and a narrow village life, coupled with ignorance, the lure of drugs and sex for those in search of a non-traditional, personal identity, and the seduction of designer goods that can only be acquired through risky economic activities – like commercial sex – can all lead towards disease.

SOURCES: Bloor (1995); *New Internationalist* (June 2002); WHO (2004)

One grisly aspect of the globalization of health is the present growing trade in body parts. The wealthy are often willing to pay a great deal for healthy organs like kidneys, corneas, eyes, lungs or hearts, even if such sales are illegal when conducted solely for commercial gain. Improved technology in the safe storage and transport of body parts and the inequalities between rich and poor countries provide poor people with strong incentives and opportunities to sell their organs. Because the trade is illegal, however, the transnational market not only relies on criminal gangs to smuggle the parts across borders, but also has to implicate hospitals in the removal and transplantation of organs (Castells 1998: 181). Much of this business involves the sale of organs from India or Egypt to wealthy patients in the oil-rich Middle East, but there is also a huge trade from South America, Russia and elsewhere to some EU countries, Japan and North America. Most people donate their organs voluntarily but there is a growing trade in organs removed without permission from recently deceased patients or, as in China, from executed state prisoners. We see here a key connection between global poverty and inequality and the development of advanced medical technology (Castells 1998: 118).

THE GLOBALIZATION OF HEALTH INEQUALITIES: POLICY EFFECTS

We now examine how globalization is shaping worldwide changes in the epidemiology of disease through the imposition of certain economic and social polices. Although these policies were designed to reduce global health inequalities, their impact has often been quite the reverse.

The WHO is composed of representatives from most nations and is a specialist UN agency based in Geneva. In 1977 it set a target to implement a new Health for All programme by 2000, after which the health of all global citizens would enable them to pursue a productive social and economic life. In the following year, WHO delegates also called for a much greater emphasis on 'primary healthcare', with disease prevention prioritized over cures that depended on expensive technologies. Much more attention would be given to public health education, the role of locally based health workers and low-cost preventive remedies such as immunization programmes, improved sanitation and clean water. Also, the focus should be on improving the basic health indicators, including reducing infant mortality rates and maternal deaths during childbirth (Curtis and Taket 1996: Chapter 9; Hall and Midgley 2004: Chapter 6.).

Unfortunately, some health experts and Western governments soon argued that such goals were impractical, given the limited health infrastructures available to many poor countries and the fact that probably around 80 per cent of their national health budgets was spent on salaries. Accordingly, a greater focus on specific health targets replaced this 'broad, social justice approach to primary healthcare' (Werner 2001: 22). For example, oral rehydration therapy was widely introduced. This provided a very low-cost remedy for lost body fluids where young children have dysentery or cholera. At the same time, powerful agents came to dominate global health agendas. We now briefly consider the changes they have wrought since the late 1970s.

THE GLOBAL IMPOSITION OF NEOLIBERAL ECONOMICS

Largely because of their inability to service their debts, especially after the second huge increase in world oil prices in 1979 and then the deep world recession that began in 1981, many indebted countries had to accept the imposition of structural adjustment programmes (SAPs) by the IMF and World Bank (WB) during the 1980s. These were economic policies that complied with the neoliberal economic policy agenda the rich countries had already accepted for their own countries (see Chapter 7). They included opening up national economies to free trade, removing barriers to the movement of capital in and out of countries, cutting government spending, reducing subsidies on foodstuffs and other essential commodities, and privatizing state and public enterprises. Eventually, the US government was able to impose a neoliberal economic agenda – the so-called 'Washington Consensus' – more or less worldwide because of its ability to threaten aid reductions or close its huge home market to countries failing to adopt its approved economic policies. Moreover, as the largest financial contributor to the IMF and WB, the USA could shape their global policy initiatives. Among other consequences, all this led to cuts in many public health programmes.

THE WORLD BANK AND GLOBAL HEALTH POLICY

During the 1980s, the WB became the leading source of funding for health investment. In effect, it also became the major force shaping WHO policy-making (Hall and Midgley 2004: 179). In this role, it placed economic considerations at the centre of global health concerns. Thus, in its 1993 *World Development Report* – interestingly subtitled *Investment in Health* – it emphasized three priorities. First, as we have seen, governments should operate neoliberal economic policies that would promote economic growth and so enable families to take responsibility for improving their own health as a result of reduced poverty. Second, much government spending on health provision was seen as inefficient and wasteful. Henceforth, public provision should be reduced and would concentrate on specific problems, such as HIV/AIDS or malarial control, where private medicine would be unable to make a profit. In addition, citizens should pay for their own medical needs through fees – 'user charges'. Third, a market-driven healthcare system operated by private companies would now cater for some health provision alongside the state. Here, market competition and privatization would reduce the waste supposedly typical in the public sector caused by 'overprovision' (Curtis and Taket 1996: 272–7; Werner 2001: 22–3). President Bush nominated the openly neoconservative Paul Wolfowitz to be president of the World Bank in March 2005, so few changes to these policies are expected.

GLOBAL HEALTH ALLIANCES AND CORPORATE INVOLVEMENT

Since the mid-1990s, many more health programmes in poor countries have been funded through their governments' partnerships with UN agencies like the WHO and UNICEF, and the WB, but also in conjunction with private companies. For example, the WB, some UN sponsoring agencies, private laboratories, several governmental development agencies, the Bill and Melinda Gates Foundation, academics and various companies – including Levi Strauss and GlaxoSmithKline – all support the International AIDS Vaccine Initiative established in 1996 (Buse and Walt 2002: 45–7). The Global Compact initiative of January 1999 emphasized, among other goals, the need for collaboration between capitalist corporations and IGOs to improve health provision worldwide. Put in place by UN Secretary-General Kofi Annan, this project specifically calls for commercial companies to improve the lives of global citizens. However, there is a fear that these global public–private partnerships will tilt the balance even further towards the massive powers already exercised by private companies (Buse and Walt 2002). The norms and priorities of global health provision may shift to reflect the needs of private corporations rather than those of the poor majority whose spending power is limited. Thus, although many health products may be 'perceived by the public sector as worthy of societal investment … the market fails to allocate resources to their discovery and development … because the potential returns do not justify the investment' (Buse and Walt: 2002: 46). We return to this theme below.

THE CONSEQUENCES OF CHANGING GLOBAL ECONOMIC AND HEALTH POLICIES

The effects of these policies are summarized as follows:

- A continuing debt burden, SAPs, economic recession (repeated in early 1990 and in Southeast Asia between 1997 and 1999), falling export earnings and

WB-led health policies drove many governments to cut their health budgets and in many countries user charges became the main revenue for healthcare. The poor were of course the hardest hit, but the rising cost of private treatment also hurt the slightly more prosperous. In India, for example, the higher private hospitalization costs impoverished many people who had not previously been poor (Hall and Midgley 2004: 185).

■ The demand for some government health services has fallen in many countries (Hall and Midgley 2004: 186–7). In the least economically developed regions of Africa and Asia, more than half the populations continue to lack access to the most basic drugs (Hall and Midgley 2004: 194).

■ Since paying for private healthcare obviously depends on income, user charges have increased inequality in health provision. Indeed, in the rich countries, the issue over public tax-funded healthcare as against private payment has always been hotly debated. A private system eliminates the cross-subsidy between citizens and so increases the risks and insecurities involved in obtaining healthcare. Through redistributive taxation, the better off subsidize the poor but the healthy also pay for the treatments required by those who are currently sick yet gain the same benefits when they are ill. In the highly individualized American private system, healthcare costs twice as much as in any other country and is often of a poor quality.

■ The inequality in healthcare between rich and poor countries has risen despite claims that market-driven policies would reduce it. Thus, in the 1990s, 88 per cent of health spending was made by the OECD industrial countries, which together constitute 15 per cent of the world's population. Meanwhile, the proportion of GDP spent by poor countries continues to be around 1 per cent and much more of this is now directly paid by citizens without any intervening redistributive tax system to soften the burden.

■ The relative shift towards private health provision means that even some of the most common diseases posing severe threats to public health are now dealt with by private practice. This includes treatment for malaria and TB (Hall and Midgley 2004: 192). In the case of TB, it is feared that pressures to reduce public spending on disease prevention will increase its incidence (Porter et al. 2002: 186). Moreover, private treatment for TB sufferers tends to be of poor quality, thus failing to halt the disease (Hall and Midgley 2004: 192).

■ Certain social groups have been especially hurt by these policies. People living in rural areas where health provision was already limited and women and children generally often experienced drastic reductions in access to basic healthcare. In some countries – especially in sub-Saharan Africa where the HIV/AIDS epidemic has recently added massively to health problems – after years of steady improvement, mortality rates and life expectancy began to fall again in the 1980s.

■ Women have always been especially vulnerable to health problems because of the risks attached to childbirth and their subordinate position in many societies. The latter often means less access to food, lower wages and a lack of education. However, it is estimated that somewhere between one-third and a quarter of households across the world are now headed by women. Together with public health cuts, user charges and falling incomes, women in poor countries have often responded by diverting scarce family income towards general household spending, thereby sacrificing their own nutritional and personal health needs even further (Jacobson 1993: 7).

▪▪▪▪▪▪▪ NORTH–SOUTH HEALTH PARADOXES AND DIVISIONS

We now consider how their very different experiences of modernization affect health patterns in poor countries compared with rich countries, while simultaneously exploring the growing similarities in all countries in terms of chronic diseases.

In its 2004 report, the WHO reminded us that we live in an increasingly divided world. This global inequality is vividly revealed in Table 11.1. The WHO neatly captures this division when it contrasts the world's poor, who suffer from 'undernutrition', with the better off, both in the North and South but mostly in the North, who experience 'overnutrition'. Thus, it estimates that approximately 26 per cent of children under the age of five worldwide are underweight and that malnourishment caused by poverty contributes to 60 per cent of child deaths in developing countries each year.

TABLE 11.1	Global divisions: contrasting health/life chances in two countries (2000)		
		Canada	Ethiopia
Annual population growth (%)		1.0	2.8
Government expenditure on health as a % of total government spending		15.5	3.2
Per capita GDP in US dollars		28,472	350
Child mortality per 1,000 males in first year of birth		6	187
Under-five mortality rate for both sexes per 1,000 live births		6.0	178.7
Per capita total expenditure on health in US dollars		2,580	11
Percentage of population aged 60+		16.7	4.7
Male life expectancy at birth in years		76.0	42.8
Female life expectancy at birth in years		81.5	44.7

SOURCE: WHO (2004)

The 2004 WHO report also shows how obesity now afflicts nearly one-third of adults in the USA, while an estimated 540,000 people across 22 Western countries die each year from diseases directly attributable to lack of exercise and diets high in fats, sugar and salt. Another lifestyle killer is tobacco and in 2000, 4.9 million people died from diseases related to this drug. Such deaths increasingly include people living in developing countries where cigarette consumption has been rising fast. One of the paradoxes of global health is that infectious and other diseases of poverty continue to exist in poor countries alongside the rise of the chronic diseases we associate with affluence. McMurray and Smith (2001) try to explain this in the following terms:

1. Because of modern medical technology, including immunization and effective drugs, mortality rates have declined more rapidly in the South than they did during the West's nineteenth- and early twentieth-century demographic transition.
2. Moreover, the falling death rates in the West prior to the twentieth-century leap in medical science were largely due to rising incomes generated by industrialization and investments in public health systems. Economic growth and industrialization, by contrast, have been slower to generate significant rises in incomes for most Southern people, though minorities have gained.
3. At the same time, birth rates have fallen more slowly than mortality rates, which also happened earlier in the West. This results partly from continuing poverty linked to the slow economic development alluded to above. But poor quality public healthcare provision means that many families still regard having many children as the best guarantee of help in old age, while inadequate birth control programmes and insufficient support for women have further slowed the decline in fertility rates.
4. The net result has been that in many countries the population has continued to grow in absolute terms – though at a slower rate than previously – and this has further obstructed economic growth and undermined the ability of governments to fund improved health provision.
5. Moreover, many citizens in poor countries, especially in urban areas where there is high unemployment, rely on irregular, poorly paid service jobs with limited prospects, thus condemning them to live in slums and shantytowns. Modernization processes marginalize them, while they also experience the stresses caused by disease, crime, fluctuating incomes, pollution and overcrowding. Yet, they are also exposed through education, the media and urban life to commercial advertising and all the attractions of a Western, consumer-oriented lifestyle.
6. Consequently, consumerist attractions draw many impoverished people, especially the young, into buying Western brand foodstuffs, beverages, cigarettes and alcohol, or their local equivalents. In adopting this lifestyle, they are following a similar path to that taken by many young, relatively less well-off and sometimes poorly educated Westerners but also other marginalized groups such as Native Americans and Australian Aborigines.

The end result of the last two points is what WHO calls 'globesity'. Thus, the non-communicable diseases linked to prosperity, longevity and sedentary lifestyles, now commonplace in the West, are spreading fast to social groups in the South. Globalizing processes shape world health in complex ways.

▪ ▪ ▪ ▪ ▪ ▪ ▪ ▪ ▪ CORPORATE CAPITAL AND THE DIFFUSION OF WESTERN LIFESTYLES

Corporate capital exerts an enormous influence over world health patterns through its influence over governments and IGOs and its ability to shape the lifestyle choices of global consumers. Unintentionally, the latter skew the distribution of diseases and the resources needed for overcoming health problems in poor countries. We now examine this theme through a case study of the pharmaceutical companies and draw your attention to the case we discussed in Chapter 7.

THE PHARMACEUTICAL COMPANIES

Pharmaceutical companies spend huge amounts on research and development (R&D), making new drugs or improving existing ones. It takes a long time before a drug is finally marketable. The companies therefore argue that they need to make good profits so they can generate sufficient revenue to continue R&D. For similar reasons, they also insist on taking out international patent rights on new products for a period of 20 years to enable them to recoup their colossal investments by restricting other companies from manufacturing what are called 'generic', non-brand name replicas. The latter can be produced more cheaply because the copycat companies did not need to engage in years of product development.

So important is the need for this international protection that, in 1996, the top pharmaceutical companies played a leading role in persuading the WTO that the Agreement on Trade-Related Aspects of Intellectual Property Rights (TRIPS) was built into the new rules for world trade. Any country joining the WTO has to agree to enforce these rules in their home market. The WTO is liable to fine any company or country that disregards TRIPS law. The poorest countries are especially frightened of breaking these rules, even though their populations would obviously benefit from being able to purchase cheaper generic drugs. This is because they risk trade retaliation from the more powerful governments of the rich countries, where the large pharmaceutical giants are based, and other 'punishments' such as reduced aid or the refusal to reschedule or reduce debts.

INGOs, academics, UN agencies and other groups trying to win a better deal for the world's poor with respect to cheaper, effective drugs have, however, mounted some powerful counter-arguments against the pharmaceutical industry.

First, the world's largest pharmaceutical companies are extremely rich. In 2002, the 10 largest each enjoyed a sales turnover of between US$11.5 billion and US$27 billion and this economic sector enjoyed worldwide sales of US$430 billion. Profits in 2002 were higher than for any other business sector, including commercial banking. In itself, such economic power is neither inherently damaging nor undesirable (*New Internationalist*, November 2003: 18–19). However, ownership in this industry during the 1990s became even more concentrated through mergers and takeovers and included the absorption of many new biotechnology firms researching the medical implications of genetics. This has produced a globally powerful network of mega-companies that enjoy a monopoly of world knowledge and control most of the world's market. Consequently, they can determine the prices of medicines. They are also increasingly able to influence the health and other policies of governments and IGOs like the WHO and the WTO (Buse et al 2002: 260).

Second, despite their claims that only through high prices and protection from cheap competition can they afford investment in R&D, in reality, the pharmaceutical companies spend far less on this than on sales promotion and advertising. In 2002, for example, for every US dollar they spent on R&D, the top US companies spent nearly US$2.50 on sales promotion, including lobbying politicians and healthcare professionals, consumer advertising and marketing (*New Internationalist*, November 2003: 19).

Third, as capitalist enterprises, their primary goal is to maximize sales and profits. Not surprisingly, therefore, they concentrate on developing products destined for markets in rich countries, where consumers can afford to pay high prices, and on fuelling the demand for medicines designed to treat the chronic diseases of old age, affluence and overindulgence (high blood pressure, diabetes and high cholesterol) and those that enhance consumers' hedonistic lifestyles (antidepressants, Viagra and body-building stimulants). Of all the new chemical substances developed and marketed between 1975 and 1997, only 1 per cent had a therapeutic use for treating tropical diseases (*New Internationalist*, November 2003: 29). Even more starkly, only 0.2 per cent of annual R&D spending by the big companies goes on drugs designed to treat TB, pneumonia and diarrhoea, even though these account for 18 per cent of the incidence of disease worldwide (*New Internationalist*, November 2003: 30). Malaria demonstrates this situation very clearly. It is responsible for the deaths of more than a million children each year, mostly in Africa but, with global warming and increased mobility, it is also spreading to Europe and North America. It also causes widespread debilitating illness, which reduces the capacity of adults and children to work effectively and thus further contributes to poverty. It is estimated that 45 per cent of the world's population is affected by this disease to a greater or lesser extent (*New Internationalist*, January 2001: 24–5). However, funding by the pharmaceutical companies for research on the prevention and treatment of malaria in 2001 was only one-twentieth of that channelled into asthma and 80 times less than that spent on HIV/AIDS (*New Internationalist*, November 2003: 18). In 2000, Glaxo Wellcome (now GlaxoSmithKline) launched the first anti-malarial drug produced by a major drug company for 40 years, but it is aimed at tourists and others travelling to malaria-prone areas and not those already living in those regions (Godrej 2003: 11) who would be mostly too poor to buy it (Buse and Walt 2002: 45).

A final worry about the pharmaceutical industry is that it has resisted attempts by concerned INGOs and governments of poor countries to counter the effects of TRIPS in keeping the prices of many essential drugs artificially high. This is especially crucial in the case of the HIV/AIDS pandemic and the need for much cheaper antiretroviral drugs, without which the mostly young victims of the disease will die. This situation has become more complicated in recent years because Southern industrially advanced countries such as India, Brazil and Thailand can now reverse-engineer and then mass reproduce a growing range of sophisticated drugs. This includes antiretroviral drugs that can be exported to other middle and low-income developing countries at much lower prices than those demanded by the Western drug giants.

South Africa has the highest number of HIV/AIDS victims in Africa. In 1997, it ordered the issue of a fast-track compulsory licence – which the WTO permitted in special cases – allowing its ministry of health to import cheaper medicines, including antiretroviral drugs. In response, 42 pharmaceutical companies instigated a law suit against South Africa's government in 1998. These moves were followed by a vigorous global campaign on behalf of South Africa's actions. In March 2001, demonstrations occurred in 30 cities around the world. Eventually, in November 2001, at the WTO conference in Doha, the system that allowed countries to relax drug patenting laws in cases of extreme threats to public health was simplified, thus making it easier to import generic drugs. By 2003, the WTO had consolidated this agreement.

REVIEW

We have examined some of the reasons why sociologists have become increasingly interested in health, disease and the body, but we have also linked this to the different ways in which globalization contributes to the worldwide transformation of the incidence and patterns of disease. Although trade and other forms of exchange between societies have always had this effect, the growing economic integration of the world, coupled with recent technological developments and climate change, has increased the speed with which diseases can spread and their ability to penetrate new regions. Globalization has also contributed to the changing epidemiology of diseases because of the shift towards neoliberal economic regimes since 1980, which have compelled governments to reduce health spending and adopt more privatized systems. Also significant has been the growing influence of the worldwide reach of commercial advertising, the media and corporate capital on consumer lifestyle choices. These provide tantalizing images of a Westernized way of life, whose promise can be realized by purchasing appropriate consumer products and pursuing the fantasized body – lean, sexually desirable, fit and enduring.

Several interesting but perplexing contradictions are evident. First, the body's inescapable 'fleshliness' – something that some religions associate with sin and that modernizing governments have identified as a source of production – gives it a double quality. It tends to become a locus for external surveillance by priests, governments and medical professionals, who seek to regulate and 'improve' it. But as a source of pleasure and self-presentation, the individual may also seek to preserve it through adopting self-imposed health disciplines, or concentrate on increasing its capacity for enjoyment, or perhaps both simultaneously. Clearly, lifestyle choices are central to these processes and this means that there are opportunities for individuals to either abuse or enhance their bodies and health, though some are clearly better equipped to do so by virtue of their superior access to education, security and high incomes. We have also discussed the role played by companies that target these concerns by offering appropriate products.

A second contradiction concerns the now dual nature of the epidemiology of diseases increasingly evident in poor countries. The cruel incidence of infectious and waterborne diseases associated with poverty and economic backwardness fell significantly in most poor countries between around 1900 and 1980. Recently, however, some of these improvements have gone into reverse, particularly among the least advantaged groups. Yet, at the same time, the chronic Western diseases of affluence have also become established, especially among those exposed to strong modernizing influences but whose poor incomes and education make it difficult for them to exercise healthy consumer and lifestyle choices.

FURTHER READING

- Both textbooks mentioned in this chapter on the sociology of health provide excellent introductions, for example K. White's *An Introduction to the Sociology of Health and Illness* (2002).

- Foucault is not easy to read. However, A. Sheridan's 1980 analysis of Foucault, *Michel Foucault: The Will to Truth*, is useful and accessible. Similarly, the discussion of Foucault in Chapter 6 of S. Seidman's book on contemporary sociology, *Contested Knowledge: Social Theory in the Postmodern Era* (1998), is excellent.

- Both books written by B. Turner and used in this chapter are highly recommended. He manages to make complex, theoretical issues seem eminently readable and fascinating. Try *Regulating Bodies: Essays in Medical Sociology* (1992).

- For up-to-date information, it is necessary to keep checking quality broadsheets and magazines such as *The Economist* or *New Internationalist* as well as websites and WHO reports. In book form, *Diseases of Globalization* (2001) by C. McMurray and R. Smith is quite useful.

GROUP WORK

- Arrange several groups to regularly check various websites such as the WHO's and assign each a topic relating to health problems caused mostly by space–time compression, for example the spread of malaria. After two months, each group will report the ongoing situation.

- Drawing on students' experiences and interpersonal knowledge, set up a class debate on the topic: 'Medicalization processes and the biomedical model of health continue to be more important than the sociology of health has suggested.'

- Split the class into three groups. Each will prepare a report from newspapers, books and websites to defend *one* of the following arguments concerning the main causes of chronic diseases: (a) moral/personal weakness, (b) consumer lifestyles or (c) the stresses of modern life. Whose case wins the most converts?

QUESTIONS TO
THINK ABOUT

1. How far can Foucault's ideas about the twin operation of internalized discipline and external surveillance/control be usefully applied to today's consumer–leisure society, for example in the case of dieting?

2. What priorities *should* be set by the WHO and other organizations trying to reduce health problems in underdeveloped countries?

3. What exactly is the sociological relationship between lifestyle and health in (a) the rich countries and (b) the poorer developing ones?

4. What role does corporate power play in world health problems and can anything be done about it?

WHAT'S ON
THE WEB

- http://dept.kent.edu/sociology/asamedsoc/ This is the page titled Research and Data Resources for Medical Sociologists, one of the sub-pages of the medical sociology section of the American Sociological Association hosted by the Department of Sociology at Kent State University. Some useful links, but some have been broken and, last time we checked (health warning!), one of the links had been intercepted by a porn downloading site.

- http://www.latrobe.edu.au/telehealth/esochealth/Links.html This is the comprehensive links page of the health sociology section of the Australian Sociological Association. It runs an electronic journal *eSocHealth* as its official newsletter and website hosted and maintained at the School of Public Health, La Trobe University, Melbourne, Australia.

- http://www.britsoc.co.uk/new_site/index.php?area=specialisms&id=52 This is the site for the Medical Sociology Study Group of the British Sociological Association. Not much that is directly downloadable, but the Abstract Book of each annual conference provides a summary of the many papers given. It is a little more work, but if you find something interesting, a Google search for the author or title usually yields something.

- http://www.socsocmed.org.uk/ The homepage of the Society for Social Medicine. Although rather more directed to public health and epidemiology than sociology, it has some useful UK and European links.

- http://www.blackwell-synergy.com/toc/shil/1/2 Through the good offices of Blackwell, the publishers, all the issues of their journal *The Sociology of Health and Illness* from 1976 to 1989 are available free online. If your library does not have this journal in hard copy or through digital access, this is a good resource to capture while it's still going free.

PART THREE
Experiences

CHAPTER 12

Tourism: Social and Cultural Effects

CONTENTS

During the twentieth century, leisure has become widely available to ordinary people and now forms an increasingly significant part of all our life experiences. In this chapter, we concentrate on one major leisure activity, international tourism. First, we consider the ways in which international tourism contributes to globalization. Second, we examine how various sociologists have tried to understand the social construction of tourist behaviour. Third, we show that international tourism also contributes to the growth of globality – a more intense feeling of common membership of the human collectivity. It does this by exposing us directly to a multicultural world in which the boundaries between societies and between insiders and outsiders (or, if you like, between hosts and guests) are becoming increasingly blurred.

The development of mass tourism requires those who wish to attract visitors to their sites of 'play' (Sheller and Urry 2004: 1) to rethink their own unique identities and then package and promote them as products that will, one hopes, attract people from other cultures (Perkins and Thorns 2001: 189). However, they must also be able to keep these sites as 'places in play' since, as Sheller and Urry also suggest, tourism now takes place very much on a 'global stage'. On 'that stage, towns, cities, islands, and countries appear, compete, mobilize themselves as spectacle, develop their own brand and attract visitors, related businesses, and "status"' (Sheller and Urry 2004: 8). These sites of play also bring together the local and the global and this is not without certain dangers. Using case studies, we will trace the evolving debate among sociologists concerning the supposed harm that contact with global forces may wreak on the autonomy of traditional cultures. Overlapping this, is a fourth theme. Tourism has compelled us all to become global performers, putting on presentations designed to project our own cultural heritage. This has led some sociologists to re-evaluate how we should understand what is meant by 'culture' and 'tradition'.

INTERNATIONAL TOURISM AND GLOBALIZATION

The World Tourism Organization (WTO), based in Madrid, collates statistics on the worldwide flows of people who holiday abroad. It defines 'international tourists' as those who remain in a country for at least 24 hours. The WTO includes people who visit in search of leisure and those engaged in business, because the two categories often coincide. It is intrinsic to the definition that both groups are financed from outside the host country. By contrast, workers commuting across local borders from nearby countries and visiting nationals who normally live abroad are not usually counted as tourists.

Greenwood (1989: 171) suggests that international tourism involves 'the largest scale movement of goods, services and people that humanity has perhaps ever seen', certainly outside wartime. The sheer numbers of overseas holiday-makers have increased at a breathtaking pace since the 1950s. Thus, international tourist arrivals grew by an astonishing 17 times between 1950 and 1990, though admittedly from a low base. As can be seen from Figure 12.1, between 1990 and 2004, international tourism rose again by approximately two-thirds (though it also fell slightly during 2001 and 2002 – especially for the USA – because of the worldwide fear of terrorist attacks on aircraft and tourist sites following the events of 9/11 in New York). Moreover, if the WTO's future projections are to be believed, the figure will probably breach the 1,000 million level in 2010, and by 2020 will be more than three times higher than the 1990 figure. In terms of its contribution to the global economy, in 2003 tourist earnings from all sources were equivalent in value to around 6 per cent of world exports or nearly one-third of the total world earnings from the service industries (WTO 2005). In actual figures, this amounted to more than US$9 trillion and this does not include transport earnings such as air fares. Few other industries can match such sustained rates of growth.

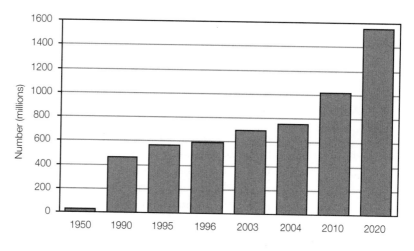

Figure 12.1 **International tourist movements (selected years and projections)**
SOURCE: WTO (2005)

There are clearly global implications to movements on the scale indicated in Figure 12.1. However, there are seven specific reasons why international tourism and globalization are intimately connected:

1. As we have indicated, tourism is now big business. Until recently it was regarded as the third largest industry in the global economy after oil and vehicle production (Sinclair and Tsegaye 1990), but some observers believe that during the 1990s it became the world's largest, legal, money-spinner.
2. This huge growth in business potential has been accompanied by the increased involvement of TNCs competing as specialist tourist operators or subsidiaries of larger corporations in the hotel business, resort development, transport provision or theme parks. By 2004, the hotel chain Accor, for example, had nearly 4,000 hotels in 140 countries, with 168,500 employees (Accor 2005).
3. Like other forms of modernization, international tourism involves assigning a market price to a hitherto free good. 'Culture' is now wrapped and sold to tourists in the shape of ancient sites, ritual ceremonies and folk customs. Even

the everyday life of ordinary people has been turned into a commodity to be sold to tourists.

4. In any single year, the sheer number of international travellers who holiday abroad has become vast and dwarfs all other comparable forms of transnational mobility, including long-term migrants, religious pilgrims, refugees from oppression or seasonal workers.

5. International tourism clearly demonstrates what Sheller and Urry (2004: 6) call 'multiple networked mobilities'. Thus, for these vast numbers of tourists to be moved across borders and their numerous cultural, biological, physical, sensuous, emotional, sexual, communicative and other demands catered for, vast armies of people have be to deployed and mobilized, along with vehicles, signs, images, money and capital, information, foodstuffs, entertainments, sites of heritage and amusement, numerous artefacts such as surfboards and beachwear and much else besides.

6. International tourism has become a worldwide phenomenon, an inescapable 'international fact'. It encompasses virtually every country and penetrates most national regions and localities, however remote and inaccessible, while it 'makes itself felt at every level and in all sectors of collective life' (Lanfant et al. 1995: 25, 26). In recent decades, even the declining, industrial rustbelt zones of North America and Europe have turned their run-down mills and furnaces, warehouses, canals and streets into veritable industrial tourist sites.

7. Unlike the other fast-growing leisure industries (consumerism, the mass media, the arts and sports), international tourism necessarily involves the mass mobility of people who engage in direct social exchanges with hosts and who experience other societies at first hand.

The combined impact of these features is that international tourism has become what Lanfant (1995: 25) called a 'transmission belt' between different ways of life and a vehicle for increased global integration. It is possible to argue that tourism may also exercise a cumulative effect that is considerably greater than any other single agent of globalization. While a similar claim has been made about the TNCs, which have rightly been seen as carriers of technology, capital and the 'culture-ideology of consumerism' (Sklair 2002), the TNCs' social impact can often be contained. By contrast, as Hannerz (1990: 239) argues, international tourism increasingly involves extensive interactions and social relationships unconfined by territorial boundaries. Wherever cultures are free to coexist and 'overlap and mingle' through transnational social networks, globalization is fostered. Many international tourists contribute to this growth of genuine multicultural understanding and the growing diversity of cultural choice.

THE INCREASE AND DISTRIBUTION OF TOURISTS

There are several explanations for the increase in tourist numbers. As Harrison (1995) argues in the case of Britain, improved standards of living for sections of the working class in the nineteenth century first produced the idea of a 'day out', then the idea of a seaside holiday at the coast. Sea water and sea air were depicted by doctors as good for you. With increasing affluence and paid leisure time, holidays and foreign travel have long ceased to be a luxury confined to aristocratic and commercial elites, as was the case until the late nineteenth century. Instead, the twentieth century witnessed the emergence of 'the holiday' as a social institution along with the 'democratization of tourism' (Sharpley 1994: 83).

Internationalization has been fostered by the rise of cheaper cruise ships and especially long-haul air travel from the 1960s, the advent of the low-cost package holiday and the attempt by ever more governments to promote national tourist industries. A further explanation for the growth of international tourism lies in the postmodern yearning to weave personal lifestyle identities around the signs and symbols associated with different leisure and consumerist activities. Foreign travel is seen as evidence of affluence, sophistication and an adventure-seeking spirit. Foreign landscapes, climates, cuisine and customs offer new arenas and opportunities for people to 'score' sexually or socially, live out their particular fantasies and assume 'diverse social roles in exotic settings' (Turner 1994: 185).

Since 1970, international tourism has become increasingly globalized. Until recently, a small number of rich Western countries dominated as the leading destinations for visitors, with the USA, Spain, France, Italy and the UK competing for rank order in the top five places. However, by 2003, China had overtaken the UK, taking fifth place after Italy in the top five. Also in 2003, WTO statistics (2004) revealed that, including China, there were seven non-Western countries among the top twenty tourist destinations: Mexico was eighth, Hong Kong – though part of China by that time – came twelfth, Turkey was fifteenth with Malaysia, Thailand and the Russian Federation placed seventeenth, eighteenth and twentieth respectively. Moreover, the combined share of world tourist arrivals for the rich Western countries slipped substantially between 1960 and 1994 from 92 to 74 per cent and this trend is set to continue, especially for Europe, as Table 12.1 shows. According to Harrison (1992: 8), both tourist arrivals and earnings by the developing countries rose substantially during the 1980s, especially in the case of the countries of East Asia and the Asia Pacific region. This trend has continued since the mid-1990s. Thus, while the annual rate of international tourist growth for the world as a whole averaged out at around 6.5 per cent between 1950 and 2003, the annual growth rate for the Asia Pacific region has been 13 per cent, while that for the Middle East was 10 per cent during the same period (WTO 2004). In the coming years, Africa and South Asia are also predicted to increase their share of a growing overall total. As can also be seen from Table 12.1, by no means all these 'new' tourists are intent on visiting Europe, North America and Japan, though many do. Instead, large numbers wish to visit other rapidly developing countries located within their own or another world region.

TABLE 12.1	Tourist destinations to selected regions, 1995–2020 (projected)				
Region	Base year 1995 (millions of visitors)	Forecast year 2020 (millions of visitors)	% Market share (1995)	% Market share (2020)	Average annual growth rate %
The Americas	110	282	19.3	18.1	3.8
East Asia and Asia Pacific	81	397	14.4	24.4	6.5
Europe	336	717	59.8	45.9	3.1
Middle East	14	69	2.2	4.4	6.7
South Asia	4	19	0.7	1.2	6.2
Africa	20	77	3.6	5.0	5.5

SOURCE: Adapted from WTO (2005)

THE SOCIOLOGY OF TOURISM

How have sociologists tried to understand tourism? First, just like any other activity, the tourist experience is socially constructed. For example, holiday-makers may score more status points in the eyes of their peers if they can afford to take their vacations in an expensive hotel on the French Rivera – once the exclusive playground of the European aristocracy and wealthy bourgeoisie – rather than in a modern holiday flat on the Costa del Sol. The year-to-year popularity of different resorts is also a matter of changing fashion. Armies of travel experts, media programmers, theme park organizers and many others cater for all tourist needs. Like prospective parents, tourists normally engage in careful preparation and planning long before their anticipated experience. This may involve consultation with friends and family, perusing brochures and travel guides, watching TV holiday programmes and buying all the necessary para-phernalia, like suntan lotion, florid shirts and camping gear. Moreover, the return to normal life is marked by various social events at which the inescapable souvenirs and photos can be displayed, while memories are shared with other pilgrims. Thus, tourism is firmly embedded in social life.

Second, holidays and tourism involve 'a leisure activity which presupposes its opposite, namely regulated and organized work' (Urry 1990a: 2). This separation between the routine, work sphere of everyday life and that of leisure and recre-ation is not new. It echoes the distinction between the **SACRED** and the **PROFANE** to which Durkheim (1976) drew attention in his study of religious life.

key concept	
	The **SACRED** and the **PROFANE**. In *The Elementary Forms of Religious Life* (1976), Durkheim argued that religious practices and beliefs require a sharp separation between ordinary mundane activities and objects and those regarded as sacred. The latter are treated with awe and veneration. They bring members of communities together in the pursuit of shared

ceremonial activities and group affirmation of deeply held convictions. Whereas the profane is knowable through everyday observable things, the sacred is known only through extraordinary experiences (see Chapter 16).

In premodern societies, the transition from everyday to extraordinary events and experiences was usually linked to important changes in the cycles of religious and social life – saints' days, Christmas, births, marriages and deaths – as well as the seasons and years (Graburn 1989: 24–5). The risks and expense incurred by travel, for example pilgrimages to holy places, meant that most poor people enjoyed such religious festivals and social rituals and transitions at home or in their local place of worship. Churches and temples were often built on a much larger scale than the villagers' houses to emphasize that they were meant to be awe-inspiring. Local celebrations constituted the nearest equivalent to what we now regard as 'the holiday'. (You will perhaps have noticed the etymological similarity between 'holiday' and 'holy day'). Industrialization and rising mass affluence have enabled the sphere of non-work to become separated from home and identified with travel to distant venues. Yet, some semblance of the excitement and anticipation formally associated with religious concerns and the sacred has survived, though it is mostly detached from its original moorings. Instead, it has become attached to the experiences we now associate with holidays. Accordingly, modern tourism involves what Graburn (1989) calls 'the sacred journey'.

This connection between holidays and the sacred journey leads us to a third interesting and influential attempt to understand tourism. This originated with MacCannell's (1976) argument that modern people living in industrial societies tend to experience life as heavily commercialized, emptied of its earlier, unique cultural content and distinctly lacking in exoticism. Particularly for those who are middle class and educated, tourism has become a sort of 'pilgrim's progress of the alienated' (Meethan 2001: 91), spurred on by the search for the authenticity, 'realness' and spirituality that only traditional societies supposedly provide. At the same time, however, 'in discovering new sources of authenticity in premodern societies, tourists inevitably pollute that which they seek to preserve' (Harrison 1995: 240). We return to this last theme later.

Fourth, Urry's work on tourism (1990a, 1990b) has been extremely influential and continues to evolve (Urry 1995, 2004). In part, he continued MacCannell's (1976) theme on tourism as the search by middle-class individuals for authenticity, but he did this by introducing the idea that holiday travel involves 'the tourist gaze'. He explains this suggestive phrase by suggesting that while travelling we seek and collect a series of new landscapes. Normally, these are 'captured through photographs, postcards, films, models and so on' (Urry 1990a: 3). Meanwhile, national or regional tourist promoters, along with commercial tour operators and other professionals, construct a series of elaborate representations of different sites and tourist phenomenon through glossy brochures, advertising and other media facilities. The tourist gaze is 'signposted [by] … markers which identify the things and places worthy of our gaze' (Urry 1990a: 47), while the tourists themselves are trained to decipher these precise meanings. Among others, Urry offers the following examples. 'When tourists see two people kissing in Paris what they capture in the gaze is "timeless romantic Paris" whereas when a small village in England is seen, what they gaze upon is the "real olde England"' (Urry 1990a: 3). We can see here that, for commercial reasons, the tourist industry is engaged in promoting particular places as tourist sites through the representations they construct and the striking and repetitive visual signs they offer. At the same time, they often create carefully staged events and fake authentic experiences, as in theme parks.

Although Urry (1990a: 45–6) suggested that the urge to collect visual experiences through various gazes was important for all kinds of tourists, he distinguished between the collective and romantic tourist gaze. The collective gazers generally seek holiday locations such as seaside resorts, theme parks or campsites where there are lots of people. But the presence of large crowds generates congestion and environmental stress – endless car parks, sewerage and piles of rubbish – and attracts a multiplicity of businesses from souvenir shops, restaurants and ice cream stalls to amusement arcades. Nevertheless, the collective gazer enjoys this melange and only feels comfortable in a thoroughly commercialized milieu. The romantic gaze is sought by those more discerning travellers who seek to discover areas of supposedly untouched natural beauty well away from the beaten track, or 'traditional' village, farm, craft or religious life that is believed to survive unspoiled and unique, perhaps in faraway countries and regions. They are more active than the collective gazers and are trying to escape from the mass spectacles and commercialism of much tourism today, while searching for more idiosyncratic, differentiated and personal experiences that offer more prospects of authenticity and emotional depth. In this way, a growing minority of tourists are seeking to break the earlier mould of mass commercial tourism.

Figure 12.2 **Nearly one million pilgrims faced the Kaaba, the holiest shrine in Islam, in prayer at the Grand Mosque at Mecca, Saudi Arabia during sunset, 27 February 2001**
Over two million pilgrims arrived in Mecca that year.

Figure 12.3 **Has Mickey Mouse, dressed here in a space helmet, assumed the status of a religious icon?**

■ ■

Global Thinkers 12 **JOHN URRY (1947–)**

Urry's contribution to the sociology of tourism has already been discussed in this chapter. Here, we consider his work on the nature of capitalism under late or postmodern conditions, which he developed with Scott Lash. We also consider his more recent work on globalization.

From 'organized' to 'disorganized capitalism'

Like others, Urry and Lash discerned a major shift taking place from the 1960s away from nationally based economies where most wealth came from manufacturing carried out in vast integrated companies and urbanized regions. Businesses were supported by government protection, an expanding science and a middle-class technocracy. They existed alongside a huge manual labour force organized in trade unions and increasingly protected by state welfare. This increasingly gave way to a far less organized economy, an economy of signs and spaces, *with several key characteristics:*

■ *Far more countries than the original few Western ones moved towards industrialization.*
■ *Capital, whether as money and shares, investments, products or components, became increasingly free from national control.*
■ *Companies increasingly downsized their main operations while outsourcing and subcontracting.*

■ *Economic life shifted towards relative dematerialization as the labour and physical content of many commodities shrank and the knowledge, design and sign content (see Chapter 13) increased. A growing number of goods (like popular music, films and holidays) had an almost entirely aesthetic, expressive appeal.*

■ *This led to the growing importance of lifestyle, leisure and consumption activities for most people in the advanced societies and the rise of the new informational economy based on knowledge and the fusion of communications and computerization technologies.*

Like Giddens, Beck and Bauman, Urry and Lash also pointed to the individualization process brought by the new economy as the controlling possibilities inherent in previous social structures, such as class and family, diminished, thereby liberating human agents to construct their own lives.

The central components of globalization

Recently Urry has expanded some of these ideas while incorporating many new and interesting arguments. These have the potential to improve our understanding of globalization. Thus, at the core of global life, we find:

■ *Massive increases in the speed, intensity and quantity of mobilities, of people (such as tourists, migrants and criminals), goods, images, money and signs. These are extremely diverse and they breach borders and spread in all directions.*

■ *Accordingly, networks rather than territories and places provide a more useful metaphor for exploring and explaining social life today.*

■ *Mobilities are especially striking with respect to cultural flows. Fragments of cultures flow or are carried readily along the technological pathways provided by IT, travel and the media, but also through migration and investment flows.*

■ *But flows also have a much wider reference. Urry adopts and applies the concept of fluidity to globalization. Thus, entities such as diseases, environmental waste, website messages, company brand images, icons and advertising images spread, seep and infiltrate everywhere like spilt liquids. Fluids are largely uncontainable and unpredictable.*

■ *Social life is increasingly inconceivable without our dependence on technologies like the internet, mobile phones, Walkmans, satellite TV, cars and aircraft. Indeed, the exercise of human agency now needs to be seen as inextricably coupled with technology.*

Consequently, global life has no centre, is hugely complex, cannot easily be steered and could move, unpredictably, in many directions. Meanwhile, the notion of 'society' is now highly dubious.

SOURCES: Lash and Urry (1987, 1994); Urry (2000, 2003)

■ ■ ■ ■ ■ ■ ■ ■ **RETHINKING TOURIST CLASSIFICATIONS**

Various attempts have been made to distinguish between the different kinds of tourists, for example Urry's useful contribution to this discussion outlined above. Another fundamental contrast is between 'mass charter' tourism and individual or small group holidays (Smith 1989: 12–13). Each basic type has also been identified with one of the two main ingredients of the now secularized and residual sphere of the sacred:

■ the escape to recreation, recuperation and fun
■ the rather more 'acceptable' desire for adventure, spiritual renewal or authenticity.

This dichotomy is significant because mass charter tourists are usually regarded as more likely to generate a huge economic and social impact on host societies. Mass tourists create a demand for vast resort facilities and services. In addition, this kind of tourist demands as a right that they will enjoy exactly the same standard of Western-style amenities as they are used to at home, from modern plumbing to TVs in their rooms, locals who speak their language and home cooking. Smith (1989: 13–14) describes mass tourism in this way:

> Charter tourists arrive en masse … and for every 747 planeload, there is a fleet of at least ten big buses waiting to transfer them from the airport to the designated hotel, in the lobby of which is a special Tour Desk to provide itineraries and other group services … Charter tourists wear name tags, are assigned to numbered buses, counted aboard, and continually reminded: 'Be sure to get on the right bus.' Given the requisite organization that makes Charter tourism a high-volume business, to avoid complaints tour operators and hotels have standardized the services to Western (or Japanese) tastes, and there are 'ice machines and soft drinks on every floor'. For Charter tourists, even the destination may be of little importance.

Like other commentators, Smith (1989: 11–12) contrasts these mass tourists with various categories of rarer and presumably more discerning visitors, travelling individually or in small groups. This species may comprise 'explorers' (in search of new experiences and unspoilt terrain) or 'offbeat' tourists (hoping to sample the exotic customs practised by remote societies) or people seeking their roots (see Box 12.1). Such groups either 'accept fully' or 'adapt well' to local customs, food and amenities (or the lack of them). Indeed, endeavouring to 'fit in' may provide much of the attraction.

Box 12.1	**Tourist development in Ghana: paying homage to a grim legacy**

Since the mid-1980s, the West African country of Ghana – once called the Gold Coast because it supplied gold to Europe and the Middle East for hundreds of years – has developed a new industry. This has involved utilizing the country's bitter legacy, associated with the Atlantic slave trade, as a way of fostering a rather remarkable kind of historical or cultural tourism. Thus, the number of tourist arrivals to Ghana grew from 85,000 in 1985 to 335,000 in 1994. In fact, by the mid-1990s, international tourism had become Ghana's third most important earner of foreign exchange after gold and cocoa exports. Moreover, it is anticipated that the tourist sector will grow in significance as the government gradually improves the standards of the country's hotels, airports and roads and invests in improving its forest wildlife parks.

At present, Ghana's most significant tourist 'attraction' remains the many Atlantic coastal forts built at different times from the end of the fifteenth century by the Dutch, Portuguese, British and French, among others. These forts had a sinister and brutal purpose. Their dungeons were used to hold the captured and branded peoples brought from the West African interior while they waited to be shipped – manacled in dark, cramped and unhealthy conditions – as slaves to the plantations of the Americas. In all, it is thought that about 10 million Africans were enslaved and transported across the Atlantic to Brazil, the Caribbean and North America from African locations. Beginning in the early sixteenth century, this appalling trade in human life peaked around 1700 but continued until the middle of the nineteenth century.

One of the most famous – or infamous – of Ghana's coastal forts is based at Cape Coast, the administrative centre for British colonial rule until 1877. Cape Coast, in particular, tends to provide a point of focus for many tourists. A considerable and growing proportion of such visitors are African-Americans. They come to rediscover their homeland and the cultural heritage their enslaved ancestors lost. But they also arrive as pilgrims mourning the suffering imposed on the original slaves. Many visitors are visibly moved, often to tears, by the haunting memories evoked as the guides conduct them through the dark dungeons.

On a happier note, the Ghana tourist industry also offers many African-Americans the opportunity to visit local people, including chiefs, and participate in ancient ceremonies that re-endow the visitors with their lost African names.

SOURCE: *Financial Times* (4 August 1995)

Other writers have also commented on the characteristics of these two different types of tourist. For example, most mass tourists have been labelled as 'accidental tourists' (Tyler 1985) who would much rather remain at home with all its reassuring amenities. However, their desire to escape from routine by experiencing fun and recreation – particularly the 'four Ss' of sun, sand, sea and sex – induces them to travel to distant venues. In a similar vein, Theroux (1986) observed that, when on vacation, most tourists seek all the familiar comforts of home life but hope to encounter an additional magical ingredient – home-plus-coconut-palm-beaches-by-moonlight. Another example of this phenomenon might be the case of sex tourism (see Box 12.2), which forms a significant part of the holiday industry in countries like Thailand and the Philippines (Hall 1992; Kruhse-Mount Burton 1995). Here, Western men may seek home plus temporary sexual liaisons with local women, sometimes even children, who appear to represent 'the quintessence of the exotic' (Enloe 1989: 28).

Box 12.2

Sex tourism in Asia

Tourism does not always bring advantages to local people, particularly in poor countries. Sex tourism is one such case. Since the 1980s, this has involved European paedophile rings organizing tour parties of gay men to the Philippines and Sri Lanka seeking sex with young boys. However, sex tourism is mainly associated with the exploitation of women and girls. This has been evident far longer and involves huge numbers of visitors.

In Thailand, tourism is the second highest foreign exchange earner. But many visitors arrive specifically for the cheap and readily available sex. Once Phuket Island in southern Thailand was a 'paradise beach', but the image soon turned sour when, in January 1984, a brothel was burned to the ground. The bodies of five young girls aged between nine and fourteen were found in a locked basement. Subsequently it was revealed that brothel-keepers were in the habit of locking up or chaining young girls from the poor northern districts of the country for the delectation of Western, Japanese and Chinese tourists. The parents of two of the girls were eventually tracked down. The mother said in a low voice: 'We have ten children and we cannot feed them all. We had to send them to town; there was no other way' (Matsui 1989: 63).

The parents sell their children to 'flesh merchants', who drag them off to 'teahouses' in Chinatown, 'massage parlours' in Patpong Street (Bangkok) or Phuket. A virginal premenstrual girl brings a high price around Chinese New Year when Chinese superstition holds that having sex with a child makes men younger. Thereafter, the young women are on a production line, force-fed birth control pills and typically serving about 1,000 customers a year. They are truly described as 'sex workers'.

Helping young women to escape from this fate is not easy. The government and police forces characteristically 'turn a blind eye' and the poor areas of Thailand are dependent on the trade. Chantawipa Apisuk, a Thai sociologist, tried to empower sex workers by giving them education and training. Some of the brothel-keepers reluctantly complied. Ms Apisuk reasoned that with better English their foreign customers would not cheat the women. A prostitute could progress to being a go-go dancer, then to a waitress – the latter a steady job with a regular salary. Some of the sex workers published a newsletter to publicize their plight and a number migrated abroad or moved into salaried employment (Matsui 1989: 66–7).

Manila in the Philippines, particularly under the Marcos regime, also competed for the title of International Sex City. Here, tour advertisements leave little room for doubt that sex is part of the 'all-inclusive' package. Moreover, the prostitutes are only minor beneficiaries. The industry contains many 'middlemen', each taking their rake-off. One estimate is that the sex worker receives only about 10 per cent of the price received.

Sex tourism also shades into the mail-order bride business. Potential 'husbands' arrive on package tours to examine 'the goods'. Often, these men are fixated by the most reactionary pre-feminist attitudes. Ordering a bride from the Philippines is a statement that they prefer what they believe to be submissive Asian women to their more feisty Westernized counterparts. Undoubtedly, there are cultural differences between many Asian and Western women, but desperation to get out of poverty and help one's family should not be mistaken for a cultural norm of obedience.

TABLE 12.2	**Types of tourist and their likely impact on host societies**	
	The mass, traditional or 'bad' tourist	The 'good' or alternative tourist
Tourist flows and numbers involved	Large, steady or continuous flows (often seasonal) and may arrive en masse. High volume capacity	Small flows and numbers; usually travel individually or in family/friendship groups
Primary motivation for the 'sacred journey'	Recreation, recuperation, pleasure, fun. The 'four Ss' plus tropical beaches, unclouded skies, cheap alcohol	Discovery of the self or values believed lost in home/industrial society. A search for authenticity, spiritual renewal and contact with nature
Specific goals and intentions	Seeks public places and crowds; the collective gaze. Home plus the magical 'X' ingredient. Sport activities: swimming, surfing, water-skiing. Sex tourism	Seeks out the romantic gaze. Yearns to sample exotic cultures, peasant life and ancient sites; the 'culture', 'ethnic' or 'historical' tourist' (Graburn 1989). Desires the curative properties of wilderness, remote regions; 'nature' tourism, 'offbeat' (trekking, canoeing). 'Unusual' tourism, for example stays in Indian village (Smith 1989)
Tourist needs and expectations	Must have full quota of Western-type amenities as a 'right'. Desires the familiarities of home living as much as possible	Needs are relatively few and desires the unfamiliar, but may nevertheless hope for basic facilities and something to remind them of home (E. Cohen 1972). Mostly tolerates rather poor local conditions and may prefer 'primitiveness' as part of the experience
Main orientation	Passive. Not very sensitive to host society. Social interaction with hosts is mostly confined to tipping the chambermaid or barman or bargaining with the souvenir traders. Relies heavily on the Westernized tour guide	Active, probing, well prepared. Highly reflexive, knowledgeable and perceptive of host problems. Participates in local culture and society where possible
Likely impact on host economy and society	Huge economic investment required for numbers and needs of visitors; hotel and beach complexes, airports. Disrupts local cultures because introduces new 'vices' (alcohol, drugs, beach nudity, gambling) and offers Western hedonistic role models likely to appeal especially to young people employed in tourist services. Large resorts engender adverse environmental effects	Tourist facilities needed are more evenly and thinly dispersed across host economy and more low-key. Disposed to interact directly with locals and show interest in traditional culture. Fosters transnational exchange, cultural diversity and under-standing. Generally supposed to create few undesirable environmental effects

Ironically, by discovering untapped tourist venues and then championing these to others, the romantic gazers unwittingly blaze the trails that the masses will then follow (Urry 1990b: 32). Thus, the romantic gaze is frequently destroyed and replaced by the collective gaze. We summarize this discussion in Table 12.2. In doing so, we have utilized Sharpley's (1994: 84–5) rather tongue-in-cheek formulation of the 'good' and 'bad' tourist, with the implication that the latter is synonymous with mass tourism.

Increasingly, many writers have questioned this basic distinction. As you will see in Chapter 13 on consumer culture, in just the same way that we have become more discerning and demanding in the everyday purchase of cars, clothing, films and other consumer goods throughout the working year, craving difference and choice, so too, as holidaymakers, many of us need and demand growing diversity. Thus, tourist markets are fragmenting, with promoters catering for a growing number of post-Fordist-type flexible, specialist niche markets (see Chapter 4), such as the 'pink'/gay holiday (Binnie 2004), tours for the elderly, the under-30s, family holidays for those with young children and so on. Linked to this is the reality that more and more people now live alone and travel singly. Many others prefer to divide their paid leave into short breaks including several long weekend trips or they split their holiday ration between a winter skiing week, an early spring break in a tropical resort via a cheap jet flight and perhaps a more adventurous summer vacation canoeing down a foreign river valley (Meethan 2001: Chapter 4). Backpacking over a period of months or years by young adults, especially during their gap year between school and university – perhaps 50,000 do this each year from Britain alone (McVeigh 2002) – has also grown rapidly in recent years and constitutes another example of a specialized, marketized experience, where among the key motives are the urge to explore other cultures and participate in cross-national friendships with backpackers from other nations (Huxley 2005).

This segmentation of tourism often means that it is not so much social class that determines holiday preferences but rather cultural meanings that shape people's hobbies, interests and lifestyle choices (Meethan 2001: 70). Indeed, since the 1980s, a growing minority of tourists has begun to seek more challenging holiday experiences, which can be loosely called 'alternative tourism'. Krippendorf (1987: 38, 174–5) argued that this had already 'developed into big business' and would rise from approximately one-quarter of all international tourists in 1986 to between one-third and two-fifths by the year 2000. His projections seem broadly correct. One form of alternative tourism is what Hall and Weiler (1992: 4–6) describe as 'special interest tourism' – including educational holidays, adventure, health and sport tourism – for example hang-gliding, rock climbing or yachting, or vacations built around archaeological digs or the attendance at festivals of fine arts. All such special interest holidays share certain common features, especially the desire for self-development and knowledge and a conscious concern to enjoy holidays without inflicting permanent damage on the local culture, society or environment.

Another critique hinges on the rise of what Feifer (1985) deems the 'post-tourist' – someone who has acquired the reflexive capacity we described in Chapter 2. Feifer observes that other places and cultures metaphorically leap out of our TV sets virtually every day. Consequently, we are well informed about the many sites available to us and we realize we can experience these without necessarily visiting them in person. Indeed, we revel in choice and wish to experiment with different holiday experiences. This means that post-tourists have become more self-aware. They are inclined to regard tourism as a game in which they are players who have the advantage of being able to read from a variety of ever changing scripts. All this involves 'playfulness', an ironic awareness of being participants in an essentially 'pseudo-event', for example at theme parks and museums (Sharpley 1994: 87).

Returning to Urry's notion of tourism as consisting largely of gazes, his influential work in this area has been criticized partly because it relies on too clear a distinction between two types of tourist. Moreover, according to Meethan (2001: 83–5), in doing so he places too much emphasis on the visual nature of tourism and depicts the majority of collective gazers as mostly content to accept passively the commercial promotions the tourist industry provides. Furthermore, Perkins and Thorns (2001) have argued that his theory concentrates on a Eurocentric view of the typical tourist orientation and ignores the very different needs and demands of tourists in other world regions, who may not only be more active but also keen to be involved in the performance mounted on their behalf by the hosts. In New Zealand, for example, large numbers of city dwellers organize their holidays around highly active outdoor pursuits such as mountaineering, horse riding, white-water canoeing or caving. But many others – both international and domestic tourists – stay near Maori communities where, for a while, they become immersed in the latter's ancestral, cultural, spiritual and everyday life (Taylor 2001). While the rituals that their Maori hosts perform for their benefit are obviously staged and therefore lack authenticity, both parties to the experience compensate for this by seeking interpersonal interaction behind the scenes where hosts and guests meet on equal terms and tourists are encouraged to 'reveal themselves' (Taylor 2001: 24).

More recently, Urry has responded to these criticisms and now argues that both hosts and guests 'are engaged in multiple performances as their bodies move through dwelling places, airport lounges, beaches, bars, restaurants, cities or museums, and as they communicate with each other via embodied gestures, written texts, translations and other forms' (Sheller and Urry 2004: 7). This means that the apparent dichotomy between the sacred journey as the pursuit of pure enjoyment by the non-reflexive masses and the quest for self-realization and authenticity by the knowledgeable few has broken down. Most tourists now understand that to different degrees they are simultaneously participants in both experiences and are themselves part of the activity.

INTERNATIONAL TOURISM AND 'TRADITIONAL' CULTURAL IDENTITIES

To attract visitors and compete in the growing global tourist market, governments and their agents need to give an account of what is special about their particular cultures and natural landscapes. Thus, everywhere 'there has been a frantic forging of signs of identity' (Lanfant 1995: 32), an attempt to create and present appealing and easily recognizable images; through skilful advertising, brochures and films, paradise regained appears on the beaches of Barbados, while a tropical, ancient, exotic wonderland emerges in Malaysia (King 1993: 108).

By the early 1970s, this tendency to sell local or national cultures had begun to alarm many observers including some social scientists (Greenwood 1972;

Turner and Ash 1975). Their concern was that the business of promoting packaged, local cultures for economic gain, along with the influx of ever growing numbers of foreign tourists, threatened to degrade those very identities that attracted visitors in the first place. We have seen that mass tourism may be especially culpable here.

A further likely consequence might be that shared ancient meanings, religious beliefs and established social relations, which enable people to know who they are and feel a pride in where they belong, were at risk of disintegrating. Moreover, they were being replaced, allegedly, by a socially divisive, homogenizing Western materialist ethos. Some observers argued that all this could be especially alarming in the case of already marginalized and sometimes repressed minorities. Such groups might be pushed by governments or driven by poverty to open their doors reluctantly to foreign guests. But this exposure to alien commercial contamination might be especially damaging, given that their traditional cultures provided just about the only resource and protection available to them. In exploring this question, we will see how the issues that scholars have raised about international tourism have shifted over time.

A CASE STUDY IN THE BASQUE PROVINCE, SPAIN

Greenwood's (1972, 1989) studies of an annual public ritual, the Alarde, in Fuenterrabia – a town in the Basque province of northern Spain – demonstrate some of these points. Once a year virtually all the inhabitants come together to perform an elaborate pageant. This commemorates the victory of their ancestors over the French in 1638 when, following a siege lasting 69 days, the invaders were finally overcome. Most social groups and wards in the town either contribute to the elaborate, costumed parades, the march to the town plaza and the mass firing in unison by contingents of armed men with shotguns, or simply cheer as onlookers. According to Greenwood, the Alarde's ritual significance lies in its ability to re-enact the ancient solidarity of the townspeople that had made victory possible. Originally, the pageant was performed by and for the locals, not for outsiders, and it provided 'an enactment of the "sacred history" of Fuenterrabia'.

The event takes place in summer and so coincides with the presence of numerous tourists. In 1969, the municipality decided that steps must be taken to ensure the tourist onlookers could also view the pageant and so insisted that the event should be staged twice rather than once as before. When Greenwood returned to the town two years later, he discovered that this once 'vital and exciting event had become an obligation to be avoided' (Greenwood 1972: 178). The decision by the municipality to promote this communal ritual as a commercial show for outsiders robbed it of much of its cultural meaning. Greenwood (1989) later reported that the Alarde has survived and has become imbued with political significance, as part of the Basque struggle for greater regional autonomy within Spain. Nevertheless, this example illustrates what may happen when tourism becomes a form of 'cultural exploitation'.

Map 12.1 **Indonesia, showing the location of the Toraja people**

THE REVIVAL OF TORAJA CULTURE, INDONESIA

From the late 1970s, however, many observers of international tourism increasingly began to interpret its cultural consequences for host societies in a different light. Instead of destroying local cultural meanings and social relationships, it appeared that in certain situations domestic and international tourism actually helped to preserve them. Thus, for the most part, the tourists who visited remote societies and ancient cultures were not mass charter tourists but were proactive, reflexive, sensitive to local needs, and motivated primarily by the search for authentic traditions.

This fascination with exotic customs, along with the new spending power brought by visitors to their community, encouraged the locals to rediscover a pride in their cultural identity – previously threatened by modernization – and to revive many of their ancient skills. One of the most interesting examples is the case of the Toraja people living in the central highlands of the island of Sulawesi, part of Indonesia.

The Toraja people number around 300,000. Over the centuries, they have been exposed, like most of the other peoples in Indonesia, to Hindu, Islamic and Christian influences among others (Volkman 1984: 153). Nevertheless, until recently, the Toraja retained their ancient religious beliefs based on ancestor worship and the idea that the gods (their dead relatives), nature, living humans and the as yet unborn were linked together in one symbolic system. Simplifying the analysis somewhat, we can say that everyday life was built around four main pillars: the common bonds based on blood (kinship) and marriage ties; the attachment of each kinship group to its colourful, ancestral houses; the enormous importance of elaborate and often lengthy funeral ceremonies, accompanied by singing, processions and dance; and the ritual slaughter of quantities of pigs and buffalo during funerals. Families invited to share the meat had to repay their 'debt' obligation in kind at some future time or risk a loss of social standing (Crystal 1989: 142–3).

The arrival of Dutch missionaries from 1906 onwards meant that many of the funeral rituals continued to be performed but they were increasingly relegated to the status of customs and lost much of their earlier deep, religious content (Volkman 1984: 156–7). Moreover, after Indonesia achieved independence from the Netherlands in 1949, additional changes began to reinforce the effects of Christianity: the spread of schools and education; the determination of the government to modernize Indonesia and create a new sense of national unity; and the migration of many younger people to Indonesia's growth centres in search of employment from the 1970s. Migration rapidly linked the Toraja to the wider world. It also brought new wealth through the earnings brought by returning migrants. Now, even poor, low-status families could engage in funeral ceremonies on a much greater scale than had previously been economically possible or thought socially appropriate (Volkman 1984: 159). This 'ritual renaissance' meant that ceremonial practices were becoming more expensive and elaborate as well as 'more central to Toraja identity' even before the first tourists arrived (Wood 1993: 61).

In 1975, roughly 2,500 tourists visited the Toraja region, but by 1985 this had risen to approximately 40,000. In 1986, the Toraja district was second only to Bali as Indonesia's most important tourist development region. By the mid-1980s, a small airport had been opened, while bus services, hotels and restaurants mushroomed across the island and tour operators were ferrying in visitors from across the world and other parts of Indonesia. How has international tourism further altered Toraja society? We can summarize these changes in several ways:

1. Toraja society has been placed firmly on the international tourist and cultural map, with growing interest shown in its traditions not only by tourists but also by museums, archaeologists, antique dealers and TV companies around the world.
2. Tourist interest in gazing at exotic ceremonies and burial sites has promoted a 'pride in Toraja's unique and valuable heritage' and a self-conscious attempt to revive ancient religious identity 'as an image through which the outside world can perceive and come to know [the] Toraja' (Volkman 1984: 164).
3. Declining traditional crafts like basket weaving, wood carving and beadwork have been revived, bringing additional sources of wealth to local people, along with the attempt to protect burial sites, rediscover funeral chants and develop a historical and archaeological interest in Toraja culture.
4. Other groups in Indonesia once derided Toraja culture, but now regard it as a vibrant component of national culture. Moreover, neighbouring peoples who once regarded the Toraja as 'savages' (Wood 1993: 62) now treat them with more respect. Thus, the wealth that has flowed into the Toraja economy has helped strengthen the wider political influence of this previously neglected region within Indonesia.

5. Tourism has also brought less desirable consequences. Family heirlooms are stolen. Ancient burial sites are desecrated. Also, the less educated, poor residents and religious specialists who continue to participate in traditional life and culture normally derive few commercial advantages from tourism (Crystal 1989: 166–8).

The Toraja case is far from being untypical. International tourism seems to have stimulated a similar reawakening on the part of many other cultures or ethnic groups, once threatened by modernization, political marginalization, regional neglect or some combination of these. You can read about such cases in the following sources: McKean (1989) and Picard (1995) for the case of Bali; de Vidas' (1995) discussion of the Andean Indians; Friedman's (1990: 319–23) discussion of the Ainu people of northern Japan; Rozenberg's (1995) account of the inhabitants of the Spanish island of Ibiza; and Taylor's analysis of the New Zealand Maori heritage tours (2001).

THE INTERACTING LOCAL AND GLOBAL ON THE WORLD TOURIST STAGE

The literature on international tourism and how it affects host societies has encouraged some social scientists to re-evaluate what we mean by 'culture' and 'tradition'. These categories cannot be regarded as fixed. They are neither internalized through childhood socialization once and for all nor reinforced by unchanging 'external' social pressures that can never be challenged – as some social scientists previously believed. Culture and tradition also do not have clearly defined boundaries.

Instead of invading and then dominating social actors from outside, culture provides 'a "tool kit" of symbols, stories, ritual and world views, which people may use in varying configurations in order to solve different kinds of problems' (Swidler 1986: 273). It provides scope for inventiveness and negotiation by the members of particular societies. It is also constantly evolving and is capable of overlapping with alternative cultures (Clifford 1988). Similarly, the alternative conception of tradition championed by writers like Hoben and Hefner (1991: 18) suggests that it consists of meanings that are 'renewed, modified and remade in each generation. Far from being self-perpetuating, they require creative effort and investment.' Thus, tradition cannot provide fixed standards against which alternatives or changes can be measured. Accordingly, there can be no such thing as 'authenticity', only ideas that always need to be reinterpreted in the present.

International tourism provides additional reasons for rethinking what we understand by tradition, authenticity and culture. As we have seen, to profit from attracting visitors, government-promoted tourism has to construct 'representations' or signs of the local. But international tourism also exposes host societies to the outside world through the tourist gaze. Both aspects begin to alter the nature of host identities (Lanfant et al. 1995: 30–40). Partly, this is because the hosts attain greater self-awareness and reflexivity. This is hardly surprising given that they are now in the business, literally, of recasting their identities. In effect, as we have seen, they perform selected aspects of their way of life and project a version of their locality onto the world stage. Several interesting consequences are likely to follow from this.

One is that a continuous process of interaction may take place between the locals involved in tourist promotion and various agents – not just visitors – from the outside world. Here, the locals strive to retain their place in the global tourist market by adjusting to the inevitable changes in fashion and technology that constantly reshape tourist flows and the concerns and perhaps demands of international organizations. One example from India is provided by Edensor (2004) who refers to 'reconstituting the Taj Mahal'. This has involved various interested local parties in an endless process of reinventing and rebranding a Muslim mausoleum built for the favourite wife of a Mogul emperor in the seventeenth century. The process involves the authorities in the city of Agra where the monument is situated and the Archaeological Survey of India who are jointly responsible for the site; the government in Delhi; and pressures from a host of local interest groups that depend on the visitors for their livelihood – the hotels, craft shops, markets and operators offering 'whistle stop tours' (Edensor 2004: 104) of the adjacent areas of historical interest.

At the same time, the locals are responding to a series of signals and demands from the wider world. Partly this requires the need to compete with other key Asian tourist sites both in India, such as urban areas, Hindu sacred sites and the beaches of Goa – which many backpackers now prefer to visit – and locations such as Thailand and Bali in Indonesia. But, in addition, UNESCO's World Heritage Convention, supported by India's supreme court, maintains a strong interest in the management and presentation of the Taj Mahal as a world site of enormous historical significance and has been placing strong pressure on the local authorities to reduce 'the polluting effects of local factories and traffic' (Edensor 2004: 108). Among the many responses by locals to these 'global networks' and the 'ever more tightly and mutually intertwined … national and global concerns' (Edensor 2004: 111) have been the following: the entrance fee for foreign visitors was increased in 2000 from 20 to 750 rupees, ostensibly to fund conservation work at this and other local historical sites, and traders have tried to find alternative viewpoints from which tourists, who cannot afford to pay this much higher entrance fee, can still gaze at the monument while buying their products.

Another consequence of constructing and projecting a local brand 'product' in the global tourist market and then successfully attracting international visitors is that the hosts increasingly begin to see a reflection of themselves in the onlookers' gaze. And what they see is yet another version of the idealized and simplified representation of their culture. This second image partly mirrors what they have created for commercial reasons. It may also express their visitors' yearnings for spiritual renewal, which might enable them to replace the meanings and traditions they fear have been lost in their own, far more commercialized society. In effect, therefore, these cultural idealizations of traditional culture only exist in the different but linked imaginations of host and guest and they become ever more distorted by the performances and interactions that take place between tourist and host. Three important implications follow from all this:

■ *The reinvention of tradition:* Although tourism enables societies to retain something we might label as 'tradition' and even to regain a once threatened pride in their own identity, the 'traditions' that survive are ones that have been reinvented. They are not the same as the original prototype.
■ *The inescapable tourist gaze:* At least potentially, everyone in the world has become a tourist product. There is no escape for any of us from the gaze of tourist visitors. But, by the same token, this means that everyone is now dependent, in part, on the tourist gaze in order to affirm and perpetuate his or her own identity.
■ *Retaining some kind of local identity despite embeddedness in global flows:* Not only does the tourist presence generate employment and valuable foreign exchange earnings, it also enables each country to 'guarantee … [its] paternity in the midst of an accelerating process of globalization … securing its present to its past' (Lanfant et al. 1995: 40).

REVIEW

Tourists are of global significance in terms of the steep rise in their numbers, their economic contribution and their cultural penetration of other societies. Through a series of case studies and summaries of current debates, we have presented the 'good' and 'bad' sides of international tourism. Clearly, it is difficult to generalize too wildly in this area – in 2004 around about 700 million tourists of very different dispositions and interests travelled each year to about 190 countries. Nonetheless, we can ask some suggestive sociological questions.

Does the differential impact of tourism have something to do with the character of the tourists themselves? Or is the distinction between the 'mass' and the 'alternative' tourist too cut and dried? Many travellers act like the cultural battering rams of the rich, powerful states, others are like the pilgrims of old. Yet others, like sex tourists, simply exploit weaker, poorer people. However, some tourists may enhance multicultural understanding and awareness. In short, tourism may destroy local cultures or revive them. As tourists and their hosts become aware of these capacities, they become actors in the tourist transaction, sometimes turning their own cultures into a pantomime, sometimes recognizing the risible irony in so doing. To parody William Shakespeare: 'All the world's a stage but tourism lets us all come to the performance.'

FURTHER READING

- K. Meethan's *Tourism in Global Society* (2001) provides excellent coverage of all the key debates on the sociology of international tourism and is detailed, thoughtful and analytical, while remaining thoroughly accessible to student readers.

- For a recent re-evaluation and update of the thinking on tourism's impact on traditional societies, see the useful chapters by Pi-Sunyer et al. and van Broeck and Puijk in V. Smith and M. Brent (eds) (2001) *Hosts and Guests Revisited: Tourism Issues of the 21st Century*.

- M. Sheller and J. Urry's co-edited volume *Tourist Mobilities: Places to Play, Places in Play* (2004) offers a generous compendium of lively research findings from many different countries, while exploring a range of different tourist styles from ecotourism to websites and surfing.

- Edited by M. F. Lanfant, J. B. Allcock and E. M. Bruner, *International Tourism: Identity and Change* (1995) is excellent. It contains some difficult material but you will find the introduction and Chapters 1, 2, 3, 4 and 9 challenging and enjoyable.

GROUP WORK

1. International tourist promotion – one class group will investigate special interest tourism and cultural/ethnic/nature holidays, while the other will investigate mass charter tourism. Using brochures collected from travel agents and brief interviews with managers, each team will report on the following questions. How far does the presentation of the two types of holiday differ (in terms of images and styles)? How far is it apparent that quite different kinds of clients are being attracted? Is there any evidence that the distinction between the two types of holiday is breaking down?

2. A survey of personal holiday experiences abroad – each class member will interview five people who have taken at least two holidays abroad during the past five years and will collate their answers. You should elicit the following information. Where did they go and why? What holiday package or arrangements were involved? Do they think that their foreign holiday preferences have changed over time and why? Did they think that the locals gained or lost from tourism and in what ways? What overall conclusions are suggested by these findings?

QUESTIONS TO THINK ABOUT

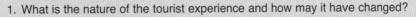

1. What is the nature of the tourist experience and how may it have changed?

2. Evaluate the different ways in which tourism acts as a globalizing force.

3. How far does tourism destroy host societies?

4. 'We are all objects of a tourist gaze now.' What does this statement tell us about the relation between the local and the global?

WHAT'S ON THE WEB

- http://www.lancs.ac.uk/fss/sociology/cemore/index.htm This is the homepage of the Centre for Mobilities Research at the Department of Sociology, University of Lancaster. Although devoted to the wider notion of 'mobilities', there is a strong interest in tourism and the department is home to key researchers in the field like John Urry and Mimi Sheller.

- http://www.ratztamara.com/tourism.html Some hot stuff on tourism in Hungary on suitably decorative web pages, with some side glances at Finland and a good general bibliography on the impact of tourism worldwide.

- http://www.odi.org.uk/rpeg/research/pro-poor_tourism/index.html In an attempt to promote tourism that will benefit poor people, a number of agencies have set up 'pro-poor' or 'responsible tourism' initiatives. This one, from the Overseas Development Institute in London, is a good portal to others and offers some original research papers.

- http://www.world-tourism.org/ This is the official UN body concerned with tourism and an excellent source of up-to-date statistics, with regional breakdowns.

CHAPTER 13

Consuming Culture

CONTENTS

Drink a cup of coffee or tea and you instantly connect to the global marketplace. The list of world goods that arrives in this casual way is formidable and grows all the time. World goods are simultaneously produced in a multiplicity of locations while being purchased and experienced by people living in many different societies. According to Firat (1995: 115), fortunate consumers in the late twentieth century are 'ready to have Italian for lunch and Chinese for dinner, to wear Levi's 501 blue jeans for the outdoor party in the afternoon and to try the Gucci suit at night'. Our experience of living in the global marketplace is revealed particularly well in the case of food and beverages. Here are just a few examples:

- By 1993 in the British fast-food sector, fish and chip shops were outnumbered by Indian takeaways (James 1996: 81). Similarly, pizza and pasta have become 'the most global of global foods' (James 1996: 76), though both have only recently become recognized as national foods in Italy and many ingredients in Italian cuisine arrived initially from China (pasta) or the Americas (tomatoes and peppers).
- Global cuisine can also be widely found in restaurants located in cities from New York to Manamah, Bahrain, in the Persian Gulf. In the latter, according to Chase (1994: 84), one restaurant offers 'Arabic (Lebanese and Gulf items), Chinese, Indian, pizza and hamburger, and grills', all delivered by Filipina employees to the accompaniment of Greek music.
- The worldwide popularity of brand name foods/beverages such as Pizza Hut, Kentucky Fried Chicken and the famous McDonald's burger – which now has restaurants in approximately 130 nations (Ritzer 2004b) – is well known. For example, by 1996 Coca-Cola was selling 13.7 billion unit cases of their various beverages in 135 countries (Coca-Cola Company 1997: 27) and this included eight billion bottles and cans in China (Hooper: 2000: 441).

In this chapter, we explore the globalization of consumption and consider its implications for how we now experience social and cultural life. Our central theme is on the impact of what Sklair (2002: Chapter 7) calls 'the culture-ideology of consumerism' evidenced by many in the rich countries, but especially those living in the developing countries. The adoption of this ideology has led some observers to fear that continued Western and more especially US domination of many industries, along with advertising and the mass media, are giving rise to a new kind of imperialism, one based not on political but cultural control.

This same process is also said to be creating an increasingly homogeneous world, in which Western lifestyles and branded goods are in danger of obliterating countless, unique local cultures. To examine this theory, we need first to explore not only the multidimensional character of consumerism as a universal activity but also its special features under global capitalism. Similarly, we need to consider the very different perspectives – both pessimistic and optimistic – from which sociologists have viewed its contemporary implications.

■ ■ ■ ■ ■ ■ ■ ■ CONSUMERISM AND EVERYDAY LIFE

As a central part of human experience, consumption has one foot squarely planted in the spheres of politics and economics and another firmly rooted in social life and culture. This has always been the case, but capitalist industrialization and globalization have deepened and accentuated these linkages in several ways:

1. The organization of production, transport and distribution through numerous companies and networks of exchange can only function because it is underpinned by certain national and worldwide institutional arrangements. These facilitate financial investment and currency management, guarantee ownership rights and freedom of movement and provide adequate systems of communication. Worldwide production and consumption further cement a more interdependent global economy.
2. Our consumption preferences and practices are shaped by social life. We demonstrate our loyalties to others through such things as wearing special uniforms, public displays of hospitality, or generosity through gift giving. Our consumer preferences and styles in everything from clothes and cars to household decorations say important things about who we are or what claims to social status we would like to make.
3. Our possessions also carry various meanings. These are associated with the wider cultural beliefs, values and orientations we share with others. Drawing on this pool of common meanings enables us to communicate, make sense of the world around us and express our shared identities and values.

This bridging quality at the societal level is paralleled by the dualistic nature possessed by all goods (Douglas and Isherwood 1978), irrespective of whether we are talking about a premodern or capitalist society. On the one hand, goods constitute the 'hardware' of social and cultural life. They possess an intrinsic materiality and utility or what Marx called their 'use-value'; eating rice keeps you alive and clothes protect you from the weather. On the other hand, even the most basic goods simultaneously act as the 'software' of everyday life. They express the meanings with which we have endowed them; they exercise a symbolic significance. Because these meanings are shared, our consumer practices can be read and decoded by others. Archaeological evidence indicates that even the most basic utensils used by prehistoric peoples – such as clay water pots – were invariably embellished with decorations. These probably expressed family affiliations, social position or respect for religious deities. They also gave aesthetic pleasure.

In capitalist economies, this *universal* duality between function and form acquires a further characteristic because goods become commodities and assume an exchange value in the market. Moreover, as we shall see, the cultural meanings that inhere in all goods become highly desirable forms of merchandise in their own right. Finally, because all goods contain symbolic as well as material qualities, it is virtually impossible, as some earlier writers suggested, to make a distinction between those that fulfil our 'real' survival *needs* and those that cater merely to our 'inessential' *wants*. No goods are inessential in cultural terms.

THE MEANING OF CONSUMERISM

In premodern societies, religion and custom provided the chief sources of the meanings 'attached' to goods. Many, such as heirlooms, ceremonial artefacts, houses and tools circulated within families and communities through inheritance and shared ownership. They served as markers of social belonging and of important differences concerning time (the seasons, religious festivals), place, social status and gender. Contemporary advertising companies sometimes imbue goods with seductive meanings borrowed from the global cultural reservoir provided by ancient religions, customs or ethnic identities. Nevertheless, consumption practices today are essentially different from those experienced in the past.

In contemporary successful economies, we enjoy a superfluity of goods compared with the past and most are acquired through the market. Normally, private ownership defines our access to these goods. Also, in place of the rather durable non-commercialized meanings that formerly adhered to products – derived from an accumulated cultural legacy – the meanings they hold today are often contrived, transitory and placed there for the purposes of profit. To understand how and why this happens we need to understand the **semiotic** or symbolic nature of goods. Contemporary sociological discussion of consumption often draws on the study of semiotics developed by Saussure (1857–1913) and Barthes (1915–80). In his lifetime, Saussure was a rather obscure professor of linguistics who taught Sanskrit, Gothic and Old High German in France, Germany and Switzerland. But when he died, his colleagues and students put together his lecture notes, published in English as *Course in General Linguistics* (1974), which became a classic work on semiotics. Saussure was mainly interested in *language* – written words or spoken sounds – which carry or signify meanings (see Box 13.1).

Semiotics The study of signs and symbols in language and other means of communication.

Box 13.1

Saussure's thinking about language and semiotics

In studying language, one of Saussure's key distinctions was between:

- The *signifier*, the vehicle or form by which meanings are conveyed. In language, signifiers are the actual words we either hear as sounds or read as particular letter combinations

- The *signified*, the mental image or concept that is carried by the signifier.

- Together, the signifier and signified form the *sign*. We carry around learned knowledge of signs in our heads and this allows us to decode them.

- Our ability to read signs enables us to engage in processes of *signification*, that is, to attribute signs with meaning.

In language, the relationship between the actual words, or signifiers, and the meanings they convey, the signifieds, is arbitrary. The word for 'bird' could just as easily be 'splift' or 'mnenk'. The image conveyed of a feathery flying creature remains the same whatever 'sound image' (Strinati 1995: 91) we decide to use, providing we share it in common. Thus, the meanings of words do not derive from the actual objects to which they refer but from the overall structure of grammatical rules and elaborate systems of word differences that we call 'language'.

> Contemporary sociologists and semiologists study all forms of representation in order to 'read' or decode their meanings, for example in art, photographs, sounds, advertisements, logos, even the assortment of clothes worn by different subcultures – like the teddy boys, hippies, punks and goths (Hebdige 1988; Hall and Jefferson 1993). In doing so, they have adapted Saussure's crucial notion that the sign combines a signifier and a signified.
>
> SOURCES: Thwaites et al. (1994); Strinati (1995)

Barthes added to our understanding of signification. You can find excellent analyses of his ideas in Thwaites et al. (1994: Chapters 1, 2 and 3) and Strinati (1995: Chapter 3). Barthes argued that in other forms of cultural representation, such as advertisements and clothing, the link between the signifier and the signified is not arbitrary. This is because, unlike in language, signifiers are manifested through visible cultural items: national flags, a particular style of shoes, a photograph of model X car or a famous TV celebrity. The messages carried and our ability to read them are not random happenings because those exposed to the same culture have learned the similar codes, social conventions or ideologies. Cultural meanings cluster together and tend to crystallize around certain dominant, clear messages. At the same time, they are embedded in particular shared histories and social conditions. In Britain, for example, a bouquet of white carnations usually means 'a wedding' and carries the message of fond congratulations. Other flowers and colours may suggest quite different things. For instance, red roses act as a signifier for an intimate declaration of romantic love.

But Barthes also insisted that many signs have been deliberately manufactured and spread by dominant interest groups and social classes – the Church, aristocratic elites or the rising capitalist bourgeoisie. One way or another and especially outside language, signs are rarely innocent. Thus, the messages they carry incorporate *value preferences*. We watch a TV news clip showing the coffin of a US marine draped in the Stars and Stripes being carried from a military plane amid a sombre scene. The president comforts bereaved relatives, ranks of uniformed dignitaries pay their respects, all accompanied by suitably doleful music. The decoded message is: America and its citizens are proud to pay the price of exercising the power and global responsibility necessary to guarantee peace and civilized values in a troubled, disorderly world.

However, such images and the powerful messages they convey work to suppress alternative interpretations. These might lead us to ask: why did the USA engage in military confrontations in Vietnam, Grenada, Somalia or Iraq? And who benefited most from these activities? Thus, such signs as the military funeral prompt us to think that they depict unavoidable and 'natural' realities, but in fact they preclude other possible lines of enquiry and explanation. When this happens, the processes of signification assume the character of myth-making. Myths acquire the status of timeless truths, but they also inhibit our ability to interpret cultural meanings.

For our purposes, two important questions arise from this discussion:

1. First, how do we read the meanings that advertisers attach to the commodities they want us to buy? On the one hand, we may be *cultural dupes* or *dopes* who passively decode these messages or signs exactly as the advertisers hope. On the other hand, we may be *cultural heroes* who are perfectly capable of disregarding such messages altogether or who impose our own meanings irrespective of the advertisers' intentions (Slater 1997: 33–4).

2. Second, what are the effects on our lives of the relentless volume of swirling messages, images and symbols to which we are subjected? They assail us every time we walk down the street, read a magazine, watch TV, visit the cinema or attend a rock concert or football match, where, inevitably, we are also exposed to advertising slogans and **BRANDS**.

key concept	A **BRAND** is more powerful than an advertisement because it refers not to one product but to an entire range of goods sold by a company. It also promises consumers access to a whole way of life modelled on the vibrant grassroots cultures found in street life, among ethnic minorities, the urban poor, youth gangs and so on (see Klein 2001).

 **A PESSIMISTIC SCENARIO: CONSUMERS AS DOPES**

For purposes of brevity and clarity, we now address some of the key arguments about consumption by focusing on these two opposed viewpoints. In this section, we discuss the idea that consumers are innocents in the face of the onslaught of producers, advertisers and market managers. In the next, we consider how consumers can strike back and, to some degree at least, assert their autonomy and innovativeness.

COMMODITY FETISHISM

Employing one of his most powerful concepts, **COMMODITY FETISHISM**, Marx argued that commodity production creates a depersonalized economy. Clusters of unknown, hired workers and machines in different locations produce goods for unknown buyers. The system constructed by capitalism is so complex and impersonal that it is virtually impossible to understand or identify with it. The surface world of commodity exchange thereby conceals the hidden, real world of work and production, while creating a 'barrier between exchange and production' (Rabine 2002: 4). At the same time, the opportunity for self-realization available to humankind through creative work and social cooperation is simultaneously denied and compensated for by the attractive possessions on sale in the bazaar and shopping mall. We tend therefore to imbue our purchases with a meaning and significance they cannot possess. We fetishize them – turn them into objects of devotion and magicality – when, in fact, a bottle of expensive perfume, for example, is only processed whale blubber with added spots of scent-essence derived from skunks.

COMMODITY FETISHISM According to Marx, this occurs when an inanimate object is treated as if it required a religious, or even sexual, devotion. In premodern societies, fetishes were handmade or rare natural objects thought to embody a spirit that protected the owner from misfortune or disease. Commodity fetishism arises under capitalism because the market system has become more real and immediate to us than the underlying social relationships (based on inequality and exploitation) that made goods sold on the market possible in the first place.

MASS CONSUMPTION

Throughout the twentieth century, many writers were highly critical of the era of mass consumption associated with the rise of Fordist production (a theme we discussed in Chapter 4). Adorno and Horkheimer (1972), for example, argued that expanding Fordist production compelled businesses as never before to feed our desire for more goods, while persuading us to abandon still useful products in favour of newer ones. Here, the advertising industry played a major role by producing an endless stream of new meanings – images of exotica, nostalgia, desire, romance, beauty or the good life. These meanings were then embedded in mundane products such as vacuum cleaners, soft drinks and soaps.

When they 'fell for it', consumers were seduced by false needs and impossible hopes, since these products were quite incapable of fulfilling their promises. Brand 'Y' shampoos cannot actually improve your love life much and refitting your living room with fashionable furniture is unlikely to fill a lonely life without friends. Also, the meanings employed in mass consumer culture need to be simple and instantly accessible so that they speed up the turnover of huge volumes of goods. As a result, the distinction between 'high' culture (for example classical music, Renaissance art) and the less sophisticated but immediately recognizable images offered by popular culture (like comic strips, TV soaps and pop music charts) is eroded. The end result, the harshest critics say, is to create a homogenized world of standardized mass products and a bland, stupefying culture, lacking substance.

SIGNIFYING CULTURE

In consumer culture, the subtle meanings implanted in goods by advertising and seductive packaging – what Baudrillard (1988) called their 'sign-values' – become more important to us than their material properties. Indeed, the intrinsic use-value of goods may become detached from the advertisers' meanings altogether, the latter becoming free-floating. Either way, increasingly we live in a 'signifying culture', one that abounds with disconnected messages; it is supposedly this rather than the functionality of goods themselves that we seek. In this scenario, what we buy bears less and less relation to our actual needs.

Figure 13.1 Yucatan Peninsula, Mexico
Blocks of *chicle* (chewing gum) are collected
in remote parts of Latin America to feed the
endless appetites of Western consumers. The
borough of Lambeth in London spent
£60,000 in 2004 cleaning degraded chewing
gum off its streets and pavements.

DEPTHLESSNESS

Another problem is the sheer quantity of signs circulating in our consumer
culture. Moreover, signs are inherently volatile. Their meanings often mutate or
break free from the object or context they were originally intended to represent.
They are also subject to media manipulation. Thus, despite the media and advertisers' emphasis on creating meanings in order to attract our attention, meaning
actually eludes us. When it comes down to it, we are unable to find self-
realization or ourselves on the supermarket shelves. According to Jameson
(1984), all this destabilizes our lives and gives to them a quality of depthlessness.
We lose our bearings and become disorientated.

FANTASY BECOMES REALITY

The media-inspired fantasy world of TV soaps, films and adverts, where messages
and symbols flourish, often seems more alive to us than the actual social world we
inhabit. The latter shrinks in significance and becomes in a curious way far less
real. Indeed, we may seek to imitate and build our lives around one or more
SIMULACRA. When such fake or fantasy experiences become more real to us than
our concrete everyday world, Baudrillard (1988) calls this condition 'hyperreality'.

SIMULACRA (singular simulacrum) are entities that have no original or surviving original in the actual world, but are thought nonetheless to be 'real'. Cult followers, for example of Elvis Presley or characters in certain TV soaps, seek to emulate their simulacra perhaps by copying their appearance or supposed lifestyles, writing to them for personal advice or even proposing marriage.

Apart from the followings that grow up around certain films and TV programmes, another excellent example of hyperreality is the enormous popularity of Disney parks in the USA, Japan and France. In 1996, the six Disneyland centres topped the list of theme parks in the world as a whole and together attracted almost one-quarter of the 320 million global visitors to such venues (Meikle 1997). In September 2005, Disneyland Hong Kong opened with expectations of gathering 3.6 million visitors in its first year, thus opening out the massive Chinese market. Disney parks offer spectacles based on a largely mythical or fairy-tale world of handsome princes and animals, such as Mickey Mouse, imbued with heroic or comical human characteristics. In Disney parks, visitors often mistake living birds and animals for plastic ones; the line between reality and fantasy has been lost. Bryman (1995: 172) speculated that 'the fake worlds of the Disney parks, which represent a non-existent reality, become models for American society, so that a hyperreal America is being constructed which is based on a simulacrum'.

THE GLOBAL CONSUMPTION OF NOTHING

In Chapter 4, we discussed Ritzer's (2004a) work on the predictable, standardized character of the fast-food and other service industries and how this McDonaldization process has spread rapidly worldwide. More recently, Ritzer (2004b: 3–10) has adapted this argument by suggesting that a vast number of products – from cars and watches to consumer services such as credit cards, entertainment and, of course, fast foods – are now relatively empty of the specific, detailed content and uniqueness that once came from their embeddedness in particular local traditions and individualized production systems. Instead, they are bland, have little substantive content and lack distinction. Their production and merchandizing is invented, directed and controlled centrally by vast corporations, advertising agencies and banks. These 'non-things' (Ritzer 2004b: 55) tend to be consumed in 'non-places' (Augé 1995) such as shopping malls, airport lounges and supermarkets, which are similarly anonymous, standardized locations to which it is impossible to feel any sense of personal attachment. Such 'nothing' consumer products and experiences lend themselves to being globalized – sold in vast quantities from huge emporia across many countries. This is in stark contrast to the traditional, individualized jewellery or original, localized clothing produced by highly skilled artisans in tin shacks in Kenya, Senegal or Ghana, which are then transported in suitcases by air and bus – through the informal 'African fashion network' (Augé

1995: 13) of individual marketers, designers and diasporic kin connections – to locations such as the Los Angeles African market for sale, perhaps, to African-Americans (Rabine 2002: Chapter 1).

▪▪▪▪▪▪▪▪▪ AN OPTIMISTIC SCENARIO: CONSUMERS AS CREATIVE HEROES

The chief difficulty with the negative scenario is that it leaves little space for human agency in the form of consumer autonomy, creativity or reflexivity. It also strongly implies that there is something inherently artificial and trivial about the meanings carried by goods under capitalism, precisely because they are produced and sold for profit and obtained through market exchange. This renders them inferior as cultural forms and implicates them deeply in exploitation. There are several counter-arguments to this view.

PRODUCT DIFFERENTIATION

One of the most striking things about capitalist marketing techniques is the attempt by companies to promote distinctive products. Consumers belong to quite different groups according to their class, education, religion, ethnicity, sexual orientation and type of family responsibilities. Each of these identities may generate marked variations in need and taste. Then there is the question of what stage people have arrived at in their life course – whether they are adolescents, single people, couples with young children, middle-aged 'empty nesters' or the elderly. Thus, the preferences of different groups not only vary but each person's needs evolve and change over time. Further, people crave difference and distinction and expect the market to provide this. In other words, product differentiation and niche marketing are at the heart of contemporary capitalism.

ADVERTISING AND ITS LIMITATIONS

According to Sinclair (1987: 63), those employed in advertising are often highly sceptical about their influence on consumers and 'have learned to doubt the usefulness of advertising'. For one thing, income remains a major constraint on our ability to respond to advertising; 'people (can only) play with the signs that they can afford' (Warde 1992: 27). Our purchases are often determined by habit and time constraints. However appealing the images attached to goods, it seems absurd to suggest that we purchase them *solely* for their sign value. Can openers, shoes and cars are useful objects and fulfil specific functions. Adverts may attract some people who never buy the goods, while others who buy have paid little attention to them. Many people adopt a playful attitude towards adverts and enjoy 'sending them up'. In short, there is 'no necessary connection between the symbolic or ideological meaning of advertising and the behavioural responses which people make to it' (Sinclair 1987: 63). Thus, more often than not there is a mismatch of codes; the messages transmitted are not necessarily the same as those received by actual consumers.

THE SOCIAL SIEVE

In Global Thinkers 13, we say much more about the key ideas of the leading late twentieth-century French sociologist Bourdieu. Here, however, it is important to mention his influential study of French lifestyles (Bourdieu 1984), where he argued that every aspect of consumer behaviour – from holidays and choice of wallpaper to food preferences and clothing styles – says important things about where we belong in society. 'Belonging' in this sense refers especially to our class, education, ethnicity, religion, generation and the place we live (whether city, suburbia, region, small town or village). Shared tastes also provide access to membership of desired groups. Thus, each subgroup expresses its own special **HABITUS**.

HABITUS In its Latin origins, habitus refers to a typical or habitual condition. For Bourdieu, it comprised a set of cultural orientations or dispositions, as a result of each individual's specific life experiences and membership of a particular social subgroup. Through these, they lean strongly towards displaying preferences for a cluster of distinctive tastes in consumption and lifestyles, though these are not completely fixed by social background; we have some room for autonomy.

Here are some examples of how habitus might be manifested:

- Urban factory workers may display art that sentimentalizes family life or romanticizes the rural past.
- Socially mobile business groups who enjoy first-generation wealth but little education may attend the opera and acquire antiques in an attempt to legitimize their economic gains and rub shoulders with more sophisticated people.
- Educated professionals are often relatively poor in terms of wealth, income and property but they are able to compensate for this through their acquisition of cultural capital – an acquired body of discerning knowledge and taste, perhaps in jazz, nineteenth-century literature or cubist art.

Some researchers argue that the rise of TNCs and the globalization of economic life are increasingly producing a transnational class of 'denationalized' (Sassen 2000: 24) professionals and business managers who often display a new global lifestyle habitus (Featherstone 1990). Others, however, suggest that this results in a fake 'consumerist cosmopolitanism' (Calhoun 2002: 105), whereby these privileged individuals search 'the world for cultural knick-knacks with which to adorn their expensive lives and abodes' (Kennedy 2005: 91) as they move from one air-conditioned, wealthy venue and milieu to another. Clearly, consumption patterns are deeply rooted in the soil of social life. The sign-values attached to goods are not free to shape our needs without the mediation of strong countervailing forces.

CONSUMPTION AS LIFE ENHANCING

Many writers have pointed to the rise of a postmodern society and its links to another fairly recent transition – the move towards post-Fordist economies. Postmodern consumers, it is argued, crave distinctiveness, personal service, originality and diversity. In part, this is what has compelled businesses to move towards niche marketing and far more flexible systems of manufacturing. The rise of postmodern sensibilities also means that consumption and leisure play a more important role in the lives of contemporary citizens than during the era of early industrialization. Then, people were much poorer and work, class consciousness, nationalism and deep loyalties to family and community figured more largely in people's lives.

CONSUMER CREATIVITY

Returning to the present, Featherstone (1987, 1990), Tomlinson (1991, 1999) and others offer a celebratory brand of postmodern thinking. Far from being consumer dopes, they argue that we have become skilled practitioners who have learned how constantly to decode messages and alter their meanings by imposing our own interpretations. We also negotiate these meanings with others through the social webs in which we are entangled. Increasingly, we revel in plurality and difference. In these ways, we weave meanings into changing patterns of personal identity. Consumerism has therefore become a vehicle for projecting our particular selves and group affiliations into social space. Certainly, numerous subcultural youth groups appear to have done this ever since the 1950s by adopting a **bricolage** of clothing styles and a variety of fashions in the perpetually changing pop and rock scene. Thus, we have become the liberated masters, not the servants of the consumer society. But the positive potentialities of consumerism go beyond individual capacities for aesthetic self-creativity. Thus, writers such as Bennett (2004) suggest that consumerism has not only become a central area of citizen concern but for some it offers opportunities for displaying moral and ethical awareness, knowledge and power as informed consumers who engage in various degrees and kinds of boycotts and similar actions. We say more about this in Chapter 18. Moreover, and despite the previous allusion to the possibly fake global consumerism sought by elites, it can be argued that the shared lifestyles made possible by consumerism across the world may partly help to neutralize some of the divisions, cultural as well as economic, that currently undermine the formation of a stronger sense of global citizenship (Urry 2000: 187).

Such postmodern arguments concerning the diverse opportunities that shopping provides for 'ordinary people … to generate and to satisfy their multiple

Bricolage An assembly of various, apparently unconnected, elements.

wants', and the fact that shopping and 'social justice are not mutually exclusive values' but can 'coexist alongside each other' (Hutton 2005: 26), reassure us that we are not consumer dopes. However, in displacing the earlier one-sided obsession with the compulsions of production and work as the primary source of meaning in people's lives, the postmodernists seem to have substituted another, equally skewed scenario in its place. Human creativity in the workplace seems to have been denied or devalued and reassigned almost entirely to the spheres of consumption and leisure. This could be said to play rather conveniently into the hands of capitalist interests and to exclude those without the material means to enjoy consumer culture.

■ ■

Global Thinkers 13   **PIERRE BOURDIEU (1930–2002)**

Agent–structure debates

Much of sociology has involved a debate between structuralists and constructivists. Bourdieu rejects both these approaches. Structuralism ignores how agents consciously interpret and sometimes resist the external structures they encounter while investing their lives with meaning, thereby often reinforcing those same structures, but not passively. In seeing society merely as an aggregate of millions of individual ways of thinking, constructivism neither explains the durability of social relations over time nor makes clear how agents obtained their thought categories in the first place (or why some agents are more influential than others in determining these).

Bourdieu's key concepts – creating a bidimensional view of society

1. ***Social fields.*** *Social life consists of many overlapping fields and subfields of social relations like religion, politics, art, production and education. Each field is rather like a game in which the players more or less know the rules and find it worthwhile to join in order to pursue their own interests.*
2. ***Unequal access to different types of capital.*** *Fields of social activity are also regions of power, where those who possess different degrees of resources struggle to improve or retain their position. These resources consist of different kinds of capital:* economic *(wealth, income),* social *(membership of clubs, networks, acquaintanceships),* cultural *(artistic knowledge, educational credentials, technical/professional qualifications) or* symbolic *(the ability to legitimize privileges by persuading others you have a right to these).*
3. ***Habitus.*** *Through their cumulative social experiences, agents internalize an understanding of the inequalities they encounter and learn how to 'play' the social cards dealt them (by family life, place of birth, type of school, or access to different kinds of capital). They therefore develop a set of* dispositions *– attitudes, orientations – that not only reflect (or roughly correspond with) their particular social situation but also enable them to play the game within each social field to the greatest extent their endowment of capital will permit. These dispositions constitute their habitus and bring together agent and structure. Thus, actors are formed by society and tend to act in ways that reproduce its structures of inequality, but they do so as knowing agents simultaneously*

exercising some autonomy and whose lives are partly governed by the way they interpret and act out the meanings they carry.

In late capitalist-industrial societies the following occur:

■ *With the relative shift to a service and knowledge-based economy, cultural capital becomes more important. Many with little economic capital are able to succeed.*
■ *Thus, type, source and level of education become critical to class position.*
■ *Similarly, the rise of consumerism means that actors compete for social position as much through lifestyle pursuits as in the sphere of production.*
■ *In general, therefore, culture in all its forms (aesthetic taste and distinction, qualifications and symbolic knowledge) and the struggle to control or redefine the overarching codes, dominant meanings and systems of representation become central to the reproduction of class and society.*

Relevance to global society and culture?
Although he was thinking of France, Bourdieu's concepts of field, different capitals and habitus can be usefully applied to global life. So too can the idea that inequalities might be improved if they can capture and redefine the dominant themes and assumptions (symbolic systems) concerning what is and might be the nature of capitalism appropriate to a twenty-first century integrated global life.

SOURCES: Bourdieu and Wacquant (1992); Bourdieu (1993); Schwartz (1997)

TOWARDS A HOMOGENEOUS, AMERICANIZED GLOBAL CULTURE?

The spectre of world cultural domination through the spread of Western consumerism and the rise of increasingly similar materialistic societies has concerned many observers and such worries have been examined in detail by several researchers (for example Tomlinson 1991, 1999; Canclini 1995; Howes 1996). The fear of Americanization is often even more acute. Sometimes this is described as **McDONALDIZATION**, namely the delivery of standardized products and their related systems of business control that we discussed in Chapter 4 (Ritzer 1993, 2004a). The McDonald's burger franchising chain is emulated by many other concerns. Certainly, McDonald's own worldwide appeal has been enormous. During 1991, it opened two and a half times more new restaurants abroad than in the USA. In 1992, the first outlet appeared in Beijing, China, with a seating capacity of 700 (Ritzer 2004a: 2–3).

| key concept | **McDONALDIZATION** originally referred to the irresistible dissemination of business systems associated with the US fast-food industry. These aimed to achieve intense control over workers and customers and the supply of cheap, standardized, but quality products in pleasant surroundings. This |

drive for efficiency and predictability has now spread to many other economic activities and countries, so that the McDonald's burger franchising chain is merely the 'paradigm case' (Ritzer 1993: 1) of a much wider formula.

Pointing to this widespread fear not simply of US consumerist but also cultural domination, Hannerz (1992: 217) coined a similar term – the 'cocacolonization of the world'. Supposedly, what is at stake here is the destruction of once vibrant and unique religious, ethnic and national identities and not just local dietary customs and small industries. Interestingly, during the immediate postwar years, many Europeans expressed a distinct antipathy to 'Yankee culture' and US market domination. The fear of Americanization was particularly strong in France. When, for example, Coca-Cola applied for a licence to begin local bottling in 1948, the French Communist Party won much public support when it implausibly argued that Coke's incursion should be resisted because the company doubled as a US spy network. Others maintained that it represented a threat to French civilization or observed that, like earlier Nazi propaganda, coke advertising exercised an 'intoxicating' effect on the masses (Pendergrast 1993: 241–3).

More recently, research has demonstrated how the leading role played by US transnational corporations in expanding postwar markets for consumer products was soon consolidated by similar moves in the 1960s on the part of US advertising agencies and media networks. Accordingly, by the late 1970s, US advertising agencies operating abroad earned 50 per cent of their incomes from these sources (Janus 1986: 127). Indeed, until the early 1980s, they virtually controlled world advertising of consumer goods in most leading markets. Meanwhile, pushed by state initiatives, television ownership grew in many developing countries during the 1960s. The US radio and TV networks were able to sell both US programmes and the technology required to establish communication facilities in developing countries (Sinclair 1987: 103).

The net result of all this was to create the channels – either through direct TNC or advertising agency sponsorship of national radio and TV programmes and newspapers – for a vast expansion in consumer demand for US products. Much of this was especially evident in Latin America. For example, Janus (1986: 131) reported that during a single day in 1971, 84 per cent of the adverts transmitted by a popular Mexican radio station involved transnational products. Likewise, 20–50 per cent of advertising space in Latin America's 22 largest newspapers during the mid-1970s was bought by TNCs. Thus, the media 'through commercial audience-maximizing systems built around advertising … encourage … high consumption patterns and the creation of expectations which can only be met by further incorporation into the world economy' (Cruise O'Brien 1979: 129).

In the former communist countries, there is little doubt that the arrival of products like Big Mac burgers was eagerly welcomed in the 1980s. They were seen as powerful symbols that offered access to Western freedoms and consumer lifestyles as exemplified in the 'authentic taste of America' (James 1996: 83). Such instances appear to demonstrate a rather simplistic view of Western life, along with a quite explicit equation of global culture with Americanization or Westernization. Are these merely extreme examples of a general stampede towards Western culture around the world? Alternatively, are there reasons for thinking that the globalization of consumption will not necessarily lead to a homogeneous, Americanized world? We now discuss the case for taking the latter position.

THE EXPERIENCED CONSUMER

People living in advanced societies have been exposed longer and more intensively to the attractions of a consumer society than anywhere else. As we have seen, there is a good case to make that the majority has not been turned into a gaggle of consumer dopes. With some possible exceptions, perhaps among children and adolescents, most of us are perfectly able to impose our own interpretations on the goods we buy. Our membership of different groups also acts as a screening device through which meanings are negotiated and altered. This being so, it is hard to believe that people living in cultures vastly different from our own will not be equally or more capable of demonstrating creative responses. If anything, the potential for a mismatch – the imposition of uncertainty, ambivalence and innovation – between the advertisers' messages and the ways consumers read them is likely to be much greater. As Hannerz (1992: 243) argued, the meaning of any external cultural flow is 'in the eye of the beholder'. In addition, involvement in global culture offers 'access to a wider cultural inventory ... new resources of technology and symbolic expression to refashion and ... integrate with what exists of more locally rooted materials' (Hannerz 1992: 241).

THE ROOTS OF CULTURAL CHANGE

Cultural change is not new. The construction of new identities and meanings has often followed in the wake of the religious and other influences that reached societies from outside. Such processes have been going on for thousands of years. Moreover, culture in all its forms is always socially constructed. It consists of a connected body of contrived meanings subject to continuous modifications and additions. Given all this, it is rather paradoxical that many people regard the changing cultural identities of the present era with such fear and distaste simply because they are mediated by the 'forces of a commercial market' (Firat 1995: 121).

Firat suggests that the explanation for this probably lies in the association of markets and money with vulgarity. But this may not be a convincing reason for such attitudes. Indeed, the 'threat' to cultures from money and commerce may actually be 'less harmful than other forms of invasion because ... a commercial invasion allows elements from all cultures to survive as long as they are marketized' (Firat 1995: 121). In short, the gluing of cultural artefacts and experiences to money incentives and their projection into the world marketplace offers the best guarantee that they will survive. This experience may alter them but, as we have seen, cultural change is inevitable anyway. Also, military and other forms of oppression are more likely to result in the massive destruction of a cultural heritage, as the impact of slavery on African people transported to the Americas amply demonstrates.

DIVERSITY WITHIN THE HOMOGENIZING STATES

Apart from their native inhabitants, both Canada and the USA were formed out of the cultural ingredients imported from many countries. Indeed, the USA has long been described as the melting-pot society par excellence. The dominant Protestant Anglo-Saxon groups have made determined efforts since the early twentieth century to Americanize (or Anglicize) the masses arriving from Eastern Europe, Italy, Ireland, China, Japan and, more recently, other parts of Asia, the Middle East and Latin America – especially through the school system. Nevertheless, distinctive ethnic cores survive in many US cities. Most continue to celebrate their linguistic, religious and culinary legacies and retain connections through marriage and community with those descended from similar migrant backgrounds. Visitors to New York, for example, arguably the epicentre of world capitalism, may be struck by its vibrant multicultural ethos. Almost every conceivable cuisine, musical genre, ethnic art, style of dress, language, business form (complete with links into global networks), church and community can be experienced by those who have the desire to do so. Much the same is true of the much older European countries.

Figure 13.2 **Rue de Rosiers, The Marais, Paris, 1996**
Fusion food – a kosher pizzeria in the Jewish quarter.

THE SURVIVAL OF LOCAL CULTURES

American consumer culture from Disney to the TV soap *Dallas* may be strongly present in every culture across the globe but the reverse is equally the case. Several generations of migrant cultural experience have survived prolonged exposure to intensive consumerist and media influences in the wealthiest country. This being so, it is not easy to understand why the availability of Kentucky Fried Chicken in the streets of Bombay or the ability to view *Roseanne* in the villages of Egypt are liable to destroy the entire cultural traditions of these or any other developing society. On occasions, some inhabitants of Lagos or Kuala Lumpur may drink coke, wear Levi 501 jeans and listen to Madonna records. But this does not mean that they are about to abandon their customs, family and religious obligations or national identities wholesale even if they could afford to do so, which most cannot. Even where certain types of clearly Western cultural commodities are imported more or less intact, local consumers invariably impose their own partic- ular meanings, reinterpreting such products to reflect their special needs. For example, Saldanha (2002) shows how teenagers from wealthy elite families in Bangalore reject all the popular musical genres widely loved across India, including Bollywood film music (see below) and Indian pop, in favour of more or less undiluted, imported Anglo-American pop rock. However, in doing so, they are simultaneously rejecting all the signifiers of what they regard as the old Hindu, semi-colonized and still impoverished India – including the peasantry, caste, state bureaucracy, corruption and religious divisions. Moreover, they have no wish to migrate to the West to escape these constrictions. Instead, their search for an ultra-modern lifestyle, through imported pop rock, fast cars and other Western consumerist indulgences, enables them to construct an Indian sensib- ility cleansed of all the traditions and constraints they believe have so far prevented it from fulfilling its potential to be a truly great power in the modern world, while remaining completely Indian, unique and autonomous.

REVERSE CULTURAL FLOWS

Significant *reverse* cultural flows to the West from Japan and the developing countries located in all world regions are also increasingly evident. Many more are likely in the future, especially when and if more non-Western countries achieve industrialization. We have already noted some examples such as world cuisine and the Japanese management ethos and more examples are discussed later, but here we would like to mention three in particular.

The first is the spread of traditional Asian medicines, health and fitness prac- tices and approaches to mental health to sizeable sections of the middle classes in Europe and North America. Examples are yoga, t'ai chi, shiatsu, meditation, chromatherapy, acupuncture and some herbal remedies, as well as martial arts like karate, judo, t'ai kwando and kung fu.

Second is the growing popularity of the carnival, not just among the migrants and diasporic groups that originally brought its traditions, dances and musical genres to the heartlands of certain Western metropolises from their original sites in Brazil and Trinidad, but also among millions of native people and other migrants. Nurse (1999) shows how, as a result of oil revenues, the Trinidad carnival came to attract up to 40,000 visitors during the 1970s. However, since then, it has been adopted and institutionalized far more widely, so that by the 1990s there were more than 60 annual Caribbean carnivals taking place in various North American and European cities, including London's Notting Hill, Toronto's Caribbean and New York's Labor Day, partly captured since the late 1940s by various African, West Indian and Asian performers.

Finally, Jones and Leshkowich (2003) describe how traditional Asian garments have increasingly been making their mark on influential Western fashion houses. The globalization of 'Asian chic', which increased rapidly in the 1990s, was helped by the economic prosperity of many East Asian countries, the videos and films celebrating the music of Michael Jackson, Madonna and others, and the interest shown by celebrity figures like the late Diana, Princess of Wales. Consequently, indigenous dyed batik cloth from Sumatra in Indonesia, Indian saris, sarong skirts, kimono jackets, mandarin collars, the Vietnamese *ao dai* – a traditional costume consisting of a coiled hat, tight-fitting tunic and loose pants – and much else besides became key elements in the global fashion industry as well as spreading between and cross-fertilizing the garment industries in these same Asian countries.

SHAPING GLOBAL CULTURE: THE ROLE OF THE LOCAL

Drawing on case studies by empirical sociologists, in this final section we explore three types of response by local cultures to the supposedly homogenizing thrust of global consumerism.

INDIGENIZATION

Several studies have explored the ways in which the local captures global influences but in the process transposes them into forms that are compatible with indigenous traditions. The case of Japan is extremely revealing. Clammer (1992) shows how its citizens reveal strong predilections towards acquiring an endless stream of brand name consumer possessions that are soon rejected in favour of newer styles. Shopping forms an essential and relished part of leisure, especially among women. Indeed, Clammer argues that the Japanese are quintessentially postmodern in their concern to construct distinctive styles of dress and other forms of consumption and the need to express subjectivity through creating the right atmosphere at home. However, much of this is rooted in long-established Japanese traditions. These had always fostered eclecticism – a delight in selecting new avenues of cultural expression – and prized the acquisition of highly developed aesthetic skills and the ability to juggle with 'semiotically ambiguous' objects (Clammer 1992: 205). Tradition also values the cultivation of the self in everyday life through appropriate forms of presentation according to social rank, age and gender.

One way in which the preoccupation with aestheticism and presentation is evident concerns the Japanese obsession with wrapping presents. This is done with enormous care and attention to detail so that exactly the right signals are conveyed to recipients. Modern consumerism has also become locked into the ancient Japanese tradition of giving and receiving gifts, which continues to provide one of the 'essential ingredients of everyday culture' (Clammer 1992: 206). In addition to family members, gifts are widely given at different times of the year and to a vast array of people from whom favours have been received and to those whose future help may be required. Given the continued flourishing of this ancient gift economy, the Japanese have found no difficulty in incorporating the Christian festival of Christmas – despite their adherence to quite different religions – in addition to certain other Western inventions such as Mother's Day and Halloween.

Since the mass media play such an important role in disseminating cultural values – and consumerist expectations – it is worth noting that many developing countries have established their own TV and radio networks, film industries and much else besides. This has certainly been the case in Latin America. Thus, between 1972 and the early 1980s, the previous dependence of Latin American TV networks on US programmes declined. Partly, this became possible through the development and rapid popularity of 'telenovelas' – locally made TV soaps that explore national problems and themes (Rogers and Antola 1985) and are often sent to migrants and diasporic groups living overseas.

The Indian film industry was established in 1912. It offers a particularly interesting case of indigenization with respect to the mass media. Based in several cities, the Bombay production centre known as 'Bollywood' has nevertheless become the most famous. India has the largest film industry in the world and produces over 900 films a year (Kasbekar 1996). Most are exported across South Asia to Russia, Africa, Latin America and those European cities in which migrants have settled. Contemporary concerns with local themes like the survival of family life in the face of rapid economic change and how the 'poor boy' can win the 'rich girl' in a society that remains very unequal dominate Indian films. Nevertheless, traditional Hindu and other mythological matters also figure prominently – for example, the concern with dharma (duty) and kinship obligations. Similarly, the plots and creative forms draw on ancient classical theatre and aesthetic traditions, the love of epic dramas and spectacles, the use of song and emphasis on romance, and a strong emotional content.

REINVENTION AND REDISCOVERY

In Chapter 12 we explored examples of how tourism has sometimes contributed to the revival of traditional cultures. In the case of consumption, the rediscovery of declining or extinct traditions is especially obvious in the case of cuisine. Visits to most bookshops to examine the cookery section will reveal just how massive and diverse the interest in global foods has become. Similarly, on most days one can watch a TV programme that explores global cuisine. However, the need to compete with the rising popularity of restaurants offering 'authentic' foreign dishes and imported fast foods has sometimes provoked a new interest in national and local culinary traditions.

Recently, this 'resistance to heterogeneity' (James 1996: 89) has been particularly marked in the UK. Thus, once forgotten or neglected cheeses, sausages, preserves, beers and fruit or vegetable varieties, most highly specific to particular localities, have been found and reinstated in 'traditional' cookbooks. Meanwhile, such delicacies as 'steamed puddings, pies and pastries, bread and butter pudding, tripe, authentic teacakes and muffins' have once again appeared 'on the menus of the more fashionable restaurants' (James 1996: 89). Chase (1994) offers another example from Istanbul, Turkey. The first hamburgers appeared in Turkish cities in the early 1960s and offered an 'all-enveloping American environment' (Chase 1994: 75). At that time she feared this would destroy the vibrant local street trade based on Middle Eastern dishes. However, on returning 30 years later, she discovered that local foods had not only survived 'the gleaming temples of American fast-food merchandizing' (Chase 1994: 77) but that the variety, popularity and quality of local snacks and dishes had grown. Thus, demand for kebabs, koftes, aubergine with yoghurt, spicy bread appetisers and much else besides from across Turkey had burgeoned in bazaars, shops and cafés. Competition from Western foods had played a role in this revival but so, too, had the growth in the city's busy working population, searching for lunchtime sustenance at a time of rising inflation and the impossibility of returning home for midday meals in the face of growing traffic jams.

CREOLIZATION

Unlike indigenization, where the global is used to express essentially local cultural forms, the mixing of ingredients involved in **CREOLIZATION** generates altogether new, fused inventions. We can suppose that such creative blending has always occurred throughout human history. Of course, creolization has encompassed many cultural forms and not just consumerism. For example, in southern Nigeria (and elsewhere in Africa), the absorption of Christianity has led to the fusion of African music and language with standard church liturgy and the incorporation of premodern concerns with health and the desire for magical protection against the ill wishes of others into ritual activity. Consequently, many Nigerian churches are very different from their European counterparts.

 **key concept**

CREOLIZATION This term describes how cross-fertilization takes place between different cultures when they interact. The locals select particular elements from incoming cultures, endow these with meanings different from those they possessed in the original culture and then creatively merge these with indigenous traditions to create totally new forms. Although this definition serves most purposes, be warned that 'Creole' is used very inconsistently in different settings.

Two contemporary examples of creolization in clothing and music are now discussed.

Clothing

Clothing offers one arena for cultural blending as we saw in the case of Asian chic, where traditional fashions do not merely spread around the world but also tend to fuse with and absorb other national styles (Leshkowich 2003). Another example comes from Guatemala. Hendrickson (1996: 117–18) discovered that the rich Guatemalan tradition of weaving as a way of representing social identity, derived from ancient Mayan culture, had found its way into various Western mail-order catalogues. Here, among other items, she found jackets made from Guatemalan tie-dyed cloth presented in the style of Japanese kimonos and hand-woven Guatemalan fabrics offered for sale as cowboy blankets, which were supposed to express the earlier frontier ethos of the USA. In any case, the invitation to acquire worldwide ethnic craft products along with contemporary mass-produced factory goods speaks volumes about the mix-and-match consumer culture now available to us.

Music

Music is another sphere where creolization has always flourished. Indeed, music perhaps more than any other aesthetic medium fosters creolization because so much of its repertoire flourishes without necessarily requiring text – or lyrics. Freed from the constraints of language and therefore particular cultural or historical referents, it flows unstoppably across borders. Several classical composers borrowed national or regional peasant folk songs drawn from countries such as Russia, Scotland and Czechoslovakia for their symphonies. More important in terms of popular music has been the influence of Africa on the immense flowering of musical styles associated with the rise of pop and rock music in the 1950s and all its numerous variants since then. Thus, not only did early twentieth-century African-Americans living in the USA invent jazz in its various forms by drawing on African musical traditions, but the birth of rock music grew largely out of the marriage of jazz with country and western music. Such creative combinations have continued until the present and have included further black cultural infusions from West African bands, Caribbean reggae and rap from the USA.

But around the world, other cultures too have creolized various musical forms. There are many examples. One interesting example is the case of rai, a mix of gypsy flamenco music from Spain, rock and Bedouin folk songs. Rai's foremost exponent, Khaled Hadj Brahmim from Algeria, won a place in the French top 10 singles charts in 1992 and again in 1996 (Myers 1997). Another involves the popularity of hip-hop and rap among second-generation Turkish youth in Germany (Bennett 2000). Taken there originally by black soldiers serving with the US military forces stationed in the Frankfurt area, the young immigrants – and some native Germans – picked up the genre and the lyrics in nightclubs and from listening to US forces radio programmes. Like black soldiers living in

America, Turkish youths often felt like second-class citizens in white German society even though they were born there. Their music reflected this sense of alienation and rejection. Interestingly, some Turkish rappers began to import traditional music from Turkey either through cassettes or via family or business trips. They then fused this imported music with African-American rap while switching their song performances in German discos and clubs back into the Turkish language. This allowed them to rediscover their ethnic roots while remaining defiantly in a local German setting but at the same time they were creating a hybrid musical form.

REVIEW

As a preliminary to examining global consumerism, we discussed two contrasting theoretical positions concerning the nature of contemporary consumer culture. We laid particular emphasis on the more positive scenario, arguing that we are often not consumer dopes, but generally interpret and express the meanings implanted in goods by advertising in ways that reflect our personal lifestyle needs and participation in various social groups. (Of course, there are other reasons for worrying about consumerism, especially its cumulative, environmental impact on the world's biosphere. We examine this issue in Chapter 20).

We also pointed out that although there is some evidence that Western or American consumer goods, and the values they carry, are spreading rapidly to the developing world, transnational cultural flows are not one-way. Neither are they totally swamping local cultural forms. Rather, and as in the past, the local normally finds ways to capture, alter and mix external influences with indigenous ones or even to reinvent itself with the aid of new resources brought by the global.

FURTHER READING

- Mysteriously, writing on consumerism – something we all engage in every day – is not always easy to understand. However, D. Slater's book, *Consumer Culture and Modernity* (1997) is more accessible than most and provides a lively introduction to this subject. Try Chapters 1, 2 and 3.

- Similarly, T. Edwards' *Contradictions of Consumption* (2000) offers a wide-ranging exploration of the sociology of consumption and related topics.

- Edited by D. Howes, *Cross-cultural Consumption* (1996) includes some fascinating material. The introduction and Chapters 2, 4, 6 and 8 are especially useful.

- J. Tomlinson's *Globalization and Culture* (1999) explores the Americanization thesis critically, while exploring other useful themes relevant to global culture.

GROUP WORK

- Arrange a visit to two department stores and two supermarkets. By examining the labels and talking to the managers, construct a list of all the goods on sale that originate abroad and categorize them by type. In class, consider these questions. How many countries are involved? What kinds of goods come from which countries? In which areas do national goods tend to dominate over foreign ones? How can this be explained? What are your overall impressions?

■ Working in groups and pooling your knowledge, construct a rough chronology of rock and pop music since the 1960s. Establish the main types of musical genre and the lines of descent between them. Then consider two questions. Which kinds of young people mainly preferred which genres or fashions? To what extent, when and in what areas have foreign musical influences shaped your own country's tastes?

■ Arrange a class debate in advance on the proposition that: 'the globalization of consumer culture is destroying local traditions everywhere.' After the main speakers have given their prepared talks, each member of the class will give two reasons why they agree or disagree with the proposition.

QUESTIONS TO THINK ABOUT

?

1. Are we consumer dopes or consumer heroes?

2. Evaluate the main arguments for the proposition that the spread of consumerism leads to a homogeneous Americanized global culture.

3. In what ways does the local respond to the arrival of globalizing cultural forces?

4. To what extent have cultural and religious influences from outside Europe and North America affected social life since the 1970s?

WHAT'S ON THE WEB

■ http://www.indiana.edu/~wanthro/consum.htm Professor Richard Wilks, Indiana operates this site on global consumer culture. Last time we looked it had not been updated recently, but the links were still mostly valid.

■ http://www.consume.bbk.ac.uk/ This is the site of a 25-project programme on consumer behaviour, including global issues, funded by the British Economic and Social Research Council and the Arts and Humanities Research Council. Check out the really interesting project on chewing gum at http://www.consume.bbk.ac.uk/research/redclift_full.html.

■ http://homepages.gold.ac.uk/slater/consumer/index.htm This takes you to the homepages of Don Slater, Sociology Department, Goldsmiths' College, London. It has some links and some free material from his work.

■ http://www.mcdonaldization.com/ A site on the McDonaldization thesis, with over 80 articles – not all of them very good – with a real sense of engagement with the argument. Discussion forums are available if you are into that.

CHAPTER 14

Media and the Information Age

CONTENTS

'The medium is the message' was the disarmingly simple motto of the pioneer guru of contemporary media studies, Marshall McLuhan (1962). But what did he mean? Generally, systems of communication depend on a speaker or author (we can call this person 'a broadcaster'); a listener, viewer or reader ('an audience'); and a means of communication from the first to the second and sometimes back again. This third mechanism is the 'medium' or, in the plural form, the 'media', linking the broadcaster to the audience. Traditionally, the people broadcasting the message saw themselves as all-important. The impulse for inventive expression was especially lionized and celebrated. Penetrating political speakers, evocative poets, amusing after-dinner speakers or astute writers are all still accorded high prestige. Nevertheless, however brilliant and original the message, it only becomes salient if critics, readers, viewers and listeners – the audience – recognize the claims of the broadcasters and give them credibility or approval. In the past, the nature of the medium was generally disregarded as uninteresting or seen as inert.

It was McLuhan's great insight to recognize the power of the medium itself to change the message. Hitler and Goebbels had already showed how the radio could be commandeered as a propaganda device to be monopolized and manipulated for state purposes. (For the Nazis, the advantage of this 'one-way medium' was that it eliminated the kind of negative feedback that a controversial politician might expect at a public meeting.) Since the discovery of printing, the typeface and phonetic alphabet has dominated most written communication. Yet, almost without us being conscious of its supercession, the TV screen took over from the book and newspaper as the most common medium of communication. This had profound consequences. Print favoured systematic exposition and sequential, deductive thinking. TV is best suited, like many conversations, for impressionistic, contradictory or unstructured discourse (Castells 1996: 331–2). The central role of the medium can be seen in two simple examples:

1. Academics used to delivering scholarly papers to a respectful audience of colleagues or giving a lecture to an attentive class of students usually find themselves at sea in a TV studio, even though both are oral media and the intended message may be similar.
2. Listeners to a radio programme (who might be ironing, child-minding, cooking or driving while being tuned in) absorb highly selective messages. Sometimes they do this subconsciously, sometimes they choose what they want or need to hear in competition with what may be other, more important sounds, like a baby crying or the dog barking.

We can now begin to understand McLuhan's point. It matters a great deal through what means the message is conveyed, though it is probably best to consider his maxim that the medium is the message as a form of poetic licence, making a good point in an exaggerated way in order to convey his meaning more powerfully. However, that the medium structures, constrains or amplifies the message and its reception is now well established in empirical studies.

The media foster globalization just as they are themselves changed by stepping up to a global scale. In this chapter, we will provide a definition and characterization of the media and also examine issues of ownership and content in relation to the growth of electronic media. We will also discuss how the acceptance of the telephone as a mass consumer good and the arrival of linked computer networks have generated what has been described as an 'informational' or (more simply) an information society. Certainly, these developments have had profound economic and social effects. We also consider the question of whether the new possibilities for sharing information and interactive communication have promoted fresh democratic possibilities at local, national and global levels.

WHAT ARE 'THE MEDIA'?

The media are agencies and organizations that specialize in the communication of ideas, information and images of our environment, our communities and ourselves. The media also project images about 'others' and their communities. Many journalists and media workers proclaim that all they are doing is collecting and disseminating ideas, information and images. They are, they often protest, not to be blamed for the content of their reports or the consequences that might arise. 'Don't shoot the messengers if they bring you bad news' is their refrain, one copied from an ancient Greek saying when a hapless runner brought news of a military defeat.

Such observations would now be regarded as naive. Not only Marshal McLuhan, but many other commentators (and indeed many in the audience) believe that the media are doing all sorts of other things than reporting news neutrally, whether the wider effects are intentional or unintentional. The media certainly can be abused, for example by politicians who seek to monopolize them or influence their content or by terrorists using threats against hostages to propagate their grisly messages. They also can communicate more than their surface message. In other words, there is a hidden meaning, or often an unintended consequence, in effecting communication. The media, in short, communicate *values, emotions* and *opinions* as well as ideas and information.

In the case of a newspaper, there is formally a nominal difference between the editorial columns (in the broadsheet newspapers they often appear in the centre of the newspaper) and the news pages. However, tabloid newspapers often run political or promotional campaigns on the front pages of their newspapers that elide the difference between advertising, editorial opinion and news. The popular English daily, the *Sun*, has specialized in devising jingoistic and xenophobic headlines. When campaigning against the EU, the paper made a front-page plea to all its readers to attend a rally at Trafalgar Square. The campaign was headed 'Up Yours, Delors' and was a crude personal attack, with virtually no news content, on the former president of the EU. When it briefly looked like the Falklands War between Britain and Argentina might be averted, the Argentine military government were urged to 'Stick It Up Your Junta'. When the British government urged NATO to bomb Serbia in March 1999, the tabloid's front page concurred, with the headline 'Clobba Slobba'.

The UK tabloids have also taken the opportunity to exploit marital discord among the British royal family and to provide constant unsolicited advice on the future constitutional arrangements of the UK. Many newspapers paid vast sums to 'paparazzi' photographers for intimate pictures of Diana, Princess of Wales, caught in an unguarded moment. The mass waves of emotion (again communicated and amplified by the media) surrounding her untimely death for a while shamed the most populist newspaper editors from persisting in their use of intrusive photography. Many seasoned observers of the media correctly predicted that this uncharacteristic restraint would be a temporary phenomenon, with commercial considerations soon taking over again. Information, news, emotions, values and opinions are, in short, hopelessly intermingled by the media themselves and also interwoven in the minds of the audience. The consequences of this confusion may be seen, at a trivial level, by the fact that actors report that many of their fans are unable to distinguish between a fictional character in a TV serial and the actor who plays the part of that character. A more serious example occurred in late January 2006, when a Danish newspaper published a series of cartoons, one depicting Muhammad with a turban twisted into a bomb. After the cartoons were reproduced in a number of European countries, many in the Muslim world were outraged. Government policy towards Muslims, the newspapers' right to free expression and Western public opinion were hopelessly conflated in the minds of many Muslims who were aghast at the newspapers' insensitivity and ignorance (images of the Prophet are forbidden) and at 'the West's' attacks on Islam. Riots and protests in Indonesia, Gaza and elsewhere immediately followed.

Broadly, the conventional media divide into the print media (books, magazines and newspapers) and the visual/aural media (movies, radio and television). As we will see later, new and hybrid forms of media are emerging through digital means. Hybridity also characterizes the conventional media. In the press coverage of TV serials, the media are mutually parasitical, often with a sort of cannibalistic feeding frenzy taking place. Radio reports the headlines in the press or 'What the papers say'. The newspapers list and review the programmes on the television and radio. Feature movies are adapted from books. The reactionary and eccentric press mogul, William Randolph Hearst (1853–1961), provided the model for the classic movie, *Citizen Kane*. The people in the media select each other as so-called 'celebrities'. Celebrity culture has been democratized in the past by talent and beauty shows where hitherto 'unknown' people are discovered. Now 'reality shows' like *Big Brother* pit unknowns against 'B list celebs' (often fading TV personalities), usually with the plan that an unknown will triumph.

CORPORATE OWNERSHIP OF THE MEDIA

The media's conflation of fact and fiction, or reason and emotion, is important not only in a trivial sense. Large media corporations may contrive to use this facility to project images and ideas that work to their own interest rather than the national or international interest. This statement might be thought vastly exaggerated if not for the fact that some corporations have achieved an oligopolistic, complex and overlapping control of newspapers, film archives, television networks, radio stations, cable companies, book publishers, music labels and satellite stations. This is true particularly of Rupert Murdoch's News Corporation, but true also of giants like Viacom, AOL Time Warner, Disney and the German-based Bertelsmann (Table 14.1). The integration of the programming, production, marketing and broadcasting functions in the hands of a small number of media corporations is also increasingly evident. The combined ownership of different media gives such corporations a global reach that is sometimes seen as threatening democracy, diversity and freedom of expression. The media moguls are able to influence business, international agencies and national governments, which often attend to them as if they were suppliant courtiers presenting themselves for royal approval. We can allude to one example of media conglomerate power that caused considerable discussion in the USA. Early in 2004, the Walt Disney Company prevented its subsidiary Miramax from distributing Michael Moore's anti-war film, *Fahrenheit 9/11*. According to one report, the company was concerned that distributing the movie 'would have endangered Disney's tax breaks for its theme parks in Florida, where the president's brother Jeb is governor' (http://www.fepproject.org/factsheets/mediademocracy.html).

TABLE 14.1 Ownership of the mass media, 2006	
Name of corporation	**Sample of companies owned**
Viacom (USA)	Columbian Broadcasting System (CBS), Showtime, Music TeleVision (MTV), Blockbuster Video, Simon and Schuster publishers, 180 radio stations, 35 TV channels
AOL Time Warner (USA)	America Online (AOL), Cable News Network (CNN), Time-Life Books, DC Comics, and *Fortune, Sports Illustrated* and *People* magazines
The Walt Disney Company (USA)	American Broadcasting Corporation (ABC) television network, the cable channels Disney and the History Channel, Miramax Films, 10 TV stations, more than 60 radio stations around the country, the Disney theme parks
General Electric (USA)	National Broadcasting Corporation television network, Universal Pictures
News Corporation (USA)	FOX, *National Geographic*, Fox News, Fox Movies, Sky satellite systems around the world, 20th Century Fox film studios, *The New York Post*, HarperCollins publishers, 34 TV stations in the USA
Vivendi Universal (USA)	CANAL+, Cineplex Odeon Theatres, music companies Music Corporation of America (MCA), Polygram, Universal Music Group, Decca, Deutsche Grammophon, Vivendi Telecom, 26.8 million shares of AOL Time Warner
Sony (Japan)	Sony Pictures, Columbia TriStar, Animax Japan, Sony Music Publishing (joint venture with Michael Jackson)
Bertelsmann (Germany)	Radio Television Luxemburg (RTL) II, Random House, Doubleday, Alfred A. Knopf, Vintage, *Financial Times Deutschland*

SOURCES: http://www.fepproject.org/factsheets/mediademocracy.html (Free Expression Policy Project, New York University School of Law); http://www.cjr.org/tools/owners/ (Columbia Journalism Review)

The control of global communications in the hands of a limited number of players began in the nineteenth century and followed the lines of European expansion, imperialism and colonialism. The old Hollywood movies about the American West frequently illustrate the march of land-based communications technology. The stagecoach operated by companies like Wells Fargo carried mail as well as passengers and (as shown in the movies) was victim to washed-out roads, broken wheels, lame horses, hold-ups by highwaymen and attacks by Native Americans. The railways and telegraph lines slowly overcame these problems and offered a secure means of communication. However, the capital investment in railways and the reliance on them was so great that whoever owned them was immediately pivotal to the politics and economic life of the time.

A similar logic obtained when steamships superseded sailing ships. Perhaps the most important development, however, was cable communications, available from the middle half of the nineteenth century. Cables were stretched along poles, buried underground and laid on the seabed. News agencies like Reuters rapidly bought up the smaller companies. Baron von Reuter (1816–99) initially started his service by using pigeons to carry news between Germany, France and Belgium, but European governments soon became alarmed at his near-monopoly of news. Although resident in London, even the British government was so concerned at the thought that Reuter – a German national – could control telegraph lines during times of war that it developed alternative, secret lines of communications.

The dominance of Reuters plus the four other big Western news agencies also means that news stories from many parts of the world either are not broadcast, or are trivial, misleading and ethnocentric. In the 1980s, the governments of African, Latin American, Asian and Middle Eastern states sought to use the good offices of UNESCO to foster acceptance of stories emanating from their own national agencies. In response, the USA – followed meekly by the UK – walked out of the organization, refusing to pay their contributions. Although the walkout was complicated by accusations of corruption and mismanagement in UNESCO, it seems that the Western media were strongly lobbying for the walkout and were probably influential in that decision.

The ownership and control of the cables – and later the satellites – is of course strategically and diplomatically vital, but it is also commercially and culturally important. Those who own the means of communications can link together vast audiences and potentially feed them with similar and selective messages. Billions saw the rites surrounding the death of the Princess of Wales, while individual sporting events also attract enormous global viewing figures (Table 14.2).

These major 'events' are of course atypical and illustrate only the latent dangers of the control of the airwaves. More gradual and perhaps more insidious are the ways in which internationally targeted television soaps like the pioneering *Dallas* were thought to convey a narrow, individualistic and materialist message. Fortunately, as we shall see below, audience research on the 'consumption' of *Dallas* does not support such a narrow presumption.

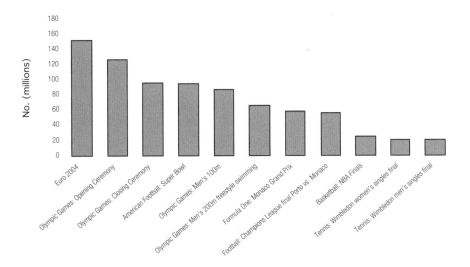

Figure 14.1 **Top 10 sporting events, by viewing numbers**
SOURCE: Adapted from *Guardian Unlimited* (23 December, 2004, http://media.guardian.co.uk/) using a survey covering 57 major TV markets, accounting for over 90 per cent of TV households globally

TELECOMMUNICATIONS

The fear of control by governments and owners of large news corporations over the global media is somewhat offset by the capacity of many people (obviously wealth and access has a lot to do with *how many* people) to circumvent the media by direct lateral communication. This is particularly true of the telephone system, and more particularly of long-distance telephones and, as we will see in a while, the internet. The global telephone network is now very dense, while the cost of calls is rapidly declining. Let us try to demonstrate this growth by reference to five developments:

1. In 1965, 85 per cent of the world's telephone lines were in Europe and North America. There was just one transatlantic telephone cable that could handle 89 calls at a time. A three-minute call from the USA to Europe or Asia typically cost US$90 at 1995 prices.
2. By 1995, however, the global network comprised more than 600 million telephone lines and over 1.2 billion telephones in 190 countries. The transatlantic cable and satellite network handled about a million simultaneous calls between the USA and Europe, at a typical cost of US$3 for a three-minute call, one-thirtieth of the price 30 years earlier.
3. Subscribers in New York can telephone London for less than the cost of calling Los Angeles.
4. Even that reduced price is massively marked up by the telephone companies whose costs per one-minute transatlantic call are a little over one US cent a minute.
5. By 2005, the Telecom Regulatory Authority of India said the country had 76 million mobile phone users and 49 million fixed-line users. Telephone usage rocketed from less than 4 per cent of the population in 2002 to 11.43 per cent.

As the Indian figures demonstrate, Cairncross (1997a) correctly predicated that the costs of connectivity would be dramatically driven down by the arrival of wireless systems (bounced off satellites) and the gathering pace of privatization of the telecoms companies. Finland, for example, has 52 companies, while more than 80 new companies entered the market in the Asia Pacific region in the 1990s. In the late 1980s, there were 190 companies routing international calls, by the late 1990s, there were 5,000. In many towns and cities globally, a residential customer has the choice of a conventional copper line from a national telephone company, a fibreoptic fixed line from a cable company, a wireless system with an aerial linking to a conventional network or one of a number of mobile wireless services. Web phones using VoIP (voice over internet protocol) will provide another alternative, marrying computer, web and telephonic technology. By 2006, VoIP technology had already been adopted by 10 per cent of Japanese telephone users.

Figure 14.2 **A cellular telephone is used alongside a remote river**
Outside South and North Africa, telephone connections in the rest of Africa were very sparse, perhaps about 4.6 million for the other 47 countries on the continent in 2001. The cost of wiring up the continent and theft of the copper were major deterrents to extending landlines. Wireless phones have allowed Africa a benign 'later developer' effect. Many people of modest means can now access mobiles.

The benefits of the revolution in telephony are not all located in the rich countries. Take the case of mobile phones. These provide a *supplement* for a well-developed telephone network in wealthy countries like Japan where, in 2005, 39.4 million of the country's 127.5 million population owned a mobile phone. But mobile phones are an *alternative* to fixed-line telephone systems in many poorer countries, where the cost of wiring dispersed rural areas may be exorbitant. Clearly, however cheaply mobile phones can be marketed, there will be many unable to take advantage of the new technology themselves. But, indirect connections via low-cost local services, small businesses or NGOs will probably greatly enhance access to a mobile phone service, even for the very poor. In South Africa, ownership of mobiles (called cell phones) has rocketed by 13 million in four years (Figure 14.3), but even in poorer African countries, small kiosks selling phone cards and providing temporary access to a mobile connection have brought technology to many.

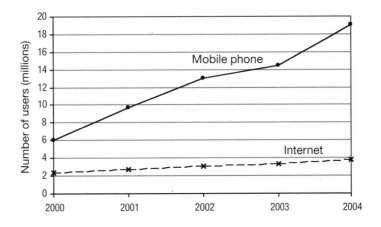

Figure 14.3 **Internet and mobile phone users in South Africa, 2000–04**
SOURCE: Brown and Molla (2005)

THE COMPUTER AND THE INTERNET

By 1995, the internet covered no more than 2 per cent of the world's population, but its exponential growth over a very short period suggests that there is plenty of room for growth. The worldwide number of internet users reached nearly 935 million in 2004 (Table 14.2) and should rise to 1.1 billion out of a global population of 6.5 billion at the end of 2005 (at the time of writing this, the final figures have not been tabulated). While the USA remains the number one user, internet usage is growing robustly in China, India, Brazil and many other places.

The arrival of the internet, which links individual computers through computer networks, broadband, wireless connections and modems, raises a number of democratic possibilities. News groups (sometimes called 'discussion groups') can be set up out of reach of the conventional media, while opinions, ideas and attitudes can be formulated in dialogue with other people linked to the internet, often on the other side of the globe. The media have attempted to get in on the act, with the production of digital versions of newspapers and digitally archived radio, but these have been notably unsuccessful in containing the explosion of information outside their control.

The democratic possibilities of the internet remain controversial. However, the very structure of decentralized control has prevented business and the media from gaining too close a control over it. This is inherent in the system, in that (at least in the folk history of the internet) the original design was intended to prevent the possibilities of a Russian attack on the Pentagon permanently disabling all military communications. Computer-to-computer connections deliberately bypassed a central switching station, a model the universities and libraries of the world replicated, and rapidly connected to each other through unusual routes. The media moguls, software companies and business interests are now trying to control access to the internet by developing specialized software, searching mechanisms ('browsers') and commercial gateways. They are also buying chunks of sensitive data and information and holding them in electronic stores that can only be accessed by codes, for which a consumer will have to pay. The success of the web browser Google looked at first as a triumph for democratic control of the web. The founders of the company had promised famously 'to do no evil', yet in January 2006, they kowtowed to Chinese government censorship of their images and pages in exchange for access to the Chinese market. The drive for more and more information to be browsed by Google has also somewhat alarmed intellectual copyright holders (authors, artists and publishers), who depend on royalties for continuing their creative work and who have accused the company of 'kleptomania'.

TABLE 14.2	Top 15 internet users, by country, 2004	
Year-end 2004	**Internet users (000s)**	**Share %**
1. USA	185,550	19.86
2. China	99,800	10.68
3. Japan	78,050	8.35
4. Germany	41,880	4.48
5. India	36,970	3.96
6. UK	33,110	3.54
7. South Korea	31,670	3.39
8. Italy	25,530	2.73
9. France	25,470	2.73
10. Brazil	22,320	2.39
11. Russia	21,230	2.27
12. Canada	20,450	2.19
13. Mexico	13,880	1.49
14. Spain	13,440	1.44
15. Australia	13,010	1.39
Top 15 countries	**662,360**	**70.88**
Worldwide total	**934,480**	**100**

SOURCE: Computer Industry Almanac (2005, http://www.c-i-a.com/pr0904.htm)

Commercial use of the internet was, at first, inhibited by the difficulties in providing secure controls to prevent the discovery of credit card numbers, bank codes, personal identification numbers (PINs) and other sensitive information. This remains a serious problem. The rise in computer fraud has not prevented the use of the internet for billions of small sales and transactions. Ordering books, buying theatre tickets, selecting groceries for delivery and interrogating bank accounts are now routine operations for many customers. Despite the increased commercialization of the internet, there is little doubt that lateral links have proliferated faster than business interests predicted and that much of the internet will escape regulation and commercialization. The anarchist spirit that underlies much of the communication on the internet has also been heartening to those who have felt oppressed by the global power of the large media corporations. Clearly, such links have provided a more democratic and less controlled form of communication between friends, families and business and professional associates across the world. The lies and half-truths of politicians can be made to look hollow when comparisons are made by those callers and bloggers (see below) with specialized experience and close familiarity with the issues being discussed. Values and social constructions of reality are also less amenable to manipulation by powerful interest groups.

THE RISE OF INFORMATIONAL SOCIETY

Futurologists extrapolate from existing trends and make more or less sophisticated predictions about the future.

Such is the level of internet activity and telecommunications traffic that the expression 'informational society' has been used to describe how important are the flows and links that criss-cross the globe. Like some sociologists, *futurologists* and computer buffs are not known for their elegant use of language. Terms such as 'the informational society', 'information superhighway', 'informatization', 'information technology', 'fourth-generation language', 'ISDN' (integrated services digital network), 'hypertext', 'VoIP' and the like are coined almost as fast as they are discarded for newer and often even more enigmatic vocabularies. Whatever the shifts in vocabulary, a persistent theme is that communication technologies and computer technologies are both developing rapidly in their own right and converging into a set of shared information technologies.

Global Thinkers 14 **MANUEL CASTELLS (1942–)**

Manuel Castells was raised in Spain but moved to France in 1963. He was an assistant professor in Paris at the time of the 'events' in May 1968, when students and workers challenged the French state in democratic and creative expressions of revolutionary zeal. 'Be realistic: ask for the impossible', said one street poster. 'It is forbidden to forbid', read another. The 'events' were too amorphous in aim to displace the government or result in lasting changes, but they informed Castells' understanding of where the challenges to the state were likely to emerge. He was particularly interested in urban social movements struggling for urban renewal, welfare entitlements and public amenities. In analysing these protests, Castells

(1983) made decisive breaks with prior understanding of urbanization and political struggle (focusing less on space than on cultures of consumption and less on class than on shifting communities of interest based on shared information).

Castells has published about 25 books, often pursuing his interest in urban processes, but undoubtedly his magnum opus is his trilogy The Information Age: Economy, Society and Culture *(1996, 1997, 1998). Here we see Castells departing from the urban question and recognizing that information networks had created a new urban space, 'the informational city', as a distinctive and further stage in the capitalist mode of production (Castells 1989). In effect, connectivity had expanded the city to a global scale and created, as he put it in two memorable phrases, 'a network society' and 'a space of flows'. In* The Rise of the Network Society *(1996: 412), Castells rather cryptically defines the space of flows as 'the material organization of time-sharing social practices that work through flows'. More concretely, he argues that the space of flows is supported by three layers: first, microelectronics, computer processing, telecommunications and the like – what we can readily understand as the hardware. Second, the nodes and hubs where information is gathered, stored, exchanged and distributed – what we can understand as the network. Third, the spatial organization of the social actors who dominate the information flows and ensure that they are tilted asymmetrically in their favour – what we can understand as organization of a new dominant class (Castells 1996: 412–18). This is an ambitious thesis, in effect updating Marxism by suggesting that whereas the ruling class in industrial society owned capital, in the networked society they command information.*

Castells readily conceded that the process was incomplete. Those who profited from prior forms of privilege and advantage were able to adapt them to the network society, as Toyota did in manufacturing (1996: 157–60) and Asian traders did in business and commerce (1996: 172–90). Nor was the information age without antagonism, between those who could 'go with the flow' and, in effect, ride on the crest of the wave and those who were still anchored in prior, often territorial-based identities and affiliations. As he suggested: 'New information technologies are integrating the world in global networks of instrumentality. Yet the distinctive social and political trend of the 1990s was the construction of social action and politics around primary identities, either ascribed, rooted in history and geography, or newly built in an anxious search for meaning and spirituality' (Castells 1996: 22). The result was to set up contradictions between cosmopolitans and locals, between virtual and place-based communities and, ultimately, between 'the net' and 'the self'.

SOURCE: Castells (1983, 1989, 1996, 1997, 1998)

The convergence of communications and computer technologies can be seen in the often bewildering overlap of hitherto separated functions. One can send a fax from a computer via a modem or network. Some fax machines have sophisticated functions like copying, scanning, automatic switching between fax and voice calls, mechanisms for correcting telephone line noise, switching to alternative telephone networks and acting as a printer for a computer. Email messages sent over the internet can contain formatted files from PCs or networked file stores. Photographic images can be scanned, digitalized, compressed, distorted, stored and transmitted. Voice, images and music are easily digitized, compressed, recorded and played back – a familiar task to the 35 million users of the iPod (2005 figures) and similar devices.

Simply getting such technologies to work seamlessly and feeling comfortable with them is more than many of us can achieve. Some people have become technophobes or **Luddites** in order to maintain their sense of self-worth in the face of the incomprehensible. Castells (1996: 22–5) goes so far as to argue that even as 'information systems and networks augment human powers of organization and integration, they simultaneously subvert the traditional Western concept of a separate independent subject'.

> **Luddites** were English artisans who rioted rather than accept mechanical and technical changes.

Communications and linked computer systems simulate in important respects a human brain. The 'artificial' in artificial intelligence is rapidly coming to resemble the real thing. It is perhaps not surprising that one patient in psychoanalysis saw in his dream an image of his head behind which was suspended a keyboard. He felt, he said, like a 'programmed head'. (We know the feeling.)

As the machine–human interface begins to naturalize through such emulative technologies as memory chips, virtual reality and artificial intelligence, humans will begin to lose the primacy of their own sensory perceptions. In the days of mass production, the notion of alienation was used to suggest that the social relations of production were artificial and that human nature was being altered to fit in with the rhythms of machines and assembly lines. Alienation in the informational society is even more profound. Whereas in the industrial age, machines mimicked a person's physical characteristics (the clanking robot with arms and legs being emblematic), in the informational age, the conscious mind itself is emulated and may eventually be relegated to a marginal status.

INFORMATIONAL SOCIETY: ECONOMIC EFFECTS

The growth of the informational society has had profound economic effects. In his *The Condition of Postmodernity* (1989), David Harvey was particularly interested in the reduction of time it takes for capital to accumulate. The days are long gone when King Midas stacked his gold in his cellar or when medieval bankers wrote longhand letters of credit. Salaries are now normally credited through automated clearance systems, while transfers of funds are virtually instantaneous. Dividends, interest and profit can be remitted relatively freely (though some states still try to prevent this), while investment, loans and credits can flow just as quickly in the opposite direction. The sale and purchase of stocks and shares is also virtually instantaneous.

The very speed and volume of these transactions make them difficult for the national authorities to track, police or tax. With the collapse of the Bretton Woods system (see Chapter 3) in the 1970s, Germany and the USA stopped trying to control the inflow and outflow of capital. This move was followed by

the incoming Thatcher government in Britain in 1979 and, later, by the deregulation and freeing of the exchange control mechanism in many other countries.
The financial market became global in character within a few years. This has
certainly profited many individuals and companies, but can provoke sudden
financial crises in particular countries. These occurred in Europe in 1992/3,
Mexico in 1994/5 and in the tiger economies of Southeast Asia in late 1997
when, for example, the bhat (the Thai currency) lost over 30 per cent of its value
in three months. Out of 91 Thai finance companies, 58 were suspended after the
government futilely spent 9 per cent of the country's 1996 GDP trying to keep
them afloat (*The Economist*, 18–24 October 1997: 131).

As the circulation of money gradually moved out of the control of national
governments, new markets in their currencies developed. Perhaps the most
notable was the Eurodollar, which trades in Europe outside the control of the
American authorities. Eurodollar deposits were particularly fuelled by 'oil money'
after 1973 and sought a home away from the uncertainties of the Middle East.
Very large sums were involved – US$50 billion in 1973 rising to US$2 trillion
in 1987, just 14 years later. The 1987 figure for Eurodollars was about the same
as the total amount of currency circulating in the USA at the same time.

As the circulation time of capital is reduced, the effective size of the globe
shrinks and it is possible to trade stocks on a 24-hour basis. If London is closed,
New York will be open. If that in turn is shut, Tokyo will be open. By linking to
the key 'global cities' (see Chapter 17), firms, TNCs and individuals can use these
different spaces instantaneously for trade, investment and banking, thus
compressing both time and space. The difficulty in immediately spotting the
illegal trading activities of Nick Leeson, the English 'rogue trader' working in
Singapore in 1995, is illustrative of this capacity. He lost his employers, Barings
Bank, US$1.3 billion. In previous decades it would be difficult to imagine that
the activities of just one currency trader could have laid low one of the most
venerable of British financial institutions.

INFORMATIONAL SOCIETY: SOCIAL EFFECTS

Despite the positive possibilities and examples described in Box 14.1 below, the
negative – or presumed negative – effects of mass media and mass communication worry many observers. Three principal effects are often mentioned, which
we list and then discuss:

1. The effects of TV on patterns of violence, sexual mores and educational
   competence.
2. The creation of a global culture that is becoming increasingly homogenized
   and ersatz, a reduction to the lowest common denominator.
3. The growth of destructive consumerism.

Box 14.1

Radios in Lebanon, blogs in Iran

While the sinister power of the media is often denounced, a number of studies in the 1960s showed that it also acts as a force for democratization and 'progressive' social change. Lerner (cited by Kornblum 1988) examined a number of remote villages in rural Lebanon. He noticed that rural villagers had developed a passion for owning radios, which allowed them to access stories and information about the world outside. He demonstrated that when connectivity increased, the power of the village patriarchs declined, in other words, there was a major shift in power relations. When television arrived, women were able to see Western women in roles other than that of filial daughters, modest sisters and devoted mothers. The number wearing a veil dropped and there were other signs of women expressing more personal freedom in their lifestyles. We must be careful not to display our normative preferences here, but it would perhaps not be going too far to describe the effects of the mass media in Lebanon as 'positive'. The media have also helped to disseminate mass education, provide some encouragement to mass literacy and provide mass entertainment on a grand scale. The recognition of other people's cultures may give rise to sentiments of common humanity or at least a recognition of cultural diversity.

A more contemporary Middle Eastern example is provided by the development of weblogs (blogs) in Iran. One of the most widely read blog on Iranian politics and society is provided by Hossein Derakshan (http://hoder.com/weblog/). As Coleman (2005: 77–8) comments, blogs in Iran have fulfilled the following functions:

- they have provided first-hand reports of events like student protests

- young people have used them as a dating service (these are not common in Iran)

- parents have got to know their children's values

- they have informed Iranians abroad about events in their home country

- some bloggers have been hired by the newspapers

- politicians and policy-holders read and have responded to blogs

- they have greatly enhanced access to Persian-language sources and information

- they have enticed some web users away from chat rooms to a more serious engagement with politics

- e-zines (web magazines) have developed, some with many readers.

We can add that with the confrontation between the EU and the USA on the one hand and Iran on the other over the development of nuclear energy (which some think could be a prelude to nuclear weaponry), this blog provides a telling insight into attitudes in Iran.

SOURCES: Lerner, cited in Kornblum (1996); Coleman (2005: 77–8)

NEGATIVE EFFECTS OF TV VIEWING

The concern about the effects of TV viewing has some intuitive support in the upward trend in TV viewing hours. In US homes, the television is turned on for an average of seven hours a day. It is estimated that by the age of 18, the average American child will have witnessed 18,000 simulated murders on TV (Watson 1998: 238). It is only reasonable that many parents, particularly those with young children, are disturbed at the thought of their children arbitrarily imitating images, ideas and behaviour patterns from the screen. However, the connection between lived violence and mediated violence is still uncertain. Some researchers point out that the most violent period in US history was between 1929 and 1933 when TV did not exist, and that in many poor countries, the level of violence experienced is high even where television ownership is low (Watson 1998: 239). Clearly, violence is not *only* caused by television. However, as Watson (1998: 238) says, the argument cannot be dismissed lightly while 80 research studies affirm the connection between television and actual violence. At the very least; 'the more we see of violence, the more we might become insensitive to it, and thus eventually immune to it. Either way it might confirm our view that out there is a dangerous and hostile world.'

Beyond the issue of violence, long hours of watching television might produce some kind of osmosis effect, in which people, children in particular, are unable to distinguish fantasy from reality. Of course some postmodernists embrace this elision of a boundary between the imaginary and the real. Fortunately, there seems to be strong evidence that despite the TV being on for so long each day, many people ignore routine programmes. The television becomes like moving wallpaper – a mildly interesting and changing pattern, rather like coloured heated oil blobs moving up and down in a lava lamp.

THE 'DUMBING DOWN' OF CULTURE

The concern about a cultural collapse to the lowest common denominator seems more likely to be soundly based. Prime-time viewing often consists of endless soaps, quiz, reality and game shows and B-quality movies. The media have also been instrumental in spreading only one global language – English, usually American English. Even significant languages like French and Spanish have had to bow to its hegemony. And although more people speak Chinese, they are concentrated in China and the China diaspora. The media have spread English as the global medium of exchange, a situation that also applies to international law, travel, business and diplomacy.

In itself, the use of English does not signify the dumbing down of culture. However, the rich tapestry of myth, storytelling and literature in other languages may gradually be lost, except to scholars working in arcane fields. Cultures depend on context for their vitality and growth. If children can see little point in learning the language of their parents and grandparents, increasingly the complexity and richness of the world will be enfeebled.

We discussed the character of global consumerism in Chapter 13, but it is worth mentioning in this context how the global media effectively diffuse consumerism. The goods that are desirable, the music that is hip, the clothes that are fashionable or the 'look' that is trendy are all rapidly absorbed through the power of the media. Perhaps surprisingly, this process of consumer imitation and emulation even had profound effects in fuelling the neoliberal opposition to state communism. The capacity of the media to suggest that there is a wonderful cornucopia of goods just waiting on the other side of the hill led many in the former communist countries to confuse the free market with political and social freedom.

The effects of mass media and mass tourism can come together in a negative sense, in that other countries and other cultures become mere objects for consumption. (Some more positive outcomes of mass consumption are also considered in Chapter 13.) The TV provides an endless stream of consumer and food programmes set in 'exotic' destinations. 'Holidays' are prizes given in fatuous competitions and dating programmes. The newspapers are full of travel writing and adverts for low-cost flights. Some companies, notably Disney (Disney World and Euro Disney) have brought together the consumption of goods, tourism and culture in a single setting. Children can graze on authentic American hamburgers, coke, ice cream and popcorn while sitting on a mechanical boat going on a so-called 'Caribbean cruise'. Segments of historical reality are reordered for the purposes of this journey – pirates wave cutlasses, black actors sing 'Ol Man River' and girls do belly dances in some sort of extraordinary pastiche of history, tradition and authenticity.

So, in short, communications do not always lead to multicultural understanding and mutual respect for other peoples. Instead, the need to annex the media to consumerism leads to an appropriation of other cultures in the greater interest of profits. This double-edged feature of democratic openness, yet commercial closure, is also seen in the case of the humble telephones. Although they can be used to foster lateral contacts outside the big media players and help to connect family members, they can also be used to cement shady business deals and for recreational purposes, not necessarily of a savoury sort. By 1997, international telephone sex chatlines had become a US$2 billion business (Cairncross 1997a: 4). This observation is also true of the internet. On 20 September 2005, Google recorded 8.2 billion sites in response to the word 'sex' (of course many were not pornographic but most, we surmise, were).

GENDER AND REPRESENTATION

Through the power of the image, the information age can also strengthen stereotypes or legitimate longstanding inequalities of class, race and gender. This likely effect has been of particular concern to feminist scholars, who have suggested that the media distorts, underrepresents or misrepresents women (Friedan 1963;

van Zoonen 1994 provide classic accounts). Women are normally narrowly portrayed in three ways:

- as wife, mother and housekeeper (thus reinforcing conventionally assigned roles and limiting women's professional horizons)
- as sexual referents who confer their sexual attractiveness onto a prosaic object (thus advertisements show chocolate bars being licked suggestively by conventionally attractive young women)
- as sex objects to be used by men (in some cases in masochistic, perverted and pornographic depictions).

As van Zoonen (1994: 30) contended, many aspects of women's lives and experiences are not properly reflected in the media: 'Many more women work than the media suggest, very few women resemble the femmes fatales of movies and TV series, and women's desires extend far beyond the hearth and home of traditional women's magazines.'

The increasing feminization of the workforce and increased recognition of domestic responsibilities by males have now significantly altered the representation of women in the media. Nonetheless, the bias remains clear. The obverse face of recognizing that images of women are a misrepresentation is the problem that advertisers and the media imply that 'real men' are strong, aggressive and in control. Particularly for working-class males who have less access to economic power or workplace authority, 'manhood' is achieved, so the media imply, through a celebration of brawn and the body's potential for strength, force and violence (Katz 1995: 135).

A more complex way of understanding why gender misrepresentation arises in the cinema, television and in advertisements is to argue that the object for nearly all visual representations of the body is that of a female, often a scantily clad or naked one. This can be seen at an obvious level in art, where male artists' depictions of the female nude are common, but where it is virtually impossible to find a female artist's painting of a male nude. In short, 'ways of seeing' are predominantly male. As Berger (1972: 47) wrote: 'Men act and women appear. Men look at women. Women watch themselves being looked at. This determines not only most relations between men and women but also the relation of women to themselves.' The result is that women become trapped in a male gaze. As Gledhill (1992: 193–4) puts it: 'The subject of [the] mainstream narrative is the patriarchal, bourgeois individual: that unified centred point from which the world is organized and given meaning.' Thus, the spectator is generally masculine while the camera appears to be held by the gaze of a male. The image is designed to flatter or console the male ego.

As we shall see also in our next section on race and the media, a critique of the representation of gender is simultaneously a demand to recognize complexity and diversity. As van Zoonen (1994: 33) insists: 'Gender should be conceived not as a fixed property of individuals, but as part of an ongoing process by which subjects are constituted, often in paradoxical ways. The identity that emerges is therefore fragmented and dynamic; gender does not determine or exhaust identity.'

▪ ▪ ▪ ▪ ▪ ▪ ▪ ▪ ▪ THE MEDIA, RACE AND SOCIAL IDENTITY

We have discussed the concentration of media ownership and the integration of the production, marketing and broadcasting functions in the hands of a few corporations. But does this inevitably lead to acceptance of the messages these corporations seek to disseminate? Morley and Robins (1995: 126–46) warn us against accepting what they call a 'hypodermic' model of media effects – the assumption that there are necessary cultural and powerful effects on all those who are 'injected' with media products.

They do not argue that the effects of the domination of the media are negligible, merely that they are more complex and more variable. Take the case of the TV soap *Dallas*, often cited as a classic example of Western media imperialism, yet different local studies have yielded a catalogue of variable responses to the programme. Morley and Robins (1995: 120) cite an important study in the Netherlands, which found that Dutch women saw the programme 'through the grid of their own feminist agenda'. Far from seeing 'JR' as successfully asserting his patriarchal power, respondents saw the women characters as making ironic jibes at the men's doomed bids for male dominance. They did not see the men as offering credible macho characters, rather they were there, the Dutch women thought, to provoke a good laugh. Australian Aborigine, American, Russian, North African and Japanese audiences all saw the programme in a different way, through the differently tinted lenses of their own cultures, kinship patterns, social preferences, religions and norms.

While different audiences are not the victims of an intrusive hypodermic needle, they also cannot be seen as 'semiotic guerrillas', accepting, discarding or refracting the message as they choose (Morley and Robins 1995: 127). The menu from which they have to choose is limited and arguably getting more restrictive despite the increasing number of TV channels and FM broadcasts. On the one hand, the proliferation of both analogue and digital channels allows the development of niche markets (for example programmes aimed at small ethnic minorities or covering hobbies from paragliding to the restoration of classic cars). On the other hand, the mainstream programming is remarkably anodyne and predictable, even when members of the audience hop from channel to channel in an increasingly futile attempt to find something to their taste.

'Complexity' is also at the heart of media consumption in a detailed ethnographic study of Punjabi young people living in Southall, London. Gillespie (1995) shows that the media had at least five distinct effects on the subjects of her study:

1. Even though the majority of her subjects were Sikhs, nearly all watched Hindu films on the VCR. Some were repelled and perhaps embarrassed by the images of poverty, but many – predominantly the girls – responded to the romantic fantasy provided by the Hindu films. 'When I watch an Indian film, after that I'm in heaven but I don't relate to the real world like I did ... they're in rose gardens and the music just springs up from nowhere', commented one girl (Gillespie 1995: 85).

2. The Hindu families (and some others) frequently watched the 'devotional soaps' together and young children were encouraged to sit up straight and show their respect to a favourite god, like Krishna, when he was depicted (Gillespie 1995: 89). TV viewing often became a form of worship as the multiple incarnations of the gods were depicted through the latest in audio-visual techniques.

3. While parents often disapproved of their children watching Western soaps, many did so, but programmes like *Neighbours* were 'embedded in family life', with aspirations for cultural change being negotiated within a context of shared family values.

4. Young people reacted to the TV News within a framework of being *both* British and Asian. When the end of Mrs Thatcher's regime was announced, three 16-year-old girls celebrated the end of the poll tax (a tax based on the number of people in a household, since replaced by council tax). 'Everyone's really pissed off with the poll tax, five people in my family have to pay it, it's crazy, where do they think we get the money from?', said one (Gillespie 1995: 128).

5. On the other hand, during the Gulf War, when the newspapers became triumphalist in tone, the Punjabis in general – but particularly those who were Muslim – were uncomfortably ambivalent. They saw through the obvious Western propaganda, yet had to thread their way uneasily through being pro-British (especially in the classroom) and not anti-Muslim (especially at home).

The conclusion one can draw from this rich study is that there is a high level of cultural survival power among many minority groups. The media provide a means of asserting a minority identity. They also provide a means of affiliating to a cosmopolitan culture, and showing loyalty to the country of settlement, but doing so without providing undue offence and provocation to the older generation's values and religious persuasions. The consumption of the media is, in short, a complex and ambiguous matter.

REVIEW

In this chapter, we have shown how the media have assumed a relatively independent life, separate from the broadcasters and audience. Of course the media cannot exist without a profusion of social actors, but the message is significantly changed through the medium of communication and this gives a special power to the technology and those who own it, work with it or understand it. The print media are, perhaps, of lesser concern in this respect, for the process of writing, editing, publishing and reviewing allows a high level of individual judgement on the part of the reader. Shall I buy this book or not? How well has it been reviewed? What do you think of it? Do I like it? These questions can still be asked of much work in the print media. On the other hand, the visual and aural media are more intrusive, more 'thrust' at the audience. It is difficult to look away when passing an offensive advertising hoarding, or not be concerned that the cars and drivers of your favourite sport, motor-racing, are plastered with tobacco sponsors. One can switch off a button on a television set, but only perhaps at the expense of annoying some other member of your household. One can walk out of a movie but few brave souls do.

These examples can be multiplied, but they all work to a common conclusion. The media have a way of 'getting to you', however reclusive or discriminating you are. This then makes it important that we understand the ownership patterns of the media and appreciate what they are not telling us, as well as what they are. Are they exercising undue influence that is distorting the democratic political order? Are they acting as the shock troops and missionaries for global capitalism, destroying other ideologies and ways of life other than those amenable to the 'free market' for goods and ideas, as Herman and McChesney (1997) suggest? Are they distorting and misrepresenting the lives and aspirations of women and ethnic minorities?

On the revolution in communications and the growth of an age of information, we have argued that the increased sophistication and use of the telephone and its adjunct technologies, as well as the internet, have many democratic possibilities that remain to be exploited. At least these developments show that powerful corporate interests cannot monopolize everything. A natural fear of media moguls and their pretensions is also offset by many detailed studies showing that we do not absorb all we are told by the 'hypodermic needle'. We ignore much, challenge some and most commonly reconstitute the message of the broadcasters according to our own shared values and cultures. Human beings have not (perhaps not *yet*) been forced to bow down to the screen, the iPod and the incessant ring of mobile phones.

FURTHER READING

- Frances Cairncross, a journalist at the *The Economist*, has been an active writer in the field of telecommunications. Her major works are 'The death of distance' (*The Economist*, 30 September 1995) and 'Telecommunications' (*The Economist*, 13 September 1997). Her book, again titled *The Death of Distance* (1997), consolidated her work.

- Edited by Edward S. Herman and Robert W. McChesney, *The Global Media* (1997) argues that the media have become the advance guard of international capital.

- Manuel Castells' major work *The Rise of the Network Society* (1996, revised 2000) has a strong prologue and the first two chapters are relevant to this chapter.

- As media studies courses have proliferated, a number of student-friendly books and readers (reprints of already published articles) have battled for market share. Two established texts are G. Branston and R. Stafford's *The Media Student's Book* (2003) and H. Sreberny-Mohammadi et al.'s *Media in Global Context: A Reader* (1997).

- Still valuable on feminist views of the media is Liesbet van Zoonen's *Feminist Media Studies* (1994).

GROUP WORK

- Two groups will watch the main news broadcast tonight. One group will look at the issue of bias: 'How is the news slanted?' The other group will speculate: 'What has been left out of the news, and why?'

- Draw up a list of the 10 most memorable movies you have seen. Why did they appeal to you?

- List the soaps you watch. Which characters relate to your personal experience?

- Find some advertisements from magazines and newspapers that, in your view, misrepresent gender, class and race. Discuss these with your group.

- Do some simple research in your library into viewing figures for the channels and the number of copies sold of the major newspapers in your region/country. Does this information give you any indication of the political and social views of the majority of people?

QUESTIONS TO THINK ABOUT

?

1. What are the democratic possibilities of the advances in telecommunications?

2. Why is it important for us to know about the patterns of media ownership?

3. Is culture going to be 'dumbed down' to the lowest common denominator?

4. Compare and contrast the 'hypodermic needle' with the 'semiotic guerrilla' model.

5. What are the effects of the global media on the social construction and reconstruction of identity?

6. Can we argue that we live in an 'informational society'?

WHAT'S ON THE WEB

- http://www.com.washington.edu/rccs/ One of the best established sites on the new digital media is the Resource Center for Cyberculture Studies, which aims to 'foster a community of students, scholars, teachers, explorers and builders of cyberculture'. Established in 1996, this is old (by internet standards).

- http://www.oii.ox.ac.uk Based at the prestigious University of Oxford, the Oxford Internet Institute talks up its credentials, but we found the site a bit thin, other than the interesting webcasts featuring interviews with eminent academics. We found that these load easily into MP4, but loading is not that seamless in other formats.

- http://www.indymedia.org/en/index.shtml By self-description, the Independent Media Center is 'a collective of independent media organizations and hundreds of journalists offering grassroots, non-corporate coverage. Indymedia is a democratic media outlet for the creation of radical, accurate, and passionate tellings of truth'. It does pick up stories not covered in the mainstream press and is delivered in an impressive array of languages.

- http://www.intute.ac.uk/socialsciences/cgi-bin/search.pl?term1=media Nearly 1,000 sites come up on this gateway. Select only the sociological ones.

CHAPTER 15

Sport in a Global Age

CONTENTS

People who are involved in sporting activities, whether as amateurs, professionals, individuals or teams, demonstrate certain universal characteristics. While sporting activities involve competition *between* players or teams, they normally arouse strong loyalties and emotions *within* the team and *among* its supporters. The latter, in turn, may help to support communal identities, whether to nations, regions, cities or districts. As Armstrong and Young (2000: 183) have said in relation to football: 'it demands partisan involvement – it isn't an "egalitarian spectacle"'. Moreover, football as a kind of ritual warfare is the 'binary expression of a symbolic power which defines "us" – our lads, in our favour – against "the other" whose defeat is our priority' (Armstrong and Young 2000: 178). What happens to these partisan affiliations when globalization and commercialization expose the local to alternative attractions while capturing its former uniqueness and selling this to a global audience?

Like music, dance and art, the enjoyment of sport does not depend on a shared language. Rather, sport comprises a kind of emotional language, the rules and procedures of which can usually be understood and appreciated by people from cultures outside the originating context. Thus, like music, dance and art, it has a potentially internationalizing quality that enables it to cross the borders between cultures and nations; sport is readily globalized.

THE ORIGINS OF SPORT

Most contemporary sports originate in traditional folk games enjoyed, mainly by men, in preindustrial societies. These folk games often combined several social dimensions. They provided amusing pastimes and offered respite from work. They brought people together in the celebration of community identity and sometimes health and fitness were also part of the experience. Games often expressed the sensuous enjoyment of the body and were closely entwined with social rituals, particularly rites of passage from adolescence to adulthood. Alternatively, they tested the capabilities of the human body, as in wrestling, throwing or running contests. Moreover, folk games were usually characteristic of specific localities, ethnic groups or nations. A study (Renson et al. 1997) of folk games in Flanders, Belgium revealed more than 1,000 associations, each pursuing a type of traditional game. Most revolved around particular drinking haunts, localities or festivals. Very similar games often flourished between villages or towns situated quite close together. For example, the study identified at least six different shooting games played with various kinds of crossbows, longbows or ball-bows and two different goose-throwing games.

All these characteristics are found in modern sports: social bonding often constructed around some notion of masculinity, maintaining collective identities, recreation, health and fitness, and friendly competition. Nevertheless, modern forms of sport are also very different from 'traditional' folk games:

■ Because sports are both intrinsically divisive and potentially unifying, governments and political elites often intervened during the era of modern nation-building to foster certain nationally 'owned' or adopted sports. Consequently, these operated, like schooling and newspapers, as another source of the common intelligibility (Anderson 1983) binding citizens into an imagined national community while projecting national identity onto the world stage (see Wagner 1990; Bale and Sang 1996; Mangan 1996).

■ Many of the games originally embedded in particular localities – such as football, cricket, running or skiing – have not only become nationally popular but over the past 150 years have also undergone a process of 'sportization' (Elias 1986; Maguire 1999), namely, being codified and standardized, then exported across the world. The celebratory, playful nature of movement cultures (Eichberg 1984) in preindustrial societies has been transformed into 'competitive, regularized, rationalized and gendered bodily exertions of achievement' (Maguire 2000: 364) that are prerequisites for participation in global sport practices today.

■ From the mid-twentieth century, we have also seen the 'corporatization' (McKay and Miller 1991; Donnelly 1996: 246) of achievement sport and a powerful process of 'turning sports into commodities' (Miller et al. 2001: 18). Thus, the American tendency to make sport dependent on business sponsorship and to turn it into an arena for multiple profit-making has come to dominate world sport in general. Since the early 1990s, the continuing revolutions in the electronic mass media, especially digitalization and satellite TV, have further revolutionized sporting contests so that they have become 'global media spectacles' (Maguire 1999: 144) relayed, and sold to billions of TV viewers worldwide.

These crucial transformations together have altered the nature of sport while contributing significantly to globalization processes. While they have brought advantages, some observers also point to powerful trends towards the possible Americanization and homogenization of sporting practices – processes we also explored in Chapter 12 – and their declining ability to engage meaningfully with the everyday lives of ordinary people. In this chapter, we evaluate these claims while exploring the key trends outlined above.

'PATRIOT GAMES': SPORT AND NATION-BUILDING

The inculcation of nationalist loyalties through sport, what Maguire (1999: 176) calls 'patriot games', was only one reason why governments chose to use it as a tool for nation-building. Others included the desire of 'muscular Christianity' (Miller et al. 2001: 4) to encourage physical activity as an alternative to 'undesirable impulses'. (We will leave you to guess what those impulses might be.) Elites also wished to divert the aggression of the lower orders into regulated sport encounters (Elias 1986). This is in some ways related to the process Foucault (1977) (see Global Thinkers 11) described, whereby, through a combination of internalized discipline and external regulation, modernizing elites employed 'biopower' to create an efficient labour force and obedient citizens. External regulation involved control by institutional regimes – prisons, factories, armies and gymnastics programmes. Thus, instilling patriotic sentiments and ensuring military readiness through exercise invariably provided key motivations for encouraging modern sport. In France, for example, until the end of the nineteenth century when cycling and rugby became the leading national sports, 'organized physical exercise' in the form of state-sponsored gymnastics in schools was the most important sporting activity and was often linked to shooting clubs (Holt 1996: 40). Moreover, the explicit intention was to foster military capability and patriotism.

BRITAIN, EMPIRE AND PLAYING THE GAME

Elias (1986) suggests that the aristocracy, the rising bourgeoisie and schoolmasters first formulated the ethos we now regard as fundamental to modern sport in mid-nineteenth-century Britain. This was taken up and eulogized by various poets and artists (Mangan 1981) and then imposed on their sons, largely through the elite school system. Thus, fostering a team spirit and ideas of gentlemanly chivalry and moral responsibility to nation and empire were first worked through on Britain's school playing fields. Many of these young men then transferred these codes of sporting practice to the top positions in the army, universities, professions and civil service. Yet, these same ideas also travelled to dominion countries like Australia, and much of Asia and Africa 'mainly on the back of British colonial expansion' (Stead and Maguire 1998: 54), through missionaries, military officers, colonial civil servants or teachers. Even where Britain had no direct imperial sway, its industrial and trading influence up until the First World War allowed its businesses and professionals to extend its national games to faraway countries. This went along with the culture of amateurism and fair play invented on the home playing fields. For example, several South American countries like Uruguay, Argentine and Brazil first discovered soccer through encounters with British railway engineers and workers engaged on construction projects in their countries (Mason 1995: 97; Archetti 1996; Giulianotti 2000: 136).

Some scholars (for example Mangan 1981; Dyreson 2003: 96) argue that British elites saw sport as a 'device' for maintaining 'British global power' and remaking 'the globe in their own image'. Indeed, their attempt to marry imperial and/or trading domination to the transmission of a unique sporting culture seems to have been extremely successful. The virtual worldwide take-up of soccer is the most outstanding example, though the adoption of rugby and cricket was more piecemeal. Nevertheless, cricket became widely adopted across Britain's dominions and South Asian and Caribbean colonies. Indeed, as early as the 1870s, the first Australian migrant cricket players came to play for English league teams, particularly in the northern county of Lancashire, while from the 1920s, black players like Learie Constantine from Trinidad arrived and soon becoming extremely popular (Hill 1994).

OTHER NATIONS AND SPORT: THE EMPIRE STRIKES BACK

The countries to which Britain had originally introduced these sports, whether colonies, dominions or other nations, eventually achieved a skill that enabled them quite literally to beat the British at their own game(s). In football, surprisingly, soon after assimilating the game, Uruguay and Argentine came to world prominence by becoming the finalists in the Olympic Games of 1928 and the first World Cup tournament of 1930, both of which Uruguay won. Britain has not managed to win the World Cup since 1966. Again, English cricket teams have fared erratically against teams from Britain's former colonies. A victory against Australia in 2005 and against the Pakistanis in 2006 broke a long run of defeats by these countries, Sri Lanka and India. During the struggle for national independence, some leading opponents of colonialism recognized the capacity of sport to stimulate national unity. In the British West Indies, for example, C. L. R. James, the great Trinidadian Trotskyite, classical scholar, historian and cricket commentator, realized that cricket could be a 'language for asserting national identity' and overcoming internal racial divisions (Dyreson 2003: 96; James 1963). During the 1957 tour of England, white players, including Goddard the captain, set themselves apart from seasoned black players like Frank Worrell and both groups were alienated from rising black stars like Garfield Sobers. The result was predictable – a crushing 3–0 defeat by England. Against the will of the West Indies Cricket Board, public opinion demanded that Frank Worrell be appointed captain for the crucial Australian tour of 1960. The result was 'the glorious seminal tied Test series that launched West Indies cricket in the new order with poise, confidence and certainty' (Beckles 1998: 131).

One of Britain's early colonies – the USA – soon became the 'biggest plunderer of the British tradition of imagining nationhood through sport' (Dyreson 2003: 96). Its political elites had always regarded national identity and patriotism as twin entities that could be fostered significantly through domestic sporting contests (Wilcox 1994). Nowhere is this more evident than in the Super Bowl football contests, which in recent decades have become the 'supreme performance' of a unique US identity and celebration of the 'aggressive masculinity' (Langman 2001: 202, 203) considered necessary for a great world power. American elites have also used their own national sports, especially basketball, volleyball, baseball and football (see Box 15.2) as vehicles for trying to make the world 'more American' (Dyreson 2003: 97) and for constructing a 'second empire' (Miller et al. 2001: 15) more influential than Britain's. Thus, baseball won over soccer in Japan for many reasons, but especially because Japan's elites were strongly influenced by American cultural diplomacy in the early twentieth century (Horne 2000) and because baseball was favoured in the top universities whose graduates then shaped the country's wider economic and cultural life.

░ ░ ▪ ▪ ▪ ▪ ■ ■ **THE OLYMPIC GAMES: UNIVERSAL HARMONY?**

Inspired by contests in ancient Greece, the first modern Olympic Games took place in Athens in 1896. The leading figure was a Frenchman, Pierre de Coubertin. He aspired to bring the youth of the world together every four years in a celebration of sporting endeavour. This would engender the goals of individual liberty and help to replace warfare between nations with mutual understanding based on peaceful competition. From the outset, therefore, the organization of the Olympic Games was based on political as well as sporting principles (Guttman 1992). However, even de Coubertin – a child of the age of the nation-state – believed that nationality was also crucial to individual identity. Despite aspirations of fostering international peace, the Olympic Games was used as a platform for pursuing nationalist rivalries and enabled politicians to manipulate patriotic sentiments. Instances of this are innumerable but here are just a few:

■ As the president of the American Olympic Association said in 1922, the primary goal in sending teams of US athletes to compete in international competitions was to 'sell the United States to the rest of the world' (cited in Dyreson 2003: 100). Other countries would perceive sporting success as an important indication of the superiority of American culture. Indeed, the US team present at the first Olympic Games in 1896 did prove to be the strongest (Guttman 1992: 18).

■ On many occasions, governments – and cities – have plotted to win the bid to host a future Olympic Games competition. Common allegations have included offering bribes, sexual services, scholarships for children and much else besides to officials of the International Olympic Committee (IOC) (Miller et al. 2001: 24).

■ During the Cold War (1947–90), the Olympic Games and other world sporting events became arenas in which the USA and USSR strove to 'prove' the superiority of their way of life by the number of medals their champions could win. On occasions they also scored political points against the other side by either boycotting or threatening to boycott the Olympic Games or other world sporting events. For example, the USA boycotted the Moscow Olympics in 1980 following the Soviet invasion of Afghanistan.

As with other international sports events such as the World Cup, Olympic ceremonies foster national feelings as much as they symbolize the ideal of a universal humanity. Miller et al. (2001: 61) demonstrate this clearly in the following description:

For many spectators, the medal ceremony … epitomizes national identification … The athletes, their bodies draped in the colours and insignia of nation and corporation, are led to the ceremony by a functionary … They bend to receive their medals as in a military service, they turn their gaze to their national flags … while the national anthem of the winning athlete/team reinforces visual supremacy with aural presence … At this point, athletes frequently cry … moved perhaps by a sense of individual … and national achievement and responsibility.

GLOBALIZATION AND SPORT IDENTITIES: LOCALITY, CLASS AND MASCULINITY

Despite their role in helping to build nationhood, sports activities and teams have also become a means for asserting a strongly held sense of local, city or neighbourhood identity and have often been especially important to men. This may have been even more significant for working-class men for whom the expression of personal support for a local team provides an opportunity for social bonding with fellow workers or neighbours and a cheap, accessible venue for celebrating the supposed virtues of masculinity – strength, courage, technical skill and comradeship. It may also provide an exciting compensation for the indignities of hard, tedious, badly paid work and low social prestige.

Examples of intense local loyalties being furthered through sports attachments are manifest everywhere and two interesting cases are outlined below. From the early years of the twentieth century, football quickly became not just a vehicle for projecting national passion in countries like Argentine, Brazil and Uruguay but also an expression of affiliation to cities, clubs within cities like Buenos Aires, and

Figure 15.1 **The heavyweight boxer, Primo Carnera (1906–67)**
Born in Udine, Italy, he moved to the USA in 1930, though he was seen as an Italian hero and depicted on an Italian stamp. He was 2.01 metres tall and for breakfast regularly had one quart of orange juice, two quarts of milk, 14 eggs, a loaf of bread, 19 slices of toast and half a pound of Virginia ham.

particular neighbourhoods (Mason 1995). Each club generated a mass following and these sometimes reflected class differences as well as local attachments. Football rivalry and club loyalty were particularly likely among recent poor immigrants and their descendants living in the *barrios* and *favelas* of Argentine and Brazil respectively. Other residents were from different national, ethnic or religious backgrounds, so ancient rivalries sometimes intermingled with interclub, inter-settlement and inter-class loyalties. Clubs and supporters organized supporting activities, whether these were linked directly to the game – pitch invasions, fights between rival club gangs, musical accompaniment or banners – or were extended to activities such as street or beach parties, family meals and outings (Mason 1995: 97–8).

| Box 15.1 | **Boxing: ethnicity and social mobility** |

What's your image of the sporting prowess of a young Jewish American male? Turning pages in a seminary or taking off a little weight at a posh gym after a hard day on Wall Street? If it were 1928, you could not be more wrong. There were more prominent Jewish boxers in the USA than from any other ethnic group. As Sammonds (1990: 2) shows, boxing was a means of social mobility for deprived immigrant groups or ethnic minorities. The 'most prominent' crown passed successively from the Irish, to Jews, to Italians, to African-Americans and then to Hispanics, as members of each group found in boxing a means of clawing their way to public recognition through hard training, body-building and sheer determination.

Boxing is not a pretty sight and, with the exception of some immensely skilled pugilists like Muhammed Ali who, as he said, 'danced like a butterfly' but 'stung like a bee', most heavyweight contests are orgies of sweat, spittle, swollen eyes, flailing arms and gore. Male testosterone levels seem to go through the roof – and that's the spectators too, not just the boxers. Wild stereotyping and primordial ethnic loyalties are galvanized and the politics of masculinity, race and nationality are never far away.

The heavyweight contests of the 1930s were particularly marked by ethnic politics. In Germany and Italy, Nazi and Fascist dictators had come to power and the powerful heavyweights Max Schmeling and Primo Carnera (Figure 15.1) became symbolic champions for the racist fantasies of Adolf Hitler and the imperial ambitions of Benito Mussolini. Max Baer had already struck a blow for Jewish-American hopes by defeating both boxers. But they rode high again and the USA lacked a 'white' contender. The colour bar was relaxed to allow Joe Louis, known as the Brown Bomber, to step into the ring. He had the classical boxer's profile, he was from a female-headed household (his father had abandoned the home), a school dropout, and a street kid before he discovered boxing. As the Louis–Carnera fight loomed (25 June 1935), internal racial tensions were augmented by an international crisis. Italy was threatening to invade Ethiopia, one of the last surviving African countries that had escaped European colonization. The boxing match was about black and white, but also about European imperialism and African freedom. After six gruelling rounds, Louis' superior skills finally toppled the Italian giant.

Louis fared less well in his first fight against Schmeling. He was poorly prepared and overconfident and Schmeling triumphed in the twelfth round. Hitler was delighted and hosted a dinner for the fighter who declared his victory was inspired by the Führer himself. Louis made no mistake the second time. He met Schmeling on 22 June 1938 in New York as war clouds loomed. Many Americans, Europeans and Africans saw the outcome of the boxing match as a rehearsal for the coming world war. Louis knocked out Schmeling in just over two minutes. The victory was celebrated across the world. Boxing had gone global and other sports soon followed.

SOURCES: Sammonds (1990); Sugden (1996: 32–58); http://www.nationmaster.com/encyclopedia /Primo-Carnera

According to Hill (1994), in many parts of Britain but especially in the northern county of Lancashire, by the late nineteenth century, playing cricket had become a major pastime for many ordinary people. Towns, villages, factories, churches and even streets often had their own teams and these became focal points around which local feelings of pride and unity could cohere while supporters' associations often tried to generate funds. As we saw earlier, some of these cricketing towns, for example Nelson, were already bringing in migrant players to boost their success as early as the 1870s. This dependence on imported 'foreigners' did not weaken the loyalties that supporters had for their own local team and their particular territories.

PARTICULARISTIC/LOCAL IDENTITIES UNDER THREAT

The twin processes of sportization (or globalization) and corporatization of competitive games may be undermining these powerful sentiments of local solidarity through sport. For example, Harvey et al. (1996) describe the increasing dependence of Canadian ice hockey teams on corporate sponsorship, as public funding declines in the face of neoliberal economic policies along with increasing commercial pressures to achieve competitive success. As a consequence some teams have lost their former attachment to local communities. Despite resistance to these processes – campaigns are organized through radio stations, public demonstrations and demands for government assistance – this de-democratization process continues. Commercial and media elites are taking control while locals lose influence.

Similar claims have been made about British football. Armstrong and Young (2000) describe how pressures for change, affecting UK football clubs since the late 1980s, have altered how people experience the game, especially its young, male, working-class supporters. One force for change came from the then Conservative government, which wanted to weaken the often noisy and sometimes violent expressions of working-class solidarity at matches, for example chanting, swearing and bodily swaying. The companies, too, wished to popularize football and squeeze more profit out of the game by widening the support for match attendance, selling coverage of key matches to media companies and generally 'extending' the football experience. The latter involved encouraging sales of club logos, replica clothing, videos and fanzine literature (Armstrong and Young 2000: 176, 202). In Britain, these changes have led to an upsurge of interest among middle-class supporters for whom going to matches, watching them on TV or becoming interested in the films, novels and 'intellectual' commentaries surrounding the game forms part of the 'style culture' they crave (Armstrong and Young 2000: 177). Family involvement has also been encouraged. All this produced a gamut of practical policy and organizational changes designed to make watching more comfortable and commercialized (more food and beverages readily available) with fewer opportunities for young, working-class fans to demonstrate occasional noisy or violent outbursts.

'Cleaning up' football matches involved reducing spectator mobility with all-seater stadiums and better surveillance – more stewards, police and CCTV cameras. Ticket prices have often increased beyond the easy reach of some low-waged spectators. Thus, the 'traditional macho-football supporter ... and old terraced culture' (Armstrong and Young 2000: 205) that provided spaces for the weekly assertion of emotional and social solidarity by mostly young men with strong roots in the locality have been largely replaced by an 'individualized, privatized, bourgeois mentality' and a 'commodified, leisure experience for the family' (Armstrong and Young 2000: 204, 205). The sale of Manchester United to a US businessman in mid-2005 was another nail in the coffin for its traditional working-class male supporters.

■ ■

Global Thinkers 15 **NORBERT ELIAS (1897–1990)**

Elias influenced many sociologists including Albrow, Bourdieu, Robertson and Maguire – whose work on global sport is used in this chapter. Elias was interested in how ways of thinking and feeling are linked to very long-term social transformations, including a civilizational process. It is for the latter that he is best known. We now indicate the outlines of his argument.

Figurations
Rather than thinking about 'society' as a system of fixed structures, we should regard behaviour as taking place within ever more overlapping and dense social networks of relationships or figurations. Humans only exist in relationships with others. These networks involve interdependency. With population growth, urbanization and a money economy, such interweaving relations become ever more complex. Elias's argument here can readily be extended to include the growing dependencies through trade, technology and cultural flows that we associate with globalization.

Processes
All social relations are ongoing, in process and unfinished and this includes the unfolding lives of individuals. Thus, it is meaningless to talk about societies as if they could attain an equilibrium state. Instead, there is continuous change. This also fits well with our understanding of globalization.

Unintended social consequences
Competition exists as individuals seize strategic opportunities for personal or group betterment. Thus, power struggles are always evident. However, the reality of

interdependency – monarchs need aristocrats to acknowledge their kingly position and rely on vast webs of economic activities going on throughout society – means that the intentions of individuals as they pursue their interests always lead to unintended consequences. The order emerging through the totality of social networks is far more compelling than that desired or planned by individuals.

The civilization process

Elias argued that over the long term individuals gradually learn to manage their emotions, their insensitive behaviour towards others and violent tendencies; they develop a set of morals and manners. As this ethos of self-restraint takes hold, the possibilities increase for ever deepening tendencies towards social interdependency, networking and social differentiation. Thus, more complex and successful – economically, culturally and politically – figurations become possible. Elias saw the origins of the civilizational process in the centralized states that emerged out of European medieval feudal societies. In seventeenth-century France, for example, in an effort to curb the warring tendencies of the nobles, the monarch established a court society and lucrative state offices. This required nobles to spend much time at court and adopt an elaborate etiquette of courteous and refined behaviour. This eventually led them to internalize and pass on to their children a habitus of self-discipline. Elias also applied the civilization process to the codification of competitive sport. He saw its origins in the rough pastimes of the British aristocracy, which later transformed these into genteel, disciplined sports.

The global spread of the civilizational process

Gradually, this habitus spread down the social system into other classes, especially the rising bourgeoisie, which adapted self-restraint as a path to capital accumulation. Later, European colonialism incorporated non-Western societies into this process. Colonial rule was based on the assertion of social superiority by the ruling elite. But, gradually the colonialists became entangled in webs of interdependency with the native population, which was required to learn skills and develop a consumer ethos so that it would be productive and more easily ruled. Imported European behaviour patterns were also imitated by subject populations.

SOURCES: Mennell (1989); Elias (1994); van Krieken (1998); Smith (2001)

THE BODY AND THE RISE OF ACHIEVEMENT SPORT CULTURE

Given that the human body is central to all sporting activities, the codification and globalization of sport rules has involved transforming the celebratory and playful nature typical of body cultures (Eichberg 1984) in preindustrial societies into a set of disciplined physical activities. Maguire (1993, 1999: 67–8) describes the processes involved in the rise of the modern sporting body. One concerns the need to train the body through intensive, regulated exercise, often requiring the use of technologies, combined with special diets. The bodies of leading sportspersons also express power and domination, certainly during competitive events, when mere spectators are awed by the strength, skill and endurance on display. The sporting body also provides a highly desirable model of perfectibility, health and perhaps beauty towards which we can aspire. The sporting body has also become a focus for several additional dilemmas associated with gender, race and sexuality. In this section, we explore some of the conflicts surrounding the sporting body and begin with the contrast between traditional and modern sport activities.

MODERN BODY CULTURE AND THE CASE OF KENYAN RUNNERS

Bale and Sang (1996) observe that athletics is the most global of all sports because it attracts more national representatives than any other sport. In 1996, 206 nations were affiliated to the International Association of Athletics Federations (IAAF). The authors describe how since the 1960s, the stunning achievements of Kenyan athletes have attracted worldwide attention. Taking into account population size, it is possible to calculate each nation's per capita output of world-class athletes. In 1993, the Kenyan index was 9.87 compared with the male per capita index of 1.52 for Africa as a whole and 2.8 for the continent of America (Bale and Sang 1996: 26, 33). Unfortunately, this huge achievement has so far been so strongly gendered that the global index for Kenyan women was only 1.52 in 1993 (though this was above the per capita average for African women as a whole of 0.84).

The first Kenyan men began to compete in world events in 1954 and by the mid-1960s were promising to become world beaters. However, Kenyan competition needed to make a gigantic leap before that became possible because the traditional sporting activities in precolonial Kenya were very different from those associated with modern world sport. Although this may reflect a bit of historical myth-making, Bale and Sang (1996) argue that the games younger men played before colonial times involved activities such as spear throwing or negotiating obstacles during running matches. These were often closely linked to hunting and keeping wild animals at bay and tested military skills or were associated with initiation ceremonies into adult life or clan affiliation. Often these activities merged with dancing and other sensuous cultural pursuits. Adventure, play and amusement were normally key elements, while the competitive events were not recorded, standardized or regulated.

All this changed dramatically when Britain colonized Kenya in the 1900s. Then, administrators, educators, missionaries, police and military personnel seized every opportunity to encourage Kenyan schoolchildren, college students, police cadets, soldiers in training and educated young employees to accept modernity, including learning the culture of modern sport. Between the 1920s and 1950s, they brought about a transition from traditional to modern sport culture, though for a long time African and British sports coexisted uneasily. They also instilled a very British version of modernity, the team spirit, a respect for friendly competitive rivalry, an understanding of the need for strict discipline and the importance of setting high sporting standards of achievement.

Bale and Sang (1996) argue that becoming socialized into the ideology of achievement sport constructed around a particular body movement culture is inescapable, because without this regulated and standardized character countries cannot participate in global sport. Also, this creates the possibility of shared experiences in mega-sport events like the World Cup for spectators and champions (Bale and Sang 1996: 107). How did traditional Kenyan body movement culture change between the 1920s and 1950s?

- Bodily movements associated with sports-like activities were transferred from the homestead, forest and village to the specially delineated sports field. Here, they were carefully demarcated and separated in terms of time, space and kind of activity from the rest of social life.
- The athletics running track and playing area constitute a 'territorialized space' that is identical to all other such modern sport spaces across the world. Accordingly, traditional African spatiality was replaced by a monolithic 'athletics space' (Bale and Sang 1996: 98).
- This new space also required the imposition of 'starting and finishing lines' and 'geometrically arranged lane markings' (Bale and Sang 1996: 98–9). Thus, the previous freedom of bodily movement was replaced by severe restrictions and the 'captured' body.
- To this was added the new 'temporal tyranny of the stopwatch with races timed to a tenth of a second' (Bale and Sang 1996: 99) and the need to fit in with a prearranged schedule of different and specialized events.
- Careful records had to be kept so that individual and team events could be measured against national or global indicators and new targets could be set. This contrasted markedly with the oral traditions dependent on memory typical of premodern societies.
- Inculcating a modern sport ethos also required instilling the goal of 'maximum effort' and the desire to set high and continuously improving standards of individual achievement. This replaced the orientation towards pleasure, adventure and social solidarity.
- Kenyan athletes who aspired to attain world-class competence had to learn the importance of obedience, drill and fitness while imposing on themselves relentless and punishing disciplines designed to raise their achievement to global levels. In effect, these amount to a loss of individuality and a continuous submission of one's body to systems of both internal and external (coaches, agents, rivals, media observers and so on) surveillance.

We can see from this that modern body movement culture imposes an individualized, highly focused, regimented and instrumental format that contrasts starkly with that found in earlier times.

RACIALIZED SPORTING BODIES: CHANGES UNDERWAY?

Despite the supposed ability of sport to express the genius of each nation's distinctive identity, a glance at any newspaper or television soon reveals that even if true in the past, many 'national' sports today depend on importing 'foreign' sporting bodies from other countries. The national distinctiveness of players, managers and others is diminishing. However, national sports have also been highly gendered activities and, until recently, mainly the preserve of white heterosexuals. The inequalities and stereotypes that persist in relation to what is thought to be the 'appropriate' gendered, racial and sexual character of sporting bodies – to reflect the national character – is a huge topic. Here we briefly explore one of these dimensions, namely the racialized nature of national and global sports.

Racism in both sport and other activities has often been expressed and enforced through bodily movements. In strongly segregated societies such as the deep South in the USA until the 1960s, and South Africa for most of the twentieth century, racialized social order was enforced through such things as the demand that black people show marked deference towards whites – though many resisted – that they live separate lives and, in the case of sport, their virtual exclusion from any delineated as 'white'. Racial segregation in sport was enforced so rigidly in South Africa that black people were not allowed to participate in sports competitions where whites were playing (Nauright 1997: 45). In the West Indies – where until 1960 no black player captained a team on international tours – such practices were socially enforced, though not as rigidly. In New Zealand, though, Maoris could and did play in provincial and national rugby teams (Nauright 1997: 45).

Of course, significant exceptions to racialized sports became increasingly common during the twentieth century, as the list of outstanding black performers increased across a range of sports, one notable case being the African-American Jesse Owens. At the Berlin Olympic Games of 1936, his outstanding achievements on the track alarmed the German Nazi government by undermining their absurd theories of white racial superiority in front of their very eyes, a feat the Nazis sought to diminish by lionizing the German boxer, Max Schmeling (see Box 15.1 above). Today, of course, footballers from West and North Africa, Brazil and other South American countries, as well as many of Caribbean origin, play leading roles in many European city teams and the latter's dependence on them is now widely recognized. According to Lanfranci (1994: 66), in France between 1931 and 1960, around 63 per cent of professional team players in one city club were born outside France and nearly one-third of these were from France's former colonies in West and North Africa. Black American players now dominate basketball, as well as many field and track events in the US Olympic team. There is also an increasing flow of successful Asian and African world-class players into tennis and cricket.

Despite these welcome signs of change, there remain a number of ways in which sport continues to be racialized, not least in the expressions of racial prejudice that are sometimes directed against black footballers or cricketers by their own or rival spectators in some countries. Then there is a tendency to explain outstanding achievements by black sportsmen and sportswomen as produced by 'natural' ability (Miller et al. 2001: 87), with the scarcely hidden presumption that an inherent biological difference explains their sporting success rather than their own discipline, hard work and effort. Similarly, Miller et al. (2001) point to the pressures (also felt acutely by women and gay people) that those who represent their nation at world sporting events must not undermine the carefully constructed 'unified notions about the nation' (Miller et al. 2001: 87) staged for a world audience and designed to conceal home inequalities. Two medal-winning African-American athletes deviated from this expectation at the 1968 Olympics in Mexico City, when they averted their eyes from the US flag and raised their fists in recognition of their support for the Black Power movement. Their actions, seen around the world on TV and in newspaper photographs, were not well received in the USA (Miller et al. 2001: 69). Black sporting bodies also challenged the myth of American national unity. Clearly, the body can be a site of both oppression and protest.

GLOBALIZATION, AMERICANIZATION OR HOMOGENIZATION

A key question in sport studies has been whether the spread of modern sport cultures – sportization – is best described as 'genuine' globalization or more accurately depicted as yet another case of US cultural imperialism. Moreover, while globalization implies growing similarities between societies linked to modernization – but accompanied by growing variety, complexity and difference – US cultural imperialism raises the spectre of the homogenization of sporting practices worldwide. To examine this issue sensibly requires us to separate the arguments into three overlapping questions. How dominant have US sport and sport cultures become in different countries? How has the increased commodification of sport altered spectators' experience and where did these pressures originate? What has been the impact of the mass media, especially television, on contemporary sport worldwide? As we shall see, in some respects, there seems to be an Americanization of global sports but in others there does not.

AMERICAN SPORT DOMINANCE: AN EVALUATION

American sports have spread widely and been adopted by many countries. US businesses brought baseball to Central and South American countries in the late nineteenth century (Miller et al. 2001) and it arrived in Japan in the 1870s through US missionaries, though it only became a major national sport during the 1930s. Basketball, too, which Wagner (1990: 401) described as 'the quintessential American sport', spread rapidly between 1890 and 1910 and in most countries is now one of the five most popular world sports, along with volleyball – another US sport – swimming, running and soccer. We also saw earlier how American political leaders often saw US sports and their cultures as major vehicles for shaping the modernization processes in other countries.

More recently, there have been instances of US sporting interests like the National Football League (NFL) or National Basketball Association (NBA) deliberately trying to popularize their sports abroad. From the early 1980s, for example, the NFL began to promote American football in the UK – a game previously 'virtually unknown on the British cultural landscape' (Maguire 1999: 158). The details of this unfolding process are explored in Box 15.2 below. The promoters of US football in Britain also decided to adopt US-style television coverage, 'with the emphasis on "entertainment" and away from a British "journalistic" style' (Maguire 1999: 159), and to this end they deployed the commentary and coverage used by US television networks such as CBS and NBC. Not only US sports but also US cultural sporting practices and styles have invaded other countries.

Ice hockey is another example. The game is widely played in Canada, the USA, Russia, Scandinavia, other European countries and Asia. Leading Canadian players have been migrating in large numbers since the mid-1990s, especially to the USA and Britain, though, increasingly, so have migrant players from countries like Sweden, Germany and Russia (Maguire 1999: 107–11). In Canada, however, there has been a strong tendency for some leading ice hockey teams to move wholesale to the USA. This is because the Canadian local and federal government can no longer provide the subsidies demanded by the businesses owning these clubs and the financial rewards available for players and entrepreneurs are so considerable in the USA (Harvey et al. 1996: 269–70). Thus, in 1995, the owners of the Winnipeg Jets finally sold their club to a consortium in Arizona, while the Quebec Nordiques team moved to Colorado.

Box 15.2	**American football's attempted invasion of British sport**

Before 1982 American football in the UK was hardly known or played except on US air-force bases. However, in 1982 Channel 4 TV, the NFL and Anheuser-Busch, the company that brews Budweiser beer, combined forces to foster the game. In that year American football and basketball were the only sports Channel 4 televised. The year 1983 saw the first live broadcast of a Super Bowl game in the UK. In that year viewing figures for some NFL and Super Bowl matches reached 4.7 million, though this was exceptional and tiny compared with the USA. However, the promoters boosted the game's UK popularity in several ways:

- Magazines were produced publicizing American football. For example, the British newspaper the *Daily Telegraph* began to produce a weekly magazine with a readership of 100,000 at its peak in 1988. The readership of these special publications was similar to that in the USA – teenage boys from mainly middle-class backgrounds, most of whom had never attended a live game.

- Anheuser-Busch paid some of the costs of televising American games in Britain and included famous US footballers in its Budweiser TV adverts. In 1986 it established the Budweiser League to organize the growing number of British teams and by 1987 there were 105.

- British interest in the game was also helped by a combined commercial

> sponsorship arrangement that brought two leading Super Bowl teams – the Dallas Cowboys and Chicago Bears – to play in London, in 1986. Some 80,000 tickets were sold.
>
> ■ The NFL applied its US marketing experience to the British situation. It did this by agreeing with Channel 4 to import the US-approach to match presentations and pushing the sale of NFL-branded products, targeted mainly at teenage boys, such as roller skates, key rings, NFL replica helmets, chocolate bars and bubble gum. A survey in 1988 revealed that 50 per cent of UK households with boys aged 10–15 liked the game and most of them believed that goods carrying the NFL logo were superior.
>
> Despite these promotional techniques, by 1993, American football gained only 71 viewing hours compared with soccer's 421 hours. In 1996, American football received only 2.4 per cent of total terrestrial TV sport coverage in the UK.
>
> SOURCE: Maguire (1999: 158–70)

On the other hand, this picture of American domination also needs to be qualified by several counter-trends and arguments:

1. American sports have spread worldwide but so have many other sports that are clearly not 'owned' by the USA, including tennis, swimming, soccer, cricket, athletics and boxing. In addition, two of America's leading sports, American football and baseball, are not widely played outside the USA.

2. While American sports are becoming widely adopted, we are also seeing reverse cultural flows. Various martial arts from Asia are now extremely popular everywhere, while knife and stick fighting from parts of Africa and cockfighting from several world regions are now found in the USA and Central America (Wagner 1990: 401). Polo, which originated in India and is now played in many countries, offers another interesting example.

3. Indeed, we are seeing the 'blending of many sport traditions ... modern and traditional ... a joining of like interests' (Wagner 1990: 400). Maguire (1999) observes a revival of folk games in some countries and the variety of games available keeps growing. With widely played sports such as soccer and athletics, it is more sensible to regard them as 'truly international' (Donnelly 1996: 245) and their diffusion as involving a process of 'internationalization' (Wagner 1990: 400) rather than Americanization or Westernization.

4. As we saw in Chapter 13, people filter and interpret the messages they receive from American cultural products, including sports events, according to their own language and national heritage. Thus, there is no 'single monolithic ideology' (Maguire 1999: 153) and 'no dominant culture flowing in a single direction to uncritical viewers, but ... multiple forms and meanings given to messages by audiences' (Miller et al. 2001: 85).

5. National sporting interests have sometimes resisted Americanization, often by campaigning for government protection and financial assistance, as with Canadian ice hockey teams (see above). In New Zealand, the growing exposure of national television, sport and the consumer culture to global influences from the late 1980s, when the country was reinventing its national identity,

generated a public outcry against the supposed threat to 'cultural sovereignty' from American imagery in the media (Andrews et al. 1996: 439). In 1995 this spilled into a debate over non-pay versus pay satellite television with respect to access to the national sport of rugby. This was because rugby teams such as the Auckland Warriors were becoming paid professionals, underwritten by selling match broadcasting rights to Rupert Murdoch's Sky TV, whose services were only available to subscribers. Eventually, this conflict was resolved when local groups realized that while globalizing media forces threatened national sports and culture, they could also project New Zealand rugby onto the world stage (Andrews et al. 1996: 437–8). Perhaps, too, some believed, this might enable national sports heroes to challenge the supremacy of Michael Jordan as the most popular and widely recognized global sports star. (Jordan's iconic worldwide fame has probably since been usurped by Britain's David Beckham.)

6. Where US sports practices are adopted, there is invariably a process of indigenization or glocalization. Here the borrowed item becomes embedded in the local scene and may be used to reimagine national culture. For example, English rugby became absorbed into American sport in the nineteenth century but re-emerged as American football. Moreover, as we saw in Box 15.2, there have been attempts to reintroduce the now transformed 'English' game back into the UK, though with limited success (Maguire 1999: 172). Andrews et al. (1996) also examined the impact of Michael Jordan on post-communist Polish youth in the early 1990s. There too he was immensely

Figure 15.2 **Tiger Woods at a tournament in Florida, USA, March 2006**
He described himself as Cablinasian (a mixture of Caucasian, black, Indian and Asian). His ethnic ambiguity appears to have enhanced his international celebrity appeal.

popular, as were the sporting goods and other American products that companies like Nike and McDonald's promoted and to whom Jordan was linked through his endorsement of them. Such products and the 'carefully fashioned stars of NBA basketball' (Andrews et al. 1996: 444) were attractive to many young Poles because they identified these with 'personal liberation' and the 'realm of pleasure' as against the drab and 'de-individualizing economic realities of life in Eastern Europe' (Andrews et al. 1996: 443, 441). Yet, these symbols of personal freedom and an idealized America were also helping young people to create a post-communist national identity.

COMMERCIALIZATION OF GLOBAL SPORT AND AMERICAN INFLUENCE

Since at least the 1980s, the process of 'turning sports into commodities' (Miller et al. 2001: 18) has been called 'corporatization'. America's Michael Jordan, his endorsement of various products and the advertising campaigns to promote him as a global sports icon provides one vivid example. There are several aspects to corporatization, which McKay and Miller (1991: 87) first identified in relation to Australian sports and on whose article we now draw:

- The amateur ethos surrounding sports, which 'gentlemen' played not for money but for enjoyment, has been increasingly supplanted by the reorganization of all sports into full-time salaried occupations. Thus, leading sports activities have become professionalized.
- The kinds of management techniques long commonplace in most businesses and based on specialist functionaries, executive directors, public relations and so on have now been widely adopted by the leading teams and organizations in most sports.
- Most amateur, semi-professional and fully professional sports interests increasingly have to rely on various kinds of sponsorship from businesses for coaching, equipment and team promotion. Advertising corporate products on playing fields, team shirts and over the media is of course central to this process. The adoption of neoliberal economic policies in most countries, with the reduction in government spending it implies, including subsidies for amateur and professional sports, has accentuated this growing reliance on business funding.
- Individual sports performers are increasingly able to make large amounts of money from agreeing to endorse company products and making celebrity appearances in the media, though the 'celebritization' of popular culture is not confined to sports stars. Large earnings can be made from prize money and appearances at events. Consequently, a lot of energy and time is now channelled into legally protecting royalty rights over logos, sports clothing, media access and sponsorship. Also, sports news is being carried in magazines and newspapers where it had never previously been reported, such as in the business and marketing sections of various newspapers.

To this list, we can add the following additional items that relate to the commod-ification of sports:

- Many sports organizations and teams have invested in their own business promotion activities, including arranging for the manufacture and marketing of team replica kits, flags, literature, videos and other local products, while some clubs have floated themselves as independent companies with shareholders.
- The sale of match broadcasting rights to public or private media companies has now become commonplace and a crucial source of revenue. We discuss this more fully later.
- Then there is the huge 'business' involved in sports migration. This now encompasses virtually every sport and nation from young African athletes recruited by American universities, South American footballers moving to Italian and French clubs and Canadian ice hockey players. In the latter case, 433 leading Canadian players migrated to Germany, Britain, Japan or else-where during the 1994–95 season alone (Maguire 1999: 107).
- A vast international division of labour has also been created to serve the sports goods industry. This makes huge profits for the companies immediately involved in its worldwide organization, while its products advertise and draw attention to sports practices. The industry is organized through numerous global commodity chains (see Chapter 4). These link homeworkers, mini-subcontractors and small to large enterprises distributed across many countries to huge designing and marketing distributors based in the West, such as Wal-Mart. In the early 1990s the sports goods industry generated US$20 billion each year in America and, despite their 'all-American image', increasing amounts of these products were being manufactured in the Caribbean, Central America and Asia, including 90 per cent of the sports shoes used by the major baseball league players (Sage 1994: 39).

Returning to the Americanization theme, we know that the USA has increas-ingly shaped world affairs since the 1920s and particularly since 1945. As it has done so, its particular style of business culture has dominated the global economy, including sport. This had three overlapping consequences. First, sport has been turned into a highly individualized and competitive 'enterprise', with the key emphasis on the very few stars who win. In most areas of sport, the amateur ethos based on respect for the game as an end in itself, once identified with the playing fields of Britain, has become less prevalent. Winning is now everything. Second, every aspect of sport is systematically organized to maximize profit-making in the ways indicated. Wilcox (1994: 74) argues that in the USA sport has always been a 'big business' as well as entertainment at some levels. Moreover, the USA has no 'organized equivalent of egalitarian "Sport for All" programs as may be found else-where in the world'. Thus, 'the American style of sport has become the internat-ional benchmark for corporate sport' (Donnelly 1996: 246) and this has driven capitalism everywhere in the direction of corporatization.

The commercial and competitive nature of sport means that most big events have become noisy spectacles (Maguire 1999: 149–50), driven by the demands of glamorous 'show-biz'-type commentators and audiences demanding 'record-setting superstar athletes' (Donnelly 1996: 246). It is therefore probable that sport is now more Americanized than other leisure activities, including films, television and music (Donnelly 1996: 246).

TELEVISUALIZATION OF GLOBAL SPORT AND ITS CONSEQUENCES

Miller et al. (2001: 4) use the term 'televisualization' to describe global sport because they regard television as the 'prime motor' (Miller et al. 2001: 68) in its development since the Second World War. This seems extremely likely, given two factors. First, the rapid spread of television worldwide has created vast potential audiences both for TV programmes and advertised products. Estimates vary, but according to one observer, (Barker 1999), in 1995 there were 850 million TV sets owned in 160 countries and watched by 2.5 billion people. Second, the continuing technological revolution in the electronic mass media of communications, which is linked to digitalization and satellite TV, has freed live sport broadcasting from the limitations of space and time. At the same time, expanding commercial networks like Sky TV provide a growing range of sports products, videoed or live, to households everywhere. Accordingly, while sport has been 'spectacularized by commerce' and 'employed to deliver audiences to sponsors', it has also been 'increasingly shaped by the media' (Miller et al. 2001: 24). Similarly, Maguire (1999) suggests that we have seen the rise of an immensely powerful 'global media-sport complex', which more than any other factor has turned contests into media mega-events. Who or what is pulling the strings in this global media complex and how does the latter shape sports experience?

In most sports, revenue from ticket sales has steadily fallen, along with subsidies from governments and private local patronage. To survive, sports found other sources of revenue and this is what has partly driven them into the world of corporate sponsorship. According to Maguire (1999: 149–51), the economics of contemporary sport involve two other powerful dynamics. Competition between different sports for audiences – with some sports interests such as the NFL and NBA in America being much more proactive than others – has compelled the less successful to follow the 'glitz and spectacle' (Maguire 1999: 150) pursued so successfully by the 'hegemonic' sports. Second, the expanding audiences brought by satellite television provide immense opportunities for sports organizations to seek further commercial compensation for dwindling ticket sales and to expand the popularity of their sport by selling match broadcasting rights to the various media companies. Indeed, sports organizations have little choice if they wish to survive.

In turn, greater media exposure increases revenue and security, but it also tempts sports to become more professional, for the ability to employ full-time, paid performers as well as to attract migrant stars from other teams is likely to increase standards and the spectacular nature of the play (Miller et al. 2001: 68). As a team's capacity to draw crowds and viewers increases, so it attracts more interest from media companies and thus gains further advertising revenue and sponsorship. Therefore, step by step, sports organizations and teams are drawn into cycles of increasing dependence on media coverage. As this happens, the media companies become increasingly dictatorial until 'sports organizations have little or no control over the nature and form in which their sport is televised, reported or covered' (Maguire 1999: 150).

Returning to our original question about Americanization, we can see that while US businesses have clearly led the way in constructing the whole global media complex since the 1920s, it would be misleading to claim that the ability of media companies to shape today's global sport constitutes overwhelming evidence for Americanization. Audiences are not passive; they ultimately decide what is popular (Wagner 1990). While some Americanization is undeniable, it has been a 'two-way process in which the recipients have interpretive and resistant powers' (Donnelly 1996: 248). Sports organizations and interests like the IOC, IAAF and NBA exercise some autonomy and try to reflect their members' interests. Commercial interests create technologies but, once available, these generate their own momentum and uses. In some countries and regions, such as the EU, governments are trying to reclaim some public influence over the media. The media corporations are not all owned by American capital, as we saw in Chapter 14, but European, Japanese, Asian and other commercial interests are also strongly involved. Meanwhile, individual media entrepreneurs like Rupert Murdoch cannot easily be labelled as belonging to any 'national' capitalist interest. Indeed, increasingly, media and other corporations involve diverse 'ownership' streams feeding into them.

Perhaps, therefore, it is more accurate to suggest that whether through the logic arising from the media sports complex and pushed by the media corporations or the sponsorship powers exercised by other TNCs, it is global capitalism per se – partly following and partly attempting to lead global audiences – that increasingly determines the character of world sport.

REVIEW

A tug-of-war exists between the corporate giants, including media corporations, driven to transform sport into a vast arena for profit, and the various national and international sports organizations, struggling to promote wider support for their particular game. This leaves the mass of ordinary sports enthusiasts and players lost somewhere in the middle trying to influence events but equipped with few resources. Moreover, these struggles may reinforce 'racial and gender systems of inequality' (Maguire 1999: 154) in sport. For example, in its search for the spectacular, media coverage can trivialize and marginalize women's sports achievements by concentrating on issues that are irrelevant to performance, such as private relationships or taste in clothes, though female sports groups have fought back (see Harvey et al. 1996: 268). Consequently, the modernization and globalization of sport practices have created some disadvantages for sport lovers. These might include the following:

- the denationalization and delocalization of sport, leaving many supporters feeling they have lost their team and place identities
- falling club standards and growing discrepancies between popular and less successful teams, as the latter find their best players migrate, their ability to sell match tickets declines and their activities are not attractive to the media
- the possible bourgeoisification of some sports such as football as working-class male support diminishes with rising ticket prices and the need to sanitize game culture so as to cater for middle-class, family and global TV audiences
- the rise of stateless teams/clubs/players among the international superstars who have less need to demonstrate loyalty to their nations and cities of origin
- the possible further consolidation of the hegemonic male sporting body
- the narrowing of sporting interests as money and resources flow towards the already popular, most profitable and spectacular sports.

On the other side of the balance sheet, however, modern globalized sport provides advantages. It helps create a more multicultural world in which the intermeshing of local and global sporting personalities, for example through sports migration and the consolidation of ethnic diasporas, brings together different cultural interests and experiences and, it is hoped, knits the nations of the world into greater interdependence. Commercial forces and competition generate greater resources and generally these raise standards of performance and hopefully, therefore, provide more pleasure. Despite strong globalizing trends, sport continues to enable some nations to strengthen patriotic sentiments. Moreover, in some instances, national sports interests can turn globalizing media opportunities into effective vehicles for projecting local/national sports identities and traditions into the global arena. Last, but not least, the mass world audiences that participate in mega-sporting events like the Olympic Games may experience a kind of unity of feeling that contributes towards globality – our consciousness of the world as a single shared place.

FURTHER READING

- J. Maguire's *Global Sport: Identities, Societies, Civilizations* (1999) provides an accessible and clear overview of all the main themes relating to globalization and sport.
- Edited by G. P. T. Finn and R. Giulianotti, *Football Culture: Local Contests, Global Visions* (2000) contains some excellent chapters and spans a range of countries.
- The extremely interesting book by J. Bale and J. Sang, *Kenyan Running: Movement Culture, Geography and Global Change* (1996), explores in vivid detail all aspects of the rise of a modern achievement culture in an African context.
- J. A. Mangan's edited volume, *Tribal Identities: Nationalism, Europe and Sport* (1996), contains a lively and readable spread of chapters, examining many aspects of sport in relation to national identities and patriotic games.
- J. Sugden's *Boxing and Society: An International Analysis* (1996) provides a readable historical and comparative sociology of boxing, with case studies

in Northern Ireland, the USA and Cuba. His account of the dangers of doing ethnographies in his chosen field sites is amusing and instructive.

GROUP WORK

1. Several students will examine a selection of tabloid and broadsheet newspapers over a certain period. Each will note examples of the following: (a) the role of migrant sports personnel in any sport and the evaluations of their performance and demeanour on and off the field; and (b) the ways in which national sporting achievement becomes an indicator of wider national success or failure. How important does a global frame of reference appear to be in the enjoyment and evaluation of national sport?

2. Drawing on the personal experiences of family and friends, develop a discussion on how local identities and affiliations are being reinforced, altered or undermined by changes in sport.

3. Think about the concept of 'corporatization' in sport and what it involves and why. Are its consequences positive or negative for our experiences of local, national and global sport.

QUESTIONS TO THINK ABOUT

?

1. What are the main reasons why many sports have become globalized?

2. List the ways in which sport body movement culture has changed with modernization. Then consider how and why this has also happened in other areas of social experience such as public comportment in streets and neighbourhoods, at work and on holiday.

3. To what extent and why is the pull of patriotic games gradually weakening?

4. In what ways have the mass media transformed sport?

WHAT'S ON THE WEB

■ www.le.ac.uk/sociology/css The University of Leicester's Centre for the Sociology of Sport has some helpful downloadable 'Fact sheets' focusing mainly on football.

■ www.uwm.edu/~aycock/nasss/nasss.html The homepage for the North American Society for the Sociology of Sport. It is mainly designed for professional sociologists, but there are pointers for students, including a hotlink called 'Links to other sport sociology websites'.

■ http://u2.u-strasbg.fr/issa The site for the International Sociology of Sport Association (hosted in 2004 by the University of Strasburg). Again this is directed to the sociology profession but the 'Links' button will lead to some other useful places.

■ www.fifa.com The governing body for world football has its own site. News stories and some great images abound, but of course you need to exercise your sociological imagination in interpreting the information provided.

CHAPTER 16

Global Religion

CONTENTS

It is often difficult to separate strictly religious phenomena from other similar types of belief and behaviour. Rites, public ceremonials, superstitions, magic (and its subcategories of 'black magic' and sorcery) and myth are all closely associated with religion. For sociologists, the key issue is not whether religion is 'true' or 'false', but why it is manifested in all societies, what meanings are invested in religion and what social functions it provides. Other pertinent questions that may be asked by a sociologist include:

- What particular faiths or sects are gaining or losing adherents and for what reasons?
- Are particular religious convictions associated with particular forms of conduct in the secular world?
- Is there a long-term growth in secularization or is this thesis refuted by the apparent revival of religiosity?
- Why do many people still retain their religious affiliations to prophets whose prophecies have failed?
- Is Islam in general a threat to 'Western civilization'? And why have Islamic jihadists turned to terrorism to express their fervent beliefs?

In this chapter, we will also review what sociologists have contributed to the study of religion, why religion has claimed so powerful a place in contemporary life, how the global claims of religion are advanced and whether the practice of religion provides a threat to social cohesion or one means of attaining that condition? We will also continue the general discussion of terrorism initiated in Chapter 9, this time concentrating on the revival of violent forms of Islam.

EARLY SOCIOLOGISTS AND RELIGION: COMTE AND MARX

Historically, a number of sociologists were impatient with religious ideas and practices, seeing them as part of a pre-Enlightenment culture that would fade with the establishment of a secular rational culture. As we explained in Chapter 1, Auguste Comte reasoned that human thought passed through three historical stages. The first was a theological stage, seen in primitive and early society. The second was a metaphysical stage found in medieval society, while a positive stage was seen in modern (for Comte, nineteenth-century) society. Animism gave way to monotheism, which, in turn, would give way to scientific, rational thinking based on logical presuppositions, experiment and evidence. In this way of thinking, religion could be seen as an irrational diversion or a residual survival of an outdated mode of seeing the world.

For Karl Marx, religion was similarly consigned to the category of 'false consciousness' and 'ideology'. He drew his major insight from the German materialist philosopher Ludwig Feuerbach (1804–72) who argued in *The Essence of Christianity* (1957) that God is the exterior projection of human beings' interior nature. God did not invent human beings, Feuerbach argued, rather *they*

invented God. By comparison with his extensive writing on the workings of capitalism, Marx wrote very little on religion. However, he did fully appreciate that
poor, subordinated people turned to religion for solace, writing, in 1844, that:

> Religious distress is at the same time the expression of real distress and the protest
> against real distress. Religion is the sigh of the oppressed creature, the heart of a
> heartless world, just as it is the spirit of a spiritless situation. It is the opium of the
> people. (quoted in Bocock and Thompson 1985: 11)

Although the phrase 'religion is the opium of the people' is widely cited, it is
worth just pausing briefly to analyse Marx's comment. He did not mean that
religion caused euphoria, but rather that it dulled the pain of existence (Aldridge
2000: 62). Moreover, in the earlier part of the quote, Marx shows rather more
empathy with the need for religious expression than in viewpoints that have
sometimes been ascribed to him.

Comte also drew back from his secular conclusions in later work and sought
to construct what we might nowadays see as a social movement in support of
'religious humanism', seeing the need to weld the 'warm' force of social cohesion
that religion provided to his 'cold' quest for scientific understanding. Nonetheless, Comte decisively opposed religion to science. This turned into a much
wider debate that caught fire in the other life sciences after the publication of
Charles Darwin's book *On the Origin of Species* (first published in 1859).
Darwin's work provided a body blow to those who believed in the literal truth of
the biblical account, in Genesis, of how humankind emerged. His account of
natural selection was based on plant, animal, bird, insect and fish life, which he
observed in considerable variation through his international voyages and careful
botanical studies. Darwin's prodigious powers of observation and analysis still,
however, do not impress 'fundamentalists' and 'creationists', who continue to
believe in the literal truth of the Bible. The angry debates that have accompanied
this opposition between religion and science have not diminished in 150 years.
Even scientists like Gould (1999), who call for dialogue or at least coexistence
between what he called the 'nonoverlapping magisteria' of science and religion,
are vigorously opposed by other biologists, like Dawkins (1991), who insist on
the basic incompatibility of the two. Perhaps it is best to withdraw gracefully
from this angry debate. Sociologists are neither theologians nor evolutionary
biologists, so we are unlikely to provide any major breakthroughs in the contes-
tations between science and religion. We need to turn our attention instead to
more overtly sociological questions.

UNDERSTANDING RELIGIOUS EXPRESSION: RITUAL, TOTEM AND TABOO

In our opening remarks, we asserted that religion manifests itself in all societies.
We can demonstrate this in two ways. First, it has proved impossible to suppress
religion, even when determined efforts are made to do so. Take the case of the

Communist Party of the Soviet Union, which in the five years after the Russian Revolution of 1917 executed 28 Russian Orthodox bishops and 1,200 priests of the same faith. In conformity with state ideology, churches were closed, there was no religious instruction in schools and atheism was accepted as state ideology. Yet, even Stalin turned to the church in the Second World War to ask for help in arousing national patriotism in the fight against the Nazis. When state communism ended (roughly in 1989), the old Orthodox churches openly re-emerged, this time in competition with evangelists, Jehovah's Witnesses and many other missionaries who found a ready audience in Russia and its former partners. Even the militantly atheistic Fidel Castro showed he was ready for a compromise, if not quite ready to throw in the atheist towel. He invited Pope John Paul II to visit communist Cuba in 1998 while asserting that he respected both those who do believe in God and those who do not.

A second demonstration of the pervasive quality of religion demands a deeper understanding of the phenomenon itself. 'Religion' should not be narrowly conflated either with the church (or mosque, synagogue, temple or gurdwara) or doctrine. The former is merely where religion is expressed or institutionalized. Increasing numbers of people claim that they are religious or spiritual, but do not attend a place of worship or claim allegiance to a particular faith. The latter, doctrine, is the elaborated theology or system of ideas that scholars and religious thinkers have developed, often after centuries of discussions and arguments about sacred texts. To give one example, the most revered holy book of the Jewish religion is the Torah, which comprises nearly 80,000 words (not even half as long as this book), but the Babylonian Talmud – the extended commentary on the Torah – took 2,000 rabbis 1,200 years to complete and is over 2.5 million words in length.

If we are to understand the ubiquity and importance of religion, we should not confine ourselves to 'church' (which we use as a synonym for all similar religious buildings/institutions) or doctrine. Instead, as one prescient Scottish sociologist William Robertson Smith (1894) insisted, religions were to be understood through rituals, totems and taboos, which are universally found. Through our discussion of ritual, totem and taboo below, we can appreciate some of the deeper structures of religion that are sedimented in every society, whatever the formal expressions of religion or its doctrine.

By *rituals* we mean the moments when collective expressions of thanks, forgiveness, celebration or dedication are made. The naming of a newborn infant, the coming of age of a young man or woman, marriage, death, a funeral, military victory, the planting or harvesting of crops, the appearance or cessation of rain, lightning, earthquakes or volcanic activity – all these have been the objects of simple or elaborated rituals. Because these events are sometimes terrifying or gratifying and often joyful, they are invested 'with the reverence and awe that characterize religious behaviour' (Chinoy 1967: 353). Of course, the church often gets in on the act and seeks to appropriate such conduct to its doctrine and practices. Take, for instance, the harvest festivals celebrated in September in Christian churches all over Europe. Celebrating the bringing in of the harvest is clearly a pre-Christian pagan ritual and now and again this becomes apparent – as in the making of the Kornwolf by festival goers. Although sanitized in many places as the 'corn dolly', the Kornwolf is the wolf spirit captured in the last sheaf of corn and imprisoned there as a life force until the next season. Such a notion is wholly alien to Christian doctrine, but has been firmly incorporated into the Christian harvest festival

Figure 16.1 **A Mongolian man pours vodka onto an Ovoo (a sacred monument) in the Taijga forest, northern Mongolia–Russian border**
The tree branches are covered in religious writings. Libation rituals were also common in ancient Greece and Rome and in Africa and its diaspora. In general, libation rituals are a way of connecting to the ancestors or other worlds.

The idea of *totem* is a more contested notion and its significance was questioned by the French social anthropologist Lévi-Strauss (1963), who thought early anthropologists did not understand what they saw. Like ritual, the idea of a totem was advanced by early ethnographers working mainly with Melanesian and Polynesian islanders, Australian Aborigines and Native Americans. These scholars observed that animals (sometimes domesticated, sometimes dangerous to humans), plants, fish and even natural phenomena (rocky crags, ice, water) were often treated with a high degree of deference and endowed with supernatural qualities. The flesh of totem animals was either not eaten or only eaten in elaborate ceremonies. The totems were seen as both protecting the group and differentiating it from its enemies. This 'marker' function of the totem was often mistaken for deeper ties of sociality, habit, ritual and kinship that bound groups together and it was this exaggerated role assigned to totemism that so alarmed Lévi-Strauss. He was right in suggesting that symbol was often mistaken for substance. Perhaps one can illustrate the point by suggesting that, other than if they have imbibed too freely, few Americans actually believe that they are grizzlies, hornets, tigers, bulls, timberwolves, panthers, bears, longhorns or coyotes. Yet, fearsome animals like these feature in over one-third of the names of US sports teams and undoubtedly provide symbols of group identification and figurative threats to the opposing teams. Totemism also thrives in contemporary society in the guise of amulets, charms and tokens. One good example, imported to the US South by African-Americans, is the belief in the potency of rabbit feet. There are currently 10 million sold each year in the USA. There and in Wales, China, Mexico, Egypt and elsewhere, rabbit feet are associated with luck, quick-wittedness, the warding off of evil spirits, fertility and good fortune (Desai 2004). Totems can, in short, be understood too literally and should be seen from an interpretative point of view (see Chapter 1 on Weber's interpretative sociology).

Finally, we consider *taboo*, a word introduced into English by Captain Cook who, in his voyages to Polynesia, was told by the islanders that certain objects or actions were 'taboo', that is, forbidden, inaccessible or off limits. This notion is found in the food prohibitions of many faiths. Pork and shellfish are prohibited to religious Jews; Muslims share the notion that pork is unclean, but add a fierce condemnation of alcohol in nearly all its forms (but see below). Like the Jews, Mormons prohibit shellfish; like the Muslims, they reject alcohol (to which they add other stimulants like tea and coffee). Catholics, by contrast, drink wine and ingest a wafer to symbolize the blood and flesh of Christ. Jews, Christians and Muslims all eat beef, which orthodox Hindus rebuff, treating the cow instead as sacred, a totem. By showing how some of these taboos are shared, while some markedly differ between faiths, we see that taboos are to do with the meanings ascribed to the act of rejection and even perhaps to the discipline required for self-abnegation. We would fall into Comte's trap of super-rationality if we try to explain the prohibition on pork by Jews and Muslims by alluding to the days when refrigeration was unavailable and rotting pork harboured dangerous diseases. In the twenty-first century, Jews and Muslims living in affluent societies in the West can observe others eating breakfasts of bacon and eggs, apparently with relish and without harming anything but their cholesterol counts. Yet they are likely to retain their taboo not because they are trying to eat healthy diets but because taboos have acquired a spiritual and religious significance, not merely a utilitarian purpose.

Whatever the doubts about detailed interpretations of ritual, totem and taboo, they have provided a way of understanding the underlying sentiments, the building blocks so to speak, of religious attachments and convictions. They have even been used to explain the roots of religious dissent, particularly by Freud. He was strongly influenced by the force of William Robertson Smith's writings. He described reading Smith's elegant prose as 'gliding on a gondola' and quotes him extensively in his own book *Totem and Taboo* (1946, first published 1913). What Freud argued was that when a taboo is violated, the individual or group wages an internal war on their psychological anxieties. When retribution did not rain down, further and more extensive violations of taboos are ventured, until eventually a secular outlook emerges. We discuss below more sociological explanations for the growth of secularization.

Global Thinkers 16 **EMILE DURKHEIM (1858–1917)**

Emile Durkheim is one of the founding figures of sociology. He established a formidable reputation on the basis of three books – The Division of Labour in Society *(English edition, 1933),* The Rules of Sociological Method *(English edition, 1938) and his famous study of* Suicide *(1952). In his early works, he set the ground rules by which most sociologists continue to operate. For example, in his* Rules *he carefully distinguished economics, biology and psychology from sociology. In distancing sociology from psychology, (Durkheim 1938: 103) argued that:*

> *Society is not a mere sum of individuals. Rather, the system formed by their association represents a specific reality that has its own characteristics. Of course, nothing collective can be produced if individual consciousnesses are not assumed, but this necessary condition is by itself insufficient. These consciousnesses must be combined in a certain way; social life results from this combination and is, consequently, explained by it.*

This core idea led to three of his guiding concepts:

- *Societies evolved from a common set of ideas, norms and expectations that were largely shared by their members. This he called the 'collective consciousness' (the French expression* la conscience collective *is also used, even in English texts).*
- *In the early forms of society, prehistoric or agricultural, social cohesion was built on a common set of superstitions, social practices and rituals, often religious, resulting in what he deemed 'mechanical solidarity'. ('Mechanical' is to be understood as 'accepted' or 'unquestioned'.)*
- *In more advanced, urban and industrial societies, mechanical solidarity was replaced by 'organic solidarity' based on a more complex division of labour between individuals. Contract, impersonality and self-interest became more common, but Durkheim still strongly insisted that there was a powerful moral order underpinning modern societies.*

Durkheim's work on suicide made a radical break with the traditions of abnormal psychology. Using groundbreaking techniques in comparative sociological statistics, he found that Protestants were prone to a higher rate of 'egotistical suicides' (one of his four types) than Catholics. The former, he surmised, were influenced by an individualistic ethos, the latter were tied together by a theology that stressed collective attitudes.

Despite being an atheist, Durkheim was vitally interested in religion, not because he wanted to know whether it was 'right' or 'wrong', 'true' or 'false', but because he was certain that religion played a vital function in social life. In The Elementary Forms of Religious Life *(1976: 427) he concluded: 'There can be no society which does not feel the need of upholding and reaffirming at regular intervals the collective sentiments and collective ideas which make its unity and its personality.' Of course, Durkheim acknowledges, this can be done through meetings, reunions, assemblies and the like. But where this becomes routinized and everyday, such behaviour is simply utilitarian and adaptive. Such behaviour Durkheim labelled 'profane' and he distinguished it from the 'sacred' – a sphere of human experience that involved expressing attitudes of awe and reverence. In his idea of the sacred, he compared the religion practised by Australian Aborigines (one of his crucial cases) with contemporary Christianity. For him religions were not 'primitive' or 'revealed truths', but systems of beliefs and practices, punctuated and cemented by rituals that drew believers into a moral community. This is why sociologists had to understand them.*

SOURCE: Durkheim (1933, 1938, 1952, 1976)

RELIGION AND CAPITALISM

Whereas Comte and Marx contrasted the practice of religion with secular, rational and scientific pursuits, Max Weber wondered whether there might be an important link between the world of mammon and the world of God. In his incisive book first published in 1905, *The Protestant Ethic and the Spirit of Capitalism* (1977), Weber suggested that the pursuit of material gain could be supported by particular religious convictions. Turning this around, he saw that Calvinist notions of predestination (in particular) could prompt hard work and generate patterns of accumulation consistent with successful entrepreneurship. Predestination suggested that God had already marked out the 'elect' for worldly success, but people who thought (or hoped) they were members of the elect could only demonstrate this to their family and peers by acquiring enough riches to do good works and show themselves to be chosen by God. Rather than resulting in passivity, predestination – and certain other Protestant beliefs – resulted in a ceaseless quest for material achievement.

Weber's thesis has provided grist to the sociological mill for a century. It was suitably subtly presented; he did not say that Protestantism causes capitalism or the other way around, but rather that there was 'an elective affinity' between the two (namely they went hand in hand). In his further studies of ancient Judaism, China and India, he made clear it was not Protestantism per se that was important. Jainism and Zoroastrianism appealed to Indian traders and entrepreneurs, whereas orthodox Hinduism constrained capitalism by its stress on religious obedience and a passive acceptance of one's place in the caste hierarchy (which allowed only intergenerational social mobility and then at a snail's pace). Equivalent arguments were made for Buddhism, Confucianism, Judaism and Islam. In each case, Weber was careful (or perhaps vague enough) to allow deviant possibilities and 'protestant-like' elements to emerge: thus permitting an explanation of why, for example, India is currently such a resounding capitalist success. The role of the Tokugawa religion in providing the preconditions for Japanese industrialization is also consistent with a broad reading of the Weberian thesis (Bellah 1985).

Finally, the thesis seems to have gained more confirmation in the rise of evangelical Christianity in many parts of the world experiencing economic growth, and more particularly in Latin America. There, Pentecostalism has often had to combine the values of community solidarity that inhere in the revival of indigenous ethnic identities with the Weberian tradition of 'exalting the individual, personal choice and an ascetic ethic of work, saving and accumulation'. Amazingly, these two apparently inconsistent tendencies have been conjoined in the highlands of Ecuador (Gros 1999: 185).

THE SECULARIZATION THESIS

Despite his deep and abiding interest in the elective affinity between religion and capitalism, Weber also saw the future role of religion as reducing when the 'legal-rational' claims of the bureaucracy of the modern state began to take over 'traditional' (by virtue of inherited office) and 'charismatic' (by virtue of personality) forms of authority. The 'iron cage' of bureaucracy was pitiless precisely because the modern state operated without passion or discrimination. Bryan Wilson (1966), who is the most widely cited proponent of what is known as 'the secularization thesis', also highlighted this role of bureaucracy. Drawing on Weber, Wilson thought 'rationalization would sweep aside tradition and marginalize charisma' (quoted in Aldridge 2000: 73). Wilson's observations rested particularly on the case of Anglicanism in England in the 1950s and 1960s, though he made far wider claims for his arguments. He used a number of statistical indicators to develop his thesis that Anglicanism was failing, but also set them in a context of wider debates about the future of the Church.

Wilson was particularly scathing about any attempt to try to accommodate secular society through what he saw as empty, trendy gestures. The ordination of women, the deference to laity and ecumenical dialogues with other faiths he depicted as indicators of weakness not strength and doomed attempts to gain popularity in the face of declining church attendances, particularly in the UK. Wilson continued his gloomy account by showing that clerical salaries were declining, the prestige of the parish priest was diminishing, while dwindling congregations were reluctant to pay up for a professional service. At a social level, the connection between a faith and its following depended on personal contact between priest and parishioners in stable communities. But local crafts, dialects and customs were disappearing, forcing religion to retreat to the private sphere. Under challenge, when confronted with the high rates of church attendance in the USA, Wilson (1966: 76) replied that he was not only interested in statistics of attendance. High participation rates in the USA did not compensate for the shallowness of religious conviction and the indirect forms of secularization that took place within formal religious adherence.

There have been a number of challenges to the secularization thesis. As Wilson reluctantly conceded, in the USA, the most affluent nation on earth, religious beliefs, practices and institutions were on the ascendant. Indeed, by the turn of the twenty-first century so important had the organized Christian Right become that many commentators have credited it with the election and re-election of George Bush Jnr. However, this is something of a double-edged argument. It is more plausible to argue that the Church has been mobilized for certain ideological purposes (for example to support a candidate who stood on an anti-abortion platform or who supported 'family values'). It is less clear that there has been a growth in profound religious sentiment and spirituality among the adherents of the conventional churches.

Stark and Bainbridge (1985) have also echoed Wilson's notion of a hidden secular consciousness that has underpinned the rise in church participation. Congregants are, in effect, using rational choice theory, which suggests that human beings seek to maximize their rewards and minimize their risks. Why shouldn't they believe? Contemporary Americans are simply following Pascal's famous wager, which posited that belief is a sensible bet or prudent investment. If God exists, the faithful win, the sceptics go to hell. If God does not exist, the faithful lose little, but the unfaithful still lose. The unfaithful lose both ways (Stark and Bainbridge 1985: 97). In other words, the logic of the casino and the stock market has been brought to religion.

Also compelling is the argument that the churches have welded together a series of concrete benefits for their congregants – superior educational opportunities, support in sickness, old age and misfortune (areas evacuated by the neoliberal state) and a network of fellow members 'who look after each other' and provide a warm circle of social acceptance. This more instrumental attitude to church membership is reinforced by quite fierce attacks on 'free-riders', who do not pull their weight in respect of the collection plate or rendering favours to other members. In the British context, where high-quality, state-supported schooling is at a premium, supported Church schools (which are generally of better quality) have insisted that parents attend church if their children are to be considered for admission. Dutiful attendance at their local Anglican church for years on end by ambitious parents does not, however, prove that they have found the way of the Lord in significant numbers.

Although also accepting that more is at stake than simply the naive growth of belief and faith, Wuthnow (1996) has assembled some reasonably robust statistical evidence to suggest that small group formation in the USA (which we discuss in Chapter 21 as the search for local community) is more important than had previously been realized. Bible study meetings, prayer fellowship, self-help groups, **twelve-step gatherings**, therapy sessions, recovery groups, youth and discussion groups are all sources of emotional support (Wuthnow 1996: ix). He suggests that as many as 40 per cent of US citizens may be involved in regular meetings of small groups; 48 per cent have been involved for more than five years (Wuthnow 1996: 47). Although many of these groups are not explicitly religious in their ethos and objectives, Wuthnow argues that they provide sympathetic environments in which religiosity is created, rekindled or nurtured.

Twelve-step gatherings
Somewhat akin to the procedures used in Alcoholics Anonymous, though with a more explicit Christian content. In a series of steps, those who are floundering are asked to admit their faults, turn to Jesus, make amends to those they have injured, embrace prayer and turn to a more positive lifestyle.

THE REVIVAL OF RELIGION

Even if the challenges to the secularization thesis among the established religions are somewhat tinged by the strong impress of instrumentality and rationality, there is no doubt that there has been a notable growth of religious sentiment among the non-established churches. Take the case of the Mormons (the Church of Jesus Christ of Latter-Day Saints). Founded in 1830, by 1997 it had recruited 9,700,000 members, while its scripture, *The Book of Mormon*, revealed to Joseph Smith in La Fayette, New York, had sold 78 million copies. A second example is the Jehovah's Witnesses, embraced by about six million followers worldwide, often after having read their publications, *Watchtower* and *Awake*. In the case of the Jehovah's Witnesses, their doctrine proclaims that Christ returned for his Second Coming in 1874, and was enthroned as King in 1878. All governments and churches were to be destroyed in 1914 and a worldwide paradise was to be ushered in.

At first sight, it is difficult to understand why a doctrine that has been refuted so decisively by known history (there were no reported sightings of Christ in 1878 and the outbreak of a bloody world war in 1914 hardly seemed to signal the arrival of paradise) has nonetheless managed to survive and even thrive. To explain this we need to turn to a classic study of failed prophecy combining psychological and sociological insights. Festinger et al. (1956) looked at a number of failed prophecies including one involving a flood of biblical proportions, followed by the rescue of believers by flying saucers. Those who proclaimed the prophecy and whose jobs and reputations were on the line would, normal rationality obtaining, be best advised to reduce their 'cognitive dissonance' (the difference between their prediction and what happened) by quietly accepting they were wrong and returning to their jobs. Instead, prophets and believers often went the other way, robustly reasserting their convictions and proselytizing with even more fervour. Festinger and his colleagues (1956: 28) explained this unexpected outcome in this way:

> The dissonance cannot be eliminated completely by denying or rationalizing the disconfirmation. But there is a way in which the remaining dissonance can be reduced. *If more and more people can be persuaded that the system of belief is correct, then clearly it must, after all, be correct* … If the proselytizing proves successful, then by gathering more adherents and effectively surrounding himself with supporters, the believer reduces dissonance to the point where he can live with it.

The mental mechanism of denial thus works in an extraordinary way. Truth is defined in terms of the absoluteness of a conviction and the number who agree with you, rather than the objective evidence visible and verifiable around you. Preaching to and converting the unbeliever takes on a fresh urgency; rejection is seen not as refutation, but as confirmation of the message. As Stone (2000: 6) explains: 'the reasoning becomes circular: those who hear and believe will be saved, but those who do not believe are already lost'. A similar cognitive process underlies the revival of fortune of the Jehovah's Witnesses, whose predictions failed so spectacularly in 1914. Some 60 per cent of the movement's followers have joined after 1975. The passage of time blurred the exact nature of the prophecies; '1914' was instead turned into an *omen* of disaster to be followed by the arrival of paradise. If paradise was indeed to happen as predicted, preaching and conversion had to be stepped up to new heights and addressed with ever more certainty. In this way, a failed prophecy was turned into a reason for further devotion, not disillusionment.

NEW RELIGIOUS MOVEMENTS

Beyond the established faiths and religious movements like the Mormons and Jehovah's Witnesses are many expressions of religion that are sometimes called 'sects', 'cults', 'alternative religions' or 'new religious movements'. There are clearly great definitional problems in comparing, defining and classifying such religious organizations (see Beckford 1985; Barker 1989). Is one person's religion simply another person's cult? Do cults and sects gradually gain acceptance as religions with the passage of time? One somewhat hazy line of distinction is that some of these alternative forms of religion have been associated with radical acts of political dissent, chiliastic (millenial) enthusiasms and strange, even bizarre acts of sacrifice and extreme conduct (see Box 16.1 for one example). The expressions 'cult' and 'sect' have particularly negative connotations. The conversion of young people, in particular, has been associated by concerned parents and policy-makers with 'brainwashing' and sometimes with satanic practices.

| Box 16.1 | **The Jonestown mass suicide** |

The government of Guyana (former British Guiana) on the northern coast of South America was anxious to develop the interior of the country, which was underpopulated. So perhaps it did not look as carefully as it might have at the background of a religious community, called the People's Temple, which in 1974 asked for a lease to develop 4,000 acres in the remote northwest of the country. Had they done so, they would have uncovered an unusual story. The People's Temple was led by Jim (James Warren) Jones, born 13 May 1931, in Indiana. He had all the marks of a charismatic leader – a humble origin, an early interest in emotional religion (in this case Pentecostalism) and an ability to attract both devotion and mistrust. He established a new religious movement in 1955, ultimately to be called the People's Temple Christian Church.

As it developed, the People's Temple began to resemble a political movement as much as a church. It drew together radical whites, often from affluent backgrounds, and marginal blacks to deliver social care and support to mentally disturbed and poor people. The movement left Indiana for the more hospitable political climate of northern California, but fell foul of the tax authorities who were determined to challenge its tax-exempt status. As Jones began to lose his erstwhile political supporters, in 1977 he decided to decamp with about 1,000 followers to the agricultural colony in Guyana, which had been precariously established three years earlier by his lieutenants. After Jones arrived, the settlement was renamed 'Jonestown'.

Jones advocated an eclectic mix of faith-healing, utopianism, Pentecostalism, communism (*Pravda*, the organ of the Communist Party of the Soviet Union, was adopted as a sacred text) and anti-racism, directed mainly at the USA. He demanded absolute obedience to his pronouncements and retained his authority by claiming divine inspiration, haranguing the community on the public address system and playing on its fears and sense of isolation. Anyone who left the community was denounced as an apostate and dismissed. One defector, Tim Stoen, who was an attorney and the Temple's legal adviser, returned to the USA and was able to organize concerned relatives who accused Jim Jones of brainwashing their loved ones. They demanded a congressional investigation. It perhaps did not help to calm the waters that Stoen's wife had a sexual liaison with Jones and the paternity and custody of Grace Stoen's child was in dispute between the two men.

Stoen was finally able to interest Congressman Leo Ryan who agreed to a site visit on behalf of the relatives. When Ryan arrived in Jonestown, he was first able to persuade the community that he was on a neutral fact-finding mission, but paranoia and confusion soon set in and Ryan was stabbed then fatally shot along with three members of the media and a community member who wanted to leave with the visiting party. Others were wounded. Jones and his lieutenants realized that the US government was certain to intervene, shutting the community and no doubt demanding extradition of those responsible for the shooting. The residents assembled in the central pavilion in a grim mood. Jones proclaimed that the only option was 'revolutionary suicide'. Against some dissent, this was agreed. A sweet drink, Kool-Aid, mixed with potassium cyanide and a variety of sedatives and tranquilizers was prepared. Parents gave the drink to infants and children; many mothers poured the poison down their children's throats (Hall 1987: 285). Jones did not drink the poison, but died of a gunshot wound to the right temple; an autopsy could not determine whether his death had been murder or suicide. On 17 November 1978, the final death toll in Jonestown was 909, a third of them minors.

Even looking at these horrific events nearly three decades later, it is difficult to come to a final interpretation of the events at Jonestown. There was a good deal of idealism underlying the People's Temple. Members, many from poor backgrounds, worked 11-hour days in difficult conditions to acquire agricultural, construction, healthcare and educational skills. Like the Puritans who founded European settlements on the east coast of the USA, they thought that God had led them to a Promised Land. The story also shows the danger of following a delusional leader, however convinced he or she is of their rationality or divinity. Finally, Jonestown provides a sombre lesson in intolerance – the media, government and self-appointed moral guardians can whip up such a climate of hatred and fear that mentally and socially vulnerable people can be driven to acts of desperation and madness.

SOURCES: Hall (1987); Chidester (2004); Moore et al. (2004); http://religiousmovements. lib.virginia.edu/nrms/Jonestwn.html

Although the events at Jonestown described in Box 16.1 must stand as a constant reminder of the dangers of absolute obedience or the suspension of disbelief, two leading sociologists have been more phlegmatic in their overall assessment of the nature of new religious movements. Beckford (1986: xv) sees the growth of such movements partly as forms of critique and renewal of older religions and partly as a response to the rapidity and ubiquity of social change, including globalization:

Rapid social change in the twentieth century is associated with the rise of a large number of new religious movements. They are both a response to change and a means of contributing to it ... They are also interesting attempts to come to terms with rapid social change by imposing new interpretations on it and by experimenting with practical responses. They amount to social and cultural laboratories where experiments in ideas, feeling and social relations are carried out.

For her part, Barker (1989), who had been commissioned to undertake a semi-official investigation into new religious movements on behalf of the British government, acknowledged that there were fears of 'brainwashing' and 'mind control' in certain sections of the British public. However, she found it difficult to distinguish between the techniques of recruitment and retention among the 500 new religious movements she studied and those forms of persuasion and socialization occurring in the family, schools, the army or indeed traditional religions (Barker 1989: 19). The self-expressed reasons for joining and staying in a new religious movement – building a successful career, improving health, gaining a sense of community, promoting self-development, changing the world or participating in a deep religious experience – did not seem to her unduly out of line with the activities of other organizations and associations. Undoubtedly, the blissful experiences that a number of adherents reported were unusual in more traditional church settings, but did correspond to the more demonstrative forms of religious expression – such as Pentecostalism – that had already gained acceptance and legitimation. One British convert to the Unification Church (founded in 1954 by a North Korean minister Sun Myung Moon and whose followers are sometimes known as 'Moonies') described her experience like this:

> When I actually heard 'conclusion' for the first time I had a rebirth experience completely intoxicated in love and joy – I even inspired my parents about God – in fact the whole week after the rebirth all I was talking about was God – my parents thought I'd gone crazy. But actually I was just so full of spirit, happy, singing, full of love. Amazing experience – I still feel it to this moment. (Barker 1989: 30)

OTHER FORMS OF RELIGIOUS REVIVAL: PILGRIMAGES

The religious revival of the past 30–40 years has also taken the form of the rediscovery and revival of religious quests, or pilgrimages. Perhaps the most famous example of this is the case of Lourdes, a small town in the French Pyrenees. Each year, Smither (2004: 28) explains, millions of people travel to Lourdes. The town only has a permanent population of 15,000 but it has 270 hotels and is second to Paris in terms of the number of tourist beds available. As is often the case with places of pilgrimage, the religious aura surrounding Lourdes arose from the appearance of a religious figure; in this case a 14-year-old girl saw the Virgin Mary 18 times in 1854. The water of Lourdes is said to be blessed and many who are sick (some in wheelchairs or on hospital trolleys) come to the town in the hope of emulating the 66 officially recognized miracle cures.

A similar example is the case of the black Madonna of Einsiedeln in northern Switzerland, a country that is often seen as the heartland of capitalist rationality. About a million pilgrims a year now visit Einsiedeln to be healed or find comfort in kneeling before the Virgin's sculpture, a wooden object turned black by the smoke of oil lamps. The Einsiedeln is just one of some 450 black Madonnas in Europe, many of which have been turned into shrines. In the matter of miracle healings, black Madonnas (made of smoked or painted wood, basalt or marble) are apparently much more effective than their white counterparts. This raises intriguing questions about whether (as the psychoanalyst Jung argued) the black Madonnas are the linear descendants of the southern Egyptian goddess Isis (who is credited with great therapeutic powers). Another possible spiritual progenitor was the Hindu Shakti, the female personification of the Divine (see Beg 1996).

Pilgrimages have also acquired new importance in the more conventional religions. Increasing numbers of Buddhists and Taoists are returning to Mount Tai in northeast China, where the shrines were vandalized by Maoist Red Guards but restored after 1976. Christians, particularly from the fundamentalist denominations, retrace the steps of the Crusaders to 'the Holy Land' to try to recreate the lives of Jesus and his apostles. Shinto priests hold at least 15 festivals each year to welcome pilgrims to Taisha, Japan. Finally, the annual haj to Medina – where able-bodied Muslims are expected to visit as least once in their lifetimes – is a source of inspiration and bonding for the Islamic world community, the umma. Occasionally, the facilities are overwhelmed by the enthusiastic crowd. In 2006, 345 pilgrims on the haj lost their lives in a stampede near the three pillars where the devil appeared to Abraham and where they are enjoined to throw stones.

THE 'THREAT' FROM ISLAM

Embraced by just over one-fifth of humankind (see Figure 16.2), the expansion of Islam and the revival of militant versions of political Islam (we will call these 'jihadists') is viewed with considerable alarm, particularly in Western political circles. This notion of an Islamic threat to Western economic and political interests has gained particular credibility in the wake of the terrorist attacks in New York, Madrid and London since 9/11.

In a climate marked by extreme ideological and military conflict, it is difficult to separate out myth and reality (it has wisely been said that 'truth is the first casualty of war'), so we must be particularly careful to assess the strength of the arguments and evidence sustaining the idea that Western and Islamic interests are on a headlong course of confrontation. The most prominent advocate of this idea was the conservative American writer Samuel Huntington (1993), whose arguments have been echoed by presidents, politicians and editorial writers. Huntington forecast a future consisting of cultural conflict and bloody wars between rival 'civilizations'. His argument can be summarized as follows:

1. A 'civilization' consists of the broadest level of cultural identity shared by clusters of ethnic groups, nations or peoples based on common experiences, especially history, religion, language and customs. On this definition, there are perhaps seven or eight such civilizations in the world today, though each contains important subdivisions.

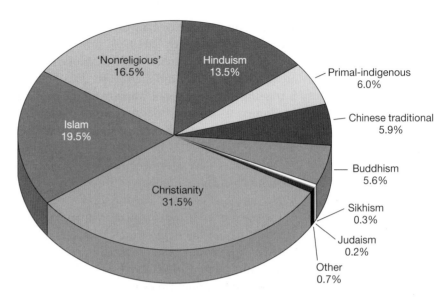

Figure 16.2 **Global shares of religious adherents and atheists**

NOTES: Christianity includes Catholic, Protestant, Eastern Orthodox, Pentecostal, Anglican, Monophysite, AICs, Latter-Day Saints, Evangelical, SDAs, Jehovah's Witnesses, Quakers, AOG, nominal, etc.
Islam includes Shi'ite, Sunni, etc.
'Nonreligious' includes agnostic, atheist, secular humanist and people with no religious preference. Half of this group is theistic but do not describe themselves as religious.
Primal-indigenous includes African traditional including diasporic expressions.

SOURCE: http://www.adherents.com/Religions_By_Adherents.html

2. In the post-Cold War era, neither ideological conflicts, as for example between communism and capitalist democracy, nor the struggles between nation-states will continue to shape global politics to the same extent as in the past, though the latter remain powerful actors. Rather, future conflicts will increasingly develop along the 'fault lines' (Huntington 1993: 29) between civilizations, sometimes exploited by political leaders and groups as a means of enhancing their own interests.

3. Chief among such confrontations may be the one between the West, now at the zenith of its global leadership and power, and a coalition of non-Western civilizations probably focused around an Islamic–Confucianist axis. The countries drawn together within the Muslim and East Asian civilizations are rapidly increasing their military capability either through imports or by developing their own arms industries linked to industrialization.

4. What binds these and other non-Western civilizations together – though much also divides them – is a shared resentment about the West's past. They see the West as continuing to impose its version of modernity on the world and using its current control of international institutions such as the World Bank and the UN to further its own interests. Western concern to prevent the spread of military capability and arms, especially nuclear weapons, to the rest of the world can be readily understood against this background.

5. Several worldwide changes are working to accelerate and intensify this

growing sense of 'civilizational consciousness' (Huntington 1993: 25). However, the most powerful of these are probably linked to globalization and modernization, especially the increased interactions between different countries and cultures arising from time–space compression and the yearning gap created in people's lives by the resulting loss of local identities. This gap is increasingly being filled by the revival of various forms of religious and cultural fundamentalism.

In August 1998, President Clinton ordered a missile attack on alleged Islamic terrorist sites located in Sudan and Afghanistan. This followed the bombing of US embassies in Kenya and Tanzania earlier that month by jihadist groups. Surely, these events and the even more dramatic bombings by jihadist terrorists in New York, Madrid and London were clear demonstrations of Huntington's predicted civilizational wars? Certainly, Huntington publicly declared his thesis had been demonstrated. However, there are some important holes in the argument that we discuss below, the first three listed being derived from Halliday's (1996) trenchant criticisms:

1. The very validity of the notion of civilization can be questioned. Like the idea of nationhood, it is based on the assumption that it is possible to identify and represent a set of timeless traditions. In reality, however, it makes more sense to regard traditions as based on different and conflicting interpretations arising out of cultural creations concocted largely to suit the political interests and purposes of different elites. Thus, the case for an actual or potential confrontation between civilizations is largely a myth because no such clearly demarcated and distinctive entities can be identified.

2. The idea of clearly differentiated civilizations with distinctive cultural boundaries is further thrown into disarray when we remember the extent to which cultures and peoples have always borrowed and mixed each other's technologies, art forms, religious symbolism and much else besides. Indeed, it seems more likely that with globalization these processes will intensify, not diminish as Huntington's argument implies.

3. The fragmentation and conflicts that have occurred within civilizations, based on inter-ethnic or state divisions, have been just as marked as those between them and often more so. This has certainly been the case in Europe, wracked for centuries by religious, civil and interstate wars, despite the apparent overarching Christian legacy. Moreover, if we count the recent bloody conflicts in the Basque region of Spain, Northern Ireland and especially the former Yugoslavia, this era did not end in 1945. The Islamic world, too, continues to be deeply divided along national and sectarian lines, among others, notwithstanding the brazen attempts by some Westerners to present the alternative image of a 'green peril' – a united Islam bent on destroying its ancient enemy (Hadar 1993).

4. The idea of an Islamic–Confucianist axis seems particularly unsustainable. Confucius had defined five key relationships (between ruler and ruled, husband and wife, parents and children, older and younger brothers, and

between friends), which stressed duty and obligation. Passivity, knowing your place and obedience to parents are at the heart of Confucian doctrine. It is difficult to square this with militant Islam or see the basis for some strategic alliance. We cannot but surmise that Huntington (correctly) saw the rise of China and militant Islam as two threats to US interests and opportunistically yoked them together. This interpretation seems to be upheld by the quiet disappearance of Confucianism in those who seek to sustain the idea of a war between civilizations.

THE COMPLEXITY OF ISLAM

The core problem for Western commentators is that they often fail to distinguish between the many varieties of Islam, an error they generally do not make in considering the many variants of Christianity. There is even some doubt among Islamic scholars whether Islam should be considered a religious faith, a political ideology, a personal conviction or a group identity (Ruthven 2000: 2). However, without beating about the bush, we must start by making a clear statement that, within the diversity that is Islam, there are a significant number of armed and trained jihadists (perhaps tens of thousands) who wish to defend and advance their faith by terrorist activities. Strictly, 'jihad' (meaning exertion or struggle) can be undertaken by the heart, the tongue, the hand or (here is the crucial one) *the sword* (Ruthven 2000: 116). So, when Muslims protest that their religion is a peaceful one and sometimes that terrorist jihadists are not Muslims at all, it is quite legitimate to respond that a peaceful disposition may be true of their case and most other cases, but classic Islamic doctrine *does allow* armed jihad against enemies who refuse to submit to persuasion.

Beyond this explicit recognition of the doctrinal support for violence, we must immediately recognize the quite contrary elements in Islamic historical practice. The Islamic record of government from the seventh to the twentieth century showed considerable levels of tolerance. The people of the Book (Jews and Christians) were often left alone to practise their own faiths, while minorities in the Ottoman Empire and elsewhere were often given considerable autonomy (see Hourani 1991). Again there are many strands in Islam, some pulling in different directions. The list below provides a partial indication of the fragmentation of Islam. This started with a split between Sunni and Shia (or Shi'ite) in the decades following the death of the Prophet in 632:

■ *Sunnis* account for 85–90 per cent of all Muslims, and are divided between various schools. There are also independent sects like the Wahhabis, Mutazilites, Qadiyanis and Kharjis (Osama bin Laden, for example, is a Wahhabi.) The Sunnis are somewhat akin to Protestants in that they rejected the attempts to fuse religious and political authority in the person of the Caliph (just as Protestants rejected a similar synthesis by the Pope) and instead turned to religious scholars (ulema) to interpret the sacred texts.

- *Shia* are the next largest segment, but are also split into groups like the Nusayris, Zaydis and the Ismailis. The Shia imam has come to be imbued with Pope-like infallibility, while the Shia religious hierarchy is not dissimilar in structure to that of the Catholic church.
- *Ismailis* (part of the Shia as noted) are further divided, but most accept the leadership of the Aga Khan. It is perhaps counterintuitive that the Aga Khan is socially accepted by the British aristocracy. He was once married to a German princess and an English model. Owning 600 racehorses, private jets and properties in five continents, he is seen as broadly sympathetic to Western ideas.
- *Sufis* express the inner mystical, psychospiritual dimension of Islam. Their priests are ascetics who have turned away from public pursuits and found inner conviction through abstinence, poverty, purification and repentence. To this list, the Whirling Dervishes, who are also Sufis, have added ritual dancing (see Figure 16.3).

Figure 16.3 **Whirling Dervishes performing a ritual dance in Sydney, Australia, October 2003**
Known to readers of the charming folk tales, *The Arabian Nights*, they tend to intervene on behalf of the underdog. They are also against jihad by the sword. During the Ottoman attack against the Habsburg Empire in 1690, they told Muslim troops to desert as the Ottoman emperor and Frankish king were simply enjoying themselves at their troops' expense.

THE WEST'S INVASION OF 'MUSLIM LANDS'

For a religion that has expanded worldwide and has a strong deterritorialized notion of its religious community, the umma, it is perhaps remarkable that many in the Muslim world have an unshakeable determination to ensure that all non-Islamic elements are expunged from 'Muslim lands'. Perhaps the key threat, in considering the contemporary Muslim world, was the foundation of the Israeli state in 1948, the recognition of which could hardly be resisted by Europe and the USA, given the stunning horrors of the recent Holocaust. The Israeli state was nonetheless a dagger in the heart of Islam, particularly since its leaders made clear that Jerusalem (a holy place for all three Abrahamic faiths) was to be the permanent capital. The arrival of French and, later, American troops in Lebanon, the British and French at Suez and the successful expansions of Israel from its 1948 borders rubbed salt in the wound. The list continued: Afghanistan was invaded by the Soviets, followed more recently by the USA. While few Muslims were enthusiastic about Iraq's occupation of Kuwait, the US-led counterstrike, from its nearby bases in Saudi Arabia, gave the 'infidel' an even stronger hold in the region. The 'US coalition of the willing' attacking and then occupying Iraq seemed the final piece of the puzzle. 'The West' (demonized as a single entity) was seen as mounting a sustained war against Islamic countries. When, in the wake of the events of 9/11, Bush warned that 'this **crusade**, this war on terrorism, is going to take a while' he could hardly have said something more tactless. For many Muslims this evoked their historical humiliation at the hands of Christian knights.

The **Crusades** took place between the eleventh and thirteenth centuries and were a generally successful attempt to drive out Muslims from Christian holy places in the Holy Land. Many Christian feudal lords (knights), with their followers, responded to Pope Urban II's call to arms following his indignant outburst in 1095 that 'The Muslims have conquered Jerusalem.'

The anger of militant Muslims against the West is also copiously extended to those rulers in Arab and Muslim countries who are seen as conniving with Western interests. The Muslim Brotherhood in Egypt, the Islamic Renaissance Party in Tunisia, the Islamic Salvation Front in Algeria, Hezbollah in Lebanon, Hamas in the West Bank and Gaza, and the shadowy al-Qaeda networks organized by Osama bin Laden in Saudi Arabia and elsewhere are just some of the organizations that have grown up in the Muslim world to urge Arab rulers on to a more militant path. That such organizations are capable of achieving political power can be seen most notably in the Iranian revolution of 1979 when a Shia cleric, the Ayatollah Khomeini, returned from his exile in Paris to install what looked superficially like an example of a medieval Islamic theocracy. The appearance of an atavistic return to an old Islamic world is, however, deceptive. Iran's ayatollahs revere the past, but are dependent on advanced technology to fight their cause – from television, to jet travel, to selling their oil on the world market, to sophisticated armaments (Hadar 1993). The desire to advance their capacity for nuclear power generation (perhaps for the purpose of producing nuclear weapons) is rapidly becoming a new source of contention between Iran and the USA and Europe.

CAN THE WEST LIVE WITH ISLAM?

While this question cannot be answered definitively, some of the parameters of the way forward are, we propose, now apparent. First, it is essential that Western political leaders are able to distinguish in theory and practice between the minority committed to violent jihad and those, the vast majority, who see Islam as a peaceful religion able to coexist with other faiths and to accept a degree of internal pluralism. Esposito (1995: 250) puts this well:

[The] focus on 'Islamic fundamentalism' as a global threat has reinforced a tendency to equate violence with Islam [and] fails to distinguish between illegitimate use of religion by individuals and the face and practice of the majority of the world's Muslims who, like believers in other religious traditions, wish to live in peace. To uncritically equate Islam and Islamic fundamentalism with extremism is to judge Islam only by those who wreck havoc, a standard not applied to Judaism or Christianity.

Second, Western political leaders need to avoid sending out mixed signals in contexts where peaceful electoral competitions have resulted in victories for Islamic parties. Notable examples of this were the case of the Islamic Salvation Front in Algeria in 1991 when the election was clearly won by an Islamic party against the expectations of the secular leaders of Algeria and their strategic partners in France, and the election of Hamas in Palestine in January 2006. The overturning of the Algerian result by the secular army and the reluctance by Western leaders to accept the Hamas victory led many in the Muslim world to accuse the West of hypocrisy; when democracy did not suit Western interests, it was abandoned.

Third, more positively, NATO's attack on Serbia in defence of the Muslim Kosovars in March 1999 showed that Western leaders were able to take a principled stance on behalf of victimized Muslims. Indeed, this was noted by a number of editorials in the Pakistan daily newspaper *Dawn* in March 1999 that called on the Muslim world to acknowledge that the leading Western powers were defending Muslims against Christians. Western powers giving generous donations to Muslim East Asians who were victims of the tsunami or Muslim Kashmiris who suffered in the earthquakes of 2005 provide other positive examples of Western humanitarian intervention.

Fourth, there are some indications that forms of modern 'civil Islam' allied closely to liberal democratic values are emerging in at least two strategically important countries. Hefner (2000) asks whether democracy and civil society can gain a foothold in Muslim societies. Can they develop independent associations, and a balance of powers between state and society? Can a public culture emerge promoting tolerance, pluralism and public competition for office (Hefner 2000: 215)? He is properly cautious in his answers, but finds some ground for optimism in Indonesia, the country with the largest number of Muslims:

In the independence era [Muslims] learned the language of democracy and constitutionality, and took enthusiastically to its forms. In matters of civic association, Muslims showed themselves second to no one. None of their rivals could match the breadth and vitality of their associations. Even under the New Order, Muslims were better able than others to resist state controls and nurture alternative ideas of the public good. (Hefner 2000: 217)

There are also grounds for cautious optimism in the case of Turkey where, of course, secularism was vigorously promoted by Ataturk as a means of modernizing the country. Turkey stands poised on the cusp between Europe and Asia, between a return to a dogmatic Islam or the evolution of a civil Islam. European politicians who need to decide whether or not to admit Turkey to the EU have a grave responsibility because their deliberations could determine which way Turkey turns.

Fifth, and finally, civil society organizations, other faiths and others have an opportunity to work with dissenting voices that need support to return to or further develop an Islamic cosmopolitanism. There are many such voices, but one, Irshad Manji, has made a dramatic impact with her book, *The Trouble with Islam Today* (Manji 2004). She calls the book 'an open letter from me, a Muslim voice of reform, to concerned citizens worldwide – Muslim and not. It's about why my faith community needs to come to terms with the diversity of ideas, beliefs and people in our universe, and why non-Muslims have a pivotal role in helping us get there' (http://www.muslim-refusenik.com/thebook.html). She wants to return to the pluralist traditions of eleventh-century Islam (when 135 varieties were on offer) and faces issues of Islamic anti-Semitism and women's rights in Muslim societies. Of course, one must be wary of only lending support to those ideas that have been taken up by the media; there are many interfaith organizations and Muslim intellectuals, writers and artists who are making their own statements in a quiet way.

REVIEW

As we have shown, religion is welded into the very fabric of human history from the earliest days when humans first interacted and formed communities to our current global age. But, as we have explained, by 'religion' we do not mean a particular faith, church or doctrine. Rather, we have been concerned to explain how 'the building blocks' of religious sentiment and behaviour emerge from understanding rituals, totems and taboos.

Some sociologists were at first sceptical of the need for religion and saw the likelihood of religion declining as the secular, rational, scientific ways of the Enlightenment took hold. However, sociologists soon realized that religion had a powerful and necessary role as a form of social cement. Durkheim was particularly clear on this point, though others, like Comte, wondered whether it might be possible to develop a sort of spiritual humanism, without the theology. Turner also emphasized the socially integrative role of religion, but saw the emergence of a secular 'civil religion' as unlikely. Instead, Turner (1991: 38–62) argued that Christianity had (in particular) accommodated itself to the separation of church and state. Christian churches in the USA, for example, provided the familiar institutions carried over from the old world, but are now giving direction and location in the new. At the same time, they retreated from any attack on the 'American way of life', choosing instead to celebrate the constitution, secular education, democracy, individualism and market capitalism.

Perhaps the crucial aspect of organized religion that has ensured its survival is its adaptation to ethnicity, nationalism and now globalization. As Robertson (1994: 128) puts it: 'The long-term adaptation of religion to society … is one of the most significant general features of the history of religion(s) and certainly of the analysis of religion.' At the same time, it has to be admitted that more unorthodox forms of traditions and new religious movements seem to be gaining adherents at the expense of the established faiths. We have tried to indicate why these movements are both successful and appealing even when they have been associated with unusual practices and failed prophecies.

We have been concerned, finally, with the resurgence of militant forms of Islam. That is not to say, of course, that fundamental sects have not emerged in all the world's major religions. Part of the response to the uncertainties of the global, postmodern world seems to have been a reaffirmation of earlier, usually invented, traditions. But armed jihadists have without doubt created the most frontal assault on the liberal, pluralist, democratic values promoted by many (even if they are not always consistent in their own policies). We do not think we are naive to say that there are ways forward if a more careful appreciation of the diversity within Islam is recognized and we begin to talk and cooperate with the many Muslims who are in favour of peaceful dialogue.

FURTHER READING

- B. Wilson's *Religion in Secular Society: a Sociological Comment* (1966) is the classic account of the secularization thesis.

- There are a number of excellent reference books on religion. In M. P. Fisher's (1997) encyclopedia of the world's faiths, *Living Religions*, she includes substantive chapters on Hinduism, Jainism, Buddhism, Taoism and Confucianism, Shinto, Zoroastrianism, Judaism, Christianity, Islam and Sikhism, a list that is not dissimilar from that provided in J. R. Hinnells' (1997) *A New Handbook of Living Religion*, though Hinnells' contains some more ambitious essays.

- Such reference books generally provide poor coverage of new religious movements. James Beckford is one of the leading scholars worldwide on this theme. See, for example, his *Cult Controversies: The Societal Response to New Religious Movements* (1985).

- We are not generally keen on the short handbooks that have become so popular among students, but M. Ruthven's *Islam: A Very Short Introduction* (2000) packs an awful lot into a small number of words.

- Jon R. Stone's edited collection, *Expecting Armageddon: Essential Readings in Failed Prophecy* (2000), provides a good introduction to the subject, together with some extracts from classical accounts and some arresting case studies.

GROUP WORK

1. Split into two groups. Both groups will provide one-paragraph definitions of ritual, totem and taboo using reference sources other than this book. Each group will list three examples under each category and describe the context.

2. Split into four groups. Using the internet and reference books, each group will try to explain the history and distinctive doctrines of a different strand of Islam, reporting their findings to the class.

3. Arrange a debate between a team designated to take a secular viewpoint and another team asked to take a religious viewpoint about the *function* of religion in society.

4. Split into three groups. Each group will undertake an imaginary pilgrimage to a major site. Describe why you went, who you were housed with and what your experiences were.

QUESTIONS TO THINK ABOUT

1. Why do many followers of prophetic religions continue to believe, even though the core prophecies of their faith have not come true?

2. Using some of the references provided as additional material, how you explain the tragic events at Jonestown?

3. Is the secularization thesis finally discredited?

4. How do we learn to live with violent forms of Islam?

WHAT'S ON THE WEB

- http://www.intute.ac.uk/socialsciences/cgi-bin/search.pl?term1=religion&gateway= Sociology&limit=0 The Intute gateway link to the sociology of religion.

- http://web.uni-marburg.de/religionswissenschaft/journal/mjr/ Ten years of full-text scholarly articles on the study of religion are available at the internet *Journal of Religion* edited by our colleagues at Marburg. The articles are not always sociological, but many are of great interest and the editorial standard is high.

- http://religiousmovements.lib.virginia.edu/nrms/Jonestwn.html This website covers the Jonestown events.

- http://www2.asanet.org/section34/newsletter.html Mainly designed for sociologists professionally interested in the study of the sociology of religion, this American Sociological Association subsection also contains a useful newsletter with short articles suitable for student use.

CHAPTER 17

Urban Life

CONTENTS

For much of human history, life was based in the rural world. In the year 1800, 97 per cent of the world's population lived in rural settlements of fewer than 5,000 people. In the year 2000, 200 years later and after a period of massive urbanization, 254 cities had emerged, each containing more than one million people. These 254 cites are very different in character, but many fall into the basic categories listed below:

1. *Ancient* cities like Baghdad, Cairo, Mexico City, Athens or Rome, which were built on the ruins of settlements that formed the basis of the great urban civilizations of the past. The remains of these great urban cultures are now picked over by tourists trying to capture some of the mysteries and glories of the past.
2. *Colonial* cities like Caracas, Lagos, São Paulo or Bombay which accompanied or followed colonial expansion. The business districts and wealthy suburbs of these cities are often like islands surrounded by seas of poverty.
3. *Industrial* cities like Birmingham, Toronto, Frankfurt, Johannesburg, Chicago or Sydney, which became centres of industrial, commercial or financial activity during the period of modernity and the construction of the nation-state system. They were also centres of major social change and immigration.
4. *Global* cities like London, Paris, Tokyo or New York, which were equally important during the modern period but have now also assumed a particular social character and distinctive role in the processes of global change and integration.

Cities are, by definition, meeting places where new settlers arrive, new marketplaces spring up, new vocations are practised and new sensibilities are formed. The culturally diverse cities in the ancient world, like Athens, gave us the name 'cosmopolis', while it was to Rome that all roads supposedly led. There were cities in the Chinese, Aztec, Ottoman and Holy Roman Empires. There were hundreds of cities before there were nation-states. Indeed, for many years there were tensions between European cities and European states. Venice, Antwerp, Genoa and Amsterdam were often economic and political rivals of kingdoms like Portugal, England and France. Eventually, some degree of 'mutuality' developed, which allowed big cities to play important administrative, military and economic roles in the evolution of the nation-state system (Taylor 1995: 48–62). Their 'mutuality' was associated only with the period of modernity and essentially depended on the capacity of the state to act to secure its external boundaries, thereby protecting the functions of the major cities located within those boundaries.

Given their importance, urban forms of settlement and the ways people lived in them became the terrains of study by some of the world's most eminent sociologists. Durkheim (1933), for example, described the rural–urban transition as the movement from 'mechanical' to 'organic' forms of solidarity. The first was marked by customary, habitual modes of interaction, the second by social relations based on anonymity, impersonality and contract. Simmel (1950a) saw the city as a place where a distinctively modern culture emerged, with new forms of 'mental life' and a complex interwoven web of group affiliations. High levels of individualism were not entirely counteracted by these social relations, so conflict and social pathologies were likely to erupt (see Global Thinkers 17).

The heyday of urban sociology was between the 1910s and the 1930s when it was pivotal to the development of the discipline (Savage and Warde 1993: 7). The central role of urban sociology was reasserted in the 1970s with the recognition of the important global functions of certain cities. In this chapter, we will consider the colonial and industrial cities, discussing in the second case the famous Chicago School of sociology, which developed a distinctive method of understanding the 'ecological patterning' and spatial distribution of urban groups. We will then look at the evolution and analysis of global cities.

THE COLONIAL CITY

Perhaps the most obvious observation to make about colonial cities is that they are characterized by extreme and often bizarre juxtapositions. As Roberts (1978: 5) puts it: 'Modern skyscrapers, sumptuous shopping, office and banking facilities coexist with unpaved streets, squatter settlements and open sewage … the elegantly dressed are waylaid by beggars and street vendors; their shoes are shined and their cars are guarded by urchins from an inner-city slum' – or, we would add, a squatter settlement.

In the colonial city there is no necessary association between urbanity and modernity. Unemployment is common, indeed normal, and self-employed forms of economic activity predominant. Although there is some full-time, blue-collar

Figure 17.1 **Arresting juxtaposition in a colonial city (1)**
Men using a laptop in Marrakech, Morocco.

Figure 17.2 **Arresting juxtaposition in a colonial city (2)**
Here a white woman pumps iron in an advertisement for a local gym, while a black man gets his exercise in another way in Lusaka, Zambia.

employment in factories and white-collar employment in government offices, banks and insurance companies, the bulk of people are located in what is known as the 'bazaar economy', or the **INFORMAL SECTOR**. Self-employed craftsmen, carpenters, masons, tailors, taxi drivers, mechanics, 'market mammies' (women traders in cheap commodities) and even farmers raising small livestock are some typical occupations. When one of the current authors lived in Nigeria, a self-proclaimed 'Doctor of Volkswagen' located at the side of the road serviced his car. Picking up the car at the end of the day was always a lengthy business, as the friendly mechanic took the opportunity of extending his 'test drive' into a prolonged taxi service for the locals.

key concept	**INFORMAL SECTOR** That part of urban society characterized by small-scale, labour-intensive, self-generated economic activity. There are minimal capital requirements in joining the informal sector and it relies on unregulated markets and skills acquired outside the formal education system. The sector is rarely controlled by government inspectors, so working conditions, safety checks and environmental standards are minimal. Exploitation and self-exploitation are rife.

In short, people survive in the best way they can. While the rich enjoy lifestyles similar to privileged groups in advanced industrialized countries, the urban poor in colonial cities often face a combination of low incomes, minimal public services and poor housing. Many live in run-down public apartments, crowded tenements and shantytowns made from cardboard, scrap wood, tin and thatch. Given the difficult life circumstances of the urban poor, sociologists have carefully investigated how far their social and political attitudes provide a threat to the established order.

Research on Latin American cities has generated surprising evidence of a more 'conservative' stance on the part of the urban poor than might perhaps be inferred from the extent of their deprivation. Those living in the shantytowns may either work in the formal sector or aspire to find a job there. Their shacks are often improved incrementally as bricks and corrugated iron roofs gradually replace the earlier rough materials. The urban poor also use the cultural and social resources at their disposal to improve their lives in creative ways (Roberts 1978: 141). Religious affiliations might provide emotional support, new ethnicities formed in the slums might be the basis for economic credit and political mobilization, while occasional forays by the conventional political parties in search of votes might provide a route into more conventional politics. Such is the weight of this push to the mainstream that Perlman (1976) has insisted that the 'marginality' of the urban poor is a myth.

THE INDUSTRIAL CITY AND THE CHICAGO SCHOOL

Robert Park, Ernest Burgess and their colleagues and successors at the University of Chicago, starting in the 1920s, undertook the most famous and far-reaching studies of industrial cities. Chicago itself provided the backdrop to their theories and field studies. For Park, writing in 1925 (cited in Kornblum 1988: 548–9),

> The city is more than a set of social conveniences – streets, buildings, electric lights, tramways, and telephones, etc., something more, also than a mere constellation of ... courts, hospitals, schools, police, and civic functionaries of various sorts. The city is, rather, a state of mind, a body of customs and traditions ... it is involved in the vital processes of the people who compose it; it is a product of nature and particularly of human nature.

As this quotation indicates, the members of the Chicago School were vitally interested in the *meaning* of the city, or how an urban culture became constituted. Was the city the source of great evil or the fount of human civilization? What moral compromises would be necessary to live there and what conflicts arose between the longstanding residents and newcomers? How were the rival claims of individual achievement and community affiliation to be played out in the new setting? As Castells (1977: 77–8) recalls in a generous tribute to one of the key figures of the Chicago School, Louis Wirth, the key insights made were that the new forms of social life were structured around the key axes of dimension, density and heterogeneity:

- *Dimension:* The bigger the city, the wider is its spectrum of individual variation and social differentiation. This leads to the loosening of community ties, increased social competition, anonymity and a multiplication of interactions, often at low levels of intensity and trust. Direct participation and involvement in social affairs is no longer possible; instead, systems of representation have to evolve.
- *Density:* This reinforces differentiation as, paradoxically, the closer one is physically to one's fellow city dwellers, the more distant are one's social contacts. There is an increasing indifference to anything that does not fulfill individual objectives and this can lead to combative, aggressive attitudes.
- *Heterogeneity:* Echoing Durkheim's observations, Wirth suggested that social heterogeneity, in ethnic and class terms, promotes rapid social mobility. Membership of groups is unstable as it is linked to the temporary interests of each individual. There is therefore a predominance of *association* (people linking up to further their rational goals) over *community* (a grouping based on descent, other affinities or long-held status).

In addition to its work on the character of urban culture, the Chicago School is also famous for its notion of the 'zoning' or 'ecology' (not what we would nowadays call ecology) of the city. Essentially, what Park, Burgess and their colleagues sought to do was to show how physical space was related to social space. Their model was based on a set of concentric rings:

- In the centre, large stores, office blocks, theatres and hotels marked the central business district.
- The next ring was the 'zone of transition', with inner-city slums, small industry and areas of extreme urban decay (known in the USA as 'skid row').
- Moving out one ring and we have the zone of the respectable working class, with corner shops, modest but clean dwellings and schools.
- Better family residences and attractive, middle-priced apartment blocks marked the next ring.
- Finally, in a looser, surrounding zone, wealthier commuters lived in suburban settings with detached plots, often with big gardens.

■ ■

Global Thinkers 17 GEORG SIMMEL (1858–1918)

Simmel is often declared to be one of the founders of sociology, yet undoubtedly he is the least well known. He predicted this outcome, saying 'I know I shall die without spiritual heirs' (quoted in Frisby 1978: 4). Why did this happen? First, he suffered from late and partial translation of his work, whereas Marx wrote a good deal in English, and both Durkheim and Weber had early advocates and translators in the Anglophone world. Second, he experienced anti-Semitism in his professional life, only securing a full professorial position at Strasbourg in 1914, just four years before his death. Other major German professors had cohorts of doctoral students

who spread their ideas. He wrote in an oddly disconnected way, drawing together grand generalizations, unusual examples and personal touches that suggested a profound pessimism and recognition of the ultimate futility of human striving.

It is this last quality that seems to have touched a contemporary chord among some scholars and students. He can connect personal intimacy and interpersonal relations. In a wider view, he is a bridge between cultural and literary studies, psychology, philosophy and mainstream sociology. Since the full translation of his major work The Philosophy of Money *(Simmel 1978), his reputation has soared. There are large claims made for the complexity and depth of* The Philosophy of Money *and we cannot summarize it fully. Suffice to say that he saw that money could be understood in a far more profound way than simply as capital or as the means to exchange value. Money, he foresaw, leads to atomization and the fragmentation of experience as it leaches into social and cultural life. In his hands, money becomes anthropomorphic. It never rests; it speaks to 'the solitary ego', 'the deeply lonely soul' at the heart of industrial and metropolitan life (quoted in Frisby 1978: 29).*

This is all quite heady stuff, but we found we could relate to the book more easily by looking at his fascinating examples. Take the case of the Buddhist monk who is constrained to reject gifts of gold and silver. Money has become an 'object of fear and horror', while poverty has become 'a jealously guarded possession, a precious part of the inventory of value' (Simmel 1978: 253–4). Or consider his discussion of prostitution. 'We experience in the nature of money itself something of the essence of prostitution' (Simmel 1978: 376–7). Kant's moral imperative never to use humans as 'mere means' is 'blatantly disregarded by both parties'. It is the 'nadir of human dignity' and the 'fullest and most distressing incongruity between giving and taking'.

These views resonate very closely with a twenty-first century awareness that the commodification of everything reaches into the heart of our being and may destroy what we are. He explores this dynamic in a brilliant essay on 'The metropolis and mental life', showing how goods sent to the metropolis are supplied almost entirely by producers for entirely unknown purchasers

who never personally enter the producers' actual field of vision. Through this anonymity, the interest of each party acquires an unmerciful matter-of-factness; and the intellectually calculating economic egoism of both parties need not fear any deflection because of the imponderables of personal relationships. (Simmel 1950b: 411–2)

As this quotation reveals, Simmel shows how strangeness and sociation, intimacy and anonymity, are held in a permanent and unbearable tension.

SOURCES: Simmel (1950a, 1950b, 1978); Frisby (1978)

The model developed by various members of the Chicago School is not to be read too literally. Not every industrial city has exactly the same profile. For example, urban planners often augment other pressures to counteract inner-city decay by encouraging the building of high-income apartments in the central business district, a process known as **GENTRIFICATION**. Nonetheless, with some adaptation, the Chicago School's ecological zone model has continued to provide a useful sociological tool for understanding how big cities work and develop.

key concept	

GENTRIFICATION is the process whereby run-down inner-city areas experience physical and economic regeneration – with a growth of small businesses, theatres, cafés and improved living areas. This may result either from the influx of 'trendy' middle-class intellectuals and professionals in the media, the arts or education who then refurbish the old housing stock (see Zukin's 1981 study of loft living in Greenwich Village, New York). Alternatively, the process can arise from the deliberate attempt by landlords, property developers and governments to push new capital investment into entire areas.

Box 17.1

African-American migration to the North

Northern US cities like Chicago and Detroit gained their importance at the turn of the twentieth century because of their industrial strengths – Chicago was the centre of the railways, the stockyards and meat-packing industries, while Detroit evolved into the main site of the motorcar and associated industries.

The social heterogeneity of such cities was based on immigration from many European countries and also from the US South. African-Americans leaving the South are one of 'the largest and most rapid mass internal movements of people in history – perhaps the greatest not caused by the immediate threat of execution or starvation' (Lemann 1991: 6).

1865–1900	Jim Crow laws promoting segregation were passed after the civil war in the South. (Jim Crow was a derogatory name for a feeble-minded African-American.) The basic mechanism for production (slavery) was destroyed, while embryonic cities in the South were devastated.
1900–1930	This was the beginning of the boll-weevil infestation, which affected cotton plants. The disease hit black farmers particularly hard as most were tenants not owners and found it difficult to switch to alternative crops. Most African-Americans were driven off their land – to the newly emerging cities of the South, to non-infested areas and finally to the North.
1920–1930	Severe agricultural depression due to overproduction of cotton worldwide. Both blacks and whites were affected.
1930–1950	Precipitous decline of agriculture. Bankruptcy for many farmers and even the big plantation owners. Tenants become part-time hands, or had to migrate North.
1950s–1970s	Displacement of agricultural workers through the spread of mechanical cotton picking.

Fortunately for the departing migrants from the South, during the First World War there was a labour shortage in the industrial North – particularly in the stock-yards, the meat-packing industries in Chicago, in transport (where blacks were employed on the Pullman cars) and in the steelyards. African-American songs of this period described the 'great black migration'. Here are verses from two:

> Some are coming on the passenger
> Some are coming on the freight
> Others will be found walking
> For none have time to wait.

> I'm tired of this Jim Crow; gonna leave this Jim Crow town
> Doggone my black soul, I'm sweet Chicago bound ...

Of the 109,000 African-Americans in Chicago in 1920, 90,000 had been born in other states, most in the South. Culturally, this migration led to the most important and influential musical expression since the development of European classical music. Think, for example, of jazz, bop, bebop, Motown (after the 'motor town' of Detroit) and urban blues – including the distinctive sounds of Chicago and Kansas City blues.

SOURCES: Fligstein (1981); Lemann (1991)

THE NOTION OF A GLOBAL CITY

Power has become spatially redistributed through the emergence of what is called the 'global city'. There is no significant distinction between the term 'world city', preferred by some authors, and 'global city' preferred by others, though the latter is now more common. John Friedman (1986) first helped to delineate the key characteristics of a world city. He argued that the spatial organization of the new international division of labour required a new way of understanding the role of certain cities. In particular, they embodied a key contradiction between politics, which still operated on a territorial basis, and economics, which increasingly functioned at a global level. Social conflict arose within cities as a consequence of this tug of war. These initial ideas led Friedman to develop what he called a 'world city hypothesis', an intervention better described as a set of seven propositions:

1. The extent to which a city is integrated into the global economy affects the physical form of the city and the nature of its labour and capital markets.
2. Key cities throughout the world are used as 'basing points' by global capital, the cities themselves being arranged in a 'complex spatial hierarchy'.
3. World cities perform different 'control functions'.
4. World cities are sites for the concentration and accumulation of capital.
5. World cities are destination points for internal and international migrants.
6. Spatial and class polarization is likely in a world city.
7. The social costs generated in world cities exceed the fiscal (tax-raising) capacity of the domestic state.

Map 17.1 shows the connections and tiered relationships between world cities as proposed by Friedman.

The world city hypothesis has generated considerable discussion in the liter-

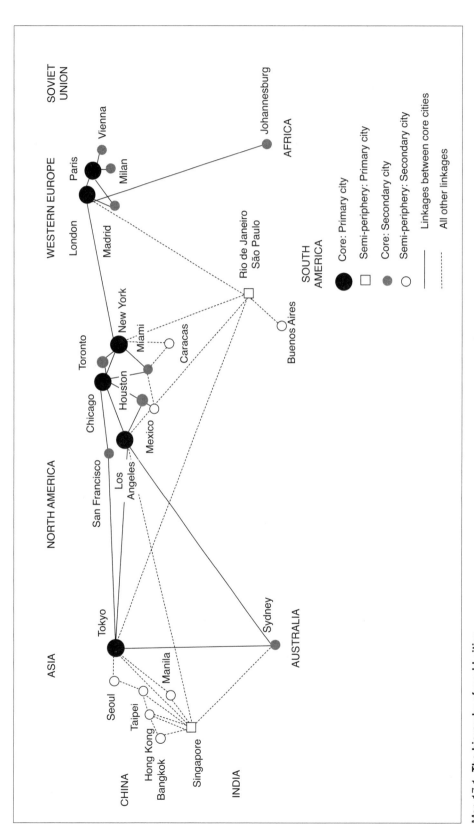

Map 17.1 **The hierarchy of world cities**
SOURCE: Friedman (1986)

ature, notably in Sassen (1991, 1995) and Knox and Taylor (1995). These authors have also considerably extended the notion of a global city in new directions. Their views can be summarized in the following propositions:

1. The corporate headquarters of the major TNCs are based in the global cities. Although, as we have seen earlier in this book, TNCs are freeing themselves from their territorial origins, there are nonetheless important advantages for a city hosting TNC headquarters. The employment that TNCs provide is valuable; they attract important clients for conferences and business meetings and there is a general political payoff in having another centre of power in a particular city.

2. All the primary cities are based in rich industrial countries. Perhaps the most notable examples are New York, London and Tokyo, which form a West–East axis of tremendous financial power through the strength of their markets.

3. The setting of corporate headquarters and stock exchanges is paralleled by the location of the major banks, insurance houses and pension fund managers. A mutually reinforcing economic agglomeration develops in a global city.

4. Within each regional cluster (American, Asian, European), there is a relatively clear relationship between a primary city and its surrounding cluster of small cities. The American cluster comprises the core cities of Los Angles, New York and Chicago. The Asian core is on an axis between Tokyo and Singapore. The European system is London–Paris and the Rhine Valley. Other cities are arranged in a complex hierarchy in relation to these major centres.

5. Global cities are assigned a specialized place in the global international division of labour. This place is sometimes, but not necessarily, coincidental with their administrative centrality. For example, London, Paris, Tokyo, Seoul, Geneva, Stockholm, Copenhagen and Mexico City are global cities and capital cities. However, the global city in Australia is Sydney not Canberra. In South Africa, it is Johannesburg not Pretoria; in Canada, Toronto and Montreal are global cities, not Ottawa; in Italy, Milan qualifies but Rome does not. These disjunctures are important as they show the capacity of global capital to depart from the old political, religious and administrative logic that informed the choice of the capital city and instead affect an intimate tie with the city with the most appropriate global features.

6. Some cities primarily serve the function of corporate headquarters, some are financial centres, some are political capitals and some are key national centres of economic activity. However, in the long run global cities bring these functions together.

7. Global cities are centres of global transport. A number like Hong Kong, Sydney, Singapore and New York evolved from their old mercantile functions as natural harbours and ports. But air transport has largely superseded this constraint and some cities have developed as turnpikes for the principal airlines.

8. All global cities are densely connected by air to other global cities. The easiest way to comprehend this is to imagine you are in an aircraft and have just opened the airline map lodged in the pocket in front of you. You notice the thin filaments that arc over the globe. If you overlaid 10 such maps of the leading carriers, you would then have an effective map of the global cities. Of course, United Airlines would cluster in Chicago, British Airways in London, Cathy Pacific in Hong Kong – but the collective effect would be to show intense clumping around certain points. Traffic is extraordinarily dense. In the case of London, planes leave Heathrow (the biggest of three airports) every two to three minutes while, on 18 July 2006, the airport recorded its biggest ever daily turnstile figure of 226,208 passengers – about a third of these people using Heathrow as the transit and switching point to other destinations.

9. Global cities are centres of communications. Again it is possible to measure this through the density of traffic on the phone, fax, telex and internet lines, and again the same pattern occurs. Starting in 1985, London's six digit telephones became seven; by 1996 you needed to push 11 digits to reach your friend's line, as the volume and density of traffic increased.

10. Global cities are centres of information, news bureaux and agencies, entertainment and cultural products. TV and recording studios are there, as are many of the major book, magazine and newspaper publishers.

11. As well as being centres for the accumulation of domestic capital, the global city becomes the centre for the attraction of foreign, though rarely speculative, capital. Typically, the financial institutions of a global city do not compete too brazenly with the known harbours for 'hot money' (like the Cayman Islands, Bermuda or Curaçao), lest they lose their reputation for stability and probity. Rather, global cities tend to attract long-term capital investments from all over the world.

The outcome of these further 11 features is, as Friedman has already suggested, that global cities become progressively more integrated into other global cities, usually at the expense of their relationship with their hinterland. As transactions and interactions between the global cities intensify, they lose their roles as administrative capitals while assuming more global, financial and cultural roles.

The integration of the global cities one with another and relative lack of connection with their provincial cities and hinterlands was made possible by technological changes as well as by the dwindling importance of the military function of the nation-state system. The first factor refers to issues we discuss elsewhere in this book – the enhancement of electronic communications, the development of cheap travel, the capacity to deskill and internationalize certain jobs through relocation and subcontracting and the consolidation of a global financial market. The second is more nuanced. Of course there are still many powerful cities located within militarily powerful nation-states. But, at the end of the Second World War, it became apparent that there was another crucial means of world expansion – through economic might alone. Both Japan and Germany had been forbidden to rearm, yet both have attained a considerable hold on world markets without the threat of force. Austria, Switzerland and Singapore have voluntarily refused to arm. The most powerful TNCs have also accomplished their economic feats without military muscle. These highly visible precedents of economic might without the expense and dangers of a military arsenal have created a pathway for others to follow. And first in line are the global cities that may reaffirm the economic role of the city-states of old.

MIGRATION TO GLOBAL CITIES

The broadest change is that global cities have become even more international and cosmopolitan than they already were. The languages spoken, the religions practised, the outlooks, consumption patterns, forms of dress and entertainment are drawn more from a multiplicity of cultures than from the national culture alone. Restaurants, music and theatre are all designed to appeal to the transitory visitors and short-term residents who populate the global cities.

International migration of a particular kind develops. 'Denizens' (privileged foreigners) arrive from other countries. Some are professional workers and managers, undertaking contract work for limited periods under the sponsorship of a TNC. Others are entrepreneurs who may be seeking a base for their operations but continue to hold dual (or multiple) citizenships and have residence rights in more than one country. Some of these denizen entrepreneurs have become spectacularly successful in their countries of adoption. Egyptian-born Mohammed Al Fayed, whose son dated the late Princess Diana and was killed in a car accident with her, owns the famous store Harrods in London's Knightsbridge. Other notable denizens operating in London are Dickson Poon and David Tang (Box 17.2).

Box 17.2

Messrs Poon and Tang take London by storm

Members of the new Chinese elite in London rather look down on the people of Chinatown as being of an unsophisticated earlier generation who sometimes cannot speak English. Their own English was learnt in the posh schools of Hong Kong or the public (that is, private) schools of England, where, it is said, there is a quota on the Chinese entrants knocking at the doors.

Thomson (1997) reported that one of the leading Chinese cosmopolitans is *Dickson Poon*, the grandson of a rice farmer, the son of stockbrokers and a graduate of Uppingham public school and the University of California. After borrowing half a million pounds from his father, he established the exclusive rights to import certain Western luxury goods to Hong Kong. In the dog days of empire, the wealthy residents of Hong Kong feared an austere mood from Beijing on the return of the colony. They spent money with wild abandon. By 1987, Poon, the owner of S. T. Dupont, the French manufacturer of gold pens and lighters, had profited mightily from this mood.

In 1991, he made his boldest move, buying the upper-class but loss-making British firm, Harvey Nichols. With its distinctively restrained British style, the store has always been a Mecca for Hong Kongers of Poon's background. Turning this 'frayed-at-the-edges' store into 'Europe's most slickly packaged emporium in the middle of the recession is one of the great retail feats of the

1990s. It is also the work of a man who glides effortlessly between two worlds.'

Poon has also started a chain of restaurants in London named after himself. Conspicuously, he has avoided Chinatown, preferring instead to set out his wares in Covent Garden and near the City, where he can cater to high-spending 'City oafs'.

Someone with an even higher profile is *David Tang*, the grandson of one of Hong Kong's greatest magnates, S. K. Tang. While he was still a student in London in the 1970s, he lost his flat gambling in one of London's smart clubs, the Clermont. By 1996, he had opened his own club in Beijing, which catered to the local yuppies. To launch the club in style, he flew out 'the cream of London society'. He has more substantial talents too, having taught philosophy at Beijing University and given classical piano recitals for charity.

Tang also managed to create a London fashion in colourful Mao Zedong jackets, made in velvet, which he sells in the Shanghai Tang shop in Hong Kong.

SOURCE AND ALL QUOTATIONS: Thomson (1997)

However, by no means all immigrants from abroad are highly skilled or privileged. Entertainers, waiters and waitresses, prostitutes, maids, chauffeurs and nurses are also attracted to global cities. The indigenous labour force has deserted some of these occupations, but employers often prefer foreign workers because they can exploit them more. Students and visitors 'overstay' or ignore the entry conditions on their visas. Illegal entrants and asylum-seekers may also be desperate to secure any kind of employment, however demeaning or badly paid. The fear that they may be reported to the immigration authorities gives the employers the whip hand in demanding compliance to their demands. Sometimes illegal migrants work in conditions little better than slavery.

CHANGES IN THE OCCUPATIONAL STRUCTURE

The new international division of labour generates important changes in the occupational structure in all regions, but many of these changes are more visible and more marked in global cities. In general, we see a strong shift from industrial to service- and information-related employment.

Work is often informalized and subcontracted in increasing conformity to the fluid, flexible work arrangements required by the global economy. By contrast, work in the unionized, high-wage sectors is either gradually or dramatically destroyed. One example of the sudden collapse of an occupational sector is the case of the workers in the newspaper industry in London. In the 1980s, print workers were highly organized, demanded a high level of control over the allocation of tasks and were beneficiaries of generous wages and working conditions. Nonetheless, they were destroyed by Rupert Murdoch's organization, News Corporation. Using a combination of guile and force, the company moved most of its titles from Fleet Street to Wapping, adopted new technologies (with the effect of eliminating the role of the compositors and typesetters) and subcontracted the distribution of the papers to a non-unionized transport company.

Other changes are seen in the running down of the nationalized or municipalized industries and public services in favour of consumer-led and insurance-supported services. These include private transport, healthcare and housing. Even schools and universities are forced to bow to the unyielding impress of the global marketplace. Many schools have to secure business sponsorship to provide basic facilities like laboratories, while universities have to recruit fee-paying overseas students to maintain their libraries and pay their lecturers. Such is the extent of denationalization that in several countries prison and immigration services are subcontracted. One police force in England persuaded McDonald's to sponsor its patrol vehicles, while highly trained and state-certified air traffic controllers in the USA were fired to make way for cheaper, less qualified colleagues.

The cumulative effect of these occupational changes became particularly visible in the global cities from the 1970s onwards, when substantial losses in manufacturing were accompanied by substantial gains in services (Table 17.1).

TABLE 17.1	Distribution of employment in New York, London and Tokyo, 1970s and 1980s (% of total)		
New York	1977	1981	1985
Manufacturing	21.9	18.7	15.4
Services	28.4	31.8	36.3
Wholesale/retail	19.4	20.2	20.2
London	1977	1981	1985
Manufacturing	22.0	19.2	16.0
Services	49.6	40.1	39.8
Wholesale/retail	13.5	19.2	20.5
Tokyo	1975	1980	1985
Manufacturing	25.1	23.5	22.0
Services	20.6	22.7	25.3
Wholesale/retail	27.5	28.5	28.4

SOURCE: Sassen (1991: 109)

THE FEMINIZATION OF EMPLOYMENT

As we have seen, the increased entry of women into the labour market is a feature of the global post-Fordist environment, but it is particularly notable in the global cities where the fashion, clerical and service occupations are concentrated. Even though they have gained a stronger foothold in employment, many women workers are paid less than their male equivalents and have highly insecure conditions of employment. One important example of the feminization of employment is in the garment and fashion industries, an activity that feeds off an international clientele. It is no coincidence that Hong Kong, Paris, London, New York and Milan are all global cities and the key global fashion centres with the most prestigious catwalks. The glamorous pictures of models reproduced in women's magazines are supported by a seamy underside of sweatshops, low pay, exploitation (normally of women workers) and the hiring of illegal workers to reduce costs. Homeworkers who, Phizacklea (1992: 109) notes, occupy the lowest rung in the clothing industry

> serve a buffer function for contractors with an erratic flow of work. If there is a rush order or a full book they will receive work, if there is not, they receive nothing. Their rate of pay is exceedingly low … The vast majority of homeworkers are women confined to the home because of domestic responsibilities, particularly the care of pre-school children. Most fail to recognize the hidden costs involved in homeworking, which include the purchase or hire of their own machine and running costs. Most homeworking is 'off the book' and a completely precarious occupation.

Homeworkers also address envelopes, perform routine clerical tasks via the internet or act as remote outposts of 'call centres'. (Call centres are linked telephone networks providing directory enquiries and information on timetables, flight prices and products for sale.) Because the 'real' cost of telephone calls (as opposed to what the consumer pays) is now equalizing internationally, calls for big businesses are now often stacked globally, with homeworkers' numbers being activated in sequence wherever they happen to be. Bemused customers using their telephone in Milan and wanting to travel on British Airways from Bristol to Newcastle may find their bookings dealt with by a homeworker in New York or Bombay.

The ubiquitous forms of service employment, which are statistically increasingly significant, tend to concentrate employment in the global cities. Low-paid domestic workers – acting as cleaners, hotel and restaurant workers or at checkout counters – are often female. Somewhat better white-collar employment is also available to women as sales personnel in department stores and boutiques, office workers (particularly entering data) and in estate agencies, banks and advertising. Because women historically colonized office work (as typists, telephonists and clerks), with the switch to more information-related employment they are often at an advantage in the labour market. Although their pay and conditions do not often match male workers, in a number of global cities there are now more females than males in paid employment.

REGIONALIZATION AND THE GLOBAL CITY

There is tendency for the *regional* role of certain major cities to be augmented, an enhancement that is often overlooked in the discussion of *global* cities. At least in the medium term, geography is not yet history for many cities. Los Angeles remains the dominant entry point for trans-Pacific migrants, Mexicans and South

Americans. New York receives many immigrants from the Caribbean archipelago. Berlin, particularly after the massive redevelopment of the city, will form the hinge between Western and Eastern Europe, while 81 per cent of Finnish emigrants head for Sweden, most of them for Stockholm. With the Channel Tunnel, London and Paris are conjoining in a single axial point in Northern Europe, adding a new dimension to their roles as capital cities. Brussels links the Benelux countries. Miami has become the shopping capital and most desirable entry point for migrants from the Caribbean area, especially from the Spanish-speaking Caribbean – Latinos have more than doubled their share of the city's population in the last half-century and now form the majority. As Grosfoguel (1995: 164) ironically notes: 'Today Miami is a bilingual city where you can find more stores with signs saying "We speak English" than those saying "*Se habla español*".'

Just as some cities are regionalizing across frontiers, others are blending their functions and dissolving their boundaries with countries. This is partly because of the accident of geographical proximity, partly because of conscious design. Randstad (the grouping of Amsterdam, Rotterdam, Utrecht and The Hague) is a good example of this development. The addition of Orange, San Bernadino, Riverside and Ventura counties to the core of Los Angeles provides another. Los Angeles now extends over 53,136 square kilometres (Waldinger and Bozorgmehr 1996: 5). The cities of Leeds, Bradford, Sheffield and Manchester in the north of England also form a continuous urban chain linked by motorways. We consider the regional roles of Los Angeles and Johannesburg in more detail.

LOS ANGELES: THE FRAGMENTED METROPOLIS

Los Angeles, 'the City of Angels', is almost twice as large as New York, San Francisco, Chicago and Philadelphia and almost four times the size of Miami. The city has been described as a 'fragmented metropolis' because of its immense sprawl. Tourism, the Hollywood film industry, and thereafter a heavy manufacturing base – often depending on defence contracts – started the flow of immigrants to the city from other parts of the USA, from neighbouring Mexico, but also from across the Pacific. In population terms the result was spectacular. At the turn of the century, Los Angeles had 100,000 residents, by 1930 it had added another 2.2 million people. Then, 30 years on in 1960, there were 6 million people, while at the last census in 1990 there were 14.5 million. In population terms, Los Angeles is just behind New York, but if the growth continues, the population will soon exceed New York's.

The city partly evolved, and was partly designed, as a chain of low-density suburban settlements linking the valleys that mark the topography of the area. Leading architects were fascinated by this form of urban settlement and praised it for its human scale. However, the logic of a global city soon took over and a 'downtown' developed, with insurance companies and banks moving in to create new skyscrapers. Much of this investment came from Japanese firms that were riding a massive boom in the 1980s. The old height restrictions of the area were ignored and new high-rise buildings proliferated. One Japanese company, Shuwa, purchased a billion US dollars' worth of property in a two-and-a-half-month buying spree. The directors of Shuwa, 'following the tradition of bringing gifts to new neighbours', made massive donations to the Ronald Reagan library and to a political campaign run by Major Bradley. He reciprocated by denouncing anyone who objected to the assertion of Japanese economic muscle as a 'racist'. In an allusion to Japan's wartime effort to turn the Asian countries it had conquered into a Japanese 'co-prosperity zone', Davis (1991: 134–40) refers to the Japanese financial involvement in Los Angeles as a 'Pacific co-prosperity zone'.

Although the economic downturn in Japan during the 1990s has mitigated fears of Japanese domination, there is no doubt that Los Angeles provides a key bridge from America across the Pacific to the global cities of Tokyo, Taipei, Hong Kong, Shanghai and Singapore. This is reflected in the changing ethnic composition of the city. For many years the city has been a magnet for migrants from Mexico, to which were added other Central Americans tempted by the lure of *el norte*. From the 1980s, however, the city began to attract highly skilled, foreign-born arrivals (denizens), often from Asia. Waldinger and Bozorgmehr (1996: 16) describe the ethnic mix as follows:

> Starting from a relatively small base in 1970 the Asian population skyrocketed; as immigrants from China, the Philippines, Korea, Vietnam, and India (in that order) poured into the region. Asians emerged as LA's third largest group, outnumbering the previously established African American population. The newcomers transformed Los Angeles into the capital of contemporary Asian America, pushing it well beyond the other major Asian American centers of New York, San Francisco–Oakland and Honolulu … The new Asians became a source of extraordinary high-skilled labor, importing school levels that left natives far behind as well as other endowments like capital and entrepreneurial talents that gave them a competitive edge.

JOHANNESBURG: THE ELUSIVE METROPOLIS

No one is quite sure which of several possible 'Johanns' gave his name to Johannesburg. All that is known for sure is that it was named quickly, in response to the sudden influx of prospectors and 'get-rich-quick-merchants' who poured into the newly designated municipality from many European origins after the discovery of gold in 1886. Africans in the vicinity at first thrived by supplying them with meat and vegetables (Bundy 1979). The dominant Boers (descendants of Dutch settlers who had trekked into the interior to escape the British government of the Cape Colony) did not know what to do. They maintained a rough form of law and order by mounting some guns on ramparts trained on the miners' camp below but, in some disgust at the spectacle provided by the godless invaders, retreated to their new capital at Pretoria, 50 kilometres north.

This did not trouble the neophyte urban dwellers unduly, who got on with what they were best at – making money and spending it in as spectacular a way as possible. There is barely a scholar or observer who has a good thing to say about the rapid development of Johannesburg. The historian van Onselen (quoted in Mbembe and Nuttall 2004: 354, 345) described the city as a 'concrete encrustation on a set of rocky ridges'. It lacked 'fertile soil, striking natural vegetation, a lake, a mountain, a valley, a river or even an attractive perennial stream'. He described Johannesburg's white burghers as a 'shallowly-rooted, first-generation bourgeoisie' who were 'crassly *nouveau riche*' and 'always more comfortable in the bank, the stock exchange, and the sports stadium' than 'in attending a church, sitting in a concert hall or even serving in the ranks of their city council'.

As if this were not bad enough, for blacks the city became the heartland of the exploitative gold industry where hundreds of thousands laboured underground in dreadful conditions to extract the precious ore, which underwrote so many of the world's transactions and (in a way too mysterious to describe here) rendered 'value' and a 'standard' to global capital. For black Africans in the servants' quarters, in the slums along the railway line, in the mining compounds and in the newly fashioned townships like Soweto (Southwestern Township), Johannesburg was fashioned from the hellish fires of violence, squalor, oppression and racism.

Despite this extraordinary history, Mbembe and Nuttall (2004: 347–72) have had a brave stab at redefining Johannesburg in a more positive light. Simmel's 'culture of things' was on display there – in the daring architechture (sometimes rivalling that found in Chicago), the love of fashion and technology, lavish displays of goods in the increasingly kitsch shopping malls (so bad they are good), flashy restaurants and public and private extravagances. And blacks were not totally left out of this, even in the brutal apartheid years. The world of black Joburgers was brilliantly depicted in the magazine, *Drum*, bought by the son of a mining magnate (a 'randlord') and handed in 1951 to a 25-year-old Englishman, Anthony Sampson, to edit. As Sampson (1956) explained, he set out to recruit a whole generation of black writers and photographers. They told of the making of new jazz sounds (like 'kwela'), beauty contests, boxing fights and the evolution of creative languages and art forms in shebeens (like the famous Back of the Moon) and dancehalls. Later, when a black area of free-holders, Sophiatown, was demolished and the Defiance Campaign began, the magazine charted the activities of black popular political movements, like the African National Congress and the Pan African Congress.

Post-apartheid Johannesburg has seen another turn of the wheel. The shopping malls, casinos and health clinics now play host to the richer elements in the rest of sub-Saharan Africa who prefer Johannesburg's distinctive style, good climate and lower prices to London, Paris or Milan. The global circuits of capital – insurance houses, corporations, new technology enterprises – advertise their presence on huge hoardings that shield the 'concrete encrustations' and encase the highways. The rapidly rising South African black elite – in politics and business – is there too, now meeting their chums on the golf courses while taking their places alongside their white compatriots in the lush suburban properties. The last words must go to Mbembe and Nuttall (2004: 367):

> [Johannesburg] is an *elusive* metropolis because either it is denigrated as being a set of ugly urban agglomerations, a crime city, or a security-obsessed dystopia, or

it is elevated as place of rapacious 'making do', and chance encounters. It is an elusive metropolis because of the multiplicity of registers in which it is African (or perhaps not at all, or not enough); European (or perhaps not, or no longer), or even American (by virtue of its embeddedness in commodity exchange and its culture of consumption). Its very elusiveness makes it especially compelling as an object of study.

▪▪▪▪▪▪▪▪ RACE, THE CITY AND THE US UNDERCLASS

In cities like Los Angeles and Miami, newcomers often edge out or further constrain established minorities like the African-Americans (See Box 17.1 for a description of why African-Americans migrated to the US industrial cities.) Some of this last group are often called an 'underclass' – referring to a notion that there is a stratum below that of the proletariat. Many post-Marxist writers have advanced this idea. As we saw in Chapter 8, for example, Fanon (1967), writing about the anti-colonial struggles in Africa, argued that Marx had underestimated the persistence of the peasantry, but more particularly those who had moved into the colonial towns and capitals as unemployed and underemployed jobseekers. Unlike Marx (who thought of the urban unemployed as a rabble, a lumpen-proletariat), Fanon thought that the urban underclass could be the spearhead of a revolutionary movement.

BLACK POWER

Fanon's ideas resonated in the Black Power movement in the USA in the 1970s. The movement saw the black population as in a quasi-colonial state, with the black ghettos being functional equivalents to the European colonies abroad. There, as in the USA, people of African descent were treated as a racially inferior species. There too blacks were treated as a labour reservoir that could be drawn on only as and when needed – and otherwise left to rot. The only difference was that the colonies were *internal* rather than external. Huey Newton, Malcolm X, Bobby Seale and Angela Davis – leaders of the Black Power and Black Panther movements in the USA – were all influenced by this view to a greater or lesser extent. The movement turned to violence, but this was contained with the use of considerable force. Instead, Black Power engaged in parades in black berets, training in unarmed combat and bellicose posturing with the authorities (and with truculent whites) on the street.

BLACK MUSLIMS

A different response, but one stemming from a similar view of the issues confronting the urban black population, was seen in the creation of the Nation of Islam, the Detroit Temple having been founded in 1932 by Elijah

Mohammed. Adherents rejected Christianity in general, which was identified with slavery, missionaries and colonialism. However, the Black Muslims, as they were known, objected in particular to the passive ('turn the other cheek') and deferred ('pie in the sky when you die') forms of Christianity. Many blacks changed the names they had inherited from the slave owners to Islamic names. The boxer Cassius Clay, for example, became Muhammad Ali and he later converted to orthodox Sunni Islam. Mosques were established in most of the black ghettos and highly disciplined congregants and believers collected money for community projects, self-improvement classes and black enterprises. Those on the political Left were wary of this response to urban deprivation and denounced it as 'black capitalism'. It was nonetheless a powerful means of gaining dignity and self-respect for a small minority of the African-American population. The movement probably gained its apogee in the Million Man March in Washington in October 1995, which was led by Louis Farrakhan, the Black Muslim leader.

THE US DEBATE: AULETTA'S VIEWS

The terms of the US debate about race and urban deprivation have been set by Ken Auletta's book *The Underclass* (1982), and by William J. Wilson in his influential books *The Declining Significance of Race* (1978) and *The Truly Disadvantaged* (1987). The common theme in these accounts is that race and racism play a small or at least declining role in the formation of a black underclass. All are agreed that there is a persistent, growing, unemployed black underclass, which most authors suggest numbers about a third of the black population.

How is this phenomenon to be explained? Auletta (1982) asserts that deviant and criminal tendencies are common in the urban black underclass, that there is apathy towards training, education and vocational guidance and hostility towards self-improvement and the work ethic. Young women in the black underclass are, he claims, prone to producing large numbers of children at a disproportionately young age. Males and females are generally dependent on welfare or charity. There is something in this argument that resembles earlier arguments by Oscar Lewis (1968), who had intensively studied a poor family's life in San Juan, Puerto Rico – out of which study had been generated the famous, some would say notorious, notion of a 'culture of poverty'.

There are many problems with this line of argument. One is that even if the observations are true, researchers can easily confuse cause with consequence. Culture may be a dependent, not an independent variable (in other words, it could be an outcome of other non-considered factors). Long-term unemployment may condition attitudes and generate feelings of resignation, acceptance or despair. Racial discrimination may likewise generate such attitudes. The lack of motivation and the work ethic may in fact be relatively healthy responses to an impossible situation of rejection and restricted or non-existent opportunities. To turn the argument on its head, if many members of the underclass had optimistic, driving, ambitious, competitive attitudes, they could be in the grip of a pathological condition, that is, holding an ideology that had no relationship to reality. A culture or subculture of poverty may therefore be a healthy and adaptive response to an irremediable situation.

WILSON'S VIEWS ON THE UNDERCLASS

A more influential line of argument was initiated by William J. Wilson, who was the first to show systematically the extent to which the black community in the USA had become bifurcated along class lines (thus his expression 'the declining significance of race'). He talks, for example, of a 'deepening economic schism' in the black community – leading to two outcomes:

1. Talented and educated blacks experience rapid upward mobility, comparable to that of whites with similar qualifications. He is not so naive as to suggest that the experience of racism is totally absent from this group. He is also happy to concede that affirmative action (or 'equal opportunities') programmes have helped this top band in its goals. However, he insists that it is *outcome* that is important. Either through their determined efforts to resist discrimination or through the help of affirmative action, the black elite is 'making it'.
2. With regard to the bottom third of the black urban population, the underclass, Wilson documents the increasing rates of crime, the increasing number of families headed by low-earning or non-earning females, the rising number on welfare, the large number who lack formal training and skills, and the consequent extent of black unemployment.

If we take this list of negative attributes, he continues, the black underclass shows more in common with the white underclass rather than with the rest of the black community. This is the second sense in which there is a 'declining significance of race'. In short, the top band of blacks resembles its white counterparts, just as the bottom band does.

FAINSTEIN'S CRITIQUE OF WILSON

Wilson happens to be black and was formerly a distinguished member of the sociology department at the University of Chicago. The only significance of his background is that his views created a storm of counter-arguments, particularly among black scholars, who saw him as denying the significance of racial discrimination, denying his own background and indeed painting the situation with 'whitewash'. Nearly all this criticism tended to be misplaced, for it was based on ideological, not sociological, premises. However, Norman Fainstein (1992), who sought to challenge the empirical basis of Wilson's argument, provided a more powerful critique. Using complex statistical data from the US census, he advances two suggestions:

1. Over the period 1960–1983, there was a slow convergence between black and white in educational attainments, though a gap remained. The high achievers were not closing the gap at the rate we would expect from Wilson's thesis, while the low achievers (for example the percentage with fewer than four years of high school) were narrowing the gap with their white counterparts.

2. With respect to income, the data lend support to Wilson's thesis. Between 1960 and 1983, the poorest African-Americans got poorer and the richest got richer, but the trend was gradual rather than, as Wilson implied, a sharp bifurcation.

MISMATCH THEORY

Is the persistence of a black underclass due to a *mismatch* between the skills that black people have and the available opportunities? The theory is that an important proportion of the African-American population are in the wrong place with the wrong skills and experience. Kasarda (cited in Fainstein 1992: 297–8) is particularly associated with the four-pronged argument that:

1. Jobs with low educational requirements are disappearing from the city centre, but blacks in the inner city are particularly dependent on such jobs.

2. They do not have the educational attainments to compete in the knowledge-intensive industries.

3. They cannot get to low-paying suburban jobs, for these are dependent on having cars because public transport is poorly developed.

4. They are unwilling to move south or southwest where there are jobs because they want to retain their benefit dependency in the high-benefit cities of the northeast (where they are partly protected by black politicians).

Fainstein (1992) again questions this argument in fine detail, but more generally suggests that it is inconsistent with the actual structure of black employment. In fact, blacks are not overrepresented in the construction, manufacturing and retail trades as the mismatch theorists had argued. They are no more dependent than whites are on manufacturing and are considerably less dependent on construction and the retail trade. They are, on the other hand, overrepresented in services including hospitals, healthcare, schools and colleges. This clearly would expose African-Americans to the cuts in public service associated with neoliberalism. Despite this dangerous dependence on jobs in the public sector, Fainstein is of the view that the problems of gaining employment at all are more important than black underrepresentation or overrepresentation in any one segment of the labour market. In short, when all is said and done black underperformance and the continued and even growing underclass have to be explained by racism and racial discrimination. Blacks are not getting jobs because they are black.

▪▪▪▪▪▪▪▪▪ REVIEW

While many cities owe their significance to the rise of modernity in Europe, others were developed – warts and all – in the wake of colonial expansion. As people were pushed or walked off the land, the cities of the colonial world swelled, but often failed to provide the employment opportunities associated with mass industrialization: these 'cities of peasants', as well as the successful industrial cites like Chicago, have provided the grist to many a sociologist's mill. It may be that the economic, political and technological conditions characteristic of the cities of the global age will provide similarly important sites for sociological analysis. The regional roles of global cities are also important – in this chapter we have shown how Los Angeles has evolved to serve the Asia Pacific region, while post-apartheid Johannesburg has found its place as the continent's cosmopolis.

Global cities are not only important phenomena in their own right; they are where certain distinctive patterns of employment emerge – in particular the move from manufacturing to services. Employment often becomes 'feminized' as old male-dominated skills are discarded and new labour markets are formed. New kinds of people, from different ethnic backgrounds and with cosmopolitan outlooks and connections with several countries, enter the global city and often succeed in their quest for social mobility. By contrast, established racial minorities are often marginalized and turned into a so-called 'underclass'. The persistence of deprivation in the midst of successful immigrant entrepreneurship often fuels urban discontent expressed in the form of riots and demonstrations.

FURTHER READING

- ▪ Bryan Roberts' *Cities of Peasants* (1978) provides a good account of cities in Latin America.

- ▪ John Friedman's classic article in *Development and Change* (1986) on 'The world city hypothesis' was what started the debate on global cities.

- ▪ The most accomplished and extensive work on the theme of global cities is Saskia Sassen's (1991) *The Global City*, which has a lot of detail on New York, Tokyo and London. Although lengthy, the book is not difficult and contains excellent data.

- ▪ One of the USA's most eminent sociologists is William J. Wilson, whose books *The Declining Significance of Race* (1978) and *The Truly Disadvantaged* (1987) are landmarks in the study of deprivation in US cities.

- ▪ Mike Davis's *City of Quartz* (1991) provides a prophetic left-wing critique of urban development in Los Angeles. A data-rich account of LA is given in R. Waldinger and M. Bozorgmehr's edited book, *Ethnic Los Angeles* (1996).

- ▪ Achille Mbembe and Sarah Nuttall edited a special issue of *Public Culture* in 2004, which contains 10 challenging articles on Johannesburg, including their excellent introductory chapter.

GROUP WORK

1. Using the 'ecological' method of the Chicago School and a large photocopy of a map of a nearby city, describe and demarcate its different zones.

2. Split into three groups. Each group will draw up a list of 'global cities' in Europe, Asia or the Americas. Why did you include some and exclude others?

3. Draw up a list of which occupations women (a) dominate or (b) might dominate in the future. Why do you suppose this is the case?

4. What images do you have of Los Angeles? Studying one of the key chapter references on the city (or any recent book you can find in your library), list the ways in which your image differs from the account consulted.

5. Spilt into three groups to engage in the 'black underclass debate'. Group A will look at cultural explanations, group B will look at the views of William J. Wilson and group C will advance a 'mismatch theory'.

QUESTIONS TO THINK ABOUT

?

1. What are the main differences between a colonial, industrial and global city (bearing in mind that individual cities might have 'migrated' across these categories)?

2. Why were cities so important to the pre-1945 sociologists?

3. Can global cities become detached from the national states in which they are found?

4. Why is employment becoming 'feminized' in some cities?

5. What accounts for the continuing underperformance of about a third of African-Americans?

WHAT'S ON THE WEB

■ The Intute gateway to sites on urban sociology is http://www.intute.ac.uk/cgi-bin/search.pl?term1=urban+sociology&limit=0&subject=socialsciences A lot of the important work linking urban themes to globalization and the evolution of world cities has been undertaken by geographers. This is the Intute gateway via geography.

■ http://www.lboro.ac.uk/gawc/ The Globalization and World Cities Study Group and Network is very active and up to date. There is a stunning amount of material that can be accessed from this site and we thank our colleagues at Loughborough University for providing this excellent resource to the scholarly community.

■ http://www.joburg.org.za/ The official website of the city of Johannesburg is remarkably lively. http://www.ci.la.ca.us/ That of Los Angeles could learn a thing or two.

PART FOUR

Dynamics and Challenges

CHAPTER 18

Global Civil Society

CONTENTS

We start this chapter by looking at various attempts to theorize the general nature of social movements, especially as they evolved from the 1960s, and provide some concrete examples. We then examine why and in what ways some social movements have become increasingly transnational in orientation – what we call 'global social movements' – and how in this capacity they are increasingly contributing to the formation of a global civil society. This involves building a global society from below through a succession of worldwide campaigns and transnational actions by ordinary individuals. We refer to some recent and highly significant examples, such as the anti-debt campaign Jubilee 2000, the global justice movement against poverty and inequality, and the worldwide resistance to the Iraq War of 2003. We also briefly consider three other themes closely related to questions about global civil society: the relationship between global social movements and INGOs; the growing importance of the human rights discourse; and the question of whether the highly nationalist responses to the terrorist attacks in New York and Washington on 11 September 2001 have affected the evolution of global civil society. Our comparative analysis of social movements in this chapter will also provide an introduction to the next two chapters in which we consider the women's and green movements in detail.

Figure 18.1 **Jubilee 2000 campaign for debt relief, Paris, April 2000**
The campaign to relieve the poorest countries of their debts gained the support of the G8 countries in 2005.

DEFINING SOCIAL MOVEMENTS

Social movements are agencies of social transformation that emerge in response to certain social changes and conditions. They are also manifestations of popular sentiment and in this respect they overlap with numerous other kinds of social activities. Not surprisingly, therefore, there are a plethora of definitions and descriptions. We can start with Wilson's (1973: 8) rather prosaic one. He claims that 'a social movement is a conscious, collective, organized attempt to bring about or resist large-scale change in the social order by non-institutionalized means' and adds, more graphically, that those who join social movements go 'beyond the customary resources of the social order to launch their own crusade against the evils of society. Such actions may enable them to reach beyond themselves and become new men and women' (Wilson 1973: 5).

Byrne (1997: 10–11), however, defines social movements as:

- unpredictable (for example women's movements do not always arise where women are most oppressed)
- irrational (adherents do not act out of self-interest)
- unreasonable (adherents think they are justified in flouting the law)
- disorganized (some avoid formalizing their organization even when it seems like a good idea to do so).

Zirakzadeh (1997: 4–5), on the other hand, suggests that a social movement:

- is a group of people who consciously attempt to build a radically new social order
- involves people of a broad range of social backgrounds
- deploys politically confrontational and socially disruptive tactics.

Figure 18.2 **Anti-war protesters gathered in London, February 2003**
The USA-led invasion of Iraq has mobilized the biggest protests since the Vietnam War and undermined the political support of President Bush and Prime Minister Blair.

▪▪▪▪▪▪▪▪ THE CHANGING NATURE OF SOCIAL MOVEMENTS SINCE THE 1960S

Many scholars who have written about social movements in advanced countries argue that they underwent a sea change from the late 1960s onwards. As with all social movements, this was apparently linked to certain underlying changes evident in industrialized countries from around that time. Touraine (1981) tried to capture the outcome of these changes with the term **POSTINDUSTRIAL SOCIETY**, which saw an occupational shift away from manual work to the knowledge and service sectors, including IT, the media, fashion, design and even therapy and counselling services.

> **key concept**
>
> **POSTINDUSTRIAL SOCIETY** refers to societies where the service industries – including the knowledge, media and information-based sectors – have become the most important source of wealth and employment. Accompanying this, therefore, is a relative decline in the contribution of manufacturing industry to national wealth, a fall in the numbers of manual workers, a huge expansion of university or tertiary education and a growing middle class.

A related feature of postindustrial society was a growing middle class of public and private sector employees, many working in the rising cultural, media and knowledge industries. Touraine contrasted the 'old' labour and political movements with the 'new' social movements that represented the interests of those working in emerging occupations. The question of whether there was a clear distinction between 'old' and 'new' movements was a lively debate for a while, but we are content with the view that nearly all the changes were more those of degree than of kind. Naturally, social movements respond to new realities and new social demands, but this is a different argument from the idea that they are totally new phenomena. Keeping this important point in mind, we now discuss four ways in which social movements have changed their orientations over recent decades – the switch to identity politics, the rise of 'countercultures', the questioning of authority and the elevation of grassroots activities.

THE SWITCH TO IDENTITY POLITICS

According to Giddens (1991: Chapter 7), throughout most of the period of modernization until the mid-twentieth century, social movements were generally concerned with what he calls 'emancipatory politics'. These were struggles against those structures and inequalities that constrained people's freedom to choose their own life experiences. Chief among these compulsions were the heavy weight of tradition (such as religious and customary obligations), material scarcity and poverty and people's exclusion from access to legal and political rights or the same opportunities to attain wealth enjoyed by ruling groups.

Important examples of emancipatory politics include the struggles to obtain universal suffrage, freedom of movement, assembly and opinion; the abolition of slavery in the USA and the European colonies; and the rights of workers to engage in free collective bargaining and to curb the worst excesses of exploitation by constructing a welfare state. In all these struggles, social movements were used to gain some degree of direct control over state power. Workers and socialist movements not only formed trade unions, which could bargain more effectively with capitalists in the workplace, but they also established political parties that were capable of taking over the reins of government. Armed with such weapons, the working classes eventually succeeded in curbing the excesses of capitalism so that the interests of the majority were met more fairly.

Contemporary social movements, by contrast, have been less interested in directly controlling or gaining access to state power. Nevertheless, since the 1960s, struggles to extend the full rights and opportunities already won by the majority of citizens to previously disadvantaged or excluded groups have continued to be fought everywhere, but especially in developing countries. Sometimes these demands have involved confrontations with the state. Social movements in advanced societies are often associated with the demands of women, religious or ethnic minorities (like the civil rights movement in the USA during the 1960s), the needs of children and young people, and the struggles of gay and disabled people.

Giddens, however, pointed to a more important difference between the earlier and more recent social movements. In *Modernity and Self-identity*, Giddens (1991: 214–27) observed that by the 1980s the main focus of social movements had shifted to causes to do with what he called 'life politics'. These raise the question of how exactly we might prefer to use emancipatory freedoms once they have been won – what kind of personal and community life we might wish to construct – and what responsibilities individuals must exercise if the guarantee of universal freedom is to continue. Since we all depend on interpersonal relationships and each individual's freedom hinges on exactly how these are arranged, issues of self-realization and questions of personal identity inevitably come to the forefront of our concerns.

This has been particularly evident in the contemporary feminist movement, which originated in the USA, swept across the Western world in the early 1970s and has now penetrated most societies. As we have seen, feminism challenged patriarchy, which relegated women to roles defined as culturally inferior. However, it has also gone much further than this by compelling women to confront questions about what sort of lives they wish to lead, what values and personal identities they wish to uphold. Pressing questions for contemporary feminists include: the nature of sexuality and preferred sexual orientations; the control of biological reproduction (including abortion); who should be entitled to exercise rights over children; the terms on which marriage and other kinds of intimate relationships should be founded; and issues of representation and freedom of expression, such as pornography. Thus, political conflicts and processes have started to dissolve the boundaries between the private and public spheres.

NON-MATERIAL VALUES AND 'COUNTERCULTURES'

According to Inglehart (1990) and others, growing affluence and material security, associated with economic growth after the Second World War and the welfare reforms implemented by the social democracies at that time, encouraged many people to become more concerned with the pursuit of non-material values and to place more emphasis on their personal fulfilment and identities. This development of a **COUNTERCULTURE** also accounts for the declining appeal of radical, socialist ideas among many workers and others during the same period. Although they may have opposed the pro-capitalist parties, they were still seen as 'part of the system'.

key concept	**COUNTERCULTURE** was predominantly seen in the richer Western countries in the 1960s and 1970s. Those involved in its development opposed the dull, unreflective, self-congratulatory uniformity of conventional political values. They displayed a growing desire for more control over personal development, greater equity and fluidity in social relationships, a heightened respect for nature and the revival of more decentralized, autonomous communities. A turn away from established religion towards Eastern philosophies, experimentation with drugs, adventurous popular music and 'way out' dress codes were also characteristic of the period.

Students were particularly associated with the counterculture movement. A groundswell of student unrest, initially associated with the civil rights movement in the USA, became evident from the early 1960s. This student movement spread to Europe and probably reached its high point during the events of May 1968 in France. These 'events' appeared to validate Inglehart's thesis. Across Europe, workers, intellectuals and students held strikes, occupied college campuses and factories. They appeared to demonstrate against a society that produced what Marcuse (1964) – a Marxist intellectual living in the USA – called 'one-dimensional man'. In the eyes of many intellectuals, this protest involved an attack on two features of industrial society:

■ The dehumanizing consequences of the bureaucratization of industry, government and higher education.
■ The 'bargain' offered by postwar Fordist economies, namely the distorting emphasis placed on economic prosperity and acquisitiveness bought at the cost of relentless disempowerment in the workplace and the decline of community and cultural autonomy.

Box 18.1

Battles in cyberspace: Greenpeace against French nuclear testing

Background events

In June 1995, the French government decided to resume testing nuclear weapons in the South Pacific despite its earlier commitment to respect an international agreement on nuclear non-proliferation. Greenpeace had long campaigned against the French government's adherence to an outdated view of national security needs fuelled by 'great power' aspirations. For example, Greenpeace had crossed swords with the French government in 1985, culminating in the sinking of the *Rainbow Warrior* ship by the French navy.

Greenpeace's worldwide campaign: July 1995 to early 1996

During its campaign against the resumption of nuclear testing, Greenpeace operated on many fronts:

- A petition was signed by more than five million people.

- Demonstrations were organized around the world, including one involving more than 15,000 people in Tahiti who blocked roads and demanded that Greenpeace's leading ship be allowed to dock against the wishes of the French government.

- Networks of supporting groups formed coalitions in many countries to influence world public opinion.

- Australian public opinion was especially targeted. Here, past admiration for the bravery of Greenpeace warriors and proximity to the nuclear testing zone could be expected to generate strong pressure on the government to use diplomacy to oppose French activities.

- Greenpeace sailed its fleet of five ships into the test area along with its helicopter, divers and several inflatable boats.

Greenpeace also exploited the then latest techniques in communications technology:

- Numerous faxes were sent and satellite telephones kept the various campaign messages flowing constantly across the world.

- Three ships were equipped with the most up-to-date communication systems and so were able to relay powerful images, including colour photos, via satellite.

- Events were also filmed by helicopter, adding to the dramatic footage that was fed into the global media.

- Meanwhile, the leading ship sent out messages on the internet. This enabled individuals, groups and the media to pick up the information relayed by Greenpeace's on-the-spot warriors via its website, established in 1994.

When the action began, with French commandos boarding *Rainbow Warrior II* and using tear gas against the protesters, observers were left in no doubt about the intensity of the South Pacific struggle. A global social movement had beaten one of the world's most powerful nation-states, at least in the propaganda war.

SOURCE: Cooper (1997)

Student discontent fed directly into an upsurge of counterculture movements that soon spread across the Western world, including the hippie and drug cultures, the anti-Vietnam War movement of the late 1960s and early 1970s and the early stirrings of the green movement. A retreat from the repressive and materialistic lifestyles offered by mainstream consumerist capitalism also involved such things as the establishment of communes and cooperatives, an interest in organic farming and foods and experimenting with Eastern philosophy and health practices.

Whether or not all or most students and others who participated in the events following May 1968 perceived it as a struggle against materialist values quite to the same degree as the intellectuals involved is open to debate. Again, in the light of more recent changes, the argument that most people's lives are no longer plagued by endemic economic insecurities now seems distinctly premature.

QUESTIONING AUTHORITY

According to Giddens (1991) and Beck (1992), the spread of higher education and developments in communication technology, among other changes, allowed people in advanced societies to become more knowledgeable than they had previously been about science, technology and the management of economic life. At the same time, the dangers associated with nuclear energy and weaponry, as well as with chemical and biological warfare, spurred many citizens to insist that governments, the military and business corporations relinquish their right to monopolize control over these areas. The realization that some scientists and technologists had placed their expertise and public prestige at the service of such narrow and unaccountable interests further deepened these demands. The campaigns against the dangers of nuclear energy in North America and Europe, which gathered pace in the 1970s, can be regarded as a concrete expression of such sentiments (Joppke 1993). They also provided a foundation both for the peace movement, which erupted in a new form in the early 1980s in Europe, North America and the Soviet Union, and for the wider green movement we shall discuss in Chapter 20.

Even the buttoned-up world of markets and business management, once regarded as out of bounds to ordinary citizens (except in their limited capacities as individual consumers or shareholders), has become increasingly exposed to detailed public scrutiny and liable to substantial criticism. This has become particularly evident among large companies that decide to market green or ethical products (Kennedy 1996). Making such commercial claims both invites external validation by relevant campaigning groups and requires it. Indeed, such companies may become inexorably sucked into engaging in green and ethical consciousness-raising activities in order to inform public opinion about their products. Moreover, responding to both public pressure and market opportunities, some of the many companies engaged in actively developing energy-saving or emission-reducing technologies have positively demanded tougher government regulations. Thus, without an even playing field created by government intervention, competitors who do not invest in, or adopt, green technologies will gain a cost advantage over more innovative and concerned companies (Oliviero and Simmons 2002; Monbiot 2005).

European public anxiety about GM crops and foods in the late 1990s is another case in point and we discuss this in more detail in Chapter 20. Similarly, since the 1990s, there has been an upsurge of local, national and global criticism, along with various campaigns, against the neoliberal economic policies and priorities imposed by the G7 countries and IGOs such as the World

Bank, IMF and WTO in their dealings with developing countries (see, for example, Desai and Said 2001; Kiely 2005b: Chapters 7 and 8). Thus, there has been a demand for the democratization of decision-making in every sphere. Although such demands have not always been met, many citizens have made it clear that they are no longer prepared to accept that there are legitimate areas of decision-making where they do not have every right to be fully informed and amply consulted.

THE ELEVATION OF GRASSROOTS ACTIVITY

The post-1960s social movements have tended to be decentralized and non-hierarchical in mobilizing members for collective action, though there are exceptions to this such as Greenpeace (see Box 18.1) and the African National Congress (ANC) in South Africa. Normally, social movements form loose federations of semi-autonomous groups, rely very much on grassroots support based on networking activities and usually permit members to arrange their own priorities and strategies of protest. Of course, such practices may also lead to divisiveness within movements, indecision, lack of focus and poorly organized campaigns. Nevertheless, these characteristics allow social movements rapidly to adjust their mode of operations, respond to the constant rush of events, select new targets for mobilization and draw upon a heterogeneous and ever changing mix of supporters. By the same token, each social movement's focus of concern and body of support tends to coalesce and overlap with those of others. For example, many animal rights' supporters are also likely to feel strongly about road-building programmes that threaten wildlife conservation areas and this may simultaneously place them among the various radical green groups. Frequently, one kind of commitment leads quite naturally to another.

Three factors largely explain the emphasis on democratic, decentralized and participatory forms of organization and action:

1. Contemporary social movements are not interested in winning direct control over state power and so they have no need to construct vast, centralized organizations capable of assuming the reins of government.
2. Their aims involve trying to persuade broad sections of the population to adopt new agendas for deep changes in social and cultural life, while compelling businesses and other powerful bodies to alter their priorities. Particularly in democratic societies, such goals call for a multiplicity of dispersed and highly diverse grassroots activities that involve consciousness-raising and exposing the failures of the existing system. Accordingly, the following actions are likely to be effective: demonstrations, petitions, consumer or investment boycotts, land occupations, road actions such as blockades and sit-ins, conferences, high-profile media events, neighbourhood action groups or mass letter-writing to politicians and company directors. Such actions embarrass politicians, undermine their electoral support and threaten the sales, profits, investment sources and reputations of commercial interests.

3. Those who tend to be attracted to social movements are often educated, informed and used to exercising personal autonomy. As such, they would be unlikely to tolerate permanent exclusion from policy-making by impersonal, bureaucratic cliques of largely unaccountable movement leaders. After all, this would fly in the face of the very ethos of self-realization and the need to empower people and civil society, which prompted such individuals to join social movements in the first place.

■ ■

Global Thinkers 18   JÜRGEN HABERMAS (1929–)

Jürgen Habermas is one of the world's most eminent contemporary sociologists and works in the tradition of the Frankfurt School of Critical Theory. The word 'critical' was essential to this group of scholars for two reasons. First, it was a signal that, while they drew on core insights by Marx, they also were preoccupied with issues arising from mass media, mass societies, mass cultures and the psychological insights generated by Freud and others. Second, 'critical' implied a preference for the interpretative understanding (Verstehen) *of social affairs rather than a narrow belief in scientific and positivist methods. For members of the School, rationality and irrationality were interlaced in human affairs. Habermas later became preoccupied with how to attain 'a rational society' and what rationality meant.*

It was hardly surprising that the members of the Frankfurt School (established in 1923) became concerned about irrationality. As Nazis seized the German state and mass rallies affirmed Hitler's wild theories, the Frankfurt School, many of them Jews, Marxists or both, had to disperse. From 1931 to 1949 it was largely based in New York. After the Second World War, two famous scholars Theodor Adorno and Max Horkheimer re-established the School in Germany. In 1956, Habermas, then 27, became Adorno's assistant. This was the beginning of a stream of powerful sociological works. In any full account of Habermas, there are perhaps 15 major works to consider, so we have to be especially selective in what follows.

Let us first mention Habermas's contribution to understanding 'the public sphere' and 'rationality'. In his first major book, The Structural Transformation of the Public Sphere *(1989), he shows how an emerging European bourgeoisie began to take an interest in public affairs by starting up newspapers and constituting an informed reading public. However, in the twentieth century, the public sphere became fragmented and politicians were able to manipulate public opinion rather than be subject to its strictures (Outhwaite 1996: 7–8). Despite a strong tendency towards public passivity, Habermas argues that there is a strong potential for rationality, in that human beings have an extended capacity for communicative competence. In* Towards a Rational Society *(1971) and* Communication and the Evolution of Society *(1979), he uses political theory, the study of language and linguistics, and notions of sociality and social action to show how people can oppose attempts to make them subject to the whims of elites. This more positive form of rationality may be deemed a 'humanizing rationality' – one that is different from the 'instrumental rationality' of states, the market, large organizations, corporations and the media.*

We see here how Habermas wants to recover a role for the 'public sphere', 'civil society' and 'moral consciousness'. He sees all states as experiencing a 'legitimation crisis' (where they cannot easily defend the morality of their actions). This results in the withdrawal of public support or, more positively, its deflection into civil society. Unlike some radical advocates of global civic action (described elsewhere in this chapter), Habermas sees civil society as a complement rather than an alternative to formal politics. Students often struggle with his abstract language, but his philosophical reasoning conceals a strong commitment to democracy and a fierce opposition to the tyranny of illegitimate state power. He took a hard-hitting stance in opposition to the 'war on terror' and the US invasion of Iraq.

SOURCES: Habermas (1971, 1979, 1989); McCarthy (1978); Braaten (1991); Outhwaite (1994, 1996)

GLOBALIZATION OF SOCIAL MOVEMENTS: CONSTRAINTS AND OPPORTUNITIES

Transnational cooperation between social movements is not new. Ever since the nineteenth century, peace, anti-slavery, women's, conservationist and workers' movements have sometimes drawn strength from collaborating with similar groups in other countries. During the 1960s, civil rights, anti-Vietnam and student movements, as well as the Campaign for Nuclear Disarmament (CND), spread across national borders. It is helpful to distinguish here between occasional collaboration between largely separate national groups and campaigns specifically designed to be globally focused that use national support as one resource in the pursuit of worldwide goals. For example, before the 1980s, apart from a few attempts to protect international wildlife, green groups in the USA mostly campaigned on domestic environmental issues (Bramble and Porter 1992: 324). By contrast, the peace movement that erupted across Europe, the USA and elsewhere from 1981 was more self-consciously globalizing in its effectiveness and thinking about nuclear war than any previous anti-war movement (Taylor and Young 1987). Indeed, according to Kaldor (1999: 198), with around five million individuals demonstrating in many different towns and cities across Europe in October 1981 and October 1983, it 'was probably the largest transnational movement in history' up until that time.

Until recently, most of the theoretical work on social movements by sociologists and others was based on the presumption that the nation-state was the natural and obvious location in which movements would seek to operate (Princen and Finger 1994: Chapter 3). In fact, various constraints existed that made global activity more difficult than corresponding actions at the national level, so most social movements had to be rooted first and foremost in national struggles dependent on domestic support. However, as the contributors to Cohen and Rai (2000) show, certain social movements such as those concerned with labour, women, peace, the environment, human rights and universalizing religion are intrinsically global, or at least international. There are now excellent opportunities as well as good reasons to choose to operate transnationally; in fact, in some ways, social movements are better equipped to do so than states (see Box 18.2).

Box 18.2

Global civil society actors: constraints and opportunities for mobilization

Opportunities and motivations

Unlike states:

1. They are not tied to territories, national interests or diplomatic practices for stabilizing inter-state relations.

2. They can operate without secrecy and are not accountable to electorates.

3. They are not guilty of such things as human rights abuses, environmental threats or poverty.

4. The concerns they articulate are widely shared by disadvantaged and/or discontented people and so support spills naturally across borders.

5. Accordingly, they can cooperate and generate alternative ideas and solutions more easily than states.

Unlike business corporations:

6. They do not represent narrow interests and have no fixed investments to protect. And they do not engage in market competition (although they compete for members and media attention).

7. They are decentralized and relatively unbureaucratic.

In contrast, they share certain unique features:

8. They earn public support by virtue of their altruism, openness and willingness to risk their lives.

9. They are adaptable, versatile, in touch with ordinary people and cheap.

Constraints

Unlike states and business corporations:

1. They have limited funds, yet the costs of global action are often high – cross-national communication, translations and travel to conferences or to lobby IGOs and governments.

2. Engaging media attention may require stunts that involve access to equipment (for example Greenpeace ships) and costly operations.

3. Family and work commitments and the costs of long-distance travel inhibit individual participation in transnational actions.

4. Language barriers and problems of intercultural communication may undermine cooperation between different national groups despite shared goals.

They often have special needs and problems:

5. Many global social movements and INGOs need technical expertise so that they can be taken seriously by scientists, governments and the public, while being sufficiently prepared to argue their case. For this they need a core of full-time professionals and reliable databases.

6. Southern groups may only be able to act or collaborate in transnational events if they are subsidized by Northern partners. This can lead to charges of 'paternalism'.

10. They mobilize support at many levels.

11. The diversity of movements and NGOs enables each to draw on the specialist resources of others.

12. The revolution in ICT has massively reduced the costs of cross-border collaboration and increased information sharing.

13. The extension of democracy in many parts of the world, the end of the Cold War and rising economic prosperity in some countries have all extended the possibilities for free association by individuals and groups.

7. Southern NGOs and social movements often have different priorities from those in the North. They are more concerned with human rights and the need to overcome poverty among the most deprived groups. Global environmental concerns often take second place. This has given rise to disagreements in the past.

SOURCES: Ghils (1992); Fisher (1993); Princen and Finger (1994); Riddell-Dixon (1995); Anheier and Themudo (2002)

You will notice in Box 18.2 that we have included INGOs in the discussion. Although estimates of how many INGOs there are vary, it is thought that there were around 17,000 in the mid-1980s (Scholte 1993: 44), 23,000 in the early 1990s (Ghils 1992: 419) and more than 47,000 in 2000 (Held and McGrew 2002: 18). There are two important points to note about these organizations. First, far more non-governmental organizations operate at a local, grassroots or national level than exist globally. According to Fisher (1993: xi), by the early 1990s, there were more than 100,000 such groups in the developing countries (the South), probably serving the needs of more than 100 million people. Most are geared towards ameliorating economic hardship and promoting human rights among women, the urban poor living in shantytowns or tribal peoples whose livelihoods are being threatened by large development projects such as dams. Alternatively, they seek substitutes for the top-down, commercially oriented structural adjustment programmes and development initiatives that Southern governments tend to promote, often with the backing of Western states, investors and IGOs like the World Bank. In turn, approximately another 35,000 'grassroots support organizations' (Fisher 1993: viii) assist these NGOs. Often these grassroots and national NGOs are staffed by young professionals who either out of a sense of commitment to their fellow citizens or because they are unemployed decide to work in a semi-voluntary capacity for these bodies. Many of these NGOs in the South also enjoy links with INGOs that provide them with funds, technical expertise, international media coverage and other kinds of external support.

The second point to note about INGOs is that they fit into a general category that includes far more associations, networks and activities than just non-profit-

making organizations like Oxfam or Amnesty International. 'True' INGOs like
the latter typically employ a core staff of permanent officials, have a large
network of volunteer supporters, and operate worldwide through a federation of
nationally based but globally cooperating offices and sister organizations that
share global aims and concerns. Their numbers have more than doubled in the
past two decades, rising from nearly 10,000 in 1981 to more than 25,000 by
2000 (Lechner and Boli 2005: 132). Moreover, in addition to their regular work
of providing famine relief, building up professional expertise and knowledge
banks, or publicizing human rights abuses, they are often closely associated with
and/or overlap other kinds of global social actors, including global social movements. And, like the latter, they often run or participate in campaigns designed
to shape government policies and public opinion in the struggle to win a fairer,
safer and more humane world and they sometimes engage in overt protest (see
Box 18.1 above). In this regard, they may provide a core around which such
groups and networks cluster; they may nest within broader global social movements while attempting to give some direction to the latter's campaigns; or they
may simply work alongside but partly separately from the latter. This brings us
to the concept of **GLOBAL CIVIL SOCIETY**.

---

key concept

GLOBAL CIVIL SOCIETY While civil society (see Chapter 3) is made up of the
networks of groups between the family and the state that try to influence
political opinion and policy-making within the confines of nation-states, a
global civil society includes all those social agents whose joint concerns
and struggles stretch beyond the borders of their nation-states, as they try
to shape the actions of a variety of powerful actors such as governments,
IGOs and TNCs over issues and problems that cannot be tackled
adequately, or at all, at any level other than the regional or global.

Recent definitions provided by scholars working in this field differ slightly, but
many draw on the classic work of Habermas (see Global Thinker 18). For
example, Anheier and Themudo (2002) and Anheier et al. (2005: 17) see the
activities that contribute to global civil society as taking place in the space
between the threefold structures of family, states and market. Keane (2003: 65),
on the other hand, includes the global economy and global economic actors like
large businesses in his definition, or what he calls 'turbo capitalism'. Because
markets are always firmly entrenched in sociopolitical structures and relations,
global civil society could not exist without a money economy or the technological investments that large corporations make to provide the communications
and other resources that enable it to flourish. In any case, the main struggle in
global civil society in recent years has been focused on debates about how to
reform, abolish or humanize the way in which the global economy currently
operates. Despite these differences in emphasis, there is also considerable agreement. Thus, global civil society agents:

■ Conduct 'cross-border social activities' and operate 'outside the boundaries of
governmental structures' (Keane 2003: 8, 9), irrespective of whether the inter-

connections they establish create 'thick' or 'thinly stretched networks, pyramids and hub-and-spoke clusters'.

■ Although their activities have many historical precedents, what is new is their 'sheer scale and scope', while the 'range and type of fields in which they operate has never been wider' (Anheier et al. 2005: 4).

■ As active involvement in conventional political activities at the national level seems to be diminishing in many countries, especially the rich ones, perhaps global civil society activism has become a way of calling governments, TNCs and IGOs 'to account' (Anheier et al. 2005: 16).

■ It may also play a role in 'revitalizing democracy' (Anheier et al. 2005: 15) by creating transnational advocacy networks – worldwide coalitions of informed public opinion and political pressure groups – that exert pressure on oppressive governments from the outside (Keck and Sikkink 1998). For example, in the mid-1990s, the Zapatistas rebelled against the Mexican government because they believed that the neoliberal economic policies it was promoting were destroying their local economic and social life (Kiely 2005b: 205–6).

■ Global civil society is made up of a vast range of agents. Some engage in activities that prove to be temporary, short-lived or intermittent, while others, such as 'true' INGOs, set up permanent organizations. In between are information networks, foundations, funds, 'grassroots organizations' such as diasporic groups, immigrant associations, 'internet-based organizations' operating mostly in cyberspace, social movements focused on specific issues like the environment, and numerous informal hybrid associations (Anheier and Themudo 2002: 196).

■ Economic globalization provides an especially powerful force that simultaneously increases global civil society activity – because of the growing ease with which connectivities can be made to work across vast distances – and encourages global political coalitions as 'a reaction' to the inequalities, insecurities and injustices it has caused, or deepened, particularly among poorer countries and social groups (Anheier et al. 2005: 7). We explore this in more detail in the next section where we discuss the global justice movement.

■ Parallel summits occur when coalitions of groups within civil society organize mass participation at large public events in the expectation of gaining international media attention. The action is often timed to coincide with the official summit meetings of governments, IGOs or big business. These are not new but their incidence has drastically increased since the late 1980s and especially since 1999; also, the international mix of the protestors involved has tended to become more radical. Thus, in 2000 and 2001 alone, the incidence of parallel summits grew by nearly 40 per cent. The social protest organized by global activists and timed to take place alongside the World Economic Forum of global business interests at Davos, Switzerland, in 2000, and the first alternative World Social Forum held at Porto Alegre, Brazil, in 2001, are just two examples (Pianta 2001: 177).

In Table 18.1 we provide a brief snapshot of the incidence, range and spread of global civil society activities that took place in just one month in January 2003. And, as you will see if you examine the chronology put together by Timms (2005), this was by no means an atypical month.

TABLE 18.1 Global civil society events in January 2003	
Social forums/alternative summits	Protests, rallies, sit-ins
Hyderabad, India: First Asian Social Forum attended by 15,000	Bahrain: sit-in at the Ministry of Justice over calls for full civil rights for women
Addis Ababa, Ethiopia: Second African Social Forum with representatives from 40 countries	San Francisco: multiethnic/religious protests against arrests of immigrants for failing to comply with US residency requirements
Belem, Brazil: Second Pan-Amazonic Social Forum focused on environmental issues	Rabat, Morocco: NGO mass anti-Iraq War march and sit-in at UN HQ plus solidarity with Palestine. Supported by trade unions
Porto Alegre, Brazil: First Global Assembly of Peasant Farmers' Organizations	Success of international boycott campaign against Nestlé to drop its US$6 million claim against Ethiopia
Porto Alegre, Brazil: Third World Social Forum with 100,000 attending from 123 countries	Grenoble, France: 8,000 protestors demonstrate against treatment of activists who tried to destroy GM plants

GLOBAL SOCIAL MOVEMENTS: RESOURCES AND CHALLENGES

We have seen global civil society activities of many kinds explode onto the national and world political stage in the past 10–15 years, though they go back much earlier than this. We now explore three overlapping changes that have increased the concrete opportunities for effective transnational communication, mobilization and collaboration: problems generated by economic globalization coupled with neoliberal policies; shifts in thinking by supporters of social movements and INGOs; and changes in communications technology that have widened the repertoire of actions available to global actors.

PROBLEMS RELATED TO ECONOMIC GLOBALIZATION AND NEOLIBERAL POLICIES

The rise of neoliberal economic thinking in advanced countries, initiated by the USA and the UK in the early 1980s, led to the implementation of stringent financial measures designed to reduce public spending and check inflationary pressures. In their dealings with developing countries, the OECD, the World Bank and the IMF insisted that the former adopt similar measures. There was also relentless pressure to increase foreign earnings for debt payment by expanding the export of raw materials such as forest products. This further accentuated the extent of the environmental deterioration in many developing countries while threatening the livelihoods of tribal, forest and other marginalized groups. According to Korton (1990: 6), these events have provoked a widespread demand for a more autonomous and 'people-centred vision' of economic development among many people living in the South.

As we saw in Chapters 4 and 8, neoliberal economic policies, coupled with the globalization of manufacturing and other changes, also reduced job security in the North, especially among manual workers and the less well educated. Thus, the virtual exclusion of huge numbers of people from the benefits of economic growth became a worldwide not just a Southern phenomenon. Indeed, the Indian sociologist Oommen (1997: 51–2) argues that, compared with previous upsurges of political action by excluded groups, the present one is 'truly transnational in its scale and scope [and] multidimensional in its thrust, because the marginalized are the victims of cumulative dominance and inequality'.

The spread of various forms of collective action and protest to the South, especially the demand for greater economic justice, human rights and more attention to the needs of women, has also been enhanced by the worldwide upsurge of democratization (Lindberg and Sverrisson 1997: 5–11). Partly, this was linked to the collapse of communism in the Soviet Union and Eastern Europe between 1989 and 1992, but the abysmal failure of many governments in the South to provide viable development programmes – especially in Africa – forced disadvantaged people, often with the assistance of INGOs, to reassert direct control over their own economic life. This, in turn, helped to strengthen civil society and generate internal pressures for democracy.

THE SHIFTING ETHOS: TOWARDS GLOBAL THINKING

According to Hegedus (1989: 19), since the 1980s, many individuals throughout the world, especially those inclined towards supporting agendas for change, have undergone a 'planetization' of understanding, with virtually everything needing to be radically rethought. This is similar to Robertson's concept of globality – the emergence of a global consciousness – discussed in Chapter 2. Empowering people in rich Western societies is thus only meaningful if poor people in the South are helped to assert their rights as well, an argument that is especially relevant to environmental problems. In fact, from the early 1980s, supporters of the peace movement in Europe and North America began to realize that simply putting pressure on one's own government to relinquish nuclear arms or curtail military expenditure was not enough. The range of actions had to be much wider, for example compelling arms-exporting countries to curtail their sales to repressive regimes and to divert arms industries into peaceful activities.

Many supporters of social movements also stopped focusing exclusively on self-realization and the reconstruction of cultural identities, though they still considered them important. Rather, they assumed a strong sense of 'personal responsibility for a collective future at a local, national and planetary level'

(Hegedus 1989: 22). This links up with our earlier discussion of Giddens' notion of life politics, in which political matters invade the sphere of domestic/personal lives and relationships. But this can be a two-way process. When a myriad of tiny individual or household decisions are aggregated together they may lend their weight to the attainment of much broader, radical changes. The relative success of Jubilee 2000, outlined in Box 18.3, offers one example of this process.

Thus, our very dependence on national and global economic life as consumers, investors, taxpayers or television viewers, coupled with our rights as voting citizens, equips us with ready-to-hand and formidable weapons. We can use these as devices for invading the arena of collective politics and protest if we so wish. Moreover, because so much of our cultural, media and especially economic life has become so globalized and interconnected, it is perfectly possible for such individual market and voting preferences to engage with transnational movements and not just local or national ones. The example of ethical and green consumerism is an obvious case in point. Here, a growing number of people have refused to buy products from companies that engage in activities of which they morally disapprove.

Box 18.3

The Jubilee 2000 campaign for debt relief

How the debt arose

1. Dollar surpluses: During the 1970s there was a surfeit of dollars flowing into the recently deregulated international commercial banks, mostly because of US trade deficits, the currency portfolios accumulated by TNCs and the huge increase in dollar earnings by the OPEC countries, which pushed up oil prices by four times in 1974 and another three times again in 1979 (oil is usually paid for in dollars). Much of this was deposited in the international banks.

2. International support from 'responsible' agents: With strong support from the G7 governments, the World Bank and the IMF, international banks were encouraged to lend this cash to indebted countries in order to recycle cash through the global economy. Meanwhile, the former were providing non-commercial loans to the poorer countries.

3. Poor spending or corruption: Unfortunately, many governments spent these loans on unnecessary 'white elephant' development/status projects or military hardware. The returns from such projects were insufficient to repay the debt. Some funds also disappeared into the Western private bank accounts of corrupt politicians and officials.

The origins and development of the campaign

Jubilee 2000 began in 1996. It campaigned for debt relief on behalf of the 52 poorest countries – the so-called heavily indebted poor countries (HIPCs), whose debts were mostly to multilateral agencies like the IMF and World Bank and the G7 governments. The aim was to reduce these debts by the millennium year of 2000. In 1998 it brought together 50,000 people in Birmingham, UK, to form a human chain around a G8 (the G7 plus its new member, Russia) meeting while a UK poll revealed that 69 per cent supported debt cancellation in preference to building the London millennium dome. By 2000 there were groups in 68 countries – from Japan and the USA to Angola and Colombia. Global coordination was helped by using the internet.

Campaign organization and strategy

The organizers adopted the form of a social movement rather than a centralized organization. Accordingly, they encouraged country groups to form autonomously rather than try to organize them from the outside. This flexibility proved successful in enabling Jubilee 2000 eventually to mobilize around 24 million people worldwide to sign a petition. However, the lack of centralization made it difficult to reconcile the differences between more and less radical supporters and a rift between Southern groups, which wanted a much broader agenda for world poverty, and supporters in the North.

The impact and successes of Jubilee 2000

The campaign has succeeded in placing debt relief high on G8 governmental agendas and educating the public. However, real debt reduction has proved difficult and has often been accompanied by conditions that make compliance difficult, such as further privatizations of public utilities and spending cuts. By 2003, only US$29 billion of a commitment to reduce debt by US$62 billion had actually been met. In 2005, the G8 nations agreed to cancel all IMF debt for 18 of the poorest HIPCs, while future cancellations will be partly offset against aid reduction. Another 10 countries could also benefit within two years. The struggle continues.

SOURCES: Pettifor (2001); Anheier and Themudo (2002); http://www.jubileedebtcampaign. org.uk/; Kiely (2005b)

According to Hegedus (1989: 33) many citizens have realized that what threatens or concerns one person equally implicates everyone else; solutions are only meaningful if they involve joint struggles. Thus, social movements increasingly involve not only '*a new ethic of responsibility*' but also '*a new practice of self-determination and solidarity*' between concrete individuals irrespective of culture or nationality. This was symbolized by the Live Aid rock song, 'We are the world' and the involvement of many rock groups in raising funds for poverty and famine relief in Africa in the 1980s. Moreover, this process was repeated with the Live8 and Make Poverty History campaigns held simultaneously around the world in summer 2005. It is estimated that more than a million people jammed into live music events at venues held in eight countries in July 2005, while perhaps two billion watched these global shows live on TV. Indeed, Hegedus observed that several social movements had already manifested these qualities by the 1980s, for example Solidarity in Poland, the peace movement across Europe, North America and the Soviet Union, and the anti-apartheid movement in and outside South Africa.

CHANGES IN COMMUNICATIONS TECHNOLOGY

The contribution of communications technology to our emerging sense of a common global identity can be traced back to the late 1960s when important developments in satellite communications enabled vast numbers of people across the world to view images of planet earth for the first time on their home TVs.

This coincided with various US voyages to the moon, which culminated in the first actual landing by humans in June 1969. Many people have since argued that these powerful images signalled a fundamental turning point in human experience. We became aware of the beauty of our planet and the need to preserve it at all costs as our only source of mutual sustenance in an otherwise bleak and infinitely vast universe. Similar emotions were activated in the early and mid-1980s when a series of computer-enhanced images taken from space gradually provided a body of clear and incontrovertible evidence of the extent to which the **ozone layer** surrounding the planet had become depleted, giving rise to the 'holes' that are especially noticeable over the polar regions in spring.

> **The ozone layer** is a band of gas encircling the planet 20–50 kilometres above the earth's surface.

In Chapter 14 we saw how recent developments in electronic communications and IT have given individuals and grassroots organizations new opportunities to achieve greater autonomy. PCs allow small groups to produce and circulate their own literature very cheaply, as well as to build up the data banks that are essential if they are to challenge the claims and legitimacy of states and other powerful institutions. The internet not only makes it possible to send messages and disseminate information instantaneously, but it also allows groups and individuals separated by vast distances to share their individual insights with ease and feed these into a kind of rapid cumulative learning experience. In Box 18.1 we cited a recent example of how cyberspace can provide an INGO such as Greenpeace with a useful weapon in its global struggle, and we shall see this further in the case of the global justice movement.

Other tactics may include galvanizing the support of consumers worldwide, capturing media attention and lobbying sympathetic groups at the UN or other IGOs. Boxes 18.2 and 18.3 both demonstrate just such a cocktail of transnational protest. The multiplicity of levels through which global social movements and INGOs now operate helps explain their much stronger presence in the world today. Assisted by the media and their close links to INGOs, global social movements can short-circuit the cumbersome processes that might otherwise be required to mount huge protests by millions of people simultaneously across the word.

INTO THE TWENTY-FIRST CENTURY: ACTIONS, CHALLENGES AND DIVISIONS

As we have seen, global civil society and social movements have proliferated hugely in recent years in the attempt to shape or alter world dialogues and to influence the exercise of **GLOBAL GOVERNANCE**. We end this chapter by briefly considering the global justice movement as a recent important case study of these ongoing struggles.

> **key concept**
>
> **GLOBAL GOVERNANCE** is the fragile, inchoate and contested cluster of agreements, agendas, laws and institutional arrangements that have been put together by states, IGOs, INGOs, TNCs, global social movements, citizen networks, professional associations and others. It is the attempt to

> establish viable systems for managing world affairs, for no global sovereign government currently exists that is capable of attaining the same degree of order at the world level that individual states can guarantee within their own territories.

Although there have been other occasions when global activists came together to challenge official government and IGO agendas – the street parties to protest against the G8 meeting in Cologne, Germany, in June 1999 and demonstrations when the WTO met in Hong Kong in December 2005 are such examples – the global justice movement (also called the anti-globalization movement) first crystallized in the eyes of the world and the media as a global force to be reckoned with in December 1999. Over a period of five days, 50,000 protestors from many countries succeeded in shutting down a major WTO conference in Seattle, USA. The protestors also received tacit support from some of the officials representing governments in Africa, Asia and Latin America, who felt that the trade agreement being negotiated at the conference was unlikely to benefit poor countries and that the agenda was dominated by the interests of wealthy G8 and OECD nations. Between December 1999 and early 2002, there were 18 separate and major mass protests against different IGO, EU or G8 agendas around the world involving demonstrations by various global justice movement supporters, and this does not include events that had a more specific national focus. Two of the most momentous of these occurred during the IMF meeting in Prague in September 2000 and the G8 meeting in Genoa in July 2001, which was attended by an estimated 300,000 protestors and accompanied by running street battles between some violent protestors and the Italian police.

The global justice movement is interesting for a number of reasons, but its emergence as a specific reaction to economic globalization is especially notable. It consists of a loose coalition of groups and networks that are willing to forge temporary alliances to oppose the 'global neoliberal project' (Kiely 2005b: 223) that the G8 governments, especially the USA, have imposed on the world. Anheier et al. (2005: 7–10) list four possible responses to current forms of globalization: one can support them, reject them, advocate reform or offer alternatives. (We discuss these positions further in Chapter 22.) Ignoring the first position, this classification now allows us to identify more clearly the different and sometimes divergent elements included in the global justice movement and to make some observations:

1. All the many groups advocating the second, third and fourth responses have participated in the global justice movement, apart from those with strong right-wing religious and nationalist leanings.
2. The majority of 'true' INGOs, and many of the remaining actors in global civil society, have campaigned as reformers; their intention is to transform global capitalism rather than to abolish or escape from it.
3. We can see that strong strands of socialism, anarchism and environmentalism – each in turn breaking down into numerous subgroupings – have

flourished within the global justice movement alongside a wide spectrum of pro- and anti-globalization groups from both the North and South.

4. Both local and global inclinations are also found there, sometimes pulling together and sometimes against each other.

One criticism of the global justice movement has been that its very diversity, flexibility, lack of hierarchy and openness – demonstrated by its reliance on networking, the accessible and interactive nature of its websites and the ever changing constituent elements feeding into it – can be a source of weakness as well as strength. This is because these characteristics also mean that it often lacks coherence and is less effective in fighting for global justice than it might otherwise be (Kiely 2005b; Waterman and Timms 2005).

Another major challenge to the global justice movement came from the destruction of the twin towers in New York in September 2001, the spread of terrorism and the Bush government in America's increasingly concentrated assertion, in the face of widespread global opposition, of unilateral military and political power. These events have highlighted the limits of global social movements in opposing determined and armed forces, state and non-state. Anderson and Rieff (2005: 35) argue that post 9/11, the issue of 'national security is back on the table and with it the value of sovereignty'. Consequently, 'the love affair between global civil society and international organizations' like the UN, which seemed to dominate much of international life during the 1990s and made global civil society seem more influential than perhaps it actually was, 'has given way to an international system under a specific challenge from the world's superpower'. Anderson and Rieff (2005: 36–7) claim that the USA's actions 'have taken centre stage' in world affairs, often making the conduct of INGOs seem 'frankly irrelevant'. Kiely (2005b: 242) also suggests that these events have forced the global justice movement to 'more forcefully address the question of the nation-state, both generally and in relation to war'. He points to another criticism in that not only have these events slightly sidelined issues of global economic justice in the past few years, but the global justice and anti-war movements have often appeared confused about war, human rights and justice. Thus, being opposed to imperialist, self-seeking wars by an arrogant global superpower is one thing. However, simply refusing to counter any moves whatsoever against regimes that oppress their people in hideous ways if this happens to coincide with the views held by the USA undermines the 'principle of global solidarity' in the search for universal justice (Kiely 2005b: 248–9).

▪▪▪▪▪▪▪▪▪ REVIEW

Although still resembling earlier models, social movements have undergone several important changes since the late 1960s. In advanced countries, they have developed a potential to incorporate much larger numbers of people. The latter are engaged in an ever widening repertoire of activities designed to challenge established interests and reconstruct society by continuously broadening the range of contested issues. Social movements have also become more widespread in the South even though the political climate and available economic resources are considerably less favourable than in the North. Important cross-national, cross-issue and North–South linkages have been established between global social movements since the 1980s, often with the help of INGOs. Increasingly, a global civil society has emerged and flourished from the conjunction of all these currents of change. This, in turn, is closely linked to the growing compulsion to recognize the interconnected and universal nature of the problems we all now confront, coupled with enhanced opportunities to engage in more effective strategies for global cooperation.

As we have noted, although global social movements continue to flourish, several key events and their various repercussions have created dilemmas for the global justice movement, particularly over the past few years. Western imperialism, vicious regimes and fundamentalist terrorist networks are all equally unacceptable in that they lead to or perpetuate militaristic, patriarchal and anti-democratic politics that endanger everyone. The global justice movement and other civil society actors must find ways to combat these challenges. Their understanding of the nature and activities of global social movements has given sociologists the tools with which to examine how global society is emerging from below. In a subsequent chapter, we will explore this process in relation to particular movements.

FURTHER READING

- *Social Movements in Development: The Challenges of Globalization and Democratization*, edited by S. Lindberg and A. Sverrisson (1997), contains some valuable material. Pay particular attention to Chapters 1, 3, 7, 12 and 13.

- R. Cohen and S. Rai's edited collection *Global Social Movements* (2000) contains articles on a number of different movements – peace, women's, religious, labour, human rights and environmental – which, they argue in their editors' introduction, have all become significantly more global.

- *Global Civil Society*, the series of books edited by H. Anheier et al. and published each year since 2001, provides a mine of detailed and interesting information with up-to-date explanations for and debates on a host of themes and issues relating to global civil society.

- R. Kiely's book, *The Clash of Globalizations* (2005), also offers a thoughtful and accessible exploration of the impact of neoliberalism on people worldwide and the struggles going on between the pro- and anti-globalizing forces in the world at present.

GROUP WORK

1. Arranged in advance, the students in each of three groups will assume responsibility for contacting and building up a file either on Oxfam, Amnesty International or Jubilee 2000 and its more recent organizations (or similar INGOs). Each group will report on the following: (a) their INGO's current membership, (b) recent objectives and campaigns, (c) affiliated sister groups abroad and (d) forms of transnational collaboration.

2. Students will read this chapter before the class. They will then divide into three groups and each will prepare a brief report on the proposition: 'Opportunities for effective transnational action by global social movements and INGOs are now much greater than the obstacles they face.'

3. Students will collect information from websites and newspapers on the activities of the global justice movement since 1999. This task can be shared out in advance by year of issue. They will then form small class groups and pool their information to construct a list showing (a) the strengths and achievements and (b) the weaknesses of the movement.

QUESTIONS TO THINK ABOUT

?

1. In what ways did social movements in advanced societies change from the late 1960s and why?

2. What factors explain the tendency over the past 15 or so years for social movements and NGOs to 'go global'? Assess their relative significance.

3. Why is it so important for people who want to elaborate a global sociology to study global social movements?

WHAT'S ON THE WEB

■ www.jubileedebtcampaign.org.uk It is in some ways surprising that the anti-debt campaign was so successful. The organizers were adept at making alliances with the churches and were able to win reforming politicians like UK Chancellor Gordon Brown to their side. The story is found here on this website.

■ http://www.ifg.org/ The International Forum on Globalization is the principal site for 'scholar activists' to document their organization against the WTO. The protests were ushered in spectacularly by the 'Battle of Seattle' in 1999 and have continued until December 2005 with trade talks in Hong Kong.

■ http://www.indymedia.org/en/index.shtml The Independent Media Center covers stories on a wide range of social movements in many countries.

■ http://www.citizen.org/trade/ Global Trade Watch is part of 'a coalition of labour, environmental, religious, family, farm and consumer organizations united in the pursuit of socially and environmentally just trade policy'.

■ http://www.intute.ac.uk/socialsciences/cgi-bin/search.pl?term1=social+movements &gateway=Sociology&limit=0&submit.x=9&submit.y=9 Our old friend the Intute gateway comes through again with some good links and papers on social movements.

CHAPTER 19

Challenging a Gendered World

CONTENTS

In Chapter 6 we explored the multiple forms of oppression to which women in most societies have been historically subjected. Here, we chart the course of some struggles by the women's movement to improve their situation, giving special emphasis to those that have assumed a global dimension. There is a growing literature on the far more numerous local actions by women's groups in ever more countries, including those based in the developing world and you can read about these struggles in the books edited by Basu (1995) and Afshar (1996) or in Molyneux's (2001) book on Latin America.

As we mentioned in Chapter 6, women were involved in political campaigns in the nineteenth and first half of the twentieth centuries, including attempts to secure international peace. The history of non-violent collective action by women remains to be properly explored. However, there is evidence that, even in ancient and medieval times, it was not unknown for women to lead street demonstrations against high food prices, or to use group singing and dancing as a vehicle through which to express their discontent (Carroll 1989). Certainly, from the late eighteenth century onwards, women increasingly made important and sometimes initiating contributions to revolutionary protest, as in the moves against the monarchy in the summer and autumn of 1789 in France. They also resisted slavery in the USA, reacted against colonialism and joined or led strikes. Women agitated for better working conditions in factories and textile mills across the world, including Lancashire in the UK and cities in North America and tsarist Russia (Carroll 1989: 4–9). For the most part, this first wave of feminist struggle can be regarded as an attempt to secure for women the same liberal freedoms and opportunities that were available to men. Second-wave feminism from the late 1960s was more radical and led many women to conclude that they had every right to challenge and reconstruct the patriarchal world. As Enloe (1989: 17) suggested, 'the world is something that has been made; therefore, it can be remade'.

WOMEN IN THE GLOBAL ORDER: AN OVERVIEW

At first sight, gender relationships appear to have little intrinsic relevance to the workings of the world order. Yet, further analysis soon reveals a different picture. Enloe (1989: 7), whose ideas are explored in Global Thinkers 19 below, holds that gender relations actually make 'the world go round'. Governments need more than secrecy and intelligence agencies to conduct foreign affairs; they also rely on private relationships. They need wives who are willing to entertain for their diplomatic husbands so that they can develop trusting relationships with other diplomatic husbands. Governments require not only military hardware at military bases, but also a steady supply of women to convince their soldiers that they are manly. In short, governments rely on notions of masculine dignity and feminine sacrifice to sustain their sense of autonomous nationhood in their quest for formal recognition of their sovereignty (Enloe 1989: 196–7).

Enloe gives several other examples of the weighty contributions that armies of women make to global political and economic life – ones that are obscured by the accepted notions of feminine and masculine roles:

■ Behind the mainly male officials and leaders who decide national and inter-national affairs lie countless female secretaries, personal assistants, clerks and middle-level personnel who provide everyday continuity and maintain the detailed, routine transactions without which the males would be impotent.

■ As a leading sector in the global economy, the success of tourism often hinges on huge numbers of badly paid female employees like hotel chambermaids, waitresses, barmaids, airline hostesses, tour guides, local employees engaged in food preparation and women who provide sexual services for tourists.

■ The crucial roles that women play at every link in the commodity chains that bind together the global system of food production and consumption often go unacknowledged. At one end of the food chain, along with the women employed as occasional seasonal farm workers on large plantations are the unpaid wives who on local plots grow subsistence crops with which to feed their families while their husbands migrate to work on distant commercial farms for low wages. Somewhere in the middle are those who do piecework in food factories, perhaps cleaning and packing vegetables or fruit. Yet further along the chain are the women who work as supermarket checkout assistants selling the final products. Finally, it is the world's housewives who mainly assume the role of consumers.

■ We can add that women also play a central role in social and biological reprod-uction in child-rearing, childcare and later preparation of young adults for the marketplace.

CONSTRAINTS ON WOMEN'S MOVEMENTS

In many situations, women face more constraints than men when they engage in social movements. Moreover, involvement in social protests often becomes progressively more difficult for women as actions move away from specific local-ities and contexts. There are several reasons for this dual state of affairs:

■ In many societies, women are less likely to have easy access to money and land; they are more likely to live in poverty and tend to be less well educated than men. They are also more likely to be tied down by customary obligations and daily routines that bind them to a host of domestic and productive services of an intrinsically local and fixed kind.

■ Patriarchal social relations reduce women's capacity for autonomy and render them vulnerable and dependent. In some societies, they may even be prohib-ited from participating in any kind of public activity without their husband's permission, including voting or engaging in outside employment, and may be virtually confined to the domestic compound.

■ All these eventualities curtail freedom of movement. Unless protests are highly local in orientation and are not perceived as a threat to established male rights, women's participation may be difficult and dangerous.

■ Where women in the South join protests, these are rarely concerned solely with feminist issues. Rather, their actions are likely to be intertwined either with wider struggles against oppression such as nationalist movements for independence and the demand for democratization (Basu 1995: 9–11) or with environmental threats or peace issues.

■ As the number of women engaged in various kinds of protests worldwide rapidly increased, divisions quickly emerged or soon intensified (Jacobs 2004). Of course, these differences can also be seen as a rich source of diversity, offering opportunities to exchange ideas and experiences. Yet, there is general agreement that they also inhibited progress towards greater world unity, particularly in the period 1975–1985 and probably beyond.

Box 19.1

Power, wealth, work and women: the gender deficits

Inequalities of politics and power

In the mid-1990s, women formed half the electorate in all countries but held a global average of only 13 per cent of parliamentary seats and 7 per cent of government posts.

In 1992 the countries with the highest share of parliamentary seats held by women were Finland with 38 per cent and Norway with 37 per cent. In the USA, France, Russia and Brazil, this share was less than 10 per cent. The global average was pulled up by China, with between 20 and 30 per cent.

On the other hand, a few women have stood out as presidents or prime ministers and were associated with important national policy changes and/or operated successfully in the role of world 'statesmen'. Some highly successful women political leaders include the following:

■ Indira Gandhi, prime minister in India throughout much of the 1960s, 1970s and early 1980s

■ Margaret Thatcher, prime minister in Britain from 1979 to 1990

■ Mary Robinson, president of Ireland from 1992–96

■ Sirimavo R. D. Bandaranaike, prime minister of Sri Lanka 1960–65, 1970–75, reappointed 1994

■ Angela Merkel, chancellor of Germany, leading a coalition government after the elections in autumn 2005

■ Ellen Johnson-Sirleaf, Liberia's 'Iron Lady', took office in January 2006 as Africa's first elected female president.

Wealth and production: women's burdens

Based originally on data presented to the UN Committee on the Status of Women in 1981, it has long been demonstrated that across the world women constitute half the population, provide one-third of the paid labour force and two-thirds of all the hours spent working. *Yet, they earn only one-tenth of the world's income and own less than 1 per cent of all the world's property.* This situation has probably changed little since 1981, except that since then the proportion of women in the global paid labour force has certainly grown considerably.

Women grow half the world's food and rather more than this in many African countries. Yet, strangely, in many regions of the world most agricultural advisers are men. For example, in Asia during the mid-1980s, women provided 40 per cent of the agricultural labour force but made up less than 1 per cent of agricultural advisers. Comparable figures for sub-Saharan Africa were 47 and 3 per cent respectively.

Employment injustices

During the 1980s, the percentages of top management positions held by women at the UN and World Bank were 3 and 5 per cent respectively. By contrast, the same figures for women employed in secretarial or clerical capacities at these same institutions were 80 per cent and over 90 per cent. In 1989, less than 20 per cent of the members of the diplomatic missions from all the world's governments based permanently at the UN were women. Only eight women among this 20 per cent had ambassadorial status.

Women often fare little better in the private sector. In 1992, only 1 per cent of the highest executive positions in leading French companies were held by women, while the comparable figure for the 1,000 wealthiest companies in the USA in 1989 was lower. Even in less elevated professional positions, women made up only one-fifth of the lawyers and around 17 per cent of the doctors in 1990 in the USA.

SOURCES: Tickner (1992); Peterson and Runyan (1993); Kidron and Segal (1995); UN Development Programme (1997)

The three main overlapping sources of difference are outlined in Table 19.1 below. By the mid-1980s, these divisions, especially those defined by racial, historical and North–South differences, were on the way to being overcome. All the following helped to heal earlier wounds:

- increased personal familiarity through contacts established at conferences and other venues
- more humility among Western feminists about their assumed right to define the terms of the global struggle against patriarchy
- a realization that global trust and cooperation required a willingness to respect the autonomy of each country's movement.

National differences arise in a number of respects. For example, during the 1970s, women in Zimbabwe, Mozambique and Vietnam were caught up in national liberation struggles against colonial or foreign domination, while women in other Southern countries had shared similar experiences during earlier anti-colonial struggles. Since men in these situations experience just as much oppression as women, many Southern women were persuaded by the need for unity in the struggle to assign lower priority to gender issues.

While feminists in the USA and Europe might have sound reasons to demand abortion rights for all women or campaign against the sexual exploitation of women through media trivialization, beauty shows or pornography, Southern feminists may have quite different priorities. They are more likely to be having to deal with repressive forms of state birth control that bear down most heavily on the poorest groups, rapes committed by police and other state officials against those within their jurisdiction (Radford 2000), or, as in India, the widespread so-called 'dowry deaths' (Kumar 1995) when young wives become the victims of pressure from in-laws for dowry payments after marriage.

Clearly, Southern women are aware of the endemic gender inequalities they face within their societies and are unwilling to overlook them indefinitely in the interests of national unity. Their strategy is more one of postponement. Women in poor countries differ most from their Northern counterparts in that they recognize that patriarchy is an aspect of inequality that has to be confronted alongside other injustices: all forms of inequality need to be tackled simultaneously as part of the same struggle. In any case, numerous Southern groups were soon finding ways to express their own concerns both at national and regional levels.

TABLE 19.1 Diverging goals and interests in women's movements, 1960–90			
Main reason for division	Key concerns and goals	Main sources of support	Preferred type of organization
1. Liberal versus more radical, second-wave feminists (from the late 1960s)	Liberals pushed for equal citizen rights at state level and tried to raise the status of women at UN and other IGOs. Not trying to change women's wider conditions New-wave feminism wished to remove all forms of male oppression, even in domestic life. Celebrated female strengths and values	Mainly older, educated, middle-class Western women. Some were involved in pre-Second World War peace movements and worked for equal recognition for women in the 1948 UN Declaration of Human Rights A younger generation, reflecting the broader class base of educational attainment. Influenced by 1960s' idea that politics is personal	Prepared to work within conservative, male-dominated state institutions or IGOs and through global networks of change through personal influence On stream from late 1960s. Sought change through a broad spectrum of activities including own media/ publications, research and independent forums
2. Established mainstreamers working in IGOs versus an emergent more disengaged group (from the early 1970s)	Mainstreamers worked to extend state and UN awareness of women's needs mostly in 'traditional' areas such as health, food and education. Also worked to increase knowledge of gender relations at UN Outsiders were more focused on specific issues linked to a wider feminist agenda such as male violence against women, prostitution and the right to choose one's sexual orientation	As above Mostly Western women, as above, but beginning to include flows of educated women from the South and/or those previously involved in struggles for national independence	Lobbied states and key UN agencies via consultative status (right to observe and submit statements at some UN forums and other IGOs). Also worked through the UN Commission on the Status of Women Exercised pressure mainly outside formal institutions, especially via networking and own separate groups. Preferred cooperative and non-hierarchical organizat-ions and direct links with grass roots
3. Rising Southern women's groups versus those with a Western membership as in 1 and 2 (from the mid-1970s)	Concerned with the limited benefits of economic development for poor women. Carving out own versions of feminism reflecting local non-Western needs. Some rifts with Northern women over their alleged ignorance of South and racist paternalism	Despite disputes with Northern women, came from rather similar backgrounds, namely privileged, educated, academic and middle class. Not always representative of the interests of poor rural and urban groups, though trying to bridge this class gap	Linked to more radical Western networks but also forming own regional and global groups, for example Development Alternatives with Women for a New Era (DAWN), launched in 1984 by Southern activists from Asia, Africa and Latin America. Partly dependent on financial assistance from the North

SOURCES: Bystdzienski (1992); Stienstra (1994); Miles (1996)

By the early 1990s, it was evident that these streams feeding into the global flow of women's struggles were becoming stronger and more diverse. Moreover, those contributing to this flow were more and more interested in participating in worldwide as well as purely local feminist debates. What helped to make this easier for Southern women was precisely that they had previously worked to carve out their own areas of independence (Miles 1996: 57–60).

■ ■

Global Thinkers 19 CYNTHIA ENLOE (1938–)

Cynthia Enloe has pioneered the use of feminist perspectives in many aspects of international affairs. In particular she shows how the military uses women's emotional and physical labour to sustain activities that are often conceived of as purely masculine pursuits.

In Bananas, Beaches and Bases *(1989), Enloe provides a number of loosely connected, but intriguing case studies, including women in the global tourism industry, wives of the diplomatic corps/women diplomats, domestic servants and nannies, women in the military and on US bases. In each of these spheres, women play underrecorded roles. Their roles in the tourism industry include acting as travel agents, travel writers, flight attendants, producers/purveyors of arts and crafts, chambermaids and in the sex industry. While attitudes are changing now, historically, independent women travellers were seen as so deviant that they often dressed as men. Even today women's roles in tourism are subordinated. In adverts, the usual assumption is that business travellers are male, flight attendants female. Playing into this and another stereotype of demure Asian women was a Singapore Airlines ad titled 'Singapore Girl ... You're a great way to Fly' (Enloe 1989: 33). As Enloe (1989: 41) argues: 'The very structure of international tourism needs patriarchy to survive. Men's capacity to control women's sense of their security and self-worth has been central to the evolution of tourism politics.'*

Enloe examines the fascinating case of Carmen Miranda, using a methodology that allows the interpretation of broader social contradictions through their embodiment in a single person. In the 1930s, the Hollywood moguls turned Miranda, a popular Brazilian singer and dancer, into a mega-movie star. Dressed in outrageous hats festooned with bananas and tropical fruit, she became wildly popular and was used as the inspiration for a cartoon character, 'Chiquita Banana'. This little ditty was played 376 times daily on US radio stations: 'I'm Chiquita Banana/And I've come to say/Bananas have to ripen/In a certain way.' It was all very innocent except that there were sly sexual nuances and that United Fruit used the character to help Americans to consume two million bananas a day. The expression 'banana republic' alluded to countries that both depended on exports of bananas and were controlled by US corporations, not local politicians. Carmen Miranda smoothed the way for American regional influence in Central and Latin America, while 'Chiquita Banana' helped to create consumer loyalty for a product that netted huge profits (Enloe 1989: 149). Meanwhile, the real women of Latin America were marginalized in the banana packing sheds.

Enloe provides a full analysis of women soldiers in Does Khaki Become You? *(1988) and a more complex discussion of surrounding issues in* Maneuvers *(2000), where she considers how military wives, military nurses, militarized prostitution (disguised as 'rest and recreation') and rape (in prisons and on battlefields) become ideologically functional and even necessary. Her case studies make for uncomfortable reading, vividly showing how men and women can become brutalized. Her ideas were to become all too relevant in the case of Private Lynndie England, who in 2005 was given a three-year sentence for abusing prisoners at Iraq's Abu Ghraib prison. She appeared in photographs holding a leash around a naked detainee's neck and pointing at detainees as they were forced to masturbate. This disturbing episode considerably hardened Muslim attitudes to the US presence in Iraq.*

SOURCE: Enloe (1988, 1989; 2000)

GROWTH OF THE WORLDWIDE MOVEMENT

Three significant changes and tendencies, which we discuss in more detail below, boosted women's movements from the 1970s and contributed to greater unity and mutual understanding:

- the UN and the older generation of liberal feminists who worked within its institutions helped to create a framework for increased networking
- the rise of second-wave radical feminism, mainly in the North, invigorated the women's movement worldwide and women's groups emerging in the South
- women worked to create their own autonomous facilities for representing women's views and achieving effective communications.

THE UN FRAMEWORK FOR NETWORKING

Partly because of earlier contributions to the peace process during and after the First World War by an older generation of rather privileged liberal feminists, international women's groups were able to influence the UN from 1945 onwards. Thus, the UN Charter of 1945 specifically referred to the equal eligibility of women to participate in all UN debates and organizations. It also granted consultative status to the representatives of several international women's organizations, which included the right to attend certain UN sessions and submit documentation. Further, it set up the Commission on the Status of Women to consider the special needs of women worldwide (Stienstra 1994: 75–86). In addition, the 1948 UN Universal Declaration of Human Rights clearly stated such rights could not be denied on any grounds, including sex.

Few radical feminists believed these gains were sufficient to meet women's real needs, yet they provided a platform for making the case for additional changes while continuing to infiltrate male-dominated institutions. Together with the rising tide of women's discontent associated with second-wave feminism, these pressures created a powerful momentum for further change led by the UN. The result was the 1975–85 UN Decade for Women built primarily around three conferences, though others were organized both during and after these years (see Box 19.2).

In some respects, the direct results of these three conferences have been meagre. For example, the first two exposed problematic divisions among women from different world regions and cultural backgrounds and the more radical feminists preferred to work outside these official forums until the mid-1980s. Nevertheless, the UN decade was a 'watershed' because it pushed women's concerns onto the agendas of IGOs and facilitated cooperation (Friedman 1995: 23). Gradually, too, as women from different cultures and regions of the world came into closer personal contact with each other at conferences and other venues, they learnt how to network more effectively – often empowered by the internet – and to gain and share new knowledge. Working together across cultural and regional divides has been especially successful in the area of women's human rights. Consequently, 'women's networking has developed a model that affirms the universality of human rights while respecting the diversity of particular experiences' (Bunch et al. 2001: 228).

Box 19.2

The global women's movement: key events and selected achievements

The UN Decade for Women, 1975–85, key UN-sponsored conferences

- 1st World Conference on Women, 1975, Mexico City, attended by 6,000 delegates.

- 2nd World Conference on Women, 1980, Copenhagen, with 7,000 delegates.

- 3rd World Conference on Women, 1985, Nairobi, with 15,000 delegates from 150 countries, and in which 2,000 workshops were held.

- 4th World Conference on Women, 1995, Beijing, attended by 8,000 delegates.

Key consequences of Nairobi conference (1985)

- Many more representatives came from developing countries and they were much more inclined to declare their own aims. The animosity between delegates from the North and South that was evident at the previous two conferences diminished.

- Several new regional and international networks were formed as a result of this conference. These included the Latin American Committee for the Defence of Women's Rights (CLADEM); the Asia-Pacific Forum on Women, Law and Development (APWD); and Women Living Under Muslim Laws (WLUML), which was formed by representatives from eight Muslim countries. All sought to facilitate exchanges of information on legal matters pertaining to human and legal rights.

- The International Women's Rights Action Watch (IWRAW), launched after the Nairobi conference in 1986, also focused on women and human rights. While promoting and monitoring the progress of the UN's work, it lobbied governments and international bodies, including NGOs, on the issue of human rights and women.

Other important conferences and events

■ UN General Assembly (UNGA), 1979, when worldwide pressure from groups demanding change to protect women from discrimination contributed to the UNGA's decision to support the Convention on the Elimination of All Forms of Discrimination against Women (CEDAW). States accepting the convention have to take whatever steps are needed to prevent discrimination. By 1994, 133 countries had ratified CEDAW, though 40 of these had made 91 reservations, mostly on religious or cultural grounds.

■ The UN Second International Conference on Human Rights was held in Vienna in 1993. Building on earlier dialogues about women and human rights, the women's groups were well organized and successfully lobbied 160 governments present at the conference. They also called for an end to gender bias brought about by religious extremism.

SOURCES: Stienstra (1994); Peters and Wolper (1995); Miles (1996)

SECOND-WAVE AND SOUTHERN FEMINISM

Second-wave feminism consisted of no less than an all-out attack on patriarchy and a rejection of male pretensions to superiority in all spheres, not simply at the level of formal institutions. The focus of its critique and challenge was thus more comprehensive than anything any earlier feminist ideas had offered. All this created a sense of intellectual and moral coherence that few could ignore and its impetus led new-wave feminists to explore many new avenues with energy and confidence. They sought to invade or seek alliances with all previously male-dominated organizations, including NGOs, trade unions, churches and religious bodies, sports and arts organizations, local and national politics, the professions (especially health, medicine and law) and all knowledge-creating centres such as universities.

Women's groups in developing countries increasingly joined the second-wave feminists. Among the issues included in this widening agenda were:

■ sex tourism and prostitution across the world
■ all forms of public and private violence against women
■ the need to persuade governments and the UN to accept that women's rights must be firmly incorporated within the human rights agenda
■ the often adverse working conditions experienced by the growing number of women worldwide employed in the export-processing manufacturing industries outlined later
■ the urgent need to rethink the development aims and priorities promoted by states in developing countries and by powerful IGOs like the IMF and World Bank.

WOMEN REPRESENTING THEMSELVES: INDEPENDENT COMMUNICATIONS

From 1975 onwards women's groups challenged the male-owned and male-oriented world media industries. They knew that how women and their needs are represented – or perhaps misrepresented and trivialized – in the media was critical to any attempt to assert autonomy and counter patriarchy. For example, during the 1970s, less than 2 per cent of the items included in world news programmes were about women or related to their needs (Byerly 1995: 106).

The first communications network to be established was the International Women's Information and Communication Service (ISIS). The International Women's Tribune Centre (IWTC) was founded in 1976. In the early 1990s, IWTC provided communication and technical services to groups in 160 countries (Miles 1996: 111). With UNESCO's assistance, feminists also set up their own press service in 1978, the Women's Feature Service (WFS), and eventually this became a permanent organization based in New Delhi. It supplies information on the environment, social customs, health and politics. Since the 1970s, feminists have also set up study and research centres and have founded women's publishing houses and organized global events in the arts.

STATES, WAR AND VIOLENCE AGAINST WOMEN

We examine below the theme of domestic and often state-sanctioned violence against women and the ways in which this affects women's mental and physical health. Here, we consider institutionalized or 'public sector' male violence and its consequences for women. Historically, women and children have always tended to become the victims of violence through war. However, recent changes, sometimes linked to globalization, have generated an increasing number of situations in which women have been exposed to violence directly or indirectly as a result of war. These include:

- the declining control that states now exert over their borders
- the escalation of regional conflicts and civil wars, as in the Balkans in the aftermath of the Cold War
- the declining capacity of states to control or prevent armed conflict, as in Somalia, Liberia, Central Africa and the drug-fuelled wars between army and various gangs in Colombia
- the changing nature of warfare itself. Thus, certain types of weaponry such as rocket-propelled grenades, landmines, mortars and small arms have become more easily accessible and widely dispersed.

All this, in turn, seems to have altered the rules governing warfare because previous codes of conduct that at least tried to minimize harm to non-combatants, especially women and children, have been abandoned (Jacobson et al. 2000). One consequence of this has been that women and children now make up between 70 and 80 per cent of the world's refugees (Kelly 2000: 53).

We saw earlier in Enloe's work that the highly gendered nature of state institutions and the way in which militarized masculinity creates a basis for organized violence have often placed women in difficult and subordinate situations. One of the most appalling ways in which this set of circumstances has been played out in recent years, and on a huge scale, has been the deployment of sexual violence against women as a deliberate strategy of war either by states or other armed forces. According to many feminists (for example Kelly 2000; Radford 2000), this is partly linked to the fact that women are seen as the carriers of a nation's or tribe's culture. We say more about this in the next section on fundamentalist religions. When this is combined with the persistence of deeply patriarchal cultures and widely held misogynist attitudes of contempt or even hatred towards women on the part of some men, which the tensions of war intensify, there is a danger that 'women's bodies and women as a group' (Kelly 2000: 50) will be seen as targets of military aggression.

In war the hatred of the enemy is 'expressed through and transformed into the hatred and violation of women' (Radford 2000: 177). Rape and other forms of violence against women in war become ways of humiliating the enemy, of capturing and dominating its territory, for 'women's bodies are constructed as … territory to be conquered' (Kelly 2000: 50). Because of the children that may result from multiple rapes, however, they are also a means of destroying the enemy's culture and replacing it with that of the victor. All this was clearly and terribly manifested in Bosnia in the early 1990s and, according to Radford (2000), distressingly similar reasoning has been evident at times in the communal violence that Hindu extremists pursued against Muslims.

WOMEN, HEALTH AND DOMESTIC VIOLENCE: A MULTI-COUNTRY STUDY

In Chapter 9, we saw that one of the most common ways women contract HIV/AIDS is from their husbands who demand unprotected sex after contracting the disease when working away from home. Here, we summarize some of the key findings on women's health linked to other aspects of their relations with male partners and male relatives. The material is drawn from a WHO (2005) study covering urban and rural areas in 10 countries – Bangladesh, Brazil, Ethiopia, Japan, Peru, Namibia, Samoa, Serbia, Thailand and Tanzania.

We tend to assume that people are safest when at home but this turns out to be far from the case. The effects of physical and sexual violence in the home are amplified because:

■ Governments and official organizations are often reluctant to interfere in domestic/family life or challenge patriarchal cultures and relations. Consequently, a great deal of domestic and sexual violence against women and children goes unreported and is never tackled.

■ Such violence also directly causes or aggravates diseases, especially long-term physical damage, reproductive illnesses (including miscarriages), memory loss, mental illness, dizziness and AIDS.

■ Violence against women is a central aspect of gender inequality both as a cause and an effect.

■ Unfortunately, much of this remains widespread despite the emphasis on women and human rights at the UN Vienna conference in 1993 and the Declaration on the Elimination of Violence Against Women (DEVAW) adopted by the UNGA, also in 1993.

The WHO (2005) study also demonstrated that the greatest risk to women from violence occurs in their intimate relationships with husbands and to a lesser extent with other male relatives, taking the following four forms:

1. The experience of physical violence against women by intimate partners in the course of a lifetime ranged from between 13 and 61 per cent depending on the site, while between 4 and 49 per cent reported severe violence. The incidence was often higher in rural than urban areas and was especially pronounced in parts of Peru, Ethiopia, Tanzania and Bangladesh. It was lowest in Japan.
2. Acts of sexual violence involving husbands or partners were between 6 and 59 per cent. Sometimes this was related to very young women being forced into early marriages.
3. Often the two types of violence were linked, for example it frequently began during pregnancy, and women exposed to violence were often abused repeatedly.
4. Emotional or psychological abuse was also commonplace and was reported by between 20 and 75 per cent of women in the sample; between 12 and 58 per cent reported it having occurred within the 12 months prior to the survey. Examples of such controlling behaviour included restricting contact with family and friends, demanding permission before being allowed to seek healthcare or being consistently ignored.

UNIFICATION IN THE FACE OF COMMON PROBLEMS

Increasingly, women have realized that they face common problems in private and public life, including that of male violence. These and other issues have encouraged some women's groups to sink their differences and seek various forms of collaboration designed to influence governments, IGOs and other powerful elite institutions. What are these common difficulties?

RELIGIOUS FUNDAMENTALISM

The resurgence of various forms of religious orthodoxy and right-wing thinking over the past 15 years, with the two often being synchronous, has presented a unifying threat to some women, especially in the USA, India, various Muslim countries in the Middle East, Israel and parts of the former Soviet Union. In the USA, right-wing religious fundamentalism has played a leading role in trying to encourage women to stay at home rather than seek personal fulfilment and relative autonomy through careers, and 'pro-life' campaigns have opposed, sometimes violently, a woman's entitlement to control her own reproduction through legalized abortion. The desire to restore fundamentalist religious values and social practices is associated with the fear that any real increase in women's freedom of choice and action will undermine the foundations of tradition, religion, morality, and – it could be argued – male control. Women as homemakers and child-rearers have cemented the main links between respecting a deity and upholding religious belief on one hand and reproducing society's moral codes from one generation to another on the other. Because this leads fundamentalists to regard women as both embodying and preserving all that is most sacred and valued in society, they have often insisted on ruthlessly conserving or reinstating women's traditional positions. This also contributes to male violence both domestically and by states and their agents.

India's case starkly illustrates the dilemmas that women's movements there face. Despite a resurgence of Hindu fundamentalism, India is usually and rightly respected as a tolerant country with a cherished regard for the pursuit of democracy and a long history of social reform and modernization. However, even before the recent rise of religious fundamentalism, governments found it difficult to tolerate or encourage the extension of some constitutional freedoms to women and family life. Thus, while the Indian constitution allows government to intervene to prevent discrimination against members of certain lower castes, it does not permit such state interference in customary law where this relates to family life and the domestic position of women (Jaising 1995; Kumar 1995; Radford 2000). Women's movements in India have consequently found it necessary to politicize the private realm of husband–wife relations, marriage and family life.

ACCELERATING ECONOMIC GLOBALIZATION

A further recent cause for global concern has been rapid economic globalization. As we saw in earlier chapters, capital has become increasingly footloose. TNCs, for example, have become much freer to move plant, technology and goods across the globe, while fragmenting production operations between sites located in different countries. Because states are often anxious to attract investment from TNCs, the corporations have remained relatively unencumbered by global or state regulation. At the same time, competition for market share between growing numbers of industrializing economies has risen dramatically. Globalization has further highlighted the plight of women worldwide and the need for women's groups to cooperate – including across the North–South divide – in order to construct forces capable of countering the power of mobile capitalism (Basu 1995: 19). We discuss examples of such actions later.

Figure 19.1 **Professor Wangari Maathai, winner of the 2004 Nobel Peace Prize**
One of the founders of the Green Belt movement in Kenya, an organization that campaigns for social, environmental and women's issues in Kenya. She was imprisoned, beaten unconscious and went on hunger strike to demand the release of political prisoners. The Kenyan government finally stopped their campaign of harassment and offered her the post of assistant minister in the Ministry of the Environment.

NEOLIBERAL IDEOLOGY AND ECONOMIC POLICIES

Alongside economic globalization, there has been a rise and spread of neoliberal economic policies prioritizing government spending and tax cuts, the privatization of industry, the deregulation of markets – including reduced protection for local industries and jobs – and an emphasis on creating 'flexible' labour markets. The purpose of such reforms is to make employees cheaper and more efficient, while increasing the power of capital over labour. Since the mid-1980s, the IMF and World Bank have imposed neoliberal reforms on many Southern countries as a condition for helping to arrange debt rescheduling and further loans. The effect of such policies, which have forced governments to reduce their spending and abolish subsidies, has been higher food prices, increased unemployment and widespread cuts in welfare spending on things such as rural clinics. Much of this has hit the poorer groups hardest and a large proportion of the most disadvantaged consists of single-parent households headed by women.

The combination of economic globalization and neoliberal policies has increased pressure on women to seek work in the global economy. New job opportunities are created wherever the businesses, in their search for cheap, flexible labour, relocate, usually far from their original national bases. Moreover, much of the global economy is now organized through global supply chains (see Chapter 7) and again women tend to supply much of the labour in some of these industries, especially in garment making, electronics and fresh produce like grapes, tomatoes and flowers, which depend on these chains. Women at present provide between 60 and 90 per cent of the workforce in the garment and fresh food industries. In fact, in the garment industries of Morocco, Bangladesh and Cambodia, they make up 70, 85 and 90 per cent of the employees respectively. The corresponding percentages in fresh foods in Colombia, Kenya and Zimbabwe are 65, 75 and 87 (cited in Raworth 2005: 16–17). Unfortunately, many of these jobs are insecure, temporary and poorly paid, there are few prospects for promotion and health and safety standards are not always enforced. In addition, women are compelled to work very long hours – making childcare difficult – and overtime is often unpaid; they also frequently have to endure bullying and sexual harassment from male overseers, for without the protection of trade unions, they are likely to lose their jobs if they protest.

Ultimately, many of these dilemmas are only solved if local women's movements struggle to confront them in their own way and on their own terms. Nevertheless, the spread of right-wing nationalism and religious fundamentalism across many societies has given women yet another reason to seek global collaboration (Basu 1995: 19).

PROTECTING HOMEWORKERS

As we saw in Chapter 5 and again in this chapter, economic globalization and neoliberal policies have, through the creation of an ever larger worldwide, casual labour force, combined to weaken labour's bargaining power and increase economic insecurity. Women are not alone in being exposed to these changes, but they have, however, often taken the brunt of them.

Historically, women have always made a significant contribution to manufacturing, but much of this has been hidden from view because many have worked in tiny unregulated enterprises or at home. The 'sweatshop' conditions that are typical of these activities leave much to be desired. Homeworkers, who earn very low rates of pay, work under poor and sometimes dangerous conditions, need to meet employer deadlines and have no legal rights, find it difficult to organize because they are dispersed and the work can easily be shifted elsewhere. Moreover, poverty and the absence of alternative work – especially for women with young children – make workers dependent on their employers. Employers are also able to reduce the costs of training the workforce because, in industries like garment manufacturing, the teenage girls have usually already acquired the skills they need from within the family.

The growth of homeworking has been most pronounced in garment manufacturing and is not confined to the developing world. In fact, it has spread widely across the cities of the North and is often a source of employment for illegal immigrants (Ross 1997: 13). Homeworking has also spread to other industries, including carpets, shoes, toys, consumer electronics and automobile parts (Rowbotham 1993: 9–24). The retailers who sell on such goods increasingly operate as 'hollow companies' (Mitter 1994: 20), because they break production down into numerous specialized work tasks and then subcontract these as vast orders to integrated global supply chains of firms across the world. These, in turn, then employ millions of homeworkers. The ability to attain greater producer flexibility and cheaper costs partly through the increased use of homeworkers has made it easier for retailers to compete successfully. Their power also enables them to earn large profits by placing huge mark-ups on the imported price of the final products.

However, it appears that not all the cards are stacked in favour of these powerful retailing companies. Their business strategy carries several risks, probably the most serious of which stems from the fact that these goods mostly carry designer labels, which are much prized by consumers and so command high prices. But, by the same token, this exposes companies to 'potentially embarrassing ... human rights violations'. They 'cannot afford to have the names of their designers, endorsers, or merchandizing labels publicly sullied [or be] embarrassed by revelations about the exploited labour behind their labels' (Ross 1997: 25). Thus, the public esteem in which a brand name image is held is worth a great deal of money. Increasingly, the various groups campaigning on behalf of women employed as homeworkers have sought to educate consumers into the principles of ethical or fair trading.

While organizing homeworkers into trade unions at the point of production is difficult, persuading consumers to join boycotts against companies that condone exploitative work conditions used by their subcontractors can be highly effective, as evidenced by the partly successful 1995 campaign in the USA against the clothes retailer, Gap. Then, a coalition of university, consumer, trade union, human rights, church and other groups obtained the company's agreement to impose and monitor codes of conduct with respect to the labour conditions prevailing in one of its Central American subcontracting firms (Cavanagh 1997: 40–1; Ross 1997: 26–7). Unfortunately, Gap and other companies depend on such subcontracting relations with many hundreds of similar firms in Central America and elsewhere and the 1995 campaign was unable to improve conditions in these.

Feminist groups and some homeworkers are also contributing to fair trade and other campaigns (Boris and Prugl 1996: 6). Despite the enormous obstacles they face, homeworkers have formed effective organizations in several countries and in some instances these have also engaged in useful international networking activities. For example, the International Labour organization (ILO), an arm of the UN based in Geneva, tries among other things to establish worldwide standards for the treatment of workers while monitoring the conditions that pertain in different countries. At a conference under ILO auspices in June 1996, an international coalition of feminists, trade unions, homeworker associations, NGOs and fair trade organizations were successful in obtaining a new ILO convention for home-based workers, though much more work still needs to be done in this area. However, in the words of Ela Bhatt, a long-term fighter for homeworkers' rights and general secretary of the Self-Employed Asian Women's Association (SEWA), 'homeworkers are no more invisible' (cited in Shaw 1998: 5).

WOMEN AND GLOBAL CARE CHAINS

Until recently, researchers have concentrated on studying global supply chains in manufacturing and agriculture and have ignored another kind of global supply chain, namely, **GLOBAL CARE CHAINS**, a phenomenon that has been considered in a number of innovative studies, notably Sontag (1993), Chang (2000), Hochschild (2000) and Yeates (2004).

---

key concept

GLOBAL CARE CHAINS comprise women who cross boundaries from poorer to richer countries to work in occupations such as nannying, nursing and domestic work. The care chain involves interconnected nodes of migration between rural and urban areas and between poor and rich countries. The links tend to reinforce, rather than obviate, existing global inequalities. An unpaid family member at the bottom of the chain tends ultimately to replace the emotional labour expended. (See Hochschild 2000 who is credited with developing the concept.)

Instead of producing finished goods, millions of women are involved in 'producing' services. They supply both physical labour, like cleaning, cooking, nursing and washing, but also emotional care involving affection and concern for others. Increasingly, the arrangements for shipping these migrant care workers from the South to the rich countries, where they are mostly employed, are managed by various service intermediaries. These include:

- governments, like that of the Philippines, which sees the export of Filipino service workers to Western or other Asian countries as a major source of export revenue
- national public institutions like the British National Health Service
- thousands of legal or illegal recruitment agencies for nannies, nurses, cleaners and others, sometimes linked to international criminal gangs
- corporate cleaning companies such as Kelly Services, which are mostly based in North America.

As indicated in our definition, care workers are engaged in a number of different occupations, including the following:

- *nurses* or *paramedics* working in hospitals or residential nursing homes. In the Philippines, for example, there are around 100,000 registered nurses but most work overseas in European, Middle Eastern, Japanese or North American hospitals and homes
- *carers* who nurse sick or elderly people in their own homes as part of local, state or federal health systems. In the USA, home healthcare workers look after four million people and are organized by 10,000 home health agencies
- *housemaids* and *nannies* working in middle-class private households, whether with legal visas/permits or as illegal workers
- *cleaners*, working in hospitals, government offices or company buildings.

SOME WIDER IMPLICATIONS OF CARE CHAINS

Although a relatively new concept, the notion of a global care chain has given impetus to a number of new lines of enquiry:

■ Most care workers remit part of their earnings to support their own children or other family members at home. The quantity of these remittances now vastly exceeds foreign aid programmes and we need to know the extent to which they are being effective in delivering welfare and development goals, as opposed to fuelling consumption and increased dependency on migrant labour.

■ Rich countries benefit hugely from the supply of cheap and often skilled care workers without the necessity – as in the case of their own nationals – to pay towards the reproductive cost of rearing and educating them in the first place since these were borne by governments and families far away. Are these clear economic advantages going to overcome the xenophobic fears of the host populations?

■ It is paradoxical that middle-class Western women can hire Southern nannies to look after their children so they can continue their high-paid careers while the latter have to forgo the experience of caring for their own children left behind at home. Will gender solidarity be relevant where there are such large social class as well as North–South inequalities between women?

■ Most foreign care workers are deprived of equal welfare rights, face uncertainties over whether or not their visas and/or work permits will be renewed and are required to work long hours for poor pay. A large proportion, however, is illegal and so faces added difficulties, including much lower pay. A survey of 18 New York agencies in 1993 found that illegal care workers averaged around US$175 a week, whereas legal employees could earn as much as US$600. What are the relations between care workers in the legal and illegal sectors?

REVIEW

Women's struggles, or at least those that bind individuals and groups together irrespective of their national or cultural identities, have made important contributions to the growth of an emergent global society from below. The women's movement satisfies the primary criterion of a global social movement, namely 'global reach'. There is hardly a country in the world where gender relations have not been profoundly altered by its impact. Moreover, the timescale for this transformation is impressively short, with most of the force of the movement only evident since the 1970s. The movement spread so fast partly because it adopted participatory forms of grassroots organization and partly because the speed and density of communications facilitated the global transmission of positive images of women.

Like other social movements, the women's movement has been partly borne along by its more or less universal appeal. However, in common with other movements, its expansion has also been propelled by the compulsion to respond to vast and sometimes threatening forces for change. These appear to be encompassing all the world's inhabitants, especially the less well off. But perhaps these global changes offer an even greater challenge to women. Partly this is because the patriarchal oppression and economic disadvantage most women face create an almost unprecedented potential for unity of thought and action. However, the resources associated with globalization – communications technologies, faster and easier travel, and with these the ever more rapid dissemination of all kinds of knowledge – offer women particularly exciting opportunities to benefit from shared experiences and pooling their acquired knowledge.

FURTHER READING

- *Bananas, Beaches and Bases: Making Feminist Sense of International Politics* by C. Enloe (1989) is not meant to provide an especially sociological analysis. However, it is witty and accessible and offers a useful way into theorizing about gender.

- In *Women's Movements in International Perspective* (2001), M. Molyneux looks at women's movements in Latin America, especially in Cuba, Nicaragua and Argentina, though she also explores more general themes that are relevant to women's struggles.

- S. Rowbotham is a central figure in the development of feminist thought. In *Homeworkers Worldwide* (1993), she gives a lively and simple introduction to this topic.

- In an edited book called *States of Conflict: Gender, Violence and Resistance*, S. Jacobs et al. (2000) include some excellent chapters on the forms of violence to which women have been exposed at the hands of states and military authorities.

GROUP WORK

1. Students will read this chapter before the seminar. Working in two groups and drawing on the text, one group will compose a list showing all the feminist directions and priorities pursued by women in the North since the 1960s, and the other will conduct a similar exercise for Southern women. After hearing each group's arguments, the class will try to explain the differences.

2. Adopt the same procedure as in 1. While one group compiles a list of the women's organizations and networks that have been mentioned and then tries to categorize them under different headings, the other will assemble a picture of all the different ways in which various IGOs have played a role in facilitating global feminism since 1945.

3. Four students will agree to prepare a debate on the topic: 'Northern women have more to learn from their sisters in the South than vice versa.' After hearing both sides, each class member will give two reasons why they agree or disagree with this proposition.

QUESTIONS TO THINK ABOUT

?

1. What have been the constraints on women's actions and to what extent has globalization provided opportunities to overcome them?

2. Assess the relative significance of the UN and its associated institutions in strengthening the world feminist movement compared with other factors.

3. Drawing on case study material, assess the impact of recent worldwide changes in encouraging women to collaborate transnationally.

WHAT'S ON THE WEB

- http://www.oxfam.org.uk/what_we_do/issues/trade/trading_rights.htm The charity Oxfam has done some pioneering work on women working in global supply chains. A useful 97-page report, *Trading our Rights Away*, can be downloaded in full on this site.

- http://www.intute.ac.uk/socialsciences/womensstudies/ This Intute gateway provides a comprehensive listing of women's studies sites. To link to our discussion of Enloe's work pay particular regard to the sub-link on Women and War.

- http://feminism.eserver.org/about/about.html This site is number 2 in Google searches for 'feminism' and number 4 in Google searches for 'women's studies', and currently reaches approximately 25,000 visitors a month. Its continuous updating is impressive.

CHAPTER 20

Towards a Sustainable Future: The Green Movement

CONTENTS

Environmentalism is a global social movement that functions to protect nature or the biosphere. In this chapter, we examine its various claims and goals and ask how valid these are. We also explore the sometimes contradictory forms of protest in which the environmental or green movement is engaged, considering too the reasons why its actions have become increasingly transnational. We begin, however, with a brief discussion of our complex relationship with nature and the role it has played in creating environmental problems.

Until recently, the viability of nature, or the biosphere, was not especially at risk from humans. However, our exploitation of the planet's resources in our relentless scramble for greater wealth is damaging the very conditions that ultimately make material progress and indeed life itself possible. It is hardly surprising therefore that what the green movement seeks to protect the environment from is us, in other words, 'from the harmful effects of human activities' (Milton 1996: 27). Both human agency and structural forces interrelate in complex ways in the impact that society has on the environment.

A SOCIOLOGY OF NATURE

Sociologists tend to view nature as both an objective reality governed by its own physical laws – though increasingly affected by our actions – and as an entity subject to the social constructions imposed by human actors. In terms of the first view, it is widely accepted that the health of the biosphere is a precondition for the survival of all life. If, by contrast, we think of nature as socially constructed, then it becomes difficult to draw a distinction between how we choose to conceptualize it and how we act towards and feel about it. Similarly, we tend to imbue nature with different meanings over time and depending on our varying interests at a given moment.

Accordingly, nature and the meaning of nature are frequently contested and manipulated. For example, one study of a public enquiry into a planning dispute showed how green groups opposed to the development of a new landfill site for municipal waste disposal employed a definition of nature that emphasized its untouched, wilderness-like qualities and the need to preserve this. The commercial developers, by contrast, argued that the countryside had already been altered by generations of human activity. They were simply proposing to extend this process of 'managing' the land in a caring way (MacNaghten 1993).

How have the deeply rooted conceptualizations of nature present in different kinds of societies altered over time and how have these changes shaped the ways we treat nature? Merchant (1990) has identified two crucial historical periods with respect to our attitudes to nature:

1. *Preindustrial societies:* Most preindustrial societies imagined nature as active, alive and nurturing, akin to a caring mother. It allowed humans to enjoy its bounty but also demanded respect, which was demonstrated through religious ceremonies and sacrifices. People shared an organic view of the universe in which the human and non-human, inanimate and living were all seen as part

of the same seamless structure created by God. Similarly, they accepted the idea of ethical restrictions on the exploitation of nature that should be respected. Despite the Christian doctrine insisting on the worship of one transcendental God, most people in Christian societies continued to believe that numerous spirits resided in hills, woods and other wild places – a survival from a pre-Christian era.

2. *Nature and modernity:* The Western view of nature underwent a massive transformation. Scientists, particularly Isaac Newton, saw nature as inert, passive, accessible to human understanding and therefore capable of serving human needs. Meanwhile, other changes, such as the spread of Protestantism and the rise of a more commercialized, individualistic ethos in socioeconomic relations, reinforced the view of nature as something that should be privately owned and could be controlled and managed for profitable and productive purposes. Nature became tamed. This reconceptualization of nature also became entwined with prevailing ways of thinking about women and gender relations. Both women and nature were considered to be passive, primitive, emotional forces requiring manipulation and control by the rational, 'higher' masculine forces embodied in science, industry and notions of human progress. Eventually, capitalist modernity – partly a product of this altered perspective – enabled more and more societies to conquer nature and make human life virtually independent of it.

The contrast between this new Western concept of nature and that upheld by people from other cultures was vividly and prophetically portrayed by Chief Seattle of the Sugumish Indians in North America (his name survives in the name of the city). He is said to have made the following comment on land grabbing by white settlers in 1855:

> We know that the white man does not understand our ways. He is a stranger who comes in the night and takes from the land whatever he needs. The earth is not his friend but his enemy, and when he has conquered it he moves on. He kidnaps the earth from his children. His appetite will devour the earth and leave behind a desert. If all the beasts were gone, we would die from a great loneliness of the spirit, for whatever happens to the beasts, happens also to us. All things are connected. Whatever befalls the earth befalls the children of the earth. (quoted in Kirkby et al. 1995: 17)

More recently, observers have suggested that our thinking is undergoing yet another transformation. Now we are apparently becoming more ambivalent and uncertain about nature. Thus, we have come to realize how much our past and present pursuit of material development may be harming nature irrevocably. For example, the commercialization of nature for profit through chemical-intensive, high-tech agriculture has led to the extensive 'refashioning' of farming and the 'denaturalization' of foods (Goodman and Redclift 1991). Similarly, our desire to extract pleasure from nature through activities like tourism, commercial game parks, outdoor hobbies and theme parks has turned it into little more than a series of consumer products (Strathern 1992). Yet, just as we are becoming increasingly aware of our adverse impact on nature, we are developing a powerful yearning to protect it, to rediscover the wild, pristine beauty we imagine it once possessed and to reunite with it as closely as possible. These yearnings are demonstrated by such things as our growing thirst for organic foods, 'natural', 'healthy' lifestyles and simple, eco-friendly holidays in remote locations such as Belize (Duffy 2004).

It seems then that we demand lifestyles that presuppose the continuing command over and perhaps eventual destruction of nature and yet simultaneously we wish to respect and resuscitate it. Similarly, we are engaged in trying to protect the environment both because we have come to believe in its intrinsic worth and because we have realized that the threat to nature means that our own futures require nothing less. Sociological insights can, it is hoped, help us to deal more critically and sensitively with these conflicting views and expectations.

THE CHANGING NATURE OF ENVIRONMENTALISM

In Europe, expressions of concern about the human threat to nature have roots in the nineteenth century. Romantic poets like William Wordsworth eulogized remote regions and country life and depicted them as sources of spiritual regeneration. When the first environmental organizations were set up in the mid-nineteenth century, they mostly focused on conservation, their main concerns being the preservation of areas of outstanding natural beauty and/or the protection of animals and birds. Early 'greens' mounted campaigns to discourage people from buying fur coats and hats decorated with feathers. Interestingly, the first effective international conservationist NGO, the International Committee for Bird Protection established in 1922, was concerned with European bird life (McCormick 1989: 23).

Since the Second World War, environmental concerns have undergone three important changes, which are considered further below:

- a shift in the issues covered
- a growth in the number of people involved in the green movement
- greater participation by NGOs in the South.

Although wildlife and nature preservation continue to attract huge memberships, for example the World Wide Fund for Nature, environmentalism now encompasses a much wider range of problems. These include the growing threats posed by various kinds of pollution and the fear that diminishing biodiversity, along with long-term climate change caused by global warming, will harm future generations.

There has been a vast growth in the number of people joining various environmental NGOs since the late 1960s, with an especially rapid increase in the 1980s. In the USA, for example, the combined memberships of the 12 leading national organizations rose from an estimated four million in 1981 to 11 million in 1990, with overall revenues totalling US$300 million a year (Bramble and Porter 1992: 317). Worldwide, the number of environmental NGOs has also grown rapidly. Princen and Finger (1994: Chapter 1) claim that there were 176 in 1909 but more than 4,500 by the late 1980s, with most of these being established during the 1980s. The number of INGOs with specifically global goals grew from nearly 980 in 1990 to 1,170 in 2000, an increase of nearly 20 per cent (Anheier et al. 2001: 300). By 2003, this number had risen to 1,781 (Anheier et al. 2005: 320).

Another change is that environmentalism is no longer confined primarily to the North. In many developing countries, the destruction of forests, the displacement of people by dam building, particularly in India, China, Malaysia and parts of Africa, and mounting industrial pollution are causing increasing alarm. One striking example of an environmental disaster in the South erupted in September 1997 when thousands of planters and farmers in Indonesia lit fires to clear the bush for cash-crop cultivation. This followed the previous mass clearance of forests by international logging companies. During a period of drought, perhaps caused by global warming, these fires raged out of control over an area of 100 square miles and the vast cloud of smoke they caused affected more than 70 million people in six countries (Harrison 1997).

TABLE 20.1 **The rise of three leading green INGOs**		
Organization and date founded	Affiliated national groups and worldwide membership in December 2005	Examples of campaigns and projects
World Wildlife Fund, now known as World Wide Fund for Nature, 1961	Has affiliated groups in more than 100 countries including 24 in the South and five million members. It is currently working on about 2,000 conservation projects, which between them employ 4,000 people worldwide	Cooperates with local groups and governments on conservation projects, for example elephant and rhino protection in Tanzania and support for an environmental education programme in Pakistan
Greenpeace International, 1971	Operates through member groups in 42 countries, of which 18 are in the South or in the territories of the former USSR. More than three million paid-up members and an annual budget of around US$30 million	First achieved media and international acclaim in the early 1970s with campaigns against US and French nuclear testing and in 1975 confronted the Soviet whaling fleet. Campaigned to turn Antarctica into a world wilderness park in 1991
Friends of the Earth, 1971	Has independent member groups in 71 countries, plus affiliated groups in a further 11 countries, 41 of which are in the South (18 in South America, 11 in Africa, 9 in Asia and 3 in the Middle East). Approximately a million members	One of many campaigns (launched in 1992) was the Mahogany is Murder project to encourage consumers to boycott Brazilian rainforest timber. By 1994 the six largest DIY chains in the UK had agreed to stop selling mahogany and imports fell by 68 per cent between 1992 and 1996

Other instances of rapid economic change in the South have also provoked organized protest, one arresting example being that of the Kenyan Green Belt movement started by Wangari Maathai. By 2004, its members, of whom there were 250,000, had planted 20 million trees. The movement had also refused to go along with government building plans in Nairobi and had formed links with similar groups in 30 other African countries, including six that are now copying the Green Belt experiment. President Moi of Kenya often threatened to have Maathai arrested, until he lost the 2002 election and she became a member of parliament. In 2004, she became the first African woman to receive the Nobel Peace Prize (Friends of the Earth 2004: 17). Environmental campaigns in the developing world are often linked to wider concerns about human rights, women's issues, poverty and extreme inequality. The protests are often also provoked by the failure of many large-scale, commercial projects to bring employment to or improve the lifestyles of the poorest people (Kothari 1996).

SPEAKING FOR HUMANITY: THE CLAIMS OF ENVIRONMENTALISM

With environmentalism increasingly claiming to represent the interests of all humanity, Milton (1996: 170) refers to it as a 'transcultural discourse' that is 'not tied to any particular group or location'. Similarly, Yearley (1996a: 151) argues that: 'Environmentalism surely counts as one of the best candidates we have for a global ideology and globalizing movement.' He suggests that the green move-ment is more likely than other social movements to succeed in its attempt to unite people irrespective of their national affiliations. We consider three factors that appear to validate such a claim before discussing some reasons for regarding it with a degree of scepticism.

THE TRANSBOUNDARY NATURE OF MANY ENVIRONMENTAL PROBLEMS

Some environmental crises are more or less confined to one location. A shocking instance of this was the release of poisonous gas from a plant in Bhopal, India, in 1984 (see Chapter 7). Others occur in one place but have a transnational impact – like the nuclear explosion at the Chernobyl plant in the Ukraine in 1986, which spread radioactive material over much of Europe. Increasingly, however, we know that many problems are caused not by a single event but by a multiplicity of human activities across the world. Moreover, they do not respect national boundaries but impact on everyone. Thus, acting alone, states can no longer protect their citizens from environmental damage. The main examples of these transnational environmental problems are global warming, ozone deple-tion, transboundary air pollution (especially **acid rain**) and the loss of biodiver-sity, namely the declining variety of species able to survive on our planet.

Acid rain is caused by the emission of toxic gases such as sulphur and nitrogen oxides, which are then carried by winds and rain.

Let us take the case of global warming. Some indications of this are partly anecdotal, but many prestigious scientists, like those associated with the Inter-governmental Panel on Climate Change (IPCC), argue that the accumulations of carbon found in ice-core samples from past centuries compared with recent deposits from the build-up of carbon dioxide in the atmosphere strongly suggest that global warming has already begun. The IPCC was established in 1988 to advise governments on whether or not there was evidence of global warming. By 1995 it included nearly 2,500 eminent scientists from about 40 countries. Although a minority of scientists – many funded by right-wing think tanks and/or heavy industries, including producers of fossil fuels (Rowell 1996) – continue to dispute the arguments put forward by the IPCC and environmental groups, evidence of global warming now seems irrefutable (Bunyard 2004: 55–6), as the following indications suggest:

- carbon dioxide emission levels are currently about one-third higher than they were in the preindustrial era (375 compared with 280 parts of carbon dioxide per million parts of the atmosphere) and are expected to rise much further
- satellite data indicate that approximately 10 per cent of the earth's snow cover has disappeared since the 1960s and the Arctic ice has thinned by 40 per cent since the 1950s, while the area it covers during spring and summer has shrunk by perhaps 15 per cent
- ten of the warmest years since records began have occurred since 1990
- freak storms, hurricanes, tornadoes, unprecedented floods and other climatic events – including forest fires, droughts and heat waves – seem to have become everyday news items
- between 1960 and 2002, worldwide consumption of coal, oil and natural gas increased nearly five times and carbon dioxide levels rose by 18 per cent in this period alone (Gardner et al. 2004: 3).

Declining biodiversity is another problem. It occurs because widespread deforestation and other kinds of commercial developments are gradually eliminating the unique habitats in which insect, animal, bird and plant species have evolved. The relentless logging of tropical rainforests is especially worrying. They cover only 7 per cent of the world's land but contain approximately half its species (Seager 1995: 16). As species diminish, so too does the storehouse of possible life forms we may need in future for medical or other purposes, while our aesthetic delight in the planet's infinite variety is undermined and despoiled.

These problems are becoming global partly because natural phenomena like winds, sea currents and tides are transporting particles, gases and minute amounts of toxic poisons or radioactivity from nuclear power stations located in different parts of the world. The pollution-generating and energy-intensive activities in which most people engage – especially members of what Durning (1992) calls the 'consuming class' (see Box 20.1) – endlessly push wastes, toxins and gases into rivers, seas, landfill sites and the atmosphere. However, as Beck (1992: 38, 23) points out, in this game the perpetrators become the victims through what he calls the 'boomerang effect'. For example, chemical-intensive agriculture eventually leads to declining soil fertility and soil erosion and the disappearance of wild plants and animals. Meanwhile, the lead that is put in our petrol along with numerous other chemical traces may turn up in breast milk consumed by babies in distant cities.

Box 20.1

Consumer desires create a world of luxury consumption and waste

Durning (1992) estimated that the world's *consuming class* consisted of 1.1 billion people, defined as such because they enjoyed per capita incomes in excess of US$7,500 a year. Most lived in the advanced countries but the number also included about one-fifth of people living in the South who were also wealthy. The consuming class eats meat and processed/packaged foods, depends on numerous energy-intensive gadgets, lives in climate-controlled buildings supplied with abundant hot water and travels in private cars and jet aeroplanes. Mostly, it consumes goods that are soon thrown away when fashions change. In sharp contrast, the 1.1 billion *poorest global inhabitants* in 1992 mostly travel on foot, rely on local resources for shelter (stone, wood, mud), eat mainly root crops, beans and lentils and frequently drink unsafe water.

Both these groups were and are deeply implicated in global pollution though for very different reasons. Poverty and necessity rather than greed give the global poor little choice but to increase the pressure on already fragile ecosystems such as semi-deserts and steep hillsides. Between these two groups comes what Durning calls the *middle income group* of 3.3 billion people. They mostly eat vegetables and cereals but are normally well fed and have access to clean water. They also use bicycles and public transport and their possessions are made to last.

The changing picture by 2003

In 2003 and building on Durning's work, Bentley slightly recast the earlier definition and defined the global consuming class as those living on the purchasing power parity or equivalent of US$7,000. According to this view, it now consists of 1.7 billion members – around one-quarter of the world – but virtually half of these live in developing nations (48 per cent). China and India alone provide over 20 per cent of this group – 362 million individuals compared with 350 million in Western Europe. On the other hand, only two million of the consuming class live in Africa.

Increased worldwide consumption:

- From 1960 to 1995: there was a 2.5 fold increase in the price of minerals; a 2.1 fold increase in metals; a 2.3 fold increase in wood products and a 5.5 fold increase in synthetics such as plastics.

- From 2000 to 2004: private car purchases in China increased from 5 million to 24 million and this will go through the roof in the coming years, given China's high economic growth rate.

- From 1950 to 2002: expenditure on advertising (which spurs consumerism) rose nine times to reach US$446 billion.

The throwaway economy

Created by the consuming class, this generates huge amounts of waste, including the release of toxic poisons from farmlands and factories (linked partly to the more than 70,000 synthetic materials created by chemical industries); the emission of greenhouse gases; and the dumping of 'obsolescent' household goods. Thus, in the USA, a total of 3,200 kilos of waste is created for every 100 kilos of manufactured products. Disposing of all this waste is expensive and may inflict permanent damage on the environment. Again in the USA, the total cost of dealing with all the consequences of waste – from disposal and air and water pollution to traffic jams, obesity and crime – was equal to at least US$2 trillion, or more than one-fifth of the entire value of the economy.

Luxury consumption compared with spending on basic needs

While annual world spending on makeup in 2003 and pet foods (in Europe and the USA in 1998) equalled US$18 billion and US$17 billion respectively, the additional annual spending required to achieve the goal of universal literacy, the elimination of hunger and malnutrition, and clean drinking water across the world was US$5 billion, US$19 billion and US$10 billion respectively.

SOURCES: Durning (1992); Baird (1997); Bentley (2003); Gardner et al. (2004)

THE GLOBALIZATION OF INDUSTRIAL DEVELOPMENT

The number of locations contributing to environmental degradation across the world is increasing fast. With its huge population and rapid economic growth, China is particularly striking in this respect. For a start, 300 of China's cities are currently short of water and four-fifths of its rivers and lakes are badly polluted. And these are not its only environmental problems. Between 1992 and 1993, 100,000 people were poisoned by pesticides or fertilizers (Smith 1993: 19–21). Then, in November 2005, a spill from a state factory explosion in Harbin, northeast China, discharged a toxin-releasing chemical called benzene into a major river; the pollution levels in the river remained high for 50 miles and nearly reached the Russian border (Watts 2005: 16). Moreover, 30 per cent of China's population has already joined the global consumer class and its continued rapid economic development may mean that many more of its present population of 1.2 billion people will soon do likewise. If so, we will see a virtual doubling of the present stress on the biosphere caused by industrialization.

Meanwhile, growing international trade increases the volume of tankers and ships discharging oil and other substances into the oceans and fills up the skies with air-polluting traffic. Some developing countries, for example in West Africa, have accepted hazardous wastes from rich, environmentally conscious countries although recent international regulations and agreements (in 1989 and 1991) have reduced these practices to some extent. Moreover, the need to generate foreign exchange for debt repayment has encouraged some developing countries to accelerate the rate at which their forests are being cut down. This, in turn, is reducing the planet's capacity to absorb carbon dioxide.

COMMUNICATIONS TECHNOLOGY AND THE VIEW FROM SPACE

Since the mid-1960s, space travel and the increased sophistication of communications technology have yielded ever more vivid images of planet earth. Satellites are able to provide more accurate and compelling evidence than ever before of the increasingly global rather than purely local extent of environmental destruction (Milton 1996: 177). The effects of relentless logging in tropical rainforests is a clear case in point, as is the probable damage that chemical pollution and ozone depletion inflict on the huge concentrations of minute plant life or sea algae found around many of the world's coasts. The latter also play a major role in absorbing carbon dioxide.

Global Thinkers 20   **ULRICH BECK (1944–)**

The risk society and different modernities
Beck's main themes are the changing nature of social action and reflexivity as modernity unfolds and risk and globalization are enhanced. He argues as follows.

The era of the first or simple modernity
Capitalist industrialization involved detraditionalization – breaking with past institutions – but also the establishment of others such as the nuclear family, class solidarity, multigenerational working-class communities, nationhood and, eventually, social welfare. The prevailing logic involved overcoming scarcity through scientific rationality and capitalist efficiency and the struggle to achieve a more equitable redistribution of resources. Actors respected science, while most risks generated by modernity were local and insurable through the calculation of probability.

The second/reflexive modernity and the world ecological risk society
From, perhaps, the 1960s, it became increasingly obvious that the cumulative consequences of industrialization – involving the relentless application of rationality by business and government to the goal of national economic 'progress' – had spawned huge environmental 'side effects' such as nuclear contamination, chemical pollutions, increasing greenhouse gas emissions and their link to global warming, the release of biogenetic organisms into farming and a series of food scares such as 'mad cow disease'. None of these were predicted, their possible long-term impact is unknowable, they are often global in scope and they are uninsurable.

The wider scope of risk
Thus, the main logic of the second modernity became one of escaping from the 'bads' of modernity rather than continuing to scramble for further material 'goods'. However, Beck has explored a much wider set of transformations and risks that have accompanied the environmental risk society:

- *World social risk society and individualization: The safe social structures of class loyalty, protected jobs, local communities, marriage and family life – established during the first modernity – have weakened their grip, leaving actors liberated from social control but simultaneously compelled to construct their own life biographies. The self-making, choosing individual rather than collectivities, becomes the key social unit.*
- *Women and gender relations: Nowhere is the above more evident than through the 'gender revolution' of the past 30 years. Now, most women expect to work and their ability to determine their own identity and economic autonomy means*

they can demand more equitable relationships or leave partners who are unwilling to provide these.

■ **The world economic risk society:** *Continuing technological changes such as robotization and computerization have reduced jobs in all economic sectors and/or relegated more and more people to insecure, badly paid work. The transition to post-Fordist flexible, casualized regimes of employment accompanied by the downward pressure on wage levels because of economic globalization have intensified this trend towards economic insecurity.*

Reflexive modernity and a new bottom-up politics

Coping with multirisk society requires actors to develop a type of reflexivity – based on 'self-confrontation' – that enables them to take personal responsibility for their private lives and the wider consequences of modernity. Thus, Beck situates the individual against a backdrop of vast global structural forces that must somehow be tamed and reformed. Globalization and individualization are like the two ends of a telescope; lone individuals across the world and their actions interpenetrate and shape each other's lives through interconnecting global forces. Dealing with all this requires new social solidarities and the invention of a more radical, grassroots, transnational politics – confronting old institutions from both inside and outside.

SOURCES: Beck (1999a, 1999b, 2000a, 2000b); Beck and Beck-Gernsheim (2002)

REASONS FOR SCEPTICISM

According to Yearley (1996b: 66), green groups have a strong interest in claiming to work for 'a global mission' on behalf of all humanity. This is because groups that engage in such appeals find it boosts their membership. They may also experience more media attention and greater access to governments and IGOs (Yearley 1996b: 86–92). In effect, adopting a global perspective and mission becomes a path to success. The global claims of green activists also elide important differences in impact between countries and regions. In particular, environmental problems do not threaten all human life to the same degree. Islands such as the Maldives or lowland areas in countries like Bangladesh, for example, may be flooded if predictions about global warming prove to be correct. However, people living at higher elevations will escape this effect, though they may experience other consequences of climate change such as increased droughts. Similarly, wealthy countries will be better equipped than poor countries to cope with problems such as rising sea levels (Yearley 1996a: 78).

Sceptics point to deep divisions in the environmental movement. According to Milton (1996: 187), an important minority among the radical or 'deep' greens shares 'an anti-globalist perspective', one example here being an NGO that emerged in the USA during the 1980s called Earth First! It has become famous for its direct action campaigns involving strategies like disabling bulldozers and spiking trees with iron bars to deter building projects and forest logging. Such activists see the relentless worldwide drive for material prosperity and the global linking of national economies together through investment and trade as the main problem. Indeed, they advocate deglobalization – the recovery of lost cultural and local self-sufficiencies – and a return to simpler, more self-reliant, decentralized economies. Dobson (2000: 2) also sees a clear difference between environmentalists and supporters of ecologism. Environmentalists adopt a 'managerial approach'; they seek solutions to environmental problems through reforms and practical, consensual policies rather than demanding huge changes in our current lifestyles and economic system. Many proponents of ecologism, however, argue that there are finite limits to economic growth, which, if pushed much further, will irreparably damage the biosphere and, therefore, ultimately, human life as well. These more radical green groups also tend to be highly critical of all or most of the theory of sustainable development discussed in the next section.

Figure 20.1 **Children greet a mascot of the world at the Earth Summit in Rio de Janeiro in June 1992**

Deep divisions are also apparent between governments. Thus, not only are most states reluctant to surrender part of their sovereignty to supranational regulatory bodies in the pursuit of global solutions but conflicts of interest have arisen on some issues. The differences between the richer countries and the developing world are probably the most serious. They became particularly obvious during the Earth Summit at Rio in 1992 and they have continued to impede international action ever since, particularly on global warming. The four main issues that divide the North and South are the following:

1. The leaders of the South argue that the North's historical culpability for environmental problems is undeniably greater. In the mid-1990s, the North used up 70 per cent of the world's energy, three-quarters of its metals, three-fifths

of its food and 85 per cent of its wood. Yet, it contained barely a quarter of the global population (Athanasiou 1997: 53). With less than 5 per cent of the world's population, the USA alone consumed one-quarter of its energy. Partly, this was linked to the fact that it has the highest propensity for air travel (Seager 1995: 30) and used 31 per cent of the world's total vehicles. Not surprisingly, at a share of 19 per cent, it was also by far the largest single country emitting greenhouse gases (Kidron and Segal 1995: 18–23). By contrast, India, with over 16 per cent of the world's population, then consumed only 3 per cent of the world's energy (Seager 1995: 72). By 2002, however, the situation had gradually begun to change. While the industrial countries were consuming 62 per cent of the world's oil, in terms of energy consumption from all sources China and India accounted for 13 per cent, mainly from coal (70 and 50 per cent respectively) rather than oil (Sawin 2004: 26–7). Moreover, as we have seen, rapid economic growth in both these countries will quickly mean a vast rise in vehicle consumption and this will push up their need for oil as well. Nevertheless, for the time being, the South's allegation of Northern culpability retains considerable validity.

2. The South further claims that high living standards in the North are partly a consequence of cheap labour in the South and an unfair international trading system that underpays poor countries for their raw materials. Governments and NGOs in the South have been further angered by the huge transfers of funds that they have had to make to Northern governments and banks since the 1970s as debt repayments.

3. Southern countries expect the North to subsidize cleaner technologies in poorer countries so that they can industrialize without losing economic momentum or adding massively to global pollution. The North recognizes the validity of this argument and the Kyoto protocol of 1997 included a provision for this with the 'clean development mechanism' (Newell 2006: 95). Similarly, they expect the North to create 'space' in the world economy for Southern development by reducing its own consumption levels. They have also asked for compensation in return for agreeing to slow down the rate of deforestation or taking steps to preserve biodiversity.

4. A final source of North–South disagreement often creates more divisions within the green movement than between governments, namely, what should be the primary focus for protest and action? Whereas Northern environmental groups and technical experts have tended to prioritize climate change, Southern campaigners acknowledge its importance but prefer to place more emphasis on the differences that in their view perpetuate their economic disadvantage – poverty and the world inequalities created by economic glob-alization, unfair trade and so on (Pettit 2004). These issues are discussed earlier in this book. Southern groups have also at times felt underrepresented at international meetings and therefore excluded from debates compared with their much better resourced Northern counterparts.

North–South differences over the question of global warming surfaced fiercely at Rio in 1992 and at Kyoto in 1997 (see Table 20.2 below). Led by the USA, the advanced countries argued that future Southern industrialization posed the greatest threat to the biosphere, especially in countries with huge populations and considerable reserves of fossil fuels like China and India. They argued that it made no sense to impose tough environmental standards on rich countries without insisting that equally sweeping constraints be adopted by the South. Moreover, at the Rio conference, the North agreed to find the resources to operationalize Agenda 21 – 'an international programme of action for achieving sustainable development in the twenty-first century' (Grubb et al. 1995: 97). It was calculated that the South would need to spend US$625 billion a year, one-fifth of which was expected to come from the North. By the mid-1990s, there was little sign that the idea would materialize (Dodds 1997: 192).

North–South disagreements in the green movement have been partly lessened by the adoption of the idea of environmental justice and the establishment of ties between the broader global justice movement – discussed in Chapter 18 – and groups that link green issues to the idea of 'climate justice' (Pettit 2004: 103). The Environmental Justice and Climate Change Initiative (www.ejcc.org) is one such group. It argues that climate change caused by global warming and manifested in rising sea levels, decreasing rainfall, storm damage and floods is already harming the poorest people in the world more than those who live in rich countries. These effects will accelerate in the future if emission levels are not tackled much more stringently than at present. Interestingly, around 80 per cent of 'people of colour and indigenous peoples' (Newell 2006: 113) in the USA live in coastal regions. Indeed, this inequality was evident in 2005, when hurricane Katrina hit the area surrounding New Orleans and the people worst hit were those, mainly African-Americans, who were too poor to escape because they did not own cars and/or occupied houses in low-lying areas adjacent to the coastline. The Inuit people of Canada and Alaska and many Hispanics living in poor areas near coastlines face similar hazards.

Newell (2006: 117) is hopeful that, despite these only partially resolved North–South differences within the green movement, this increased focus on the link between climate change and politics, between 'social justice … and global injustice', will provide a way to 're-energise efforts' in the struggle to confront the enormous task of dealing with climate change.

FRIENDS OF THE GREEN MOVEMENT?

While environmentalism's claim to represent the interests of all humanity may or may not be entirely valid, the movement does seem to have achieved a nearly universal appeal and in this sense it evinces a certain global dimension. In this section, we consider the support for environmentalism that has come from the top-down actions spearheaded by powerful elite groups, states and international organizations.

STATE AND UN INVOLVEMENT IN ENVIRONMENTALISM SINCE 1972

As you can see from Table 20.2, governments have sometimes been prepared to act on environmental matters through the auspices of the United Nations General Assembly (UNGA). The United Nations Environment Programme (UNEP) and the World Commission on Environment and Development (WCED) have also become important foci for change.

TABLE 20.2	State and UN involvement in environmentalism: key events	
Event/venue and date	Main initiator and representation (if any)	Key outcomes
Stockholm, 1972	Swedish government, leading politicians from 113 countries and more than 250 NGOs	The UNGA voted to establish the UNEP
New York, 1983	The UNGA called for the establishment of the WCED to investigate how economic development and environmental safety could be pursued simultaneously	Gro Harlem (Norway's prime minister) chaired the WCED and in 1987 it published *Our Common Future*. This became the basis for thinking about sustainable development (SD)
New York, 1989	The UNGA called for the United Nations Conference on Environment and Development (UNCED) in 1992 to debate SD	
Rio de Janeiro, the Earth Summit, 1992	UNGA, UNEP, WCED. Attended by delegations from 178 countries including 120 heads of state, 5,000 journalists and attended by representatives from 9,000 green NGOs and INGOs	Various agreements, but mostly declarations of principle on issues such as climate change and biodiversity, not binding commitments. Agenda 21 offered practical guidelines on how countries could implement SD
Kyoto, Japan, 1997	UNEP, UNCED. Government leaders and officials from 159 countries plus 10,000 journalists, green activists and industrial lobbyists	An agreement that 38 already industrial nations would together cut greenhouse gas emissions by an overall 5.5 per cent (on 1990 levels) by 2012 but with varying targets. Australia refused. President Clinton agreed but Bush government in 2001 and Congress refused to ratify. To come into force required ratification by 55 countries including those developed nations responsible for 55 per cent of emissions
Johannesburg, South Africa, 2002	UNGA, WCED. Reaffirmed the commitment of states to SD and prioritized the need to tackle world poverty as part of SD. For example, there was a commitment that by 2015 all children would complete primary school	Over 300 partnership agreements reached on the environment involving women and youth groups, trade unions, farmers, Aboriginal peoples, businesses, NGOs and states. Johannesburg was said to have revealed a stronger sense of a 'world community'
Montreal, Canada, December 2005	UNGA, WCED. Attended by delegates of 156 countries who had by now ratified the Kyoto protocol, except Australia and USA. Russia finally did in 2004 and so it became legally binding on all signatories in February 2005	Those present agreed to start urgent negotiations in 2006 towards setting stronger targets for emission cuts ready for the second stage of Kyoto from 2013 to 2017. Also agreed on a five-year plan of action to help developing countries cope with climate change via clean technology transfers and other means

SOURCES: McCormick (1989: 101); Princen and Finger (1994); Willetts (1996: 69); Dodds (1997: 4–5); www.Greenpeace.org/ international

According to McCormick (1989: 88), the UN conference at Stockholm in 1972 'was the first occasion on which the … problems of the global environment were discussed at an intergovernmental forum with a view to actually taking corrective action'. Most of the initiative for instigating the 1972 conference came from the Swedish government. However, several leading scientific bodies and green INGOs also supported it strongly. This set a crucial precedent for future world conferences where INGOs later became more prominent (Willetts 1996: 69). The developing countries also participated despite their suspicions that Northern green concerns might be a ploy to slow down Southern development.

The 1972 Stockholm conference set in train an important sequence of global activities, especially the establishment of the UN Environmental Programme. Its role was to safeguard the world's environment and cooperate with relevant agencies. Although the UNEP has been underfunded, growing evidence of environmental problems and grassroots pressure has boosted its influence. Between Stockholm 1972 and Kyoto 1997, there have been many other world environmental conferences too numerous to mention. Some have given rise to international agreements such as those reached at Montreal in 1987 and Copenhagen in 1992 on phasing out the production and use of CFCs and other dangerous ozone-destroying chemicals. But the lineage of world events briefly outlined in Table 20.2 is probably the most significant.

SUSTAINABLE DEVELOPMENT: A MANUAL FOR GREEN REFORM?

The concept of 'sustainable development' offered by the World Commission on Environment and Development in 1987 offered inspiration as well as a set of clear environmental guidelines. Its central tenet is that the pursuit of economic development is perfectly compatible with greater environmental safety. There are two key reasons for linking these goals together. First, given the South's primary concern with overcoming national poverty, it might have been unwilling to cooperate without a parallel commitment to the goal of development. Second, since poverty has been widely recognized as a major cause of global environmental devastation in its own right, reducing it through economic development should simultaneously help the environment. The WCED report argued that three principles must be followed:

1. A commitment to better environmental management must be incorporated into all future economic decision-making, whether by states, companies or households. This means requiring all farms, factories and other businesses to stop using the seas, rivers or atmosphere as a free dumping ground for their waste. It also involves giving priority to the development of new technologies that will reduce the amount of energy and materials used in every sphere of economic life.

2. Overcoming worldwide environmental problems requires an inescapable moral pledge to the idea of greater equity. Thus, each generation should desist

from squandering the environmental capital it inherits but try to leave the planet in a fit state for their children to use. Similarly, the rich countries should agree to assist the poorer South in its attempts to attain economic development without imperilling the goal of environmental safety.

3. Sustainability also demands that in future we prioritize quality of life rather than higher material living standards measured solely in monetary terms. Instead of the obsession with acquiring a second or larger car, we would do well to worry more about our ability to breathe city air without contracting asthma or the availability of unspoiled scenery along with sufficient leisure time to enjoy it.

CRITIQUE OF SUSTAINABLE DEVELOPMENT

The idea of sustainable development has been widely criticized. According to Lele (1991: 613), the chief difficulty is that it tries to offer a 'metafix' that will unite everybody from green activists, conservationists and poor farmers in the South to development-oriented governments and large companies. It therefore fails to provide much of real substance for anyone. For example, as we have seen, the proponents of sustainable development claim that reducing poverty through further economic growth will make an essential contribution to reducing environmental devastation. However, Lele (1991: 614) states that, by itself, economic growth has never been sufficient to reduce poverty or inequality. It is difficult to see, therefore, how it can contribute to environmental sustainability in the absence of additional policies aimed at overcoming poverty through redistributing incomes in favour of deprived groups.

Box 20.2.

The resistance to GM crops/foods

What are GM crops?

These are crops like soya, maize and oilseed rape that have had their genetic structures modified in laboratories by introducing specific genes (taken from unrelated life forms such as bacteria) into the genetic code of the crops. The two most common modifications, which in 2003 accounted for most of the 59 million hectares in commercial cultivation, involve either the implantation of a gene that gives crops resistance to certain insects without the use of chemical pesticides or one that enables plants to remain healthy when exposed to herbicides so that only weeds are killed when these are applied.

Who produces GM seeds and where are they being grown?

In 2003, GM crops were being grown in 16 countries, but 99 per cent were cultivated in only four countries – the USA (66 per cent), Argentina (23 per cent), Canada (6 per cent) and China (4 per cent). The agricultural biotech industry is dominated by four TNCs – Syngenta, Bayer CropScience, Monsanto and Du Pont. Previous revolutions in agriculture, such as the post-Second World War Green Revolution, harnessed science to farming by breeding higher yielding seeds and linking this to fertilizers and irrigation but they did not use genetic modification.

The debate over GM crops

The biotech industry and its supporters argue that GM seeds make farmers' work easier and cheaper because they will need to spend less on pesticides and herbicides. It is also claimed that GM seeds can help to overcome poverty if grown by farmers in the South because crops would be more abundant and cheaper to grow. What is clear is that these companies have cleverly linked their seeds – which can only be produced in laboratories, under licence, and so must be bought anew each year – to their production of herbicides and pesticides. If widely used, they would gain a monopolistic and powerful hold over the world's farmers and consumers.

Opponents are consumer groups and most green campaigners. Among their counter-arguments are:

■ GM cultivation creates huge risks, especially the possibility that cross-pollination by insects will spread the new genes and their properties uncontrollably into the wider environment. No one can be sure what the long-term impact may be, for example the emergence of powerful herbicide-resistant weeds, or threats to the health of the people who eat GM foods or the animals to which the crops are fed.

■ The biotech industry is unlikely ever to be seriously interested in the crops that poor farmers grow in the South compared with the highly commercial crops like soya and maize grown for the meat industry or for processed foods consumed by the better off. In fact, little research on poor farmers' crops has so far been carried out.

■ The gains to consumers or farmers in terms of cost reductions have been small and certainly insufficient to justify the risks involved, though they clearly benefit the biotech companies.

Mass resistance and its impact

Ever since GM crops first appeared in the EU and other countries in the late 1990s, their introduction has been widely opposed not only by green campaigners and organic farmers but also by schoolchildren, housewives, local government councillors and many others. Campaigners have often broken the law by destroying GM crops, especially in EU countries:

■ So considerable was consumer opposition to GM foods that the EU placed a six-year moratorium on the import or cultivation of GM foods, though some governments, as in the UK, are reluctant to allow their national biotech industry to lose out in competition with the USA and have continued to support field trials and encourage public investigations.

■ Similarly, some supermarkets refused to stock food containing GM ingredients.

■ This opposition angered the US government and its agro-industry. By 2003, it threatened to take its complaint against the EU to the WTO on the grounds that the EU rules interfered with free trade.

■ Anti-GM activism has continued to ebb and flow while consumer unpopularity has continued more or less unabated across the EU.

■ In the UK, the Welsh Assembly declared the areas under their jurisdiction a GM-free zone. Indeed, in the summer of 2005, more than 100 GM-free regions existed across the EU, with around 3,500 similar actions undertaken by local authorities.

SOURCES: *The Economist* (26 July 2003: 25); Rowell (2003); Lynas (2004); Friends of the Earth (2005: 8)

Sachs (1993), another major critic, fears that the concept of sustainability and its related ethos of environmental managerialism have generated a new breed of elite, global 'eco-crats'. This group has 'hijacked' the green agenda from the more radical groups. Unlike many individuals and green activists, the eco-crats do not regard the biosphere as a fragile heritage that needs to be protected for posterity. Rather, they regard it as a 'commercial asset in danger' (Sachs 1993: xvii). The earth's dwindling resources require worldwide management by, and on behalf of, the rich and powerful.

COLLABORATION WITH ELITE INSTITUTIONS: RISKS AND NEW PATHS

Green INGOs and global social movements have often collaborated with elite agents to their mutual advantage. The former have gained because the willingness of UN agencies and states to provide increasing access to important global events has given green activists a platform on which to express grassroots concerns and an opportunity to influence global policy-making. However, nation-states and UN agencies also benefit because green groups have resources that may facilitate the search for environmental solutions. These include technical expertise, a reputation for integrity, an intimate knowledge of local peoples and wide-ranging support from the grass roots, the media, and professional groups. All these give green groups considerable bargaining power. In the late 1980s, 10–15 per cent of the development funding that OECD countries sent to the South was routed through NGOs (Princen and Finger 1994: 34).

While collaboration with governments on green issues has generally been positive, even governments with excellent environmental records may, on occasion, find they have to respond to national economic interests rather than transnational causes. Norway's reluctance to sign the international moratorium on commercial whaling in the 1980s is a case in point. At the same time, the absence of a world government and the current reluctance of the USA – the nearest thing we have to a hegemonic power – to do much about green issues mean that reaching effective global agreements is fraught with difficulties. In addition, growing competition to attract foreign investment along with the increasingly footloose nature of capital means that governments are less and less willing to take steps that might deter investment by TNCs (Clapp 1997: 127). Indeed, the unwillingness of states to place too many environmental constraints on TNCs has recently led many green NGOs and global social movements to switch the targets of their campaigning to the large global corporations. The aim here has been to fill the void in international regulation left by government reluctance to frustrate or annoy business (Newall 1998).

There are always likely to be situations in which nation-states, businesses and other elite interests are unwilling to enforce necessary environmental policies. Green NGOs and global social movements often respond by seeking to mobilize pressure from below to compel states and others to accept the need for more radical agendas. The Rainforest Action Network (RAN) is an example of this. Alarmed by the continuing deforestation of the Amazon region (which Brazil's need to service huge debts was exacerbating) and its growing threat to wildlife and local peoples, Northern green groups began to oppose further Amazonian development schemes. In 1983, a US coalition of green NGOs forced the World Bank and other big multilateral development banks (MDBs) to recognize what impact their lending schemes were having on local people and the environment. (MDBs provide low-interest loans for large-scale works like Brazil's gigantic Polonoroeste and highway projects.) In 1985, a number of US university groups formed the RAN and by 1990 it had 150 branches plus another 100 worldwide, which supported the coalition to alter MDB lending policies. RAN also led a consumer boycott of leading restaurant chains like Burger King because their beef imports came from ranches carved out of South American rainforests. The World Bank eventually agreed to take more account of green issues when deciding future loans. Green INGOs learnt much from this episode. It helped to blaze the trail for a number of similar transnational alliances in Malaysia, Bolivia, India and Indonesia (see Scarce 1990: Chapter 8; Bramble and Porter 1992: 325–34; various issues of the *Ecologist* in 1994).

MOBILIZING BOTTOM-UP SUPPORT FOR LOCAL AND GLOBAL ACTION

When it comes to activating grassroots support, green groups may have several aims. One involves the need to mobilize supporters to engage in controversial protests and political struggles, perhaps initially little understood or supported. Sometimes, these are directed against clearly identifiable and powerful agents of environmental destruction, such as governments intent on implementing massive development projects, oil companies, timber importers or agricultural companies like Monsanto that are trying to persuade governments, farmers and consumers to accept GM foods. On other occasions, actions are more likely to draw attention to the complicity of ordinary members of the public. Thus, as Newell (2006) observes, while some environmental issues, for example killing whales or the dangers CFCs pose to the ozone layer, can catch the public imagination with relative ease and require little change in everyday behaviour, winning public support on many other issues can be problematic. The reason for this is that to different degrees we all act in ways that contribute towards environmental deterioration, though often unwittingly. As such, we are all potential targets of green criticism.

Newell (2006) points to two factors that complicate this situation. First, there are intergenerational implications when 'benefits of action will be felt in years to come but sacrifices have to be made now'. Second, with the really 'big' issue of how to deal with climate change, it is hard for campaigners to 'package measures … in appealing and attractive terms where there are perceived threats to people's standards of living or freedom of choice' (Newell 2006: 90, 109). Examples of the sacrifices that consumers are being asked to make would include a preference for cheap food despite dangerous chemical contamination or cruel methods of factory farming, reducing their use of private cars or paying more for fuel. The organizers of the protest against fuel taxes in the UK during 2000 attracted a lot of public support despite the obvious long-term environmental benefits of measures designed to reduce petrol consumption and greenhouse gas emissions. We might call this the 'hard' or fighting edge of the green movement.

The previous point demonstrates the need for environmental groups to work consistently towards raising the consciousness of ordinary citizens. Not only do we all *need* to contribute to making a greener world, but, with a little assistance and education, most of us, perhaps, are quite *capable* of doing so. On the other hand, not all lifestyle activities require us to make large sacrifices and not everything linked to environmentalism requires radical collective action. Examples include recycling household rubbish or buying furniture produced from environmentally managed forests. If large numbers of people adopt ordinary, everyday lifestyle changes, they may make a critical contribution to the attainment of green objectives. We might regard such actions as the 'soft' side of environmentalism. Mostly, they have deep roots in individual and domestic life and prompt the need steadily to alter opinion over time.

Somewhere in between the two extremes of 'hard' and 'soft' environmental commitment is a cluster of activities for which green groups can count on dedicated minorities to support specific campaigns. These might involve joining a mass public protest like a march or picket. Equally, however, the decision by sympathizers – each mostly working in isolation – to exercise their right to make selective choices as consumers, shareholders, taxpayers or users of various facilities, can sometimes be very effective. In this case, the products or services provided by one bank, company or institution are boycotted while those provided by others are favoured. Ethical share investment provides a similar example.

In Chapter 18, we argued that because so much social movement activity is embedded in life politics and personal identity, global social movements and INGOs are able to transcend purely local protests. Local struggles can then be thrown into the maelstrom of transnational action in the pursuit of global goals. Selective buying campaigns are likely to play a particularly important role because they are relatively easy to activate and coordinate simultaneously across countries. Thus, while there are many situations for which the most practical option is to seek global support to solve *local* problems – 'act locally, think globally' – increasingly it is both necessary and possible to mobilize local support to solve *global* problems.

There are three other factors that have enabled global social movements and INGOs to undertake successful transnational actions:

1. Their skill in focusing worldwide media attention on different environmental crises through various kinds of stunts and the ability to harness the opportunities provided by recent advances in electronic communications.
2. Their bargaining power with respect to elite agents because of their reputation, close ties to sympathetic scientists, their acquisition of technical expertise and their role in educating the public.
3. Their access to numerous cross-issue and transnational networks, coalitions and alliances in which groups may participate and the growing repertoire of techniques available for political protest.

The ability of green groups to utilize some or all these resources simultaneously may empower them to lobby elite groups directly. Failing this, they may wield the 'implicit threat of embarrassing delinquent governments' (Clapp 1997: 135) or other agents such as TNCs whose environmental record is unacceptable. INGOs are especially effective in activating transnational pressures for change because in addition to political activities as campaigners, they are also organizations run by semi-permanent officials. Consequently, they enjoy continuity, access to regular sources of information and links with other relevant organizations. Many can also fall back on regular financial resources through membership subscriptions. All this gives INGOs considerable flexibility with respect to synchronizing actions across distances and between events and issues.

REVIEW

Environmentalism may have a potentially universal appeal because we all bear some responsibility for green problems and most of us can and perhaps need to contribute to finding solutions through accepting personal lifestyle changes while supporting appropriate public policies. Presumably, we also stand to gain from the preservation of a safe, vibrant natural world. In any case, as many countries in the South rush headlong towards industrialization, so environmental distress is becoming globalized.

Because global problems demand global solutions, it is hardly surprising that the green movement has increasingly sought to operate transnationally. Partly what enables green groups to be globally effective is their capacity to construct viable linkages between different countries, groups and issues. But what also empowers them is their growing ability to collaborate with states and powerful elite interests when that appears useful, while activating transnational grassroots support for more radical agendas whenever the opposition to change displayed by the former makes this necessary. By and large, we should welcome top-down initiatives. Actions by TNCs, IGOs and above all by nation-states are usually helpful because they can affect the structural constraints on social behaviour in far-reaching ways. For example, only states can introduce the green taxes, financial incentives and national policies that encourage or compel individuals, corporations and others to adopt more environmentally friendly practices. Moreover, states 'remain the only actors who can legally reach international environmental accords, and ... are ultimately held responsible for those agreements' (Clapp 1997: 137).

However, such collaboration may undermine the autonomy of green groups and their capacity to demand radical change by activating grassroots pressure. Anything that weakens their capacity to shape global opinion and influence policy-making effectively could jeopardize our future. This is not because green INGOs and global social movements are always right and nation-states or TNCs are invariably wrong, although the public is usually more inclined to trust the former than the latter. Rather, the difficulty is that governments face constraints that may undermine their ability to lead in the environmental arena. In part this is because the primary duty of states is to protect national sovereignty, for example by guaranteeing military security. This makes them reluctant to delegate their powers to supranational regulatory bodies for global environmental purposes, an outcome that may become more urgent as our fragile earth lurches from one environmental crisis to the next.

For their part, NGOs and global social movements must avoid becoming compromised by elite interests. Above all, they must do nothing to lose, indeed they need to expand, their grassroots support wherever possible. Despite this need to protest their mass support, activists need to collaborate with governments, IGOs and business interests wherever possible because the latters' potential role in fostering the conditions for environmental improvement is often paramount. Negotiating a path through this political minefield is difficult and risky.

FURTHER READING

- R. Scarce's *Eco-warriors: Understanding the Radical Environmental Movement* (1900) offers a lively introduction to green radicalism. Chapter 8 deals with international movements.

- S. Yearley's *Sociology, Environmentalism, Globalization* (1996) assesses environmentalism's global claims and the debate on sustainable development from a thoroughly sociological perspective.

- The Worldwatch Institute's *State of the World 2004* focuses specifically on how contemporary consumer behaviour is linked to environmental problems, but some chapters also consider what can be done to alleviate these through adopting simple lifestyle changes.

- A. Dobson's *Green Political Thought* (2000) provides a clear and interesting exposition of green thinking; try especially Chapters 1, 3 and 4.

- The chapter by P. Newell, in *Global Civil Society 2005/06,* offers an excellent, lively and thoughtful analysis of recent changes in the green movement.

GROUP WORK

1. Refer to your library's copy of the *Ecologist*, published six times each year. Most issues run a feature called Campaigns. A group of students could agree in advance to check the back issues for Campaigns, listing the various types of green protests discussed and following through how they developed. To what extent did these protests become transnational? What kinds of global connections were established?

2. Arrange a debate on the proposition that 'The global nature and claims of the environmental movement have been greatly exaggerated.' After the speakers have been heard, each remaining class member will give two reasons why they either agree or disagree.

3. Access two or more of the following websites and, using them as a resource, construct a debate around the following theme: 'Achieving real gains on greenhouse gas emissions worldwide will only be possible if the issues of climate injustice and North–South inequalities are closely linked': www. risingtide.org.uk; www.ejcc.org; www.indiaresource.org; www.ejrc.cau.edu.

QUESTIONS TO THINK ABOUT

?

1. Many environmental activists claim that they represent the interests of all humanity. Evaluate the validity of such claims.

2. On balance, who gains most from collaboration, environmental groups or elite interests such as states, IGOs and TNCs? Explain your answer.

3. Examine the obstacles that made it difficult to implement the principle of sustainable development on a realistic basis worldwide?

4. 'We may all be culpable where global environmental problems are concerned but some are much more responsible than others.' Discuss.

WHAT'S ON THE WEB

- www.risingtide.org.uk; www.ejcc.org; www.indiaresource.org; www.ejrc.cau.edu Linking the environmental movement to the global justice movement is discussed on these sites.

- http://www.earthrights.org/ EarthRights International is a non-profit group comprised of lawyers and activists concerned with human rights, government accountability and the environment. There are some useful articles found there too.

- http://egj.lib.uidaho.edu/backis.html The University of Idaho has been publishing an electronic green journal, with full-text access since 1994. The first issues seem rather amateurish, but the journal is now fully professional, refereed and of good quality.

- http://www.rachelcarson.org/ Sometimes nominated as one of the 10 books that changed the world is Rachel Carson's *Silent Spring* (1963), which anticipated many of the concerns of the green movement. This website is perhaps a little too reverential, but gives a good sense of the history of the green movement.

Identities and Belonging

CONTENTS

A major theme of this book has been that of commonality and difference. In various places we have talked about the ways in which people are pushed apart, treated in unequal ways or socially excluded. In this chapter, we are concerned with social *inclusion* – how social ties are generated and sustained at different levels. Scheff has proposed that the maintenance of social bonds is 'our most crucial human motive' (1990: 4). The relationship between closeness and distance, he continues, gives rise to a theoretically optimal level of differentiation, 'which balances the needs of the individual and the needs of the self. It involves being able to maintain ties with others who are different from self.' These bonds are often formalized in associations, but are usually more loosely expressed in **COMMUNITIES** or other units of belonging.

key **concept**	**COMMUNITIES** are marked by deep, familiar and cooperative ties between members. In this sense, 'community' is close to Durkheim's idea of social solidarity, which emerges from commitment to a shared set of values. He calls this 'the collective conscience'. A formal definition is given by Nisbet (1970: 47). For him, community 'encompasses all forms of relationship which are characterized by a high degree of personal intimacy, emotional depth, moral commitment, social cohesion and continuity in time'.

There are many units of social solidarity – the family, organizations including work and voluntary associations, ethnicity, religion, or nation. Given the main theme of the book, we are also interested in the possibilities of creating communities at a global level. These different expressions of community can be seen simply as indicating differences in scale, starting from the most immediate and intimate and ending at the most macroscopic and remote. It might be tempting to assume that the ties that bind people most strongly are the most immediate and intimate and those that seem most abstract are the weakest or of little value. However, this view is much too simple, as can be seen in the following examples:

■ *The nuclear family:* Some of the previously most intimate of social bonds, like the nuclear family in industrial societies, are undergoing massive changes. In the USA, for example, over the period 1970–95 the marriage rate fell by 30 per cent, the number of never married people doubled, the divorce rate increased by 40 per cent, unmarried couple households increased sevenfold, while half of all children expected to spend at least part of their childhood in single-parent homes (Tischler 1999: 353–4). A more relaxed attitude to gay and lesbian partnerships has also altered the marriage figures, though in some countries, 'civil partnerships' between gay couples are now permitted. By 2000, there were 957,200 divorces each year in the USA, just over four out of every ten marriages. Such data partly reflect changing gender expectations, the restructuring of the labour market and more relaxed attitudes to sexual norms. In all, there is no doubt that family life, as conventionally conceived, has radically altered in a significant number of countries in the West.

■ *Transnational communities:* By contrast, 'space–time compression' has encouraged an increasing volume and intensity of ties (for example through tourism, family visits and migration) of people who were previously less intimately linked. Further interconnections and interdependencies have been promoted mainly by the spread of a worldwide economic market and a network of increasingly powerful transnational actors and organizations, such as the TNCs. A sense of global community has also been fostered by common challenges facing all the world's inhabitants – from threats to the biosphere to poorly policed nuclear arsenals. These planetary problems have generated an awareness of global issues (we have called this 'globality') and a form of worldwide politics, seen in the growth and support for global social movements like the 'greens' and feminists, discussed in earlier chapters.

The bonds that social actors feel and experience at these different levels are not mutually exclusive. Rather, they are reactive, contradictory and complementary. On the one hand, the scale, pace and intensity of global changes have led to fears of atomization and anonymization. A powerful set of reactions has reasserted the salience and continued viability of local communities and forms of belonging. On the other hand, some intimate characteristics of small, old communities have been transferred to a larger scale. A nation, for example, you will remember from Chapter 5, was memorably described as an 'imagined community'. Again, Faist (1998: 221) and others have shown how transnational communities are 'connected by dense and strong social and symbolic ties over time and across space [by] patterns of networks and circuits'. They are 'communities without propinquity, in which community and spatial proximity are decoupled'. Some communities, for example religious ones, seem to have discovered a way of incorporating two or more levels of appeal.

Using the criterion of 'level of appeal', we propose loosely to classify 'communities' under three headings:

1. *Localism* – the behaviour of communities that act on a relatively small scale (this covers all movements based on family, kin, ethnic and subnational sentiments).
2. *Nationalism* – seeks to create anew, reassert or reform the nation-state as a continuing focus of loyalty and association.
3. *Transnationalism and multi-level identity* – working, as they see it, *with* the grain of history are those states, groups, organizations and individuals that recognize diversity and difference and seek to foster creative and positive bonds between peoples of different national backgrounds or seek to appeal across local, national and global levels.

THE RESURGENCE OF LOCALISM

Despite, or perhaps because of, all the global forces acting to make people come together, fierce struggles have ensued to continue to keep people apart. Notwithstanding the end of the Cold War and increased economic globalization, we have been confronted by many localized ethnic and religious conflicts. As the bipolar ideological struggle between capitalism and communism has evaporated, it has partly been replaced by the politics of identity and community. Premdas (1996) estimated that there were 4,000 'ethnocultural' groups worldwide, uneasily enclosed in (at that time) 185 states. With migration, commerce and travel, nearly all states are now multiethnic to some degree: the few exceptions include Somalia, Korea, Botswana and Swaziland. Some 40 per cent of the world's states have more than five significant ethnic communities. Just seven years after the collapse of the Berlin Wall (the symbolic end of the Cold War), there were 100 ongoing subnational conflicts, about 20 classified as 'high intensity'. To contain these conflicts, some of the peace dividend had to be spent on 70,000 UN peace-keepers costing US$4 billion each year to maintain.

Many observers have been alarmed at the increasingly militant demands for ethnic exclusivity, minority language education, religious separatism and exclusive territorial entities. The conflicts between Kosovars and Serbs in the Balkans, Hutu and Tutsi in Rwanda, Christians and Muslims in Lebanon, Jews and Arabs in the Middle East, Tamils and Sinhalese in Sri Lanka, Protestants and Catholics in Northern Ireland, and rival clans in Somalia – these examples and many more show the persistence, tenacity or re-emergence of ethnic and religious differences.

This phenomenon presents a paradox to the theorists of globalization. If social, political, cultural and economic changes are all thought to be moving in a global or macro direction, why do we see throughout the world evidence of the contrary tendency – namely the assertion, or sometimes the reassertion, of local identities? A partial solution to this paradox may be found in the writings of Stuart Hall. He suggests that globalization at the cultural level has also brought about the frag-mentation and multiplication of identities and this may require, paradoxically, a return to the familiar. Hall (1991: 35–6) described the process like this:

> The face-to-face communities that are knowable, that are locatable, one can give them a place. One knows what the voices are. One knows what the faces are. The recreation, the reconstruction of imaginary, knowable places in the face of the global post-modern which has, as it were, destroyed the identities of specific places, absorbed them into this post-modern flux of diversity. So one understands the moment when people reach for those groundings, as it were, and the reach for those groundings is what we call ethnicity.

In other words, ethnicity is not an irrelevant anachronism to the gathering pace of globalization but a necessary reaction to it. It is true that we are becoming increasingly interdependent in economic and cultural terms, that there is an increased awareness that we are 'one world' facing common ecological, political and security problems. Yet this very process of globalization, the very rapidity of the dissolution of the known world, creates an unexpected effect. People reach out to the habitual, to the communities where they find familiar faces, voices, sounds, smells, tastes and places. Confronted by the pace of globalization, they often need ethnicity *more* not less. Confused by the effects of postmodernity, relativism and the deconstruction of their known world, they reaffirm and reify what they believe to be true.

■ ■

Global Thinkers 21 ZYGMUNT BAUMAN (1925–)

Zygmunt Bauman is Emeritus Professor of Sociology at Leeds. He is a marvellous example of the phenomenon of a 'second wind', having produced over 20 books since his retirement. The sociologist Richard Sennett suggests that Bauman (born in Poland) made the right decision not to settle in the USA: 'He would have felt very marginal there. He is one of those displaced intellectuals who has come home to Britain; they never assimilate, but at the same time they are very comfortable. They all dwell on the great crises of central European culture – the Second World War, Holocaust, communism and its collapse. It speaks well for Britain that these men could work out this crisis of European humanism here' (Sennett quoted by Bunting 2003). As Bauman's writing moves seamlessly between Russian, Polish, French, German and English sources, one does indeed sense that all Europe's predicaments – war, displacement, fragile boundaries, extermination, loss and resettlement – are steeped in his bones and saturated his mind.

The focus of this chapter is on 'identities and belonging', on which themes Bauman has made some important contributions, but before covering these, we must record that Bauman is a general social theorist of modernity and postmodernity. His most controversial book was Modernity and the Holocaust *(1991) in which he discounts as explanations for the Holocaust the peculiarities of German history and culture, the notion that Germans had an authoritarian character or that the horrific events were an atavistic reversion to some barbarian and irrational past (Bauman 1991: 211–12). Instead, 'the Holocaust was as much a product, as it was a failure, of modern civilization. Like everything else done in the modern – rational, planned, scientifically informed, expert, efficiently managed, coordinated – way, the Holocaust left behind and put to shame all its alleged premodern equivalents, exposing them as primitive, wasteful and ineffective by comparison' (Bauman 1991: 89).*

The book caused a sensation in Germany and in Jewish studies, for it was interpreted somehow as displacing 'blame' to a system and letting the Germans 'off the hook'. This is something of a misinterpretation of Bauman's intentions. He was clear that the ultra-modernist Nazis adopted a sinister intent to Gypsies and Jews because of their 'permanent and irremedial homelessness', which formed such an integral part of Jewish identity 'from the beginning of their diasporic history' (Bauman 1991: 35). The homeless nature of identity becomes a more general characteristic in the postmodern period. It becomes 'light' or 'liquid'. 'The search for identity', he argues, 'is the ongoing struggle to arrest or slow down the flow, to solidify the fluid, to give form to the formless … Yet far from slowing the flow, let alone stopping it, identities are more like the spots of crust hardening time and time again on the top of volcanic lava which melt and dissolve again before they have time to cool and set' (Bauman 2000: 82–3).

Elsewhere, Bauman suggests that 'the problem of identity' is radically different under conditions of modernity and postmodernity. In the former, typified, say, by nation-building, the problem is 'how to construct an identity and keep it solid and stable'. Under postmodernity, the problem is to 'avoid fixation and keep the options open' (Bauman 1995: 81). One thinks of identity, he continues, when you are not sure where you belong: it is an 'escape from uncertainty' (Bauman 1995: 82).

SOURCES: Bauman (1991, 1995, 2000); Bunting (2003)

For many people, ethnic ties are a matter of loyalty, pride, location, belonging, refuge, identity, trust, acceptance and security. It is the type of attachment that most parents feel for their children and most siblings feel for one another. As Allahar (1994) suggested, such ties imply an unquestioned affinity and devotion purely on the basis of the intimacy of the tie. It is the closest form of association that can be achieved by a collectivity of humans. It expresses their gregariousness and preference for group membership rather than the social rejection of a misfit or the isolation of a hermit. By embracing an ethnic identity (or some similar group affiliation), groups of human beings acknowledge that they are part of society and that their survival depends on forces bigger than the individual. The locality into which they were born and that has nurtured them is an object of affection – in that place are others who share their origin and their likely fate.

MARGINALIZING LOCAL IDENTITIES

We have ventured some arguments about why ethnic ties are more resilient than many observers predicted. Their continuing strength accounts for the simultaneity of globalization and localization. However, we also need to clarify why the force of ethnicity was (relatively speaking) neglected in social theory until the 1980s. There is no doubt that those who believed that only one global future was possible overlooked the continuing power of ethnicity, race and religion. In the postwar world, the two dominant interpretations of social change, modernization theory and Marxism, which we will discuss in turn, also marginalized ethnicity.

MODERNIZATION THEORISTS

Derived from eighteenth- and nineteenth-century notions of progress, modernization theorists posited increasing secularization, urbanization, industrialization and rationalization – spread by the emerging state bureaucracies. Ethnicity and nation were things of the past – a receding reality. It had, of course, to be conceded that even modern nations, such as Nazi Germany, had experienced massive upsurges of a dangerous nationalist spirit. But this had been defeated and many of the characterizations of the phenomenon used the language of primitivism to describe National Socialism. For example, it was denounced as 'abnormal', 'deviant', or 'atavistic'. The implication was that that since Nazism had been vanquished, Germany could be normalized and returned to the modern fold. Educators who were sent into Germany after the war specifically had the task of 'de-Nazifying' the state. Ultimately, rationalism, secularization, constitutionalism and liberal democracy would prevail. This package had, in turn, to be sold to the 'emerging nations'.

The second dominant interpretation of social change was Marxism, which, like modernization theory, was largely dismissive of ethnic and national loyalties. As we mentioned in Chapter 6, Marxists argued that dominant or rising classes used ethnicity and nationalism cynically for instrumental purposes of their own. Competing elites need the masses for raw street power and ethnic appeals worked to arouse the poor and uninformed. Marxists sought to abolish ethnicity as merely an **epiphenomenon** or an instance of 'false consciousness'. For Marxists the only form of true consciousness was class consciousness. But while class may indeed be a powerful form of association, powerful enough sometimes to rival or overdetermine ethnic consciousness, it makes little sense to call the one 'true' and dismiss the other as 'false' consciousness.

> An **epiphenomenon** is something that appears to be of great causal significance, but is really derived from some other primary basis. In overvaluing an epiphenomenon, observers mistake a symptom for a reason.

Class consciousness arises, as Marx stated, from objectively different relationships to the means of production, distribution and exchange shared by those who sell their labour power, own capital or trade in commodities or services. These different positions give them different interests. As is now generally accepted, contemporary capitalism has produced the conditions in which these interests have become overlapping and thereby diluted. However, a more fundamental critique of the idea of a superordinate class consciousness is that class awareness is predominantly an awareness of *interest*. And, despite the mantras of the Marxists and the free marketeers alike, people live not just by interests alone, but by their emotions. They live by anger, grief, anxiety, jealousy, affection, fear and devotion – precisely those emotions harnessed by localism. As we have seen in Chapter 16, despite determined attempts by communist governments in the Soviet Union and Cuba to abolish religion, religious sentiment remains strong and enduring.

HOW DOES LOCALISM ARISE?

We have argued so far that kinship, ethnicity and religion are more powerful forces than many would, perhaps, like to accept. We have also suggested that localism does not disappear when confronted with the rival claims of class interest, the demands of nation-building, state-promoted atheism, or the impelling force of globalization. The Marxist charge of false consciousness is contradicted by the weight of historical evidence that many more people are prepared to fight and die for their ethnic group, nation and religion than for their class. Perhaps we should spell this out. Class war takes the form of strikes, marches and meetings (very rarely are the barricades of class revolution raised). By contrast, the stakes seem to be higher in ethnic, religious and national wars, which often take the form of mass destruction, ethnic cleansing, saturation bombing, genocide, nuclear attack, defoliation, inquisitions and terrorism.

Figure 21.1 **Drumcree, Northern Ireland, July 1999**
Members of the Orange Order commemorate the defeat of the Irish at the Battle of the Boyne in 1690.
Their hostility to 'Popish plots' remains largely undiminished, despite some years of peace.

Even if we accept that ethnicity, race and religion are uncomfortably powerful *subjective* forces, can we explain how ethnic differences arise *objectively*? There are four ways, discussed in turn, in which structural factors and established patterns of social behaviour can mould ethnicity:

■ legal and political restrictions that force differences to remain or create them for the first time
■ a history of coerced labour that has moulded ethnic work hierarchies
■ differences in appearance
■ the forms of belief that pattern people's responses to difference.

LEGAL AND POLITICAL RESTRICTIONS

In many settings there were legal and political restrictions on which occupations and activities were permitted to subordinated groups. We will give just one, admittedly extreme, example. Until the end of legal apartheid in South Africa in 1989, people designated as 'Bantu', 'white', 'Coloured and 'Asian' were legally separated from one another, while the Bantu (black African) section of the population was subdivided into ethnicities like the Zulu, Tswana, Venda and Xhosa. While we can all recognize the artificiality of a number of these distinctions, the argument has to be pressed one stage further. Legalized ethnic distinctions were given force in economic, educational, residential and occupational terms and this determined the limits of opportunity in terms of access to good housing, jobs or healthcare. Ethnic identities were, in short, not freely selected but *imposed* by law, regulation, police action and the threat of state violence.

HISTORY OF COERCED MIGRATION

Ethnic, racial and religious differences also arose through various kinds of coerced migration. Colonial and mercantile powers often brought different peoples to new settings for work on their plantations or to further their commercial interests. For example, 10 million African slaves were shipped across the Atlantic, while 1.4 million Indian indentured workers were sent to the sugar plantations. The governor of Dutch Indonesia even sent warships to capture Chinese on the mainland to help develop his colony. These patterns of involuntary migration led to complex, often three-way, interactions as indigenous people faced outsiders, who faced other outsiders, who all faced representatives of the colonial powers. Alluding to the time and circumstances in which immigrants were brought in, we can see how occupational categories fused with ethnic identities. Thus, we have an evolution of paired 'ethno-occupations', a phenomenon evoked by these familiar descriptions: 'Chinese traders', 'Indian "coolies"', 'Sikh soldiers', 'Irish navvies', 'Lebanese middlemen' or 'Scottish engineers'.

DIFFERENCES IN APPEARANCE

A third objective factor to limit how ethnicity is subjectively constructed is the one that is both obvious yet uncomfortable to state openly. Quite often people look rather different one to another. In popular language they are white, brown, black or yellow, dark- or light-skinned, Nordic-, Mediterranean-, Latin American- or Asian-looking. Of course, these are absurdly unscientific categories and we fully accept that the human species overwhelmingly shares a common set of characteristics and traits. We do not want to engage in ridiculous exercises in racial typology. Rather, we want simply to affirm that appearance – technically phenotype – can provide constraints on how far one can imagine oneself into another ethnicity. There are, in other words, bodily limits to the manipulative use of identity changes, although many inventive and adventurous individuals have managed to push those limits quite far (Box 21.1).

Box 21.1	**Changing identities: Barry Cox becomes Gok Pak-wing**

Gregg Zachary (1999), an American journalist, described how Barry Cox, a 21-year-old man from Liverpool, pushed at the limits of how far he could change his own social identity. Mr Cox has an English working-class background, eats meat pies and likes cricket. At high school he became fascinated by Chinese popular culture. He experimented with martial arts and enjoyed the soundtracks to the Jackie Chan movies. Hanging around his local fish and chip shops, he met many of Liverpool's own Chinese community, some of whom run the local 'chippies'.

Frustrated that he could not understand those Chinese who did not speak

English, he studied Cantonese and found he could understand and learn it. He worked as a waiter in a Chinese restaurant so that he could practise his language skills and now works in a Chinese grocery store. He has a Chinese name, Gok Pak-wing (meaning 'long life'), and dates a British-born Chinese woman. Gok Pak-wing and his partner's Shanghai-born parents are concerned that she can't speak Chinese.

Although working in a grocery store, Gok's ambition is to be a Chinese pop star. He has already won some local contests, singing such 'Canto-pop' songs in Cantonese as 'Kiss under the moon', 'Kiss once more' and 'Ten words of an angel'. The title of his original song, which his fans love, translates as 'I think I am Chinese. I want to be Chinese'. Despite his obviously English appearance, he seems to have convinced some of his fans. One asked him 'Are you English or Chinese?' Another insisted that his intonation was so good 'his father must be Chinese'.

Cox/Gok's English mother, Valerie, says: 'He lives, breathes and sleeps Chinese. I think he'd actually be Chinese if he could.' Cox/Gok concurs: 'If I didn't mix with Chinese and sing Chinese, what would I be doing now? I'd just be a normal person, nothing special about me. Although I know I'm not Chinese, I'm trying to put myself in a Chinese body.'

SOURCE AND ALL QUOTES: Zachary (1999)

ETHNIC SUBJECTIVITIES

The fourth factor driving the strength of ethnicity derives from an appreciation of social behaviour. What is the meaning of ethnicity to the actors themselves and how do they respond? The visibility (or sometimes the fevered imagining) of ethnic differences allows them to be seen as 'primordial' or fundamental, reaching to the very heart of one's social being. An outside observer may not share this perception, but the participants in ethnic interactions and conflicts may firmly believe they are describing reality. As Weber notably reminded us, sociologists must start from an acceptance of the gap between the observer's view of reality and the subjective and often irrational meanings that people use to make sense of their worlds. We need to accept that distinction because people act out what is in their heads, not in ours. 'What is real in the mind, is real in its consequences' is a tried and tested sociological adage.

Let us illustrate this idea with a simple example in a social setting. If, say, Serbs believe that the Croats are about to bomb their cities, loot their property, rape their women and murder their children, they will seek to defend themselves or will anticipate an attack by initiating one themselves. The Croats respond in kind, thus reinforcing the Serb's original perception that Croats are bombers, looters, rapists and murderers. Fiercer attacks are therefore justified. Within a short time, historical battles are recalled, vengeance is afoot and further recrimination and atrocities transpire.

The mechanisms involved in these encounters are certainly irrational, but they are not inexplicable. Fear of the unknown and **heterophobia** are both marked by a psychological state of unease, extreme anxiety, discomfort and a

Heterophobia is the fear of difference.

sense of loss of control (Bauman 1991: 62–82). Competition over jobs, desirable sexual partners, housing, status, or territory compounds psychological angst, driving it into a higher gear. Sensing attack, people seek a bond with their friends and a clearer definition of their enemies.

This bonding is sometimes so powerful that some people think it is sacred. The ethnic or racial group, a religious faith, sometimes even a whole nation, become objects of worship – civil religions for which some are prepared to die. Slogans and expressions like 'White is right', 'For king and country', 'Deutschland über alles', 'Christ died for you', 'black power', 'mad mullahs' or 'white trash' may seem paltry enough ideas to a 'laid-back' student or an intellectual sophisticate, but they are real enough to the many people who believe in them.

Box 21.2 — Islamophobia and how to recognize it

Heterophobia and ethnocentrism are part and parcel of the same phenomenon – fear of an unknown group leads to anger and misapprehension. Like the pioneer white settlers in the USA featured in Hollywood westerns, the group draws the wagons around itself and prepares to repel all invaders. This 'clannishness' leads to further disparagement, further defensiveness and so on, in a dispiriting downward spiral. One of the most virulent of all recent hate campaigns is directed against people of Islamic origin. 'Islamophobia' is a newly coined world and means the dread and horror (from the Greek word 'phobia') of Muslim people.

Examples of Islamophobia include reports by two experienced and, to many readers, respectable English journalists. In the wake of the Oklahoma bombing, in which numerous lives were lost, there was an immediate and unwarranted suspicion in the USA and UK that this was the work of 'Muslim fanatics'. Bernard Levin, a columnist in *The Times* (21 April 1995) wrote: 'Do you realize that in perhaps half a century not more, and perhaps a good deal less, there will be wars in which fanatical Muslims will be winning? As for Oklahoma, it will be called Khartoum-on-the-Mississippi, and woe betide anyone who calls it anything else.' Charles Moore, then editor of the *Spectator* and subsequently editor of the highly respectable *Daily Telegraph*, supplied another doom-laden warning, with social Malthusian overtones (see Chapter 10). Moore opined: 'Because of our obstinate refusal to have enough babies, Western European civilization will start to die at the point when it could have been revived with new blood. Then the hooded hordes will win, and the Koran will be taught, as Gibbon famously imagined, in the schools of Oxford' (*Spectator*, 9 October 1991).

The Runnymede Trust in the UK, set up to promote good race relations and the understanding of cultural diversity, established a special commission of academics, writers and religious figures to study the rise of Islamophobia (Stubbs 1997). They argued that unreasonable fear of Islam had seven telltale features:

- Muslim cultures are seen as monolithic and unchanging

- Muslim cultures are regarded as wholly different from other cultures

- Islam is seen as implacably threatening

- The Islamic faith is used, it is alleged, mainly for political or military advantage

- Muslim criticisms of Western cultures are rejected out of hand

- Racist immigration restrictions are associated with Islam

- Islamophobia is assumed to be natural and unproblematic.

Each one of these supposed 'features' can be challenged by historical and comparative evidence. For example, as we explain in Chapter 16, Islam as practised in Iraq or Egypt is very different from the religion in Chechenia, Indonesia, Iran and Malaysia. There are also different interpretations of the Koran. As in the history of Christianity, different sects abounded. Moreover, Islamic civilization has closely interacted with Western civilization and made contributions in such diverse areas as architecture, philosophical thought, medicine and the numerals (1, 2, 3, 4) we all use in our daily life.

This is no place for a detailed refutation of Western images of Islam. Rather, as sociologists, we need to be critically aware of the structures of power that underpin different discourses and always question 'commonsense' and stereotypical thinking in order to disclose the social structures and processes that inform them.

NATIONALISM AS A REACTION TO GLOBAL CHANGE

Like localism, nationalism also seems to be on the increase while globalization runs apace. As we saw in Table 5.1, the number of recognized nation-states has proliferated since the foundation of the UN in 1945; from 51 states at the outset, the UN recognized 191 states in 2005. Despite this formal increase in the number of nation-states, a number of observers, as we have shown in Chapter 5, suggest that the autonomy of many nation-states has weakened. The nation-state may become the 'piggy in the middle', rushing from the global to the local level in an attempt to keep in the game. Others argue that the fears arising from global terrorism have forced us to recognize that we can only derive our security ultimately from strengthening the intelligence services, police and armed forces of existing nation-states and giving greater weight to the need for nationwide social cohesion.

The unity of the nation-state rests on a myth of a continuous legitimate authority of a single people. But, in practice, most nation-states are diverse, multi-stranded, richly layered and plural. Indeed, it is part of the achievement of the modern nation-state that this complex history has been ideologically suppressed. Mechanisms were developed for dealing with cultural diversity. Religious wars were resolved. Dissidents often emigrated or were expelled. Different languages were reconciled into a single lingua franca. Flags, anthems, sporting teams, capital cities, grand buildings, icons and symbols reinforced the nation-builders' message. War, trade competition and imperialist rivalries consolidated the processes of national unification. Despite the impress of this history, several limitations to the national project remain:

1. The concept of a homogenizing nation means that some features of the national heritage are arbitrarily selected while others are rejected or sidelined.
2. The notion of an essential national character is seriously flawed. Parekh (1995: 141–2) claims that 'the very language of nationality, nationhood and even national identity is deeply suspect. It cannot avoid offering a homogenized, reified and ideologically biased abridgement of a rich, complex and fluid way

of life, and drawing false contrasts and setting up impregnable walls between different ways of life.'

3. The nation is sometimes presented as the lowest common denominator. Yet, given its fluidity, it is better represented as a series of 'add-on' elements that arrive with each new wave of immigrants.

4. The nation is offered as an object of affection. One is enjoined to love one's country, to revere its institutions, even to fight and die for it in war. In these claims, the nation is a rival form of identification to the subnational ethnic group. But the nation-state is often too large and too amorphous an entity to be the object of intimate affection. One can marry a spouse of one's own kind and feel the warm embrace of kinship; one can kneel in common prayer with one's co-religionists; one can effect easier friendships with those of a common background; one can eat one's own ethnic cuisine and, in a sense, ingest one's ethnicity. (The reference by African-Americans to 'soul food' conveys this idea.)

THE LIMITS OF A MULTICULTURAL NATIONHOOD: THE USA

The inherent difficulty of making something as large as a nation-state an object of common affection does not mean that many national political leaders have not tried in the past to pull off this trick or still see it as a priority. The best known example of an attempt to create a nation from people of diverse cultural backgrounds is the case of the USA. Other nations (like Australia, Canada, Brazil and South Africa) have sought to embrace people of different backgrounds, either because their territories include several groups each claiming a territorial right, or because they were settled by successive waves of immigrants. These 'immigrant countries' comprise some of the most powerful and dynamic nation-states in the world. For the nation-builders in these countries the challenge was to create one nation from a multitude of different components. The Latin slogan *Ex pluribus unum* ('from many, one') became the organizing principle. Speaking for the USA at the end of the nineteenth century, Theodore Roosevelt put in bluntly: 'There can be no fifty-fifty Americanism in this country … there is room here only for 100 per cent Americanism, only for those who are American and nothing else' (cited in Rumbaut 1997).

This idea of 'Americanism' can be understood both as a state **IDEOLOGY** and as something that was diffused from the bottom as well as the top – in night school classes, newspapers, neighbourhood schools and even from church pulpits. Perhaps the most memorable version of this popular message was provided by the American playwright Israel Zangwill, who in 1908 wrote a Broadway hit called *The Melting Pot*. In his play, one of the characters, a refugee from the pogroms of Eastern Europe, makes this impassioned speech:

America is God's crucible, the great melting pot where all the races of Europe are melting and reforming! Here you stand, good folk, think I, when we see them at Ellis Island, here you stand in your fifty groups with your fifty languages and histories, and your fifty blood hatreds and rivalries, but you won't be long like that brothers, for these are the fires of God you've come to – these are the fires of God. A fig for your feuds and vendettas! Germans and Frenchmen, Irishmen and Englishmen, Jews and Russians – into the crucible with you all. God is making the American. (Glazer and Moynihan 1963: 89–90)

key concept	**IDEOLOGY** refers, at a loose level, to a reasonably coherent set of assumptions and convictions shared by a particular social group. Pacifists and vegetarians share an ideology in this sense. Where ideologies are totalizing and universal in their claims (for example communism), they are sometimes referred to as meta-narratives. For some social theorists, ideologies can be contrasted with reason or science, and are used deliberately by ruling groups to obscure real power relations in their own interest.

Although he did not invent the phrase, after Zangwill's play, the expression 'the melting pot' subsequently became a slogan for all those who believed that civic nationalism, modernization, education, class allegiances or better communications would dissolve prior ethnic loyalties. Probably the best known sociological discussion of melting pot theory was Milton Gordon's *Assimilation in American Life* (1964), which, though published over a generation ago, is still widely read. Gordon argued that there was an 'assimilation sequence', whereby people moved from cultural assimilation to structural assimilation and intermarriage and finally to 'identificational assimilation' (namely, they consciously chose to assimilate).

As Rumbaut (1997) notes, it was perhaps difficult for Gordon to imagine what a furore his rather innocent use of the idea of assimilation would cause. For many sociologists at the time, as well as many immigrants to the USA, assimilation merely expressed the process of 'learning the ropes' and 'fitting in'. The bulk of the 35 million immigrants over the period 1870–1914 were Europeans, who appeared to be only too pleased to be escaping the squalor of the great industrial cities and depressed agricultural conditions of countries such as Ireland, Italy and Greece. Loud declarations of loyalty to the USA were heard from many of these European immigrants.

Yet doubts soon began to set in. Just before Gordon's book was published, his fellow sociologists Glazer and Moynihan (1963) had questioned whether the process of assimilation in the USA had gone as far as was commonly believed. The great exceptions to the assimilation process were the African-Americans, who were still trying to assert their basic civil rights, let alone assimilate. The history of coerced (rather than free) migration and slavery had a great deal to do with this outcome, but Native Americans, Asians and others also suffered a high level of discrimination. Even the European groups were highly differentiated in the extent to which they were assimilated, and in their private and social lives, certainly, but also in their capacity to compete for public goods, they often remained stubbornly unmeltable.

A more fundamental critique of assimilation revolved around the question:

'What are immigrants supposed to assimilate to?' Clearly not all cultures were regarded by the powerful elites as enjoying equal status. Many immigrants found they were being asked to assimilate to an 'Anglo' norm, in terms of language, education, political institutions, religious convictions, social conventions and public expectations. It is now three generations on from the staging of Zangwill's play and we are still waiting for the contents of the pot to melt. If anything, there is an increased conviction and even fear on the part of political commentators that the nation-building project is in serious danger of falling apart (Schlesinger 1992).

These fears were given renewed force in the wake of the 9/11 terrorist attacks in New York. In political discourse, the neoconservative and conservative Right in the USA and Europe has questioned the degree of recognition afforded to migrants' home cultures, religions, languages and social practices. The attack on diversity and difference has been particularly fierce in the USA. Perhaps the most powerful academic voice on this question is that of Samuel Huntington (2004), a professor of politics at Harvard and the director of security planning for the National Security Council in the Carter administration. In his *cri de coeur* titled *Who Are We?*, he angrily denounces those in the USA who had discarded earlier notions that the USA was a 'melting pot' or 'tomato soup' and proposed instead that it was more like a 'mosaic' or 'salad bowl' of diverse peoples. He insists on the primacy of the English-speaking, Protestant, eastern seaboard and deplores the 'deconstructionists' who sought to 'enhance the status and influence of subnational racial, ethnic and cultural groups', which, Huntington (2004: 142–3) claims, had deleterious effects on democratic values and liberties:

> They downgraded the centrality of English in American life and pushed bilingual education and linguistic diversity. They advocated legal recognition of group rights and racial preferences over the individual rights central to the American Creed. They justified their actions by theories of multiculturalism and the idea that diversity rather than unity or community should be America's overriding value. The combined effect of these efforts was to promote the deconstruction of the American identity that had been gradually created over three centuries.

Despite these angry words, it seems that because of the extent of travel, migration and global interdependency, the nation-state is going to have to adapt to a more complex mosaic of cultures, religions, languages and citizenships. Often an official declaration of 'multiculturalism', 'cultural pluralism' or 'a rainbow nationhood' signals the end of the attempt by policy-makers to assimilate all elements of the population. Canada, Australia and post-apartheid South Africa have probably gone furthest in welcoming this outcome, while the authorities and many commentators in the USA have remained rather wary. However, detailed empirical work by sociologists like Rumbaut (1997) demonstrates that although assimilation is incomplete, this does not necessarily lead to alienation from the core institutions of the USA. Assimilation takes a selective form among the children of recent immigrants. For example, Hispanics may continue to speak Spanish in community settings, are likely to practise Catholicism and will have close links to their home countries. However, they will use the conventional ladders of social mobility and will don their 'straight' Brooks Brothers suits and speak standard American English when interviewing for a job with the American Federal Bank.

▪▪▪▪▪▪▪▪▪ TRANSNATIONALISM AND MULTI-LEVEL IDENTITY

We have talked of how those expressing local and national identities have reacted and adapted to global change. But perhaps the most innovative forms of response arise at the translocal and transnational level. We are referring particularly to the revival and development of complex forms of cosmopolitanism, diasporic identities and multi-level religious identities, which we discuss further below.

COSMOPOLITANISM AND THE CITY

The important role of the city as the reception point to people from many parts of the world can be inferred from the classical Greek roots of the word – *kosmos* (world) and *polis* (city). As we have discussed the functions of global cities at length in Chapter 17, we will just remind you of the argument made there. Cities (we argued) predated the nation-state system and even during modernity continued as places where diversity rather than ethnic uniformity obtained. It may be that the city-state concept will be renewed in the global age (places like Singapore and Hong Kong play a comparable role with earlier city-states like Venice). But even if the city-state form does not take hold universally, 'the global city' *within* existing nation-states will increasingly contain the disparate elements moving from place to place, as travel, tourism, business links and the labour market become more organized on a global scale.

The social structure of these global cities has indeed already been reshaped to accommodate their new position in the international division of labour. In those cities, identities will be more fluid, more situational, more ambiguous and more open. People may move through different zones or planes of belonging, perhaps combining residual attachments to a local community, a cross-ethnic partnership or marriage, and a transnational lifestyle in respect of leisure and cultural pursuits. As a practice and preference, cosmopolitanism is clearly a massive threat to those who assert that the only way to respond to globalization is to assert a determined loyalty to their ethnic group, nation or religion. The Nazis hated the Jews and sought to massacre them precisely because of their multifaceted identity. To be a critic of cosmopolitanism from a position of such extreme nationalism is perhaps only to be expected. Far less predictable is a critique mounted by a liberal American historian. In his posthumous collection of essays, Lasch (1995) talks of 'the darker side of cosmopolitanism'. The loosely defined 'privileged classes' or 'elites' are said to be in revolt against the nation-state. This is because they no longer identify with it. 'In the borderless global economy, money has lost its links to nationality ... The privileged classes in Los Angeles feel more kinship with their counterparts in Japan, Singapore, and Korea than with most of their countrymen' (Lasch 1995: 46). This detachment from the state means that they regard themselves as 'world citizens' without any of the normal obligations of national citizenship.

The identification of the elites across frontiers is paralleled by a concern only for their immediate neighbourhood:

> The cosmopolitanism of the favoured few ... turns out to be a higher form of parochialism. Instead of supporting public services, the new elites put their money into the improvement of their own self-enclosed enclaves. They gladly pay for private healthcare and suburban private schools, private police and private systems of garbage collection; but they have managed to relieve themselves, to a remarkable extent, of the obligation to contribute to the national treasury. [This is] a striking instance of the revolt of the elites against the constraints of time and place. (Lasch 1995: 47)

Lasch's concern is a legitimate one, particularly in the context of the USA. He is impressed by the virtues of 'small-town democracy' and the traditions of *noblesse oblige,* whereby the rich, powerful and fortunate assumed their civic responsibility to look after the less privileged. In a country where (compared with a number of European countries and neighbouring Canada) welfare systems are underdeveloped, there was a particular reliance on voluntary and charitable support for the sick, poor and elderly. However, one should not imagine that Lasch's arguments apply purely to the USA. In global cities everywhere, the attachment of the denizens (privileged foreigners) to the state in which they find themselves often can only be described as minimal. This alienation clearly can have dangerous social consequences.

If Lasch sees the danger of cosmopolitanism, Beck (1998: 30) sees its opportunities. Cosmopolitan movements can transcend the appeal to national traditions, values and solidarities in favour of human values and traditions in every culture and religion. Such movements can address planetary concerns through new concepts, structures and organizations that can support the need to create transnationalism from below. For Beck, the notion of 'world citizenship' is to be embraced not feared. New forms of 'post-national understanding, responsibility, the state, justice, art, science and public understanding' (Beck 1998: 30) can emerge. This in turn can lead to more advanced forms of democracy, toleration, liberty and mutuality.

DIASPORAS

While global cities have provided important spatial vessels to contain plurality, the revival of a long-established social organization, a transnational diaspora, has come to symbolize how people are subverting, transcending or perhaps just paralleling the nation-state system. You will remember that previously we defined diasporas as the dispersion of peoples to a number of countries. They constitute a diaspora if they continue to evince a common concern for their 'homeland' (sometimes an imagined community) and come to share a sense of a common purpose with their own people, wherever they happen to be. The word 'diaspora' has particular associations with the Jewish (and later Armenian and African) peoples living out of their natal lands. These associations particularly evoke the idea of 'victims' – groups that were forcibly dispersed at one moment in history when a cataclysmic event happened. Nowadays the concept is used more widely and imaginatively to include groups that are essentially voluntary migrants (Cohen 1997).

A diasporic consciousness is revived when a community still has links with its place of origin and does not feel the need for 'indentificational assimilation' with the nation-state in which it currently resides. For many, reaffirming their diasporic connections is a positive choice but, in some cases, the welcome accorded to them in a place of destination is so hostile or lukewarm that they feel impelled to reattach themselves to a transnational link. This is made easier by the ways in which 'home' and 'away' are connected by rapid transport, electronic communications and cultural sharing – part of the phenomena of globalization and transnationalism. It is now possible to have multiple localities and multiple identities.

While smoother, deeper and cheaper connectivity provides a facilitating role, the revival of diasporas is also based on a renewed search for 'roots', what Hall (quoted above) called a 'reach for groundings'. Yet, this inclination need not imply a narrow localism, a retreat from global realities or an inability to respond to the challenges of the ever widening marketplace and to the new ethical and cultural demands stemming from globalization. To meet both needs, for a meaningful identity and a flexible response to burgeoning opportunities, a double-facing type of social organization is highly advantageous. Just such an organization exists in the form of a diaspora. This is not just a contemporary function of diasporas. They have always been in a better position to act as a bridge between the particular and the universal. Among other arenas, this has allowed them to act as interlocutors in commerce and administration.

Many members of diasporic communities are bilingual or multilingual. They can spot 'what is missing' in the societies they visit or in which they settle. Often they are better able to discern what their own group shares with other groups and when its cultural norms and social practices threaten majority groups. Being 'streetwise' may affect the very survival of the group itself. It is perhaps because of this need to be sensitive to prevalent currents (the Zeitgeist) that in addition to their achievements in trade and finance, diasporic groups are typically overrepresented in the arts, cinema, media and entertainment industries. Knowledge and awareness have enlarged to the point of cosmopolitanism or humanism, but at the same time, traditional cultural values, which sustain solidarity and have always supported the search for education and enlightenment, have not been threatened.

Cosmopolitanism combined with ethnic collectivism is also an important constituent in successful business ventures. Probably the most upbeat analysis along these lines is in Kotkin's (1992) comparative study of why some peoples seem more successful as entrepreneurs than others. In his quest, he provides case studies of five 'global tribes' – the Jews, the British, the Japanese, the Chinese and the Indians. Gone, for Kotkin, are the traumas of exile, the troubled relationship

with the host culture and other negative aspects of the classical diasporic tradition. Instead, strong diasporas are the key to determine success in the global
economy. As Kotkin writes (1992: 255, 258):

> Rather than being a relic of a regressive past, the success of global tribes – from
> the Jews and British over many centuries to the Chinese, Armenians and Pales-
> tinians of today – suggests the critical importance of values, emphasis on the
> acquisition of knowledge and cosmopolitan perspectives in the emerging world
> economy. In an ever more transnational and highly competitive world economy,
> highly dependent on the flow and acquisition of knowledge, societies that nurture
> the presence of such groups seem most likely to flourish … Commercial oppor-
> tunism overwhelms the narrower economic nationalism of the past as the
> cosmopolitan global city-state takes precedence and even supplants the nation.

Diasporas score by being able to interrogate the universal with the particular and
by being able to use their transnationalism to press the limits of the local.

MULTI-LEVEL RELIGIOUS IDENTITIES

We have already seen how diasporic identities can swing backwards and forwards
from local to transnational poles. Many religious identities seem to be undergoing
a similar transmogrification. We have probed a number of aspects of religion in
Chapter 16, but here we are particularly concerned about the sense in which its
adherents are moving between local, national and transnational levels. As van de
Veer (2001: 12) observes, major secular thinkers like John Stuart Mill have often
seen religious allegiances as 'condemning the believer to parochialism, absolutism
and a lack of tolerance'. Rerendered in our terms, religious faith is a form of backward localism, inward-looking and impervious to the possibilities of doing things
in a different way. One can hardly deny that there are many examples of such
blind faith. In small villages in poor countries, the village priest is a considerable
figure – one who might have the monopoly of literacy, derive his social status from
his knowledge of the sacred texts and keeping his flock in ignorance.

However, this picture of backwardness has always been a parody of religion.
Many religions started with universal aspirations. They were there not merely to
unshackle this group of rural dwellers from their superstitions or celebrate that
nation's military victory, rather, they sought to liberate humankind. Even if these
thoughts were not explicit in the minds of the founders of many of the world's
major religions, they were developed by later theology. Thus, in the case of
Catholicism, the Apostle's Creed (formulated in the first and second century BC)
evolved the idea of the universal visible Church. Protestants later retaliated with
the idea of a universal invisible Church, while Muslim theologians developed the
idea of the umma, the worldwide community of the faith. Despite these early
universal doctrines, as van der Veer (2001: 1) states: 'religion as a category and
nationalism as an ideology emerge together in discourses of modernity in the
nineteenth century'.

We can dramatise this conjuncture of religion and nationalism if we think back to the drama surrounding the reign of Henry VIII of England in the sixteenth century. The drama was a farce. Henry was gouty and overweight but this did not prevent him wishing to marry six times. When the Pope was reluctant to annul his marriages (technically Henry, like other European monarchs, was beholden to him in religious matters), Henry broke with Rome, established the Church of England, killed a few dissident monks, seized the Catholic monasteries and set himself up at the head of the new Church (a position his royal successors still occupy). The crucial point of the drama was that henceforth the Church was subordinate to and coupled with the political authority in most parts of Europe. This was signalled by the change in names – to the Church of Ireland, the Church of Scotland, the Dutch Reformed Church and others. Sixteenth-century Germany was more fragmented, but a parallel development arose after 1555, when the Religious Peace of Augsburg fixed on the idea of *cuius regio, eius religio* (whose region, his religion). This meant that the religion of the local rulers (generally in little principalities) determined the religion of their subjects.

In the global era, the subordination of religion to nation and locality has largely been reversed, or certainly has been under challenge. Three well-known examples of this are the reassertion of papal power particularly under John Paul II, the revival of the global ambitions of certain Islamic groups and the spread of evangelical/pentecostal Christianity, notably to Latin America and Asia. These assertions of religious power and influence can work in complex and sometimes contradictory ways. Although it is an oversimplification, Catholicism in Northern Ireland was essentially a local level phenomenon, mobilizing the minority community there to assert its civil rights against the Protestant majority that was reluctant to give up its privileges. The fact that this struggle was mounted partly through armed terrorism made it difficult for outsiders unequivocally to support the Catholic cause. By contrast, Catholics in Poland were able to ally themselves to a peaceful, national, freedom struggle against the godless communists, a struggle that was sustained by the papacy. Finally, the global moral claims of the Pope were openly challenged in the Church and outside when he proclaimed that artificial contraception and abortions were sins, despite the AIDS pandemic and widespread rape during civil wars.

A more obscure case, but one with important implications, is the Vishna Hindu Parishad (VHP) founded in 1964 by militant Hindu nationalists. As van der Veer (2001: 6) explains, the VHP 'is a Hindu revivalist movement which simultaneously tries to reach out to all Hindus in the world and mobilize Hindus in India for anti-Muslim politics'. The movement succeeded in a number of ways. It persuaded Hindus to march to Ayodya to destroy the Babri Masjid, a mosque allegedly built on a Hindu site. It helped to promote the political fortunes of the Bharatiya Janata Party (BJP) to the extent that it became India's largest party and was able to form a government. It created or fostered an 'anti-Western' and 'anti-globalization' ethos, arguing that these forces were alien to the 'Hindu nation'. This last message was never proclaimed to the VHP's supporters in the Indian diaspora in the USA, who were ideologically committed to liberalism and an open international economy and also happened to bankroll the movement. Although multi-level Hindu fundamentalism is not widely discussed outside India, it is of concern that the world's largest democracy, whose leaders had crafted so admirable a multi-faith secular state, could now be undermined from within.

Figure 21.2 **Activists burn effigies of leading Bharatia Janata Party leaders in Calcutta, India, December 2000**
They are protesting again Hindu zealots who they accuse of destroying the Babri Masjid mosque in 1992. The destruction of the mosque sparked the worst communal violence in India for half a century and left 3,000 people dead. Muslim–Hindu relations are still tense in the city.

REVIEW

In assessing the different levels of community and belonging – local, national, transnational and multi-level – we have seen that the great hopes after the end of the Cold War for a 'new world order', a 'peace dividend' or the expression of 'universal values' have been sadly dashed. The world has not witnessed the emergence of a compliant, single culture in which all people learn to love one another. Perlmutter (1991) helpfully depicts the world as being organized vertically by nation-states and regions, but horizontally by an overlapping, permeable, multiple system of interaction – communities not of place but of interest, shared opinions and beliefs, tastes, ethnicities and religions. Unlike those who argue that a single homogenized global culture is emerging, Perlmutter more plausibly suggests that multiple cultures are being syncretized in a complex way. The elements of particular cultures can be drawn from a global array, but they will mix and match differently in each setting.

Nation-states can resist these tendencies and seek to arrest the emergence or strengthening of multi-level identities. Alternatively, they can 'go with the flow' and seek to adapt to the increasing mobility and complex social identities of their home populations. In practice, a double tendency seems to be emerging. In some zones (generally the more cosmopolitan parts of the global cities), there is rapid adjustment to the new pluralist or multi-level realities. Outside these zones, certain politicians seek to mobilize or exploit traditional nationalist loyalties, which still carry some conviction with threatened social groups. The cosmopolitanism of Paris and the support given to Le Pen (the leader of France's National Front) in the provincial towns and cities is illustrative of this duality.

There are also many political movements that seek to resist multi-level and transnational affiliations by creating new certainties, new states defined on the basis of a single ethno-nationality. The states that emerged from the collapse of the Soviet Union and the disintegration of Yugoslavia provide abundant examples of this inclination. Longstanding residents of many of these 'new nations' were bundled out unceremoniously and told to return to natal lands with which they may not have had an association for several generations. At worst, this drive for ethnic territorialism leads to 'ethnic cleansing' and even systematic attempts at genocide. A tendency to recognize subnational claims for devolution or autonomy is evident in the UK, Spain and elsewhere.

Nationalist appeals are also paralleled by appeals to locality, religion or ethnicity. This new insistence on ethnic and religious difference has created many dilemmas for established nation-states, which have exhibited a huge variation in the extent to which they are open to newcomers or reassertions of subnational loyalties. Even the USA, which promoted a singular idea of assimilation on the basis of cultural and social obedience and exclusive citizenship, has been forced to retreat. The world is simply not like that any more; the scope for multiple affiliations and associations has been opened up outside and beyond the nation-state. Globalization has meant that there is no longer any stability in the points of origin, no finality in the points of destination and no necessary coincidence between social and national identities (Khan 1995: 93).

Transnationalism and multi-level identities have begun to supersede nationalism. We have described how a chain of global cities and an increasing proliferation of subnational and transnational identities cannot easily be contained in the nation-state system. Among the most important of the established transnational identities are cosmopolitan cities, diasporas and world religions, social formations that preceded the age of globalization by thousands of years. Transnationalism is also evident in key shifts of attitude and behaviour; many people, not just those who can be called 'world citizens' or 'cosmopolites', are more willing to recognize and accept cultural and religious diversity. There is an increased knowledge and awareness of other cultures derived from the global media and travel. Knowledge and awareness at least sometimes leads to tolerance and the respect for difference. We remind you of Perlmutter's (1991: 901) remark that now, for the first time in history, 'we have in our possession the technology to support the choice of sharing the governance of our planet rather than fighting with one another to see who will be in charge'.

FURTHER READING

- There are many readers and textbooks on ethnicity and nationalism. Among the most significant are Anthony D. Smith's *Ethnicity and Nationalism* (1992) and his *Nations and Nationalism in a Global Era* (1995), although it is difficult to choose from among this sociologist's many works on the question.

- A well-balanced reader titled *The Ethnicity Reader: Nationalism, Multiculturalism and Migration* has been edited by J. Rex and M. Guiberrnau (1997).

- Michael Ignatieff's *Blood and Belonging* (1994) is a powerful book, based on a television series.

- S. P. Huntington's *Who are We?* (2004) is one of a number of accounts by conservative American academics and commentators decrying what they see as the excesses of multiculturalism.

- Two books on diasporas are Robin Cohen's *Global Diasporas* (1997) and a reference book with 34 previously published articles titled *Migration, Diasporas and Transnationalism* edited by S. Vertovec and R. Cohen (1999).

GROUP WORK

1. Using conventional reference books, plot out the diverse elements and sects within Islam.

2. Divide into two debating teams, one addressing the proposition that the USA is in the process of 'disuniting', the other that 'assimilation' is still working to integrate that country.

3. What indices would you use to establish who is a cosmopolitan? ('Someone who reads a magazine of that name' will be regarded as an inadequate answer!)

4. Divide into two groups. One will address the proposition that global cities can contain transnationalism. The other group will explore the way in which diasporas express transnationalism.

QUESTIONS TO THINK ABOUT

?

1. In what ways is it erroneous to group ethnicity, race and religion all under the category 'localism'?

2. Why does localism arise in the midst of globalization?

3. Why was the force of race and ethnicity so systematically undervalued?

4. To what extent have the immigrant countries failed in their quest to assimilate people of different cultures?

5. Do diasporas 'solve' the problem of bridging local sentiments and global imperatives?

WHAT'S ON THE WEB

- http://www.ceu.hu/nation/nsn.html#113005 An online full textbook titled *Studies on Nationalism* is provided by the Nationalism Studies Network. Although this book is useful, 'the network' seems little more than an advert for a Masters degree at the Central European University in Budapest.

- www.transcomm.ox.ac.uk For developments in the field of transnationalism, consult this website. Although the programme that sustained the site is now completed, it still provides some helpful information.

- For material on religious identities see the web links at the end of Chapter 16.

- http://www.intute.ac.uk/socialsciences/cgi-bin/search.pl?term1=race+and+ethnicity&gateway=Sociology&limit=0 Material and links on race and ethnicity are grouped at the Intute site.

CHAPTER 22

Contested Futures

CONTENTS

In Chapter 2 we explored two concepts – globalization (the objective worldwide processes of integration) and globality (the subjective awareness of living in 'one world' with high levels of mutual interdependency). The extent to which these two processes have advanced remains contentious and besieged by uncertainties. Some anticipate that globalization and globality will be sufficiently vibrant phenomena to usher in a new global age and promote the construction of a generally benign global society. Others are gloomier. Some scholars, the ones we might describe as 'globalization sceptics', strongly contest even the extent of globalization. The sceptical position needs enunciation, but provided we agree on what constitutes 'globalization', we can resolve the question largely by statistical and factual means. That debate should be distinguished from a political or moral debate in which people and organizations promote, advocate, oppose, reject or wish to reform aspects of globalization, which is the question we now consider.

In earlier chapters (especially Chapters 6 and 8), we probed the degree to which globalization was an uneven process, benefiting some, perhaps many, but also excluding and marginalizing others. We will examine whether these processes and dynamics of inclusion and exclusion have an underlying logic. One of the often expressed fears of globalization and globality is the idea that a vibrant cultural diversity will be replaced by a dull, homogeneous uniformity. Is this the most likely development or are there counterindications that juxtaposing cultures will lead to creative, hybrid, 'creolized' mixes? Finally, we reconsider the elements we have identified as constituting the building blocks of globality and the emergence of a global society. We can anticipate the conclusion to this chapter by indicating that while we do not yet see a fully assembled structure constituting a global society, the lattice work, scaffolding, bricks and mortar are evident and making that construction happen.

IS GLOBALIZATION NEW AND HOW EXTENSIVE IS IT?

One of the most crucial arguments developed by those with a sceptical turn of mind is that globalization is nothing new. Certainly, international trade is not new. As the leading economy for much of the nineteenth century, Britain's imports of raw materials rose by a factor of 20 between 1800 and 1875 (Dunning 1993a: 110). The development of the commercial steamship, from approximately 1850, along with the telegraph, rapidly transformed trade opportunities in the last decades of the nineteenth century by reducing the previously prohibitive costs and risks involved in the movement of people and bulk goods. Moreover, since competition is intrinsic to capitalism, Britain and its emerging industrial rivals – the USA, Germany, France and eventually others – increasingly sought to export finished goods to each other's markets.

These countries also required reliable supplies of foodstuffs, raw materials and fuels for their expanding home markets and growing populations. This need for raw materials led to the scramble for captive colonies, imperial conquest and the division of the world into rival spheres of trading interests, which each country then tried to monopolize. The net result of all this was that by 1914, on the eve of the First World War, a highly internationalized global economy had already emerged. Indeed, Hirst and Thompson's (1996: Chapter 2) boldest claim is that it was hardly less internationalized and open than the current world economy.

A similar case has been made for transnational flows of capital. Thus, foreign direct investment (FDI) by established home companies grew rapidly from about 1870. According to Dunning (1993b: 116), by 1913 it had obtained an importance, proportionately, in the global economy that was not reached again until the mid-1950s. From about 1870, FDI also increasingly supplemented the investment role played by portfolio investment (where finance raised in a home country is used to acquire shareholding interests in a foreign government's or company's own projects rather than directly owned and managed businesses). Moreover, compared with the 1980s and 1990s, when developing countries only received about 20 per cent of FDI, before 1913 such flows were more geographically dispersed – with two-thirds of the total directed to the colonies and dominions, especially Britain's (Dunning 1993a: 117–18).

So, the basic argument these sceptics make is that economic globalization is an old story and nothing special. However, there are several good reasons to doubt if the world economy was as open and integrated before the First World War as in the past four decades. We will also present data showing the rapid acceleration in many indices of globalization since 1982. Considering only the economic dimension of globalization, we offer the following observations:

1. Far fewer countries were involved in international trade and FDI as major actors. For example, as Hirst and Thompson (1996: 22) concede, between them Britain and Germany supplied over half the world's manufactured exports in 1913.

2. According to Dicken (1992: 27), whereas in the first quarter of the twentieth century, only eight countries supplied 95 per cent of the world's manufacturing output, by 1986, the number producing this same share had risen to twenty-five.

3. Similarly, before the First World War only a handful of countries were significant overseas investors. One country, Britain, provided the lion's share, with 45 per cent of the world total, including both portfolio investment and FDI.

4. By contrast, the TNCs headquartered in many more developed countries are now engaged in FDI (for example in Italy, Canada, Denmark and Switzerland). Their counterparts in developing countries (including India, China, Taiwan, South Korea, Hong Kong, Singapore, Brazil, Argentine and Mexico) have also become significant sources of capital flows.

5. Measured in terms of volume, both international trade (from the 1950s) and overseas investment (from the 1960s) increased dramatically and soon dwarfed the corresponding amounts for any previous era.

6. According to Dicken (1992: 51), the average number of subsidiary manufacturing plants the largest TNCs established overseas each year between 1965 and 1967 was more than ten times greater than at any point in the period 1920–1929 and nearly seven times higher than in the years just after the Second World War.

7. The lion's share of the capital outflows through FDI before 1914 was invested in such a way as to facilitate the export of raw materials, especially from the former colonies. Very little, only 15 per cent, was directed towards manufacturing and most of this was located in Europe, America, Russia and Britain's dominions (Dunning 1993b: Chapter 5).

8. The share invested in services – especially those relating to businesses like banking, insurance and trade distribution networks – has also risen considerably from only 15 per cent in 1914 to 47 per cent by 1988 (Dicken 1992: 59). This huge increase has contributed to furthering the market penetration of manufactured products.

9. Arguments that compare international trade in 1914 with the present period miss the point that each country's trade (imports and exports) and the capital flows associated with outward and inward FDI it experiences are fast becoming indistinguishable (Julius 1990). This is because their integrated global operations compel TNCs to engage in intra-firm exchanges. A good part of a country's official declared imports and exports actually consists of the cross-border movement of components, semi-finished goods, production-related services and other 'products' between the various subsidiaries of foreign and locally based TNCs.

Although we readily accept that there were high levels of international trade in the period just before the First World War, we do not believe this significantly dents the argument that we are witnessing a new era of economic globalization. For one thing, prior to 1914 and for several decades after, states were driven by overt and strongly nationalist pressures towards protecting their home economies while seeking to dominate overseas spheres of imperialist influence. But protectionism and imperialism have been declining rather rapidly since the 1950s in most countries. (The USA is a notable exception in respect of its newly articulated imperial mission.) Also, in terms of scale, complexity, the number of actors involved (both state and non-state) and the integration of finance, manufacturing, services and investment, the economic globalization commencing in the late twentieth century has gone well beyond anything that existed in 1914.

RECENT MEASURES OF GLOBALIZATION

Is it possible to measure the changes to and extent of globalization in a systematic way? This was the challenge taken up by two researchers at the University of Warwick. Lockwood and Redoano (2005) first divided the forms of globalization into three kinds – economic, social and political. Next they sought to find reliable data sets that measured various variables within the three types of globalization. Thus:

1. *Economic globalization* was measured by these variables:
   - *trade* (exports plus imports of goods and services expressed as a proportion of GDP)

- *foreign direct investment* (inflows plus outflows as a proportion of GDP)
- *portfolio investment* (inflows and outflows as a proportion of GDP)
- *income* (the amount crossing frontiers as a proportion of GDP).

2. *Social globalization* comprised two elements:
   - the 'people' variables were *stocks of foreigners* (as a proportion of a country's total population), *flows of foreigners* (again, as a proportion of total population), *worker remittances* and *tourist arrivals*
   - the 'ideas' variables were *phone calls*, *internet users*, *films* (the number imported and exported), *books/newspapers* (value imported and exported) and *mail* (the number of international letters per capita).

3. *Political globalization* was measured by the following variables:
   - *embassies* (the number of foreign embassies in a country)
   - *UN missions* (the number of UN peacekeeping missions in which a country participates)
   - *organizations* (the number of memberships of international organizations).

The results of calculating and weighting all these variables are presented in many tables, but the crucial aggregated information is summarized in Table 22.1.

TABLE 22.1 Warwick world globalization index			
	1982	2001	% increase
Economic globalization	0.176	0.223	26.7
Social globalization	0.070	0.335	378.6
Political globalization	0.721	1.065	47.7
Overall globalization	0.182	0.406	123.1

SOURCES: Lockwood and Redoano (2005); Adapted from data available at http://www2.warwick.ac.uk/fac/soc/csgr/index/

Of course statistical measures are not everything. There are certain activities that cannot be measured, or have only been measured in a sporadic fashion and therefore are not included. There may be disputes over the methodology, the selection of variables and the weighting between them. Perhaps more damagingly, because the researchers were forced to use country-based statistics (which is how they are collected), the data are stronger indications of the extent to which each country has become *internationalized* rather than the extent to which the world has become *globalized*. Nonetheless, by clustering the data both regionally and globally, we are able to get the best measure yet of the extent to which globalization has indeed occurred, rather than has been said to have occurred by commentators and politicians. Within the stated parameters, the results are conclusive and even startling. While economic and political globalization has proceeded apace, the growth of social globalization is staggering and generally unrecognized. The headline news is that, by 2001, the world as a whole was over 2.2 times more globalized than it was 20 years earlier. When global change has happened to that degree, over that scope and within so short a period, to state that globalization is a 'new' and 'extensive' phenomenon seems to us a valid statement, whatever the doubts of the sceptics.

MORAL AND POLITICAL POSITIONS ON GLOBALIZATION

Clearly, the massive changes accompanying the various processes of globalization we have talked about throughout this book have produced differing responses from people and organizations. These responses are contested and derive from contested political and ideological positions. Freely adapting Anheier et al.'s (2001: 7–10) account and relabelling three of their categories, these responses may be classified into four clusters.

SUPPORTERS

Supporters of current forms of globalization consist of TNCs and others who directly benefit from open economies. The 'others' may include highly skilled transnational migrants who are able to command high salaries and favourable conditions of work by treating the world as a single labour market. The World Bank and WTO are just two of the bodies promoting free trade and an open global capitalist economy. Banks and insurance and investment companies are also in favour of open borders because they profit by selling their services globally. At the social level, there is probably a consensus that student mobility, the global sharing of scientific data and the transmission of films, DVDs, books and journals are 'a good thing'. A similarly positive view attaches to the internet and the opportunities for blogging, which have led to the democratization and internationalization of information and ideas. Finally, at the political level, supporters of globalization may also be prepared to endorse interventions by strong states to enforce preferred regimes and protect human rights.

DETRACTORS

Detractors seek to reverse globalization, preferring to return to a world in which nation-states exercise full sovereignty over the economic and political destinies of their own citizens. Such detractors include left-wing groups that are opposed to capitalism and wish to introduce some kind of socialist, collectivized economic life at the national level, largely decoupled from global financial flows. Also included are right-wing nationalist and religious interests that want to protect local markets, businesses and jobs from international competition and capital movements or 'foreign' faiths. Both Left and Right are suspicious of open borders, the growth of global governance and giving increased power to the UN or its specialist agencies. Both also tend to romanticize or idealize the past. At the cultural and social level, enhanced intercourse with non-nationals is seen as threatening to national cultures and social cohesion, so detractors tend to be fiercely anti-immigration.

REFORMERS

Reformers see globalization as potentially beneficial because it can provide the technological means for fostering increased connectivity between different peoples and bringing prosperity to more individuals, but they insist that these will remain only possibilities unless global capitalism is civilized or reformed. Thus, they demand fairer economic institutions and rules that are more clearly dedicated to spreading the benefits of economic development to the less advantaged. Politically, they demand much greater participation by ordinary people in setting global agendas at national and global levels with respect to such issues as technological progress, debt relief, fair trade, controls on international business and representation in international bodies. They are also likely to want stronger environmental protection, increased and more democratic global governance and an international system for policing human rights. Unlike the 'supporters', the reformers would want the UN to be the sole body authorizing humanitarian interventions in support of human rights.

OUTSIDERS

Outsiders see globalization as happening at one remove from them. They want to opt out and develop their own separate courses of action 'independently of government, international institutions and transnational corporations' (Anheier et al. 2001: 10). Such individuals or groups tend to operate very much at a local and grassroots level and are likely to prefer economic autarky derived from small-scale organic farming. Characteristically, outsiders will reject innovations like GM foods, will be strongly committed to a simpler, less consumer-driven way of life and are opposed to the powers wielded by TNCs and strong governments. When involved in protests and wider social movements, they tend to engage in striking and colourful activities with a strong central theme of reclaiming public spaces from all kinds of authority. Anarchists and those with strong green commitments are intertwined with global outsiders.

This fourfold division of reactions to globalization is imperfect, even crude. However, it serves to reinforce the point, already made in Chapter 2, that social actors are not simply helpless chaff, victims of the tornado of globalization that blows across the world. Individuals, groups, movements, institutions and governments can promote, defend and advance their own causes and preferences and so help to shape the nature and characteristics of globalization and globality. We will see below that human agency is also important in determining who is included and who is excluded from the current global order.

GLOBAL EXCLUSION AND INCLUSION

In Chapter 8, we showed that despite the claims by many writers that 'globalization works' (Wolf 2005), the contemporary world remains characterized by sharp inequalities and uneven development. Particular countries and regions and selected groups – rural producers, refugees, famine victims, workers in deindustrializing areas and the urban poor – were the focus of our attention. There are other groups – the disabled, those with major ailments like HIV/AIDS and the elderly – that could also have been singled out for detailed discussion. Here we ask whether there is some underlying logic or central insight that explains why social exclusion arises, why some get pushed to the edge of existence and why others, at best, benefit only to a small degree from economic development.

To keep you in suspense no longer, our hypothesis is that social exclusion is more likely to occur when the adoption of neoliberal economic practices is disengaged from social policy and forms of political governance. Put more simply, a free market alone is neither an ethical good nor a practical solution to inequality or marginality if there is no simultaneous social reform or if dictatorial, inefficient or corrupt forms of politics are allowed to continue. This point can be illustrated at a country level, but more importantly it also forms the basis of a global discussion of social inclusion and exclusion – who wins and who loses. Let us take just one single country example, namely Russia. There the enthusiastic adoption of neoliberal economic blueprints triggered a near disintegration of society for at least a decade. Of course some people benefited. Instead of lining up at the drab communist GUM (state department store), the wealthy elite can visit the 'Petrovsky Passage' in Moscow. There they will find boutiques selling labels like Moschino, Marina Rinaldi, Max Mara, La Perla, Nina Ricci, Mandarina Duck, Kenzo, Etro, Pomellato, Ermanno Scervino, Bosco Women and Bosco Men. However, other social indicators of the new Russia are less impressive. Without the protection of the old Soviet welfare state, the life expectancy of men fell to 58 years, while suicide rates climbed 60 per cent in the period 1989–99 (Ciment 1999). The population is rapidly declining, from 148 million in 1991 to a projected 130 million by 2030 (*The Economist* 2005: 107).

In moving from the country level to a broadbrush global treatment of social exclusion, we will refer to Munck's (2005) work on globalization and social exclusion. Munck is not alone in spotting the renewed significance of Polanyi's (2002) work *The Great Transformation*, first published in 1957. The reissued version of the work has a laudatory foreword by the Nobel laureate, former World Bank's chief economist (and now principal gadfly) Joseph Stiglitz (Polanyi 2002). In brief, Polanyi's central insight was that there was no innate attribute explaining the rise of nineteenth-century economic liberalism. The invisible hand of the market did *not* arise spontaneously or freely. As Polanyi wrote:

> There was nothing natural about laissez faire; free markets could never have come into being merely by allowing things to take their course ... the road to the free market was opened up and kept open by an enormous increase in continuous, centrally organized and controlled interventionism. (Polanyi, cited in Munck 2005: 146)

This apparently simple point carries enormous explanatory punch in our contemporary world. At a national level, it helps to explain farm subsidies to midwest farmers and tax breaks to oil giants in the USA; it illuminates the official banking–civil service–TNC alliance in Japan; it sheds light on 'Asian capitalism' in Singapore and Malaysia. At a global level, we can understand the salience of the structural adjustment programmes (SAPs), GATT rules and TRIPS. All these national and international measures were bribes to particular interests or threats imposed by powerful governments lobbied by powerful companies and, in the case of SAPs, at the cost of considerable violence (Walton and Seddon 1994). As in the case of nineteenth-century liberalism, late twentieth-century neoliberalism, generally termed 'economic globalization', has come not because of the mysterious workings of the free market but because key social and political actors have determined that it should do so. Equally, as nineteenth-century liberalism was opposed by what Polanyi called a welfarist 'countermovment', current neoliberalism has generated its own countermovement, the global social justice movement. Although there is some evidence that Polanyi continued to be attracted by socialist ideas, the strength of his position – and its continuing relevance – is that he did not get trapped into a conventional leftist class position. In other words, wicked capitalists with large cigars and big bellies are not the only people who impose liberalism and neoliberalism, and the heroic, horny-handed sons and daughters of toil are not the only ones who oppose these forces.

Let us focus in more detail on the countermovement. What Polanyi emphasizes is that liberalism/neoliberalism tends to destroy important socialities and cherished community values. Need is replaced by greed, social cohesion is replaced by individualism, caring is replaced by neglect or indifference, and charity is replaced by contempt for the poor. We can see contemporary examples of a number of states evacuating the social space needed to hold the fabric of society together. In some cases, this is a matter of choice or ideology; in others, where spending patterns are determined by external forces, national elites might reduce welfare spending with a good deal of reluctance. Social exclusion is derivative of these large structural logics and forces. In particular, Munck (2005: 25–6) argues that the notion of social exclusion can be used as a 'unifying perspective' on global deprivation, marginality and inequality for three reasons:

- globalization has brought all under the sway of capitalist market relations
- North and South are interpenetrated, with the South (comprising poor immigrants and locals) found in urban slums in rich countries, and the North found in financial centres and gated communities in the South
- neoliberalism has spread the ideology of the self-regulating market to all societies (even, we add, nominally communist ones like China).

Those arguing for social inclusion and seeking to advance the countermovement are therefore faced with the need to operate on a broad front. There is some ambiguity (given its structural starting point) about whether Polanyi's countermovement operates as an inevitable opposing force, rather along the lines of a Hegelian dialectic, or whether there needs to be organization to bring the countermovement into being and advance its course. We take the latter view, for it is consistent with Polanyi's prior argument that neoliberalism was imposed and did not drop mysteriously from the skies. The countermovement (or, if you like, the movement for social inclusion) would then comprise these and other active social agents:

1. Progressive governments demanding reform of the international trading regime (for example, those pushing for 'fair trade, not free trade').
2. Churches organizing programmes to protect the poor.
3. Social movements seeking to secure debt relief for poor countries.
4. Consumer groups promoting the purchase of fair trade and ecologically friendly goods, as well as goods produced in factories where good labour conditions obtain.
5. Governments reinvigorating social welfare expenditure and policies.
6. Corporations signing up to and actually delivering 'social responsibility' programmes (as opposed to simply massaging their public relations profile).
7. Labour/trade unions protecting their members from exploitation and helping to organize internationally.
8. Migrant organizations and those working on behalf of migrant organizations.
9. The global movement for social justice (often misleadingly called the 'anti-globalization movement') pressing for general reforms to the global order.
10. Intellectuals and journalists exposing the deficiencies of neoliberalism in theory and practice.

In short, what we are witnessing is a countermovement to neoliberalism that has a variety of supporters and activists and operates on local, national and global scales. It seeks – if one could meaningfully anthropomorphize it into having a common purpose – to recover or advance the cause of social inclusion. It is difficult to study such a global and dispersed countermovement, but we have shown through this book that social movements like the green and women's movements have sought to organize the marginalized, dispossessed and excluded, drawing them into the mainstream through a process of confronting the established order and empowering the hitherto powerless.

CULTURAL GLOBALIZATION: UNIFORMITY OR CREOLIZATION

So far we have argued that current forms of globalization tend to unevenness and inequality, but that a countermovement in the opposite direction can ameliorate these features. At the cultural level, dominant forms of globalization tend not so much to unevenness but, some suggest, to a condition of bland sameness. Sachs (1992: 102) put it dramatically when he maintained that 'the homogenization of the world is in full swing. A global monoculture spreads like an oil slick over the entire planet.' What are the sources of this supposed global monoculture and is there the cultural equivalent of a social and political countermovement acting as a rival force?

Until recently, the overwhelming force for universalization in world affairs was the Western-inspired view that progress meant greater humanism and international peace linked to the spread of science, the creation of a unified world market and the pursuit of material improvement for all. In the days of formal imperialism and colonialism, such views enabled the West to legitimize its mission to impose its culture and its political and social institutions on much of the world. The 'trade-off' for the colonized was access to new markets and new commodities. Borne at first by colonialism and imperialism, the source of contemporary cultural homogenization (see Figure 22.1) arises largely from the global marketplace, led and often controlled by US corporations. Along with this, critics say, comes the all-pervasive and seductive imagery peddled worldwide through media influence, also largely monopolized by the USA. Barber (1995), to take just one view, fears that the 'McWorld' market system will lead to the standardization of cultures and consumption practices. The TNCs, he thinks, will raise people's expectations through advertising, encouraging consumers to believe that their purchases open new avenues to a better life of opportunity and freedom. This is the now familiar 'McWorld' of consumer culture and its brand name icons – Levi's 501 jeans, Coca-Cola, Reebok trainers, fast foods including the famous McDonald's burger itself – that are now desired even by the world's poorest inhabitants living in slums and rural backwaters.

Figure 22.1 **US troops in Olongapo, Luzon Island, the Philippines, near the largest US base outside the USA itself**
During the Vietnam War, the troops in Olongapo left the killing fields on rotation to engage in what is called 'rest and recreation'. Is this one way to create the cultural homogenization of the world, or will the troops escape their monocultural past and become creolized as they interact with other cultures?

In Chapter 13, we showed how cheap, standardized products have come to dominate consumer choices in a number of arenas. In an extension to his argument, Ritzer (1998), the originator of the McDonalidization thesis, adds that to fast-food restaurants, the other consumer practices exported by the USA include credit cards, the supermarket, the shopping mall, TV shopping channels and the emergence of 'cybermalls' on the internet. The attraction of these modes of consumption is that they have subtlety fused with notions of well-being (shopping as 'retail therapy') and entertainment. In earlier epochs, the fusion with entertainment was visible at fairs where a carnival tradition was found. But, Ritzer (1998: 92) proposes, the fusion of consumption and amusement has now became more pervasive, ordered, sanitized and homogenized. Ritzer (1998: 92) continues:

> Amusement parks like Disneyland and Disney World, while they are ostensibly about entertainment, can be seen as really shopping malls for the vast array of Disney products ... Shopping malls themselves are coming to look more and more like amusement parks: the huge malls in Bloomington, Minnesota and Edmonton, Canada, literally encompass amusement parks complete with rollercoasters and ferris wheels. Lured to the malls by the amusements, many consumers stay to shop, eat, drink, see a movie, visit a fitness center, and so on.

Ritzer and others working in the field have made an important contribution to our understanding of contemporary capitalism, in particular by recognizing the salience of the means of consumption rather than the means of production, emphasized by Marx. However, most products are quite clearly unable to deliver the kind of personal self-fulfilment promised in the adverts. Nor is the purchasing power for consumer goods any substitute for secure employment opportunities, strong community values or the ability of citizens to influence the political process through democratic institutions. Accordingly, the vista of abundant market choice holds out promises it cannot keep.

In fact, generally, the TNCs have no interest in improving people's real lives or encouraging the strengthening of civil society. Nor do they intend to promote the kind of meaningful transnational solidarity that might empower global citizens to cooperate in overcoming common problems. Sklair (1995: 174, 280) echoes this view, maintaining that capitalism invariably engenders a powerful and understandable popular appeal among ordinary citizens that is difficult to counter or replace with a fairer, democratic, socialist alternative. Other alternatives are in effect precluded.

Meanwhile, even those lucky enough to afford to participate in consumerism may ultimately experience dissatisfaction. This is because consumerism cannot cater for people's additional needs for community involvement, personal development and meaningful social relationships. Instead of fostering community and solidarity, shopping malls merely provide a site for what Albrow (1996) describes as disconnected flows of social life forming something like a cavalcade (see Global Thinkers 22).

We share many of the anxieties that Sklair and Albrow raise. Certainly, it would be foolish to deny or ignore the enormous influence TNCs exert over all aspects of our lives. However, although the dangers posed by TNCs and the spread of capitalism are formidable, the concrete evidence for suggesting that together these produce an irresistible, disempowering and homogeneous culture dominated by US consumerist values is often more apparent than real. Indeed, as has been seen in Chapters 12 and 13 on tourism and consumerism, there are powerful grounds for arguing that, under capitalism consumers retain far more opportunities for personal creativity and autonomy than these arguments suggest. Moreover, as we suggest below, a countermovement to cultural homogeneity expressed through hybridity and creolization is showing vigorous growth.

■ ■

Global Thinkers 22 **MARTIN ALBROW (1942–)**

Globality and the end of modernity

For 200 years modernity and its assumptions – material progress steered by the nation-state and pursued through science and rational organization – have dominated our lives. But, like Beck, Albrow argues that the pursuit of modernity has unleashed worldwide forces that take us into a totally different situation. In particular, he highlights:

- *the environmental limits to economic development*
- *the spread of weaponry that is too dangerous to use*
- *global systems of communication that overwhelm local cultures*
- *an integrated global economy*
- *increasingly reflexive individuals, critically aware of the consequences of their own and others' actions.*

The consequences of these five elements mean that:

- *the nation-state no longer 'contains' all our aspirations or 'monopolizes' our attention*
- *for more and more people the world is becoming the frame of reference, the object of concern and the reality that dominates our awareness (what we call 'globality')*
- *a world (though not yet a global) society is emerging, consisting of the totality of social relations that directly or indirectly involve actions having a global scope and intention*
- *we begin jointly to share values and take actions that are specifically designed to shape the global order.*

Globalization liberates human social relations from imprisonment

Globalizing processes have released and renewed human sociality from its confinement within the artificial boundaries imposed by modernizing nation-state societies. The sociology formulated during the period of modernity also buried the social by locating causation in the 'social system', with its roles and institutions, leaving human beings outside their analysis. Now, the qualities of people as social/human beings have a chance to cross national boundaries and transcend social systems.

Understanding everyday global life: sociospheres

Albrow also provides some useful concepts for making sense of global life. For example, we can conceptualize the totality of relations each person has under global conditions – spread over several locations and operated through virtual, imaginary and/or co-present relations – in terms of a sociosphere. Each person's sociosphere is unique to them and many of those included in it may not know each other (your school and university friends are probably different from your work friends or your family). This concept is especially useful for analysing global life.

Socioscapes

He then adapts Appadurai's (1990) concept of 'scapes'. These are disjointed fragments of ethnic, media, technical, financial or ethical resources that flow around the world and out of which we build our own imagined lives. Albrow adds the idea of socioscapes to this repertoire. Wherever a cluster of individual sociospheres come together in a particular location, we get a series of probably disconnected flows of social life forming something like a cavalcade (the people eating in the café when you are, those attending the same pop concert or strolling along a shopping mall). Like Appadurai's other scapes, technologies bring together a disjunctive set of social actors in a probably temporary but significant flow.

Disconnected contiguity

This is another of the interesting possibilities that can arise with globalization. Here, we can live within a few metres of many other people – in a block of flats and/or in the middle of a large city – yet know virtually none of them personally. Meanwhile, we enjoy close relations via our mobile, letters and the internet with many friends and family scattered across the world.

SOURCE: Albrow (1987, 1996, 1997)

CREOLIZATION AND HYBRIDITY

There are a number of possible responses to the oil slick of cultural homogeneity. They include acceptance and assimilation of the idea of a consumer-led culture of consumption. Another response is a turning back to an old culture, often reinforced by the reinvigoration of orthodox notions within religions. This response can be described as indigenization or, in a religious setting, fundamentalism. A much cited account of how the globalized world of consumer culture is opposed by religious fundamentalism is provided by Barber's (1995) work, with the unequivocal title *Jihad vs. McWorld*. In the global cities, enclave cultures can survive and even thrive under the banner of pluralism or multiculturalism, though arguably there is much less tolerance of this response in the wake of recent revivals of nationalism. Again, some groups can seek to move between local, historical and transnational cultural affinities, a process we described in our discussion of diasporas and multi-level identities in Chapter 21.

While some of these responses have been discussed elsewhere in the book, here we want to focus on **HYBRIDITY** and **CREOLIZATION**, two rather underexplored, yet pervasive responses to global cultural homogenization. They are closely related terms and are often used interchangeably, though the intellectual provenance of the terms has meant that cultural theorists tend to use the first term and linguists, sociologists and anthropologists tend to use the second. Both terms rest on the predicate that the arrival of unfamiliar goods, ideas or artistic forms generally enriches rather than narrows the local repertoire of cultural resources by extending the opportunities to express indigenous 'traditions' and lifestyles. In such situations, people exercise selectivity and consciously mix the old with the new to create alternative (hybridized or creolized) forms of culture.

key concept	**HYBRIDITY** refers principally to the creation of dynamic mixed cultures. Cultural theorists have developed the idea of a 'third space', the evolution of commingled cultures from two or more parent cultures, often a colonial and indigenous pair. Using literature and other cultural expressions, Bhabha (1986) adds that hybridity is a transgressive act, challenging the colonizers' authority, values and representations and thereby constituting an act of self-empowerment and defiance.

Increasingly, too, this process of cultural borrowing and mixing works in reverse because Western societies are increasingly absorbing a widening range of cultural experiences from the non-Western world. This is readily apparent in a variety of activities, stretching from culinary, musical and artistic ones to practices and philosophies associated with health, sport and methods of business organization, to name but a few. The evidence so far does not bear out the contention that non-Western people have no defences – and wish to have none – against the onslaught of Americanized material culture.

key concept	In linguistics **CREOLIZATION** is the process whereby the language of the superordinate group is mixed with an indigenous or other imported language to create a new mother tongue. More recently, sociologists and anthropologists use creolization in a much richer sense, alluding to all kinds of cross-fertilization that takes place between different cultures when they interact. When creolizing, participants select particular elements from incoming or inherited cultures, endow these with meanings different from those they possessed in the original culture and then imaginatively merge these to create totally new varieties that supersede the prior forms.

The words 'Creole' and 'creolization' have been used in many different contexts and generally in an inconsistent way. 'Creole' was possibly derived from the Latin *creare* ('created originally'). The most common historical use was the Spanish *criollo*, which described the children of Spanish colonizers born in the Caribbean. The French transformed the word to '*créole*'. However, the racially exclusive definition, which confined the term to whites in colonial societies, had already been challenged in the early eighteenth century and referred also to indigenous people and other immigrants who had acquired metropolitan manners, cultures and sensibilities. Creolization has escaped its colonial cage, a development that was signalled in the work of the Martinican writer and cultural theorist Edouard Glissant (1981, 1998). Glissant suggests that creolization grows from the situation of displaced African slaves having to rebuild their lives in new settings but that now 'perhaps creolization is becoming one of our present day goals', not just 'on behalf of the Americas but of the entire world' (cited in Stoddard and Cornwell 1999: 349). Elsewhere Glissant (1998) asks whether we should favour an identity that would not be the projection of a single sectarian root, but rather a rhizome identity with a multiplicity of extensions in all directions. This would not kill all around it, but instead would establish communication and relations with other cultures.

Equally significant is the work of the Swedish social and cultural anthropologist Ulf Hannerz (see Global Thinkers 10), who in a number of important articles and books (notably Hannerz 1987, 1992) has suggested that the 'world is in creolization'. In his discussion of the global ecumene (cultural zone) – (Hannerz 1992: 217–63) – he argues that cultures are no longer as bounded or autonomous as they once were and that complex and asymmetrical flows have reshaped them, which, given existing forms and meanings of culture, are unlikely to result in global homogenization. He is clear that 'emerging hybridized webs of meaning' (Hannerz 1992: 264) are not spurious or inauthentic cultures. While these Creole cultures may be relatively unformed, because they are recent they can and do take on a complex character, often because the periphery is stronger than it may appear:

> Creolization also increasingly allows the periphery to talk back. As it creates a greater affinity between the cultures of the center and the periphery, and as the latter increasingly uses the same organizational forms and the same technology as the center … some of its new cultural commodities become increasingly attractive on a global market. Third World music of a creolized kind becomes world music … Creolization thought is open-ended; the tendencies towards maturation and saturation are understood as quite possibly going on side by side, or interleaving. (Hannerz 1992: 265–6)

The creolization of the world in the sense described by Glissant and Hannerz has provided a space in which many people can create a home, a locus, to express their uniqueness in the face of cultural fundamentalisms and imperialism. The flowering of this possibility, this opening to a cultural countermovement, depends on:

- an increasing volume of cultural interactions
- growing interconnections and interdependencies
- a collapse of the solidity of ethnic and racial categories
- a growing incongruence between biological appearance and social prestige (expressed in language, religion, lifestyle, attitudes and behaviour)
- the weakening and more complex rendering of identity politics.

If these elements grow, cross-fertilization will take place between different cultures as they interact. As those predicting the creolization of the world propose, the locals will select particular elements from incoming cultures, endow these with meanings different from those they possessed in the original culture and then creatively merge these with indigenous and other imported traditions to create totally new forms. In short, the flows and movements of ideas, images, capital and people will generate a new wave of mixtures, new cultures, new hybridities, in short a creolization of the world.

THE MAKING OF GLOBAL SOCIETY

We have considered the extent and scope of globalization and suggested that the impressive growth of social globalization remains to be fully appreciated and realized. There are at least seven other major gains at a social level to be realized from globalization and globality:

1. An extension of democratic, civil and human rights.
2. The spread of education and literacy.
3. Information and access to communications for all the world's inhabitants.
4. The growth of multicultural understanding and awareness.
5. The empowering of women and other historically disadvantaged groups.
6. The promotion of environment-friendly production systems.
7. The growth of leisure, creativity and freedom from want.

Can any of these dreams be realized? There are those who still pin their hopes on a 'positive nationalism'. Bienefeld, for example, while recognizing the malign as well as the benign aspects of nationalism, nonetheless says that we have little alternative but to rely on a reformed nation-state. In what other form, Bienefeld (1994: 122) asks:

> can we realistically hope, at the end of the twentieth century to redefine and reconstruct political entities that would allow us to manage the increasingly destructive forces of global competition while providing individuals with the capacity to define themselves as social beings and while containing the risk of political conflict between such political entities?

The question is a good one, but we feel that those who wish to reform the nation-state do not adequately recognize how far disillusionment has already set in. In some 'hollowed out' or 'broken-backed' states, for example Liberia, Sierra Leone, Myanmar or Somalia, the state has imploded – leaving its former citizens to the mercies of gangs and warlords. But even in the industrialized states, the belief in nationhood and formal democracy has eroded. The former appears increasingly as parochial and irrelevant, while democracy seems to offer little more than a hollow administrative system for reaching decisions that do not begin to address the needs or tap the energies of citizens living in the rapidly changing world. Besides, as we argued in Chapter 5, the cultural pluralism characteristic of the global age undermines the idea of territoriality and sovereignty, the historical building blocks of the nation-state. Where the nation-state has been visibly strengthened, as in the USA during the Bush Jnr administration, its global stance has taken a unilateral and imperial turn that is quite some distance from 'positive nationalism'.

That said, there clearly is still a need to develop more active national democracies with flourishing civil societies. However, in addition to and in some respects superseding the nation-state are other sites of political encounter and engagement. Let us just mention again eight of these sites, which were discussed at greater length elsewhere in this book:

1. At the international level, courts, particularly those dealing with human rights and genocide, have begun to make effective judgements that transcend domestic legislation.
2. The international governmental organizations, such as the UN and its agencies, have made some advances in acting on behalf of a global community, though the UN is still crucially dependent on the members of the Security Council and especially the USA.
3. A proliferation of regional bodies has developed, admittedly with a highly variable level of power and authority.
4. TNCs have generated immense resources and power and are effectively out of the control of the nation-state. In Chapter 7 we showed how some accept their corporate social responsibilities.
5. Transnational communities have developed through enhanced travel and communications.
6. Global cities have evolved to service the needs of the world economy and its cosmopolitan citizens, a development discussed in Chapter 17.
7. Global diasporas and religions have resurfaced to bridge the gap between universalism and the need to link to one's past (Chapters 16 and 21).
8. Global social movements have arisen to help to build the global society of the future (Chapters 18, 19 and 20).

We need to say just a little more about global social movements. In sociology there has always been a creative tension between 'structure' and 'agency' – what happens to one and what one makes happen. Social movements are the key agents for progressive and humanitarian social change. Even if they only achieve a few of the tasks they have set for themselves, their struggles will have been worthwhile. The environment and women's movements have merited our special attention as they both have considerable transformatory potential but other social movements are also potentially significant in the slow construction of a relatively benign and functioning global society.

■ ■ ■ ■ ■ ■ ■ ■ REVIEW AND FINAL REMARKS

In this concluding chapter, we have partly concurred with those who argue that not everything connected with the making of a global society brings advantages and gains to the human condition. A more integrated world is not necessarily a more harmonious or a more equal one. We are faced with greater risks as well as opportunities. As we have seen throughout this book, much transnational activity is atavistic and potentially damaging to others, as in the case of neo-Nazi cells, crime gangs, terrorist networks or drug syndicates that operate on an international basis. Some transnational movements and groups may evoke a common universal purpose, yet are divided and made ineffective by internal squabbles.

There are also plausible concerns about the ways in which global homogenization could eventually dilute local and national particularities, about environmental problems, a demographic explosion, joblessness and poverty, the emergence of terrorism, drug trafficking and the spread of epidemics throughout the world. Globalization has so far done little to diminish the blight of poverty and wretchedness in which about half the world's inhabitants are forced to live. And social movements have yet to prove effective in mobilizing efforts to reduce global inequalities. Thus, we are not dealing with a utopian, unilinear process that will inevitably take us to a better world.

Despite these concessions to the sceptics and critics, we nonetheless argue that globalization has become irreversible and is taking on new forms not previously encountered. Moreover, although the direction in which it may evolve is unclear and certainly not fixed, some global changes are very positive. They provide a greater potential than ever before for the world's inhabitants to forge new understandings, alliances and structures – both from below and in alliance with elite institutions – in the pursuit of more harmonious, environmentally sustainable and humanitarian solutions to local and global problems. The world of work has been transformed and for many lucky citizens the possibilities for a creative engagement with global changes are much enhanced. In itself globalization will lead neither to a dystopia or a utopia. The future directions of global society depend on us as ordinary world citizens, on what moral positions we choose and what battles we are prepared to fight.

A 'global ecumene', 'a universal humanism', a 'shared planet', a 'cosmopolitan democracy' or 'a creolized culture' – these notions are not fully developed realities, but possibilities and aspirations. The world remains lopsided. Many powerful and wealthy actors profit disproportionately from global changes. Throughout this book we have shown how 'global winners' use their privileged access to power, wealth and opportunity to feather their own nests. The TNCs, crime syndicates, rich tourists, skilled migrants and others are all major beneficiaries of the opportunities for transnational activity. It behoves us to remind you as we end our text of the many 'global losers' – the refugees, poor peasants, famine and AIDS victims, and the underclasses of the collapsing cities – who still peer through the bars at the gilded cages of the rich and powerful.

The key social challenge of the twenty-first century is to prise open the bars for these disadvantaged people so that they can discover the transformatory possibilities that globalization has generated. A vibrant civil society, creative cultural achievements and active global social movements provide far-off glimpses of that benign future. However distant, we hope we have encouraged you to envisage some of the many possibilities for social engagement, cooperation and positive change.

FURTHER READING

- An articulate and coherent critique of globalization from a Marxist point of view is provided in Roger Burbach et al. (1997) *Globalization and its Discontents: The Rise of Postmodern Socialisms*.

- Although written by an anthropologist rather than a sociologist, Hannerz's *Cultural Complexity* (1992) provides an insightful account of cultural and social change in many settings.

- Benjamin Barber's *Jihad vs. McWorld* (1995) speaks to the gloomy visions of a clash of civilizations and a homogenized global consumer culture.

- Martin Albrow's *The Global Age* (1996) remains an incisive introduction to global thinking.

GROUP WORK

- Divide into two groups: Group A, who are statistically minded and Group B, whose eyes swim when they see a number larger than ten. Group B will visit the Warwick world globalization index at http://www2.warwick.ac.uk/fac/soc/csgr/index/. Look at the social globalization indicators. How good are they? Can you think of others? Group A will respond to a presentation by Group B.

- The class will divide into groups of five who will either recall visiting large shopping malls or will set out on a fresh expedition to unfamiliar palaces of consumption. Report on the fusion between shopping and entertainment and shopping and well-being. How successful were the malls you visited in joining these activities?

- Some critics of globalization express anxiety at the disquieting sense of lost local or national identity that many individuals may feel. Drawing on your own personal experiences, what are the perceptions of the class members themselves on this question and how can you account for them?

QUESTIONS TO THINK ABOUT

?

1. 'The degree to which the world economy has become integrated is no greater than it was before the First World War.' Discuss.

2. How can socially marginalized and excluded people improve their situation?

3. Is the world likely to become more culturally homogeneous or more creolized?

4. Using the material in this chapter and any other sources you like, construct (a) an optimistic scenario for an emergent global society followed by (b) a critique that traces the possible parallel dangers and difficulties.

**WHAT'S ON
THE WEB**

- http://www.monde-diplomatique.fr/dossiers/ft/ Is globalization inevitable and desirable? This was the topic of a debate convened by the French newspaper *Le Monde Diplomatique* in 1997. Although a little while ago, the issues are still very live. And, by the way, the debate is in English.

- http://www.indiana.edu/~wanthro/consum.htm A small site developed by Richard Wilks on global consumer culture, with about 25 links.

- http://www2.warwick.ac.uk/fac/soc/sociology/research/cscs/ A site on creolization being developed by one of the current authors.

- http://gsociology.icaap.org/reports.html Statistical and other hard data on global trends can be accessed here.

References

Abella, M. A. (1993) 'Labor mobility, trade and structural change: the Philippine experience', *Asian and Pacific Migration Journal*, **2**(3), 249–68.

Abu-Lughod, J. (1989) *Before European Hegemony: The World System, AD 1250–1350*, New York: Oxford University Press.

Accor (2005) Web page of the Accor Group <http://www.accorservices.co.uk/en/aboutus/accorgroupprofile/accorgroupprofile.asp>.

Adorno, T. and Horkheimer, M. (1972) *Dialectic of Enlightenment*, New York: Herder.

Afshar, H. (ed.) (1996) *Women and Politics in the Third World*, London: Routledge.

Aglietta, M. (1979) *A Theory of Capitalist Regulation*, London: New Left Books.

Agostinelli, G. (1991) *Migration–Development Interrelationships: The Case of the Philippines*, New York: Center for Migration Studies.

Ahmed, A. S. (1992) *Postmodernism and Islam: Predicament and Promise*, London: Routledge.

Alavi, H. (1972) 'The state in post-colonial societies: Pakistan and Bangladesh', *New Left Review*, 74, 59–81.

Albrow, M. (1987) 'Sociology for one world', *International Sociology*, **2**, 1–12.

Albrow, M. (1990) 'Globalization, knowledge and society: an introduction', in Albrow, M. and King, E. (eds) *Globalization, Knowledge and Society*, London: Sage, 3–13.

Albrow, M. (1996) *The Global Age*, Cambridge: Polity Press.

Albrow, M. (1997) 'Travelling beyond local cultures: socioscapes in a global city', in Eade, J. (ed.) *Living the Global City: Globalization as a Local Process*, London: Routledge, 37–55.

Alcock, P. (1997) *Understanding Poverty* (2nd edn) Basingstoke: Macmillan.

Aldridge, A. (2000) *Religion in the Contemporary World: A Sociological Introduction*, Cambridge: Polity Press.

Alexander, D. (2002) 'Nature's impartiality, man's inhumanity: reflections on terrorism and world crisis in a context of historical disaster', *Disasters*, **26**(1), 1–9.

Allahar, A. (1994) 'More than an oxymoron: ethnicity and the social construction of primordial attachment', unpublished paper, Department of Sociology, University of Western Ontario, Canada.

Allen, J., Braham, P. and Lewis, P. (eds) (1992) *Political and Economic Forms of Modernity*, Cambridge: Polity Press.

Amin, A. (ed.) (1994) *Post-Fordism: A Reader*, Oxford: Blackwell.

Amin, S. (1974) *Accumulation on a World Scale* (2 vols) New York: Monthly Review Press.

Anderson, B. (1983) *Imagined Communities: Reflections on the Origins and Spread of Nationalism*, London: Verso.

Anderson, K. and Rieff, D. (2005) '"Global civil society": a sceptical view', in Anheier, H., Glasius, M. and Kaldor, M. (eds) *Global Civil Society 2004/05*, London: Sage, 26–39.

Andrae, G. and Beckman, B. (1985) *The Wheat Trap: Bread and Underdevelopment in Nigeria*, London: Zed Books/Scandinavian Institute of African Studies.

Andrews, D. L., Carrington, B., Jackson, S. L. and Mazur, Z. (1996) 'Jordanscapes: a preliminary analysis of the global popular', *Sociology of Sport Journal*, **14**, 428–57.

Anheier, H. and Themudo, N. (2002) 'Organisational forms of global civil society: implications of going global', in Glasius, M., Kaldor, M. and Anheier, H. (eds) *Global Civil Society Yearbook 2002*, Oxford: Oxford University Press, 191–216.

Anheier, H., Glasius, M. and Kaldor, M. (eds) (2001) *Global Civil Society Yearbook 2001*, Oxford: Oxford University Press.

Anheier, H., Glasius, M. and Kaldor, M. (eds) (2002) *Global Civil Society Yearbook 2002*, Oxford: Oxford University Press.

Anheier, H., Glasius M. and Kaldor, M. (2005) 'Introducing global civil society', in Anheier, H., Glasius, M. and Kaldor, M. (eds) *Global Civil Society 2004/05*, London: Sage, 3–22.

Appadurai, A. (1990) 'Disjuncture and difference in the global cultural economy', in Featherstone, M. (ed.) *Global Culture: Nationalism, Globalization and Modernity*, London: Sage, 295–310.

Archetti, P. E. (1996) 'In search of national identity: Argentinian football and Europe', in Mangan, J. A. (ed.) *Tribal Identities: Nationalism, Sport and Europe*, London: Frank Cass, 201–19.

Armstrong, G. and Young, M. (2000) 'Fanatical football chants: creating and controlling carnival', in Finn, G. P. T. and Giulianotti, R. (eds) *Football Culture: Local Contests, Global Visions*, London: Frank Cass, 173–211.

Arrighi, G. (1994) *The Long Twentieth Century*, New York: Verso.

Athanasiou, T. (1997) *Slow Reckoning: The Ecology of a Divided Planet*, London: Secker & Warburg.

Augé, M. (1995) *Non-Places*, London: Verso.

Auletta, K. (1982) *The Underclass*, New York: Random House.

Avineri, S. (1968) *The Social and Political Thought of Karl Marx*, Cambridge: Cambridge University Press.

Badham, R. (1986) *Theories of Industrial Society*, London: Croom Helm.

Bagchi, A. K. (1982) *The Political Economy of Underdevelopment*, Cambridge: Cambridge University Press.

Baird, V. (1997) 'Trash: inside the heap', *New Internationalist*, (295), 7–10.

Bale, J. and Sang, J. (1996) *Kenyan Running: Movement Culture, Geography and Global Change*, London: Frank Cass.

Banton, M. (1994) 'UNESCO', in Ellis Cashmore, E. (ed.) *Dictionary of Race and Ethnic Relations* (3rd edn) London: Routledge, 336–7.

Barber, B. (1995) *Jihad vs. McWorld*, New York: Ballantine Books.

Barker, C. (1999) *Television, Globalisation and Cultural Identities*, Buckingham: Open University Press.

Barker, E. (1989) *New Religious Movements: A Practical Introduction*, London: Stationery Office.

Barry, A.-M. and Yuill, C. (2002) *Understanding Health: A Sociological Introduction*, London: Sage.

Basu, A. (ed.) (1995) *The Challenge of Local Feminisms*, Boulder, CO: Westview Press.

Baudrillard, J. (1988) *Selected Writings*, ed. by M. Poster, Cambridge: Polity Press.

Bauman, Z. (1991) *Modernity and the Holocaust*, Cambridge: Polity Press.

Bauman, Z. (1995) *Life in Fragments: Essays in Postmodern Morality*, Oxford: Blackwell.

Bauman, Z. (2000) *Liquid Modernity*, Cambridge: Polity Press.

Beck, U. (1992) *The Risk Society: Towards a New Modernity*, London: Sage.

Beck, U. (1998) 'The cosmopolitan manifesto', *New Statesman*, 20 March, 28–30.

Beck, U. (1999a) *World Risk Society*, Cambridge: Polity Press.

Beck, U. (1999b) *The Reinvention of Politics: Rethinking Modernity in the Global Social Order*, Cambridge: Polity Press.

Beck, U. (2000a) *Brave New World of Work*, Cambridge: Polity Press.

Beck, U. (2000b) *What is Globalization?* Cambridge: Polity Press.

Beck, U. and Beck-Gernsheim, E. (2002) *Individualization: Institutionalized Individualism and its Social and Political Consequences*, London: Sage.

Beck, U., Giddens, A. and Lash, S. (eds) (1994) *Reflexive Modernization: Politics, Tradition and Aesthetics in the Modern Social Order*, Cambridge: Polity Press.

Becker, H. S. (1963) *Outsiders: Studies in the Sociology of Deviance*, New York: Free Press.

Becker, H. S. (2005) Introduction to the Danish edition of *Outsiders: Studies in the Sociology of Deviance* posted on 'Howie's home page' http://home.earthlink.net/~hsbecker/danishintro.htm.

Beckford, J. A. (1985) *Cult Controversies: The Societal*

Response to New Religious Movements, London: Tavistock.

Beckford, J. A. (1986) *New Religious Movements and Rapid Social Change*, London: Sage for UNESCO.

Beckles, H. McD. (1998) *The Development of West Indies Cricket*, vol. 2, *The Age of Globalization*, Barbados: The Press, University of the West Indies.

Beg, E. (1996) *The Cult of the Black Virgin*, Harmondsworth: Penguin.

Bell, D. (1973) *The Coming of Post-industrial Society: A Venture in Social Forecasting*, Harmondsworth: Penguin.

Bellah, R. N. (1985) *Tokugawa Religion: The Cultural Roots of Modern Japan*, New York: Free Press.

Bello, W. (1994) *Dark Victory: The United States, Structural Adjustment and Global Poverty*, London: Pluto Press.

Bello, W. (2001) *The Future in the Balance: Essays on Globalization and Resistance*, Oakland, CA: Food First Books.

Bello, W. (2002) *Deglobalization: Ideas for a New World Economy*, London: Zed Books.

Bennett, A. S. (2000) *Popular Music and Youth Culture: Music, Identity and Place*, Basingstoke: Macmillan.

Bennett, W. L. (2004) 'Branded political communication: lifestyle politics, logo campaigns, and the rise of global citizenship', in Føllesdal, A., Micheletti, M. and Stolle, D. (eds) *Politics, Products and Markets: Exploring Political Consumerism Past and Present*, New Brunswick, NJ: Transaction Books, 101–25.

Bentley, M. (2003) 'Sustainable consumption: ethics, national indices and international relations', unpublished Ph.D, American Graduate School of International Relations and Diplomacy, Paris.

Berger, J. (1972) *Ways of Seeing*, Harmondsworth: Penguin/BBC.

Bergesen, A. J. and Lizardo, O. (2004) 'International terrorism and the world-system', *Sociological Theory*, **22**(1), 38–52.

Bergeson, A. (1990) 'Turning world-system theory on its head', in Featherstone, M. (ed.) *Global Culture: Nationalism, Globalization and Modernity*, London: Sage, 67–82.

Beynon, H. (1973) *Working for Ford*, Harmondsworth: Allen Lane.

Bhabha, H. K. (1986) 'Signs taken for wonders: questions of ambivalence and authority under a tree outside Delhi, May 1817', in Gates, H. L. Jr (ed.) *'Race', Writing and Difference*, Chicago: University of Chicago Press, 173–83.

Bienefeld, M. (1994) 'Capitalism and the nation state in the dog days of the twentieth century', in Miliband, R. and Panitch, L. (eds) *Socialist Register: Between Globalism and Nationalism*, London: Merlin Press, 94–129.

Binnie, J. (2004) *The Globalization of Sexuality*, London: Sage.

Bloor, M. (1995) *The Sociology of HIV Transmission*, London: Sage.

Bluestone, B. and Harrison, B. (1987) 'The impact of private disinvestment on workers and their communities', in Peet, R. (ed.) *International Capitalism and Industrial Restructuring*, London: Allen & Unwin, 72–104.

Bocock, R. and Thompson, K. (1985) *Religion and Ideology: A Reader*, Manchester: Open University Press.

Booth, C. (1967) *Life and Labour of the People of London*, London: Macmillan.

Boris, E. and Prugl, E. (eds) (1996) *Homeworkers in Global Perspective: Invisible No More*, New York: Routledge.

Boserup, E. (1970) *Women's Role in Economic Development*, London: Allen & Unwin.

Bourdieu, P. (1984) *Distinction: A Social Critique of the Judgement of Taste*, Cambridge, MA: Harvard University Press.

Bourdieu, P. (1993) *Sociology in Question*, London: Sage.

Bourdieu, P. and Wacquant, L. J. D. (1992) *An Invitation to Reflexive Sociology*, Cambridge: Polity Press.

Bové, J., Dufour, F. and de Casparis, A. (2001) *The World is Not for Sale: Farmers against Junk Food*, London: Verso.

Braaten, J. (1991) *Habermas's Critical Theory of Society*, Albany, NY: State University of New York Press.

Bramble, B. J. and Porter, G. (1992) 'Non-governmental organizations and the making of US international environmental policy', in Hurrell, A. and Kingsbury, B. (eds) *The Inter national Politics of the Environment*, Oxford: Clarendon Press, 313–53.

Branston, G. and Stafford, R. (2003) *The Media Student's Book*, London: Routledge.

Braverman, H. (1974) *Labour and Monopoly Capital*, New York: Monthly Review Press.

Brenner, R. (2002) *The Boom and the Bubble: The US in the World Economy*, London: Verso.

Brett, E. A. (1985) *The World Economy since the War: The Politics of Uneven Development*, Basingstoke: Macmillan.

Brown, I. and Molla, A. (2005) 'Determinants of Internet and cell phone banking adoption in South Africa', <http://www.arraydev.com/commerce/jibc/2005-02/brown.HTM>.

Brubaker, R. (1991) *The Limits of Rationality: An Essay on the Social and Moral Thought of Max Weber*, London: Routledge.

Bruegel, I. (1988) 'Sex and race in the labour market', a paper given at the Socialist Feminist Forum, London.

Bryman, A. (1995) *Disney and his World*, London: Routledge.

Bunch, C., Antrobus, P., Frost, S. and Reilly, N. (2001) 'International networking for women's human rights', in Edwards, M. and Gaventa, J. (eds) *Global Citizen Action*, London: Earthscan, 217–30.

Bundy, C. (1979) *The Rise and Fall of the South African Peasantry*, London: Heinemann Educational Books.

Bunting, M. (2003) 'Passion and pessimism', *Guardian*, 5 April (a profile of Zygmunt Bauman).

Bunyard, P. (2004) 'Crossing the threshold', *Ecologist*, **34**(1), 55–9.

Burawoy, M. (2005) '2004 American Sociological Association presidential address: for public sociology', *British Journal of Sociology*, **56**(2), 259–94.

Burbach, R., Núñez, O. and Kagarlitsky, B. (1997) *Globalization and its Discontents: The Rise of Postmodern Socialisms*, London: Pluto Press.

Burton, J. (1972) *World Society*, Cambridge: Cambridge University Press.

Buse, K. and Walt, G. (2002) 'Globalisation and multilateral public–private health partnerships: issues for health policy', in Lee, K., Buse, K. and Fustukian, S. (eds) *Health Policy in a Globalising World*, Cambridge: Cambridge University Press, 41–62.

Buse, K., Drager, N., Fustukian, S. and Lee, K. (2002) 'Globalisation and health policy: trends and opportunities', in Lee, K., Buse, K. and Fustukian, S. (eds) *Health Policy in a Globalising World*, Cambridge: Cambridge University Press, 251–80.

Bush, R. (1996) 'The politics of food and starvation', *Review of African Political Economy*, **23**(68), 169–95.

Byerly, C. M. (1995) 'News, consciousness and social participation: the role of Women's Feature Service in world news', in Valdivia, A. N. (ed.) *Feminism, Multiculturalism and the Media: Global Diversities*, London: Sage, 105–22.

Byrne, P. (1997) *Social Movements in Britain*, London: Routledge.

Bystdzienski, J. M. (ed.) (1992) *Women Transforming Politics: Worldwide Strategies for Empowerment*, Bloomington: Indiana University Press.

Cairncross, F. (1995) 'The death of distance', *The Economist*, 30 September.

Cairncross, F. (1997a) 'Telecommunications', *The Economist*, 13 September.

Cairncross, F. (1997b) *The Death of Distance*, Boston, MA: Harvard Business School Press.

Calhoun, C. (2002) 'The class consciousness of frequent travellers: towards a critique of actually existing cosmopolitanism', in Vertovec, S. and Cohen, R. (eds) *Conceiving Cosmopolitanism: Theory, Context and Practice*, Oxford: Oxford University Press, 86–119.

Camilleri, J. and Falk, J. (1992) *The End of Sovereignty? The Politics of a Shrinking and Fragmenting World*, Cheltenham: Edward Elgar.

Campani, G. (1995) 'Women migrants: from marginal subjects to social actors', in Cohen, R. (ed.) *The Cambridge Survey of World Migration*, Cambridge: Cambridge University Press, 536–50.

Campbell, D. (2004) 'Lost in transit', *New Internationalist*, (369), 20–2.

Canclini N. G. (1995) *Hybrid Cultures: Strategies for Entering and Leaving Modernity*, Minneapolis: University of Minneapolis Press.

Caneles, A. (1999) 'Industrialization, urbanization and population growth on the border', *Borderlines*, 7(7), 1–15.

Cardoso, F. H. and Falletto, E. (1969) *Dependency*

and Development in Latin America, Berkeley: University of California Press.

Carroll, B. A. (1989) '"Women take action!" Women's direct action and social change', *Women's Studies International Forum*, **12**(1), 3–24.

Carroll, W. K. and Carson, C. (2003) 'The network of global corporations and elite policy groups: a structure for transnational capitalist formation?' *Global Networks: A Journal of Transnational Affairs*, **3**(1), 29–58.

Carson, R. (1963) *Silent Spring*, London: Hamish Hamilton.

Cashmore, E. (ed.) (1994) *Dictionary of Race and Ethnic Relations* (3rd edn) London: Routledge.

Cass, N., Shrove, E. and Urry, J. (2005) 'Social exclusion, mobility and class', *Sociological Review*, **53**(3), 539–55.

Castells, M. (1977) *The Urban Question: A Marxist Approach*, London: Edward Arnold.

Castells, M. (1983) *The City and the Grassroots: A Cross-cultural Theory of Urban Social Movements*, London: Edward Arnold.

Castells, M. (1989) *The Informational City: Information Technology, Economic Restructuring and the Urban–Regional Process*, Oxford: Blackwell.

Castells, M. (1996) *The Rise of the Network Society* (vol. 1 of Castells, M., *The Information Age: Economy, Society and Culture*), Oxford: Blackwell (rev. edn 2000).

Castells, M. (1997) *The Power of Identity* (vol. 2 of *The Information Age: Economy, Society and Culture*) Oxford: Blackwell (rev. edn 2000).

Castells, M. (1998) *End of Millennium* (vol. 3 of *The Information Age: Economy, Society and Culture*) Oxford: Blackwell (rev. edn 2000).

Castles, S. and Miller, M. (2003) *The Age of Migration: International Population Movements in the Modern World* (3rd edn) Basingstoke: Palgrave Macmillan.

Cavanagh, J. (1997) 'The global resistance to sweatshops', in Ross, A. (ed.) *No Sweat*, London: Verso, 39–50.

Chang, G. (2000) *Disposable Domestics: Immigrant Women Workers in the Global Economy*, Cambridge, MA: South End Press.

Chase, H. (1994) 'The *Meyhane* or the McDonald's? Changes in eating habits and the evolution of fast food in Istanbul', in Zubaida, S. and Tapper, R. (eds) *Culinary Cultures of the Middle East*, London: I.B. Tauris, 73–86.

Chidester, D. (2004) *Salvation and Suicide: An Interpretation of Jim Jones, the People's Temple, and Jonestown*, Bloomington: Indiana University Press (first published 1988).

Chinoy, E. (1967) *Society: An Introduction to Sociology*, New York: Random House.

Chomsky, N. (2004) *Hegemony or Survival: America's Quest for Global Dominance*, London: Penguin.

Ciment, J. (1999) 'Life expectancy of Russian males falls to 58',<http://bmj. bmjjournals.com/cgi/content/full/319/7208/468/a>.

Clammer, J. (1992) 'Shopping in Japan', in Shields, R. (ed.) *Lifestyle Shopping*, London: Routledge, 195–213.

Clapp, J. (1997) 'Threats to the environment in an era of globalization: an end to state sovereignty?' in Schrecker, T. (ed.) *Surviving Globalism*, Basingstoke: Macmillan, 123–40.

Clifford, J. (1988) *The Predicament of Culture: Twentieth Century Ethnography, Literature and Art*, Cambridge, MA: Harvard University Press.

Coca-Cola Company (1997) *Annual Report*, Atlanta, GA.

Cohen, E. (1972) 'Towards a sociology of international tourism', *Social Research*, **39**, 164–82.

Cohen, G. A. (1978) *Karl Marx's Theory of History: A Defence*, Oxford: Oxford University Press.

Cohen, R. (1987) *The New Helots: Migrants in the International Division of Labour*, Aldershot: Gower.

Cohen, R. (ed.) (1995) *The Cambridge Survey of World Migration*, Cambridge: Cambridge University Press.

Cohen, R. (1997) *Global Diasporas: An Introduction*, London: UCL Press.

Cohen, R. (2006) *Migration and its Enemies: Global Capital, Migrant Labour and the Nation-state*, Aldershot: Ashgate.

Cohen, R. and Rai, S. (eds) (2000) *Global Social Movements*, London: Athlone.

Cohen, S. (1972) *Folk Devils and Moral Panics*, London: MacGibben & Kee.

Cohen, S. (1985) *Visions of Social Control: Crime Punishment and Classification*, Cambridge: Polity Press.

Coleman, S. (2005) 'Blogs and the new politics of listening', *Political Quarterly*, **76**(2), 273–80.

Comte, A. (1853) *The Positive Philosophy of Auguste Comte, Freely Translated and Condensed by Harriet Martineau*, London: John Chapman.

Cooper, A. F. (1997) 'Snapshots of cyber-diplomacy: Greenpeace against French nuclear testing and the Spain–Canada "fish war"', discussion paper no. 36, *Diplomatic Studies Programme*, Leicester University.

Cooper, R. (1985) *The Baha'is of Iran*, London: Minority Rights Group.

Coser, L. A. and Rosenberg, B. (1976) *Sociological Theory: A Book of Readings* (4th edn) New York: Macmillan Publishing.

Coward, R. (1978) 'Sexual liberation and the family', *m/f*, 1, 7–24.

Crow, G. (1997) *Comparative Sociology and Social Theory*, Basingstoke: Macmillan.

Cruise O'Brien, R. (1979) 'Mass communications: social mechanisms of incorporation and dependence', in Villamil, J. (ed.) *Transnational Capitalism and National Development*, New Jersey: Humanities Press, 129–43.

Crystal, D. (1995) *The Cambridge Encyclopedia of Language*, Cambridge: Cambridge University Press.

Crystal, E, (1989) 'Tourism in Toraja (Sulawesi, Indonesia)', in Smith, V. L. (ed.) *Hosts and Guests* (2nd edn) Philadelphia, PA: University of Pennsylvania Press, 139–67.

Curtis, S. and Taket, A. (1996) *Health and Societies*, London: Arnold.

Davis, M. (1991) *City of Quartz*, London: Verso.

Dawkins, R. (1991) *The Blind Watchmaker*, Harmondsworth: Penguin.

Delanty, G. (2000) *Citizenship in a Global Age: Society, Culture, Politics*, Buckingham: Open University Press.

Desai, M. and Said, Y. (2001) 'The new anti-capitalist movement: money and global civil society', in Anheier, H., Glasius, M. and Kaldor, M. (eds) *Global Civil Society 2001*, Oxford: Oxford University Press, 51–78.

Desai, S. (2004) 'Lucky foot? Unlucky rabbit', http://www.buzzle.com/editorials/5-16-2004-54202.asp.

De Vidas, A. A. (1995) 'Textiles, memory and the souvenir industry in the Andes', in Lanfant, M. F., Allcock, J. B. and Bruner, E. M. (eds) *International Tourism: Identity and Change*, London: Sage, 67–83.

Dicken, P. (1992) *Global Shift: The Internationalization of Economic Activity*, London: Paul Chapman.

Dicken, P. (2003) *Global Shift: Reshaping the Global Economic Map in the 21st Century*, London: Sage.

Dobson, A. (2000) *Green Political Thought* (3rd edn) London: Routledge.

Dodds, F. (ed.) (1997) *The Way Forward: Beyond Agenda 21*, London: Earthscan.

Dohse, K., Jürgens, U. and Malsch, T. (1985) 'From Fordism to Toyotism', *Politics and Society*, 14(2), 115–46.

Donnelly, P. (1996) 'The local and the global: globalization in the sociology of sport', *Journal of Sport and Social Issues*, (23), 239–57.

Dore, R. (1958) *City Life in Japan: A Study of a Tokyo Ward*, London: Routledge & Kegan Paul.

Dore, R. (1959) *Land Reform in Japan*, London: Oxford University Press.

Dore, R. (1965) *Education in Tokugawa Japan*, London: Routledge & Kegan Paul.

Dore, R. (1986) *Flexible Rigidities: Industrial Policy and Structural Adjustment in the Japanese Economy, 1970–80*, London: Athlone Press.

Douglas, M. and Isherwood, B. (1978) *The World of Goods: Towards an Anthropology of Consumption*, New York: W. W. Norton.

Dreze, J. and Sen, A. (1989) *Hunger and Public Action*, Oxford: Clarendon Press.

Drucker, P. (1989) *The New Realities: In Government and Politics, in Economy and Business, in Society and in World View*, Oxford: Heinemann.

Duffy, R. (2004) 'Ecotourists on the beach', in Sheller, M. and Urry, J. (eds) *Tourism Mobilities: Places to Play, Places in Play*, London: Routledge, 32–41.

Dunning, J. H. (1993a) *Multinational Enterprises in a Global Economy*, Wokingham: Addison-Wesley.

Dunning, J. H. (1993b) *The Globalization of Business*, London: Routledge.

Durkheim, E. (1933) *The Division of Labor in Society* (2nd edn) New York: Macmillan.

Durkheim, E. (1938) *The Rules of Sociological Method*, Chicago: Chicago University Press.

Durkheim, E. (1952) *Suicide: A Study in Sociology*, London: Routledge.

Durkheim, E. (1976) *The Elementary Forms of Religious Life*, London: George Allen & Unwin (first published 1915)

Durning, A. T. (1992) *How Much is Enough? The Consumer Society and the Future of the Earth*, London: Earthscan.

Dyreson, M. (2003) 'Globalizing the nation-making process: modern sport in world history', *International Journal of the History of Sport*, **20**(1), 99–106.

Dyson, T. M. (1996) *Population and Food: Global Trends and Future Prospects*, London: Routledge.

Edensor, T. (2004) 'Reconstituting the Taj Mahal: tourist flows and glocalization', in Sheller, M. and Urry, J. (eds) *Tourism Mobilities: Places to Play, Places in Play*, London: Routledge, 103–15.

Edgell, S. (2005) *Sociological Analysis of Work: Change and Continuity in Paid and Unpaid Work*, London: Sage.

Edwards, T. (2000) *Contradictions of Consumption: Concepts, Policies and Politics in Consumer Society*, Buckingham: Open University Press.

Eichberg, H. (1984) 'Olympic sport: neocolonialism and alternatives', *International Review for the Sociology of Sport*, **19**, 97–105.

Elger, T. and Smith, C. (eds) (1994) *Global Japanization? The Transnational Transformation of the Labour Process*, London: Routledge.

Elias, N. (1978) *What is Sociology?* London: Hutchinson.

Elias, N. (1986) 'Introduction', in Elias, N. and Dunning, E., *Quest for Excitement: Sport and the Civilizing Process*, Oxford: Basil Blackwell, 19–62.

Elias, N. (1994) *The Civilizing Process*, Oxford: Blackwell.

Enloe, C. (1988) *Does Khaki Become You? The Militarization of Women's Lives*, San Francisco: HarperCollins.

Enloe, C. (1989) *Bananas, Beaches and Bases: Making Feminist Sense of International Politics*, Berkeley: University of California Press.

Enloe, C. (2000) *Maneuvers: The International Politics of Militarizing Women's Lives*, Berkeley: University of California Press.

Esposito, J. L (1995) *The Islamic Threat: Myth or Reality?* Oxford: Oxford University Press.

Evans, M. and Lee, E. (eds) (2002) *Real Bodies: A Sociological Introduction*, Basingstoke: Palgrave Macmillan.

Fainstein, N. (1992) 'The urban underclass and mismatch theory re-examined', in Cross, M. (ed.) *Ethnic Minorities and Industrial Change in Europe and North America*, Cambridge: Cambridge University Press, 276–312.

Faist, T. (1998) 'Transnational social spaces out of international migration: evolution, significance and future prospects', *Archives of European Sociology*, **39**(2), 213–47.

Faist, T. (2000) *The Volume and Dynamics of International Migration and Transnational Society*, Oxford: Clarendon Press.

Fanon, F. (1967) *The Wretched of the Earth*, Harmondsworth: Penguin.

Featherstone, M. (1987) 'Lifestyle and consumer culture', *Theory, Culture and Society*, **4**, 55–70.

Featherstone, M. (1990) 'Global culture: an introduction', in Featherstone, M. (ed.) *Global Culture: Nationalism, Globalization and Modernity*, London: Sage, 1–14.

Featherstone, M. (1992) *Consumer Culture and Postmodernism*, London: Sage.

Feifer, M. (1985) *Going Places: The Ways of the Tourist from Imperial Rome to the Present*, Basingstoke: Macmillan.

Festingher, L., Riecken, H. W. and Schachter, S. (1956) *When Prophecy Fails: A Social and Psychological Study of a Modern Group that Predicted the End of the World*, New York: Harper & Row.

Feuerbach, L. (1957) *The Essence of Christianity*, New York: Harper & Row.

Finn, G. P. T. and Giulianotti, R. (eds) (2000) *Football Culture: Local Contests, Global Visions*, London: Frank Cass.

Firat, A. F. (1995) 'Consumer culture or culture consumed?', in Costa, J. A. and Bamossy, G. J. (eds) *Marketing in a Multicultural World*, London: Sage, 105–25.

Fisher, J. (1993) *The Road from Rio: Sustainable Development and the Non-Governmental Movement in the Third World*, Westport, CN: Praeger.

Fisher, M. P. (1997) *Living Religions*, London: Prentice Hall.

Fligstein, N. (1981) *Going North: Migration of Blacks and Whites from the South, 1900–1950*, New York: Academic Press.

Foucault, M. (1973) *Birth of the Clinic*, London: Routledge.

Foucault, M. (1977) *Discipline and Punish: The Birth of the Prison*, London: Allen Lane.

France, P. (1996) *Hermits: The Insights of Solitude*, London: Chatto & Windus.

Frank, A. G. (1967) *Capitalism and Underdevelopment in Latin America*, New York: Monthly Review Press.

Frank, A. G. (1969) *Latin America: Undevelopment or Revolution*, New York: Monthly Review Press.

Freedland, J. (1999) 'Shangri-la. It's quite a European place-name, the way it splits in two', *Guardian*, 24 March.

Freidberg, S. (2001) 'On the trail of the global green bean: methodological considerations in multi-site ethnography', *Global Networks*, 1(4), 353–68.

Freud, S. (1946) *Totem and Taboo: Resemblances between the Psychic Lives of Savages and Neurotics*, New York: Vintage.

Friburg, M. and Hettne, B. (1988) 'Local mobilization and world system politics', *International Journal of Social Science*, 40(117), 341–60.

Friedan, B. (1963) *The Feminine Mystique*, London: Gollanz.

Friedman, E. (1995) 'Women's human rights: the emergence of a movement', in Peters, J. and Wolper, A. (eds) *Women's Rights, Human Rights: International Feminist Perspectives*, New York: Routledge, 18–35.

Friedman, J. (1986) 'The world city hypothesis', *Development and Change*, 17 (2), January, 69–83.

Friedman, J. (1990) 'Being in the world: globalization and localization', in Featherstone, M. (ed.) *Global Culture: Nationalism, Globalization and Modernity*, London: Sage, 311–28.

Friends of the Earth (2004) 'Ear to the ground: Right Hon Sister', *Earthmatters*, (59).

Friends of the Earth (2005) 'Sweet harmony', *Earthmatters*, (61).

Frisby, D. (1978) 'Translator's introduction', in Simmel, G., *The Philosophy of Money*, London: Routledge & Kegan Paul (translated from the German by Bottomore, T. and Frisby, D.).

Fröbel, F., Heinrich, J. and Kreye, O. (1980) *The New International Division of Labour*, Cambridge: Cambridge University Press.

Gardner, G., Assadourian, E. and Sarin, R. (2004) 'The state of consumption today', in *Worldwatch Institute State of the World 2004: Progress towards a Sustainable Society*, London: Earthscan, 3–21.

GCIM (2005) *Migration in an Interconnected World: New Directions for Action: Report of the Global Commission on International Migration*, Geneva: Global Commission on International Migration.

Gerschenkron, A. (1966) *Economic Backwardness in Historical Perspective*, Cambridge, MA: Harvard University Press.

Gerth, H. H. and Mills, C. W. (1946) *From Max Weber: Essays in Sociology*, New York: Oxford University Press.

Ghils, P. (1992) 'International civil society: international non-governmental organizations in the international system', *International Social Science Journal*, (133), 417–29.

Giddens, A. (1985) *The Nation State and Violence*, Cambridge: Polity Press.

Giddens, A. (1990) *The Consequences of Modernity*, Cambridge: Polity Press.

Giddens, A. (1991) *Modernity and Self-identity*, Cambridge: Polity Press.

Giddens, A. (1992) *The Transformation of Intimacy*, Cambridge: Polity Press.

Giddens, A. (1994) 'Living in a post-traditional society', in Beck, U., Giddens, A. and Lash, S. (eds) *Reflexive Modernization: Politics, Tradition and Aesthetics in the Modern Social Order*, Cambridge: Polity Press, 56–108.

Giddens, A. (2002) *Runaway World: How Globalisation is Reshaping Our Lives*, London: Profile Books.

Gilbert, A. and Gugler, J. (1992) *Cities, Poverty and Development: Urbanization in the Third World*, Oxford: Oxford University Press.

Gillespie, M. (1995) *Television, Ethnicity and Cultural Change*, London: Routledge.

Giulianotti, R. (2000) 'Built by the two Varelas: the rise and fall of football culture and national identity in Uruguay', in Finn, G. P. T. and Giulianotti, R. (eds) *Football Culture: Local Contests, Global Visions*, London: Frank Cass, 134–54.

Glazer, N. and Moynihan, D. (1963) *Beyond the Melting Pot: The Negroes, Puerto Ricans, Jews, Italians and Irish of New York City*, Cambridge, MA: MIT Press.

Gledhill, C. (1992) 'Pleasurable negotiations', in Bonner, F., Goodman, L., Allen, R., Janes, L. and King, C. (eds) *Imagining Women: Cultural Representations and Gender*, Cambridge: Polity Press/Open University, 193–209.

Glissant, E. (1981) *Le discourse antillais*, Paris: Seuil.

Glissant, E, (1998) 'Creolization du monde', in Ruano-Borbalan, J. C. (ed.) *L'identité: L'individu, le groupe, la société*, Auxerre: Sciences Humaines Editions.

Godrej, D. (2003) 'The great health grab', *New Internationalist*, (362).

Godrej, D. (2004) 'Smoke gets in your eyes', *New Internationalist*, (369).

Goldthorpe, J. H., with Llewellyn, C. and Payne, C. (1980) *Social Mobility and Class Structure in Modern Britain*, Oxford: Clarendon.

Goodman, D. and Redclift, M. (1991) *Refashioning Nature: Food, Ecology and Culture*, London: Routledge.

Gordon, M. (1964) *Assimilation in American Life: The Role of Race, Religion and National Life*, New York: Oxford University Press.

Gould, S. J. (1999) *Rocks of Ages: Science and Religion in the Fullness of Life*, New York: Ballantine.

Gowan, P. (1999) *The Global Gamble: Washington's Faustian Bid for World Dominance*, London: Verso.

Graburn, N. H. H. (1989) 'The sacred journey', in Smith, V. L. (ed.) *Hosts and Guests: The Anthropology of Tourism* (2nd edn) Philadelphia, PA: University of Pennsylvania Press, 21–36.

Greenwood, D. J. (1972) 'Tourism as an agent of change: a Spanish Basque case', *Ethnology*, **11**, 80–91.

Greenwood, D. J. (1989) 'Culture by the pound: an anthropological perspective on tourism as cultural commoditization', in Smith, V. L. (ed.) *Hosts and Guests: The Anthropology of Tourism* (2nd edn) Philadelphia, PA: University of Pennsylvania Press, 171–86.

Gros, C. (1999) 'Evangelical Protestantism and indigenous population', *Bulletin of Latin American Research*, **18**(2), 175–97.

Grosfoguel, R. (1995) 'Global logics in the Caribbean city system: the case of Miami', in Knox, P. L. and Taylor, P. J. (eds) *World Cities in a World System*, Cambridge: Cambridge University Press, 156–170.

Grubb, M., Koch, M., Munson, A., Sullivan, F. and Thompson, K. (1995) *The Earth Summit Agreements: A Guide and Assessment*, London: Earthscan.

Gugler, J. (1995) 'The urbanization of the globe', in Cohen, R. (ed.) *The Cambridge Survey of World Migration*, Cambridge: Cambridge University Press, 541–5.

Gunson, P. (1996) 'Indians run for their lives', *Observer*, 29 September.

Guttman, A. (1992) *The Olympics: A History of the Modern Games*, Urban, IL: University of Illinois Press.

Habermas, J. (1971) *Towards a Rational Society*, London: Heinemann Educational Books.

Habermas, J. (1979) *Communication and the Evolution of Society*, London: Heinemann Educational Books.

Habermas, J. (1989) *The Structural Transformation of the Public Sphere*, Cambridge: Polity Press.

Hadar, L. T. (1993) 'What green peril?' *Foreign Affairs*, **72**(2), 27–42.

Hall, A. and Midgley, J. (2004) *Social Policy for Development*, London: Sage.

Hall, C. M. and Weiler, B. (1992) *Special Interest Tourism*, London: Belhaven Press.

Hall, J. R. (1987) *Gone from the Promised Land: Jonestown in American Cultural History*, New Brunswick: Transaction Books (reissued 2004).

Hall, S. (1991) 'The local and the global: globalization and ethnicity', in King, A. D. (ed.) *Culture, Globalization and the World System: Contemporary Conditions for the Representations of Identity*, Basingstoke: Macmillan.

Hall, S. (1992) 'New ethnicities', in Donals, J. and Rattansi, A. (eds) *Race, Culture and Difference*, London: Sage/Open University Press, 252–9.

Hall, S. and Gieben, B. (eds) (1992) *Formations of Modernity*, Cambridge: Polity Press for the Open University.

Hall, S. and Jefferson, T. (1993) *Resistance through Rituals: Youth Subcultures in Post-war Britain*, London: HarperCollins.

Hall, T. D. (1996) 'World-system theory', in Kuper, A. and Kuper, J. (eds) *The Social Science Encyclopaedia* (2nd edn) London, Routledge, 922–3.

Halliday, F. (1994) *Rethinking International Relations*, Basingstoke: Macmillan.

Halliday, F. (1996) *Islam and the Myth of Confrontation*, London: I.B. Tauris.

Hampton, J. (1998) *Internally Displaced People: A Global Survey*, London: Earthscan/Norwegian Refugee Council.

Hannerz, U. (1969) *Soulside: Inquiries in Ghetto, Culture and Community*, New York: Columbia University Press.

Hannerz, U. (1980) *Exploring the City: Inquiries Towards an Urban Anthropology*, New York: Columbia University Press.

Hannerz, U. (1987) 'The world in creolization' *Africa*, 57, 546–59.

Hannerz, U. (1990) 'Cosmopolitans and locals in world culture', in Featherstone, M. (ed.) *Global Culture: Nationalism, Globalization and Modernity*, London: Sage, 237–53.

Hannerz, U. (1992) *Cultural Complexity: Studies in the Social Organization of Meaning*, New York: Columbia University Press.

Hannerz, U. (1996) *Transnational Connections: Culture, People, Places*, London: Routledge.

Harding, L. (2005) 'Forgotten victims of East German doping take their battle to court' *Guardian*, 1 November.

Hargreaves, C. (1992) *Snowfields: The War on Cocaine in the Andes*, London: Zed Books.

Harris, N. (1983) *Of Bread and Guns: The World Economy in Crisis*, Harmondsworth: Penguin.

Harris, N. (2004) 'What will drive international migration? Response', in Global Commission on International Migration, *Report on the Migration Futures Workshop held at St Antony's College, Oxford*, Geneva: GCIM.

Harrison, D. (ed.) (1992) *Tourism in the Less Developed Countries*, London: Bellhaven Press.

Harrison, D. (1995) 'Tourism, capitalism and development in less developed countries', in Sklair, L. (ed.) *Capitalism and Development*, London: Routledge, 232–57.

Harrison, D. (1997) 'Asia's heart of darkness', *Observer*, 28 September.

Harrison, P. (1981) *Inside the Third World*, Harmondsworth: Penguin.

Harvey, D. (1982) *The Limits to Capital*, Oxford: Blackwell.

Harvey, D. (1985) *Consciousness and the Urban Experience*, Oxford: Blackwell.

Harvey, D. (1989) *The Condition of Postmodernity: An Enquiry into the Origins of Cultural Change*, Oxford: Blackwell.

Harvey, D. (2003) *The New Imperialism,* Oxford: Oxford University Press.

Harvey, J., Rail, G. and Thibault, L. (1996) 'Globalization and sport: sketching theoretical models for empirical analyses', *Journal of Sport and Social Issues*, **23**, 358–77.

Hebdige, D. (1988) *Subcultures: The Meaning of Style*, London: Routledge.

Hefner, R. W. (2000) *Civil Islam: Muslims and Democratization in Indonesia*, Princeton: Princeton University Press.

Hegedus, Z. (1989) 'Social movements and social change in self-creative society: new civil initiatives in the international arena', *International Sociology*, 4(1), 19–36.

Held, D. (1989) 'The decline of the nation state', in Hall, S. and Jacques, M. (eds) *New Times*, London: Lawrence & Wishart, 191–204.

Held, D. (1995) 'Democracy and the international order', in Held, D. and Archibugi, D. (eds) *Cosmopolitan Democracy: An Agenda for a New World Order*, Cambridge: Polity Press, 96–118.

Held, D. and Archibugi, D. (eds) (1995) *Cosmopolitan Democracy: An Agenda for a New World Order*, Cambridge: Polity Press.

Held, D. and McGrew, A. (2002) *Globalization/Anti-Globalization*, Cambridge: Polity Press.

Held, D., McGrew, A., Goldblatt, D. and Perraton, J. (1999) *Global Transformations: Politics, Economics and Culture*, Cambridge: Polity Press.

Hendrickson, C. (1996) 'Selling Guatemala: Maya export products in US mail-order catalogues', in Howes, D. (ed.) *Cross-cultural Consumption: Global Markets, Local Realities*, London: Routledge, 106–24.

Herman, E. S. and McChesney, R. W. (1997) *The Global Media: The New Missionaries of Global Capitalism*, London: Cassell.

Herrnstein, R. J and Murray, C. (1994) *The Bell Curve: Intelligence and Class Structure in American Life*, New York: Free Press.

Hill, J. (1994) 'Cricket and the imperial connection: overseas players in Lancashire in the interwar years', in Bale, J. and Maguire, J. (eds) *The Global Sports Arena: Athletic Talent Migration in an Interdependent World*, London: Frank Cass, 49–62.

Hinnells, J. R. (ed.) (1997) *A New Handbook of Living Religion*, Oxford: Blackwell.

Hirst, P. and Thompson, G. (1996) *Globalization in Question: The International Economy and the Possibilities of Governance,* Cambridge: Polity Press.

Hoben, A. and Hefner, R. (1991) 'The integrative revolution revisited', *World Development*, **19**(2), 17–30.

Hobhouse, L. T. (1922) *The Elements of Social Justice*, London: Allen & Unwin.

Hobsbawm, E. J. (1994) *Age of Extremes: The Short Twentieth Century, 1914–1991*, London: Michael Joseph.

Hochschild, A. R. (2000) 'Global care chains and emotional surplus value', in Hutton, W. and Giddens, A. (eds) *On the Edge: Living with Global Capitalism*, London: Jonathan Cape, 130–46.

Hoggart, S. (1996) 'The hollow state', *Guardian*, 26 October.

Holt, R. (1996) 'Contrasting nationalisms: sport, militarism and the unitary state in Britain and France', in Mangan, J. A. (ed.) *Tribal Identities: Nationalism, Sport and Europe*, London: Frank Cass, 39–54.

Hoogvelt, A. M. (1997) *Globalization and the Post-Colonial World: The New Political Economy of Development*, Basingstoke: Macmillan.

Hooker, C. (1997) 'Ford's sociology department and the Americanization campaign and the manufacture of popular culture among assembly line workers, c.1910–1917', *Journal of American and Comparative Cultures*, **20**(1), 47–53.

Hooper, B. (2000) 'Globalization and resistance in post-Mao China: the case of foreign consumer products', *Asian Studies Review*, **24**(4), 439–70.

Hopkins, A. G. (1973) *An Economic History of West Africa*, London: Longman.

Horne, J. (2000) 'Soccer in Japan: is *Wa* all you need?' in Finn, G. P. T. and Giulianotti, R. (eds) *Football Culture: Local Contests, Global Visions*, London: Frank Cass, 212–29.

Hourani, A. H. (1991) *A History of the Arab Peoples*, London: Faber.

Howes, D. (ed.) (1996) *Cross-cultural Consumption: Global Market, Local Realities*, London: Routledge.

Huntington, S. P. (1993) 'The clash of civilizations', *Foreign Affairs*, **72**(3), 22–49.

Huntington, S. P. (2004) *Who Are We? America's Great Debate*, London: Simon & Schuster.

Hutton, W. (1998) 'World must wake up to this disaster', *Observer*, 30 August.

Hutton, W. (2005) 'Shopping and tut-tutting', *Observer*, 4 September.

Huxley, L. (2005) 'Western backpackers and the global experience: an exploration of young people's interactions with local cultures', *Tourism, Culture and Communications*, **5**(1), 37–44.

Ignatieff, M. (1994) *Blood and Belonging: Journeys into the New Nationalism*, London: Vintage.

Inglehart, R. (1990) *Culture Shift in Advanced Industrial Society*, Princeton, NJ: Princeton University Press.

Iyer, P. (2001) *The Global Soul: Jet-lag, Shopping Malls and the Search for Home*, London: Bloomsbury.

Jacobs, S. (2004) 'New forms, longstanding issues, and some successes: feminist networks and organizing in a globalising era', *Journal of Interdisciplinary Gender Studies*, **8**(1 and 2), 171–93.

Jacobs, S., Jacobson, R. and Marchbank, J. (eds) (2000) *States of Conflict: Gender, Violence and Resistance*, London: Zed Books.

Jacobson, J. L. (1993) 'Women's health: the price of poverty', in Koblinsky, M., Timyan, J. and Gay, J. (eds) *The Health of Women: A Global Perspective*, Boulder, CO: Westview Press, 3–32.

Jacobson, R., Jacobs, S. and Marchbank, J. (2000), 'Introduction: states of conflict', in Jacobs, S., Jacobson, R. and Marchbank, J. (eds) *States of Conflict: Gender, Violence and Resistance*, London: Zed Books.

Jaising, I. (1995) 'Violence against women: the Indian perspective', in Peters, J. and Wolper, A. (eds) *Women's Rights, Human Rights: International Perspectives*, New York: Routledge, 51–6.

James, A. (1996) 'Cooking the books: global or local identities in contemporary food cultures', in Howes, D. (ed.) *Cross-cultural Consumption: Global Markets, Local Realities*, London: Routledge, 77–92.

James, C. L. R. (1963) *Beyond a Boundary*, London: Stanley Paul.

Jameson, F. (1984) 'Postmodernism or the cultural logic of late capitalism', *New Left Review*, (146), 53–92.

Janus, N. (1986) 'Transnational advertising: some considerations on the impact of peripheral societies', in Atwood, R. and McAnany, E. G. (eds) *Communications and Latin American Society: Trends in Critical Research 1960–85*, Madison, WI: University of Wisconsin Press, 127–42.

Jenson, A. (1969) 'How much can we boost IQ and scholastic achievement', *Harvard Educational Review*, **39**, 1–123.

Jones, C. and Leshkowich, A. M. (2003) 'Introduction: the globalization of Asian dress: re-orienting fashion or re-orientalizing Asia?' in Niessen, S., Leshkowich, A. M. and Jones, C. (eds) *The Globalization of Asian Dress: Re-Orienting Fashion*, Oxford: Berg, 1–48.

Jones, E. L. (1988) *Growth Recurring: Economic*

Change in World History, Oxford: Clarendon Press.

Jones, S. (1993) *The Language of the Genes: Biology, History and the Evolutionary Future*, London: HarperCollins.

Joppke, C. (1993) *Mobilizing Against Nuclear Energy*, Berkeley: University of California Press.

Jordan, B. and Duvell, F. (2003) *Migration: Boundaries of Equality and Justice*, Cambridge: Polity Press.

Jubilee Debt Campaign (2005) London: Jubilee Debt Campaign.

Juergensmeyer, M. (2003) *Terror in the Mind of God: The Global Rise of Religious Violence*, Berkeley: University of California Press.

Julius, D. (1990) *Global Companies and Public Policy*, London: Pinter.

Kaldor, M. (1999) 'Transnational civil society', in Dunne, T. and Wheeler, N. J. (eds) *Human Rights in Global Politics*, Cambridge: Cambridge University Press, 195–213.

Kandiyoti, D. (1997) 'Bargaining with patriarchy', in Visvanathan, N., Duggan, L., Nissonoff, L. and Wiegersmal, N. (eds) *The Women, Gender and Development Reader*, London: Zed Books, 86–99.

Kasbekar, A. (1996) 'An introduction to Indian cinema', in Nelmes, J. (ed.) *An Introduction to Film Studies*, London: Routledge, 365–92.

Katz, J. (1995) 'Advertising and the construction of violent male masculinity', in Dines, G. and Humez, J. M. (eds) *Gender, Race and Class in Media: A Text-Reader*, Thousand Oaks, CA: Sage, 133–41.

Keane, J. (2003) *Global Civil Society?* Cambridge: Cambridge University Press.

Keck, M. E. and Sikkink, K. (1998) *Activists Beyond Borders: Advocacy Networks in International Politics*, Ithaca, NY: Cornell University Press.

Keen, D. (1994) *The Benefits of Famine: A Political Economy of Famine and Relief in Southwestern Sudan, 1983–89*, Princeton, NJ: Princeton University Press.

Kegley, C. W. and Wittkopf, E. R. (2004) *World Politics: Trend and Transformation*, Belmont, CA: Thomson & Wadsworth.

Kelly, L. (2000) 'Wars against women: sexual violence, sexual politics and the militarized state', in Jacobs, S., Jacobson, R. and Marchbank, J. (eds) *States of Conflict: Gender, Violence and Resistance*, London: Zed Books, 45–65.

Kennedy, P. (1996) 'Business enterprises as agents of cultural and political change: the case of green/ethical marketing', in Barker, C. and Kennedy, P. (eds) *To Make Another World: Studies in Protest and Collective Action*, Aldershot: Avebury.

Kennedy, P. (2004) 'Making global society: friendship networks among transnational professionals in the building design industry', *Global Networks: A Journal of Transnational Affairs,* 4(2), 157–79.

Kennedy, P. (2005) 'Informal sociality, cosmopolitanism and gender among transnational professionals: unravelling some of the linkages between the global economy and civil society', in Eade, J. and O'Byrne, D. (eds) *Global Ethics and Civil Society*, Aldershot: Ashgate, 89–107.

Kenny, M. and Florida, R. (1988) 'Beyond mass production: production and the labour process in Japan', *Politics and Society,* 16(1), 121–58.

Kerr, C. (1983) *The Future of Industrial Societies: Convergence or Continuing Diversity*, Cambridge, MA: Harvard University Press.

Khan, A. (1995) 'Homeland, motherland: authenticity legitimacy and ideologies of place among Muslims in Trinidad', in van der Veer, P. (ed.) *Nation and Migration: The Politics of Space in the South Asian Diaspora*, Philadelphia, PA: University of Pennsylvania Press, 93–131.

Kidron, M. and Segal, R. (1995) *The State of the World Atlas*, London: Penguin.

Kiely, R. (2005a) *Empire in the Age of Globalisation: US Hegemony and the Neoliberal Disorder*, London: Pluto Press.

Kiely, R. (2005b) *The Clash of Globalizations: Neoliberalism, the Third Way and Anti-globalization*, Leiden: Brill.

King, V. T. (1993) 'Tourism and culture in Malaysia', in Hitchcock, M., King, V. T. and Parnwell, J. G. (eds) *Tourism in South-east Asia*, London: Routledge, 99–116.

Kirkby, J., O'Keefe, P. and Timberlake, L. (eds) (1995) *The Earthscan Reader in Sustainable Development*, London: Earthscan.

Klein, N. (2001) *No Logo: No Space, No Choice, No Jobs*, London: Flamingo.

Knox, P. L. and Taylor, P. J. (eds) (1995) *World Cities in a World-System*, Cambridge: Cambridge University Press.

Kornblum, W. (1998) *Sociology in a Changing World*, New York: Holt, Rinehart & Winston.

Korton, D. (1990) *Getting to the 21st Century*, West Hartford, CN: Kumarian Press.

Kothari, S. (1996) 'Social movements, ecology and justice', in Osler Hampson, F. and Reppy, J. (eds) *Earthly Goods: Environmental Change and Social Justice*, Ithaca, NY: Cornell University Press, 154–72.

Kotkin, J. (1992) *Tribes: How Race, Religion and Identity Determine Success in the Global Economy*, New York: Random House.

Kreis, S. (2000) 'The age of ideologies: the world of Auguste Comte', http://www.historyguide.org/intellect/lecture25a.html.

Krippendorf, J. (1987) *The Holiday Makers*, London: Heinemann.

Kruhse-Mount Burton, S. (1995) 'Sex tourism and traditional Australian male identity', in Lanfant, M. F., Allcock, J. B. and Bruner, E. M. (eds) *International Tourism: Identity and Change*, London: Sage, 192–204.

Kumar, R. (1995) 'From Chipko to Sati: the contemporary Indian women's movement', in Basu, A. (ed.) *The Challenge of Local Feminisms*, Boulder, CO: Westview Press, 58–86.

Kumaranayake, L. and Lake, S. (2002) 'Global approaches to private sector provision: where is the evidence?', in Lee, K., Buse, K. and Fustukian, S. (eds) *Health Policy in a Globalising World*, Cambridge: Cambridge University Press, 78–96.

Lanfant, M. F. (1995) 'International tourism, internationalisation and the challenge to identity', in Lanfant, M. F., Allcock, J. B. and Bruner, E. M. (eds) *International Tourism: Identity and Change*. London: Sage.

Lanfant, M. F., Allcock, J. B. and Bruner, E. M. (eds) (1995) *International Tourism: Identity and Change*, London: Sage.

Lanfranchi, P. (1994) 'The migration of footballers: the case of France, 1932–1982', in Bale, J. and Maguire J. (eds) *The Global Sports Arena: Athletic Talent Migration in an Interdependent World*, London: Frank Cass, 63–77.

Langman, L. (2001) 'Globalization and national identity rituals in Brazil and the USA: the politics of pleasure versus the politics of protest', in Kennedy, P. and Danks, C. J. (eds) *Globalization and National Identities: Crisis or Opportunity?* Basingstoke: Palgrave Macmillan, 190–209.

Lasch, C. (1995) *The Revolt of the Elites and the Betrayal of Democracy*, New York: W. W. Norton.

Lash, S. and Urry, J. (1987) *The End of Organised Capitalism*, Cambridge: Polity Press.

Lash, S. and Urry, J. (1994) *Economies of Signs and Space*, London: Sage.

Lechner, F. J. and Boli, J. (2005) *World Culture: Origins and Consequences*, Oxford: Blackwell.

Lee, E. and Jackson, E. (2002) 'The pregnant body', in Evans, M. and Lee, E. (eds) *Real Bodies: A Sociological Introduction*, Basingstoke: Palgrave Macmillan, 115–32.

Lee, K. and Dodgson, R. (2000) 'Globalization and cholera: implications for global governance', *Global Governance*, **6**(2), 213–36.

Lele, S. M. (1991) 'Sustainable development: a critical review', *World Development*, **19**(6), 607–21.

Lemann, N. (1991) *The Promised Land: The Great Black Migration and How it Changed America*, New York: Alfred S. Knopf.

Leshkowich, A. M. (2003) 'The *Ao Dai* goes global: how international influences and female entrepreneurs have shaped Vietnam's "national costume"', in Niessen, S., Leshkowich, A. M. and Jones, C. (eds) *The Globalization of Asian Dress: Reorienting Fashion*, Oxford: Berg, 49–79.

Lévi-Strauss C. (1963) *Totemism*, trans. by Needham, R., Boston: Beacon Press

Lewis, O. (1968) *La Vida: A Puerto Rican Family in the Culture of Poverty – San Juan and New York*, New York: Vintage Books.

Lewis, P. (1992) 'Democracy in modern societies', in Allen, J., Braham, P. and Lewis, P. (eds) *Political and Economic Forms of Modernity*, Cambridge: Polity Press, 89–96.

Lindberg, S. and Sverrisson, A. (eds) (1997) *Social Movements in Development: The Challenges of Globalization and Democratization*, Basingstoke: Macmillan.

Lipietz, A. (1987) *Mirages and Miracles: The Crisis of Global Fordism*, trans. D. Macey, London: Verso.

Lister, R. (1997) *Citizenship: Feminist Perspectives*, Basingstoke: Macmillan.

Lockwood, B. and Redoano, M. (2005) 'The CSGR globalisation index: an introductory guide', Centre for the Study of Globalisation and Regionalisation, University of Warwick, Working Paper 155/04.

Lynas, M. (2004) 'If they plant them, we'll pull them up', *Ecologist*, **34**(3), 26–30.

Lyon, D. (2005) 'Forced labour – global problem',

<http://news.bbc.co.uk/1/hi/world/europe/4521921.stm>.

MacCannell, D. (1976) *The Tourist: A New Theory of the Leisure Class*, New York: Schocken Books.

McCarthy, T. (1978) *The Critical Theory of Jürgen Habermas*, Cambridge: Polity Press.

McCormick, J. (1989) *The Global Environmental Movement*, London: Bellhaven.

Macionis, J. J. and Plummer, K. (2005) *Sociology: A Global Introduction*, Harlow: Pearson.

McKay, J. and Miller, T. (1991) 'From old boys to men and women of the corporation: the Americanization and commodification of Australian sport', *Sociology of Sport Journal*, **8**, 86–94.

McKean, P. F. (1989) 'Towards a theoretical analysis of tourism: economic dualism and cultural involution in Bali', in Smith, V. L. (ed.) *Hosts and Guests: The Anthropology of Tourism* (2nd edn) Philadelphia, PA: University of Pennsylvania Press, 119–38.

McKie, R. (2000) 'Killer bug spreads West', *Observer*, 24 September.

McLuhan, M. (1962) *The Gutenberg Galaxy: The Making of Typographical Man*, Toronto: University of Toronto Press.

McMichael, P. (2000) *Development and Social Change: A Global Perspective* (2nd edn) Thousand Oaks, CA: Pine Forge.

McMurray, C. and Smith, R. (2001) *Diseases of Globalization: Socioeconomic Transitions and Health*, London: Earthscan.

MacNaghten, P. (1993) 'Discourses of nature: argumentation and power', in Burman, E. and Parks, I. (eds) *Discourse Analytical Research*, London: Routledge, 52–71.

McNeill, W. H. (1971) *A World History*, Oxford: Oxford University Press.

McVeigh, T. (2002) 'A-level fiasco leads to gap-year boom', *Observer*, 6 October.

Maguire, J. (1993) 'Bodies, sportscultures and societies: a critical review of some theories in the sociology of the body', *International Review for the Sociology of Sport*, **28**, 33–52.

Maguire, J. (1999) *Global Sport: Identities, Societies, Civilizations*, Cambridge: Polity Press.

Maguire, J. (2000) 'Sport and globalization', in, Oakley, J. and Dunning, E. (eds) *Handbook of Sport Studies*, London: Sage, 356–69.

Malik, K. (1996) *The Meaning of Race: Race History and Culture in Western Society*, Basingstoke: Macmillan.

Mangan, J. A. (1981) *Athleticism in the Victorian and Edwardian Public Schools*, Cambridge: Cambridge University Press.

Mangan, J. A. (ed.) (1996) *Tribal Identities: Nationalism, Sport and Europe*, London: Frank Cass.

Manji, I. (2004) *The Trouble with Islam Today: A Muslim's Call for Reform in her Faith*, New York: St Martin's Press.

Mann, M. (1988) *States, War and Capitalism: Studies in Political Sociology*, Oxford: Blackwell.

Mann, M. (1996) 'Ruling class strategies and citizenship', in Bulmer, M. and Rees, A. M. (eds) *Citizenship Today: The Contemporary Relevance of T. H. Marshall*, London: UCL Press, 125–44.

Marcus, G. E. (ed.) (1998) *Corporate Futures: The Diffusion of the Culturally Sensitive Firm*, Chicago: University of Chicago Press.

Marcuse, H. (1964) *One-Dimensional Man*, London: Routledge & Kegan Paul.

Marsh, I., Keating, M., Eyre, A., Campbell, R. and McKenzie, J. (ed.) (1996) *Making Sense of Society: An Introduction to Sociology*, Harlow: Addison Wesley Longman.

Marshall, T. H. (1950) *Citizenship and Social Class*, Cambridge: Cambridge University Press.

Martin, H. P. and Schuman, H. (1997) *The Global Trap: Globalization and the Assault on Democracy and Prosperity*, London: Zed Books.

Marx, K. (1954) *The Eighteenth Brumaire of Louis Bonaparte*, Moscow: Progress Publishers (first published 1852).

Marx, K. (1976) *Capital: A Critique of Political Economy*, vol. 1, Harmondsworth: Penguin.

Marx, K. and Engels, F. (1967) *The Communist Manifesto*, Harmondsworth: Penguin (first published 1848).

Mason, T. (1995) *Passion of the People? Football in South America*, London: Verso.

Massey, D. S. and Denton, N. A. (1993) *American Apartheid: Segregation and the Making of the Underclass*, Cambridge, MA: Harvard University Press.

Matsui, Y. (1989) *Women's Asia*, London: Zed Books.

Mayer, J. A. (1983) 'Notes towards a working definition of social control in historical analysis', in Cohen, S. and Scull, A. (eds) *Social Control and the State*, Oxford: Martin Robertson, 17–38.

Mbembe, A. and Nuttall, S. (2004) 'Writing the world from an African metropolis', in Mbembe, A. and Nuttall, S. (eds) *Johannesburg: The Elusive Metropolis*, special issue of *Public Culture*, 44, 347–72.

Medilink (2005) 'Africa: Five million grandparents looking after orphans', *Health News*, <http://medilinkz.org/news/news2.asp?page=9&NewsID=330>.

Meethan, K. (2001) *Tourism in Global Society: Place, Culture, Consumption*, New York: Palgrave.

Meikle, J. (1997) 'Disney leads in theme parks', *Guardian*, 11 September.

Mennell, S. (1989) *Norbert Elias*, Oxford: Blackwell.

Merchant, C. (1990) *The Death of Nature: Women, Ecology and the Scientific Revolution*, New York: Harper & Row.

Miles, A. (1996) *Integrative Feminisms: Building Global Visions, 1960s–1990s*, New York: Routledge.

Miles, R. (1989) *Racism*, London: Routledge.

Miller, T., Lawrence, G., McKay, J. and Rowe, D. (2001) *Globalization and Sport: Playing the World*, London: Sage.

Millet, K. (1977) *Sexual Politics*, London: Virago.

Milton, K. (1996) *Environmentalism and Cultural Theory*, London: Routledge.

Mishra, O., Unnikrishnan, P. V. and Martin, M. (1998) 'India', in Hampton, J. (ed.) *Internally Displaced People: A Global Survey*, London: Earthscan/Norwegian Refugee Council, 142–6.

Mitchell, K. (1995) 'Flexible circulation in the Pacific Rim: capitalism in cultural context, *Economic Geography*, 71(4), 364–82.

Mitter, S. (1994) 'On organising women in casualised work: a global overview', in Rowbotham, S. and Mitter, S. (eds) *Dignity and Daily Bread*, London: Routledge, 16–52.

Mohammed, Y. S. (2002) 'Hero worship' *BBC Focus on Africa*, February–March, 51.

Molyneux, M. (2001) *Women's Movements in International Perspective: Latin America and Beyond*, Basingstoke: Macmillan.

Monbiot, G. (2005) 'It would seem that I was wrong about big business', *Guardian*, 20 September.

Moore, B. (1967) *Social Origins of Dictatorship and Democracy: Lord and Peasant in the Making of the Modern World*, Harmondsworth: Penguin.

Moore, B. (1972) *Reflections on the Causes of Human Misery and upon Certain Proposals to Eliminate Them*, London: Allen Lane.

Moore, R., Pinn, A. B. and Sawyer, M. R. (eds) (2004) *People's Temple and Black Religion in America*, Bloomington: University of Indiana Press.

Morgenthau, H. J. (1948) *Politics among Nations: The Struggle for Power and Peace*, New York: Knopf.

Morley, D. and Robins, K. (1995) *Spaces of Identity: Global Media, Electronic Landscapes and Cultural Boundaries*, London: Routledge.

Munck, R. (2005) *Globalization and Social Exclusion: A Transformationalist Perspective*, Bloomfield, CT: Kumerian Press.

Murray, R. (1989) 'Fordism and post-Fordism', in Hall, S. and Jacques, M. (eds) *New Times*, London: Lawrence & Wishart, 38–53.

Myers, P. (1997) 'Mixing it in a mad world', *Guardian*, 16 May.

Nauright, J. (1997) *Sport, Cultures and Identities in South Africa*, London: Leicester University Press.

Neale, J. (2002) *You are the G8, We are the 6 Billion*, London: Vision Paperbacks.

Needham, J. (1969) *The Grand Titration: Science and Society in East and West*, Toronto: University of Toronto Press.

Nettle, D. and Romaine, S. (2000) *Vanishing Voices: The Extinction of the World's Languages*, New York: Oxford University Press.

Newall, P. (1998) 'Environmental NGOs, multinational corporations and the question of governance', a paper given at the conference on transnational social movements at the Department of Sociology, University of Warwick, March.

Newell, P. (2006) 'Climate for change? Civil society and the politics of global warming', in Glasius, M., Kaldor, M. and Anheier, H. (eds) *Global Civil Society 2005/06*, London: Sage, 90–120.

Nicholls, D. (1995) 'Population and process: Parson Malthus', *Anglican Theological Review*, 77(3), 321–34.

Nisbet, R. A. (1970) *The Sociological Tradition*, London: Heinemann Educational Books.

Nurse, K. (1999) 'Globalization and Trinidad carnival: diaspora, hybridity and identity in global culture', *Cultural Studies*, 13(4), 661–90.

O'Brien, M., Penna, S. and Hay, C. (eds) (1999) *Theorising Modernity: Reflexivity, Environment and Identity in Giddens' Social Theory*, New York: Longman.

O'Byrne, D. (2003) *Human Rights: An Introduction*, Harlow: Pearson Education.

O'Connor, A. (2002) 'Punk and globalization: Mexico City and Toronto', in Kennedy, P. and Roudometof, V. (eds) *Communities Across Borders: New Immigrants and Transnational Cultures*, London: Routledge, 143–55.

Ohmae, K. (1994) *The Borderless World: Power and Strategy in the International Economy*, London: Collins.

Oliviero, M. B. and Simmons, A. (2002) 'Who's minding the store? Global civil society and corporate responsibility', in Anheier, H., Glasius, M. and Kaldor, M. (eds) *Global Civil Society 2002*, Oxford: Oxford University Press, 77–108.

Oommen, T. K. (1997) 'Social movements in the Third World', in Lindberg, S. and Sverrisson, A. (eds) *Social Movements in Development: The Challenges to Globalization and Democratization*, Basingstoke: Macmillan, 46–66.

Outhwaite, W. (1994) *Habermas: A Critical Introducton*, Cambridge: Polity Press.

Outhwaite, W. (ed.) (1996) *The Habermas Reader*, Cambridge: Polity Press.

Oxfam International (2004) *Trading Away our Rights: Women in Global Supply Chains*, Oxford: Oxfam International.

Parekh, B. (1995) 'Politics of nationhood', in von Benda-Beckman, K. and Verkuyten, M. (ed.) *Nationalism, Ethnicity and Cultural Identity in Europe*, Utrecht: European Research Centre on Migration and Ethnic Relations, 122–43.

Parsons, T. (1971) *Societies: Evolutionary and Comparative Perspectives*, Englewood, Cliffs, NJ: Prentice Hall.

Passel, J. (2005) 'Unauthorised', *Migration News*, 12(2), http://migration.ucdavis. edu.

Patterson, O. (1982) *Slavery and Social Death: A Comparative Study*, Cambridge, MA: Harvard University Press.

Pearce, F. and Tombs, S. (1993) 'US capital vs. the Third World: Union Carbide and Bhopal', in Pearce, F. and Woodiwiss, M. (eds) *Global Crime Connections: Dynamics and Control*, Toronto: University of Toronto Press, 187–211.

Pearce, F. and Woodiwiss, M. (eds) (1993) *Global Crime Connections: Dynamics and Control*, Toronto: University of Toronto Press.

Pearse, A. (1980) *Seeds of Plenty, Seeds of Want: Social and Economic Implications of the Green Revolution*, Oxford: Clarendon Press.

Peet, R. (ed.) (1987) *International Capitalism and Industrial Restructuring*, Boston: Allen & Unwin.

Pendergrast, M. (1993) *For God, Country and Coca-Cola*, New York: Charles Scribner & Sons.

Perkins, H. C. and Thorns, D. C. (2001), 'Gazing or performing? Reflections on Urry's tourist gaze in the context of contemporary experience in the Antipodes', *International Sociology*, **16**(2), 185–204.

Perlman, J. E. (1976) *The Myth of Marginality: Urban Poverty and Politics in Rio de Janeiro*, Berkeley: University of California Press.

Perlmutter, H. (1991) 'On the rocky road to the first global civilization', *Human Relations*, **44**(9), 897–1010.

Peters, J. and Wolper, A. (eds) (1995) *Women's Rights, Human Rights: International Feminist Perspectives*, New York: Routledge.

Peterson, V. S. and Runyan, A. S. (1993) *Global Gender Issues*, Boulder, CO: Westview Press.

Pettifor, A. (2001) 'Why Jubilee 2000 made an impact', in Anheier, H., Glasius, M. and Kaldor, M. (eds) *Global Civil Society 2004/05*, London: Sage, 62–3.

Pettit, J. (2004) 'Climate justice: a new social movement for atmospheric rights', *IDS Bulletin*, **35**(3), 102–6.

Phizacklea, A. (1992) 'Jobs for the girls: the production of women's outerwear in the UK', in Cross, M. (ed.) *Ethnic Minorities and Industrial Change in Europe and North America*, Cambridge: Cambridge University Press, 94–110.

Pianta, M. (2001) 'Parallel summits of global civil society', in Anheier, H., Glasius M. and Kaldor, M. (eds) *Global Civil Society 2001*, Oxford: Oxford University Press, 169–94.

Picard, M. (1995) 'Cultural heritage and tourist capital: cultural tourism in Bali', in Lanfant, M. F., Allcock, J. B. and Bruner, E. M. (eds) *International Tourism: Identity and Change*, London: Sage, 44–66.

Piore, M. and Sabel, C. (1984) *The Second Industrial Divide*, New York: Basic Books.

Pi-Sunyer, O., Brooke Thomas, R. and Daltabuit, M. (2001) 'Tourism on the Maya periphery', in Smith, V. and Brent, M. (eds) *Hosts and Guests Revisited: Tourism Issues of the 21st Century*, New

York: Cognizant Communication Corporation, 122–40.

Polanyi, K. (2002) *The Great Transformation: The Political and Economic Origins of Our Time*, New York: Beacon Books. Foreword by Joseph E. Stiglitz (first published 1957).

Porter, J., Lee, K. and Ogden, J. (2002) 'The globalisation of DOTS: tuberculosis as a global emergency', in Lee, K., Buse, K. and Fustukian, S. (eds) *Health Policy in a Globalising World*, Cambridge: Cambridge University Press, 181–94.

Premdas, R. (1996) 'Ethnicity and elections in the Caribbean', working paper no. 224, Kellogg Institute, University of Notre Dame.

Princen, T. and Finger, M. (eds) (1994) *Environmental NGOs in World Politics*, London: Routledge.

Pugh, M. (2002) 'Maintaining peace and security', in Held, D. and McGrew, A. (eds) *Governing Globalization: Power, Authority and Global Governance*, Cambridge: Polity Press, 209–33.

Rabine, L. W. (2002) *The Global Circulation of African Fashion*, Oxford: Berg.

Radford, J. (2000) 'Theorizing commonalities and differences: sexual violence, law and feminist activism in India and the UK', in Radford, J., Friedberg, M. and Harne, L. (eds) *Women, Violence and Strategies for Action: Feminist Research, Policy and Practice*, Buckingham: Open University Press, 167–84.

Rajeev, D. (2005) 'India: everything gets worse with Coca-Cola', *Inter Press Service*, India, 22 August.

Raworth, K. (2005) *Trading Away Our Rights: Women Working in Global Supply Chains*, Oxford: Oxfam International.

Renson, R., de Cramer, E. and de Vroede, E. (1997) 'Local heroes: beyond the stereotype of the participants in traditional games', *International Review for the Sociology of Sport*, **32**(1), 59–68.

Reuter, P. (1983) *Disorganised Crime: The Economics of the Visible Hand*, Cambridge, MA: MIT Press.

Rex, J. (1986) *Race and Ethnicity*, Milton Keynes: Open University Press.

Rex, J. and Guibernau, M. (eds) (1997) *The Ethnicity Reader: Nationalism, Multiculturalism and Migration*, Cambridge: Polity Press.

Riddell-Dixon, E. (1995) 'Social movements and the United Nations', *International Social Science Journal*, (144), 289–303.

Riley, D. (1992) 'Citizenship and the welfare state', in Allen, J., Braham, P. and Lewis, P. (eds) *Political and Economic Forms of Modernity*, Cambridge: Polity Press.

Ritzer, G. (1993) *The McDonaldization of Society: An Investigation into the Changing Character of Social Life*, Thousand Oaks, CA: Pine Forge Press.

Ritzer, G. (1998) *The McDonaldization Thesis: Explorations and Extensions*, London: Sage.

Ritzer, G. (2004a) *The McDonaldization of Society*, Thousand Oaks, CA: Pine Forge and Sage (rev. New Century edn).

Ritzer, G. (2004b) *The Globalization of Nothing*, Thousand Oaks, CA: Pine Forge and Sage.

Roberts, B. (1978) *Cities of Peasants: The Political Economy of Urbanization in the Third World*, London: Edward Arnold.

Roberts, J. M. (1992) *History of the World*, Oxford: Helicon.

Roberts, J. M. (1994) *Shorter History of the World*, London: Quality Paperbacks Direct.

Robertson, R. (1992) *Globalization: Social Theory and Global Culture*, London: Sage.

Robertson, R. (1994) 'Religion and the global field', *Social Compass*, **41**(1), 121–35.

Robertson, R. (1995) 'Glocalization: time–space and homogeneity–heterogeneity', in Featherstone, M., Lash, S. and Robertson, R. (eds) *Global Modernities*, London: Sage, 25–44.

Robertson, R. (2001) 'Globalization theory 2000+: major problematics', in Ritzer, G. and Smart, B. (eds) *Handbook of Social Theory*, London: Sage, 458–71.

Robertson, R. and Inglis, D. (2004) 'The global *animus*: in the tracks of world consciousness', *Globalizations*, **1**(1), 38–49.

Robinson, W. I. (2002) 'Capitalist globalization and the transnationalization of the state', in Rupert, M. and Smith, H. (eds) *Historical Materialism and Globalization*, London: Routledge, 210–29.

Robinson, W. I. and Harris, J. (2000) 'Towards a global ruling class? Globalization and the transnational capitalist class', *Science and Society*, **64**(1), 11–54.

Roche, M. (1992) *Rethinking Citizenship: Welfare, Ideology and Change in Modern Society*, Cambridge: Polity Press.

Rock, P. (1996a) 'Symbolic interactionism', in

Kuper, A. and Kuper, J. (eds) *The Social Science Encylopedia*, London: Routledge, 859–60.

Rock, P. (1996b) 'Deviance', in Kuper, A. and Kuper, J. (eds) *The Social Science Encyclopaedia*, London: Routledge, 182–5.

Rogers, E. M. and Antola, L. (1985) 'Telenovelas in Latin America', *Journal of Communications*, **35**, 24–35.

Rohatyn, F. (2002) 'The betrayal of capitalism', *New York Review of Books*, **49**(3), 6–8.

Rosenau, J. N. (1990) *Turbulence in World Politics: A Theory of Change and Continuity*, Princeton, NJ: Princeton University Press.

Ross, A. (ed.) (1997) *No Sweat*, London: Verso.

Rowbotham, S. (1973) *Hidden from History: 300 Years of Women's Oppression and the Fight Against It*, London: Pluto.

Rowbotham, S. (1993) *Homeworkers Worldwide*, London: Merlin Press.

Rowbotham, S. (1995a) 'Feminist approaches to technology: women's values or a gender lens?', in Mitter, S. and Rowbotham, S. (eds) *Women Encounter Technology: Changing Patterns of Employment in the Third World*, London: Routledge, 44–69.

Rowbotham, S. (1995b) 'Afterword', in Mitter, S. and Rowbotham, S. (eds) *Women Encounter Technology: Changing Patterns of Employment in the Third World*, London: Routledge, 341–3.

Rowbotham, S. and Mitter, S. (1994) 'Introduction', in Rowbotham, S. and Mitter, S. (eds) *Dignity and Daily Bread: New Forms of Organizing Among Poor Women in the Third World and the First*, London: Routledge, 1–13.

Rowell, A. (1996) *Green Backlash: Global Subversion of the Environmental Movement*, London: Routledge.

Rowell, A. (2003) 'Debate, what debate?' *Ecologist*, **33**(6), 26–36.

Rozenberg, D. (1995) 'International tourism and utopia: the Balearic islands', in Lanfant, M. F., Allcock, J. B. and Bruner, E. M. (eds) *International Tourism: Identity and Change*, London: Sage, 159–76.

Rumbaut, R. (1997) 'Assimilation and its discontents: between rhetoric and reality', *International Migration Review*, **31**(4), 134–55.

Runciman, W. G. (1990) 'How many classes are there in contemporary society?' *Sociology*, (24), 377–96.

Ruthven, M. (2000) *Islam: A Very Short Introduction*, Oxford: Oxford University Press.

Sachs, W. (1992) 'One world', in Sachs, W. (ed.) *The Development Dictionary*, London: Zed Books, 102–15.

Sachs, W. (ed.) (1993) *Global Ecology: A New Arena of Global Conflict*, London: Fernwood Books/Zed Books.

Sage, H. G. (1994) 'Deindustrialization and the American sporting goods industry', in Wilcox, R. C. (ed.) *Sport in the Global Village*, Morgantown, WV: Fitness Information Technology, 39–51.

Saldanha, A. (2002) 'Music, space, identity: geographies of youth culture in Bangalore', *Cultural Studies*, **16** (3), 337–50.

Sammonds, J. (1990) *Beyond the Ring: The Role of Boxing in American Society*, Urbana: University of Illinois Press.

Sampson, A. (1956) *Drum: A Venture into New Africa*, London: Collins.

Sampson, E. E. (1993) *Celebrating the Other: A Dialogic Account of Human Nature*, Hemel Hempstead: Harvester Wheatsheaf.

Sanssurre, F. de (1974) *Course in General Linguistics*. London: P. Owen.

Sassen, S. (1991) *The Global City: New York, London, Tokyo*, Princeton, NJ: Princeton University Press.

Sassen, S. (1995) 'The state and the global city: notes towards a conception of place-centred governance', *Competition and Change: The Journal of Global Business and Political Economy*, **1**(1), 1–13.

Sassen, S. (2000), *Cities in a World Economy*, Thousand Oaks, CA: Pine Forge.

Savage, M. and Warde, A. (1993) *Urban Sociology, Capitalism and Modernity*, Basingstoke: Macmillan.

Sawin, J. L. (2004) 'Making better energy choices', in Worldwatch Institute, *State of the World 2004: Progress Towards a Sustainable Society*, London: Earthscan, 24–43.

Scarce, R. (1990) *Eco-warriors: Understanding the Radical Environmental Movement*, Chicago: Noble Press.

Schechter, D. (2000) *Falun Gong's Challenge to China: Spiritual Practice or 'Evil Cult'*, New York: Akashic Books.

Scheff, T. J. (1990) *Microsociology: Discourse, Emotion and Social Structure*, Chicago: University of Chicago Press.

Schlesinger, A. M. (1992) *The Disuniting of America*, New York: W. W. Norton.

Scholte, J. A. (1993) *International Relations of Social Change*, Buckingham: Open University Press.

Schwartz, D. (1997) *Culture and Power: The Sociology of Pierre Bourdieu*, Chicago: University of Chicago Press.

Scott, J. (2004) *Social Theory: Central Issues in Sociology*, London: Sage.

Seager, J. (1995) *The New State of the Earth Atlas*, New York: Simon & Schuster.

Seagrave, S. (1995) *Lords of the Rim: The Invisible Empire of the Overseas Chinese*, New York: G. P. Putnam's Sons.

Seckinelgin, H. (2002) 'Time to stop and think: HIV/AIDS, global civil society and people's politics', in Glasius, M., Kaldor, M and Anheier, H. (eds) *Global Civil Society 2002*, Oxford: Oxford University Press.

Seidman, S. (1983) *Liberalism and the Origins of European Social Theory*, Oxford: Blackwell.

Seidman, S. (1998) *Contested Knowledge: Social Theory in the Postmodern Era*, Oxford: Blackwell.

Sen, A. (1981) *Poverty and Famine: An Essay on Entitlement and Deprivation*, Oxford: Clarendon Press.

Sharpley, R. (1994) *Tourism, Tourists and Society*, Ripton, Huntington: Elm Publications.

Shaw, L. (1998) 'Labour and the label', paper given at the Conference on Global Social Movements and International Social Institutions at Warwick University, Department of Sociology, March.

Shaw, M. (1994) *Global Society and International Relations: Sociological Concepts and Political Perspective*, Cambridge: Polity Press.

Shaw, M. (1997) 'The state of globalization: towards a theory of state transformation', *Review of International Political Economy*, 4(3), 497–513.

Sheller, M. and Urry, J. (eds) (2004) *Tourism Mobilities: Places to Play, Places in Play*, London: Routledge.

Shenkar, O. (2004) *The Chinese Century*, Pennsylvania: Wharton School Publishing.

Sheridan, A. (1980) *Michel Foucault: The Will to Truth*, London: Tavistock.

Simmel, G. (1950a) *The Sociology of Georg Simmel*, trans. and ed. by Wolff, K. H., New York: Free Press.

Simmel, G. (1950b) 'The metropolis and mental life', in Wolff, K. H. (ed. and trans.) *The Sociology of Georg Simmel*, New York: Free Press, 409–24.

Simmel, G. (1978) *The Philosophy of Money*, London: Routledge & Kegan Paul (translated from the German by Tom Bottomore and David Frisby).

Sinclair, J. (1987) *Images Incorporated: Advertising as Industry and Ideology*, London: Croom Helm.

Sinclair, M. T. and Tsegaye, A. (1990) 'International tourism and export instability', *Journal of Development Studies*, **26**(3), 487–504.

Sklair, L. (1995) *Sociology of the Global System*, London: Prentice Hall/Harvester Wheatsheaf.

Sklair, L. (2001) *The Transnational Capitalist Class*, London: Blackwell.

Sklair, L. (2002) *Globalization, Capitalism and its Alternatives*, Oxford: Oxford University Press.

Skocpol, T. (1979) *States and Social Revolutions: A Comparative Analysis of France, Russia and China*, Cambridge: Cambridge University Press.

Slater, D. (1997) *Consumer Culture and Modernity*, Cambridge: Polity Press.

Smith, A. D. (1991) 'Towards a global culture?', in Featherstone, M. (ed.) *Global Culture: Nationalism, Globalization, Modernity*, London: Sage, 171–92.

Smith, A. D. (1992) *Ethnicity and Nationalism*, Leiden: Brill.

Smith, A. D. (1995) *Nations and Nationalism in a Global Era*, Cambridge: Polity Press.

Smith, D. (2001) *Norbert Elias and Modern Social Theory*, London: Sage.

Smith, D. and Bræin, A. (2003) *The State of the World Atlas*, London: Earthscan.

Smith, R. (1993) 'Creative destruction: capitalist development and China's environment', *New Left Review*, (222), 2–42.

Smith, R. C. (1998) 'Transnational localities: community, technology and the politics of membership within the context of Mexico and US migration', in Smith, M. P. and Guarnizo, L. E. (eds) *Transnationalism from Below*, New Brunswick, NJ: Transaction Publishers, 196–238.

Smith, V. L. (ed.) (1989) *Host and Guests: The Anthropology of Tourism* (2nd edn) Philadelphia, PA: University of Pennsylvania Press.

Smith, W. R. (1894) *Lectures on the Religion of the Semites*, Edinburgh: Black.

Smither, A. D. (2004) 'The business of miracle-working', *Independent*, 14 August.

Sontag, D. (1993) 'Increasingly, two-career family means illegal immigrant help', *New York Times*, 24 January.

Soros, G. (1998) *The Crisis of Global Capitalism*, London: Little, Brown.

Soros, G. (2002) *George Soros on Globalization*, New York: Public Affairs Ltd.

Spencer, H. (1902) *The Principles of Sociology*, London: Williams & Norgate.

Spicker, P. (2005) *An Introduction to Social Policy*, Aberdeen: The Robert Gordon University, <http://www2.rgu.ac.uk/publicpolicy/introduction>.

Sreberny-Mohammadi, A., Winseck, D., McKenna, J. and Boyd-Barrett, O. (1997) *Media in Global Context: A Reader*, London: Edward Arnold.

Srinivas, M. N. (1952) *Religion and Society among the Coorgs of South India*, Oxford: Oxford University Press.

Stark, R. and Bainbridge, W. S. (1985) *The Future of Religion: Secularization, Revival and Cult Formation*, Berkeley: University of California Press.

Stead, D. and Maguire, J. (1998) 'Cricket's global "finishing school": the migration of overseas cricketers into English county cricket', *European Physical Education Review*, 4(1), 54–69.

Stein, D. (1995) *People who Count: Population and Politics, Women and Children*, London: Earthscan.

Stephan, N. (1982) *The Idea of Race in Science: Great Britain, 1800–1960*, Basingstoke: Macmillan.

Stienstra, D. (1994) *Women's Movements and International Organizations*, New York: St Martin's Press.

Stiglitz, J. E. (2002) *Globalization and its Discontents*, London: Allen Lane.

Stoddard, E. and Cornwell, G. H. (1999) 'Cosmopolitan or mongrel: créolité, hybridity and "douglarisation" in Trinidad', *European Journal of Cultural Studies*, 2(3), 331–53.

Stone, J. R. (2000) 'Introduction', in Stone, J. R. (ed.) *Expecting Armageddon: Essential Readings in Failed Prophecy*, New York: Routledge, 1–29.

Strange, S. (1986) *Casino Capitalism*, Oxford: Basil Blackwell.

Strange, S. (1996) *The Retreat of the State: The Diffusion of Power in the World Economy*, Cambridge: Cambridge University Press.

Strathern, M. (1992) *After Nature: English Kinship in the Late Twentieth Century*, Cambridge: Cambridge University Press.

Strinati, D. (1995) *An Introduction to Theories of Popular Culture*, London: Routledge.

Stubbs, S. (1997) 'The hooded hordes of prejudice', *New Statesman*, 28 February.

Sugden, J. (1996) *Boxing and Society: An International Analysis*, Manchester: Manchester University Press.

Swidler, A. (1986) 'Culture in action: symbols and strategies', *American Sociological Review*, **51**, 273–86.

Taylor, J. G. (1979) *From Modernisation to Modes of Production: A Critique of the Sociologies of Development and Underdevelopment*, Basingstoke: Macmillan.

Taylor, J. P. (2001) 'Authenticity and sincerity in tourism', *Annals of Tourism Research*, **28**(1), 7–26.

Taylor, P. J. (1995) 'World cities and territorial states: the rise and fall of their mutuality', in Knox, P. L. and Taylor, P. J. (eds) *World Cities in a World System*, Cambridge: Cambridge University Press, 48–62.

Taylor, R. and Young, N. (eds) (1987) *Campaign for Peace: British Peace Movements in the Twentieth Century*, Manchester: Manchester University Press.

Teschke, B. and Heine, C. (2002) 'The dialectics of globalization: a critique of social constructivism', in Rupert, M. and Smith, H. (eds) *Historical Materialism and Globalization*, London: Routledge, 165–88.

Theroux, P. (1986) *Sunrise with Seamonsters*, Harmondsworth: Penguin.

Thomson, D. (1997) 'Hong Kong on the Thames', *Telegraph Magazine*, 12 April.

Thrift, N. (2004) 'Movement–space: the changing domains of thinking resulting from the development of new kinds of spatial awareness', *Economy and Society*, **34**(4), 582–604.

Thwaites, T., Davis, L. and Mules, W. (1994) *Tools for Cultural Studies: An Introduction*, South Melbourne: Macmillan Education.

Tickner, J. A. (1992) *Gender in International Relations*, New York: Columbia University Press.

Tilly, C. (ed.) (1975) *The Formation of Nation States in Western Europe*, Princeton, NJ: Princeton University Press.

Tilly, C. (2004) 'Terror, terrorism, terrorists', *Sociological Theory*, **22**(1), 5–13.

Timms, J. (2005) 'Chronology of global civil society events', in Anheier, H., Glasius, M. and Kaldor, M. (eds) *Global Civil Society 2004/05*, London: Sage, 350–60.

Tinker, A. (1997) *Older People in Modern Society* (4th edn) Longman, New York.

Tischler, H. L. (1999) *Introduction to Sociology* (5th edn) Fort Worth, TX: Harcourt Press.

Tomlinson, J. (1991) *Cultural Imperialism: A Critical Introduction*, London: Pinter.

Tomlinson, J. (1999) *Globalization and Culture*, Cambridge: Polity Press.

Tönnies, F. (1971) *Ferdinand Tönnies on Sociology: Pure, Applied and Empirical: Selected Writings*, Chicago: University of Chicago Press (first published 1887).

Touraine, A. (1981) *The Voice and the Eye: An Analysis of Social Movements*, Cambridge: Cambridge University Press.

Townsend, P. (1996) *A Poor Future: Can We Counter Growing Poverty in Britain and Across the World?* London: Lemos & Crane/Friendship Group.

Tuckman, J. (2005) 'Shopkeeper took on Coke – and won', *Guardian*, 17 November.

Turner, B. (1991) *Religion and Social Theory*, London: Sage.

Turner, B. (1992) *Regulating Bodies: Essays in Medical Sociology*, London: Routledge.

Turner, B. (1994) *Orientalism, Postmodernism and Globalism*, London: Routledge.

Turner, B. (1995) *Medical Power and Social Knowledge*, London: Sage.

Turner, L. and Ash, J. (1975) *The Golden Hordes: International Tourism and the Pleasure Periphery*, London: Constable.

Tyler, A. (1985) *The Accidental Tourist*, New York: Knopf.

UK Government Ministry of Defence (2005) *Joint Doctrine and Concept Centre: Strategic Trends*, www.jdcc-strategictrends.org.

UN (1995) *The Copenhagen Declaration and Programme of Action: World Summit for Social Development (6–12 March 1995)*, New York: UN Department of Publications.

UN (2004) *World Population Prospects: The 2002 Revision*, New York: UN Department of Economic and Social Affairs.

UN Development Programme (1997) *Human Development Report 1997*, Oxford: Oxford University Press.

UNHCR (2005) *Global Refugee Trends*, Geneva: UN High Commissioner for Refugees, www.unhcr.org/statistics.

UN Office on Drugs and Crime (2004) *Seventh United Nations Survey of Crime Trends and Operations of Criminal Justice Systems, covering the period 1998–2000*, New York: UN Centre for International Crime Prevention.

UN Office on Drugs and Crime (2005) *World Drug Report*, New York: UN Centre for International Crime Prevention, <http://www.unodc.org/pdf/WDR_2005/ volume_1_web.pdf>.

UNRISD (1995) *States of Disarray: The Social Effects of Globalization*, Geneva: UN Research Institute for Social Development.

Urry, J. (1990a) *The Tourist Gaze*, London: Sage.

Urry, J. (1990b) 'The "consumption" of tourism', *Sociology*, **24**(1), 23–34.

Urry, J. (1995) *Consuming Places*, London: Routledge.

Urry, J. (2000) *Sociology Beyond Societies: Mobilities for the Twenty-First Century*, London: Routledge.

Urry, J. (2003) *Global Complexity*, Cambridge: Polity Press.

Urry, J. (2004) 'The "system" of automobility', *Theory, Culture and Society*, **21**(4/5), 25–39.

US State Department (2003) *Patterns of Global Terrorism*. Annual Report. Washington, DC: Department of State.

Van Broeck, A. M. and Puijk, R. (2001) 'Pamukkale: Turkish homestay tourism', in Smith, V. and Brent, M. (eds) *Hosts and Guests Revisited: Tourism Issues of the 21st Century*, New York: Cognizant Communication Corporation.

Van den Berghe, P. (1994) 'Intelligence and race', in Cashmore, E. (ed.) *Dictionary of Race and Ethnic Relations* (3rd edn) London: Routledge.

Van de Veer, P. (2001) 'Transnational religion', working paper, Transnational Communities Programme, University of Oxford, WPTC-01-18.

Van Hear, N. (1998) *New Diasporas: The Mass Exodus, Dispersal and Regrouping of Migrant Communities*, London: UCL Press.

Van Krieken, R. (1998) *Norbert Elias*, London: Routledge.

Van Zoonen, L. (1994) *Feminist Media Studies*, London: Sage.

Vertovec, S. and Cohen, R. (eds) (1999) *Migration, Diasporas and Transnationalism*, Cheltenham: Edward Elgar.

Volkman, T. A. (1984) 'Great performances: Toraja cultural identity in the 1970s', *American Ethnologist*, 152–68.

Waddington, I. (2000) *Sport, Health and Drugs: A Critical Sociological Perspective*, London: E & FN Spon.

Wagner, E. A. (1990) 'Sport in Asia and Africa: Americanization or mundialization?' *Sociology of Sport Journal*, 7, 399–402.

Walby, S. (1990) *Theorizing Patriarchy*, Oxford: Blackwell.

Waldinger, R. and Bozorgmehr, M. (eds) (1996) *Ethnic Los Angeles*, New York: Russell Sage Foundation.

Wallerstein, I. (1974) *The Modern World System: Capitalism, Agriculture and the Origins of the European World-Economy in the Sixteenth Century*, New York: Academic Press.

Wallerstein, I. (1979) 'The rise and future demise of the world capitalist system: concepts for comparative analysis', in Wallerstein, I. (ed.) *The Capitalist World-Economy*, Cambridge: Cambridge University Press, 3–36.

Wallerstein, I. (1989) 'Culture as the ideological battleground of the modern world-system', *Hitotsubashi Journal of Social Studies*, 21(1), 5–22.

Wallerstein, I. (1991) *Geopolitics and Geoculture*, Cambridge: Cambridge University Press.

Wallerstein, I. (1996) *Open the Social Sciences: Report of the Gulbenkian Commission on the Restructuring of the Social Sciences*, (ed. Mudimbe, V. Y.) Stanford: Stanford University Press.

Walton, J. and Seddon, D. (1994) *Free Markets and Food Riots: The Politics of Global Adjustment*, Oxford: Blackwell.

Warde, A. (1992) 'Notes on the relationship between production and consumption', in Burrows, R. and Marsh, C. (eds) *Consumption and Class: Divisions and Change*, Basingstoke: Macmillan.

Waterman, P. and Timms, J. (2005) 'Trade union internationalism and a global civil society in the making', in Anheier, H., Glasius, M. and Kaldor, M. (eds) *Global Civil Society 2004/05*, London: Sage, 178–202.

Waters, M. (1995) *Globalization*, London: Routledge.

Watkins, J. (1997) *Briefing on Poverty*, Oxford: Oxfam Publications.

Watson, J. (1998) *Media Communication: An Introduction to Theory and Practice*, Basingstoke: Macmillan.

Watts, J. (2005) 'China admits toxic spill is threat to city's water', *Guardian*, 24 November.

Weber, M. (1976) 'Subjective meaning in the social situation', in Coser, L. A. and Rosenberg, B., *Sociological Theory: A Book of Readings*, New York: Macmillan, 209–20.

Weber, M. (1977) *The Protestant Ethic and the Spirit of Capitalism*, London: Allen & Unwin.

Weber, M. (1978) *Economy and Society*, Berkeley: University of California Press.

Webster, F. (2002) *Theories of the Information Society*, London: Routledge.

Weiss, L. (1998) *The Myth of the Powerless State*, Cambridge: Polity Press.

Werner, D. (2001) 'Elusive promise', *New Internationalist*, (331), 22–3.

White, K. (2002) *An Introduction to the Sociology of Health and Illness*, London: Sage.

WHO (2004) *World Health Report*, Geneva: World Health Organization Press.

WHO (2005) *WHO Multi-Country Study on Women's Health and Domestic Violence Against Women*, Geneva: World Health Organization Press.

Wight, M. (1977) *Systems of States*, Leicester: Leicester University Press.

Wilcox, R. C. (1994) 'Of fungos and fumbles: explaining the cultural uniqueness of American sport, or a paradoxical peek at sport American style', in Wilcox, R. C. (ed.) *Sport in the Global Village*, Morgantown, WV: Fitness Information Technology, 73–102.

Willetts, P. (1996) 'From Stockholm to Rio and beyond: the impact of the environmental movement on arrangements for NGOs', *Review of International Studies*, 22(1), 57–80.

Williams, K., Haslam, C., Williams, J. and Cutler, J. (1992) 'Against lean production', *Economy and Society*, 21(3), 321–54.

Wilson, B. (1966) *Religion in Secular Society: A Sociological Comment*, London: Watts.

Wilson, J. (1973) *Introduction to Social Movements*, New York: Basic Books.

Wilson, W. J. (1978) *The Declining Significance of Race*, Chicago: University of Chicago Press.

Wilson, W. J. (1987) *The Truly Disadvantaged: The Inner City, the Underclass and Public Policy*, Chicago: Chicago University Press.

Wolf, M. (2004) *Why Globalization Works: The Case for the Global Market Economy*, New Haven: Yale University Press.

Wolf, M. (2005) *Why Globalization Works*, Yale: Yale University Press.

Womack, J. P., Jones, D. T. and Roos, D. (1990) *The Machine that Changed the World*, New York: Rawson Associates.

Wood, R. E. (1993) 'Tourism, culture and the sociology of development', in Hitchcock, M., King, V. T. and Parnwell, M. J. G. (eds) *Tourism in South-east Asia*, London: Routledge, 48–70.

World Bank (2004a) *World Development Indicators*, Washington: World Bank, http://www.worldbank.org/data.

World Bank (2004b) 'Global poverty down by half since 1981 but progress uneven as economic growth eludes many countries', press release, Washington: World Bank, 23 April.

World Bank (2005a) *World Development Report*, Washington, DC: World Bank.

World Bank (2005b) *Social Indicators of Development*, Washington, DC: World Bank.

Worldwatch Institute (2004) *State of the World 2004: Progress Towards a Sustainable Society*, London: Earthscan.

Worsley, P. (1967) *The Third World*, London: Weidenfeld & Nicolson.

Wright, E. O. (1985) *Classes*, London: Verso.

WTO (2004) *Yearbook of Tourism Statistics*, Madrid: World Tourism Organization.

WTO (2005) *Yearbook of Tourism Statistics*, Madrid: World Tourism Organization.

Wuthnow, R. (1996) *Sharing the Journey: Suppo Groups and America's New Quest for Commun* New York: Free Press.

Yearley, S. (1996a) *Sociology, Environmentalis Globalization: Reinventing the Globe*, Londo Sage.

Yearley, S. (1996b) 'The local and the global: t transnational politics of the environment', Anderson, J., Brook, C. and Cochrane, A. (e *A Global World? Re-ordering Political Spa* Oxford: Oxford University Press, 209–67.

Yeates, N. (2004) 'Global care chains: critical refle tions and lines of enquiry', *International Femi ist Journal of Politics*, 6(3), 369–91.

Yuval-Davis, N. and Anthias, F. (eds) (198 *Woman–nation–state*, Basingstoke: Macmillan

Zachary, G. P. (1999) 'This singing sensation fro Liverpool longs to be in Hong Kong', *Wa Street Journal*, 1–10.

Zalewski, M. (1993) 'Feminist theory and inte national relations', in Bowker, M. and Brow R. (eds) *From Cold War to Collapse: Theory an World Politics in the 1980s*, Cambridge: Car bridge University Press, 115–44.

Zhou, Y. and Tseng, Y. F. (2001) 'Regrounding t "ungrounded empires": localization as t geographical catalyst for transnationalism *Global Networks: A Journal of Transnation. Affairs*, 1(2), 131–54.

Zirakzadeh, C. E. (1997) *Social Movements in Po itics: A Comparative Study*, London: Longmar

Zolberg, A. R., Suhrke, A. and Aguayo, S. (198 *Escape from Violence: Conflict and the Refug Crisis in the Developing World*, New Yor Oxford University Press.

Zukin, S. (1981) *Loft Living*, London: Hutchi son/Radius.

Name Index

The principal entries for Global Thinkers are shown in **bold numerals**

Subject Index

The principal entries for Key Concepts are indicated in **bold numerals**